Students! Essential Access Information for HM Video Cases

Explore Teaching in Action

Are you interested in what happens in actual classrooms? Do you want to know how in-service teachers handle a variety of situations in the classroom? Watch the Houghton Mifflin Video Cases and explore how new and experienced teachers apply concepts and strategies in real K–12 classrooms. These four- to six-minute video clips cover a variety of different topics faced by today's teachers and allow you to experience and reflect on real teaching in action.

To access the Houghton Mifflin Video Cases:

1. Using your browser go to: **college.hmco.com/pic/kaleidoscope11e**
2. Select the student website
3. Click on HM Video Cases
4. You will be prompted to enter the passkey below and to choose a username and password
5. Select a video case from the list of options

Passkey: 2ZA1UAXZ49MBP

Access is provided for free with the purchase of a new Ryan/Cooper, *Kaleidoscope: Readings in Education*, Eleventh Edition textbook and will expire six months after first use. If you have a problem accessing the website with this passkey, please contact Houghton Mifflin Technical Support at: **http://college.hmco.com/how/how_techsupp.html.**

Enhance Your Learning Experience

Houghton Mifflin Video Cases include video clips and a host of related materials to provide a comprehensive learning experience.

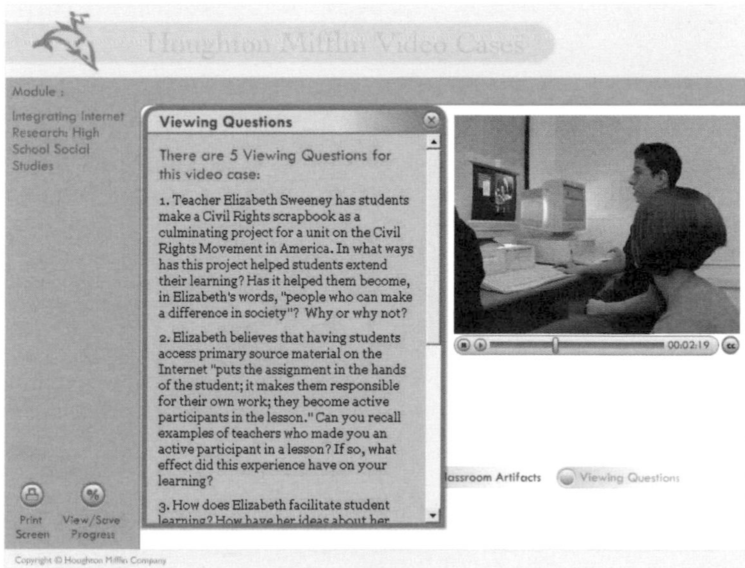

Reflect on the teacher's approach and assess how you might handle the situation by considering the **Viewing Questions.**

Watch textbook concepts come to life through video clips and bonus videos of real teachers applying teaching models and addressing key topics in their own classrooms.

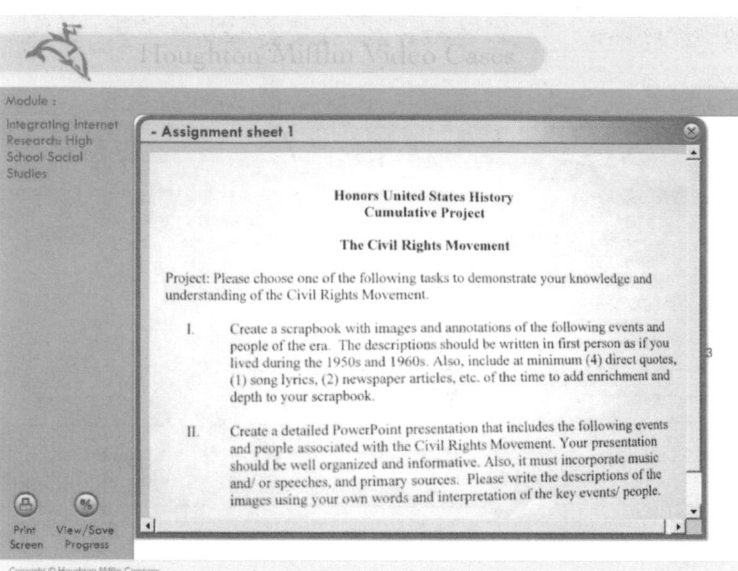

View **handouts and materials used in the class,** and gain ideas for your own portfolio.

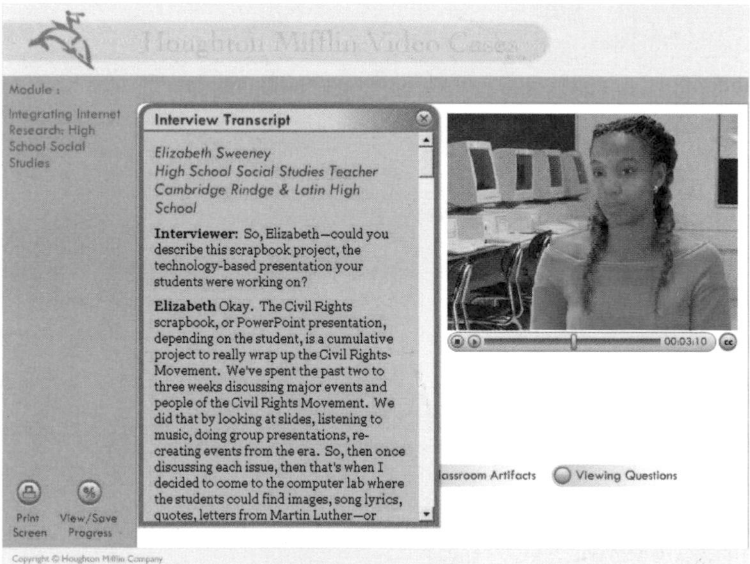

Read detailed **interviews with the teachers** as they explain their approach, how they engage students and how they resolve issues.

Topic	Author	Abbreviated Title	Kaleidoscope (pages)	Those Who Can, Teach (chapters)	Foundations of Education (chapters)
Cooperative Learning	Johnson & Johnson	*Making Cooperative Learning Work*	245–253	5	14
Curriculum	Adler	*The Paideia Proposal*	163–168	5, 9	4, 14
	Popham	*Curriculum Matters*	143–148	5, 11, 12	4
	Haycock	*Closing the Achievement Gap*	199–205	5, 6, 10, 12	11, 12, 16
	Nord	*The Relevance of Religion to the Curriculum*	180–185	5, 8, 12	3, 5, 9
	Peddiwell	*The Saber-Tooth Curriculum*	149–154	5	14
Diversity	Hardy	*The New Diversity*	399–403	3, 5, 12	10, 11, 12
Ethics of Teaching	Strike	*The Ethics of Teaching*	293–297	8, 9	4, 9
Finance	Miles	*Putting Money Where It Matters*	361–366	11	8, 16
Gender Issues	Gurian & Stevens	*With Boys and Girls in Mind*	434–440	4, 8	10
	Woods	*Hostile Hallways*	75–78	4, 8	6, 9
Gifted Education	Willard-Holt	*Raising Expectations for the Gifted*	92–97	3	12, 14, 16
Harassment	Woods	*Hostile Hallways*	75–78	4, 8	6, 9
Home Schooling	Lines	*Home Schooling Comes of Age*	137–141	8, 12	9
Homework	Hofferth and Jankuniene	*Life After School*	132–136	4	10, 11
Inclusion	Villa & Thousand	*Making Inclusive Education Work*	427–433	3	12
	Kauffman, McGee, & Brigham	*Enabling or Disabling?*	298–309	3	12
Instruction	Tomlinson	*Mapping a Route Toward Differentiated Instruction*	254–259	5	12, 14
Law and the Teacher	McDaniel	*The Teacher's Ten Commandments*	298–309	8	9
Multicultural Education	Gay	*The Importance of Multicultural Education*	411–417	3, 5	11, 12
	Hardy	*The New Diversity*	399–403	3, 5, 12	11, 12
	Ravitch	*A Considered Opinion*	404–406	3, 5	11, 12
	Stotsky	*Multicultural Illiteracy*	407–410	3, 5, 10	6, 11, 12

KALEIDOSCOPE

KALEIDOSCOPE

11

Eleventh Edition

Readings in Education

Kevin Ryan
Boston University

James M. Cooper
University of Virginia

HOUGHTON MIFFLIN COMPANY
Boston New York

Publisher: Pat Coryell
Senior Sponsoring Editor: Mary Finch
Senior Development Editor: Lisa Mafrici
Editorial Assistant: Dayna Pell
Senior Project Editor: Jane Lee
Editorial Assistant: Kristen Truncellito
Senior Art and Design Coordinator: Jill Haber
Senior Photo Editor: Jennifer Meyer Dare
Composition Buyer: Chuck Dutton
Manufacturing Buyer: Karen Fawcett
Marketing Manager: Elinor Gregory
Marketing Assistant: Evelyn Yang

Printed in the U.S.A.

Library of Congress Control Number: 2005935919

Instructor's exam copy:
ISBN 13: **978-0-618-73232-6**
ISBN 10: **0-618-73232-2**

For orders, use student text ISBNs:
ISBN 13: **978-0-618-64362-2**
ISBN 10: **0-618-64362-1**

123456789-QF-10 09 08 07 06

Contents

Preface xi

PART ONE: **Teachers** 1

1. Simon Hole and Grace Hall McEntee
Reflection Is at the Heart of Practice 2
2. Robert Fried
The Heart of the Matter 7
3. Julia E. Koppich
All Teachers Are *Not* the Same: A Multiple Approach to Teacher Compensation 11
4. Edward R. Ducharme
The Great Teacher Question: Beyond Competencies 14
5. Martin Haberman
Can Star Teachers Create Learning Communities? 21
6. Molly Ness
Lessons of a First-Year Teacher 27
7. Claudia Graziano
School's Out 31
8. Patricia Houghton
Finding Allies: Sustaining Teachers' Health and Well-Being 37
9. John C. Crowley
Letter from a Teacher 46

PART TWO: **Students** 49

10. Robert D. Barr
Who Is This Child? 50
11. Marian Wright Edelman
Leaving No Child Behind 52
12. D. Stanley Eitzen
Problem Students: The Sociocultural Roots 56
13. Thomas David Knestrict
Memories from the "Other": Lessons in Connecting with Students 63
14. Ruby K. Payne
Understanding and Working with Students and Adults from Poverty 69
15. Jacqueline Woods
Hostile Hallways 75
16. M. Mark Wasicsko and Steven M. Ross
How to Create Discipline Problems 79
17. Dennis L. Cates, Marc A. Markell, and Sherrie Bettenhausen
At Risk for Abuse: A Teacher's Guide for Recognizing and Reporting Child Neglect and Abuse 85
18. Colleen Willard-Holt
Raising Expectations for the Gifted 92

PART THREE: **Schools** 98

19. Roland S. Barth
The Culture Builder 99
20. Larry Cuban
A Tale of Two Schools 104
21. Rosetta Marantz Cohen
Schools Our Teachers Deserve 109
22. Kathleen Vail
Remaking High School 117
23. Patricia A. Wasley
Small Classes, Small Schools: The Time Is Now 121
24. Margaret Finders and Cynthia Lewis
Why Some Parents Don't Come to School 126

25. Sandra L. Hofferth and Zita Jankuniene
Life After School 132

26. Patricia M. Lines
Home Schooling Comes of Age 137

PART FOUR: Curriculum and Standards 142

27. W. James Popham
Curriculum Matters 143

28. J. Abner Peddiwell
The Saber-Tooth Curriculum 149

29. Scott Thompson
The Authentic Standards Movement and Its Evil Twin 155

30. Mortimer J. Adler
The Paideia Proposal: Rediscovering the Essence of Education 163

31. William Glasser
The Quality School Curriculum 169

32. John I. Goodlad
Teaching What We Hold to Be Sacred 176

33. Warren A. Nord
The Relevance of Religion to the Curriculum 181

34. Nel Noddings
Teaching Themes of Care 186

35. Kevin Ryan
Mining the Values in the Curriculum 194

PART FIVE: Instruction 198

36. Kati Haycock
Closing the Achievement Gap 199

37. Robert J. Marzano and Jana S. Marzano
The Key to Classroom Management 206

38. Anne Wescott Dodd
Engaging Students: What I Learned Along the Way 214

39. Margaret M. Clifford
Students Need Challenge, Not Easy Success 218

40. Jay McTighe, Elliott Seif, and Grant Wiggins
You *Can* Teach for Meaning 225

41. David Perkins
The Many Faces of Constructivism 231

42. Thomas R. Guskey
Making the Grade: What Benefits Students? 237

43. David W. Johnson and Roger T. Johnson
Making Cooperative Learning Work 245

44. Carol Ann Tomlinson
Mapping a Route Toward Differentiated Instruction 254

PART SIX: Foundations 260

45. John Dewey
My Pedagogic Creed 261

46. Carl Rogers
Personal Thoughts on Teaching and Learning 268

47. Ernest L. Boyer
The Educated Person 271

48. Robert E. Slavin
A Reader's Guide to Scientifically Based Research 279

49. James C. Carper
The Changing Landscape of U.S. Education 286

50. Kenneth A. Strike
The Ethics of Teaching 293

51. Thomas R. McDaniel
The Teacher's Ten Commandments: School Law in the Classroom 298

52. Thomas Lickona
The Return of Character Education 310

PART SEVEN: Educational Reform 317

53. Linda Darling-Hammond
What Matters Most: A Competent Teacher for Every Child 318

54. Elliot W. Eisner
The Kind of Schools We Need 332

55. Richard Rothstein
Class and the Classroom 341

56. Frederick M. Hess
The Case for Being Mean 349

57. Mary Anne Raywid
Accountability: What's Worth Measuring? 355

58. Karen Hawley Miles
Putting Money Where It Matters 361

59. Joseph P. Viteritti
Coming Around on School Choice 367

60. Timothy McDonald
The False Promise of Vouchers 373

PART EIGHT: Educational Technology 379

61. Marvin Cetron and Kimberley Cetron
A Forecast for Schools 380

62. Jane M. Healy
The Mad Dash to Compute 387

63. Paul Gow
Technology and the Culture of Learning 392

PART NINE: Diversity and Social Issues 398

64. Lawrence Hardy
The New Diversity 399

65. Diane Ravitch
A Considered Opinion: Diversity, Tragedy, and the Schools 404

66. Sandra Stotsky
Multicultural Illiteracy 407

67. Geneva Gay
The Importance of Multicultural Education 411

68. James M. Kauffman, Kathleen McGee, and Michele Brigham
Enabling or Disabling? Observations on Changes in Special Education 418

69. Richard A. Villa and Jacqueline S. Thousand
Making Inclusive Education Work 427

70. Michael Gurian and Kathy Stevens
With Boys and Girls in Mind 434

Glossary 441

Index 453

Article Review Form 461

Student Response Form 463

HM Video Cases That Accompany This Text

PART ONE: Teachers

Teaching as a Profession: What Defines Effective Teaching?

Teaching as a Profession: Collaboration with Colleagues

PART TWO: Students

Motivating Adolescent Learners: Curriculum Based on Real Life

PART THREE: Schools

Parental Involvement in School Culture: A Literacy Project

PART FOUR: Curriculum and Standards

Constructivist Teaching in Action: A High School Classroom Debate

Cooperative Learning: High School History Lesson

PART FIVE: Instruction

Classroom Management: Best Practices

Grading: Strategies and Approaches

Cooperative Learning in the Elementary Grades: Jigsaw Model

Academic Diversity: Differentiated Instruction

PART SIX: Foundations

Legal and Ethical Dimensions of Teaching: Reflections from Today's Educators

PART SEVEN: Educational Reform

Teacher Accountability: A Student Teacher's Perspective

PART EIGHT: Educational Technology

An Expanded Definition of Literacy: Meaningful Ways to Integrate Technology

Educational Technology: Issues of Equity and Access

PART NINE: Diversity and Social Issues

Culturally Responsive Teaching: A Multicultural Lesson for Elementary Students

Inclusion: Classroom Implications for the General and Special Educator

Gender Equity in the Classroom: Girls and Science

Preface

When we were children, one of our favorite toys was the kaleidoscope, the cylindrical instrument containing loose bits of colored glass between two flat plates and two mirrors so placed that shaking or rotating the cylinder causes the bits of glass to be reflected in an endless variety of patterns. We chose *Kaleidoscope* as the name of this book because it seems that education can be viewed from multiple perspectives, each showing a different pattern or set of structures.

Audience and Purpose

This is the eleventh edition of *Kaleidoscope: Readings in Education.* It is intended for use either as a supplemental book of readings to accompany any "Introduction to Education," "Foundations of Education," or "Issues in Education" textbook, or as a core textbook itself.

Today is a time of unprecedented educational debate and reform in the United States. It is our hope that this collection of seventy high-interest selections will help readers participate in these national discussions in a more informed way.

The book's wide range of sources and writers—from the classic John Dewey and Carl Rogers to the contemporary Diane Ravitch, Elliot Eisner, Linda Darling-Hammond, and Robert Slavin—makes it highly flexible and responsive to a broad variety of course needs.

The material we have selected for *Kaleidoscope* is not technical and can be understood, we believe, by people without extensive professional backgrounds in education. The articles are relatively brief and come from classroom teachers, educational researchers, journalists, and educational reformers. Some selections are summaries of research. Some are classic writings by noted educators. Some are descriptions of educational problems and proposed solutions. And, we hasten to add, we agree with some articles and do not agree with others. Our aim is to present a wide variety of philosophical and psychological positions to reflect the varied voices heard in education today.

Coverage

Kaleidoscope is divided into nine parts. Part One concentrates on teachers, with articles ranging from personal reports by teachers to an article about what constitutes great teaching. Part Two contains selections about students, dealing with topics from the changing nature of childhood in the United States to child abuse. Part Three looks at schools and describes some of their current problems as well as a number of recent recommendations for developing more effective schools. Part Four examines curriculum issues and deals with the classic question: "What is most worth knowing?" but also has a number of articles dealing with a major contemporary curricular concern—the movement for higher curricular standards. Part Five focuses on instruction and includes selections on cooperative learning, classroom management, constructivist learning, differentiated instruction, and research on effective teaching. Part Six contains articles on the foundations of education that discuss the historical, philosophical, psychological, and legal roots of contemporary education. Part Seven contains articles on contemporary educational reform efforts in the United States, with particular attention given to the national concern over school choice. Part Eight examines various aspects of how educational technology is affecting or is likely to affect teaching and learning. Finally, Part Nine focuses on various social issues affecting education in the United States today, with particular attention to ethnic and linguistic diversity as well as gender issues and special education inclusion efforts.

Features of the Revision

Given that over 30 percent of the selections are new to this edition, *Kaleidoscope* covers current topics such as multicultural education, standards-based education, professional development of teachers, teacher reflection, technology, classroom management, brain research, inclusion, school reform, and curriculum reform.

Curriculum and Standards Section

Curriculum has been a mainstay of past editions of *Kaleidoscope,* but we have revamped the section, giving more prominence to what we believe is the major curricular issue facing today's educators: content standards and their accompanying high-stakes testing and assessment. In addition, the effects of the movement to increase students' academic achievement are reflected in a number of articles in other sections.

Diversity and Social Issues Section

In the ninth edition, we inaugurated a section on diversity, and in the tenth edition we broadened the section to include additional social issues. We have continued this tradition in the eleventh edition. The articles in Part Nine examine such topics as multiculturalism, inclusion and special education issues, and issues of gender in the classroom.

Education Classics

In this edition, we have continued a feature that was introduced in the tenth edition by designating several articles as *Education Classics*. These articles, marked with special icons, provide readers with a foundation in some of the ideas that have stood the test of time and shifts in educational priorities over many years. As we explain in the postnotes for these articles, they were chosen because the article's author has been highly influential or is well known or because the article addresses an enduring idea or controversy in American education.

Online Teaching and Study Centers

The Online Teaching and Study Centers for instructors and students accompany the printed version of the eleventh edition. This edition's Online Study Center is enhanced with new Houghton Mifflin Video Cases—four- to six-minute video clips filmed in actual classrooms and accompanied by teacher interviews, classroom "artifacts," and viewing questions—that bring the topics of the textbook to life. In addition, the Online Teaching and Study Centers offer several articles from *Kaleidoscope,* annotated and enhanced with links to more information and critical thinking questions, as well as several articles that are unique to the website. Glossary flashcards, an article review form, and a student response form are also included. Also, brand new to the website is an **Education Portfolio Building Tutorial**—an interactive tool that helps preservice teachers learn about the portfolio building process, from explaining what a portfolio is to showing how to create one.

Special Features of the Book

To facilitate understanding of the selections in this book, the eleventh edition of *Kaleidoscope* includes a number of especially helpful features.

- Each of the nine major sections is introduced by a **section-opening overview** to place the readings into a broader context.
  - ***New.*** At the beginning of each article, we have introduced a **Focus Question** to guide the reader as to the most important point or issue to think about as he or she reads the article.
  - A brief **biographical sketch of each author** is presented at the beginning of each article.
- The end of each reading features a **postnote** and several **discussion questions**. The postnote comments on the issues raised by the article, and the discussion questions prompt readers to do some additional thinking about the major points made in the reading.

- **"Terms to Note."** Key terms are introduced at the beginning of each article, providing students valuable additions to their educational vocabularies and reminding them that a glossary of these terms is included at the end of the book. Students can test their knowledge of key terms with the interactive glossary flashcards on the Online Study Center.
- The **Glossary** of key terms at the end of the book is especially useful to those students taking their first course in education or those using this book as a primary text. A detailed subject index also appears at the end of the book.
- The **Article Review Form**, found at the end of the book, will help you to analyze and discuss the articles in the text.
- The **Student Response Form**, also at the end of the book, is your opportunity to comment on each of the readings and to suggest new readings or topics for the next edition. We sincerely hope that you will take the time to complete this form and mail it back to us. Your comments will be invaluable to future students and us as you help us to select the best readings.
- The **Correlating Table**, arranged alphabetically by topic, relates each *Kaleidoscope* selection to specific chapters in both *Those Who Can, Teach,* eleventh edition, by Kevin Ryan and James M. Cooper, and *Foundations of Education,* ninth edition, by Allan Ornstein and Daniel Levine. We hope this chart will serve as a handy cross-reference for users of these books. This chart is printed on the inside covers of the text for easy reference.

Acknowledgments

We are especially grateful to a number of reviewers for their excellent recommendations and suggestions, most notably:

Sally R. Beisser, Drake University
Margaret J. Emery, Erskine College
Jeffrey E. Hahn, Harwick College
Patricia K. Lowry, Jacksonville State University
Linda M. Lyons, Colorado State University
Mary Mueller, Seton Hall University
Fredna Carlson Scroggins, St. Louis Community College at Meramec
Miriam J. Singer, Fairleigh Dickinson University
Robin Loflin Smith, Salem College

In addition, we would like to offer a special note of thanks to the many users of this book who have been kind enough to share with us their impressions of it and their suggestions for how we might improve it in subsequent editions. We hope this tradition will continue as you complete and return the Student Response Form or send us your comments via the Houghton Mifflin website at **college.hmco.com/pic/kaleidoscope11e.**

Kevin Ryan and James M. Cooper

Part One

1 Teachers

Being a teacher today has special drawbacks. It is difficult to be a teacher in an age that mocks idealism. It is difficult to be a teacher without the traditional authority and respect that once came with the title. To be a teacher in a time of permissive childrearing causes special strains, given that many students and some parents are filled with anti-authoritarian attitudes. It is punishing to work at an occupation that is not keeping up economically. It is painful to be part of a profession that is continually asked to solve deep social problems and to do the essential job of educating children and is then regularly criticized for its failings. A good case can be made for discouragement, even for self-pity.

This negativism, or at least acknowledgment of the negative, obscures the fact that teaching is one of the truly great professions. These passing conditions overlook the greatness that resides in the teacher's public responsibility. Many adults struggle with the work-life question: Am I engaged in significant work? Teachers always know that they are engaged in crucial, life-shaping work.

Reflection Is at the Heart of Practice

SIMON HOLE AND GRACE HALL McENTEE

FOCUS Question

What is one habit that separates ordinary teachers from constantly-improving teachers?

Term to Note

Guided reflection protocol

The life force of teaching practice is thinking and wondering. We carry home those moments of the day that touch us, and we question decisions made. During these times of reflection, we realize when something needs to change.

A protocol, or guide, enables teachers to refine the process of reflection, alone or with colleagues. The Guided Reflection Protocol is useful for teachers who choose to reflect alone. The Critical Incidents Protocol, which we developed through our work with the Annenberg Institute for School Reform at Brown University, is used for shared reflection. The steps for each protocol are similar; both include writing.

Guided Reflection Protocol

The first step in guided reflection is to collect possible episodes for reflection. In his book *Critical Incidents in Teaching: Developing Professional Judgement* (1993), David Tripp encourages us to think about ordinary events, which often have much to tell us about the underlying trends, motives, and structures of our practice. Simon's story, "The Geese and the Blinds," exemplifies this use of an ordinary event.

Step One: What Happened?

> Wednesday, September 24, 9:30 A.M. I stand to one side of the classroom, taking the morning attendance. One student glances out the window and sees a dozen Canada geese grazing on the playground. Hopping from his seat, he calls out as he heads to the window for a better view. Within moments, six students cluster around the

---

Simon Hole is a fourth grade teacher at Narragansett Elementary School in Narragansett, Rhode Island. He has written a book entitled *Reflection: The Heart of Changing Practice* (Teachers College Press, 2002). **Grace Hall McEntee** is cofounder of Educators Writing for Change. She may be reached at Box 301, Prudence Island, RI 02872 (e-mail: Gmcente@aol.com). From Simon Hole and Grace McEntee, "Reflection Is at the Heart of Practice." *Educational Leadership,* May 1999, pp. 34–37. Reprinted by permission. The Association for Supervision and Curriculum Development is a worldwide community of educators advocating sound policies and sharing best practices to achieve the success of each learner. To learn more, visit ASCD at **www.ascd.org.**

> **Guided Reflection Protocol (For Individual Reflection)**
>
> 1. *Collect stories.* Some educators find that keeping a set of index cards or a steno book close at hand provides a way to jot down stories as they occur. Others prefer to wait until the end of the day and write in a journal.
> 2. *What happened?* Choose a story that strikes you as particularly interesting. Write it succinctly.
> 3. *Why did it happen?* Fill in enough of the context to give the story meaning. Answer the question in a way that makes sense to you.
> 4. *What might it mean?* Recognizing that there is no one answer is an important step. Explore possible meanings rather than determine the meaning.
> 5. *What are the implications for practice?* Consider how your practice might change given any new understandings that have emerged from the earlier steps.

window. Others start from their seats to join them. I call for attention and ask them to return to their desks. When none of the students respond, I walk to the window and lower the blinds.

Answering the question What happened? is more difficult than it sounds. We all have a tendency to jump into an interpretive or a judgmental mode, but it is important to begin by simply telling the story. Writing down what happened—without analysis or judgment—aids in creating a brief narrative. Only then are we ready to move to the second step.

Step Two: Why Did It Happen?

Attempting to understand why an event happened the way it did is the beginning of reflection. We must search the context within which the event occurred for explanations. Simon reflects:

> It's not hard to imagine why the students reacted to the geese as they did. As 9-year-olds, they are incredibly curious about their world. Explaining my reaction is more difficult. Even as I was lowering the blinds, I was kicking myself. Here was a natural opportunity to explore the students' interests. Had I stood at the window with them for five minutes, asking questions to see what they knew about geese, or even just listening to them, I'd be telling a story about seizing the moment or taking advantage of a learning opportunity. I knew that even as I lowered the blinds. So, why?

Searching deeper, we may find that a specific event serves as an example of a more general category of events. We need to consider the underlying structures within the school that may be a part of the event and examine deeply held values. As we search, we often find more questions than answers.

> Two key things stand out concerning that morning. First, the schedule. On Wednesdays, students leave the room at 10:00 a.m. and do not return until 15 minutes before lunch. I would be out of the classroom all afternoon attending a meeting, and so this half hour was all the time I would have with my students.
>
> Second, this is the most challenging class I've had in 22 years of teaching. The first three weeks of school had been a constant struggle as I tried strategy after strategy to hold their attention long enough to have a discussion, give directions, or conduct a lesson. The hectic schedule and the need to prepare the class for a substitute added to the difficulty I've had "controlling" the class, so I closed the blinds.

There's something satisfying about answering the question Why did it happen? Reflection often stops here. If the goal is to become a reflective practitioner, however, we need to look more deeply. The search for meaning is step three.

Step Three: What Might It Mean?

Assigning meaning to the ordinary episodes that make up our days can feel like overkill. Is there really meaning behind all those events? Wouldn't it be more productive to wait for something extraordinary to happen, an event marked with a sign: "Pay attention! Something important is happening." Guided reflection is a way to find the meaning within the mundane. Split-second decision making is a crucial aspect of teaching. Given the daily madness of life in a classroom, considering all the options and consequences is difficult. Often, it is only through reflection that we even recognize that we had a choice, that we could have done something differently.

> Like a football quarterback, I often make bad decisions because of pressure. Unlike a quarterback, I don't have an offensive line to blame for letting the pressure get to me. While it would be nice to believe that I could somehow make the pressure go away, the fact is that it will always be with me. Being a teacher means learning to live within that pressure, learning from the decisions I make and learning to make better decisions.

Our growing awareness of how all events carry some meaning is not a new concept. In *Experience and Education* (1938), John Dewey wrote about experience and its relationship to learning and teaching: "Every experience affects for better or worse the attitudes which help decide the quality of further experience" (p. 37). He believed that teachers must be aware of the "possibilities inherent in ordinary experience" (p. 89), that the "business of the educator [is] to see in what direction an experience is heading" (p. 38). Rediscovering this concept through the examination of ordinary events creates a fresh awareness of its meaning.

The search for meaning is an integral part of being human. But understanding by itself doesn't create changes in classroom practice. The last phase of guided reflection is more action oriented and involves holding our practice to the light of those new understandings.

Step Four: What Are the Implications for My Practice?

Simon continues:

> My reaction to the pressure this year has been to resort to methods of control. I seem to be forever pulling down the blinds. I'm thinking about how I might better deal with the pressure.
>
> But there is something else that needs attention. Where is the pressure coming from? I'm sensing from administration and parents that they feel I should be doing things differently. I've gotten subtle and overt messages that I need to pay more attention to "covering" the curriculum, that I should be finding a more equal balance between process and product.
>
> Maybe they're right. What I've been doing hasn't exactly been a spectacular success. But I think that what is causing the lowering of the blinds stems from my not trusting enough in the process. Controlling the class in a fairly traditional sense isn't going to work in the long run. Establishing a process that allows the class to control itself will help keep the blinds up.

Cultivating deep reflection through the use of a guiding protocol is an entry into rethinking and changing practice. Alone, each of us can proceed step-by-step through the examination of a particular event. Through the process, we gain new insights into the implications of ordinary events, as Simon did when he analyzed "The Geese and the Blinds."

Whereas Guided Reflection is for use by individuals, the Critical Incidents Protocol is used with colleagues. The goal is the same: to get to the heart of our practice, the place that pumps the lifeblood into our teaching, where we reflect, gain insight, and change what we do with our students. In addition, the Critical Incidents Protocol encourages the establishment of collegial relationships.

Critical Incidents Protocol

Schools are social places. Although too often educators think and act alone, in most schools colleagues do share daily events. Stories told in teachers' lounges are a potential source of rich insight into issues of teaching and learning and can open doors to professional dialogue.

Telling stories has the potential for changing individual practice and the culture of our schools. The Critical Incidents Protocol allows practitioners to share stories in a way that is useful to their own thinking and to that of the group.

Three to five colleagues meet for the purpose of exploring a "critical incident." For 10 minutes,

Critical Incidents Protocol (For Shared Reflection)

1. *Write stories.* Each group member writes briefly in response to the question: What happened? (10 minutes)
2. *Choose a story.* The group decides which story to use. (5 minutes)
3. *What happened?* The presenter reads the written account of what happened and sets it within the context of professional goals. (10 minutes)
4. *Why did it happen?* Colleagues ask clarifying questions. (5 minutes)
5. *What might it mean?* The group raises questions about the incident in the context of the presenter's work. They discuss it as professional, caring colleagues while the presenter listens. (15 minutes)
6. *What are the implications for practice?* The presenter responds, then the group engages in conversation about the implications for the presenter's practice and for the participants' own practice. A useful question at this stage might be, "What new insights occurred?" (15 minutes)
7. *Debrief the process.* The group talks about what just happened. How did the process work? (10 minutes)

all write a brief account of an incident. Participants should know that the sharing of their writing will be for the purpose of getting feedback on what happened rather than on the quality of the writing itself.

Next, the group decides which story to use with the protocol. The presenter for the session then reads the story while the group listens carefully to understand the incident and the context. Colleagues ask clarifying questions about what happened or why the incident occurred, then they discuss what the incident might mean in terms of the presenter's practice. During this time, the presenter listens and takes notes. The presenter then responds, and the participants discuss the implications for their own practice. To conclude, one member leads a conversation about what happened during the session, how well the process worked, and how the group might change the process.

The sharing of individual stories raises issues in the fresh air of collegial support. If open dialogue is not already part of a school's culture, however, colleagues may feel insecure about beginning. To gain confidence, they may choose to run through the protocol first with a story that is not theirs. For this purpose, Grace offers a story about an incident in the writing lab from her practice as a high school English teacher.

Step One: What Happened?

We went into the computer lab to work on essay drafts. TJ, Neptune, Ronny, and Mick sat as a foursome. Their sitting together had not worked last time. On their single printer an obscene message had appeared. All four had denied writing it.

The next day Ronny, Neptune, and Mick had already sat together. Just as TJ was about to take his seat, I asked him if he would mind sitting over at the next bay of computers. He exploded. "You think I'm the cause of the problem, don't you?"

Actually I did think he might be, but I wasn't at all certain. "No," I said, "but I do want you to sit over here for today." He got red in the face, plunked down in the chair near the three other boys, and refused to move.

I motioned for him to come with me. Out in the hall, I said to him quietly, "The bottom line is that all of you need to get your work done." Out of control, body shaking, TJ angrily spewed out, "You always pick on me. Those guys . . . You . . ." I could hardly hear his words, so fascinated was I with his intense emotion and his whole-body animation.

Contrary to my ordinary response to students who yell, I felt perfectly calm. I knew I needed to wait. Out of the corner of my eye, I saw two male teachers rise out of their chairs in the hallway about 25 feet away. They obviously thought that I, a woman of small stature, needed protection. But I did not look at them. I looked at TJ and waited.

When he had expended his wrathful energy, I said softly, "You know, TJ, you are a natural-born leader." I waited. Breathed in and out. "You did not choose to be a leader; it was thrust upon you. But there you are. People follow you. So you have a tremendous responsibility, to lead in a positive and productive way. Do you understand what I am saying?"

Like an exhalation after a long in-breath, his body visibly relaxed. He looked down at me and nodded his head. Then he held out his hand to me and said, "I'm sorry."

Back in the room, he picked up his stuff and, without a word, moved to the next bay of computers.

Step Two: Using the Critical Incidents Protocol

At first you'll think that you need more information than this, but we think that you have enough here. One member of the group will take the role of Grace. Your "Grace" can answer clarifying questions about what happened or why it happened in whatever way he or she sees fit. Work through the protocol to figure out what the incident might mean in terms of "Grace's" practice. Finally, discuss what implications the incident in the writing lab might have for her practice and for your own as reflective educators. Then, try an event of your own.

We think that you will find that whether the group uses your story or someone else's, building reflective practice together is a sure way to get to the heart of teaching and learning.

References

Dewey, J. (1938). *Experience and education.* New York: Macmillan.

Tripp, D. (1993). *Critical incidents in teaching: Developing professional judgement.* New York: Routledge.

Postnote

A common complaint of teachers is that they don't have enough time to do all the things that they either need or want to do. The day just doesn't seem to have enough hours to do everything that needs doing. When time is precious, making the time to reflect on one's teaching seems extravagant. After all, there are so many more pressing items. On the other hand, if teachers are asked if they want to improve their teaching, it's hard to imagine one saying, "No." The authors of this article make the case that teacher reflection is the key component for improving our teaching. And, if you think about it, improving your teaching without seriously reflecting on it is virtually impossible.

Reflective teaching involves a process of examination and evaluation in which you develop the habits of inquiry and reflection. By describing two structured ways of reflecting, one individually and one with colleagues, the authors give us useful protocols for conducting a reflective process. The use of journal writing, observation instruments, simulations, and videotaping can also help you examine teaching, learning, and the contexts in which they occur. Comparing your perspectives with those of fellow students, professors, and school personnel will broaden your interpretations and give you new insights. As you reflect on your experiences, you will come to distrust simple answers and explanations. Nuances and subtleties will start to become clear, and situations that once seemed simple will reveal their complexities. Moral and ethical issues are likely to be encountered and thought about. By practicing reflective teaching, you will grow and develop the attitudes and skills to become a lifelong student of teaching—you will become an effective, professional teacher.

Discussion Questions

1. What do you see as the primary benefits of reflecting on your teaching? What concerns do you have about it?
2. What case do the authors make for reflecting on ordinary, as opposed to special, events? Do you agree?
3. Are you more likely to use an individual or a cooperative form of reflection? Why?

The Heart of the Matter

ROBERT FRIED

FOCUS Question

What is the secret ingredient that helps a teacher fight through difficulties and make progress toward excellence?

When you get right down to it, every teacher faces one existential question: "What am I here for—to journey with young people into the great world of knowledge and ideas or to shepherd a bunch of mostly unwilling students through the everyday rituals of instruction and assessment?" Who among us has not sought the former and suffered through the latter time and again in our teaching?

Just maybe it's time to face this issue head-on and resolve to no longer accept an answer that defines a teacher as a "classroom manager," or "deliverer of instruction," or "assertive disciplinarian," or "keeper of the grade book."

The alternative to such roles is to assert that one is a passionate teacher: someone truly enamored of a field of knowledge, or deeply stirred by issues and ideas that challenge our world, or drawn to the crises and creativity of the young people who come into class each day—or all of these. To be a passionate teacher is to stop being isolated within a classroom, to refuse to submit to a culture of apathy or cynicism, to look beyond getting through the day.

Only when teachers bring their passions about learning and life into their daily work can they dispel the fog of passive compliance or surly disinterest that surrounds so many kids in school. I believe that we all have it within us to be passionate teachers and that nothing else will quite do the trick.

In too many classrooms, we see the sound and smoke of note-taking, answer-giving, homework-checking, test-taking, and the forgetting that so quickly follows. And in the end, there is creativity for a few, compliance for most, rebellion for some, but not much fiery engagement of the mind and spirit.

What counts is students' willing engagement. They have to want to see where their ideas and energies might take them, to follow their

---

Robert Fried is the author of *The Passionate Teacher—A Practical Guide,* published by Beacon Press. Reprinted with permission from *Teacher Magazine,* Vol. 7, Issue No. 2, October 1995. By permission of Robert Fried, author of *The Passionate Teacher: A Practical Guide* (Boston: Beacon Press, 1995).

curiosity and intuition to useful places. They have to get unshy about being smart—to stop using their brains to put each other down or to get around doing the work we assign them. Today's students need help from teachers who are more than well-prepared or genial or fair. They need teachers who have passions.

Passion itself isn't the goal of education. It's a bridge that connects us to the intensity of young people's thoughts and life experiences—things that they too rarely see as part of school. Once that connection has been made, we can help transfer passions about ideas into habits of hard work and discipline that will remain with students even when peers cajole them to "take it easy." It's not the whole story, of course, but passion is at the heart of what teaching should be if we want to be mentors for young people who sorely need (but rarely seek) heroes of the mind to balance the heroes of brute strength and exotic fashion that surround them in the media.

Yet as I look into hundreds of classrooms, watch all kinds of teachers working with a bewildering variety of students, when I ask myself what makes the greatest difference in the quality and depth of student learning—it is a teacher's passion that leaps out. More than knowledge of subject matter. More than variety of teaching techniques. More than being well-organized, or friendly, or funny, or fair.

Passionate people are the ones who make a difference in our lives. By the intensity of their beliefs and actions, they connect us with a sense of value that is within—and beyond—ourselves. Sometimes that passion burns with a quiet, refined intensity. Sometimes it bellows forth with thunder and eloquence. But in whatever style a teacher's passion emerges, students know they are in the presence of someone whose devotion to learning is exceptional. It's what makes a teacher unforgettable—this caring about ideas and values, this fascination with the potential for growth within people, this fervor about doing things well and striving for excellence.

Passion may just be the difference between being remembered as a "pretty good teacher" who made chemistry or algebra "sort of interesting"—or being the person who opened up a world of the mind to some students who had no one else to make them feel that they were capable of doing great things with test tubes, trumpets, trigonometry, or T. S. Eliot. How, then, is a teacher "passionate"?

You can be passionate about your field of knowledge: in love with the poetry of Emily Dickinson or the prose of Marcus Garvey; dazzled by the spiral of DNA or the swirl of Van Gogh's cypresses; intrigued by the origins of the Milky Way or the demise of the Soviet empire; delighted by the sound of Mozart or the sonority of French vowels.

You can be passionate about issues facing our world: active in the struggle for social justice or for the survival of the global environment; dedicated to the celebration of cultural diversity or to the search for a cure for AIDS.

You can be passionate about children: about the shocking rate of violence experienced by young black males; about including children with disabilities in regular school activities; about raising the low rate of high school completion by Latino children; about the insidious effects of sexism, racism, and social class prejudice on the spirits of all children; about the neglect of "average" kids in schools where those at the "top" and "bottom" seem to get all of the attention.

To be avowedly passionate about at least some of these things puts one apart from those who approach each day in a fog of fatigue, or who come to work wrapped in a self-protective cocoon. The passion that accompanies our attention to knowledge, values, and children is not just something we offer our students. It is a gift we grant ourselves, a way of honoring our life's work, our profession. It says: "I know why I am devoting this life to children."

Let's distinguish passionate teaching from mere idiosyncrasies. Lots of teachers have pet peeves or fixations: points of grammar, disciplinary practices, eccentricities of diction. These may, indeed, make them memorable to their students (for better or worse). But the passions I am speaking about convey much more.

What impresses me about truly passionate teachers is that there is no particular style of teaching, much less a common personality type, that epitomizes them. What unites them are the ways they approach the mission of teaching. They organize their curricula and their daily work with students in practical ways that play to their own strengths.

But how do we make passionate teaching happen? How do we shove aside all the stuff we're supposed to do and make room in our lesson plans for things we feel strongly about?

We may want to ask our students to study in depth the Cuban Missile Crisis, rather than surveying the entire Cold War history. Or study the ecology of one small nearby pond instead of covering all the chapters in the biology text. Or learn a lot about Emily Dickinson and leave other 19th-century poets to be discovered later in students' lives. Language arts teachers in an urban middle school may decide that learning to write good, clear, convincing prose is so vital to students' future success that they enlist colleagues in science and social studies and math to teach writing across the curriculum.

A high school history teacher in a rural New Hampshire town brought her intense interest in archaeology into the classroom by taking her students out into the woods in search of a long-forgotten graveyard. After watching her begin to carefully restore the site, they pitched in to clean and prop up the headstones. A week later, the class traveled to the local historical society to search for the records of the people whose graves they had tended. Each student became a 200-year-old former resident of the town and shared his or her life story in a presentation for the townspeople.

As passionate teachers, we share our commitment to active learning by showing, not just telling. We are readers, writers, researchers, explorers of new knowledge, new ideas, new techniques and technologies, new ways of looking at old facts and theories. Our very excitement about these things helps young people reach beyond their social preoccupations and self-centeredness. When we are no longer learning, we no longer teach because we have lost the power to exemplify for young people what it means to be intellectually active. Even though we may still be able to present them with information, we have become simple purveyors of subject matter, "deliverers of educational services," in the jargon of the field.

Students need us, not because we have all the answers but because we can help them discover the right questions. It's not that we always know what's good for them but that we want to protect them from having to face life's dilemmas in ignorance or in despair. Those adults to whom young people look for advice on serious life issues know how important they are to kids' futures. For all teachers, the recovery of passion can mean a recovery of our dynamic and positive influence in the lives of children.

This, I argue, is what education *is*. There simply is no education without a commitment to developing the mind and the character of learners. And in our time and culture, perhaps as never before, that commitment must be a passionate one if we want young people to heed that calling.

Postnote

The passion a teacher has for the subject that he or she teaches is often not discussed in teacher education programs. Hollywood, however, frequently employs passionate teachers as the protagonists in films: Robin Williams' character in *Dead Poets Society,* Maggie Smith's in *The Prime of Miss Jean Brodie,* and Richard Dreyfus's in *Mr. Holland's Opus* display fire and passion in their teaching.

Some of our most memorable teachers are probably the ones who cared deeply and passionately about what they taught. Equally or perhaps more important are caring and passion for one's students. Teachers who care about their students—and let those students know it in various ways—are often the ones who affect their students the most.

Discussion Questions

1. Think of two or three of the best teachers you've ever had. What was it that made them so good? How were they alike or different?
2. Have you ever had a really good teacher who didn't have passion for his or her subject?
3. Can passion for the subject be learned, or is it something one just has or doesn't have? Why do you think so?

All Teachers Are *Not* the Same: A Multiple Approach to Teacher Compensation

3

JULIA E. KOPPICH

FOCUS Question

Will changing the single salary schedule and building in financial incentives improve the education of our children?

TERMS TO NOTE

Added-value approach

Peer review

Single salary schedule

It is by now a familiar story, often told as a lament: teachers in this country continue to be paid according to the single salary schedule. They accrue better pay on the basis of years of experience and college units earned. Units may or may not be related to teaching assignment. Some districts have modestly tweaked this arrangement by paying a premium to teachers who earn certification through the National Board for Professional Teaching Standards. But by and large, in thousands of school districts across the United States, the unvarnished standard single salary schedule prevails.

Teacher unions, among the staunchest defenders of the standard compensation arrangement, are often credited—or blamed—with inventing this salary calculus. In fact, the classic teachers' salary arrangement is an artifact of civil service. Developed in the early 1920s, the system was popularized three decades later as a way of creating salary equity between elementary teachers, most of whom were women, and secondary teachers, most of whom were men. This was not a pre-feminist revolution so much as a necessary economic response to the post–World War II enrollment boom. Over time, to be sure, teacher unions have come to defend the standard single salary schedule in the name of employee equity and fairness.

The National Education Association assiduously avoids anything that might be construed as "merit pay." The position taken by the American Federation of Teachers is less rigid, yet replete with caveats to protect against anticipated slights and abuses. The unions' position is not unwarranted. Merit pay schemes that have been tried in education have an abysmal track record. . . .

Part of the problem, however, has been that merit pay systems are rarely based on objective standards, a flaw that often created unhealthy

Julia E. Koppich is an education consultant based in San Francisco. A former high school teacher and faculty member in the school of education at the University of California, Berkeley, she is also coauthor of *United Mind Workers: Unions and Teaching in the Knowledge Society.* "All Teachers Are Not the Same," by Julia E. Koppich, *Education Next,* Winter 2005, pp. 13–15. Reprinted with permission.

competition for the usually scarce resources rather than cooperation among teachers. These insufficient funds all too typically forced many teachers to take their rewards solely in the form of psychic remuneration.

Compounding the compensation dilemma, policies promoted by both districts and unions have endeavored to maintain the fiction that "a teacher is a teacher is a teacher." Compensation structures have failed to recognize that some teaching jobs are more difficult than others or that some teachers are more—or less—skilled than others.

Salaries for the Real World

The time has come for school districts and teacher unions to take a different tack. It is time to develop and implement a professional compensation arrangement that recognizes the complex nature of the work of teaching and that compensates teachers for both the difficulty of the assignment and the professional accomplishment that is part of it.

We need a compensation structure that utilizes multiple approaches. These should include paying teachers more for: 1) attaining knowledge and skills that demonstrably contribute to improving student learning; 2) mentoring newer and less skilled teachers; 3) teaching in hard-to-staff schools and choosing difficult-to-staff subjects; 4) producing higher test scores, using a value-added approach.

These ideas fly in the face of long-established tradition. But it's time to reexamine that tradition. It's time to acknowledge publicly that some teaching jobs are more difficult than others. And we must be willing to pay more for some fields than for others. In a perfect world, perhaps, a physics teacher is no more valuable than an English teacher. But we do not live in a perfect world. We live in a world in which physics teachers are at a premium, and for the foreseeable future supply and demand will need to prevail. The market must have its way.

Some will argue that what is suggested above is too complicated, that it is time to scrap the old salary schedule and pay teachers on the basis of their students' test scores alone. After all, assert proponents of this argument, isn't the true measure of a teacher's worth her students' test results? In fact, at the base of this argument lies the same fault line that threatens No Child Left Behind. Making judgments about student learning by simply examining test scores from one year to the next is hazardous at best. Tests provide a simple snapshot in time and may not be well aligned with standards or curriculum. Moreover, particularly in urban districts, given the rate of student transience, the cohort of students tested at the beginning of the year may be different from that tested at the end of the year, thus providing few useful comparative data.

The New Math for Merit

But there is a way to use test scores to gain needed information about the impact of teaching and the levels of student learning: value-added calculations. The value-added approach has the advantage of separating student effects (ethnicity, family background, socioeconomic status) from school effects (teachers, administrators, programs) since it examines test scores to determine if students are making anticipated academic gains each year. Measured on the basis of their progress from the previous year, students, in a sense, act as their own statistical control. Value-added programs calculate a projected test score for a student in a given grade or subject based on his or her previous academic achievement. The difference between the actual score and the projected score is the value added.

Value-added calculations, however, should not be used as the sole gauge of teachers' compensation. They too are an imperfect technology. But they can, and should, serve as one important measure. Consistent value-added work by William Sanders in Tennessee has shown that several consecutive years of teachers' adding measurable value to students' learning provide a foundation on which students can continue to make academic progress. After several years of ineffective teaching, students may never recover academically.

Finally, it is not possible to discuss teachers' compensation without taking up the issue of their evaluation. In most places, evaluation is done poorly, with checklists about behavior standing in for standards of good practice that should frame evaluation systems. Administrators typically in charge of the process have too little time or training to effectively help teachers improve their practice.

But there is an effective alternative to the ineffective evaluation as well. Systems of peer review, in place for a decade or more in a dozen or so districts—such as Toledo and Columbus, Ohio; Rochester, New York; and Montgomery County, Maryland—have shown remarkable promise. Beginning teachers are provided the support they need from specially selected experienced teachers, who are chosen jointly by the district and the union. Those individuals who were not meant to be teachers are soon out of the profession. Struggling tenured teachers are given the support they have long needed. Should that not prove adequate, they are encouraged to find other lines of work. Conventional wisdom notwithstanding, teachers, including unionized teachers, are able to judge their colleagues fairly but rigorously. Yes, some teachers are dismissed. More important, evaluation accomplishes the purpose for which it is intended: improving professional practice.

Working with Complexity

Marrying a well-developed system of peer review and value-added test scores could create a powerful framework for teachers' compensation. Adding pay for knowledge and skills, compensation for mentoring, and pay for teaching in hard-to-staff schools and subjects will transform a pro-forma salary schedule into a professional compensation arrangement that better recognizes the complexity of teaching and offers teachers the kinds of incentives and options that professionals deserve.

Salaries by themselves, no matter how high or competitive, will not encourage teachers to remain at schools where the working conditions are poor. Competent, supportive administrators, a decent physical plant, and requisite instructional supplies are the *sine qua non* for maintaining a quality teaching staff, regardless of the rate of pay.

In sum, it is time to construct a salary schedule that gives teachers choices, opportunities, and options—pay for knowledge and skills, pay for mentoring, added pay for hard-to-staff schools and subjects, and added compensation for test scores calculated using a value-added approach.

The hope is that progressive unions and districts will take up the challenge to shape this new salary construct. They will come to see rethinking compensation as part of their obligation to promote quality teaching, and as the next step on the road to creating a true profession.

Postnote

A counter argument to suggestions of abandoning the single salary schedule is that introducing value-added and peer review systems could introduce competitive attitudes among teachers. These often-disruptive sentiments can lead to conflicts, bad feeling, and poor morale.

While some schools surely have problems with value-added systems, it is very much in doubt that such problems always arise. Many private schools and most universities operate quite well with such systems. Nevertheless, many teachers and many of their professional associations oppose efforts to institute these competitive elements into the teaching profession.

Still strikingly absent from these discussions is the purpose of our schools. Will such changes improve the quality of education?

Discussion Questions

1. Do you see any reason why there ought to be a change in the single salary scale for teachers?
2. In your view, what would be the positive effects of getting rid of the single salary scale? What would be the negative effects?
3. What other service professions have a single salary scale?

The Great Teacher Question: Beyond Competencies

EDWARD R. DUCHARME

FOCUS Question

How can the teacher qualities mentioned by the author be learned?

TERMS TO NOTE

Aesthetic

At-homeness

Teacher competencies

I begin this essay by defining a great teacher as one who influences others in positive ways so that their lives are forever altered, and then asking a question I have asked groups many times. How many teachers fitting that description have you had in your lifetime? It is rare for anyone to claim more than five in a lifetime; the usual answer is one or two.

I ask this question of groups whose members have at least master's degrees, often doctorates. They have experienced anywhere from eighty to one hundred or more teachers in their lifetimes and usually describe no more than 2% of them as great. Those voting are among the ones who stayed in school considerably longer than most people do; one wonders how many great teachers those dropping out in the 9th or 10th grade experience in their lifetimes. My little experiment, repeated many times over the years, suggests that the number of great teachers is very limited. They should be cherished and treasured because they are so rare; we should do all that we can to develop more of them.

This paper is purely speculative; no data corrupt it; no references or citations burden it. It began as I sat with a colleague at a meeting in 1987 in Washington; we were listening to a speaker drone on about the competencies teachers need. I asked my friend: "How would you like to write a paper about qualities great teachers have that do not lend themselves to competency measurements?" The proposed shared writing exercise did not get much beyond our talking about it the next couple of times we saw each other, but I have continued to speculate on these qualities as I have read, taught, studied, talked with others, and relived my own learning experiences.

The remarks result from years of being with teachers, students, and schools; of three decades of being a teacher; of five decades of being a learner. There is no science in the remarks, no cool, objective look at teaching. These are personal reflections and observations to provoke,

---

Edward R. Ducharme is a writer and consultant living in Brewster, Massachusetts.

to get some of us thinking beyond numbers, test scores, attendance rates, and demographics, to reflect on the notion of the Great Teacher.

I am weary of competencies even though I recognize the need for specific indicators that teachers possess certain skills and knowledge. I believe, however, that good teacher preparation programs do more than a reasonable job on these and are doing better and better. Three conditions lead me to believe that most future graduates of teacher education programs will be competent. First, the overall quality of teacher candidates is improving; second, there is a great deal more known about helping to develop people to the point where they are competent; third, the level of the education professoriate has improved dramatically. Thus, I think that *most* preparation programs will be graduating competent teachers. We should begin to worry about what lies beyond competency.

My interests extend beyond competencies to qualities that I see from time to time as I visit classrooms. Few teachers possess even several of the qualities I will describe—no great teacher lacks all of them. In the remainder of this paper, I will name and describe the qualities and show what these qualities might look like in prospective teachers.

1. Penchant for and Skill in Relating One Thing with Another with Another and with Another

John Donne, the 17th century English poet and cleric, once wrote "The new science calls all into doubt." He was referring to the Copernican contention that the earth is not the center of the universe, that humankind may not be the cynosure of divine interest, countering beliefs that the old Ptolemaic system of earthcenteredness had fostered.

Donne saw relationships among things not readily apparent to many others. He recognized a new truth cancelled another belief, one that had affected attitudes and actions among his fellow Christians for a long time, and would have a dramatic effect. He knew that if something held eternally true were suddenly shown to be false, conclusively false, then other things would be questioned; nothing would be steadfast.

Many of us do not see the implications and relationships among seemingly unrelated events, people, places, works of art, scientific principles. Some great teachers have the ability to see these relationships and, equally important, help others see them. Donne saw them. His collected sermons evidence the intellectual force of great teachers.

I once took a course in which John Steinbeck's *The Sea of Cortez* and *The Grapes of Wrath* were among the readings. *The Sea of Cortez* is Steinbeck's ruminations on the vast complexity and interrelatedness of life under the water; *The Grapes of Wrath,* his ruminations on the complexities of life on land, on what happens when a natural disaster combines with human ineptness and lack of concern, one for the other. The professor used a word not much in vogue in those ancient days: ecology. He defined it as the "interrelatedness of all living things." He raised questions about the relationships of these issues to the problems of New York City and its schools, as we sat in class in Memorial Lounge at Teachers College, Columbia.

E. D. Hirsch, in *Cultural Literacy: What Every American Needs to Know,* has a series of provocative listings under each letter of the alphabet. His point is that in order to grasp the meanings of words on pages, readers must know things not part of the page. Hirsch's book contains pages of items. Under the letter C, he lists caste, cool one's heels, *Crime and Punishment,* coral reef, and czar. One would "know" such things by studying sociology, language, literature, biology, and history or, perhaps equally often, simply by living for a period of time and reading newspapers, watching movies, and so forth. Hirsch's point is that when one hears a sentence like "He runs his business as though he were the czar," one would think of autocratic, harsh rule, tyranny, Russia, lack of human rights. Some might think of how the word is sometimes spelled tsar and wonder why. Others might think of the song about the czar/tsar from *Fiddler on the Roof,* while a few would think the person incapable of pronouncing the word tsar. Hirsch has in mind one kind of "relating one field to another": that which occurs when one sees a known reference and makes the associative leap.

Edna St. Vincent Millay, in her poem on Euclid's geometry, also drew associations from seemingly unrelated things. She saw the design and texture in poetry related to the design and texture of a geometric theorem. The quality described here is the same quality that Donne and Steinbeck manifested: seeing the interrelatedness of things.

What does that quality look like in prospective teachers? Sometimes it is the person who sees the connections between sociological and educational themes; sometimes, the person who wants to introduce students to the variety of language by teaching them about snowflakes and the vast number of words Eskimos have for them; sometimes, the person who understands mathematics through music, in fact, it may be the person who says mathematics is a kind of music or that music is a kind of mathematics.

2. Lack of Fondness for Closure or, Put Another Way, Fondness for Questions over Answers

Many of us are constantly on the lookout for answers to questions. For example, we might give a great deal to know the answer to the two-part question: What makes a great teacher and how do we produce one? Of course, the answer to the first part of the question depends on who is answering it. For someone in need of specific guidance at some point in life, the great teacher may be the one pointing the way to a different kind of existence, the one making the individual feel strong. To another person, confident about life, the great teacher may be the one raising questions, challenging, making the person wonder about certitudes once held dearly.

I teach Leadership and the Creative Imagination, a course designed as a humanities experience for doctoral students in educational administration. In the course, students read twelve novels and plays, discuss them effectively, and write about them in ways related to the leadership theory literature, their own experience, and the works themselves. In the fall semester of 1987, I had what has become a redundant experience. A student in the course stopped me in the hall after class one night in November. She said that she had taken the course because her advisor had said it would be a good experience for her. And, said she, she had truly enjoyed the early readings and the discussions. But now she found the readings troubling; they were causing her to question things she does, ways she relates to people, habits of thinking. She said that she was losing a sense of assuredness of what life was all about. The books, she said, just kept raising questions. "When do we get answers?" she asked.

We talked for a while, and I reminded her of a point I had made repeatedly during the first couple of classes: there are two kinds of books, answer books and question books. Writers of answer books raise provocative questions and then provide comfortable, assuring answers. Then there are the writers who raise the provocative issues—"Thou know'st 'tis common,—all that lives must die, passing through nature into eternity," (if you get the source of that, Hirsch will like you)—and then frustrate the reader looking for facile answers by showing that the realization in the statement prompts questions: Why must all that lives die? What does it mean to pass through nature into eternity? What or when is eternity? Are we supposed to know that all that lives must die?

The predisposition to raise questions is present in all of us to varying degrees. In young, prospective teachers, the predisposition takes on various shades and hues. They ask questions like: Why do some children learn more slowly than others? Tell me, why is that, whatever that may be, a better way to do it? But how do I know they learned it? In more mature prospective teachers coming back for a fifth year and certification, it might look different: Why is this more meaningful than that? Why should we teach this instead of that? Why does my experience teach me that this is wrong? What happens next? How do I know if this is right or wrong?

Persons with fondness for questions over answers recognize that most "answers" to complex questions are but tentative, that today's answers provoke tomorrow's uneasiness. As prospective teachers, they show a disrespect for finite answers to questions about human development, the limits of knowledge, the ways of knowing, the ways of doing. They itch to know even though they have begun to believe that they can never really know, that there is always another word to be said on every subject of consequence. Often, to answer-oriented teacher educators, these students are seen as hindrances instead of prospective great teachers. In truth, they stand the chance of provoking in their future students the quest to explore, to question, to imagine, to be comfortable with the discomfort of never "really knowing," of lifelong pursuit of knowledge.

3. Growing Knowledge, Understanding, and Commitment to Some Aspect of Human Endeavor; for Example, Science, Literature, Mathematics, or Blizzards

In the last several years, the point that teachers must know something before they can teach it has been made ad nauseam. We have admonitions from the Carnegie Forum to the Holmes Group to Secretary Bennett to the person on the street to all the teachers in the field who prepared with BS degrees in education all belaboring the obvious need for knowledge, albeit with a slightly different twist than the argument had the first twenty times around: teachers must have a bachelor's degree in an academic major before being admitted to a teacher preparation program.

But we all know that to know is not enough. Merely holding a bachelor of arts does not answer the question of the relationship between teacher and knowledge. What answers the question?

Teachers are rightfully and powerfully connected with knowledge when, even early in their learning careers, they begin to make metaphors to explain their existence, their issues and dilemmas, their joys and sorrows, from the knowledge they are acquiring. I speak not of that jaded notion of students being excited by what they are learning. I get excited watching a baseball game, but it doesn't have much meaning for me the next day. I mean something including and transcending excitement. Great teachers are driven by the power, beauty, force, logic, illogic, color, vitality, relatedness, uniqueness of what they know and love. They make metaphors from it to explain the world; they are forever trying to understand the thing itself, always falling a bit short yet still urging others on. They are the teachers who make learners think what is being taught has value and meaning and may actually touch individual lives.

This quality shows itself in a variety of ways in prospective teachers. Often, it is hidden because that which captures the imagination and interest of a student may not be part of the course, may have no way of being known. I have never forgotten a young woman in a class I taught fifteen years ago. She was a freshman in one of those horrible introduction to education courses. For the last assignment, each student in the class had to teach something to the class. This young woman, who had spoken, but rarely and only when challenged during the semester, asked if the class might go to the student lounge when her turn came. I agreed; we went as a group. There was a piano in the room and she proceeded to play a piece by Chopin and explain to the class why it was an important piece of music. I suspected—and subsequent discussions with her bore out my thought—that this young woman saw the world through music, that she could explain almost anything better if she could use music as the metaphor, the carrier of her thoughts.

Most of us do not have students in our classes capable of playing a piece by Chopin, but we all have students who understand the world through a medium different from what the rest of the group may be using. Experience has taught many young people to hide this quality because it is not honored in classrooms.

4. A Sense of the Aesthetic

The development of the aesthetic domain in young people is critical to their growth and development; it is a fundamental right. The ability to grasp the beautiful makes us human; to deny that to young people is to deny their humanity. Great teachers often have an acutely developed sense of the aesthetic; they are unafraid to show their fondness for beauty in front of young people; they do so in such a manner as to make the young people themselves value beauty and their own perceptions of it.

For many young people, the world is a harsh and barren place, devoid of beauty. But in every generation, there are those who emerge spiritually changed from their schooling experiences, eager to face what is at times a hostile world. The changes are sometimes the result of a teacher with a sense of the aesthetic, one able to see beyond the everydayness and blandness of institutional life.

In a world stultified by the commercial definitions of beauty, individuals preparing to teach with this embryonic sense of the aesthetic are rare. Our own jadedness and mass-produced tastes make it difficult for us to recognize this quality in students. What does it look like? In its evolutionary phases, it might be an impulse to make the secondary methods classroom more attractive; it might be a choice of book covers; it might be in the selection of course materials for young people; it might be in the habits of an individual. I'm uncertain as to its many forms, but I am quite certain that when we see it we should treasure its existence and support its development.

5. Willingness to Assume Risks

There are teachers who say the right things, prescribe the right books, associate with the right people, but never take risks on behalf of others, beliefs, and ideas, never do more than verbalize. They are hollow shams.

The quality of risk-taking of great teachers is subtle, not necessarily that which puts people on picket lines, at the barricades, although it might be. The quality is critical to teacher modeling, for great teachers go beyond the statement of principles and ideas, beyond the endorsement of the importance of friendships, as they move students from the consideration of abstract principles to the actualization of deeds.

The 1960s and 1970s were filled with risk-taking teachers. While neither praising nor disparaging these obvious examples, I urge other instances for consideration inasmuch as the "opportunity" for collective risk-taking is a rare occurrence in the lives of most of us. While it was not easy to be a risk-taker then, it wasn't very lonely either. Other instances, some more prosaic, abound: teachers in certain parts of the country who persist in teaching evolution despite pressure to desist, teachers who assign controversial books despite adverse criticism, teachers who teach the Civil War and the Vietnam War without partisanship or chauvinism. These quiet acts of risk-taking occur daily in schools and universities; they instruct students of the importance of ideas joined with actions.

I recall my high school art teacher who took abuse from the principal because she demanded the right for her students to use the gymnasium to prepare for a dance. He rebuked and embarrassed her in front of the students for "daring to question [my] authority." His act prompted some of us to go to the superintendent to complain about him; we got the gym. But we also each had a private interview with the principal in which he shared his scorn and derision for us for having "gone over [my] head to the superintendent." We learned that acting on principles is sometimes risky, that we had to support a teacher who took risks for us, that actions have consequences, that a "good" act like defending a brave teacher can lead to punishment. But her risk-taking led us to risk-taking on behalf of another person and the resolution of a mild injustice.

Detecting this quality in the young is difficult. The young often appear cause-driven and it is hard to distinguish when students are merely following a popular, low-risk cause and when they are standing for something involving personal decisions and risk. We might see it in its evolutionary form in some quite simple instances. Many teacher educators suffer the indignity of seeing their ideas and principles distorted by the wisdom of the workplace, of having their students grow disenchanted with what they have been taught as they encounter the world of the school: "We'll knock that Ivory Tower stuff out of you here. This is the *real* world." Of course, we all know some of it should be knocked out, but much of it should remain. It is a rare student who during practical, internship, and early years of teaching remains steadfast to such principles as: all student answers, honestly given, merit serious consideration; or worksheets are rarely good instructional materials. It is risky for young pre-professionals and beginning professionals to dispute the wisdom of the workplace and maintain fidelity to earlier acquired principles. Perhaps in these seemingly small matters lies the quality to be writ large during the full career.

6. At-Homeness in the World

Great teachers live effectively in what often seems a perverse world. Acutely aware of life's unevenness, the disparities in the distribution of the world's goods, talents, and resources, they cry out for justice in their own special ways while continuing to live with a sense of equanimity and contribute to the world. They demonstrate that life is to be lived as fully as one can despite problems and issues. They show that one can be a sensitive human being caring about and doing things about the problems and issues, and, at the same time, live a life of personal fulfillment. They are not overwhelmed by the insolubility of things on the grand scale, for they are able to make sense of things on the personal level.

I once had a professor for a course in Victorian poetry. In addition to his academic accomplishments, the professor was a fine gardener, each year producing a beautifully crafted flower garden, filled with design and beauty.

We were reading "In Memoriam," the part in which Tennyson refers to nature, red in tooth and claw. All of a sudden, the professor talked about how, that morning, while eating his breakfast, he had watched his cat stalk a robin, catch it, and devour part of it. He related the incident, of course, to the poem. (Clearly he had the quality alluded to earlier, the sense on interrelatedness of things.) I am uncertain what I learned about "In Memoriam" that morning, but I know I learned that this man who earlier in the semester had pointed out the delicate beauty of some of Tennyson's lyrics had integrated death into his life while remaining sensitive to beauty, to love. It was partly through him that I began to see that the parts of life I did not like were not to be ignored nor to be paralyzed about. All this in the death of a bird? No, all this in a powerful teacher's reaction to the death of a bird in the midst of life.

And what does at-homeness in the world look like in prospective teachers? I am quite uncertain, very tentative about this one. Perhaps it shows itself in a combination of things like joy in life one day and despair over life the next as the young slowly come to grips with the enigmas of life, its vicissitudes and sorrows. The young are often studies in extremes as they make order of life, of their lives. As a consequence, one sees a few students with vast energy both to live life and to anguish over its difficulties. But one cannot arrive at the point of my professor with his lovely garden and dead robin simultaneously entertained in his head without a sense of the joyful and the tragic in life, without a constant attempt to deal with the wholeness that is life, without a sense of being at home in the world.

All prospective teachers have touches of each of these qualities which should be supported and nurtured so that their presence is ever more manifest in classrooms. But a few students have some of these qualities writ large. Buttressed by programs that guarantee competency in instructional skills, these individuals have the potential to become great teachers themselves, to be the teachers who take the students beyond knowledge acquisition and skill development to questioning, to wondering, to striving. We must, first, find these prospective teachers, help them grow and develop, treasure them, and give them to the young people of America, each one of whom deserves several great teachers during thirteen years of public schooling.

And what has all this to do with the preparation of teachers? Surely, preparing teachers to be competent in providing basic instruction to as many students as possible is enough of a major task. Clearly, the raising of reading scores, of math achievement levels, of writing skills, of thinking processes are significant accomplishments. Of course, all these things must be accomplished, and teacher preparation programs around the country are getting better and better at these matters.

But we must have more; we must have an increase in the presence of greatness in the schools, in the universities. Love for a teacher's kindness, gratitude for skills acquired, fondness for teachers—these are critically important. But equally important is the possibility that students will encounter greatness, greatness that transcends the everydayness of anyplace, that invites, cajoles, pushes, drags, drives, brings students into the possibilities that questions mean more than answers; that knowledge is interrelated; that there is joy to be had from beauty; that knowledge can affect people to the cores of their being; that ideas find their worth in actions; that life is full of potential in a sometimes perverse world.

Postnote

Ducharme's article is provocative in its challenge to go beyond competence to reach for greatness in our teaching. The characteristics that he suggests embody greatness in teaching are difficult to challenge because they ring true. They also are formidable if we dare to want to become teachers who possess these characteristics.

In an effort to ensure that prospective teachers will be "safe to practice," many teacher educators focus their instruction on the knowledge and skills (competencies) new teachers will need to function effectively in classrooms. It may be a rare instance where the focus of teacher education is on what it will take to become a *great* teacher, not merely a *competent* one.

Discussion Questions

1. Is a particular kind of teacher preparation needed to produce great, rather than just competent, teachers? Or does a prospective teacher need to earn competence before greatness can be achieved? Explain your answers.
2. Think of the great teachers you have had. Did they possess the characteristics Ducharme describes? Briefly discuss what made these teachers great.
3. Can you think of any other characteristics that great teachers possess that were not identified by Ducharme? If so, what are they?

5

Can Star Teachers Create Learning Communities?

MARTIN HABERMAN

FOCUS Question

What qualities transform regular teachers into stars?

TERMS TO NOTE

Learning communities
Star teacher
Teacher voice

Successful schools share a number of attributes—good leadership, a common vision that makes a climate of learning the highest priority, teachers who use best practices, an effective accountability system, and parent involvement. An attribute less frequently discussed is the manner in which teachers and staff pursue their professional development. Would making the school a learning community—one that encourages teachers and staff to grow personally and professionally—benefit the students? Would a school with great teachers be more likely to become a learning community?

The well-known quip attributed to Will Rogers, usually quoted incompletely as "You can't teach what you don't know," is often applied to teachers who teach content in which they are less than expert. The entire aphorism, however, conveys a significantly different meaning: "You can't teach what you don't know *about places you ain't never been.*" The full message refers to experiential knowledge rather than content knowledge.

The pursuit of learning is not a piece of content that can be taught. It is a value that teachers model. Only teachers who are avid, internally motivated learners can truly teach their students the joy of learning. The frequently espoused goal of lifelong learning for our students is hollow rhetoric unless the school is also a learning community in which teachers demonstrate engagement in meaningful learning activities. Teachers who are not "turned on" to learning themselves are trying to teach about "places they ain't never been."

A group is a learning community when members share a common vision that learning is the primary purpose for their association and the ultimate value to preserve in their workplace and that learning outcomes are the primary criteria for evaluating the success of their work. In a school learning community, teachers pursue two realms of

---

Martin Haberman is Distinguished Professor in the Department of Curriculum and Instruction, School of Education, University of Wisconsin-Milwaukee. "Can Star Teachers Create Learning Communities?" by Martin Haberman, *Educational Leadership,* May 2004, pp. 52–56. Reprinted by permission. The Association for Supervision and Curriculum Development is a worldwide community of educators advocating sound policies and sharing best practices to achieve the success of each learner. To learn more, visit ASCD at **www.ascd.org.**

knowledge: professional development and learning for the sake of learning. The importance of the former is self-evident. As for the latter, inculcating love of learning is the surest way of teaching students to become turned-on learners. Students will model behavior of teachers they respect—teachers who have strong interests, who love to learn, and who are always reading something of interest.

Attributes of a Learning Community

During the first four years of my career as a university faculty member, I had the special privilege of participating in a community of learners. The following attributes of that learning community have applications in both primary and secondary school environments:

- *Modeling.* In guiding student learning and development, teachers applied the same principles that guided their own learning and development.
- *Continual sharing of ideas.* Teachers shared ideas daily regarding vital issues of equity, instruction, curriculum, testing, school organization, and the value of specific kinds of knowledge.
- *Collaboration.* Teachers became involved in team teaching and other collaborative efforts in program development, writing, and research.
- *Egalitarianism.* Teachers dispensed with formalities. Anyone who took an interest could vote in a department meeting, especially students. The quality of ideas was more important than their source.
- *High productivity.* Teachers continually increased their workloads. No matter how high the output, they continually pressured themselves to create new programs, develop new courses, publish books and articles, and produce more research.
- *Community.* Faculty members valued community more than promotion. Finding a more stimulating learning community became the criterion that guided the movement of faculty to various institutions.
- *Practical applications.* Teachers asked themselves, "How does what we are doing help students, teachers, and schools? What did we do this week to help?"

Assuming that these seven attributes adequately describe a learning community, how can we develop such a community? And what role would star teachers play in transforming schools into learning communities?

Attributes of Star Teachers

The term *star teachers* designates teachers who are so effective that the adverse conditions of working in failing schools or school districts do not prevent them from being successful teachers. They make up approximately 8 percent of the teachers who work with seven million diverse low-income students in the United States. Several characteristics set them apart (Haberman, 1995/2004): their persistence, their physical and emotional stamina, their caring relationships with students, their commitment to acknowledging and appreciating student effort, their willingness to admit mistakes, their focus on deep learning, their commitment to inclusion, and their organization skills. They also protect student learning, translate theory and research into practice, cope with the bureaucracy, create student ownership, engage parents and caregivers as partners in student learning, and support accountability for at-risk students.

These attributes predict the effectiveness and staying power of teachers serving diverse students in low-income urban schools. More than 170 urban school districts in the United States now use the Star Teacher Interview, which evaluates these attributes, as part of their teacher hiring process (Haberman, 2004).

Star Teacher Ideology

Undergirding these attributes is the common ideology of star teachers.

- *Stars tend to be nonjudgmental.* As they interact with students and adults in school settings, star teachers try to understand the motivation behind a given behavior rather than judge the behavior.

- *Stars are not moralistic.* Star teachers know that preaching and lecturing do not equate to teaching and that those approaches neither influence behavior nor increase students' desire to learn.
- *Stars respond as professionals and are not easily shocked.* Horrific events occur in urban schools with some regularity. Star teachers ask themselves, "What can I do about this?" If they can help, they take action. If not, they get on with their work and their lives. They respond to emotionally charged situations as thoughtful professionals.
- *Stars hear what students and adults say to them.* Star teachers listen and understand. They have exceedingly sensitive communication skills. They regard everyone in the school community as a potential source of useful information.
- *Stars recognize and compensate for their weaknesses.* Star teachers are aware of their weaknesses in terms of a lack of knowledge or skills or in terms of their own biases and prejudices. They strive to overcome them.
- *Stars do not see themselves as saviors.* Star teachers have not come to rescue the system. Actually, they do not expect much from the system—except for the likelihood that it may worsen. They focus on making their students successful in spite of the system.
- *Stars do not work in isolation.* Star teachers know that burnout can affect everyone. They network and create their own support groups.
- *Stars view themselves as successful professionals rescuing students.* Star teachers see themselves as "winning" even though they know that their total influence on their students is likely to be less than that of the society, neighborhood, or even gang. They take pride in turning students on to learning and making them educationally successful in the midst of failed urban school systems.
- *Stars derive energy and well-being from their interactions with students.* Star teachers so enjoy being with students that they are even willing to put up with irrational demands of the system. Rather than always feeling exhausted, they often feel vitalized and energized from a day at work.
- *Stars see themselves as teachers of children as well as of content.* Star teachers want to encourage their students to become better people, not just higher achievers.
- *Stars are learners.* Star teachers are models of learning for students because they are vitally interested in some subject matter or avocation that keeps them continually learning.
- *Stars have no need for power.* Star teachers derive their satisfaction from effectively teaching diverse low-income students.
- *Stars recognize the imperative of student success.* Star teachers see the need for diverse low-income students to succeed in school as a matter of life and death for the students and for the survival of society.

Teacher Voice

Star teachers are avid learners. The challenge is getting them to actively participate in a schoolwide learning community. Their motivation for becoming teachers generally has little to do with serving as change agents or transforming schools. Stars will not necessarily assume leadership roles in this regard because they focus on their students. Although they seek to get along with colleagues, work positively as team members, and share their expertise when asked, they prefer to put their time to use working with individual students, gathering interesting learning materials, making home visits, and pursuing the particular interests and avocations they value. They will need to be convinced that their participation in schoolwide activities will directly benefit their students.

What will *not* convince them to participate are learning communities that they perceive have been created with an agenda, such as one that tries to convince teachers that they need the "Bumstead" reading program or the "Surefire Method" of instruction. If administrators have teachers meet to learn primarily about the mandates that the teachers need to follow, then the creation of a learning community will be stillborn.

A learning community is based on the assumption that developing the faculty is a necessary condition of school improvement. If the district or building administration operates on the assumption that teacher-proof programs can improve schools, then star teachers will detach themselves from the process. Star teachers need to be convinced that the faculty will have the major voice in determining its own professional development. This is a step-by-step trust-building process involving teachers and their school administrators. The school administration must also show genuine willingness to live with and support the results of the freedom that teachers must exercise to create a school-based learning community.

When Stars Steal the Show

Stars care about and respect students—even students whom other teachers cannot handle and do not want in their classrooms. For example, stars do not suspend students unless the law requires them to do so (for example, when a student brings a gun to school). At schools that suspend more than half of their students during the course of the school year, the positive relationships between stars and their students become obvious.

Stars do not follow mandates if they believe that the mandates will hurt student learning. Stars do not follow curriculums page by page because their expertise in the subjects they teach gives them the confidence to know what to skip. Stars do not "cover" material but rather focus their teaching on generating interest and relevance.

These teacher behaviors do not go unnoticed by other teachers and administrators. Individual teachers or teacher committees often come to principals demanding to know, "If we have to do this, why doesn't he or she [the star teacher] have to?" In middle and high schools, where each student has many teachers, a star's success with students whom other teachers are failing can become a source of faculty dissension. Other teachers often have a difficult time accepting that stars are successful and happy about their work when they themselves may be experiencing great stress and discouragement. Indeed, teachers often feel pressured by the presence of stars. The star's success makes other teachers' failures all the more obvious. The failure may be one of inadequate professional know-how, a lack of teacher effort, or the teachers' inability to establish positive working relationships with students.

Using star teachers in ways that help the school can be a challenge for principals. In many schools, the principal may be reluctant to provide stars with "space" because their success could reveal the principal's inadequacy at providing professional development activities that will bring the rest of the staff up to the stars' level. The principal must also deal with parents who want their children in star teachers' classrooms and with grievances from teachers who are concerned that stars may not be following school regulations, such as requiring silence in the lunchroom or suspending students for first-time infractions. Unfortunately, it is easier to pander to the majority than to protect the best practices of the stars. Principals sometimes even feel pressured to drive stars out, typically by assigning them to teach subjects for which they are unprepared.

The challenge to the principal, or to those seeking to create a learning community, is to use star teachers in unobtrusive, supportive ways that do not threaten the rest of the faculty and continuously remind them of their inadequacies. School administrators could use star teachers as committee members but without singling them out or designating them as chairpersons or faculty leaders. Administrators should let star teachers remain in their classrooms rather than removing them to become mentors or coaches. Star teachers should also work on the same agreed-on activities that the other teachers work on. And administrators should never request teachers to observe star teachers' classrooms unless the teachers themselves request it. Stars can have a positive impact if other teachers see that the stars are not seeking promotions out of their classrooms and are not trying to control the behavior of their peers.

School leaders must also recognize that the battle is for the hearts and minds of the teachers in the middle. This is the group that leaders must reach for the school to truly become a learning community. These are the satisfactory teachers who represent approximately 40 percent of the faculty. This middle group is as susceptible to becoming discouraged and accepting failure as they are to emulating the more positive approach of the stars.

A Portrait of Success

What if all teachers in a school were star teachers? What impact would it have on student achievement? Two failing elementary schools whose faculties were to be reconstituted provided us with the answer. One school serves low-income students of Mexican descent in Texas; the other serves predominantly low-income African American students in a depressed urban area in New York State. Using the Star Teacher Selection Interview to identify star ideology and attributes, we hired only those teachers who passed the interview. We scored candidate responses in terms of how closely they mirrored the star teacher approach. Only a small percentage passed at the star level. The principals for these reconstituted schools also needed to pass the Star Administrator Selection Interview.

These schools, which had been designated as failing, were moved out of that category within a year. The school in Texas actually became one of the highest-achieving schools in the district within this short period. Highly effective teachers, led by an effective principal, can clearly close the achievement gap.

In an in-depth study of the two schools, I identified more than 30 factors that contributed directly or indirectly to creating a learning community. For example, all the teachers focused on effort rather than ability as their explanation for school success. The teachers saw effective instruction as a matter of life and death for students. Moreover, the teachers *expected* to have problems as part of their daily work. They viewed working with English language–limited students and inclusion students as an integral, not an extra, part of their jobs. And they accepted accountability for student achievement.

The learning communities that developed in these two schools were not based on teachers necessarily liking one another, or even agreeing with one another's philosophies and methods. Teachers did mutually respect one another, however, because they firmly believed that they all put the learning of the students above the convenience of the adults. Teachers did not blame the students for not learning, nor did they define their jobs in terms of the legally required minimums. Rather, teachers defined their roles in terms of "whatever it takes" to solve the problems. Selecting both veteran teachers and beginners with star ideology created a climate that provided continual opportunities for teachers to pursue their own learning and model their commitment to learning for their students (Haberman, 1999).

At the start of the school year, the teachers trusted my contention that if they pursued these practices rather than teach for the tests, test scores would take care of themselves. And the test scores did just that. The faculty came to regard the achievement tests as minimum, not maximum, levels of what their students could achieve.

Looking to the Future

On the basis of what I have observed in approximately 200 failing school districts during the last 50 years, I can make a number of predictions. First, working conditions in schools will most likely worsen rather than improve. Second, the next generation of principals will spring from the same internal pools as the current generation and will most likely not experience greater success. Last, transformers seeking to change the culture of schools using teacher-proof methods and programs will not create learning communities.

There are effective schools in every failing district that have, against all odds, created a learning community that functions to some degree. Moreover, a great opportunity exists to create viable learning communities in schools that must be reconstituted by law or reconstituted as charter schools within the same public school district.

It makes little sense to work harder and longer at replicating strategies for changing school culture that have consistently failed in the past. What is worthy of replication is building the culture of a school that will foster and maintain a learning community, with teachers whose ideology continually moves them down the road toward becoming stars.

References

Haberman, M. (1995/2004). *Star teachers of children in poverty.* Houston, TX: Haberman Educational Foundation.

Haberman, M. (1999). Victory at Buffalo Creek: What makes a school serving Hispanic children in poverty successful? *Instructional Leader, 17*(2).

Haberman, M. (2004). Creating effective schools in failed urban districts. *Myriad.* University of Wisconsin-Milwaukee.

Postnote

Haberman makes several telling points. Among them are the several qualities that designate a truly outstanding teacher, a star teacher, from the rest. However, if teachers are to function as stars, it seems essential that they be recognized as professionals, and professionals, by definition, have some degree of control over their environment. Haberman reminds us that "the teacher voice" is crucial in gaining this sense of sharing in control. Teacher voice is not a matter of being a prima donna or winning a struggle to control what goes on in a school. It is having a voice in what goes on. Without that sense of being listened to, of being recognized as a professional, teachers become functionaries and tend to dry up.

Discussion Questions

1. Review the list of star qualities. Are there any you would add? Any that, in your opinion, do not belong?
2. In your schooling, have you encountered any real star teachers? Describe them.
3. Although star qualities are impressive, aren't some stars eccentric and quirky?

Lessons of a First-Year Teacher

MOLLY NESS

FOCUSQuestion

What can we learn from the difficulties and failures of others?

Term to Note

Teach For America

When I graduated from college, I joined Teach For America and so committed the next two years of my life to teaching in one of the nation's most underresourced school districts. Now part of the AmeriCorps service program, Teach For America has a clear mission: to give every child—regardless of race, ethnicity, background, or religion—the opportunity to attain an excellent education. Founded a decade ago, Teach For America places more than 800 college graduates every year in impoverished school districts in such urban areas as Baltimore, Los Angeles, and New York City and in such rural areas as the Mississippi Delta and the Rio Grande Valley. Teach For America teachers fill vacancies in districts that suffer from teacher shortages, most often taking the most challenging placements in the most difficult schools.

Corps members go through an intensive five-week training program before they are placed in schools. In that training, they focus on theories of education, holding children to high expectations, practical ways of becoming an effective teacher, and leveling the playing field for students who lack the educational opportunities that children from better backgrounds take for granted. Corps members are hired directly by school districts, and many complete state credentialing programs during their two years of service. Upon the completion of their two-year commitment, more than 60% of corps members continue teaching, while the others change paths and move on to graduate school or to other forms of employment.

In my first year of teaching, I was assigned to Roosevelt Middle School in East Oakland, California, an extremely overcrowded school with an annual teacher retention rate of just 60%. The student body is 50% Asian, 25% Latino, and 25% African American. Roosevelt is located in a rough area that is notorious for drug use, and gangs are an ever-present force. Most of my students were not native speakers of English.

At the time this article was written, **Molly Ness** was a second-year teacher at Roosevelt Middle School, Oakland, California. Molly Ness, "Lessons of a First-Year Teacher," *Phi Delta Kappan,* May 2001.

Indeed, in that first year, my students spoke 10 languages, including Arabic, Cambodian, Spanish, Vietnamese, and Chinese. Many were recent immigrants, and I was expected to teach them conversational and written English, as well as the state-mandated social studies curriculum.

Although I had been told before I began my Teach For America commitment that I was about to experience a harsher reality than anything I had previously known, I still believed that teaching was a 9-to-3 job and that I could leave my work at school and keep my personal and professional lives totally separate. I thought I could bring my students into my classroom, shut the door, and leave the problems of their inner-city community outside. I believed that I could instill the love of learning in my students and that they would somehow be able to forget all the turmoil they faced in their lives.

I vowed that my passion and enthusiasm for my children and for teaching would never diminish. I would never allow myself to suffer emotionally, as many first-year teachers do. I would stay positive and avoid the disillusionment that so many teachers feel. I would enter my classroom every day with the same energy and passion I started with in September. It wouldn't matter if it was a gloomy Thursday in late October or if I had been battling the flu for two weeks. I would never become the "worksheet teacher." Rather than slide grammar worksheets under my students' noses, I would have them build the pyramids out of sugar cubes. I set high expectations not only for my students, but for myself as well.

In one swift transformation, I graduated from college, packed my belongings, and drove across the country to start life anew in an entirely unfamiliar environment, without the comforts of family, friends, and home. It was an exciting adventure at first—relocating, getting my first real job, and having the responsibilities of adult life.

But by early November, the excitement had worn off, and the reality had begun to sink in. I was living in a new city, far from my home and with no connections to my past. Maintaining a positive learning environment in an otherwise depressing place was an endless challenge: the constant planning, the discipline, the paperwork, the headaches of the district bureaucracy. I felt underappreciated by my administration and abused by my students. I would come home from school, sit on my couch, and think, "I can't go back tomorrow." I felt drained. And gradually I felt that I was letting my students down; nothing I was doing in my classroom could ever be enough to make life fair for them. I was becoming the worksheet teacher that I swore I would never be. I felt that I had lost myself in this process of trying to serve my students. And so I started asking the really hard questions, about myself, about my life, and about my commitment.

Often I feel that Teach For America is too eager to dismiss the frustrations we teachers inevitably feel about our lives and our jobs. It sometimes seems as if I am just supposed to grin and bear it through the two years. Then I can pause to reflect on my experience and say, "That was an impossibly difficult experience, but I am a richer person because of it."

Given the passion and dedication of most corps members, it seems taboo to question your commitment to Teach For America and to your students. But, in fact, I question my commitment nearly every day. I have a vivid memory of calling a friend in Los Angeles, a corps member placed in Compton, to ask, "Will you quit with me?" At first I thought that doubting my commitment made me a bad person, that some omniscient Teach For America presence was frowning down on me. In fact, maybe all this questioning of my commitment is actually a positive force that makes me push to achieve more in my classroom.

When I went home for the winter break that first year, I wasn't sure exactly what to tell my friends and family about my Teach For America experience. Should I focus on the good or the bad of teaching? Should I tell them how I teach 97 students who speak little or no English? Should I tell them how there are never enough markers or scissors or even textbooks to go around? Should I tell them of my 12-year-old student who is now serving time in juvenile hall for armed robbery? Or maybe I should tell them about my 13-year-old student who cannot spell *dog* because he is a victim of social promotion.

Slowly I realized that I was mouthing platitudes that were simply untrue to the experience. I could barely make sense of the tension of opposites I felt in my life: Did I want to quit and get out, or did I want to devote all my life and energy to the vision of Teach For America? How should I characterize the way I felt, cynicism or optimism? Should I dwell on the bad experiences or dismiss them in light of the positive ones?

I began to reflect on my initial impressions of teaching. I remembered feeling overwhelmed on first entering the classroom. How would I ever begin to teach these children English and social studies? More important, how could I teach them that education could be their way out of poverty and into a better future? How could I teach them to be upstanding citizens and to practice civility in their everyday lives? How could I teach them conflict resolution, responsibility, and self-respect? When I told my father about my worries, he told me, "Do your best. You have been handed an unrealistic situation. All that anybody can ask you to do is your best. Don't beat yourself up over what you cannot accomplish."

For a long time, I believed my father's advice. I believed that I did face an unrealistic situation at Roosevelt Middle School. I believed that it was unrealistic to think that a first-year teacher could handle such a difficult placement, in such an underresourced school, with so little support.

But after a while, I came to realize that my father had it backwards. My situation was realistic—and that was exactly the problem. Far too many of our nation's children attend overcrowded schools like Roosevelt that cannot provide adequate materials, instruction, or attention. Too many of our children receive a subpar education, which seems to ensure that the cycle of poverty will not soon be broken. Too many teachers are thrown into classrooms with minimal support. In such circumstances, teachers do not receive enough concrete incentives to make teaching a lifelong profession. Our best teachers are often lost before they even start to achieve success in the classroom. It is no secret that teachers are overworked, underpaid, and underappreciated; I am living proof of that.

Upon completing my first year of teaching, I struggled to make sense of the lessons that I had learned. I truly believe that I have learned more about the world in a year of teaching than I did in several years of college.

I have learned that children are unbelievably resilient. My students have been handed immeasurable challenges and have tackled them with the courage, grace, and strength that many adults fail to demonstrate. I have learned how to make personal sacrifices for the sake of a greater good. I have learned that many people in the world today would rather let schools in places like Oakland be forgotten than try to solve the problems head-on. I have learned that it is rather easy to be idealistic in thoughts and words, but much harder to keep that idealism alive in actions every day. I have realized that not enough people in our society today devote their lives, their energy, and their souls to making this world a little better than they found it. I have learned the meaning and value of humility. And last, I have learned that I am only one person, but my power as a teacher will extend further than I could ever have guessed.

Postnote

Teach For America is based on one of those ideas that have a great deal of surface appeal. It is a quick and rather painless way to get into a classroom after going through only brief training. The program is filled with bright and idealistic people like Molly Ness, the author of this article. And, of course, we are sure that it is a great idea for some people. On the other hand, it leads many young, potentially gifted teachers into a swamp that they are totally unprepared to handle. And while this may be enormously disappointing to the young teachers involved, what about the students? What about the third-grader who only has one "third grade" and has to spend it with a teacher who is not up to the task? What about the minority high school freshman who needs a solid basis in algebra to fulfill a dream of becoming an engineer? While their ill-prepared teacher is crashing and burning, so are their opportunities.

What makes teacher preparation difficult (along with most professional training) is that the trainees all have different needs, different background experiences, and different learning styles, and are going out to apply what they learn in vastly different environments. A certain amount of seemingly unnecessary information and overtraining is part of all professional training. On the other hand, quick fixes and crash programs may be extremely costly for both prospective teachers and particularly their future students.

Discussion Questions

1. Have you ever had a teacher who was clearly incompetent? What were the causes? What were the effects?
2. What was the advice the author received from her father? Do you believe it was the right advice? Why or why not?
3. Which of the problems encountered by the author do you believe you might be vulnerable to? What can you do about it now?

School's Out

CLAUDIA GRAZIANO

FOCUS Question

Nearly half of all new teachers leave the job within five years. What is killing their spirit? How can we get them to stay?

It was late August four years ago when I sat down at a scratched wooden desk to begin my first teaching position. I was nervous. I knew that the job, if done right, wouldn't be easy. There would be long hours and little pay. But I also hoped that I could inspire kids the way my best teachers had inspired me.

What I didn't know then was that I wouldn't make it. Less than a year after facing my first classroom of 32 fidgeting tenth graders, I walked away and never came back—to that classroom or to teaching. I became a statistic.

I entered the teaching profession full of idealism. After years of working as a journalist, covering the frenetic worlds of business and technology, I felt professionally unsatisfied. I spent my days writing about underconceived companies and overpaid CEOs. I spent hours hyping the latest gadgets.

My roommate, a high school math teacher, suggested I sit in on a few of her classes. They were raucous, open, and energetic; I was fascinated. I had always loved language, and I saw teaching as a way to help kids appreciate it—perhaps even love it—as well.

By fall 2001, I made the career switch, completed much of my licensing credential, and was hired to teach tenth-grade English at Sequoia High School, in Redwood City, California, about 20 miles south of San Francisco. By the new year, I was gone.

Leaving So Soon?

Every year, U.S. schools hire more than 200,000 new teachers for that first day of class. By the time summer rolls around, at least 22,000 have quit. Even those who make it beyond the trying first year aren't likely to stay long: about 30 percent of new teachers flee the profession after just three years, and more than 45 percent leave after five. (See Figure 1.)

Claudia Graziano is a writer based in San Francisco. "School's Out," by Claudia Graziano, *Edutopia*, February/March 2005, pp. 38–44. Reprinted by permission.

FIGURE 1

First Years Are the Toughest

Percentage of teachers leaving the profession each year (approximate)

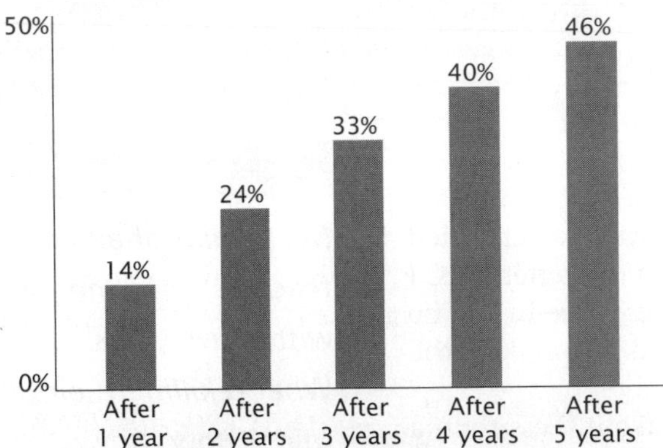

Source: Richard Ingersoll, cited in "No Dream Denied: A Pledge to America's Children," by the National Commission on Teaching and America's Future and the National Center for Education Statistics.

What's more, 37 percent of the education workforce is over 50 and considering retirement, according to the National Education Association. Suddenly, you've got a double whammy: tens of thousands of new teachers leaving the profession because they can't take it anymore, and as many or more retiring.

When teachers drop out, everyone pays. Each teacher who leaves costs a district $11,000 to replace, not including indirect costs related to schools' lost investment in professional development, curriculum, and school-specific knowledge. At least 15 percent of K–12 teachers either switch schools or leave the profession every year, so the cost to school districts nationwide is staggering—an estimated $5.8 billion.

Students from the lowest-income families suffer the most. Inexperienced teachers (those with less than three years on the job) frequently land in classrooms with the neediest and often the most challenging students. Beginning teachers frequently start their careers at hard-to-staff schools where resources may be scarce—in other words, urban schools—simply because there are more jobs available there.

It's a recipe for disaster for both teachers and students, says Barnett Berry, president of the Southeast Center for Teaching Quality, in Chapel Hill, North Carolina. Low-performing schools in high-poverty areas often cannot retain a critical mass of veteran teachers, says Berry. "Not only are teachers who are new to these schools more likely to be underprepared, they're also more likely to be underqualified."

The U.S. Department of Education confirms that teacher turnover is highest in public schools where half or more of the students receive free or reduced-price lunches. In California, for example, students in schools with large minority populations are five times more likely to face an "underprepared" teacher (someone working on an emergency credential or outside of the person's subject area) than are students in schools with low percentages of minority students, according to a study conducted by SRI International and sponsored by the Center for the Future of Teaching and Learning in conjunction with California State University and the University of California.

A Frazzling First Year

Teachers quit for several reasons, but the one you'd expect to be at the top of the list—salary—typically isn't. Even though they start their careers earning roughly $30,000 (and fork out, on average, about $500 of their own money for instructional supplies), less than 20 percent of teachers who change schools or leave the profession cite salary as their primary job complaint, according to the National Center for Education Statistics.

More frequently, the reason is dissatisfaction with administrative support (38 percent) or workplace conditions (32 percent), according to the NCES's 2001 survey of 8,400 public- and private-school teachers. Poor administrative support, lack of influence within the school system, classroom intrusion, and inadequate time are mentioned more often by teachers leaving low-income schools where working conditions are more stressful; salary is mentioned more often by teachers leaving affluent schools.

Many of these reasons are just euphemisms for one of the profession's hardest realities: Teaching can exact a considerable emotional toll. I don't know of any other professionals who have to break up fistfights, as I did, as a matter of course, or who find razor blades left on their chair, or who feel personally responsible because students in tenth-grade English class are reading at the sixth-grade level or lower and are failing hopelessly.

New teachers, however naive and idealistic, often know before they enter the profession that the salaries are paltry, the class sizes large, and the supplies scant. What they don't know is how little support from parents, school administrators, and colleagues they can expect once the door is closed and the textbooks are opened.

"We don't put attorneys just out of law school alone on their first case, yet we put new teachers alone in the classroom for their first year and expect them to shoulder the same responsibilities as veteran teachers," says Kathleen Fulton, director for reinventing schools for the 21st century at the National Commission on Teaching and America's Future. "Our induction model creates impossibly high expectations."

New teachers are expected to assume a full schedule of classes, create their own lesson plans, and develop teaching techniques and classroom-management strategies in relative isolation. They are also expected to learn quickly the administrative ins and outs of the job, from taking attendance and communicating with parents to navigating the schools' computer network and finding the faculty bathrooms. The result: New teachers must weather a frazzling first year that many veterans come to view as a rite of passage. It's also a recipe for early burnout. Attrition rates for beginning teachers who have not had strong teacher-preparation programs are much higher than for better-prepared colleagues. (See Wanted: Better Training.)

"Not a day went by that I didn't go home and cry," remembers fourth-grade teacher Sue Manley of her first year. Manley, who graduated from Northwestern University with a master's degree in education, thought she was well prepared for her first assignment, teaching at a South Side Chicago elementary school. She had completed her student teaching the previous year at a grammar school in the same neighborhood and had spent four months volunteering as a classroom aide at another urban elementary school. Working with experienced teachers while she was still a graduate student and a volunteer had made teaching look easy to Manley. "Academically, I was prepared. Socially, professionally, and emotionally, I was not."

Like any new teacher, Manley needed to hone her classroom-management skills, but the pressures of managing a classroom solo for the

Wanted: Better Training

Many educators believe that schools need to completely rethink the way new teachers are trained. "One of the real problems with schools today is that they're the schools we had yesterday," says Kathleen Fulton, the director for reinventing schools in the 21st century for the National Commission on Teaching and America's Future (NCTAF). "The existing training and recruitment model doesn't work for kids or teachers. Collaboration is key to developing good teaching skills, yet we're not set up for that in today's classrooms."

The answer, Fulton says, lies in radical change. She envisions clusters of new teachers working together in the classroom or alongside more-experienced teachers and under the supervision of a national-board-certified teacher.

Progress is being made toward that goal. The NCTAF is developing online learning communities that support novice teachers in rural and urban school districts. Called Teachers Learning in Networked Communities (T-LINC), the project will first target school districts in Washington, Colorado, Texas, and Maine. The idea is to bring together—at least virtually—new teachers, experienced mentors, and faculty members from institutions of higher learning to ensure that educators at all levels participate in the professional-development and mentoring process. —*C.G.*

first time were compounded by the lack of basic resources and administrative support. "We weren't allowed to use the copy machine [for handouts], so I had to stop at Kinko's every morning on my way to work," she explains. "There was never any toilet paper in the bathrooms for the kids, so I had to bring that, too." The last straw for Manley came in April, when she read a student's journal entry that described violent acts directed at her.

While Manley's situation may seem extreme, it's far from unusual. Other new teachers have reported similar feelings of isolation and impossible expectations.

"The amount of time I put into teaching was huge, and I still felt overwhelmed," says Pam Zabel, a former high school science teacher in Charleston, Rhode Island. Zabel, who holds a master's degree in education, says she was assigned a mentor teacher who was theoretically there for support and professional coaching, "but it was a very unstructured relationship—I met with him maybe two or three times during the school year. For the most part, I was on my own." Zabel left teaching after her first year and is now a full-time mom.

"Mentally draining" is how Jim Treman, a former ninth-grade science teacher, remembers his induction to teaching. "I had no life for two years. I was constantly working. By the time Fridays rolled around, I was dead."

Treman worked as an architect for ten years prior to entering the single-subject credential program at San Francisco State University. His decision to become a teacher grew out of an experience he'd had teaching English while traveling in South America. He completed his student teaching as an intern, working as a full-time teacher while earning his credential. "I was reluctant to take the position at first because I had no clue what I was doing," says Treman. "I was promised a ton of support, which in the end turned out to be completely untrue. I was totally on my own."

Treman struggled to motivate his students; his assigned mentor, a physical education teacher, was unable to offer Treman curriculum guidance. Other science teachers seemed unwilling to share their materials. The school district's policy of laying off teachers in the spring and rehiring them in the fall didn't help. After his second year of teaching, Treman returned to architecture.

It Started Out So Well

Zabel and Treman, like me, were on their own. I always chalked up my experience to a bad case of unrealistic expectations. Maybe I was too spoiled by the fat and happy corporate world. Maybe I shouldn't have thought I would enjoy teaching my first year.

But as a student teacher, I'd had a very positive experience. I had taught language arts to seventh graders at a middle school in the upscale suburbs of San Francisco, and I was fortunate enough to have had an excellent mentor teacher. I designed what I considered to be fun, innovative lessons. I invited journalist friends to talk to the class about the persuasive power of writing. I organized grammar games and spelling contests. I brought in music from the '30s to illustrate the concept of story setting. I researched yoga and breathing exercises to help students take the edge off pretest jitters. (The entire class broke up laughing as we all tried to balance on one leg before the SAT-9s.)

But when the semester was over, Taylor Middle School wasn't hiring. Through my university's placement program, I landed a position at Sequoia. During the interview, the principal (who would be gone by that fall, along with the vice principal) told me my limited experience teaching seventh grade was "perfect" for teaching tenth grade at Sequoia. I was so naive that I didn't even ask why.

He promised plenty of support, recounted plans for a week-long new-teacher induction program before the school year started, and described the school building's recent remodel. I was given the names and phone numbers of two other English teachers willing to serve as my mentors that first year.

In practice, the induction program turned out to be something of a pep rally for new teachers, not a training exercise. The mentor teachers who had promised to help did what they could but were either teaching different grade levels or classes, and once the semester got under way had their own teaching concerns to address. In the end, I stopped asking for help. I was sinking, yet no one in the administration noticed. The principal, a former English teacher, observed my classes a few times and offered tips on my woefully underdeveloped classroom-management style, but she seemed unconcerned by my obvious lack of experience.

She told me not to worry and that tenth grade is the year when students who aren't going to succeed drop out. "High school is still a novelty for them in 9th grade," she said. "By 11th grade, those that are left are the ones who've decided they want to graduate."

I didn't know what to make of that. Was I teaching students who were expected to drop out? As the semester progressed and I watched students struggle through assignments that were clearly beyond their ability, I grew more anxious and disheartened. I came home at the semester break and camped out on the sofa for three days, depressed and despondent. When the semester resumed, I emailed the principal my resignation.

Support Systems

There are some effective ways to soften the coarseness of the first year. What made the difference for Manley, for example, was a free two-year induction program sponsored by the University of Chicago's Center for Urban School Improvement. The New Teachers Network offers first- and second-year teachers at Chicago public schools personalized mentoring and online coaching that addresses a variety of issues, from classroom management to curriculum.

Several studies (and common sense) show that good mentoring programs can cut attrition rates by as much as half. Richard Ingersoll, a professor at the University of Pennsylvania and a respected researcher in the field of education, analyzed statistics from ten studies on mentoring and teacher induction to sort out what works and why. (See Figure 2.)

His analysis, published in the *American Educational Research Journal* last summer, concludes that new teachers who receive no induction are twice as likely to leave teaching after their first year as those who receive all six of the supports his study identifies. These supports include having a mentor from the same field, collaborating regularly with other teachers in the same subject, and being part of an external network of teachers.

Other successful induction methods include a program called INTIME (Integrating New Technologies into the Methods of Education), which provides teacher candidates with videos of accomplished teachers in the classroom. The teachers in the videos give lessons in a variety of contexts, including multiage classrooms, alternative high schools, special education students, and gifted and talented programs. Such preparation can drastically cut teacher attrition rates. For

FIGURE 2

Teacher Preparation Reduces Attrition of First-Year Teachers (2000–01)

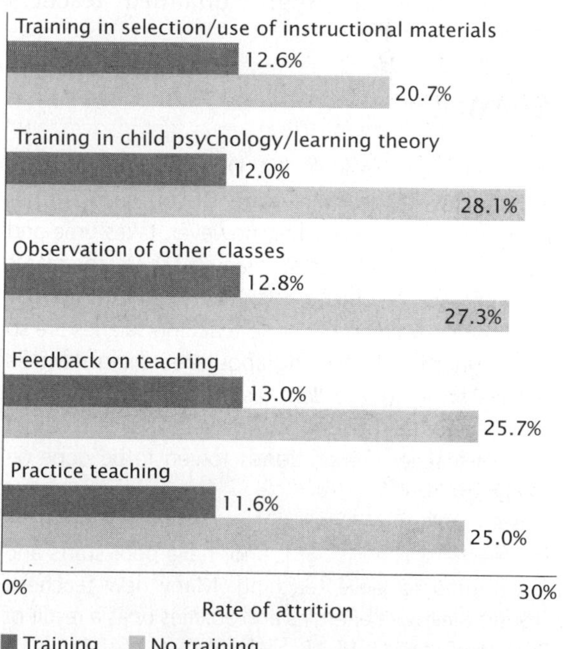

people who are changing careers to enter teaching, schools like George Washington University offer assistive programs for mid-career entrants, including former military and Peace Corps attendees. One example is the school's Transition to Teaching Partnership, a collaboration with nearby Fairfax County Public Schools in Virginia.

But while mentoring and induction programs for new teachers are a mainstay in most states, not all programs are created equal. Of the 28 states that have state-level teacher-induction programs, only 10 actually provide funding for such programs, as well as mandating them, according to Recruiting New Teachers (RNT), a nonprofit organization that advocates national reform for teacher recruitment and development. That's a big problem. "Funding is critical, because mentors need to be given the time to work closely with new teachers," says Mildred Hudson, CEO of RNT in Belmont, Massachusetts.

The regimen of the federal No Child Left Behind (NCLB) Act may help bridge the existing funding gap for some states. The first federal attempt to establish professional criteria for teachers, NCLB appropriates $2.85 billion over the next two years to help school districts recruit, develop, and retain "highly qualified" teachers (i.e., those who meet state certification requirements and demonstrate knowledge in their core subject area, according to NCLB). Indeed, last fall the U.S. Department of Education unveiled a free professional-development Web site for teachers (www.paec.org/teacher2teacher). Targeted mainly at K–8 instructors, the site offers streaming video of workshops conducted by other teachers, as well as supplementary course materials.

In addition, consideration and time must be given to professional development. For instance, seminars and lectures for beginning teachers were offered monthly at Sue Manley's school, but they were held on weekday evenings. Manley usually felt too busy and worn out after teaching all day to attend them. It's a situation many new teachers—myself included—encounter. When new teachers aren't granted release time for professional development, many end up going without. And eventually they just go.

Teachers who tough out the early years are often glad they did. Now in her seventh year of teaching, Manley has herself become a coach and a counselor for new teachers. "My advice is," she says, "don't take things personally, be firm, and be calm. And take care of yourself. It does get better."

Postnote

Education is caught in a box. Our students need talented and skilled teachers—and lots of them. Preparing a person to be a teacher, however, takes time and resources. Since we need so many teachers, the states find it difficult to come up with adequate funds to pay for elaborate training. Because teaching salaries are so modest, individuals thinking about becoming teachers are leery of going into debt (as most medical students do) to pay for the training themselves. The result is that much of teacher preparation is forced to be done on the cheap.

The result of such minimal preparation is that many new teachers, like Ms. Graziano, have poor starts and are tempted to leave teaching. Many new teachers, through their own energies and abilities or as a result of mentoring programs, are able to overcome the limitations of their preparation. Nevertheless, as this article shows, many are not. The teaching profession remains caught in a classic Catch-22.

Discussion Questions

1. What are the author's major complaints about the induction system into teaching?
2. In your view, what are the primary causes for teachers' leaving teaching for other fields?
3. Don't young people in other occupations face similar problems and switch careers? Are you convinced that teaching is unique in this matter?

Finding Allies: Sustaining Teachers' Health and Well-Being

PATRICIA HOUGHTON

FOCUS Question

Where can a new teacher look for support?

If we hope for wonderful schools for our children, then we must be concerned with the mental health and well-being of our teachers. I have often heard teachers criticized for being concerned about their own comfort and happiness as educators or even for taking care of themselves. As teachers, however, we can be effective only if we are able to maintain our own health and energy levels. Roland Barth offered a telling analogy:

> Consider the common instructions given by flight attendants to airline passengers: "For those of you traveling with small children, in the event of an oxygen failure, first place the oxygen mask on your own face and then—and only then—place the mask on your child's face." The fact of the matter is, of course, that the adult must be alive in order to help the child. In schools we spend a great deal of time placing oxygen masks on other people's faces while we ourselves are suffocating.[1]

Nel Noddings writes that "teaching requires tremendous amounts of physical and psychic energy."[2] When we as teachers can maintain a high level of energy, we can be powerful educators. We may even have the strength and the ability to change schools for the better. The question is, How do we achieve and maintain the levels of mental and physical energy that are required to sustain ourselves as teachers?

I have been searching for the answer to this question for years. I have examined my own teaching, watched other teachers, observed wonderful and not so wonderful schools, and read a variety of literature related to this topic, and I continue to talk and think about these issues with others. In my search for the answer to this question I traveled to New York City to speak with Deborah Meier, the founder of the Central Park East Schools in Harlem, and to observe her schools. She advised me to find *allies*. To be great teachers and have an impact on the system of education or the schools in which we teach, we must have the support of others. There are endless resources we can

---

Patricia Houghton is a teacher and a teacher educator at the University of Puget Sound, Tacoma, Washington. Patricia Houghton, "Sustaining Teachers' Health and Well-Being," *Phi Delta Kappan,* May 2001. Reprinted with permission of Patricia Houghton.

tap: colleagues, students, parents, professional organizations, other schools, universities, and—ultimately—ourselves.

Colleagues as Allies: Building Positive Communities of Support

During the difficult and discouraging times of teaching, it is often hard for me to recognize all the progress that my students and I are making and how much we are growing. Sometimes I stumble on the good that I had been unable to see, as I write in my journal or speak with colleagues—as I take the time to be reflective. My friend Tricia and I made a ritual of meeting each week while we were student teaching. We would begin to tell each other how hard—even terrible—the week had been. Yet soon enough, we were pointing out the good we heard in the other's story, the growth the other had missed. We began to see for ourselves that there were a lot of wonderful things happening in our classrooms. It took the telling of our stories to find the good. It took the other person to point out what we ourselves were unable to see. We need others to help us solve problems and to console, understand, celebrate, and appreciate ourselves and our students.

We as teachers tend to isolate ourselves. But the job of teaching is too big and too complex to do alone. We need one another. Even though collegial support is so vital to the lives of teachers, it can be hard to find. My friend Lori was telling me about a conversation among teachers in the staff lounge. It went something like this:

> *Teacher A:* How was your field trip?
> *Teacher B:* It was wonderful. We had a great time. Everything was great!

Lori had been on the same field trip and knew that there had been many complications and that everything had *not* been great. Many teachers have a tendency to make things sound better than they really are. The first step in building communities of teachers as allies may be just to be honest. When one person takes the risk to tell how he or she really is, it can create an atmosphere in which it is safe for others to do the same. We cannot support one another if we feel the need to hide behind a façade.

Joseph Featherstone recommends that teachers form groups to break the isolation. Such groups could meet to talk directly about teaching issues, or they could be a way for teachers just to get to know one another. "Sometimes people need to socialize before they feel able to bring up real problems."[3]

Pam Grossman and Sam Wineburg led a group of high school teachers as they read and discussed "literary and historical works and plan[ned] an interdisciplinary humanities curriculum." These teachers also helped one another improve their teaching methods. Teachers showed videos of their own classrooms, thus "opening up the act of teaching to question, comment, and elaboration by a group of supportive peers."[4] Membership in this group helped move these teachers from isolation to collaboration.

The most successful schools and programs that I have observed are characterized by teachers who support one another in a variety of ways. For example, the Central Park East Schools in Harlem were designed to allow teachers to work closely with one another. In a staff meeting at CPE II, I heard the teachers talking about how to help a new teacher who had just joined them and another teacher who had broken her toe. Other items that were discussed included the school picnic to be held at Central Park the next day, integrating science with the Harlem Meer (a body of water on the north side of the park) project, a phone tree for parents, and how to manage the number of students in the bathroom at once. The director spoke with the teachers. He did guide the discussion, but the teachers all spoke and gave input. He did not make the final decisions about anything; rather, he was a facilitator. The feeling that teachers had ownership of their school was evident when one teacher answered the phone as if she were in her own home. It was clear that staff members were working together.

Many of us already know that increased interactions with our colleagues do not always help us to be healthier. Early in my teaching career, I discovered that my attitude about students became much more negative when I began eating lunch with some of the other teachers. Their negativity was contagious, and I began to think of the relationship between teachers and students as *us* against *them*. It is important that we choose positive staff members to associate with and learn from and that we strive to be positive ourselves.

Students as Allies: Building Honest, Mutual Relationships

Our students are a valuable source of support that we often overlook. When I began my teaching career, I was cautioned not to smile for months in order to gain students' respect. One teacher suggested that I not be honest with my students about being a first-year teacher or about my age because they might respect me less. Others believed that it was important not to let students know you were unsure of something when teaching and that it was best to "bluff" instead. I found that these suggestions distanced me from my students and did not make the job of teaching easier or make me a better teacher.

In order to enlist our students as allies, it is important to be human, real, and honest with them. When I began teaching, there was so much I did not know. There is still so much that I want to learn. I was fortunate to have a clear sense of purpose as a teacher and my own philosophy of teaching. I was less knowledgeable about the subject matter. I was to teach students about Canada, Latin America, earthquakes, volcanoes, and how their own bodies worked. I knew little about these subjects. During one lesson about the respiratory system, students asked question after question while I was trying to explain how the respiratory system worked. I was having quite a hard time teaching the lesson, so I stopped and explained, "I am really excited that you are so interested in this lesson. I know how to teach, but I don't know very much about the respiratory system. I have spent a lot of time this past week trying to learn more about it so I could teach you, but it is hard for me to teach this and answer questions along the way. I was wondering if you could save your questions for the end? I probably won't be able to answer them, but I can ask Mr. Flak [another science teacher] or do some research to find the answers for you."

We had all been sitting on the rug when I said this. One of my students, Theressa, got up on her knees and exclaimed, "You know, no other teacher would ever tell us that they didn't know something. They'd just pretend." It was clear that Theressa was very proud of me for being honest with the class. She was letting me and the rest of the class know that she respected me for my honesty. I have been able to develop strong relationships with my students because of this type of honesty.

If we strive to keep ourselves distant from our students, we will tend to feel that we only give—receiving nothing in return. This is because we are not creating an environment that is reciprocal. Susan Florio-Ruane, a former teacher education professor of mine, says that when she was a teacher she sometimes began the day feeling like a wet, full, dripping sponge. By the time she left the classroom at the end of the day, she often felt like a sponge that had been sucked dry—hard and empty. Many of us can relate to this feeling all too well. Yet if we can tap into our students' energy, we may not end each day feeling dry and depleted. There can be a flow between us so that when we give, we also receive. We can receive only if we are open to what our students have to offer. It seems that we as teachers often forget to look for what our students do have to offer.

One night I was feeling quite troubled as I was trying to plan for the next day's math lesson. I was teaching third-graders about fractions. I came to a point where I felt completely hopeless. How on earth could I teach this lesson to 31 students? Their skill levels varied so greatly. I felt that the task was impossible. In the midst of these feelings of despair came what felt like a revelation: *my students could help one another!* I realized that I did not have to be the only teacher in that classroom. I could facilitate the process of students teaching and helping one another. My thoughts about teaching have not been the same since. It is not an us against them kind of game. We can do this together.

Each of us has to decide for ourselves if we want to build connections with students. In my observations of schools in which staff members and students seem happy, healthy, and productive, there is always a sense of closeness between the teachers and the students. At Seattle Public Alternative School #1, the connection between teachers and students is of primary importance. The courses offered are designed in such a way that teachers and students connect over common interests. Each teacher offers courses in an area of personal interest, such as sailing or environmental studies. Students then choose courses that are of interest to them. Thus the teacher and the student have something in common that can bring them together in a learning partnership.

At Gig Harbor (Washington) High School and Central Park East Secondary School, the staff members feel so strongly about building relationships with their students that they have advisory periods on a regular basis. Students are assigned advisors upon entering high school and see these adults weekly throughout their high school careers. The advisory periods acknowledge that students need to have adults in the school who know them and that teachers need time to get to know their students.

Parents as Allies: Joining Forces with Students' Families

Feeling alone as a teacher can be a source of stress. The more supported we feel, the healthier we are likely to be. I have been fortunate to receive help and encouragement from the parents of my students. They are a wonderful resource. Working with them has made my job easier and much less stressful. I also feel certain that a positive relationship between parents and teachers helps students do better in school. The praise and encouragement I have received have helped give me energy to push onward when I am tired and discouraged. It saddens me when teachers view parents as a hindrance. I understand that it is sometimes hard to find the time and energy to meet with parents who have concerns, and it can be easy to feel threatened or criticized when parents don't understand or like your teaching methods. However, the benefits of working with parents can far outweigh any possible negatives.

To help parents get more involved in helping their children to be more successful, we need to tell them how they can help. Within a week of my arrival in a new state to begin my first teaching job, the school had an orientation session and barbecue for students and parents. My excitement about the coming year bubbled over, although I was simultaneously overwhelmed and scared. I confided my conflicting feelings to many of the parents as we talked. Parents responded by reaching out. One grandmother gave me a big hug and said, "You're going to be just fine, just fine, honey." Another mother heard me laughing and telling someone that I was still sleeping on the floor because I didn't yet have a bed. She approached me and said that she would keep her eyes out for a bed at the thrift store where she worked. I learned quickly that allowing others to give is a way to build community and gain support. I did not keep these families at arm's length by trying to maintain a "professional" relationship. We treated one another as people—able to step outside the roles of teacher and parent.

Throughout the year, I found that the parents and I worked as a team to educate their children. We supported one another. If I was having difficulty with a student's attitude or behavior or was concerned about a child's reading, writing, or math skills, I was able to reach out to the parents and ask for help. There were many times that I called, visited, or met with parents at school to ask them to speak with their child about a problem we were having or to suggest that they have their child work on skills each day at home.

Many times the greatest help I received was when parents were candid with me. They shared some of the troubles they were having at home.

This helped me to understand where their child was coming from, and I was often able to support the child and the family. One mother, Callie, was having a hard time getting her daughter to come to school. Angela would throw temper tantrums in the morning. I began to support Callie by calling in the morning and talking with Angela. I often told Callie, "You really need to get Angela to school. I know it's hard, but you're the mom. You just need to get her here, and I'll do the rest." Callie told me that she needed this support and encouragement. I needed Callie's help as well. It was hard for me to teach Angela when she was absent so often. By getting Angela to school, Callie helped me tremendously, making my job easier. Most important, together we were able to help Angela.

Professional Groups as Allies: Entering Larger Conversations

Being a member of a professional organization and attending professional conferences can be a source of inspiration and support for teachers. These organizations and conferences allow teachers to connect with other colleagues, share ideas, and learn about new methods, materials, literature, and so on. Breaking outside of one's individual school or district can be refreshing and lead to a sense of hope. There are times when we feel alone in the school where we teach because we are unable to find others who share a common philosophy. Organizations or conferences can give us a chance to get our souls fed by others who are like-minded and to have our own beliefs affirmed.

Making a presentation or sharing personal expertise at a conference or as a member of an organization can be personally rewarding. This is particularly important if we do not feel valued in the school where we teach. I have also seen that it can be quite energizing for teachers to work with university students during their field experiences or student teaching. Taking on leadership roles such as these helps us gain some ownership over our profession. Becoming involved in these ways can elicit a sense of worth. People burn out when they don't feel valued and when their work is unrewarding.

Taking on leadership roles within our own schools can also be a way for us to feel empowered. While this option may not always seem available, there are always ways to have a positive impact on other staff members. It may be just by providing coffee in the morning and encouraging others to join in. I found it rewarding to leave articles or inspirational poems or stories in other teachers' mailboxes. As a new teacher, I shared my excitement over a reading workshop that I was implementing in my classroom. I never tried to push my ideas on anyone; I just shared what was happening in my classroom over lunch. Soon, a few of the veteran teachers asked me to help them set up a reading workshop.

It may seem strange in an article about the health of teachers to recommend doing *more* as a way to be healthy. But it is important for us to take an active role in the leadership of our schools or in professional organizations if we are to overcome the feelings of helplessness that sometimes overtake us. I have felt frustrated and even angry about all that I cannot change or cannot easily change within the schools where I teach. Looking at what I *do* have the power to affect has helped me to feel more hopeful. There is much that we can do.

Other Settings as Allies: Seeing Alternatives

Getting outside of one's own classroom is very important. Observing the classrooms of effective colleagues in our own schools, throughout the district, and in other districts can open up many possibilities we might not otherwise have considered. Observing other teachers and other schools can help us to stop and rethink the cycle we are in. Actually seeing things done differently can guide us to new places in our teaching.

Another benefit of observing other teachers is that we often discover that they have problems, too. In many cases, we feel inadequate because things don't always go smoothly in our classrooms or our students don't seem interested in the subject at hand. Finding out that all teachers have challenging days can help us be less critical of ourselves and of our students. The complex job of teaching does not always go smoothly.

Professional Literature as an Ally: Nourishing Our Inner Teacher

A helpful way to cope when feeling uninspired, alone, overwhelmed, lost, or inadequate is to read literature by or about teachers and teaching. Reading good books can be a source of inspiration, direction, and comfort. When I was reflecting on my first three years of teaching, I realized that I turned to a book about teaching every August before school started. I didn't do this consciously, but I was drawn to these books because I needed something to help prepare me for the coming year. The sustenance I received from these books was powerful.

The August before my first year of teaching I was feeling apprehensive about some of my teaching ideas and how they would be perceived by others. I was committed to creating a community of learners in a classroom that was student-centered rather than teacher-centered. I wanted students to feel a sense of belonging and a sense of ownership over *our* classroom. For these reasons, I had decided not to decorate the classroom before the students arrived. I would not put up posters or arrange the desks because I had decided that the students should be involved. Although I firmly believed this was a good idea, I began to worry that others would think I was strange or, worse, lazy. I then read William Ayers' book *To Teach: The Journey of a Teacher.* Instantly I felt I had an ally. Someone understood and affirmed what I was doing. Ayers did not talk specifically about decorating the classroom, but he did write about the importance of the environment in which one teaches.

> Questioning everything in the environment, from the bottom up, is an important task for teachers. We cannot necessarily change it all, but we can certainly become aware of the messages, the hidden as well as the obvious, the commonplace as well as the gaudy. We can peel the cover back a bit, peek underground, disclose the undisclosed—at least for ourselves. And in telling what is untold, we can become stronger in shaping our own environments, until they become places that more fully reflect what we know and value. . . . We can become better at creating what we intend for ourselves and for our students. If I am aiming to create a classroom where kids are eager to be, where they hate to leave, where I have to finally whisk them out the door, what would I do?[5]

Ayers' philosophy was much like my own. I had a wonderful feeling that someone was telling me that it was okay not to decorate the room before the students arrived. The book affirmed what I was doing, and I planned on using it as a reference if others questioned my choice. These ideas were in writing—in a book. It was a source of validation. Reading Ayers' book helped me step into my first year of teaching with a stronger hold on my beliefs about teaching. It helped me start the year believing that I had a friend beside me, and it helped me feel much more confident.

This experience may have been what led me to another book the following August. I read Lucy Calkins' *Living Between the Lines.*[6] Prior to my third year of teaching, I read *"My Posse Don't Do Homework,"* written by LouAnne Johnson.[7] The book was the story of her experiences as a teacher in a "tough" urban school. As I read, I was amazed by the similarities between Johnson's struggles and my own. Reading the book was much like sitting down to have a conversation with a fellow teacher about the joys and challenges and even the heartbreaks we face as educators. I also gained some great teaching ideas as I "watched" her solve problems. Reading these books in August and continuing to read wonderful books about teaching throughout the school year has helped inspire and sustain me.

Universities as Allies: Pursuing Further Education

A valuable step I have taken on this journey to achieve a greater level of mental health, energy, and well-being has been to take a year off from teaching to spend as a full-time learner. Spending a year as a graduate student allowed me to focus on building myself up as a professional. I was able to devote more of my energy to my own mental health and was able to return to the classroom reenergized. The university was a place for me to find all the allies I have mentioned. I had more time to get in touch with myself as an ally as I spent hours thinking and reflecting on my teaching practice and writing in a journal. I had hours to spend with colleagues, discussing issues that I am passionate about and solving problems together. I had greater access to colleagues in other schools and districts. I had more time to attend professional conferences and to observe a variety of schools, thus expanding my network of support. And, of course, I had the privilege of being immersed in wonderful literature, some of which reaffirmed previous beliefs and some of which opened me up to new ways of thinking.

A colleague of mine chose to pursue her master's degree while teaching. She was quite intimidated by the notion of returning to the university. It was hard for her to imagine being able to find the time to devote to being a student as well as a teacher. She discovered that, although she had more demands on her time, she had more energy for teaching. Her coursework at the university caused her to be more excited about teaching and allowed her to build connections with other educators. Spending time in an intensive learning program for yourself can be a way to dedicate time to your own well-being and to renew yourself and your energy supply for teaching.

Self as Ally: Befriending Ourselves

In order to be successful and healthy teachers, we must first and foremost be allies to ourselves. We can begin by teaching ourselves to think in new ways. It is easy to lose hope when teaching students who are far behind academically, who have no books at home, and who are not getting many of their physical and emotional needs met. I have spoken with several teachers who feel a sense of despair because their students are so far behind in school or have troubling home situations. It may be necessary for us to focus only on what we *can* do and to do that to the best of our ability. We must let go of those things we cannot control. Judith Deiro writes about six teachers who have "healthy connections" with their students. One way in which these teachers "ease their stress level and cope with the demands of the job" is to detach. This is not to say that the teachers do not deeply care about their students, but rather "that they do not assume responsibility for students' well-being."[8]

There are limits to what we can give to our classrooms and our students. We are responsible for taking care of ourselves physically and emotionally. During my first year of teaching, I would stay up late working on plans and reading students' work. I realized midway through the year that pushing myself so hard was actually causing me to be a less effective teacher. I was tired and frustrated instead of rested and energetic. I have learned that I can never really do enough. There is always more to do. I have to stop at some point in order to be healthy.

I have therefore created a system that works for me: I work for a certain amount of time and then go home. I try not to take my "teaching bag" home anymore so that I have a space in my life that allows another aspect of my self to grow and thrive. A colleague of mine used to joke that he just took his box full of teaching stuff for a ride each evening. He couldn't find the energy to work on it when he finally got home, but he continued to take it for a ride! If we are to be friends to ourselves, we must set limits for what we can give to our teaching and be sure to meet our own needs as well.

Another way in which I have relied on myself as an ally has been to keep a journal. Writing in my journal has been an outlet for the vast array of emotions that I feel as a teacher. I can write about and celebrate my successes. I can work through frustrating situations that arise in my classroom and in my school or system. Things often become clearer for me as I put down on paper what is happening and what I am feeling. The process of writing forces me to slow down and reflect, which often enables me to gain a new perspective.

One powerful way to help ourselves is to be mindful of all that is beautiful and glorious about being a teacher. There is much to celebrate in what we do. It is essential to work toward self-improvement, but it is also critical to forgive ourselves for mistakes we make along the way. A field instructor of mine in college encouraged us to focus on what students *can* do rather than to look at their deficiencies. She also helped us as preservice teachers to focus on our own capabilities. I find both of these activities necessary, if I am to enjoy teaching.

Taking an Active Role in Our Well-Being

Taking care of ourselves and getting support from colleagues, students, parents, professional organizations, observations, and reading are all ways to sustain ourselves as teachers. Yet even if we surround ourselves with allies, we may find that it is nearly impossible for us to be healthy in a given teaching situation. I have come to realize that there are some places where I cannot be the type of teacher—or even the type of human being—that I want and need to be. Ultimately, achieving wellness as an educator may require understanding what one absolutely needs in order to be good at one's job. I know that I have to be in a place where I can teach according to my philosophy. I have to teach in a situation that is conducive to my getting to know students on a personal level. Without these bare necessities, I am miserable and feel professionally ineffective.

The schools I have visited in which teachers show little or no signs of burnout are those in which teachers share a common philosophy and are given the encouragement and the environment that enable them to teach according to their beliefs. These schools are also places in which teachers take an active role in decision making. At the Seattle Country Day School, staff members make virtually every decision that affects them as teachers. When a new library assistant was hired, the current librarian was allowed to advertise the position and to interview and choose the person to fill it. Teachers at the school are given personal budgets to buy supplies for their classrooms. They are trusted to act as professionals, and they live up to these expectations. It is obvious that the teachers feel ownership of their school. Settings like these are conducive to being a healthy teacher. If we are teaching in situations where we are not valued or respected in such ways, we may find it difficult to sustain the levels of energy and health we need to be successful.

Teaching can be frustrating, challenging, and even infuriating. It can also be rewarding, meaningful, joyous work. I have often said to friends that teaching is too hard a job unless you have a passion for it. If we don't have a good answer to the question "Why do you teach?" we may not ever be able to achieve wellness in this profession. A passionate sense of purpose is essential.

What is it that you can do to be healthy as a teacher? How can you achieve and maintain the level of energy that is required to sustain yourself in this profession? We each need to answer these questions for ourselves. The suggestions I have put forth here are meant as guidelines to help you think about what it is that you need to be healthy and how you can meet those needs. We owe it to ourselves and to our students to take our own well-being seriously.

Notes

1. Roland Barth, *Improving Schools from Within: Teachers, Parents, and Principals Can Make a Difference* (San Francisco: Jossey-Bass, 1990), p. 42.
2. Nel Noddings, Foreword to Judith A. Deiro, *Teaching with Heart: Making Healthy Connections with Students* (Thousand Oaks, Calif.: Corwin, 1996), p. vii.
3. Joseph Featherstone, "Getting a Life: A New Teacher's Guide," in William Ayers, ed., *To Become a Teacher: Making a Difference in Children's Lives* (New York: Teachers College Press, 1995), p. 230.

4. Pam Grossman and Sam Wineburg, "Creating a Community of Learners Among High School Teachers," *Phi Delta Kappan*, January 1998, pp. 350–53.
5. Williams Ayers, *To Teach: The Journey of a Teacher* (New York: Teachers College Press, 1993), p. 53.
6. Lucy McCormick Calkins with Shelley Harwayne, *Living Between the Lines* (Portsmouth, N.H.: Heinemann, 1991).
7. LouAnne Johnson, *"My Posse Don't Do Homework"* (New York: St. Martin's, 1992).
8. Deiro, p. 77.

Postnote

For readers who have yet to experience their first year of teaching, this one is a keeper! Like the first year in many occupations (medicine, sales, the law), teaching often has a taxing break-in period. It is complicated by the fact that new teachers are shocked by the strangeness of something that is quite familiar: being in school. The issue, and the problem, is that new teachers are in an entirely different role. Being on "the other side of the desk" can be a world away. One of the most difficult aspects of the work for many new teachers is being "in charge." They know about school. They know their subjects. They know what their students should be doing. They don't, however, know how to get them to do it. They have not had much experience being the boss or "the responsible person." Neither have they had much experience with directing others or with what the military would call giving orders. Necessity, however, is still the mother of invention, and most new teachers adapt in time. This fine article is rich with insights and sources of support for struggling new teachers. Don't lose it!

Discussion Questions

1. As a student, what memorable experiences did you have with new teachers? Describe them.
2. If and when you become a new teacher, what do you believe will be your most vulnerable areas?
3. Which ideas and suggestions in this article appeal most to you, and which do you plan to put into practice?

Letter from a Teacher

JOHN C. CROWLEY

FOCUSQuestion

Doing well in student teaching is an important first step. What should be on the agenda for the next step in the teaching journey?

TERMS TO NOTE

Empathy
Philosophy
Professional teacher

Dear Bill:

Well, your baptism by fire is about over. You have passed through that vague state appropriately mislabelled as "Student Teacher." Soon you will return to the more familiar and secure world of the college campus.

I hope your teaching experience was of some value. Throughout the time we worked together I made repeated plans to sit down with you and have a long talk—a "tell it like it is" type session. Unfortunately, except for between-class chats and noontime gab sessions, our talks never did get down to the nitty-gritty. So, with due apologies for a letter instead of a talk, this will have to do.

If you leave here feeling to some degree satisfied and rewarded, accept these feelings. You have worked diligently and consistently. For your part you have a right to feel rewarded. Teaching offers many intangible bonuses; feeling satisfied when a class goes well is one of them. The day teaching no longer offers to you the feelings of satisfaction and reward is the day you should seriously consider another profession.

Mingled with these feelings is also one of discouragement. Accept this too. Accept it, learn to live with it, and be grateful for it. Of course certain classes flopped; some lesson plans were horror shows; and some kids never seemed to get involved or turned on. This is not a phenomenon experienced only by student teachers. We all encounter this. The good teacher profits from it—he investigates the reasons for the failure and seeks to correct himself, his approach, or his students. And in so doing, the good teacher further improves and gets better.

Bad teachers develop mental calluses, blame it on the kids, and sweep the failures under the rug. Always be discouraged and unsatisfied; it's the trademark of a good, professional teacher.

I don't know if you plan to make teaching your career—perhaps, at this point, you don't know yourself—but if you do, I'm sure you

---

John C. Crowley was a high school teacher in Massachusetts. He died shortly after the publication of this letter. "Letter from a Teacher" by John C. Crowley. From the *Massachusetts Teacher* (Sept.–Oct. 1970), pp. 2, 34, 38.

will do well; you have the potential. In the event you do elect a teaching career, I would offer these suggestions:

1. Develop a philosophy for yourself and your job. Why do you teach? What do you expect of yourself and your students? Do not chisel this philosophy on stone. Etch it lightly in pencil on your mind, inspect it frequently. Do not be surprised that it changes—that can be a good sign. Be more concerned with the reasons for a change rather than the change itself. Unless you base your teaching on a foundation of goals and ideals, you are wasting time. If you as the teacher-model cannot show a solid basis of beliefs, how can you expect your student-imitators to develop any definite beliefs?

2. Do not be just "a teacher," be a professional teacher. Teaching is the most rewarding, demanding, and important job in the world. We deal with the minds of men and the future of the world. It is not a task to be taken lightly. Demand professionalism of yourself and your associates. Do not shut yourself up in a classroom, isolated from and ignorant of the real world. Be prepared to teach at any time, in any place, to anyone. Ferret out ignorance with the zeal of a crusader and the compassion of a saint. Teach as if the fate of mankind rested squarely upon your shoulders and you'll know, in part, what I mean.

3. Always be a learner. Never assume you know all the answers or enough material to teach your class. Read constantly. Do not become an encapsulated specialist. Vary the material. Talk to others. Most of all, learn to listen to your students . . . not to what they say but to what they mean.

   A good teacher learns as much from his students as he teaches to them. Do not discourage dialogue. Do not be so dogmatic as to accept only your own views. Do not use the textbook as a mental crutch.

   Any fool can break a book up into 180 reading assignments and still manage to keep one section ahead of the students, but such a fool should not assume the title of teacher. At best, he would be a grossly overpaid reading instructor.

4. Develop the feeling of empathy. Try to feel how the student feels. Do not lapse into the warm complacency of a seating chart, names without faces. Do not accept the cold facts of a rank book, marks without personality.

   See the girl in the second row, homework undone because her parents fought all night. She couldn't even sleep, let alone concentrate on homework. Does that deserve an "F"?

   Or the boy in the back of the room. Bad teeth, poor complexion, shabby clothes. No known father, a promiscuous mother, and a cold-water flat in a bad part of town. Of course he acts up and appears rebellious; wouldn't you? How have we alleviated his problems by assigning detention time and writing a bad progress report? How does it feel to sit in a class day after day hungry, ill, knowing that when the last bell rings it will be back to the sewer?

   Is it any wonder that Jacksonian Democracy, the English morality plays, or Boyle's Law leaves these kids cold? But if they are to eventually move into society we must reach them, and the first step comes when we, as teachers, understand them.

   I am not advocating that you become a "softy." Do not rationalize every failure with some outside cause. But be prepared to evaluate a student on the basis of your understanding of him and his problems. A grade is something more than a mathematical total and an average. Before assigning a grade, look closely at the particular student and ask yourself, "Why?"

5. Finally, alluding to the misadventures of Don Quixote, I would counsel—"Do not be afraid of windmills!" As a conscientious, professional teacher you will find your path constantly bestraddled with windmills of one type or another.

These may come in the form of other teachers, guidance departments, administrators, department heads, school committees, parents, or heaven knows what. They will obstruct, criticize, belittle, and attack you for a variety of reasons and motives. If you think you are right, do not back down! Always be willing to go as far as necessary to defend your convictions and beliefs. Do not avoid experimentation for fear of mistakes or criticism!

If we accept the status quo and maintain a conservative view toward change, we will not progress. In fact, we'll probably regress. We have an obligation, as educators, to constantly seek better ways of doing things. If that means putting our own heads on the chopping block, so be it. Either we stand for something or we stand for nothing. If we stand for something it should be so important that any sacrifice to preserve and further it is worthwhile. And, as educators, we are under a moral and ethical responsibility to stand for something.

Well, I hope these words of advice have proved helpful. Repeating an earlier statement, you have a great deal of potential and I personally hope you put it to use as a teacher.

I know of no other job that compares with teaching. We need every promising candidate who comes along. It goes without saying of course that should you need a letter of recommendation I will be only too glad to supply it. Having participated in your student teaching experience I also feel morally obliged to assist you should you, at some future date, require and want such assistance. It's there for the asking.

With confidence in the nature of man, I remain

Very truly yours,
Jack Crowley

Postnote

"With confidence in the nature of man, I remain . . ." This letter, one of the last Jack Crowley wrote before he died, is overflowing with one of life's rarest commodities—wisdom. His closing, though, speaks to a value that stands behind the huge edifice of education. The phrase "confidence in the nature of man" captures the hope and conviction that must undergird the teacher's work. Without this confidence, teachers may find their goodwill eroding. The phrase also reminds us that as teachers, we must be dedicated to more than the status quo. We must try to bring human nature to a higher level.

Discussion Questions

1. What are your reactions to the suggestions Jack Crowley makes to Bill, the student teacher?
2. How would you feel if you received such a letter from your supervising teacher? Why?
3. What attitudes toward teaching and toward students does Jack Crowley reveal in this letter?

Students

Part Two

Teaching is one of life's most complex activities. So much is involved: knowledge, attitudes, values, and skills to be learned; the process of instruction and the management of the learning environment. To teach well, to be an effective educator, demands so much of our attention that an essential element in the teaching-learning process may be lost: the student.

The entire purpose of teaching is to make positive change in students. They are the main event, but sometimes teachers lose focus. We become so involved in the knowledge to be conveyed or in the process of instruction that we often lose sight of our students. We need to remind ourselves continually that the entire enterprise of education fails if the student is ill served. And we need to remind ourselves constantly that each student has a different set of needs, preferences, and goals.

One thing that should help us stay attuned to the student is the fact that modern life regularly requires us all to become students. No longer is the term *student* reserved for a relatively few young people receiving formal education. With the explosion of education in the last quarter century, people continually move in and out of student status. A knowledge-based and information-oriented society such as ours requires continuous education. Whether it is acquiring computer literacy or learning how to run cooperative learning groups, we all return to being students from time to time. Having to struggle with new information or trying to master a new skill may be the best thing we can do to improve our teaching.

Who Is This Child?

ROBERT D. BARR

FOCUS Question

How can one guard against overgeneralizing and stereotyping?

During my spring vacation, I visited my grandson Sam's first-grade classroom in Eugene, Oregon—home of author Ken Kesey, the University of Oregon's Fighting Ducks, and a T-shirt that proudly proclaims, "Me Tarzan, Eugene." Eager to start the day, Sam and I traded a couple of high-fives and sallied forth. He carried his books and an authentic Mighty Morphin Power Ranger lunch box; I carried a note pad and wore a sappy grin. This was the essence of grandparenting: a bright spring day in Oregon and off to school, hand-in-hand with Sam.

On arrival, Sam threw down his things and yelled over his shoulder, "Watch my stuff," as he ran off to join his friends in a soccer game. Almost immediately, I felt a small arm slide around my waist. Surprised, I looked down into the face of a little girl. "Who is this child?" I wondered. She flashed me a ragged smile that was missing half a dozen teeth. "I am from Chicago," she said and buried her head in my side. Suddenly uneasy, I looked around for some other adult. Having served on teacher licensure boards in two states and having sat through a dozen or so hearings to revoke the certification of child molesters, I was well aware of the taboos governing interactions between old guys like me and this small child.

As I tried to disentangle myself, she looked up at me with huge, longing eyes. "We don't have a father in our family," she said in her small voice. Then, as if repeating from a script, she whispered, "My father is a deadbeat dad. He ran away because he couldn't pay his bills." She blew her bangs up out of her eyes and sighed. "They found him, though. He is somewhere, I forgot . . . maybe in Portland, but I don't know where that is." She stared up at me with moist eyes. "But it's all right. My mom says we don't need him." Once again she burrowed into my side.

At the time this article was written, **Robert D. Barr** was Professor of Secondary Education, Boise State University, Boise, Idaho. He is the coauthor, with William H. Parrett, of *Hope at Last for At-Risk Youth* (Boston: Allyn and Bacon, 1995). Barr, Robert D., "Who Is This Child?" *Phi Delta Kappan,* January 1996.

The longing and need of this small child caught me off guard. Her yearning for affection was almost palpable. And suddenly I knew this child—not her name or her address, but her identity. In her ragged dress, with her dirty fingernails, she carried the staggering weight of research predictability, of statistical probability. I had pored over the data far too long; I knew where she came from, where she was bound, and where her sad journey would end. I knew that a deep yearning for denied love can soon wither into anger—perhaps even hate—and that one generation will impose its tragic story on the next.

Was there even a chance that this small child would one day graduate from the University of Oregon School of Law and walk crisply into the world, clad in a Brooks Brothers pin-striped jacket and miniskirt, swinging an Armani briefcase? More likely, she was a teenage parent in the making. I could envision a burned-out, unemployed 28-year-old, recovering from a messy second divorce and pregnant with her third child. Yes, I thought, I knew this child.

Just then a bell rang, setting off a wild rush to classes. My little friend gave me a final squeeze, waved goodbye, and skipped away. Sam ran up laughing—and, after he had gathered his things, we walked hand-in-hand into the school.

Still troubled by my encounter with the little girl, I watched her up ahead as she turned into a classroom. When I came abreast of that particular classroom door, I paused and looked in. What I saw was a teacher kneeling to hug the little girl and to say, "Melody, it's so good to see you! I'm so glad you made it to school today!" The teacher held the little girl at arm's length and gave her a thousand-watt smile that lit up the entire classroom. Then she took the little girl's hand and walked her to a desk. "Won't we have a great time today?" the teacher asked. "We'll paint today and sing—and of course we'll read some books." Bathed in the warmth of the teacher's care, the little girl seemed almost to glow.

Watching this touching tableau reminded me that researchers often jump to hasty conclusions, overgeneralizing from far too little data. I knew all the grim predictions that could be derived from the research literature, but I also knew the power of a good school and of caring and demanding teachers. I knew that schools could make a difference, could transform the lives of children, could overcome the deficiencies of the home and the dysfunctions of the family. I knew about resilient children and about the power of education, done well, to transform.

With a sigh of relief, I turned back to Sam, who was impatiently tugging at my hand. "Come on, Bob," he said. "We're gonna be late for class." With a final wave at the little girl, this 55-year-old researcher—now filled with hope—headed once again into a first-grade classroom.

Postnote

This brief, poignant article reminds us of the potential power of education to make a difference in the lives of children. Although statistical norms and stereotypical images tempt us to form expectations that can lead to self-fulfilling prophecies, this article helps us see that each child is an individual with potential to overcome the circumstances that place him or her at risk of not succeeding in life. For many of these children, education is their best chance to beat the odds and improve their lot in the world, but only if educators take it upon themselves to provide the extra care and love these children need.

Discussion Questions

1. The author uses the term "resilient children." What do you think he means by it? What research can you find on the topic?
2. What are some of the factors that put children at risk for failure? What role can or should schools play in addressing these risk factors?
3. What did you learn from the way the teacher greeted Melody?

CLASSIC

Leaving No Child Behind

MARIAN WRIGHT EDELMAN

FOCUSQuestion

The author raises a troubling question about the condition of our young. What is our moral responsibility to other people's children?

TERM TO NOTE

Values

We are living at an incredible moral moment in history. Few human beings are blessed to anticipate or experience the beginning of a new century and millennium.

How will we say thanks for the life, for the earth, for the nation, and for the children God has entrusted to our care? What legacies, principles, values, and deeds will we stand for and send to the future through our children to their children and to a spiritually confused, balkanized, and violent world desperately hungering for moral leadership?

How will progress be measured over the next thousand years if we survive them? By the kill power and number of weapons of destruction we can produce and traffic at home and abroad, or by our willingness to shrink, indeed destroy, the prison of violence constructed in the name of peace and security?

By how many material things we can manufacture, advertise, sell, and consume, or by our rediscovery of more lasting non-material measures of success—a new Dow Jones for the purpose and quality of life in our families, neighborhoods, and national community? By how rapidly technology and corporate merger-mania can render human beings and human work obsolete, or by a better balance between corporate profits and corporate caring for children, families, and communities?

By how much a few at the top can get at the expense of the many at the bottom and in the middle, or by our struggle for a concept of enough for all Americans? By the glitz, style, and banality of too much of our culture, or by the substance of our struggle to rekindle an ethic of caring, community, and justice in a world driven by money, technology, and weaponry?

Marian Wright Edelman, founder and president of the Children's Defense Fund (CDF), has been an advocate for disadvantaged Americans for her entire professional career. Under her leadership, the Washington-based CDF has become a strong national voice for children and families. The mission of the Children's Defense Fund is to "Leave No Child Behind." Marian Wright Edelman's article is excerpted from *The State of America's Children Yearbook 1996,* published by the Children's Defense Fund. "Stand for Children: Leave No Child Behind," from *The State of America's Children Yearbook 1996.* Reprinted by permission of Children's Defense Fund.

The answers lie in the values we stand for and decisions and actions we take today. What an opportunity for good and evil we Americans personally and collectively hold in our hands as parents, citizens, public school leaders, and as titular world leader in the post–Cold War and post-industrial era on the cusp of the third millennium. . . .

A thousand years ago the United States was not even a dream. Copernicus and Galileo had not told us the earth was round or revolved around the sun. Gutenberg's Bible was not printed, Wycliffe had not translated it into English, and Martin Luther had not tacked his theses on the church door. The Magna Carta did not exist, Chaucer's and Shakespeare's tales had not been spun, and Bach's, Beethoven's, and Mozart's miraculous music had not been created to inspire, soothe, and heal our spirits. European serfs struggled in bondage while African empires flourished in independence. Native Americans peopled our land free of slavery's blight, and Hitler's Holocaust had yet to show the depths human evil can reach when good women and men remain silent or indifferent.

A thousand years from now, will civilization remain and humankind survive? Will America's dream be alive, be remembered, and be worth remembering? Will the United States be a blip or a beacon in history? Can our founding principle "that all men are created equal" and "are endowed by their Creator with certain inalienable rights" withstand the test of time, the tempests of politics, and become deed and not just creed for *every* child? Is America's dream big enough for every fifth child who is poor, every sixth child who is black, every seventh child who is Latino, and every eighth child who is mentally or physically challenged?

Protecting children is the moral litmus test of our humanity and the overarching moral challenge in our world and nation where millions of child lives are ravaged by the wars, neglect, abuse, and racial, ethnic, religious, and class divisions of adults. In the last decade, UNICEF reports, 2 million children have been killed, 4.5 million disabled, 12 million left homeless, more than 1 million orphaned or sundered from parents, and some 10 million have been traumatized by armed conflicts throughout the world.

In the United States since 1979, more than 50,000 children have been killed by guns in our homes, schools, and neighborhoods in a civil war on our own young. Although we are the world's leading military power, we stand by silent and indifferent as a classroomful of children are killed violently every two days from guns. About every day and a half, gun violence kills as many children as the children killed in the tragic Oklahoma City bombing.

In the richest nation in history, we appear unashamed that a child dies from poverty every 53 minutes, that children are the poorest group of Americans, and do not express outrage as political leaders of both parties propose policies to make them poorer. We talk about family values but turn our backs on real needs of families for jobs and decent wages and child care and health care. We tolerate a child welfare system that abuses and neglects children already abused and neglected by their families. While we bemoan a few child victims of abuse like Susan Smith's young sons and beautiful Elisa Izquierdo in New York City, we do not mend our cracked child welfare system that lets an abused child die every seven hours.

How much child suffering, death, and neglect will it take for you, me, religious, civic, school, and political leaders to stand up and cry out "enough" with our hearts and voices and votes to protect our young who are our sacred trust and collective American future?

A Mass Movement

When Jesus Christ invited little children to come unto him, He did not invite only rich, middle-class, white, male children without disabilities, from two-parent families, or our own children to come. He welcomed all children. There are no illegitimate children in God's sight. James Agee eloquently reminded: "In every child who is born under no matter what circumstances and of no matter what parents, the potentiality of the human race is born again, and in him, too, once more, and each of us, our terrific responsibility toward human life: toward the utmost idea of goodness, of the horror of terrorism, and of God."

Yet every day too many of us fail our terrific responsibility toward our own children and millions of other people's children who are America's and God's potentiality.

It is not just poor or minority children who are afflicted by the breakdown of moral, family, and community values today. The pollution of our airwaves, air, food, and water; growing economic insecurity among middle-class children and young families; rampant drug and alcohol abuse, teen pregnancy, and domestic violence among rich, middle-class, and poor alike; AIDS; random gun and terrorist violence; resurging racial intolerance in our places of learning, work, and worship; and the crass, empty materialism of too much of our culture threaten every American child.

Every day in America, 2,660 children are born into poverty and 27 die from poverty. And every day 7,962 children of all races and classes are reported abused or neglected, and three die from abuse; 15 die from firearms and 2,833 drop out of school; 2,700 get pregnant; and 790 are born at low birthweight. We are first in the world in military and health technology but 18th in the industrialized world in infant mortality.

But it is poor children who suffer most. What kind of country permits this? A poor one? An undemocratic one? An uncaring one? A foolish one? One that ignores the biblical injunction to "defend the poor and fatherless and do justice to afflicted and needy"?

Our failure to place children first as parents, communities, corporate, civic, cultural, educational, and political leaders is our Achilles' heel and will be our future undoing. Indeed the present unraveling of our family fabric is a portent of what is to come if we do not correct course and regain our moral moorings.

The stresses and strains of making a living leave too many parents too little time with their children. Too many affluent parents are more preoccupied with material than with eternal things—with fun rather than faithfulness in providing the family rituals, continuity, and consistent companionship children need to grow up healthy, caring, loving, and productive. Parenting itself is not a valued calling and people who care for children get the least support in America. Too many neighbors look out just for themselves and take little or no interest in each other's children. Too many business people seem to forget they are parents and family members and treat children as consumers to whom they can market excessively violent, sexually charged messages and products they would not want their own children to see or use. And too many faith communities fail to provide the strong moral leadership parents and communities need to meet their shared responsibilities to children.

What you stand for and do now as educational leaders—and encourage our political leaders to stand for during the final years of the century—will shape our nation's fate and our children's futures in the next century and millennium. It is time to call the moral question about whether America truly values and will stand up for children not just with words but with work; not just with promises but with leadership and investment in child health, early childhood education, after-school programs, and family economic security; not just with a speech or photo opportunity, but with sustained positive commitment to meet every child's needs.

Postnote

This article by a lifelong advocate for children has earned Classic status because it both outlines the problems and calls upon the nation to act. Marian Wright Edelman has for years been America's conscience for children's welfare. As the founder and president of the Children's Defense Fund, she has forcefully reminded Americans that, as a nation, we have turned a blind eye and a deaf ear to the worlds of many of our children, particularly our children of color. She has worked tirelessly with presidents, congressional representatives, governors, and bureaucrats to better children's lives. In this article, she once again appeals to our consciences. Although the United States is the richest country in the world, it has the highest poverty rate for children among industrialized countries. Our health care system permits millions of children to fall between the cracks. About a million verified cases of child abuse occur each year. Guns kill more children in America than in all of Europe. How can this be? Who is looking out for the children?

Discussion Questions

1. What reasons can you give for the sad state of so many children living in the United States?
2. What steps would you recommend to help remedy the problems experienced by children that Edelman identifies in the article?
3. Who besides Edelman can you identify as children's advocates? What actions have they taken to improve children's lives in America?

Problem Students: The Sociocultural Roots

D. STANLEY EITZEN

FOCUS Question

Every generation of young people faces unique social conditions. What are the special problems confronting today's students?

TERM TO NOTE

Head Start

Although many of today's students are a joy to work with in the classroom, some are not. Some children are angry, alienated, and apathetic. A few are uncooperative, rude, abrasive, threatening, and even violent. Some abuse drugs. Some are sexually promiscuous. Some belong to gangs. Some are sociopaths. Why are some children such problems to themselves, to their parents, to their teachers, and to the community? Is the cause biological—a result of flawed genes? Is the source psychological—a manifestation of personalities warped by harmful experiences? My strong conviction is that children are *not* born with sociopathic tendencies; problem children are socially created.

Now you might say, "Here we go again; another bleeding-heart liberal professor is going to argue that these problem children are not to blame—the system is." Well, you are partly right. I am politically liberal, and as a social scientist I embrace a theoretical perspective that focuses on the system as the source of social problems. However, I do recognize that, while human actors are subject to powerful social forces, they make choices for which they must be held accountable. But I also believe that it is imperative that we understand the social factors that influence behavior and impel a disproportionate number of children in certain social categories to act in socially deviant ways.

Children of this generation manifest more serious behavioral problems than children of a generation ago. I believe that four social forces account for the differences between today's young people and those of 15 years ago: the changing economy, the changing racial and ethnic landscape, changing government policies, and changing families. Moreover, these structural changes have taken place within a cultural milieu, and they combine with one another and with that culture to create the problem students that we face today. We must understand this sociocultural context of social problems in order to understand problem students and what we might do to help them.

D. Stanley Eitzen is a sociologist and an emeritus professor at Colorado State University, Fort Collins. Eitzen, D. Stanley, "Problem Students: The Sociocultural Roots" from *Phi Delta Kappan,* April 1992.

The Changing Economy

I begin with the assumption that families and individuals within them are shaped fundamentally by their economic situation, which, of course, is tied directly to work. I want to consider two related features of the changing economy: 1) the structural transformation of the economy and 2) the new forms of poverty.

Transformation of the Economy

We are in the midst of one of the most profound transformations in history, similar in magnitude and consequence to the Industrial Revolution. Several powerful forces are converging to transform the U.S. economy by redesigning and redistributing jobs, exacerbating inequalities, reorganizing cities and regions, and profoundly affecting families and individuals. These forces are technological breakthroughs in microelectronics, the globalization of the economy, capital flight, and the shift from an economy based on the manufacture of goods to one based on information and services. I want to focus here on the significance of the last two factors.

The term *capital flight* refers to investment choices to maximize profit that involve the movement of corporate funds from one investment to another. This activity takes several forms: investment overseas, plant relocation within the U.S., and mergers and buyouts. These investment choices, which are directly related to the shift from manufacturing to services, have had dramatic and negative impacts on communities, families, and individuals.

Across the country such capital flight has meant the loss of millions of well-paid industrial jobs as plants have shut down and the jobs have migrated to other localities or the companies have shifted to other types of work. Similarly, there has been a dramatic downward tug on organized labor and wages. . . . Although many new jobs have been created by the shift to a service economy, . . . the large majority of these jobs are "bad" jobs—with much lower pay and fewer benefits than the manufacturing jobs that were lost. . . .

This is the first generation in American history to have more downward social mobility than upward. Downward mobility is devastating in American society, not only because of the loss of economic resources, but also because self-worth is so closely connected to occupational status and income. Individual self-esteem and family honor are bruised by downward mobility. Those affected feel the sting of embarrassment and guilt. Moreover, such a change in family circumstances impairs the chances of the children—both as young people and later as adults—to enjoy economic security and a comfortable lifestyle.

Some families find successful coping strategies to deal with their adverse situations. Others facing downward mobility experience stress, marital separation and divorce, depression, high levels of alcohol consumption, and spouse and child abuse. Children, so dependent on peer approval, often find the increasing gap in material differences between themselves and their peers intolerable. This may explain why some try to become "somebody" by acting tough, joining a gang, rejecting authority, experimenting with drugs and sex, or running away from home.

Poverty

One especially unfortunate consequence of capitalism is that a significant proportion of people—13.5% in 1990 and rising[1]—are officially poor. (Of course, many additional millions are just above the official government poverty line but poor nonetheless.) Poverty in the 1980s declined for some categories of the population (whites and the elderly) and *increased* for others: racial minorities, fully employed workers (the working poor), households headed by women, and children.

There is an important historical distinction that we must draw regarding the poor. Before 1973 the poor could hope to break out of poverty because jobs were generally available to

---

[1]The proportion of Americans living in poverty reached 12.7% by 2004.—Eds.

those who were willing to work, even if the prospective workers were immigrants or school dropouts. The "new poor," on the other hand, are much more trapped in poverty because of the economic transformation. Hard physical labor is rarely needed in a high-tech society. Moreover, those few available unskilled jobs now offer low wages and few, if any, benefits or hopes of advancement. This situation diminishes the life chances of the working class, especially blacks, Hispanics, and other racial minorities who face the added burden of institutional racism.

Consequently, poverty has become more permanent, and we now have a relatively permanent category of the poor—the underclass. These people have little hope of making it economically in legitimate ways. This lack of opportunity explains, in part, their overrepresentation in the drug trade and in other criminal activities. Moreover, their hopelessness and alienation help us to understand their abuse of alcohol and other drugs. All of these conditions stem from the absence of stable, well-paid jobs. A further consequence of this state of affairs is that it undermines the stability of families.

Poverty is especially damaging to children. Poor children are more likely to weigh less at birth, to receive little or no health care, to live in substandard housing, to be malnourished, and to be exposed to the health dangers of pollution. Let me provide one example of this last point. Poor children are much more likely than others to be exposed to lead from old paint and old plumbing fixtures and from the lead in household dust. Sixteen percent of white children and 55% of black children have high levels of lead in their blood, a condition that leads to irreversible learning disabilities and other problems. Children suffering from exposure to lead have an average I.Q. four to eight points lower than unexposed children, and they run four times the risk of having an I.Q. below 80.

The Changing Racial Landscape

American society is becoming more racially and ethnically diverse. Recent immigration (both legal and illegal), especially by Latinos and Asians, accounts for most of this change. If current trends continue, Latinos will surpass African-Americans as the largest racial minority by the year 2020. In some areas of the country, most notably in California, the new immigration has created a patchwork of barrios, Koreatowns, Little Taipeis, and Little Saigons. These changes have also created competition and conflict over scarce resources and have led to battles over disputed turf among rival gangs and intense rivalries between members of the white working class and people of color. Moreover, communities, corporations, and schools have had difficulty providing the newcomers with the services they require because of the language and cultural barriers.

We are currently experiencing a resurgence of racial antipathy in the U.S. This is clear in various forms of racial oppression and overt acts of racial hostility in communities, in schools and universities, and in the workplace. We can expect these hateful episodes to escalate further if the economy continues to worsen.

Racial and ethnic minorities—especially African-Americans, Native Americans, and Latinos—are also the objects of institutional racism, which keeps them disadvantaged. They do not fare as well in schools as white children, their performance on so-called objective tests is lower, the jobs they obtain and their chances for advancement are less good, and so on. They are negatively stereotyped and stigmatized. Their opportunities in this "land of opportunity" are drastically limited. They are blamed for their failures, even when the causes are structural. Is it any wonder that a disproportionate number of them are "problem" people?

The Changing Government Policy

One of the reasons that the disadvantaged are faring less well now than a generation ago is that government policies today are less helpful to them. At the very time that good jobs in manufacturing began disappearing, the government was reducing various forms of aid to those negatively affected by the changing economy. During the administrations of the last three presidents—Reagan, Bush, and Clinton—the funds for government programs designed for the economically disadvantaged have diminished by more than 25 percent. In 1996, for example, Congress passed legislation that: 1) ended the 61-year-old federal guarantee of cash assistance to people whose need makes them eligible; 2) reduced federal spending on food stamps by $23 billion over six years; 3) made legal immigrants ineligible for most federal benefits for their first five years in the U.S.; and 4) demanded that each of the states require at least half of all single mothers on welfare be working by 2002 or lose some federal funds. The Urban Institute estimates that among the negative consequences of these policies, the number of children in poverty will increase by more than 10 percent, adding 1.1 million to the officially impoverished and worsening the conditions for millions already below the poverty line. The bitter irony is that these disadvantaged young people will end up, disproportionately, as society's losers, and most Americans will blame them for their failure.[2]

The Changing Family

A number of recent trends regarding the family suggest a lessening of family influence on children. Let me note just a few. First, more and more families include two primary wage earners. This means, in effect, that more and more women are working outside the home. Over 50% of mothers with children under age 6 work outside the home, and about 70% of mothers with children between the ages of 6 and 17 are in the workplace. As a result, more and more children are being raised in families in which the parents have less and less time for them. This also means that more and more preschoolers are being cared for by adults who are not their parents—a situation that is not necessarily bad, though it can be.

Second, although the divorce rate has declined slightly since 1981, it remains at a historically high level. More than one million children each year experience the divorce of their parents, up from about 300,000 a year in 1950.

Third, it is estimated that 60% of today's 5-year-olds will live in a single-parent family before they reach the age of 18; 90% of them will live with their mothers, which usually means that they will exist on a decidedly lower income than in a two-parent family. Research has shown that children from one-parent families differ significantly from the children of two-parent families with regard to school behaviors. Children from single-parent families are less likely to be high achievers; they are consistently more likely to be late, truant, and subject to disciplinary action; and they are more than twice as likely to drop out of school.

Fourth, about three million children between the ages of 5 and 13 have no adult supervision after school. One study has found that these latchkey children are twice as likely to use drugs as those who come home from school to find an adult waiting.

These trends indicate widespread family instability in American society—and that instability has increased dramatically in a single generation. Many of the children facing such unstable situations cope successfully. Others do not. Rejection from one or both parents may lead some children to act out in especially hostile ways. Low self-esteem can lead to sexual promiscuity or to alcohol or drug abuse. Whatever the negative response of the children, I believe that we can conclude that the victims of family instability are not completely to blame for their misbehaviors.

The Cultural Milieu

The structural changes that I have noted occur within a cultural milieu. I will address only two aspects of that culture here: American values and the messages sent by the media. Let's begin with values. The highly valued individual in American society is the self-made person—that is, one who has achieved money, position, and privilege through his or her own efforts in a highly competitive system. Economic success, as evidenced by material possessions, is the most common indicator of who is and who is not successful.

---

[2] This paragraph was updated by Professor Eitzen in January 1997.—Eds.

Moreover, economic success has come to be the common measure of self-worth.

Competition is pervasive in American society, and we glorify the winners. That is never truer than in economic competition. What about the losers in that competition? How do they respond to failure? How do we respond to them? How do they respond to ridicule? How do they react to the shame of being poor? How do the children of the poor respond to having less than their peers? How do they respond to social ostracism for "living on the other side of the tracks"? They may respond by working harder to succeed, which is the great American myth. Alternatively, they may become apathetic, drop out, tune out with drugs, join others who are also "failures" in a fight against the system that has rejected them, or engage in various forms of social deviance to obtain the material manifestations of success.

The other aspect of culture that has special relevance here is the influence of the media, particularly the messages purveyed by television, by the movies, and by advertising. These media outlets glamorize—among other things—materialism, violence, drug and alcohol use, hedonistic lifestyles, and easy sex. The messages children receive are consistent. They are bombarded with materialism and consumerism, with what it takes to be a success, with the legitimacy of violence, and with what it takes to be "cool."

Consider the following illustrations of the power of the media. Three-year-olds watch about 30 hours of television a week, and by the time an American child graduates from high school she or he will have spent more time in front of the television set than in class. Between the ages of 2 and 18 the average American child sees 100,000 beer commercials on television, and young people see on average some 12,000 acts of televised violence a year.

A study by the University of Pennsylvania's Annenberg School of Communications revealed that children watching Saturday morning cartoons in 1988 saw an average of 26.4 violent acts each hour, up from 18.6 per hour in 1980. Two of the conclusions by the authors of this study were that: 1) in these cartoons children see a mean and dangerous world in which people are not to be trusted and disputes are legitimately settled by violence, and 2) children who see so much violence become desensitized to it. The powerful and consistent messages from television are reinforced in the movies children watch and in the toys that are spun off from them.

Given these strong cultural messages that pervade society, is it any wonder that violence is widespread among the youth of this generation? Nor should we be surprised at children using alcohol, tobacco, and other drugs and experimenting with sex as ways to act "adult." Moreover, we should not be puzzled by those young people who decide to drop out of school to work so that they can buy the clothing and the cars that will bring them immediate status.

The current generation of young people is clearly different from earlier ones. Its members manifest problems that are structural in origin. Obviously, these social problems cannot be solved by the schools alone, although the community often blames the schools when these problems surface.

Since the problems of today's young people are largely structural, solving them requires structural changes. The government must create jobs and supply job training. There must be an adequate system for delivering health care, rather than our current system that rations care according to ability to pay. There must be massive expenditures on education to equalize opportunities from state to state and from community to community. There must be equity in pay scales for women. And finally, there must be an unwavering commitment to eradicating institutional sexism and racism. Among other benefits, such a strategy will strengthen families and give children both resources and hope.

The government must also exert more control over the private sector. In particular, corporations must pay decent wages and provide adequate benefits to their employees. In addition, corporations contemplating a plant shutdown or a dramatic layoff must go beyond the present 60-day notification, so that communities and families can plan appropriate coping strategies.

These proposals seem laughable in the current political climate, where politicians are timid and citizens seem interested only in reducing their tax burden. The political agenda for meeting our social problems requires political leadership that is innovative and capable of convincing the public that sacrifices to help the disadvantaged today will pay long-term benefits to all. Such leadership will emerge from a base of educated citizens who are willing to work to challenge others to meet societal goals.

At the community level, we must reorder our priorities so that human and humane considerations are paramount. This means that community leaders must make the difficult decisions required to help the disadvantaged secure decent jobs, job training, health care, housing, and education. Schools must be committed to the education of all children. This requires a special commitment to invest extra resources in the disadvantaged, by assigning the most creative and effective teachers to them and by providing a solid preschool foundation to children through such programs as Head Start. Most important, though, all children must be shown that the school and the community want them to succeed. Then the self-fulfilling prophecy we create will be a positive one.

In 1990 Roger Wilkins presented a visual essay on the Public Broadcasting Service series "Frontline," titled "Throw-away People." This essay examined the structural reasons for the emergence in this past generation of a black underclass in Washington, D.C. His conclusion is appropriate for this discussion.

> If [the children of the underclass] are to survive, America must come back to them with imagination and generosity. These are imperiled children who need sustained services to repair the injuries that were inflicted on them before they were born. Adults need jobs, jobs that pay more than the minimum wage, that keep families together, that make connections with the outside world, and [they need] the strength to grow. We can face the humanity of these people and begin to attack their problems, or we can continue to watch the downward rush of this generation, in the middle of our civilization, eroding the core of our conscience and destroying our claim to be an honorable people.

Every day teachers are confronted by the unacceptable behaviors of students. Obviously, they must be handled. I hope that this discussion will help teachers and administrators understand the complex sources of these objectionable and seemingly irrational behaviors. We must begin with an understanding of these problem children. From my point of view, such an understanding begins with underlying social factors. Most important, we must realize that social and economic factors have battered down certain children and increased the likelihood that they will fail and that they will behave in ways that we deplore.

Everyone needs a dream. Without a dream, we become apathetic. Without a dream, we become fatalistic. Without a dream and the hope of attaining it, society becomes our enemy. We educators must realize that some young people act in antisocial ways because they have lost their dreams. And we must realize that we as a society are partly responsible for that loss. Teaching is a noble profession whose goal is to increase the success rate for *all* children. We must do everything we can to achieve this goal. If not, we—society, schools, teachers, and students—will all fail.

Sources and Recommended Readings

Eitzen, D. Stanley, and Maxine Baca Zinn, eds. *The Reshaping of America: Social Consequences of the Changing Economy.* Englewood Cliffs, N.J.: Prentice-Hall, 1989.

Ellwood, David T. *Poor Support: Poverty in the American Family.* New York: Basic Books, 1988.

Levy, Frank. *Dollars and Dreams: The Changing American Income Distribution.* New York: Russell Sage Foundation, 1987.

MacLeod, Jay. *Ain't No Makin' It: Leveled Aspirations in a Low-Income Neighborhood.* Boulder, Colo.: Westview Press, 1987.

Mattera, Philip. *Prosperity Lost: How a Decade of Greed Has Eroded Our Standard of Living and Endangered Our Children's Future.* Reading, Mass.: Addison-Wesley, 1991.

Schorr, Lisbeth B., with Daniel Schorr. *Within Our Reach: Breaking the Cycle of Disadvantage.* New York: Doubleday, 1988.

Postnote

A century and a half ago, Alexis de Tocqueville (1805–1859), one of the most perceptive commentators on American politics and culture, wrote, "America is great because it is good. When it is no longer good, it will cease to be great."

This article suggests two issues: First, adult Americans have turned away from their responsibilities as parents; and second, American children are growing up with values and behaviors that not only threaten their happiness but threaten the republic as well. All segments of society—homes, schools, churches, and communities—must devote more time and energy to our children. The stakes could not be higher.

Discussion Questions

1. Of the problems of youth identified by Eitzen, which is most serious? Why?
2. What strong and positive actions can schools take to help solve the problems of youth?
3. In what ways are schools limited in their efforts to help the young? What boundaries define schools' roles?

Memories from the "Other": Lessons in Connecting with Students

THOMAS DAVID KNESTRICT

FOCUSQuestion

How does a school's culture appear to a definite underachiever?

I hated school. I struggled with it from the moment I started kindergarten. Before that, I had been so happy as a young child. I can remember when I was 4 years old, coloring with my mom at home. I can still hear her telling me how smart I was and how much she loved me. I remember quite vividly entering Hayes Elementary School in September of 1964 and walking into the large kindergarten room. I came into the room excited about school and eager to learn. I had perfect attendance the first semester of that year and received a certificate for my achievement.

But as the year progressed, things changed. My memories of that year have faded somewhat over time, but there are certain recurrent themes that stay with me today. The first is that I very clearly was different from most of the other children. I had trouble sitting on the floor "Indian style." I needed to get up and move. The next theme I clearly recall is that I wasn't as smart as the other boys and girls. Learning to read was difficult; learning to write was even harder. In fact, anything that required me to focus for an extended period of time or to use fine motor skills was lost on me. The final general recollection I have is discovering that I was a "problem" in class. I remember being sent to the "cloak room" several times that year for "not playing nice" or "disrupting the class."

Mrs. L. came over to me and took the paper fire truck I had just completed. She peeled the wheels off of the first truck and told me that she knew I could do better. I had tried to cut out round wheels but was unable to create anything better than octagon shapes. Obviously this was not good enough.

In first grade I was placed in a class with an almost entirely new group of children. The only student I already knew was a boy named Tommy. We had been in kindergarten together, he came to first grade with me, and he was with me until my senior year of high school. But the rest of the students we had been with the previous year were placed in the two other classrooms. The children I met in first grade were to

---

Thomas David Knestrict is an assistant professor of education at Xavier University, Cincinnati, Ohio. He taught in the public schools for fifteen years. "Memories from the 'Other': Lessons in Connecting with Students," by Thomas David Knestrict, *Phi Delta Kappan,* June 2005, pp. 782–786. Reprinted by permission.

be my classmates for the next five years. Students were tracked back then, and I was in the "slow class." This was the term that Mr. P., our principal, used on more than one occasion. It was true. All of us had trouble reading, writing, and behaving. I can't imagine what the teacher must have been thinking when she received her class list in August. This might explain why many of the teachers we had did not return the following year.

Class was so boring. The print made no sense to me. So I found ways to entertain myself, especially during reading. I can remember looking for Tommy during reading group. I knew if I could catch his eye, I could make him laugh. I was always searching for a way to escape the monotony. When I got his attention I turned both of my eyelids inside out and stared at him. Pretty soon every boy in the reading group was doing the same thing. Mrs. S. became very angry and made all of us stay in for recess.

The overwhelming message I received every day was that I was different, not as good, and defective. I had different books. I completed different assignments. I was not asked to join in any of the extra activities my fellow students in the other classes participated in. There were only a few kids in our class each year who excelled. The next year they would be moved to one of the other classrooms. Their spot was always taken by a new kid—usually a kid like me or a new student who couldn't speak English. The funny thing is that after a new kid learned to speak English, he usually excelled and left our class. My grades were horrible. The school used to trust me to bring my report card home for my parents to sign. But it never found its way home. Every year my mom would have to call about the whereabouts of my report card.

I dreaded oral reading groups. My handwriting was illegible, and the teachers always claimed that I was very smart but lazy. By third grade I had discovered some "truths" about myself. The first truth was that I was stupid. This was reinforced daily by teacher comments and by the eventual absence of teacher concern—a kind of teaching boycott put into effect because of my perceived bad attitude. Second, I was different from the "cool" kids in the other classes. I was viewed by my peers and my teachers as different, and because of this I had a very limited group of people around me from whom to draw friends. Last, I did possess a significant talent. I was one funny guy. I could make people laugh. Turning my eyelids inside out was just one trick. I had a million of them. But it worked only within the context of school. Outside of the classroom, the groups were even more rigidly defined, and I had no capital.

The middle grades of elementary school were very tough. These years were marked by a tremendous lack of accomplishment. I never read a book. I never completed a book report. I rarely passed a test. I never completed any homework. But I continued to be passed to the next grade with little or no assistance for my increasing academic deficits.

In fourth grade I had Ms. S. for a teacher. She was determined to whip me into shape. I remember turning in some kind of written assignment to her and having her hand it back to me to be recopied. It was far too messy, and there were too many misspelled words. I recopied it, and she handed it back to me again. I handed it in a third time, and again she handed it back to me. I was not allowed to go to recess or gym that day. I stayed after school until 4:00. I started to cry, and she told me that if I continued to cry I would have to stay in the next day as well. I stayed inside for three consecutive days. She finally gave up. I did, too.

In fifth grade I had Mr. H. for math. It was in this class that I really learned my place in school. The pain and humiliation I and my fellow students suffered in this class were remarkable. By fifth grade you should be learning fractions, long division, pre-algebra, equations, probability. We were still on two-digit times two-digit multiplication. One day, Mr. H. caught me clowning around in class. As punishment he had me get up in front of the class to complete the following problem:

23×13

Mr. H. knew that I could complete this problem only to the point of putting the place-holding zeros down. I got lost and could not go any further. As I froze and tried to climb inside of the chalkboard, Mr. H. said these words: "Mr. Knestrict, I could teach and teach and teach, and you still would not get this. I give up." What I heard was, "You're stupid, Mr. Knestrict. You can't do math, Mr. Knestrict. You are not a capable student, Mr. Knestrict." This is a moment I would relive many times in my academic career. His is a voice I still hear today. I hear it when I bounce a check. I heard it when I took my first statistics course in college. I hear it when I am at the grocery store figuring my bill or when I am figuring the tip at a restaurant. Like so many kids with learning differences, I had these words burned into my heart, into my brain. At that moment Mr. H. verbalized 10 years of my internal dialogue. When he voiced this condemnation, it made it so for me, for my peers, and for him. At that moment I was defined.

Beth was a smart girl. She attended the same elementary school I did but was always in the "smart class." In junior high, members of my class were mixed in with the "smart kids" for art, music, and industrial arts. I sat next to Beth in music. We had to do a report together about a famous musician. We picked John Denver. We began reading some books on him, and Beth started taking notes on index cards. I asked her what she was doing, and she showed me how she would read a fact about John Denver that she thought was interesting and write it down on the card. "A different card for every fact. Then when it's time to write, we can just copy down what we wrote on the cards." I was stunned. I could do this. It took a 12-year-old girl to show me that I could complete a meaningful academic task.

In junior high, things changed a bit for me. I was still tracked with the same kids. However, several elementary schools merged, and all the "dumb kids" from each school were grouped together. At least there were some new faces. And there were the "mixed-ability" groups for some subjects. Beth was the first "smart girl" I had ever made friends with. She helped me get my first A in any class . . . ever! Our paper on John Denver was a thing of beauty. During the writing process, Beth told me that it was okay that I had trouble writing. "I'll carry us, Tom." And she did. But she also taught me that I could do a few things myself. During the research part of the assignment, she could not find some basic biographical data on Mr. Denver. I had all of his albums at home, and on one of them there was a John Denver biography. I brought this in and wrote out five fact cards to contribute to the effort. Beth was so pleased. I felt like Einstein.

I remember sitting in Mrs. A's English class. We were diagramming sentences. I could not figure out the appropriate lines to draw for the various parts of speech. So I invented my own. I brought my paper up to Mrs. A., and she looked at it and told me to sit down and reread the assignment because I had done it completely wrong. She handed the paper back to me and continued to work at her desk. She did not know I could barely read the book we were using.

I had to go to other classes in junior high. I had to take Spanish in sixth grade. I never could figure out how a kid who couldn't master English was supposed to learn Spanish. I failed. In fact, I took Spanish I three years in a row. I think it still stands as a record at Harding Junior High School. Math was still a mystery. Physical education, an enjoyable class for me in elementary school, became a daily nightmare in junior high. Taking your clothes off in front of others? Taking showers? All of the "smart" boys and all the "dumb" boys were in gym together. In one respect, the playing field was leveled in gym class. Luckily, intelligence had little to do with the tasks in Mr. S.'s gym class. It was all about testosterone. Who could withstand pain, tumble, run, jump, and wrestle? I was a good athlete, and I went into this class feeling good.

But that wouldn't last. Mr. S. had a rule. If you did not remember to bring your uniform, you had to wear the "community clothes": a pair of very dirty shorts that smelled funny and had brown stains in the seat and a smelly tank-style top with the words "Lakewood" on the front. It was a well-known fact that the girls wore the shirts that said "Lakewood" and the boys wore the shirts that said "Rangers." Because I sometimes forgot my uniform, I was now clearly a girl. I missed a record number of days during my sixth-grade year. Thirty-four to be exact.

There was a spelling bee in sixth grade. The entire sixth grade participated. I can remember standing in line, on stage, in front of all of the seventh- and eighth-graders, waiting for my word. The first round was usually seen as a practice round, and the students were given a simple word to spell in order to get comfortable. It came to me. My word was "Lakewood." Simple enough, my hometown. "L . . . a . . . k . . . w . . . o . . . o . . . d, Lakewood." Silence. "Incorrect." The auditorium erupted. I laughed and joked, but I was dying inside. I then had to sit down in the front row for the next 30 minutes until another speller made a mistake and left the competition.

In high school I attempted to take Spanish again. I failed again. But my Spanish teacher, Ms. D., referred me to the school counselor, telling me, "Thomas, you must first learn the English language before learning Spanish." She referred me for academic testing. The year was 1975, and P.L. 94-142 had just been passed. I sometimes think I was the first child identified after its ratification. I was given a tutor and had to attend certain classes in the resource room for extra help. I made sure nobody saw me go into that room. It would be social suicide. Although, given my social status, I had very little to lose.

I was told that I was learning disabled and that I had to go to special education classes. The school psychologist told me this as if it were cause for celebration. "Hooray, we finally know what is wrong with Tom." But I wasn't ready to celebrate the fact that there was yet another thing that made me different.

Sometime during my sophomore year, a counselor met with me and talked to me about vocational school. "Tom," she said, "it's clear you are not on the college track here at LHS. So I would like you to start thinking about vocational school or even the military." I was devastated. My entire family had attended Bowling Green State University. I was going to go, too. But now, it looked like I would barely get out of high school. I finished that year in special education. I was 16, low on the social ladder, attending school on the special education track. I'd been told I couldn't attend the "regular" (read "normal") high school the next year, and I could barely read and write. I became very depressed. I started to cut class and feign illness to avoid going to school. There were days I came to school just for homeroom, so I could be counted as present, and then I would leave for home. I did this easily 50% of the time and never got caught. Still, I passed to the 11th grade. Remarkable!

In my junior year, I was required to take the ACT exam. I posted a total score of 7. I have been told that you could guess and score higher than this. I didn't guess.

At the end of my senior year, I had a grade-point average of 1.7. I read at about the fourth-grade level, still had not mastered my multiplication facts, had never read a book, had developed a consistent pattern of starting and then quitting new activities, thought of myself as stupid, could not write a coherent paragraph, had few friends, and in June was handed a diploma and graduated with my class from high school. It still ranks as the most inexplicable moment of my life. I kept thinking that my fellow classmates would attack if they knew that I was getting the same piece of paper they were that stated that I, too, had completed all the requisite coursework to graduate. No, I had not!

I woke up after graduation and wondered what had just happened. School was over—they let me graduate? Huh?

Somewhere between my graduation and the following school year, I had an epiphany. During that summer I worked at a gas station and a pizza place. I was very aware of how the people I was working with had been working these jobs for most of their adult lives and didn't seem real happy. I went home that night and talked to my father, and he convinced me to try taking a class at Cuyahoga Community College, also known as Tri C. I signed up for a series of high school–level reading and writing classes affectionately known as the 0900 courses. There were adults in these classes older than I was, and somehow that fact made me feel better about myself.

I signed up for all the high school–level courses I could that year, and in my first writing course I had a professor who saved my life. He taught me how to write and how to love to read. We read *Death of a Salesman* and books by Hemingway and Poe, and then we talked and wrote about the books. It would take me forever to finish a book, and sometimes it would be a combination of reading the book, watching the movie, and using the Cliff notes that got me through the assignments, but I loved every minute of it. It was the most amazing thing I had ever experienced. I was learning about metaphor and simile, seeing how the literature gave me insight into my life, writing reflections on my feelings about these books. It was wonderful. It was life changing. I learned more in that one year at Tri C than I had learned in the previous 12 years of school.

What was different was that I was seen as capable. The professors knew I could do it and expected me to do it. Also, they wanted me to enjoy the process and worry about the products later. One professor I had during this time stated, "Process over product. If you learn the process of reading and writing, the products will follow." But most important, they knew me and I knew them. We had a relationship. They cared about me. I had never, in 12 years of school, had that before.

As I was leaving my last writing and reading class at Tri C, the professor looked at me and said, "Make sure you read the comments I wrote on your last paper." When I got to my car, I pulled the paper out and read, "Thomas, this paper was one of the most insightful and inspired papers I have ever received from a student. I am so pleased with your progress this year. Grade for the quarter: A." I cried.

Later that year I ended up being accepted "conditionally" to Kent State University. During that year I met a man who ran a camp for children with learning disabilities and behavior problems. He was at Kent to hire counselors for the summer. I started talking to him a bit about my school experience. He hired me on the spot. I worked that summer leading hikes, camping, doing crafts, and canoeing with children who were experiencing some of the same things I had gone through in school. I found I had a real talent for working with children. From that point on, I knew I would teach.

That summer, the director of the camp, Jerry Dunlap, taught me something that has become a fundamental part of my teaching philosophy: he told me that all children deserve to feel lovable and capable. He then asked me if I felt lovable and capable. And for the first time in my life, I could say yes. I had spent most of my school years believing that I was not lovable and not capable. The system had beaten me up. But thanks to the good work of some significant teachers in my life, I was on the mend, with a focus on teaching and helping kids.

During my first year of teaching in the classroom, I had a student named Dante. He was 7 years old, could not read or write, and spoke only sparingly. As I introduced myself to Dante and his parents on the first day of school, I laughed at the joke God had played on me. Dante was me, and I was quite possibly the only person able to help him. We had a wonderful year, filled with lots of loving and learning. In June I asked Dante if he felt lovable and capable. He looked at me and smiled and said, "I know you love me, Mr. Knestrict, but what does 'capable' mean?"

Postscript

As I reflect on my life in school, I am struck by the times teachers failed to connect with me on any real human level. I am a professor of education now, and I am still struck by the lack of emphasis on this human connection in education. We spend so much of our time as teachers worrying about the standards, giving tests, and focusing entirely on content that the child as a person seems to disappear. One of the fundamental theories we teach undergraduates in our education programs is Abraham Maslow's hierarchy of needs. We know that human connection is crucial to child development, but our schools fail to manifest this knowledge in practice.[1] Classes get bigger and bigger, and test scores matter more and more. Our cultural obsession with measurement and testing often serves to sort students, not help them. These values define students very early in life. Once defined, individuals begin to see themselves that way, and the perception becomes a self-fulfilling prophecy. In fact, when a child is identified with a special need and placed on an Individualized Education Plan, he or she will actually have that label for a minimum of three years—and, as research suggests, much longer emotionally.[2]

I can tell you firsthand that I still hold internalized notions of myself as a child. I still have trouble seeing myself as smart, lovable, and capable. I believe that this difficulty is a result of the damage caused by my experience in schools and in particular our education system's notion of how to help children with different needs. I am not advocating de-emphasizing content. However, it is not unreasonable to assume that we can teach a solid curriculum and at the same time treat students with dignity and care.

References

1. Joan Wink and Dawn Wink, *Teaching Passionately: What's Love Got to Do with It?* (Boston: Pearson/Allyn and Bacon, 2004).
2. John R. Weisz et al., "Cognitive Development, Helpless Behavior, and Labeling Effects in the Lives of the Mentally Retarded," *Applied Developmental Psychology,* vol. 24, 1985, pp. 672–83.

Postnote

Most teachers have had pretty good experiences in school before entering the profession. Most were solid students; some were outstanding. The author of this article was at the other end of the academic spectrum. As described here, school for him was a living hell. The article reads like an educational version of a trip through Dante's *Inferno.* Although this author may be a rarity in the teaching ranks, he is hardly a rarity in our schools. For many students, school is one long, embarrassing, and demeaning slog through the grades. For a variety of reasons, from intellectual limitations to temperamental qualities, these students are never in step with what is going on in school. Being young and never having proved themselves in other arenas, they have nothing to balance against the failures of schooling. Many are heavily scarred by such experiences. This teacher-author is a survivor, and his candid look at his own troubling educational experiences should help us see our students more fully and more sympathetically.

Discussion Questions

1. The author is now a professor of education. What specific gifts do you believe he can bring to his students?
2. What do you believe were the causes for the author's various difficulties in elementary and high school?
3. Have you known people who have had experiences of educational failures like those of this author? What were the causes? How have the difficulties resolved themselves, if they have?

Understanding and Working with Students and Adults from Poverty

RUBY K. PAYNE

FOCUS Question

Sociologists say that the American public educational system is a middle-class institution. If so, how can it serve the needs of children of poverty more effectively?

TERMS TO NOTE

Generational poverty

Hidden rules

Mediation

Situation poverty

Although this article was originally written for teachers, the information presented may be of help to those who are working with persons making the transition from welfare to work.

To understand and work with students and adults from generational poverty, a framework is needed. This analytical framework is shaped around these basic ideas:

- Each individual has eight resources which greatly influence achievement; money is only one.
- Poverty is the extent to which an individual is without these eight resources.
- The hidden rules of the middle class govern schools and work; students from generational poverty come with a completely different set of hidden rules and do not know middle-class hidden rules.
- Language issues and the story structure of casual register cause many students from generational poverty to be unmediated, and therefore, the cognitive structures needed inside the mind to learn at the levels required by state tests have not been fully developed.
- Teaching is what happens outside the head; learning is what happens inside the head. For these students to learn, direct teaching must occur to build these cognitive structures.
- Relationships are the key motivators for learning for students from generational poverty.

Key Points

Here are some key points that need to be addressed before discussing the framework:

Poverty is relative. If everyone around you has similar circumstances, the notion of poverty and wealth is vague. Poverty or wealth

---

Ruby K. Payne is the founder and president of aha! Process, Inc., and the author of over a dozen books on education and social service. "Understanding and Working with Students and Adults from Poverty," by Ruby K. Payne, *Instructional Leader,* March 1996. Reprinted by permission of the author.

only exists in relationship to the known quantities or expectation.

Poverty occurs among people of all ethnic backgrounds and in all countries. The notion of a middle class as a large segment of society is a phenomenon of this century. The percentage of the population that is poor is subject to definition and circumstance.

Economic class is a continuous line, not a clear-cut distinction. Individuals move and are stationed all along the continuum of income.

Generational poverty and situational poverty are different. Generational poverty is defined as being in poverty for two generations or longer. Situational poverty exists for a shorter time and is caused by circumstances like death, illness, or divorce.

This framework is based on patterns. All patterns have exceptions.

Individuals bring with them the hidden rules of the class in which they were raised. Even though the income of the individual may rise significantly, many patterns of thought, social interaction, cognitive strategies, and so on remain with the individual.

School and businesses operate from middle-class norms and use the hidden rules of the middle class. These norms and hidden rules are never directly taught in schools or in businesses.

We must understand our students' hidden rules and teach them the hidden middle-class rules that will make them successful at school and work. We can neither excuse them nor scold them for not knowing; we must teach them and provide support, insistence, and expectations.

To move from poverty to middle class or from middle class to wealth, an individual must give up relationships for achievement.

Resources

Poverty is defined as the "extent to which an individual does without resources." These are the resources that influence achievement:

Financial: the money to purchase goods and services.

Emotional: the ability to choose and control emotional responses, particularly to negative situations, without engaging in self-destructive behavior. This is an internal resource and shows itself through stamina, perseverance, and choices.

Mental: the necessary intellectual ability and acquired skills, such as reading, writing, and computing, to deal with everyday life.

Spiritual: a belief in divine purpose and guidance.

Physical: health and mobility.

Support systems: friends, family, backup resources and knowledge bases one can rely on in times of need. These are external resources.

Role models: frequent access to adults who are appropriate and nurturing to the child, and who do not engage in self-destructive behavior.

Knowledge of hidden rules: knowing the unspoken cues and habits of a group.

Language and Story Structure

To understand students and adults who come from a background of generational poverty, it's helpful to be acquainted with the five registers of language. These are frozen, formal, consultative, casual, and intimate. Formal register is standard business and educational language. Formal register is characterized by complete sentences and specific word choice. Casual register is characterized by a 400- to 500-word vocabulary, broken sentences, and many non-verbal assists.

Maria Montano-Harmon, a California researcher, *has found that many low-income students know only casual register.* Many discipline referrals occur because the student has spoken in casual register. When individuals have no access to the structure and specificity of formal register, their achievement lags. This is complicated by the story structure used in casual register.

In formal register, the story structure focuses on plot, has a beginning and end, and weaves sequence, cause and effect, characters, and consequences into the plot. In casual register, the focus of the story is characterization.

Typically, the story starts at the end (Joey busted his nose), proceeds with short vignettes interspersed with participatory comments from the audience (He hit him hard. BAM-BAM. You shouda' seen the blood on him), and finishes with a comment about the character. (To see this in action, watch a TV talk show where many of the participants use this structure.) The story elements that are included are those with emotional significance for the teller. This is an episodic, random approach with many omissions. It does not include sequence, cause and effect, or consequence.

Cognitive Issues

The cognitive research indicates that early memory is linked to the predominant story structure that an individual knows. Furthermore, stories are retained in the mind longer than many other memory patterns for adults. Consequently, if a person has not had access to a story structure with cause and effect, consequence, and sequence, and lives in an environment where routine and structure are not available, he or she cannot plan.

According to Reuven Feuerstein, an Israeli educator:

- Individuals who cannot plan, cannot predict.
- If they cannot predict, they cannot identify cause and effect.
- If they cannot identify cause and effect, they cannot identify consequence.
- If they cannot identify consequence, they cannot control impulsivity.
- If they cannot control impulsivity, they have an inclination to criminal behavior.

Mediation

Feuerstein refers to these students as "unmediated." Simply explained mediation happens when an adult makes a deliberate intervention and does three things:

- points out the stimulus (what needs to be paid attention to)
- gives the stimulus meaning
- provides a strategy to deal with the stimulus.

For example: Don't cross the street without looking (stimulus). You could be killed (meaning). Look twice both ways before crossing (strategy).

Mediation builds cognitive strategies for the mind. The strategies are analogous to the infrastructure of house, that is, the plumbing, electrical and heating systems. When cognitive strategies are only partially in place, the mind can only partially accept the teaching. According to Feuerstein, unmediated students may miss as much as 50 percent of text on a page.

Why are so many students unmediated? Poverty forces one's time to be spent on survival. Many students from poverty live in single-parent families. When there is only one parent, he or she does not have time and energy to both mediate the children and work to put food on the table. And if the parent is nonmediated, his or her ability to mediate the children will be significantly lessened.

To help students learn when they are only partially mediated, four structures must be built as part of direct teaching:

- the structure of the discipline,
- cognitive strategies,
- conceptual frameworks, and
- models for sorting out what is important from what is unimportant in text.

Hidden Rules

One key resource for success in school and at work is an understanding of the hidden rules. Hidden rules are the unspoken cueing system that individuals use to indicate membership in a group. One of the most important middle-class rules is that work and achievement tend to be the driving forces in decision-making. In generational poverty, the driving forces are survival, entertainment, and relationships. This is why a student may have a $30 Halloween costume but an unpaid book bill.

Hidden rules shape what happens at school. For example, if the rule a student brings to school is to laugh when disciplined and he does so, the teacher is probably going to be offended. Yet for

Hidden Class Rules

GENERATIONAL POVERTY	MIDDLE CLASS	WEALTH
The driving forces for decision-making are survival, relationships, and entertainment	The driving forces for decision-making are work and achievement.	The driving forces for decision-making are social, financial, and political connections.
People are possessions. It is worse to steal someone's girlfriend than a thing. A relationship is valued over achievement. That's why you must defend your child no matter what he or she has done. Too much education is feared because the individual might leave.	Things are possessions. If material security is threatened, often the relationship is broken.	Legacies, one-of-a-kind objects, and pedigrees are possessions.
The "world" is defined in local terms.	The "world" is defined in national terms.	The "world" is defined in international terms.
Physical fighting is how conflict is resolved. If you only know casual register, you don't have the words to negotiate a resolution. Respect is accorded to those who can physically defend themselves.	Fighting is done verbally. Physical fighting is viewed with distaste.	Fighting is done through social inclusion/exclusion and through lawyers.
Food is valued for its quantity.	Food is valued for its quality.	Food is valued for its presentation.

OTHER RULES

Generational Poverty

- You laugh when you are disciplined; it is a way to save face.
- The noise level is higher, non-verbal information is more important than verbal. Emotions are openly displayed, and the value of personality to the group is your ability to entertain.
- Destiny and fate govern. The notion of having choices is foreign. Discipline is about penance and forgiveness, not change.
- Tools are often not available. Therefore, the concepts of repair and fixing may not be present.

Middle Class

- Formal register is always used in an interview and is often an expected part of social interaction.
- Work is a daily part of life.
- Discipline is about changing behavior. To stay in the middle class, one must be self-governing and self-supporting.
- A reprimand is taken seriously (at least the pretense is there), without smiling and with some deference to authority.
- Choice is a key concept in the lifestyle. The future is very important. Formal education is seen as crucial for future success.

Wealth

- The artistic and aesthetic are key to the lifestyle and include clothing, art, interior design, seasonal decorating, food, music, social activities, etc.*
- For reasons of security and safety, virtually all contacts are dependent on connection and introductions.
- Education is for the purpose of social, financial and political connections, as well as to enhance the artistic and aesthetic.

**One of the key differences between the well-to-do and the wealthy is that the wealthy almost always are patrons to the arts and often have an individual artist(s) to whom they are patrons as well.*

the student, this is the appropriate way to deal with the situation. The recommended approach is simply to teach the student that he needs a set of rules that brings success in school and at work and a different set that brings success outside of school. So, for example, if an employee laughs at a boss when being disciplined, he will probably be fired.

Many of the greatest frustrations teachers and administrators have with students from poverty are related to knowledge of the hidden rules. These students simply do not know middle-class hidden rules nor do most educators know the hidden rules of generational poverty.

To be successful, students must be given the opportunity to learn these rules. If they choose not to use them, that is their choice. But how can they make the choice if they don't know the rules exist?

Relationships Are Key

When individuals who made it out of poverty are interviewed, virtually all cite an individual who made a significant difference for them. Not only must the relationship be present, but tasks need to be referenced in terms of relationships.

For example, rather than talk about going to college, the conversation needs to be about how the learning will impact relationships. One teacher had this conversation with a 17-year-old student who didn't do his math homework on positive and negative numbers.

"Well," she said, "I guess it will be all right with you when your friends cheat you at cards. You won't know whether they're cheating you or not because you don't know positive and negative numbers, and they aren't going to let you keep score, either." He then used a deck of cards to show her that he knew how to keep score. So she told him, "Then you know positive and negative numbers. I expect you to do your homework."

From that time on, he did his homework and kept an A average. The teacher simply couched the importance of the task according to the student's relationships.

Conclusion

Students from generational poverty need direct teaching to build cognitive structures necessary for learning. The relationships that will motivate them need to be established. The hidden rules must be taught so they can choose the appropriate responses if they desire.

Students from poverty are no less capable or intelligent. They simply have not been mediated in the strategies or hidden rules that contribute to success in school and at work.

References

Feuerstein, Reuven, et al. (1980). *Instrumental Enrichment: An Intervention Program for Cognitive Modifiability.* Glenview, IL: Scott, Foresman.

Joos, Martin (1967). The Styles of the Five Clocks. *Language and Cultural Diversity in American Education,* 1972. Abrahams, R. D. and Troike, R. C., Eds. Englewood Cliffs, NJ: Prentice-Hall.

Making Schools Work for Children in Poverty: A New Framework Prepared by the Commission on Chapter 1 (1992). Washington, DC: AASA, December.

Montano-Harmon, Maria Rosario (1991). Discourse Features of Written Mexican Spanish: Current Research in Contrastive Rhetoric and Its Implications. *Hispania,* Vol. 74, No. 2, May, 417–425.

Montano-Harmon, Maria Rosario (1994). Presentation given to Harris County Department of Education on the topic of her research findings.

Wheatley, Margaret J. (1992). *Leadership and the New Science.* San Francisco, CA: Berrett-Koehler Publishers.

Postnote

Traditionally, teachers come from the middle class or have lower-class origins and are merging into the middle class. Few of America's teachers have an intimate, first-hand experience with the entrenched generational poverty described here. The result is an educational system that is often dramatically out of sync with poor children. When educators, with the best of intentions, respond to this condition, we make one of two errors. The first is to become overly sympathetic and "understanding." This often leads to lowering or relaxing standards for economically disadvantaged children. The second error is to rigidly hold them not only to academic standards, but middle-class standards of speech, dress, and behavior, and to take infractions as a rejection. With impressive insight, Ruby Payne gives us a fresh way to think about this issue and help ways to respond.

Discussion Questions

1. What has been your direct exposure to generational poverty?
2. Do you feel well-prepared to teach the kinds of poor children described in this article? Why or why not? If not, what can you do to become better prepared?
3. In your own elementary and secondary schooling, did you see examples of the kinds of cultural misconnections described in this article?

Hostile Hallways

JACQUELINE WOODS

FOCUS Question

This report tackles a major source of disruption in our secondary schools. What is sexual harassment, and what can we do about it?

Term to Note

Sexual harassment

We all remember that high school classmate—the one whom all the other girls scorned. That girl had her phone number scrawled on every bathroom wall in the school. She endured heckles—and worse—as she walked down the halls. She suffered disapproving glances from students and teachers. In private, she wondered what she had done to deserve such treatment and if she could ever go anywhere or meet anyone without her reputation preceding her.

A 2001 American Association of University Women (AAUW) Educational Foundation report, *Hostile Hallways: Bullying, Teasing, and Sexual Harassment in School,* examines the results of a survey of public school students in grades 8–11. The survey sought to determine how physical and nonphysical harassment in school affects students' lives.[1] The report indicates that sexual harassment happens often, occurs right under teachers' noses, can begin in elementary school, and upsets both girls and boys.

What Is Sexual Harassment?

In an employment context, courts generally recognize two types of sexual harassment: quid pro quo and hostile environment. These correspond to some aspects of the school environment as well. Quid pro quo harassment occurs when, for example, a teacher offers to raise a student's grade in exchange for a sexual act. By contrast, hostile environment harassment in school includes continual sexual taunting.

The AAUW Educational Foundation survey defined sexual harassment as "unwanted and unwelcome sexual behavior that interferes with your life." Sexual harassment does not include behaviors that students like or want (for example, wanted kissing, touching, or flirting). Students responding to the survey reported hearing sexual comments or seeing graffiti, being called *gay* and *lesbian,* being touched or grabbed in a sexual way, being forced to kiss someone or perform other sexual acts, or being bullied or threatened because of their sexual orientation.

Jacqueline Woods is executive director of the American Association of University Women, 1111 Sixteenth St., NW, Washington, DC 20036. From Jacqueline Woods, "Hostile Hallways," *Educational Leadership,* December 2001/January 2002, pp. 20–23. Reprinted with permission of the Association for Supervision and Curriculum Development.

ow Pervasive and Damaging Is It?

The *Hostile Hallways* survey found that four out of five students (81 percent) experience some form of sexual harassment, and 18 percent of students fear being hurt by someone in their school. Girls and boys reported that harassment makes them feel embarrassed (53 and 32 percent respectively), self-conscious (44 and 19 percent), and less confident (32 and 16 percent). Harassed students said that they talk less in class and find it hard to pay attention. Not surprisingly, students change their behaviors to avoid harassers, including skipping school (16 percent), dropping out of a particular activity or sport (9 percent), and dropping courses (3 percent). Girls commented that being sexually harassed makes them feel "dirty—like a piece of trash," "terrible," "awkward," and "like a second-class citizen."

Is Harassment Against the Law?

Title IX of the Education Amendments of 1972 prohibits sexual discrimination, including sexual harassment, in federally funded schools, programs, and activities. States have also enacted statutes against sexual harassment in schools. The Illinois legislature, for example, passed a law requiring schools to create an anti-bullying policy.

The equal protection clause of the Fourteenth Amendment to the U.S. Constitution has been invoked by gay teens seeking relief from sexual harassment. In the case of *Nabozny* v. *Podlesny* (1996), Jamie Nabozny was constantly harassed, both verbally and physically, at school. Harassment included a mock rape in front of his classmates and a beating that left him with broken ribs. When he complained to a school official, Nabozny was told that he "had to expect that kind of stuff" because of his sexual orientation. Nabozny moved to another state to obtain a graduate equivalent degree, and, in 1995, he sued the school district in which he had been harassed. Judges for the 7th U.S. Circuit Court of Appeals ruled that they were "unable to garner any rational basis for permitting one student to assault another based on the victim's sexual orientation" (*Nabozny* v. *Podlesny,* 1996, at 458) and eventually awarded Nabozny $900,000 in damages.

In 1999, the U.S. Supreme Court ruled in *Davis* v. *Monroe County Board of Education* that a school district can be held liable in sexual harassment cases when the school knows about the harassment and fails to deal with it adequately. LaShonda Davis, a 5th grader, reported to her teacher that she had been harassed by a fellow 5th grader who attempted to fondle her breasts, said that he wanted to get in bed with her, and rubbed against her in a sexually suggestive way. Davis complained to three different teachers on several different occasions. One of the teachers told the principal, yet the harassment continued. Finally, Davis's mother pressed charges against the boy for sexual battery, to which he pled guilty. Throughout the ordeal, Davis's grades dropped, and she wrote a suicide note. Davis's mother sued the school district for deliberate indifference, alleging that the principal's inaction led to Davis's emotional distress.

What Can Schools Do?

Establish a Harassment Policy

As reported in *Hostile Hallways,* 70 percent of students know that their schools have a policy that prohibits sexual harassment, a significant increase from the 25 percent of students who knew about such policies when the first AAUW survey was conducted in 1993. One-third of students responded that their schools distribute booklets, handouts, and other literature on sexual harassment. The first step in stopping harassment must be to ensure that all schools have policies on how to handle sexual harassment and that all students understand those policies.

The U.S. Department of Education's Office of Civil Rights (1999) publishes guidelines for creating a school harassment policy. Guidelines include the following suggestions:

- Define the types of harassment—race, color, national origin, ethnicity, sex, disability, sexual orientation, and religion—covered by the policy.

- Identify the kinds of activities and sites where prohibited conduct could occur.
- Include standards for determining whether a hostile environment exists.
- Specify that the school will take remedial action to stop the harassment and prevent recurrence.
- Include specific procedures to address formal complaints of discrimination.
- Require staff to report harassment when they become aware of it.
- Prohibit retaliation against people who report harassment or participate in related proceedings.

The AAUW, in conjunction with the National Education Association, is forming a task force to develop an assessment tool that schools can use to evaluate the effectiveness of their sexual harassment policies.

A zero tolerance policy may indicate that the school does not accept sexual harassment. Such a policy may send mixed signals, however, about which behaviors are acceptable and which are prohibited. After all, sexual harassment does not include such behaviors as kissing or holding hands when these behaviors are welcomed. A zero tolerance policy may also create an adversarial relationship between students and faculty members that discourages students from reporting sexual harassment.

Discuss Harassment with Students

Once an anti-harassment policy is in place, students need more than pamphlets to help them understand sexual harassment. Students need dialogue. They need an opportunity to ask questions about sexual harassment. They need an opportunity to talk to one another about how harassment makes them feel.

Students surveyed for *Hostile Hallways* described the inadequacy of many school programs to deal with harassment. One 8th grade girl suggested,

> Instead of popping in a video and expecting the problem to be solved, teachers need to take time out and talk to us. It's a problem that one video can't fix.

A 10th grade boy said, "They should help distinguish a little more the differences between sexual harassment and accidents."

Researcher Nan Stein (1999) emphasizes that schools have an obligation to be mindful of and vigilant about harassment and peer-on-peer interactions, but that they must also take advantage of "teachable moments"—incidents of inappropriate behavior that can spark students to discuss norms and behaviors in school.

Enforce the Policy

Creating an anti-harassment policy and helping students understand harassment are not enough—the policy must be enforced. According to the AAUW survey, even though students know about school harassment policies, they report harassment in the hallways (71 percent of respondents had experienced physical harassment and 64 percent had experienced nonphysical harassment in the hallways), in the classroom (61 percent physical and 56 percent nonphysical), in the gym (45 percent physical and 43 percent nonphysical), and in the cafeteria (37 percent physical and 38 percent nonphysical). Teachers and administrators are present in all these public places and must be aware of harassment, yet victims—and harassers—know that, all too often, there will be no repercussions for harassing behavior.

All adults in schools, not just teachers, need training to identify sexual harassment and to enforce the school's sexual harassment policy. According to the Office of Civil Rights (1999),

> The lack of a strong, immediate response by a teacher or administrator who is aware of the harassment may be perceived by a student as approval of the activity or as an indication that the student deserves the harassment. (p. 25)

Several companies and individuals help schools train their staff to recognize and deal with sexual harassment.

Create a Supportive Environment

An integral part of successfully preventing sexual harassment in schools includes providing an environment in which students feel comfortable talking to adults about harassment and in which students know that staff members will take their complaints seriously. Schools need to find a middle ground between a casual, laissez-faire attitude toward harassment that may be legally defined as neglectful and an intractable zero tolerance policy that causes staff members to overreact to questionable behaviors and that discourages conversation about the topic.

Some schools have created support groups as a forum for targeted students (gay and lesbian students, for example). Support groups send a message to everyone that such students are a respected part of the student body. Although support groups may cause an uproar in some communities, schools that encourage such groups will go a long way toward creating a supportive and safe environment for all students.

Everyone knows that sexual harassment takes place; in fact, many of us have felt its sting. Nevertheless, none of us should tolerate it. Our perceptions that "boys will be boys" and that "everyone gets teased" must change so that sexual harassment is seen as a serious issue—one that directly affects students' lives and learning.

Note

1. From September through November 2000, Harris Interactive surveyed 2,064 public school students in grades 8–11; 1,559 students were surveyed during an English class, and 505 students were surveyed online. For more information about the survey, visit **www.aauw.org.**

References

Davis v. *Monroe County Board of Education,* 526 U.S. 629 (1999).

Nabozny v. *Podlesny,* 92 F.3d 446 (7th Cir. 1996).

Office of Civil Rights. (1999, January). *Protecting students from harassment and hate crime: A guide for schools.* Washington, DC: U.S. Department of Education. Available: **www.ed.gov/PDFDocs/harassment.pdf**

Stein, N. (1999). *Classrooms and courtrooms: Facing sexual harassment in K–12 schools.* New York: Teachers College Press.

Title IX of the Education Amendments, 20 U.S.C. § 1681 *et seq.* (1972).

Postnote

The author ends her article by urging educators to strike a middle ground between a casual, laissez-faire attitude and an intractable zero tolerance policy that might cause staff members to overreact and discourage conversation about the topic. "Striking a middle ground," while seeming reasonable, may be extremely difficult in the sex-saturated world of today's culture. Middle school and high school students in particular are extremely interested in sex, and most are coming into a time of peak sexual energy. Their sexual drives and curiosities are being catered to continually by much of their out-of-school life, such as popular music, TV sitcoms, movies, and Internet pornography. On the other hand, most educators and serious adults would agree that an active sex life, or even a constant preoccupation with sex, strongly interferes with being a successful student and preparing for adult responsibilities. Why not, then, a zero tolerance policy? Why not ban what used to be called "public displays of affection" in school? Why not ban crude language and sexual teasing? Why not have schools that run counter to the sexually toxic culture that has brought many students HIV and other STDs, unwanted pregnancies, and heartbreaking affairs? Why not?

Discussion Questions

1. Did you experience "hostile hallways" in your school experience?
2. Do you agree with the recommendations of the AAUW? Why or why not?
3. What sort of school policies vis-à-vis adolescent sexual behavior, language, and dress do you think educators should adopt?

How to Create Discipline Problems

M. MARK WASICSKO AND STEVEN M. ROSS

FOCUS Question

What is the classroom philosophy inherent in the authors' suggestions?

TERMS TO NOTE

Discipline problems
Teachers' expectations

Creating classroom discipline problems is easy. By following the ten simple rules listed you should be able to substantially improve your skill at this popular teacher pastime.

1. *Expect the worst from kids.* This will keep you on guard at all times.
2. *Never tell students what is expected of them.* Kids need to learn to figure things out for themselves.
3. *Punish and criticize kids often.* This better prepares them for real life.
4. *Punish the whole class when one student misbehaves.* All the other students were probably doing the same thing or at least thinking about doing it.
5. *Never give students privileges.* It makes students soft and they will just abuse privileges anyway.
6. *Punish every misbehavior you see.* If you don't, the students will take over.
7. *Threaten and warn kids often.* "If you aren't good, I'll keep you after school for the rest of your life."
8. *Use the same punishment for every student.* If it works for one it will work for all.
9. *Use school work as punishment.* "Okay, smarty, answer all the questions in the book for homework!"
10. *Maintain personal distance from students.* Familiarity breeds contempt, you know.

M. Mark Wasicsko is currently Professor and Bank of Kentucky endowed Chair in Educational Leadership at Northern Kentucky University. **Steven M. Ross** is Executive Director at The Center for Research in Educational Policy (CREP) and is a professor of Educational Psychology and Research at The University of Memphis. From M. Mark Wasicsko and Steven M. Ross, "How to Create Discipline Problems," *The Clearing House,* May/June 1994, pp. 248–251. Reprinted with permission of the Helen Dwight Reid Educational Foundation. Published by Heldref Publications, 1319 Eighteenth Street, NW, Washington, DC 20036-1802.

We doubt that teachers would deliberately follow any of these rules, but punishments are frequently dealt out without much thought about their effects. In this article we suggest that many discipline problems are caused and sustained by teachers who inadvertently use self-defeating discipline strategies. There are, we believe, several simple, concrete methods to reduce classroom discipline problems.

Expect the Best from Kids

That teachers' expectations play an important role in determining student behavior has long been known. One author remembers two teachers who, at first glance, appeared similar. Both were very strict, gave mountains of homework, and kept students busy from the first moment they entered the classroom. However, they differed in their expectations for students. One seemed to say, "I know I am hard on you, but it is because I know you can do the work." She was effective and was loved by students. The other conveyed her negative expectations, "If I don't keep these kids busy they will stab me in the back." Students did everything they could to live up to each teacher's expectations. Thus, by conveying negative attitudes toward students, many teachers create their own discipline problems.

A first step in reducing discipline problems is to demonstrate positive expectations toward students. This is relatively easy to do for "good" students but probably more necessary for the others. If you were lucky, you probably had a teacher or two who believed you were able and worthy, and expected you to be capable even when you presented evidence to the contrary. You probably looked up to these teachers and did whatever you could to please them (and possibly even became a teacher yourself as a result). Now is the time to return the favor. Expect the best from *each* of your students. Assume that *every* child, if given the chance, will act properly. And, most important, if students don't meet your expectations, *don't give up*! Some students will require much attention before they will begin to respond.

Make the Implicit Explicit

Many teachers increase the likelihood of discipline problems by not making their expectations about proper behavior clear and explicit. For example, how many times have you heard yourself saying, "Now class, BEHAVE!"? You assume everyone knows what you mean by "behave." This assumption may not be reasonable. On the playground, for example, proper behavior means running, jumping, throwing things (preferably balls, not rocks), and cooperating with other students. Classroom teachers have different notions about proper behavior, but in few cases do teachers spell out their expectations carefully. Sad to say, most students must learn the meaning of "behave" by the process of elimination: "Don't look out the window. . . . Don't put hands on fellow students. . . . Don't put feet on the desk . . . don't . . . don't . . . don't. . . ."

A preferred approach would be to present rules for *proper* conduct on the front end (and try to phrase them positively: "Students should . . ."). The teacher (or the class) could prepare a poster on which rules are listed. In that way, rules are clear, explicit, and ever present in the classroom. If you want to increase the likelihood that rules will be followed, have students help make the rules. Research shows that when students feel responsible for rules, they make greater efforts to live by them.

Rewards, Yes! Punishments, No!

A major factor in creating classroom discipline problems is the overuse of punishments as an answer to misbehavior. While most teachers would agree with this statement, recent research indicates that punishments outweigh rewards by at least 10 to 1 in the typical classroom. The types of punishments identified include such old favorites as The Trip to the Office and "Write a million times, 'I will not. . . .'" But punishments also include the almost unconscious (but frequent) responses made for minor infractions: the "evil eye" stare of disapproval and the countless pleas to "Face front," "Stop talking," "Sit down!" and so on.

Punishments (both major and minor) have at least four consequences that frequently lead to increased classroom disruption: 1) Punishment brings attention to those who misbehave. We all know the adage, "The squeaky wheel gets greased." Good behavior frequently leaves a student nameless and unnoticed, but bad behavior can bring the undivided attention of the teacher before an audience of classmates! 2) Punishment has negative side effects such as aggression, depression, anxiety, or embarrassment. At the least, when a child is punished he feels worse about himself, about you and your class, or about school in general. He may even try to reduce the negative side effects by taking it out on another child or on school equipment. 3) Punishment only temporarily suppresses bad behavior. The teacher who rules with an iron ruler can have students who never misbehave in her presence, but who misbehave the moment she leaves the room or turns her back. 4) Punishment disrupts the continuity of your lessons and reduces the time spent on productive learning. These facts, and because punishments are usually not premeditated (and frequently do not address the real problems of misbehavior such as boredom, frustration, or physical discomfort), usually work to increase classroom discipline problems rather than to reduce them.

In view of these factors, the preferred approach is to use rewards. Rewards bring attention to *good* behaviors: "Thank you for being prepared." Rewards provide an appropriate model for other students, and make students feel positive about themselves, about you, and about your class. Also, reinforcing positive behaviors reduces the inclination toward misbehavior and enhances the flow of your lesson. You stay on task, get more student participation, and accentuate the correct responses.

Let the Punishment Fit the Crime

When rewards are inappropriate, many teachers create discipline problems by using short-sighted or ineffective punishments. The classic example is the "whole class punishment." "Okay, I said if anyone talked there would be no recess, so we stay in today!" This approach frustrates students (especially the ones who were behaving properly) and causes more misbehavior.

Research indicates that punishments are most effective when they are the natural consequences of the behavior. For example, if a child breaks a window, it makes sense to punish him with clean-up responsibilities and by making him pay for damage. Having him write 1,000 times, "I will not break the window," or having him do extra math problems (!) does little to help him see the relationship between actions and consequences.

In reality, this is one of the hardest suggestions to follow. In many cases, the "natural consequences" are obscure ("Okay, Steve, you hurt Carlton's feelings by calling him fat. For your punishment, you will make him feel better."). So, finding an appropriate punishment is often difficult. We suggest that after racking your brain, you consult with the offenders. They may be able to come up with a consequence that at least appears to them to be a fit punishment. In any case, nothing is lost for trying.

If You Must Punish, Remove Privileges

In the event that there are no natural consequences that can serve as punishments, the next best approach is to withdraw privileges. This type of punishment fits in well with the actual conditions in our society. In "real life" (located somewhere outside the school walls) privileges and responsibilities go hand in hand. People who do not act responsibly quickly lose freedoms and privileges. Classrooms provide a great opportunity to teach this lesson, but there is one catch: *There must be privileges to withdraw!* Many privileges already exist in classrooms and many more should be created. For example, students who finish their work neatly and on time can play an educational game, do an extra credit math sheet, work on homework, or earn points toward fun activities and free time. The possibilities are limitless. The important point, however, is that those who break the rules lose out on the privileges.

"Ignor"ance Is Bliss

One of the most effective ways to create troubles is to reward the very behaviors you want to eliminate. Many teachers do this inadvertently by giving attention to misbehaviors. For example, while one author was observing a kindergarten class, a child uttered an expletive after dropping a box of toys. The teachers quickly surrounded him and excitedly exclaimed, "That's nasty! Shame! Shame! Don't ever say that nasty word again!" All the while the other kids looked on with studied interest. So by lunch time, many of the other students were chanting, ". . . (expletive deleted) . . ." and the teachers were in a frenzy! Teachers create similar problems by bringing attention to note passing, gum chewing, and countless other minor transgressions. Such problems can usually be avoided by ignoring minor misbehaviors and, at a later time, talking to the student individually. Some minor misbehavior is probably being committed by at least one student during every second you teach! Your choice is to spend your time trying to correct (and bring attention to) each one *or* to go about the business of teaching.

Consistency Is the Best Policy

Another good way to create discipline problems is to be inconsistent with rules, assignments, and punishments. For example, one author's daughter was given 750 math problems to complete over the Christmas holidays. She spent many hours (which she would rather have spent playing with friends) completing the task. As it turned out, no one else completed the assignment, so the teacher extended the deadline by another week. In this case, the teacher was teaching students that it is all right to skip assignments. When events like this recur, the teacher loses credibility and students are taught to procrastinate, which they may continue to do throughout their lives.

Inconsistent punishment has a similar effect. By warning and rewarning students, teachers actually cultivate misbehavior. "The next time you do that, you're going to the office!" Five minutes pass and then, "I'm warning you, one more time and you are gone!" And later, "This is your last warning!" And finally, "Okay, I have had it with you, go stand in the hall!" In this instance, a student has learned that a punishment buys him/her a number of chances to misbehave (she/he might as well use them all), and that the actual punishment will be less severe than the promised one (not a bad deal).

To avoid the pitfalls of inconsistency, mean what you say, and, when you say it, follow through.

Know Each Student Well

Discipline problems can frequently be caused by punishing students we intended to reward and vice versa. When a student is told to clean up the classroom after school, is that a reward or punishment? It's hard to tell. As we all know, "One person's pleasure is another's poison."

One author remembers the difficulty he had with reading in the fourth grade. It made him so anxious that he would become sick just before reading period in the hope that he would be sent to the clinic, home, or anywhere other than to "the circle." One day, after helping the teacher straighten out the room before school, the teacher thanked him with, "Mark, you've been so helpful, you can be the first to read today." The author made sure he was never "helpful" enough to be so severely punished again.

The opposite happens just as often. For example, there are many class clowns who delight in such "punishments" as standing in the corner, leaving the room, or being called to the blackboard. The same author recalls having to stand in the school courtyard for punishment. He missed math, social studies, and English, and by the end of the day had entertained many classmates with tales of his escapades.

The key to reducing discipline problems is to know your students well; know what is rewarding and what is punishing for each.

Use School Work as Rewards

One of the worst sins a teacher can commit is to use school work as punishments. There is something sadly humorous about the language arts teacher who punishes students with, "Write 1,000 times, I will not . . ." or the math teacher who assigns 100 problems as punishment. In cases like these we are actually punishing students with that which we want them to use and enjoy! Teachers can actually reduce discipline problems (and increase learning) by using their subjects as rewards. This is done in subtle and sometimes indirect ways, through making lessons meaningful, practical, and fun. If you are teaching about fractions, bring in pies and cakes and see how fast those kids can learn the difference between ½, ¼, and ⅛. Reading teachers should allow free reading as a reward for good behavior. Math teachers can give extra credit math sheets (points to be added to the next test) when regular assignments are completed. The possibilities are endless and the results will be less misbehavior and a greater appreciation for both teacher and subject.

Treat Students with Love and Respect

The final suggestion for reducing discipline problems is to treat students kindly. It is no secret that people tend to respond with the same kind of treatment that they are given. If students are treated in a cold or impersonal manner, they are less likely to care if they cause you grief. If they are treated with warmth and respect they will want to treat you well in return. One of the best ways to show you care (and thus reduce discipline problems) is to surprise kids. After they have worked particularly hard, give them a treat. "You kids have worked so hard you may have 30 minutes extra recess." Or have a party one day for no good reason at all. Kids will come to think, "This school stuff isn't so bad after all!" Be careful to keep the surprises unexpected. If kids come to expect them, surprises lose their effectiveness. Recently, one author heard a student pay a teacher the highest tribute. He said, "She is more than just a teacher; she is our friend." Not surprisingly, this teacher is known for having few major discipline problems.

Final Thoughts

When talking about reducing discipline problems, we need to be careful not to suggest that they can or should be totally eliminated. When children are enthusiastic about learning, involved in what they are doing, and allowed to express themselves creatively, "discipline problems" are apt to occur. Albert Einstein is one of numerous examples of highly successful people who were labeled discipline problems in school. It was said of Einstein that he was "the boy who knew not merely which monkey wrench to throw in the works, but also how best to throw it." This led to his expulsion from school because his "presence in the class is disruptive and affects the other students." For dictators and tyrants, robot-like obedience is a major goal. For teachers, however, a much more critical objective is to help a classroom full of students reach their maximum potential as individuals.

The theme of this article has been that many teachers create their own discipline problems. Just as we teach the way we were taught, we tend to discipline with the same ineffectual methods that were used on us. By becoming aware of this and by following the simple suggestions presented above, learning and teaching can become more rewarding for all involved.

Postnote

A friend of ours, Ernie Lundquist, claims that as a student he actually saw a sign on his principal's door that read, "The beatings will continue until the morale improves." While over the years Ernie has not proved to be a particularly reliable source in these matters, his reported sign-sighting underlines the point that student misbehavior often brings out the very worst in educators. In dealing with disruptive, misbehaving students, we who are supposed to stand for the use of intelligence, compassion, and imagination all too often demonstrate stupidity, insensitivity, and a complete lack of imagination.

The authors of this essay take the problem and turn it inside out, suggesting how we can create discipline problems for ourselves. But the real answer they offer us, and one the teacher frequently forgets in the heat of dealing with a discipline problem, is to *be creative!* We expect creativity from our students. Why not show a little in dealing with our discipline problems?

Discussion Questions

1. Which of the authors' "ten simple rules" have you seen demonstrated most frequently in our schools?
2. What do you believe is the central message of this article?
3. What, in your judgment, are the three most practical suggestions offered by the authors? Why?

At Risk for Abuse: A Teacher's Guide for Recognizing and Reporting Child Neglect and Abuse

DENNIS L. CATES, MARC A. MARKELL, AND SHERRIE BETTENHAUSEN

FOCUS Question

Child abuse is becoming increasingly common in our society. What exactly are the classroom teacher's responsibilities?

TERMS TO NOTE

Behavioral indicators

Child abuse of child abuse

Physical indicators of child abuse

In 1992, 2.9 million children were reported as suspected victims of abuse or neglect, an increase of 8% from 1991 (Children, Youth, & Families Department [CYFD], 1993). [Editor's note: In 2002, 3 million incidents of child abuse or neglect were reported, and 900,000 of these reported cases were sustained (*National Clearinghouse on Child Abuse and Neglect Information.* Available at: **http://nccanch.acf.hhs.gov/**).] The exact number of children who are abused is, of course, difficult to determine because many cases of abuse go unreported and the definition of abuse varies from state to state (Winters Communication, Inc. [WCI], 1988). Not only does the definition of abuse differ among states, but professionals also define abuse in different ways (Pagelow, 1984). An additional reason for the difficulty in determining an accurate rate is that there may be a failure to recognize and report child abuse among professionals. Giovannoni (1989) stated that the failure to uncover child abuse and neglect is generally a result of three factors: (a) failure to detect injury caused by abuse, particularly when parents use different medical treatment facilities each time or do not seek medical treatment; (b) failure to recognize the indicators of abuse and neglect, especially for middle- and upper-income families; and (c) failure to report the case to the appropriate agency when injury is detected and recognized as abuse or neglect.

Although exact numbers for children who are abused are not available, it is known that an alarming number of children are abused each year. These children are in our classrooms throughout the United States.

Child abuse can lead to the development of a full range of problems in children, from poor academic performance and socialization to a variety of physical and cognitive disabilities. Because children are required

---

At the time this article was written, **Dennis L. Cates** was an assistant professor in Programs in Special Education at the University of South Carolina in Columbia. **Marc A. Markell** is currently a professor in the Department of Special Education at St. Cloud State University in St. Cloud, Minnesota. **Sherrie Bettenhausen** died in August 2003. At the time this article was written, she was a professor in the Special Education Department of the University of Charleston. Dennis L. Cates, Marc A. Markell, and Sherrie Bettenhausen, "At Risk for Abuse: A Teacher's Guide for Recognizing and Reporting Child Neglect and Abuse," from *Preventing School Failure,* Vol. 39, No. 2, Winter 1995. Reprinted by permission of the authors.

to attend school, teachers and other educators are faced with the responsibility of maintaining a protective and vigilant posture in relation to their students' well-being.

Studies have shown that children with disabilities are at greater risk for abuse and neglect than are nondisabled children (Ammerman, Lubetsky, Hersen, & Van Hasselt, 1988). Meier and Sloan (1984) suggested that "most certifiably abused children have been identified as suffering from various developmental handicaps" (p. 247). They further stated that "it is seldom clear whether or not the handicapping conditions are a result of inflicted trauma or, because of a misreading of the child's abilities by parents, such disappointing delays precipitate further abuse" (pp. 247–248). Blacher (1984) suggested that children with disabilities are more likely to supply the "trigger mechanism" for abuse or neglect. It has further been indicated that parents who abuse often describe their children as being backward, hyperactive, continually crying, or difficult to control.

The premise that a disability, developmental delay, or problem adjusting to the school environment may be directly linked to an abusive home environment requires that educators must be especially vigilant in dealing with those children who are at risk for the development of educational disabilities or poor school performance. Because many children will not report abuse directly, teachers need to be aware of specific behavioral and physical indicators that may indicate that abuse has occurred (Parent Advocacy for Educational Rights [PACER], 1989). The purpose of this article is to provide teachers with potential indicators of abuse, guidelines in dealing with child abuse in at-risk children, and information related to their legal responsibilities in reporting suspected child abuse.

Definitions and Extent of the Problem

The Child Abuse Prevention and Treatment Act of 1974 defines child abuse and neglect as follows:

> the physical or mental injury, sexual abuse or exploitation, negligent treatment, or maltreatment of a child under the age of eighteen, or the age specified by the child protection law of the state in question, by a person who is responsible for the child welfare under the circumstances which indicate that the child's health or welfare is harmed or threatened thereby. (42 U.S.C. § 5102)

Maltreatment of a child can be further described in terms of neglect and physical, verbal, emotional, and sexual abuse.

Neglect typically involves a failure on the part of a parent, guardian, or other responsible party to provide for the child's basic needs, such as food, shelter, medical care, educational opportunities, or protection and supervision. Further, neglect is associated with abandonment and inadequate supervision (Campbell, 1992).

Verbal abuse may involve excessive acts of derision, taunting, teasing, and mocking. Verbal abuse also involves the frequent humiliation of the child as well as a heavy reliance on yelling to convey feelings. Physical abuse can involve shaking, beating, or burning.

Emotional abuse is a pattern of behavior that takes place over an extended period of time, characterized by intimidating, belittling, and otherwise damaging interactions that affect a child's emotional development (PACER, 1989). It may be related to an intent to withhold attention or a failure to provide adequate supervision, or relatively normal living experiences. Sensory deprivation and long periods of confinement are also related to emotional abuse. Emotional abuse is very difficult to define or categorize.

Sexual abuse of children is also referred to as child sexual abuse and child molesting. It is typically defined in terms of the criminal laws of a state and involves intent to commit sexual acts with minors or to sexually exploit children for personal gratification (Campbell, 1992). Sexual intercourse need not take place and, in fact, is rare in prepubertal children. Sexual abuse involves coercion, deceit, and manipulation to achieve power over the child (PACER, 1989).

In Table 1, we provide possible physical and behavioral indicators of neglect and physical, emotional, and sexual abuse. A child who persistently shows several of these characteristics

TABLE 1

Physical and Behavioral Indicators of Possible Neglect and Abuse

PHYSICAL INDICATORS	BEHAVIORAL INDICATORS
Emotional Abuse and Neglect	
• Height and weight significantly below age level • Inappropriate clothing for weather, scaly skin • Poor hygiene, lice, body odor • Child left unsupervised or abandoned • Lack of a safe and sanitary shelter • Unattended medical or dental needs • Developmental lags • Habit disorders	• Begging or stealing food • Constant fatigue • Poor school attendance • Chronic hunger • Dull, apathetic appearance • Running away from home • Child reports that no one cares for/looks after him/her • Sudden onset of behavioral extremes (conduct problems, depression)
Physical Abuse	
• Frequent injuries such as cuts, bruises, or burns • Wearing long sleeves in warm weather • Pain despite lack of evident injury • Inability to perform fine motor skills because of injured hands • Difficulty walking or sitting	• Poor school attendance • Refusing to change clothes for physical education • Finding reasons to stay at school and not go home • Frequent complaints of harsh treatments by parents • Fear of adults
Sexual Abuse	
• Bedwetting or soiling • Stained or bloody underclothing • Venereal disease • Blood or purulent discharge from genital or anal area • Difficulty walking or sitting • Excessive fears, clinging	• Unusual, sophisticated sexual behavior/knowledge • Sudden onset of behavioral extremes • Poor school attendance • Finding reasons to stay at school and not go home

may be experiencing the symptoms of abuse or neglect.

It is important to note that the physical and behavioral indicators of neglect and emotional, sexual, and physical abuse *suggest* or *indicate* that abuse *may* have taken place. They *do not prove* that abuse has occurred and may be indicators of other situations happening in the child's life. Additionally, educators need to be cognizant of the fact that children who are motorically delayed or impaired may be prone to accidents and as a result have bruises, scrapes, cuts, or other minor injuries. This may also be true of children with severely limited vision. Children with diagnosed medical conditions may develop symptoms that result in a change of demeanor or physical appearance. It is important that teachers who serve these children become familiar with the child's condition and be well acquainted with the child's family. Frequent meetings, by telephone and in person, will assist the teacher in keeping up to date with changing medical conditions and aid in monitoring changes in family life patterns.

A teacher who is equipped with knowledge of the symptoms of child abuse and neglect and the characteristics of the child and the family will be able to better determine whether an at-risk learner or child with a disability is a victim of abuse.

Legal Obligations

Children who are at risk for developmental delays are at greater risk for child abuse than children who are not. Teachers who work with these students should, therefore, be aware of their responsibilities relative to child abuse and neglect.

Child abuse cannot be legally ignored by school officials. Teachers and administrators are required by law in all 50 states to report suspected child abuse (Fossey, 1993; Trudell & Whatley, 1988). In most jurisdictions, it is a criminal offense for a person to fail to report abuse when he or she is required by law to do so (Fossey, 1993). Therefore, failure to act may result in the filing of criminal charges or civil suits. The courts have also ruled against teachers for delaying their actions (McCarthy & Cambron-McCabe, 1992). The possibility of criminal or civil proceedings may give many teachers pause and result in undue anxiety or overreaction to the problem. Educators must, therefore, become aware of their legal and administrative responsibilities.

The state laws governing the reporting of child abuse generally require teachers, doctors, school counselors, nurses, dentists, and police, to name a few, to report suspected child abuse to those human services agencies responsible for child welfare. Generally, teachers are required only to have a reasonable suspicion that child abuse has occurred before they are required to report it. Reasonable suspicion suggests that one is relieved of the responsibility of researching a case or of having specific facts related to the incidence of abuse. Given teachers' training in child behavior and their daily contact with children, they are in a position to recognize unusual circumstances. Exercising prudence in reporting suspected abuse will generally protect the teacher from criminal or civil action. Persons who report abuse and neglect *in good faith* to the appropriate state agency are immune from civil liability (Fossey, 1993). Laws vary from state to state in this regard, however.

Reporting laws in all states give final authority to investigate abuse charges to agencies other than the schools (Fossey, 1993). The advantage of reporting suspected abuse to agencies other than the school lies in the fact that the burden of gathering facts does not rest with the school. These agencies can research each case objectively and determine the need for action. Teachers may report child abuse to law enforcement officials; however, most states require them to report to local service agencies such as children's protective services, child abuse hotlines, local welfare departments, local social service agencies, public health authorities, school social workers, nurses, or counselors. In extreme cases, teachers may be required to report cases to hospital emergency rooms. Questions often arise, however, about the procedures for reporting abuse.

Should teachers report suspected abuse directly to the appropriate human service agency or to their building principal or immediate supervisor? These questions may be difficult to answer if specific policies and procedures have not been outlined. If no policy exists, and a teacher reports suspected abuse to the principal, and the principal fails or refuses to report the case to the proper authorities, both teacher and principal may be subject to legal action. In such a case, a teacher may be held responsible depending upon specific circumstances involved.

A specific policy or procedure for reporting abuse should protect the teacher from legal liability if those procedures are followed. A policy requiring a teacher to report to the principal or school counselor relieves the teacher of the need to second-guess the system. Teachers are encouraged to familiarize themselves with existing law as well as district policies related to child abuse. If policies do not exist or are not clear, teachers should work through their professional organizations to help promote institutionalization of such policies.

McCarthy and Cambron-McCabe (1992) suggest that low levels of reporting by teachers may be related to the lack of clearly defined administrative policy. Additionally, they recommend the development of in-service programs to acquaint teachers with their legal responsibilities as well as the signs of abuse.

Even though specific laws may require the person suspecting abuse to report specific information, the following suggestions from PACER (1989), CYFD (1992), and WCI (1988) should answer many questions a teacher may have concerning the reporting of suspected abuse.

1. *To whom should I report suspected child abuse?* If the teacher suspects that a child has been abused, she or he must report the suspected abuse to the local social service agency, the local police, or the local county sheriff's department. Reporting the suspected abuse to another teacher or the school principal may not be enough to fulfill the requirements of mandatory reporting.
2. *Should I tell the parents or alleged abuser of my suspicion of child abuse?* The teacher should not disclose the suspicion of abuse or neglect of a child to either the parents, the caregiver, or the alleged perpetrators. The teacher should report the suspected abuse to the local social service agency, the local police, or the county sheriff's department.
3. *What should I report?* The teacher should report the following information (if known):
   - identifying information about the child (name, age, grade, address, and names of parents)
   - name of the person responsible for the abuse
   - where the alleged abuse took place
   - description of the child, any relevant statements made by the child, and any observations made
   - how long ago the incident described took place
   - the reporter's name, address, and phone number
   - if the child has a disability, any information that may be helpful to the officials (i.e., if the child has difficulty with communication, uses a hearing aid, has mental retardation, emotional, or behavioral difficulties, or has a learning disability that indicates special needs)

Summary

To ensure that accurate information is reported to the appropriate human service agency, teachers who serve children at risk for the development of educational problems must be prudent in their efforts to know their children and their families well. Parents who abuse or neglect their children often exhibit characteristics that may be heightened or triggered during family crises. This is of critical importance to teachers of children at risk for developing educational problems because of the additional stress that often results from the child's presence. Parents who abuse or neglect their child may exhibit low self-esteem or appear to be isolated from the community. They typically fail to appear for parent–teacher conferences and are often defensive when questioned about their child. Their child's injuries are often blamed on others or unsatisfactorily explained. The child may relate stories of abuse or unusual behavior by his or her parents. Limited parenting skills may be a result of lack of education, experience, or maturity. Parents may lack patience and be overly demanding of a child who, because of developmental difficulties, is unable to meet their demands in a timely manner. Often, parents who abuse their children were abused themselves.

In determining whether a child is subject to abuse or neglect, the teacher should make note of consistent behaviors or physical evidence, being aware that one incident may not be evidence of child abuse. An isolated incident should be recorded for future reference but should not necessarily be reported immediately. This will depend, of course, on the severity of the injury or the effect on the child's behavior. Knowing the parents well will certainly aid in making a decision relative to reporting of abuse and neglect.

Recognizing abuse and reporting it to the appropriate agency is expected of all teachers and administrators. The experienced teacher makes the extra effort to gather information about the family, to become well acquainted with the parents, and to monitor all of his or her students' physical and behavioral conditions. Teachers must know their students if they intend to effectively deal with child abuse and neglect.

In addition to understanding the procedures for reporting abuse and neglect, teachers may also contribute to improved parent–student relations by participating in the development of parenting education programs or in setting up a more flexible schedule for parent conferences. Efforts should be made to help parents see the advances and improvements made by their children. As parents develop a more realistic view of their child's abilities and potential, they may become more patient and understanding of their child's actions. Teachers should preface a note home with a friendly telephone call or an informal letter discussing the child's overall performance in school. Given a situation in which abuse is present, a teacher's first note home detailing a disciplinary action may precipitate undue punishment. One key to reduced child abuse is improved parent–teacher communication. Teachers cannot afford to wait for the parent to initiate contact. Open lines of communication must be established and supported by the school's administration.

Children at risk for the development of educational problems are at greater risk for abuse and neglect than those children who develop normally. Teachers who serve these children must be aware of this and be able to recognize the warning signs. They must also have a complete understanding of the legal and administrative procedures for reporting abuse. Most important, they must know their students and work to establish effective parent–teacher communication. To stem the tide of abuse and neglect among disabled and at-risk children, teachers must be vigilant, understanding, observant, prudent, and effective record keepers.

Acknowledgment

We wish to thank Dr. J. David Smith and Dr. Mitchell L. Yell for their editorial assistance in the preparation of this manuscript.

References

Ammerman, R., Lubetsky, M., Hersen, M., & Van Hasselt, V. (1988). Maltreatment of children and adolescents with multiple handicaps: Five case examples. *Journal of the Multihandicapped Person, 1,* 129–139.

Blacher, J. (1984). A dynamic perspective on the impact of a severely handicapped child on the family. In J. Blacher (Ed.), *Severely handicapped young children and their families: Research in review* (pp. 3–50). New York: Academic Press.

Campbell, R. (1992). Child abuse and neglect. In L. Bullock (Ed.), *Exceptionalities in children and youth* (pp. 470–475). Boston: Allyn and Bacon.

Child Abuse Prevention and Treatment Act of 1974, 42 U.S.C. § 5101 et. seq.

Children, Youth, and Families Department (CYFD). (1993). *Stop child abuse/neglect: Prevention and reporting kit.* Available from Children, Youth and Families Department, Social Services Division, Child Abuse Prevention Unit, 300 San Mateo NE, Suite 802, Albuquerque, NM 87108-1516.

Fossey, R. (1993). Child abuse investigations in the public school: A practical guide for school administrators. *Education Law Reporter.* St. Paul, Minn.: West.

Giovannoni, J. (1989). Definitional issues in child maltreatment. In D. Cicchitti & V. Carlson (Eds.), *Child maltreatment: Theory and research on the causes and consequences of child abuse and neglect* (pp. 48–50). New York: Cambridge University Press.

McCarthy, M., & Cambron-McCabe, N. (1992). *Public school law: Teachers' and students' rights.* Boston: Allyn and Bacon.

Meier, J., & Sloan, M. (1984). The severely handicapped and child abuse. In J. Blacher (Ed.), *Severely handicapped young children and their families: Research in review* (pp. 247–272). New York: Academic Press.

Pagelow, M. D. (1984). *Family violence.* New York: Praeger Publishing.

Parent Advocacy for Educational Rights (PACER). (1989). *Let's prevent abuse: An informational guide for educators.* Available from PACER Center, Inc., 4826 Chicago Avenue South, Minneapolis, Minnesota 55407-1055.

Trudell, B., & Whatley, M. H. (1988). School sexual abuse prevention: Unintended consequences and dilemmas. *Child Abuse and Neglect, 12,* 103–113.

Winters Communication, Inc. (WCI). (1988). *Child abuse and its prevention.* Available from Winters Communication, Inc., 1007 Samy Drive, Tampa, Florida 33613.

Postnote

The abuse (or, more accurately stated, the torture) of a helpless child by an adult is one of those crimes that truly cries out for attention. The effects of abuse usually spill over into a child's school life and can make him or her impervious to the best schooling. Recently, greater attention has been given to child abuse in the hope of alerting teachers and other youth workers to the problem and of sensitizing adults to its long-term harm.

The National Clearinghouse on Child Abuse and Neglect Information (in the U.S. Department of Health and Human Services) distributes materials, collects data, and conducts research into this problem area. If you wish to obtain more information, one especially useful report from the Center is entitled, "The Role of Educators in the Prevention and Treatment of Child Abuse and Neglect," which can be found at the Clearinghouse website: **http://nccanch.acf.hhs.gov/.**

Discussion Questions

1. Describe a case of child abuse you know of personally or through media accounts. What was the outcome of the case for all parties involved?
2. What legal responsibilities do teachers have in your state for reporting child abuse? Do they have any legal protection (such as anonymity) once they have reported a case? How comfortable are you with the possibility of meeting these responsibilities?
3. What services are available in your area for children who have been abused? Consider child protection or welfare services as well as law enforcement agencies at the state, county, and city levels.

Raising Expectations for the Gifted

COLLEEN WILLARD-HOLT

FOCUS Question

One of the most demanding challenges of teaching is providing stimulating and appropriate instruction for gifted students. What are some specific strategies that teachers can employ with bright and creative students?

TERMS TO NOTE

Curriculum compacting
Flexible grouping
Multilevel learning stations
Product choice
Tiered assignment
Zone of proximal development

Most gifted students study in regular classrooms for most of their school careers and are taught using the same state standards intended for all students. Most state standards, however, do not provide sufficient intellectual challenge for gifted students.

Neuroscientific research has found that rats in unstimulating environments had thinner cortexes, the part of the brain where higher mental functions reside (Diamond & Hopson, 1998). This effect appeared after just four days!

Education research has shown that gifted students' motivation and performance also declined in the absence of mental stimulation, even leading to underachievement (Purcell, 1993; Whitmore, 1980), but that gifted students exposed to intellectually stimulating content at an accelerated pace outperformed gifted peers not in such programs (Cornell & Delcourt, 1990; Kulik, 1992). It is too great a risk to subject gifted students to a steady diet of unchallenging work.

Standards need not imply standardization of learning activities or expectations. Gifted students may need less time to master a given standard, or they may address the standard in greater depth. Classroom teachers might follow the principle of teaching all students at their optimal level of instruction—what Vygotsky would call their "zone of proximal development" (1978).

How can regular classroom teachers address the needs of their gifted students? The first step in differentiating a standards-based lesson or unit for gifted students is to identify the standards that the lesson will address. An efficient way to accomplish several tasks within one lesson is to combine content, skills, and arts standards. For example, making a poster for National Arbor Day can address science standards in environmental health, language arts standards in research and communication,

Colleen Willard-Holt is an associate professor of education in the School of Behavioral Sciences and Education at Penn State-Capital College. "Raising Expectations for the Gifted," by Colleen Willard-Holt, *Educational Leadership,* October 2003, pp. 72–75. Reprinted by permission. The Association for Supervision and Curriculum Development is a worldwide community of educators advocating sound policies and sharing best practices to achieve the success of each learner. To learn more, visit ASCD at **www.ascd.org.**

and standards regarding the elements and principles of visual art.

Teachers can then assess students' grasp of content and skills. They might pretest the students, using an end-of-chapter test that integrates skills with content, or review students' achievement on content and skills that they have previously studied. Perusing student portfolios or assessing interests and multiple intelligences profiles can also provide insight into skills and content knowledge.

Once teachers have determined students' readiness levels, they can execute differentiation strategies. Curriculum compacting, flexible grouping, product choices, tiered assignments, and multilevel learning stations are excellent strategies for differentiating instruction for gifted students in regular classrooms (see Gregory & Chapman, 2002; Maker & Nielson, 1996; Reis, Burns, & Renzulli, 1992; Tomlinson, 1999; Willard-Holt, 1994). Some of these strategies also lend themselves well to meeting the needs of gifted students with disabilities.

Curriculum Compacting

Curriculum compacting is a powerful strategy for ensuring accountability for standards while acknowledging what students already know. Curriculum compacting means streamlining what is taught to students by first assessing their prior knowledge and then modifying or eliminating work that has been partially or fully mastered. After teachers assess student mastery of a particular standard, three groups often emerge: students with poor mastery, students with partial mastery, and students with full mastery who are ready for more advanced work.[1] The first group, usually the largest, proceeds with the planned sequence of instruction; the second group may accomplish the planned sequence more quickly and then proceed to a greater challenge; the third group may begin an independent project immediately.

Consider this math standard for grade 3: "Count, compare, and make change using a collection of coins and one-dollar bills" (PA Std. 2.1.3E).[2] The first group is ready to make several combinations of pennies, nickels, and dimes for given amounts. The second group is confident of these steps and can make change, but they need help using quarters. They will join the rest of the class when the teacher provides information and practice with quarters; the rest of the time they work together on a coin-related project that they will present to the class. The project might entail making a poster of U.S. coinage from colonial times to the present, using drawings, replicas, or actual coins when available. The third group's students, who tested 85 percent or above on the pretest, are making a chart that compares currency systems for different countries. They will defend their choice of the most efficient system at the end of the unit. Such higher-order thinking projects may also satisfy language arts standards, using a similar process for compacting skill standards in reading or writing.

In middle and high school grades, gifted students may not have the technical knowledge to meet a particular content standard and therefore may not show mastery on a pretest. They may be able to learn the content quickly by reading the text and completing application exercises on their own, however, and then successfully complete a criterion-referenced posttest. For example, a life sciences course might focus on the 10th grade standard, "Identify and characterize major life forms by kingdom, phylum, class, and order" (PA Std. 3.3.10A). The teacher invites students who have performed well in previous science units to read the text and work through a packet of exercises at their own pace. This packet consists of activities crucial to understanding the topic and differs from the step-by-step exercises given to the rest of the class. When ready, students take the posttest and, if they demonstrate mastery, undertake an in-depth project, such as creating a three-dimensional clay model of a dissected starfish (Miller & Willard-Holt, 2000). This project addresses skill and arts standards simultaneously.

Teachers can also use compacting with gifted students who have disabilities. If the goal is to master content quickly while circumventing the disability, the teacher can compact in areas of weakness as well as strength. For the standard, "Identify planets in our solar system and their general characteristics" (PA Std. 3.4.4D), the class assignment might be a written report on a planet. A gifted student with a writing disability who demonstrates mastery of the characteristics of the planets on a pretest might instead research current theories about the birth of galaxies and create a PowerPoint presentation.

It is not always necessary to focus on remediation. If the goal is to develop coping strategies for the disability, compacting can focus on the area of strength.

Flexible Grouping

Flexible grouping is particularly effective when students' achievement levels in content and skills differ, as is often the case for gifted students with disabilities. The teacher groups students according to strength, need, or interest, and groups change frequently, sometimes in the course of a single class session. As an illustration, an 11th grade English class might address the standards, "Analyze the relationships, uses, and effectiveness of literary elements used by one or more authors, including characterization, setting, plot, theme, point of view, tone, and style" (PA Std. 1.3.11B) and "Write short stories, poems, and plays" (PA Std. 1.4.11A). The class has read a scene from *Romeo and Juliet,* viewed the corresponding scene from *West Side Story,* and discussed similarities and differences. In groups, students write a contemporary scene in which young people are in love despite their families' differences. Drawing on their knowledge of current events, students research the conflict between the groups that the families represent, such as Israelis versus Palestinians, big business versus environmentalists, or Shiite versus Sunni Muslims. Students could also choose groups that are at odds in their immediate community.

Students initially come together around the specific conflict that most interests them, with groups changing later as needed. Each group has students with mixed levels of ability. The teacher provides mini-lessons to address specific skills—for example, how to research the conflict using print resources, Internet, and interviews of community leaders; write authentic dialogue; punctuate dialogue correctly; or write stage directions. Later, gifted students might meet together to choose a multilayered conflict, the threads of which they must logically incorporate into the scene.

Product Choices

Another way to plan for gifted students is to allow them choices of what kind of product they will produce. In the *Romeo and Juliet* example, one group might complete a written script (verbal/linguistic intelligence); another, a videotaped dramatization of the scene (bodily/kinesthetic intelligence); and a third, a comic strip (visual/spatial intelligence). In this way, each group addresses the same content standard but uses a different skill or arts standard.

For the 6th grade standard, "Describe the human characteristics of places and regions by their cultural characteristics" (PA Std. 7.3.6B), students studying a unit on Central and South America might choose to create an authentic traditional costume, dance, food, artwork, or model of a home—developing a three-dimensional model, drawing, or verbal description. The projects appeal to different intelligences and address different skills and arts standards.

Product choices are important for gifted students with disabilities, allowing them to demonstrate their understanding of the content without their disability interfering. For example, a student with a learning disability in written expression may conduct research, make the necessary cognitive connections, and demonstrate understanding through art and oral expression, thereby circumventing writing. A blind student may conduct research by using text-to-speech interfaces on the Internet and create a three-dimensional model. In each case, the focus is on content mastery. Assignments in other areas would remediate or develop coping strategies for the disability.

Tiered Assignments

The advantage of this strategy is that the entire class studies the same content, but individual students choose assignments at different levels of complexity, with the teacher's assistance. For example, coupling a 4th grade science standard, "Know basic weather elements"(PA Std. 3.4.4C), with a math standard, "Organize and display data using pictures, tallies, tables, charts, bar graphs, and circle graphs" (PA Std. 2.6.5A), allows students to learn how to gather weather data from various sources and graph the data. Assignment choices might include

- Making a bar graph that shows the average monthly temperatures in two cities (basic level).
- Choosing two appropriate types of graphs to show the proportion of rainy days to sunny days, and the average rainfall by months in a city of your choice (average level).
- Generating two appropriate graphs on the computer to show the ratio of rain to snow, and monthly temperature and precipitation in a city of your choice (advanced level).

Students choose the assignment that sounds most interesting and best stimulates their learning. Gentle nudging might encourage students to accept the appropriate level of challenge.

Multilevel Learning Stations

Multilevel learning stations provide meaningful independent work that extends and enriches class discussions. For example, a learning station can assist 3rd grade students studying ancient civilizations by addressing history, geography, arts, and language arts standards, including the following:

- Compare similarities and differences between the earliest civilizations and life today (PA Std. 8.4.3C).
- Explain the historical, cultural, and social context of an individual work in the arts (PA Std. 9.2.3A).
- Relate works in the arts chronologically to historical events (PA Std. 9.2.3B) or geographic regions (PA Std. 9.2.3G).

Activity cards address such topics as leaders/famous people, arts, structures, ways of life, and location. In addition, the teacher codes the activity cards according to Bloom's thinking levels: red for knowledge/comprehension, blue for application, green for analysis, yellow for synthesis, and white for evaluation. On the basis of assessment data, each student receives an assignment sheet detailing the number of activities that he or she is to complete at each level. For example, Juan will do one of each color; Sarah will select five activities, all at green, yellow, or white levels; and Randy will choose five red or blue activities.

Teachers often assume that learning stations are appropriate only for the elementary grades, yet secondary students also seem to enjoy them. For example, U.S. history students addressing the Civil War might explore in depth topics relating to battles, leaders, military technology, camp life, civilian life, or the roles of women or African Americans in the war, according to their interests.

Inspiring Extraordinary Achievement

Some gifted students' capabilities and rates of learning are so far beyond their chronological ages that they would spend almost all of their time reviewing what they already knew if they followed the curriculum offered in a regular classroom. These students need a highly individualized program at an advanced level, perhaps through acceleration or mentoring. Other gifted students may be highly advanced in one subject and could benefit from acceleration or mentoring in that subject while remaining in the inclusive classroom for the remainder of the day.

Providing gifted students with instruction at the appropriate level also removes pressure that they might feel in cooperative learning situations within inclusive classrooms. It may be tempting to ask advanced students to tutor others—a strategy that is permissible on occasion, but inappropriate as a regular activity. Gifted students, like all students, come to school to encounter new learning challenges. Depending on gifted students as peer tutors also places them at risk for social isolation if other students come to view them as teacher's pets or know-it-alls (Robinson, 1990).

Teaching to standards need not mean standardization of learning activities or expectations. Simply meeting standards is not an adequate challenge for most gifted students, although that is all the law may require of them. As Tomlinson states in reference to the No Child Left Behind Act of 2001,

> There is no incentive for schools to attend to the growth of students once they attain proficiency . . . and certainly not to inspire those who far exceed proficiency. (2002, p. 36)

Don't we want more than minimal proficiency from our gifted students? By using strategies to challenge all students at their optimal levels of instruction, teachers can meet their responsibilities for accountability while inspiring extraordinary achievement.

References

Cornell, D. G., & Delcourt, M. A. B. (1990). Achievement, attitudes, and adjustment. *Communicator, 20* (5), 28.

Diamond, M., & Hopson, J. (1998). *Magic trees of the mind.* New York: Plume Books.

Gregory, G. H., & Chapman, C. (2002). *Differentiated instructional strategies: One size doesn't fit all.* Thousand Oaks, CA: Corwin Press.

Kulik, J. A. (1992). *An analysis of the research on ability grouping* (RBDM 9204). Storrs, CT: University of Connecticut, The National Research Center on the Gifted and Talented.

Maker, C. J., & Nielson, A. B. (1996). *Curriculum development and teaching strategies for gifted learners* (2nd ed.). Austin, TX: Pro-Ed.

Miller, B., & Willard-Holt, C. (2000). *Dare to differentiate: Strategies for enrichment in middle school science.* Manassas, VA: Gifted Education Press.

Purcell, J. H. (1993). The effects of the elimination of gifted and talented programs on participating students and their parents. *Gifted Child Quarterly, 37*(4), 177–187.

Reis, S. M., Burns, D. E., & Renzulli, J. S. (1992). *Curriculum compacting.* Mansfield Center, CT: Creative Learning Press.

Robinson, A. (1990). Cooperation or exploitation? The argument against cooperative learning for talented students. *Journal for the Education of the Gifted, 14* (3), 9–27, 31–36.

Tomlinson, C. A. (1999). *The differentiated classroom: Responding to the needs of all learners.* Alexandria, VA: ASCD.

Tomlinson, C. A. (2002, Nov. 6). Proficiency is not enough. *Education Week, 22* (10), 36, 38.

Vygotsky, L. S. (1978). *Mind in society: The development of higher psychological processes.* Cambridge, MA: Harvard University Press.

Whitmore, J. R. (1980). *Giftedness, conflict, and underachievement.* Boston: Allyn and Bacon.

Willard-Holt, C. (1994). Strategies for individualizing instruction in regular classrooms. *Roeper Review, 17* (1), 43–45.

Endnotes

1. A fourth group—those not yet ready to attempt the standard—is beyond the scope of this article.
2. I refer to Pennsylvania standards. The standards are available at **www.pde.state.pa.us/stateboard_ed; click Academic Standards.**

Postnote

Every child, no matter what his or her level of ability, is of immeasurable importance. The work of the teacher is to draw out and extend each child's abilities and capacities. In addition to this blanket responsibility, however, gifted students offer the teacher a particular challenge. Although most gifted students are a delight to teach, they can also be demanding, exhausting, and sometimes quite frustrating. They devour material. They often get quickly bored, which sometimes leads them into trouble. Sometimes, their intellectual development is well beyond their emotional development. Nevertheless, these students who come into our schools with great intelligence or creativity or rare abilities are a precious resource to our nation and to the world. They need to be handled with care.

Discussion Questions

1. In your own words, how would you describe "giftedness"?
2. This article and the Postnote seem to suggest that teachers need to make special plans and go to special efforts for gifted students. Do you believe this is fair? Why or why not?
3. Which two of the five strategies offered by the author appeal most to you as a learner? As a teacher?

Part Three Schools

Schools and schooling in the United States have been the object of intense scrutiny and considerable criticism in recent years. Disappointing test scores, disciplinary problems, violence, and a lack of clear direction are all points of tension. In the past few years, there has been a shift in what educators, legislators, and critics say schools must do to address these and other problems. There is a sense that schools have drifted away from their most important purpose—that is, to prepare students academically and intellectually. Schools have lost sight, some say, of a sense of excellence.

Some of the selections in this section consider this emphasis, whereas others pose alternative solutions. The topics include characteristics of good schools, school culture, the size of schools, schools that focus on teachers, and some of the new approaches to school improvement.

CLASSIC

The Culture Builder

ROLAND S. BARTH

FOCUS Question

What is a "culture" and in what ways does a school have a culture?

Terms to Note

Nondiscussables

School culture

Stakeholders

Probably the most important—and the most difficult—job of an instructional leader is to change the prevailing culture of a school. The school's culture dictates, in no uncertain terms, "the way we do things around here." A school's culture has far more influence on life and learning in the schoolhouse than the president of the country, the state department of education, the superintendent, the school board, or even the principal, teachers, and parents can ever have. One cannot, of course, change a school culture alone. But one can provide forms of leadership that invite others to join as observers of the old and architects of the new. The effect must be to transform what we did last September into what we would like to do next September.

The culture of a school is apparent to the newcomer. In one school, a beginning teacher stands up in a faculty meeting to express her views to the others on, say, pupil evaluation. Her contribution is received with mockery, cold stares, and put-downs. "Who does she think she is?" As the new teacher quickly learns, the culture at her school dictates that newcomers must not speak until they have experienced, for at least two or three years, the toil and tedium of the old-timers. "That's the way we do things around here." And she learns that cruel and unusual punishments await those who violate the cultural taboos of the school.

In another school, a high school student is tormented by his peers for studying on the day of the football game. And, indeed, the culture in many schools dictates that learning is not "cool" on Saturdays—or on any day of the week, for that matter.

In yet another school, a teacher encounters trouble managing a class full of difficult youngsters. Within a few days, every other teacher in the building knows of her problem—and volunteers to help. In the same school, when a student is experiencing difficulty with an assignment or a new concept, several fellow students step in to assist. "That's the way we do things around here."

Roland S. Barth is a former teacher, principal, and member of the faculty of Harvard University, where he founded the Harvard Principals' Center and the International Network of Principals' Centers. "The Culture Builder," by Roland S. Barth, from *Learning by Heart,* by Roland S. Barth.

A school's culture is a complex pattern of norms, attitudes, beliefs, behaviors, values, ceremonies, traditions, and myths that are deeply ingrained in the very core of the organization. It is the historically transmitted pattern of meaning that wields astonishing power in shaping what people think and how they act.

Every school has a culture. Some are hospitable, others toxic. A school's culture can work for or against improvement and reform. Some schools are populated by teachers and administrators who are reformers, others by educators who are gifted and talented at subverting reform. And many school cultures are indifferent to reform.

And all school cultures are incredibly resistant to change, which makes school improvement—from within or from without—usually futile. Unless teachers and administrators act to change the culture of a school, all innovations, high standards, and high-stakes tests will have to fit in and around existing elements of the culture. They will remain superficial window dressing, incapable of making much of a difference.

To change the culture requires that the instructional leader become aware of the culture, the way things are done here. What do you see, hear, and experience in the school? What *don't* you see and hear? What are the clues that reveal the school's culture? What behaviors get rewards and status? Which ones are greeted with reprimands? Do the adults model the behavior they expect of students? Who makes the decisions? Do parents experience welcome, suspicion, or rejection when they enter the school?

Nondiscussables

An important part of awareness is attending to "nondiscussables." Nondiscussables are subjects sufficiently important that they are talked about frequently but are so laden with anxiety and fearfulness that these conversations take place only in the parking lot, the rest rooms, the playground, the car pool, or the dinner table at home. Fear abounds that open discussion of these incendiary issues—at a faculty meeting, for example—will cause a meltdown. The nondiscussable is the elephant in the living room. Everyone knows that this huge pachyderm is there, right between the sofa and the fireplace, but we go on mopping and dusting and vacuuming around it as if it did not exist.

Each school has its own nondiscussables. For one it is "the leadership of the principal." For another, it is "the way decisions are made here." For many it is "race" or "the underperforming teacher." Schools are full of these land mines from which trip wires emanate. We walk about carefully, trying not to detonate them. Yet by giving these nondiscussables this incredible power over us, by avoiding them at all cost, we issue the underperforming teacher a license to continue this year as he did last year, taking a heavy toll on countless students and other teachers. We deprive the principal of honest, timely feedback and thereby continue to suffer from poor leadership. We condemn ourselves to live with all the debilitating tensions that surround race.

The health of a school is inversely proportional to the number of nondiscussables: the fewer nondiscussables, the healthier the school; the more nondiscussables, the more pathology in the school culture. To change the culture of the school, the instructional leader must enable its residents to name, acknowledge, and address the nondiscussables—especially those that impede learning. No mean task, for as one principal put it, "These nondiscussables are the third rail of school leadership."

Changing the Culture

It is said that a fish would be the last creature on earth to discover water, so totally and continuously immersed in it is he. The same might be said of those working within the school culture. By the time a beginning teacher waits the obligatory three years to speak in a faculty meeting, she, too, is likely to be so immersed in the culture that she will no longer be able to see with a beginner's clarity the school's cultural patterns of leadership, competition, fearfulness, self-interest, or lack of support.

To change the culture requires that more desirable qualities replace the existing unhealthy elements. Clear personal and collective visions are crucial for this enterprise. Educators Saphier and King identified a dozen healthy cultural norms: collegiality, experimentation, high expectations, trust and confidence, tangible support, reaching out to the knowledge bases, appreciation and recognition, caring celebration and humor, involvement in decision making, protection of what's important, traditions, and honest and open communication.[1] These qualities dramatically affect the capacity of a school to improve—and to promote learning.

To change a school's culture requires mustering the courage and skill to not remain victimized by the toxic elements of the school's culture and to address them instead. Culture building requires the will to transform the elements of school culture into forces that support rather than subvert the school's purposes. Of course, these acts violate the taboos of many school cultures, which is why culture changing is the most important, difficult, and perilous job of school-based reformers.

E. B. White observed, "A person must have something to cling to. Without that we are as a pea vine sprawling in search of a trellis." We educators need a trellis to keep us off the ground in the face of the cold rains and hot winds that buffet the schoolhouse. The trellis of our profession—and the most crucial element of school culture—is an ethos hospitable to the promotion of human learning.

Learning Curves off the Chart

The ability to learn prodigiously from birth to death sets human beings apart from other forms of life. The greatest purpose of school is to unlock, release, and foster this wonderful capability.

Schools exist to promote learning in all their inhabitants. Whether we are teachers, principals, professors, or parents, our primary responsibility is to promote learning in others and in ourselves. That responsibility sets educators apart from insurance salespeople, engineers, and doctors. To the extent that our activities in school are dedicated to getting learning curves off the chart, what we do is a calling. To the extent that we spend most of our time doing something else in school, we are engaged in a job.

Recent school reforms are an invitation—nay, a demand—to examine every school policy, practice, and decision and ask, What, if anything, of importance is anyone learning as a consequence of doing *that*? Who learns what from ability grouping? Who learns what from letter grades of *A, B,* and *C*? Who learns what from having 26 students in a class? Who learns what from the annual practice of principals evaluating teachers? We created the myriad school practices that now clutter a school's culture because at some time someone believed that this policy, practice, or procedure was capable of getting someone's learning curve off the chart.

The instructional leader must assist the faculty in taking continual, fresh inventory of these and other habituated practices encrusted in our schools' cultures and in categorizing them. Some—such as the practice of providing individual instruction or giving students immediate feedback on their work—seem undeniably associated with promoting learning. Keep those. Others—such as ability grouping or parent nights—we may need to study to determine just what effect, if any, they are having on people's learning. Still other practices—perhaps faculty meetings or intrusive announcements over the loudspeaker—appear to contribute to no one's learning—or may even impede learning—and need to be scrapped. A final category is for the activities that must continue but in a more successful way.

Residing in all the stakeholders in schools—parents, teachers, students, principals—are wonderful, fresh, imaginative ideas about a better way. Achieving that better way takes recognition of and moral outrage at ineffective practices, confidence that there *is* a better way, and the courage and invention to find that way and implement it. Whose learning curve goes off the chart by doing *that*? is a revolutionary question whose time has finally come.

At-Risk Students

Unhealthy school cultures tend to beget at-risk students—students who leave school before or after graduation with little possibility of continuing learning.

I remember visiting a high school just after the last spring exams and before graduation. As I approached the school grounds, I saw a group of students standing around a roaring fire, to which they were heartily contributing. I went over and asked, "What's up?"

"We're burning our notes and our books," replied one. "We're outta here!"

On further conversation, I learned that these students were not from the bottom ability group, but rather *A, B,* and *C* students, many headed for college.

That fire continues to smolder within me. I wonder how many of our students not so labeled are in fact at risk, with little possibility of continuing learning. How many of them graduate from our schools and exult in the belief that they have learned all they ever need or intend to know?

One reason that those students were burning those books, literally, and that so many more students burn their books figuratively at the end of the school year is that lurking beneath the culture of most schools is a chilling message: *Learn or we will hurt you.* Educators have taken learning—a wonderful, spontaneous capacity of all human beings—and coupled it with punitive measures. We have developed an arsenal of sanctions and punishments that we inextricably link with learning experiences. "Johnny, if you don't learn your multiplication tables, you're going to have to repeat 4th grade." "Mary, if you don't improve your compositions, I'm not going to write a favorable recommendation for college." "Tom, if your standardized test scores don't improve, you don't graduate." And so it goes. What those students burning their books are really telling us is, "You can't hurt me anymore."

But so closely have we coupled learning and punishment that the students throw one into the fire with the other. School cultures in which students submit to learning, and to the threats of punishment for not learning, generate students who want to be finished with learning when they graduate. And, of course, this applies to adults as well. The state tells the teacher or principal, "Unless you complete 15 hours of continuing education credits this year, we will not renew your certification." Learn or we will hurt you.

An immense challenge to the instructional leader—and to our profession—is to find ways to *un*couple learning and punishment. We must change the message to students—and to their educators—from "Learn or we will hurt you" to "Learn or you will hurt yourself." Students who burn their books and their notes and celebrate the conclusion of their learning will be relegated to the periphery of the 21st century. Those who will thrive in the years ahead, in contrast, will be those who have become—during their school experience—active, voracious, independent, lifelong learners. The nature of the workplace, our society, and learning dictates that we need to learn as we go along, or we won't survive.

Yearning for Learning

The most important requirement for graduation—whether from 4th, 9th, or 12th grade—is some evidence that this student is becoming or has become an independent, lifelong learner. We must look closely at what students choose to do with their own time. What evidence is there of enduring intellectual passion in this student? Is the student capable of posing questions, marshaling resources, and pursuing learning with dedication, independence, imagination, and courage?

If your school has succeeded in getting 95 percent of its students scoring at the 95th percentile on standardized tests, and if, at the same time, students are leaving a teacher, a grade, or the school "burning their books" and saying "I'm done with this stuff; I'm outta here," then you have won a battle but lost the war. The price of short-term success is long-term failure. Enhancement of performance has led to a curtailment of lifelong learning. The school has failed in its most important mission—to create and provide a culture hospitable to human learning and to make it likely that students and educators will become and remain life-long learners. This is what instructional leadership is all about.

"Our School Is a Community of Learners!" How many times do we see and hear this assertion? It is both an ambitious, welcome vision and an empty promissory note. The vision is, first, that the school will be a *community,* a place full of adults and students who care about, look after, and root for one another and who work together for the good of the whole, in times of need and in times of celebration. Every member of the community holds some responsibility for the welfare of every other and for the welfare of the community as a whole. Schools face tremendous difficulty in fulfilling this definition of a community. More are organizations, institutions, or bureaucracies.

As if community were not ambitious enough, the defining, underlying culture of this community is *learning.* The condition for membership in the community is that one learns, continues to learn, and supports the learning of others. Everyone. A tall order to fill, and one to which few schools aspire and even fewer attain.

When we come to believe that our schools should be providing a culture that creates and sustains a community of student and adult learning—that this is the trellis of our profession—then we will organize our schools, classrooms, and learning experiences differently. Show me a school where instructional leaders constantly examine the school's culture and work to transform it into one hospitable to sustained human learning, and I'll show you students who do just fine on those standardized tests.

Note

1. Saphier, J., and King, M. (1985). Good seeds grow in strong cultures. *Educational Leadership, 42*(6), 67–74.

Postnote

We have selected this article as a Classic because it points out the rarely recognized, and rarely addressed, power of a school's culture. Only rarely do we step back and acknowledge that this or that is "the way we do things around here." Except for the very wise ones, old-timers are rarely aware of the dynamics (sometimes quite bizarre) of their culture. Newcomers, on the other hand, are often surprised and sometimes quite disoriented by their new culture. As Roland Barth makes clear in his article, schools have cultures, and those cultures vary enormously. The experienced teachers in a school, the old hands, are quite accustomed to the school's culture, even if it is rather dysfunctional. A new teacher, however, sees the school and its culture with fresh eyes, particularly if it is different from the schools she has attended. Not a few first-year teachers get off on the wrong foot with veteran teachers by disparaging what they find odd or foolish or wrong about their new surroundings. Prudence recommends that new teachers hold their fire until they are fully respected by their new peers and have been able to establish themselves. The author of this Postnote was once upon a time a rather brash first-year teacher. His department chairman, a former army sergeant, gave him a tip from his military years when he said, "Don't sound off until your barracks bag stops swinging." In other words, wait a while before you start making suggestions for improvement.

Discussion Questions

1. Have you ever been in a new culture and been confused by what was going on around you? Specifically, what was different, and what did you do?
2. Reflecting on your own school experience, do you see aspects of school culture that differ significantly from what you believe would be good educational practice?
3. What would you suggest (for yourself and other teachers) to continually keep perspective on your school's culture?

CLASSIC

A Tale of Two Schools

LARRY CUBAN

FOCUS Question

Can schools with seemingly divergent philosophies of education nevertheless prepare their students to be good citizens in a democracy?

Terms to Note

Good school
Progressive school
Traditional school

For this entire century, there has been conflict among educators, public officials, researchers, and parents over whether traditionalist or progressive ways of teaching reading, math, science, and other subjects are best. Nowhere has this unrelenting search for the one best way of teaching a subject or skill been more obvious than in the search for "good" schools. Progressives and traditionalists each have scorn for those who argue that there are many versions of "good" schools. Partisan debates have consumed policymakers, parents, practitioners, and researchers, blocking consideration of the unadorned fact that there is more than one kind of "good" school.

What follows is a verbal collage of two elementary schools I know well. School A is a quiet, orderly school where the teacher's authority is openly honored by both students and parents. The principal and faculty seek out students' and parental advice when making schoolwide decisions. The professional staff sets high academic standards, establishes school rules that respect differences among students, and demands regular study habits from the culturally diverse population. Drill and practice are parts of each teacher's daily lesson. Report cards with letter grades are sent home every nine weeks. A banner in the school says: "Free Monday through Friday: Knowledge—Bring Your Own Container." These snippets describe what many would call a "traditional" school.

School B prizes freedom for students and teachers to pursue their interests. Most classrooms are multiage (6- to 9-year-olds and 7- to 11-year-olds). Every teacher encourages student-initiated projects and trusts children to make the right choices. In this school, there are no spelling bees; no accelerated reading program; no letter or numerical grades. Instead, there is a year-end narrative in which a teacher describes the personal growth of each student. Students take only those standardized tests required by the state. A banner in the classroom reads: "Children need a place to run! explore! a world to discover." This brief description describes what many would call a "progressive" school.

Larry Cuban is an emeritus professor of education at Stanford University, Stanford, California. Reprinted with permission from *Education Week,* Vol. 17, No. 20, January 28, 1998, and from the author.

I will argue that both Schools A and B are "good" schools. What parents, teachers, and students at each school value about knowledge, teaching, learning, and freedom differs. Yet both public schools have been in existence for 25 years. Parents have chosen to send their children to the schools. Both schools have staffs that volunteered to work there. And both schools enjoy unalloyed support: Annual surveys of parent and student opinion have registered praise for each school; each school has had a waiting list of parents who wish to enroll their sons and daughters; teacher turnovers at each school have been virtually nil.

Moreover, by most student-outcome measures, both schools have compiled enviable records. In academic achievement, measured by standardized tests, School A was in the top 10 schools in the entire state. School B was in the upper quartile of the state's schools.

These schools differ dramatically from one another in how teachers organize their classrooms, view learning, and teach the curriculum. Can both of them be "good"? The answer is yes.

What makes these schools "good"? They have stable staffs committed to core beliefs about what is best for students and the community, parents with beliefs that mirror those of the staffs, competent people working together, and time to make it all happen. Whether one was traditional or progressive was irrelevant. The century-long war of words over traditional vs. progressive schooling is a cul-de-sac, a dead end argument that needs to be retired once and for all.

What partisans of each fail to recognize is that this pendulum-like swing between traditional and progressive schooling is really a deeper political conflict over what role schools should play in society. Should schools in a democracy primarily concentrate on making citizens who fulfill their civic duties? Should schools focus on efficiently preparing students with skills credentials to get jobs and maintain a healthy economy? Honor individual excellence yet treat everyone equally? Or should schools do everything they can to develop the personal and social capabilities of each and every child? For almost two centuries of tax-supported public schooling in the United States, all of these goals have been viewed as both important and achievable.

The war of words between progressives and traditionalists has been a proxy for this political struggle over goals. Progressive vs. traditionalist battles over discipline in schools, national tests, tracking students by their performance, and school uniforms mask a more fundamental tension in this country over which goals for public schools should have priority.

The problem lies not in knowing how to make schools better. Many parents and educators already know what they want and possess the requisite knowledge and skills to get it. Schools A and B are examples of that knowledge in action. The problem is determining what goals public schools should pursue, given the many goals that are desired and inescapable limits on time, money, and people.

Determining priorities among school goals is a political process of making choices that involves policymakers, school officials, taxpayers, and parents. Deciding what is important and how much should be allocated to it is at the heart of the process. Political parties, lobbies, and citizen groups vie for voters' attention. Both bickering and deliberation arise from the process. Making a school "good" is not a technical problem that can be solved by experts or scientific investigation into traditional or progressive approaches. It is a struggle over values that are worked out in elections for public office, tax referendums, and open debate in civic meetings, newspapers, and TV talk shows. Yet these simple distinctions between the political and the technical, between goals for schools and the crucial importance of the democratic process determining which goals should be primary, seem to have been lost in squabbles over whether progressive or traditional schools are better.

And that is why I began with my descriptions of the two schools. They represent a way out of this futile struggle over which kind of schooling is better than the other. I argue that both these schools are "good."

One is clearly traditional in its concentration on passing on to children the best knowledge, skills, and values in society. The other is progressive in its focus on students' personal and social development. Each serves different goals, each honors different values. Yet—and this is the important point that I wish to drive home—these seemingly different goals are not inconsistent. They derive from a deeply embedded, but seldom noticed, common framework of what parents and taxpayers want their public schools to achieve.

What is different, on the surface, are the relative weights that each "good" school gives to these goals, how they go about putting into practice what they seek, and the words that they use to describe what they do. The common framework I refer to is the core duty of tax-supported public schools in a democracy to pass on to the next generation democratic attitudes, values, and behaviors. Too often we take for granted the linkage between the schools that we have and the kind of civic life that we want for ourselves and our children. What do I mean by democratic attitudes, values, and behaviors? A few examples may help:

- Open-mindedness to different opinions and a willingness to listen to such opinions.
- Respect for values that differ from one's own.
- Treating individuals decently and fairly, regardless of background.
- A commitment to talk through problems, reason, deliberate, and struggle toward openly arrived-at compromises.

I doubt whether partisans for traditional and progressive schools, such as former U.S. Secretary of Education William J. Bennett, educator Deborah Meier, and academics like Howard Gardner and E. D. Hirsch, Jr., would find this list unimportant.

Tax-supported public schools in this country were not established 150 years ago to get jobs for graduates. They were not established to replace the family or church. They were established to make sure that children grew into literate adults who respected authority, could make reasoned judgments, accept differences of opinions, and fulfill their civic duties to participate in the political life of their communities. Over time, of course, as conditions changed, other responsibilities were added to the charter of public schools. But the core duty of schools, teachers, and administrators—past and present—has been to turn students into citizens who can independently reason through difficult decisions, defend what they have decided, and honor the rule of law. Our traditional and progressive schools each have been working on these paramount and essential tasks.

Consider such democratic values as individual freedom and respect for authority. In School A, students have freedom in many activities, as long as they stay within the clear boundaries established by teachers on what students can do and what content they must learn. Staff members set rules for behavior and academic performance, but students and parents are consulted; students accept the limits easily, even enjoying the bounded freedom that such rules give them. School A's teachers and parents believe that students' self-discipline grows best by setting limits on freedom and learning what knowledge previous generations counted as important. From these will evolve students' respect for the rule of law and their growth into active citizens.

In School B, more emphasis is placed on children's individual freedom to create, diverge from the group, and work at their own pace. Students work on individually designed projects over the year. They respect teachers' authority but often ask why certain things have to be done. The teacher gives reasons and, on occasion, negotiates over what will be done and how it will be done. School B's teachers and parents believe that students' self-discipline, regard for authority, and future civic responsibility evolve out of an extended, but not total, freedom.

Thus, I would argue, both of these schools prize individual freedom and respect for authority, but they define each value differently in how they organize the school, view the curriculum, and engage in teaching. Neither value is ignored. Parents, teachers, and students accept the differences in how their schools put these values into practice. Moreover, each school, in its individual way, cultivates the deeper democratic attitudes of open-mindedness, respect for others' values, treating others decently, and making deliberate decisions.

Because no researcher could ever prove that one way of schooling is better than the other, what matters to me in judging whether schools are "good" is whether they are discharging their primary duty to help students think and act democratically. What we need to talk about openly in debates about schooling is not whether a traditional school is better or worse than a progressive one, but whether that school concentrates on instilling within children the virtues that a democratic society must have in each generation. Current talk about national goals is *not* about this core goal of schooling. It is about being first in the world in science and math achievement; it is about preparing students to use technology to get better jobs. Very little is said about the basic purpose of schooling except in occasional one-liners or a paragraph here and there in speeches by top public officials.

What are other criteria for judging goodness? I have already suggested parent, student, and teacher satisfaction as reasonable standards to use in determining how "good" a school is. I would go further and add: To what degree has a school achieved its own explicit goals? By this criterion, School A is a clear success. Parents and teachers want children to become literate, respectful of authority, and responsible. Although School B scores well on standardized tests, parents and teachers are less interested in test results. What School B wants most are students who can think on their own and work together easily with those who are different from themselves; students who, when faced with a problem, can tackle it from different vantage points and come up with solutions that are creative. Parents and teachers have plenty of stories about students' reaching these goals, but there are few existing tests or quantitative measures that capture these behaviors.

So, another standard to judge "goodness" in a school is to produce graduates who possess these democratic behaviors, values, and attitudes. This is, and always has been, the common, but often ignored, framework for our public schools. It has been lost in the battle of words and programs between public officials and educators who champion either traditional or progressive schools. A "good" school, I would argue, even in the face of the technological revolution and globalization of the U.S. economy in this century, is one that has students who display those virtues in different situations during their careers as students and afterwards as well.

My criteria, then, for determining good schools are as follows: Are parents, staff, and students satisfied with what occurs in the school? Is the school achieving the explicit goals it has set for itself? And, finally, are democratic behaviors, values, and attitudes evident in the students?

Why is it so hard to get past the idea that there is only one kind of "good" school? Varied notions of goodness have gotten mired in the endless and fruitless debate between traditionalists and progressives. The deeply buried but persistent impulse in the United States to create a "one best system," a solution for every problem, has kept progressives and traditionalists contesting which innovations are best for children, while ignoring that there are more ways than one to get "goodness" in schools.

Until Americans shed the view of a one best school for all, the squabbles over whether a traditional schooling is better than a progressive one will continue. Such a futile war of words ignores the fundamental purpose of public schooling as revitalizing democratic virtues in each generation and, most sadly, ignores the good schools that already exist.

Postnote

We select this article as a Classic because of the profound importance of its message: a call to educators to rise above ideological squabbles and get on with the serious business of educational excellence.

What one defines as a good school depends on what one values, says Larry Cuban, which makes perfectly good sense. A person's educational philosophy will determine how that person views schooling, teaching, and curriculum. Thus, many different types of good schools can and do exist.

Cuban's point argues for giving parents choices about the kind of school that their children attend. By offering different kinds of schools that represent different educational philosophies and by allowing parents to select the school of their choice, school boards can better satisfy parents' educational preferences. In this way, more parents will believe that their children attend good schools.

Discussion Questions

1. Of the two schools that Cuban describes in his article, would you prefer to teach in School A or School B? Why?
2. Describe the characteristics of the kind of school that you would consider to be "good."
3. Do you agree with Cuban's assertion that the common framework of public schools should be to "pass on to the next generation democratic attitudes, values, and behaviors"? Is there anything else that you would add to this common framework?

Schools Our Teachers Deserve

ROSETTA MARANTZ COHEN

FOCUS Question

Overwhelmingly, school reform efforts focus on curriculum or instruction or students. What would a school look like if the focus of reform were the teachers?

TERMS TO NOTE

Block scheduling
Cooperative learning
Direct instruction
Sabbatical
Site-based management
Tenure

It seems that a spate of recent books has appeared on the old, familiar subject of school reform. As always, some of these works have focused on the curriculum and call for more progressive approaches and an end to standardized testing.[1] Others have addressed the issues of low standards or parent involvement or the moral culture of the schools.[2] However, not one has focused its arguments on the one indispensable element in all successful schools—the one variable always given short shrift, it seems, whenever reformers think about school change—the teacher.

For more than five decades now, warehouses of writing on school reform have focused on the needs of the *students,* calling for the creation of "child-centered classrooms" and "learner-centered schools." Every administrator in America intones, "It's all about the kids!" And those words echo through every disaffected, demoralized student-centered high school building in the land. The whole failed history of modern education reform—from the prescriptive lesson-plan formats of the 1970s to the restructuring plans in the 1980s to the state testing and curriculum of the 1990s—has addressed the "needs of the child." It has paid hardly any attention to the work of the teacher, the one critical player in the school who makes the biggest difference.

"In this school, the teacher comes first." I would wager there isn't a public school in the land with such a motto. School reform efforts most frequently proceed *despite,* not because of, the teacher. When states impose new curricular mandates or introduce new statewide standardized tests, teachers are often viewed as stumbling blocks to implementation. Administrators try to "get the teachers on board," as if they were prisoners diving seaward to escape the shackles and whip. Even "bottom-up" reform is rarely that. In most districts that tried site-based management, it came and went a decade ago with hardly a teacher mourning

Rosetta Marantz Cohen is a professor in the Department of Education and Child Study, Smith College, Northampton, Massachusetts. Rosetta Marantz Cohen, "Schools Our Teachers Deserve: A Proposal for Teacher-Centered Reform," *Phi Delta Kappan,* March 2002. Reprinted with permission of Rosetta Marantz Cohen.

its passing. Frequently, such "teacher-centered" strategies simply burdened faculty members with the minutiae of daily governance without relieving them of any other responsibilities. The teacher's job was not redefined; rather, it was extended and expanded. Newly "empowered" teachers were burdened with clerical work and logistical concerns about building maintenance and scheduling—the very concerns that many teachers enter teaching to avoid. Indeed, such teacher-empowering reforms seemed calculated, in advance, to fail.

Everyone knows that teachers resist change.[3] Why shouldn't they? Any teacher who has spent more than a decade in the profession has already intuited what school reformers haven't gleaned in a century of tinkering: lasting and meaningful change doesn't come from fiats, whether external or internal. It doesn't have anything to do with long blocks or short blocks, cooperative learning or direct instruction. It has to do with how an individual teacher feels about his or her work and how the school perceives that teacher. If the teacher is perceived as a hero, the school will flourish. If the teacher is perceived as a pain in the ass, the school is going downhill—long blocks, cooperative learning, and all. For a school to be an intellectual center, for it to have the ethos, the sense of community, and the "spirit" that so many parents and administrators seek, it must celebrate the work of its teachers in a way that is rarely seen in public schools. It must attend to the needs of teachers, it must accommodate their sensibilities, and it must treat the teachers' contributions with as much genuine concern as it does those of any other constituency—maybe more.

Why Focus on the Teacher?

One good reason to focus on the teacher has to do with the nature of healthy institutions. Almost 20 years ago Sara Lawrence Lightfoot told us that successful high schools are those that possess powerful traditions and embedded norms. In the best schools (or hospitals or corporations), values are consistent and known; they are embodied in the experiences of everyday life.[4] How do those traditions get transferred to young people? Not by administrators. Principals have little direct contact with students and certainly not enough to transmit the subtleties of an institution's culture and beliefs. If a school is to have a powerful ethos, it is the *teachers* who must communicate it, embody it, transmit it. Indeed, teachers are the one stable influence on a culture that is, by definition, always in flux. Students seldom stay in a school longer than four years; many teachers remain in the system for 30 years or more. Because they are the fixed and tenured bearers of the school's values and ethos, it is critical that teachers feel good about the institution they are charged with representing.

This argument is even borne out in recent corporate management theory. Education policy makers have long been influenced by the models put forward by business and industry. In the 1980s, for example, corporate downsizing and bottom-line accountability certainly inspired education policy reforms in the areas of testing and teacher accountability. Cooperative learning and goals-based performance standards also have their roots in management theory.

What then is the most recent thinking about corporate competitiveness and productivity? Many of the most influential books that have been published on this subject in the last five years have shifted their primary focus away from concerns with markets and economies of scale. Instead, employee morale has become a central priority. Jeffrey Pfeffer, a professor of organizational behavior at Stanford University, reflects the new thinking in his field when he argues that a loyal, intelligent work force is the key factor in corporate competitiveness—more critical than technology or protected and regulated markets.[5] When workers are disgruntled, distracted, or poorly trained, no brilliant strategy for expanding market share will compensate for that liability. Why should it be any different for schools?

A second reason for shifting the reformers' emphasis from the student to the teacher concerns the nature of the teaching force itself.

Demographics within the profession have in recent years put schools in an unusual position. In general, the teacher population across the country is aging. In certain states, particularly in the Northeast, the average teacher's age is 40 or above. As teachers continue to age and then retire, schools will be faced with two very different challenges. First, they will have to attract excellent new people into the field. Second, they will have to figure out ways to help large numbers of older teachers stay invested in and committed to their work.

In the case of the hiring of new faculty members, schools will be confronted with the problem of incentives. What can a school offer a high-achieving college graduate to lure him or her away from business or law school? Obviously, schools will never be able to compete in terms of salary and other material benefits. But teaching holds a natural attraction for many idealistic, intelligent young people. Many students at competitive academic institutions are willing to consider teaching as a career.

Our introductory education classes at Smith College have some of the largest enrollments on campus. However, too many students are chased away from the field after their initial observations in local high schools that are part of their pre-practicum experiences. What they see when they visit schools is often demoralizing for them. Teachers work in isolation, and they work with too many students. They rarely interact with other faculty members, except over rushed lunches. They teach from books that they sometimes do not like themselves and that—to judge by their condition—seem to have been used by generations of students. By the time students at Smith become seniors, less than a handful each year are interested in becoming certified to teach high school. If schools are going to attract good new teachers, then they need to figure out ways to make the profession *look better* from the outside.

In terms of the burgeoning ranks of *veteran* teachers, the problem is even more complex. If good new teachers are hard to attract, it is even harder to reenergize those who have been victims of the system for decades. Some of these teachers, particularly those in their forties and fifties, have almost half a career ahead of them. With salaries frontloaded and no vertical advancement in the field, such teachers have little incentive to grow. As any high school student will tell you, the sullenness and exhaustion of these teachers and their cynicism and contempt for the system are the real root causes of bad schooling. Poorly written curricula, scheduling, and structural concerns are of so much lesser importance than teacher morale that they might as well not be factors at all.

Finally, the most obvious reason to focus on the teacher has to do with the nature of good teaching itself. Good teaching (as any good teacher will tell you) is not only about content and curriculum. It is also about the intersection of that content with the individual who is presenting it. For better or worse, teachers teach themselves, and any teacher who denies it is either lying or is out of touch with his or her effect on a class. School reformers almost always think in terms of *what* should be taught, how, when, and with what materials. And yet to a great extent teachers *are* the curriculum: affect, attitude, and persona have a much more powerful impact on classes than do the books they use or the pedagogical techniques they employ. One need only recall one's own best high school teachers to know how true this is. We remember the human beings and their passion or energy. The texts and techniques are secondary.

Teacher-Centered Reform

How then can a school nurture and promote the kind of teacher energy and enthusiasm that will "reform" schools? Forget the workshops on cooperative learning, the curriculum revision committees, the endless tinkering with the schedule. Focus instead on what can be done to make teachers feel better about their work. In other words, ask yourself, How can schools be made into adult-friendly places?

To answer that question, it seems logical to look to those schools that have succeeded in making teachers feel valuable: the best private schools and the best colleges. In both of these settings, money has little to do with job satisfaction. Private schools, as we all know, pay teachers less than public schools. And the salaries of assistant and even associate professors on many campuses fall below those of suburban public school teachers. Nor is workload necessarily the key. Some of the most competitive teaching jobs in the country can be found in private schools that require enormous service from their faculty members, including 24-hour, on-call availability in dormitories, extracurricular work, and lengthy written evaluations of students.

Why is it then that the best college graduates interested in teaching so often compete for the scarce jobs at Exeter and Andover, eschewing public schools even in the most affluent communities? I believe it is because these institutions hold out for bright graduates the promise of a truly intellectual life. Smart college students who choose to teach high school most frequently do so because they hope to continue to read and practice the subjects they love. Public schools, partly *because* of the very student-centered policies they persist in defending, fail to convey to these aspiring teachers the promise of such a life.

Similarly, many of the most passionately intellectual students at our college overlook the notion of high school teaching altogether. Their ambitions are set, from the start, on teaching at the college level. These students are not choosing college teaching because of a smaller workload or an easier life. Any freshman at Smith can see that introductory classes can be as large as 80 students and that the pressures to publish and the tensions associated with tenure complicate the lives of young professors. But in college teaching, these students do envision themselves respected as intellectuals, rewarded for using their minds in original ways, and capable of choosing and changing what they will teach. Good liberal arts colleges, like good private schools, really are "teacher-centered" institutions. Both seem to recognize that the way to foster excellence in students is to foster excellence in teachers. Good high schools need to prize young teachers who love their disciplines, and they need to celebrate book knowledge as an important, core value in the institutional culture.

Some may argue that a call to nurture "intellectual" teachers is a luxury in a public school system filled with so many students performing below grade level. Quite the contrary. Schools have for generations placed their least academically inclined teachers in classrooms with the lowest-ability students. No one would argue that such a strategy has raised levels of achievement among those students. If anything, a situation in which weak teachers teach weak students creates a self-fulfilling prophecy and helps perpetuate the very problems schools are trying to reverse. Teachers with intelligence, with passion and enthusiasm for their subjects, are every bit as important for at-risk students as they are for high-achieving students—and probably more so. For some low-achieving students, teachers are the one plausible role model for a life of literacy and reflection, a life in which intellect matters.

A Teacher-Centered Reform Agenda

What would a teacher-centered public high school look like? How could it be created? What follow are suggested reforms that I contend would have a powerful effect on the morale of any public high school. Many of these reforms are commonsensical. Many of them cost nothing. None of them requires radical restructuring or retraining, expensive testing, or additional personnel.

Offer Sabbaticals

The notion of a sabbatical, a paid period of leave in which a scholar can pursue scholarly ideas, stands as a key characteristic of intellectual teaching. Good colleges, of course, build periodic sabbaticals into the compensation packages for their faculty members. Many private schools also offer sabbatical leaves to faculty members on a competitive basis. Budgeting a single sabbatical leave (for which teachers would compete) into the yearly expenses of a public high school would not bankrupt any school system. Knowing that such a leave exists, however, would have an immensely salutary effect on the intellectual life of a staff. It would allow teachers to think in terms of ambitious scholarly projects; it would give them incentive to develop proposals for new classes or to outline for themselves lists of new readings they want to do—not only to enrich their curricula, but also for their own personal growth. For many years, the National Endowment for the Humanities has offered summer stipends for teachers to study literary or historical topics presented by college and university faculty. NEH studies show that teachers who take these seminars return to their classrooms energized and stimulated. The same good would emerge from the semester-long or yearlong sabbatical. It would reinforce the idea, too often ignored, that teaching is essentially an intellectual activity. Finally, the sabbatical would serve as another excellent lure for teacher candidates.

Reallocate Budgets So That More Money Is Available for Books; Let Teachers Choose What They Teach

In many good private schools and in most colleges, teachers design their own classes and choose their own books. This is rarely true in public high schools, where teachers inherit curricula and use whatever books are available—regardless of their age or the teacher's interest in a particular work. Common sense suggests that one would teach better—with more passion and enthusiasm—a class that one has had a hand in designing. Clearly, teachers must work within certain inevitable constraints: states have curricular mandates, and certain texts are not appropriate for younger students. But within those obvious boundaries there could be a good deal more creative freedom than now exists in most public schools. Book ordering needs to be a high priority for school districts, and teachers need to have a much greater say in what books get bought, how many get bought, and when.

Involve Teachers in the Evaluation Process

In no other profession do outsiders, individuals with no direct contact with the work of the professional, routinely evaluate and hire individuals within the profession. In law, for example, it would seem absurd for an outsider (one not even a practicing lawyer) to pass judgment on the work of a new lawyer in the firm. And yet this is precisely what happens in many schools and districts in which new teachers are hired without any input from faculty members in the departments in which they will teach. Teachers, too, are routinely evaluated by administrators who have not taught for decades, have never taught the particular subject under scrutiny, or have no larger context (What did the class do yesterday? Last week?) for the brief evaluation. States like Texas hire supervisors who don't even work in the school itself; they arrive unannounced from a central office and then proceed, without any first-hand knowledge of the school's culture, to evaluate its teachers.

For teaching to gain real professional status, teachers need to control hiring and firing, they need to lay out their own criteria for acceptable practice, and they need to do their own evaluating. This is certainly not a new idea; unions have supported such practice for decades. But too few school systems go to the trouble of acting on the concept, either out of laziness or out of fear that, once so empowered, teachers will become less dependent on them and so less tractable.

Change Hiring Practices

Several years ago, a gifted teacher I know, a 35-year veteran, an Advanced Placement history teacher, informed the school district in May that she was intending to retire. Then she waited to see advertisements for her position posted in professional journals or in newspapers in the two neighboring cities near her home. Nothing happened. It was not until the last week of August that the job was listed under the heading "Teacher, H.S. History" in the local newspaper, sandwiched between ads for "Tag Sale Coordinator" and "Truckdriver, Part Time."

Teaching will never be the most desirable profession in the land. In order to attract smart college graduates, districts have to work hard at it—devoting energy and ingenuity to the task. Hiring is by far the most important work of any school administrator, and it should be a high priority for the district superintendent as well. Administrators need to pound the pavement in search of top candidates; they need to visit college campuses, forge contacts with teacher education personnel in the best schools, track and follow potential teachers who have not yet graduated. Today, few districts do any of this. Hiring is perceived as a last minute catch-as-catch-can process in which having a credential is far more important than the quality of a transcript. Again, good colleges and private schools seem to understand the importance of hiring the best staff possible. They recruit actively and compete with one another for good teachers. Just knowing that you are pursued makes an enormous difference for a new teacher. It communicates the fact that the district values you. No last-minute hire—the product of an abstracted, impersonal interview—can begin his or her work with that same sense.

Make Tenure Mean Something

As long as tenure exists, it is absurd not to use this mechanism to improve the quality of teaching. If the public school system is burdened by large numbers of uninspiring or incompetent teachers, it is partly because those individuals were not weeded out in the first years of their employment. While it is unfair to evaluate the long-term success of a teacher in the first year or two, it certainly becomes less difficult after three or four years. An insightful administrator (or better, a team of talented teachers) can certainly begin to see talent or its absence by then. It is critical that poor teachers not get rehired, not slip through the cracks of an ineffectual system of supervision.

For real substantive evaluation before tenure to work, the period of probation for teachers needs to be extended. Currently, teachers have a three-year probationary period, after which time—barring grievous malfeasance—they are automatically tenured. Colleges generally require seven years before tenure, and tenure itself becomes a critical rite of passage, like the formal initiation into an exclusive club. Tenure in colleges really means something. While I'm not proposing that the criteria for high school tenure should change (I don't think high school teachers should be required to publish, for example), I do think that the quality of one's teaching should be much more carefully scrutinized—and by individuals who really *know* something about good teaching.

Reallocate the Use of Time to Protect Teachers

Long blocks, short blocks, whatever. There are good arguments for all kinds of different scheduling formats, and the students themselves don't much care. The decision on how best to structure the day should be left to the teachers, who will weigh the merits of any scheduling system according to how they feel they can best present the material. Schools that move summarily to one scheduling system or another, without prioritizing the needs and preferences of teachers, do nothing more than alienate that critical constituency.

Teachers, like any other professionals, also need opportunities to work and reflect with one another. Again, many private schools seem to understand this fact. They build large chunks of time into the weekly schedule for teacher curriculum work and consulting. While public schools cannot afford to have half-day Wednesdays, as many private institutions do, they can at least prioritize the scheduling of teachers' free periods to benefit those within a given department. Or they can schedule longer, common lunch periods (duty-free) to allow teachers time to have leisurely discussions with one another.

Administrators Should Teach

Of all the traits that characterize the very best schools, this one is perhaps the most important. Teachers have long noted a curious phenomenon: when teachers become full-time administrators, they quickly lose their capacity to empathize with their former colleagues. It is extraordinary how quickly one forgets the complex stresses and challenges of teaching once one is charged with implementing bureaucratic mandates or fielding parent complaints. The only way to avoid this sort of amnesia is for principals and assistant principals to continue to interact with students in a classroom. Even one class a day is enough to retain the flavor of the work and to maintain credibility with teachers—who often measure administrative effectiveness against what the principal seems to know about real teaching.

Finally, administrators who teach are far more likely to understand the importance of praising their teachers' best work. Teachers receive so little in the way of positive reinforcement. Unbelievable as it seems, a good teacher can spend years in the profession without hearing a single compliment about his or her work. Memos and reminders about tardy forms and report cards abound, but there is no mechanism in the profession for cataloguing and celebrating the good things that happen daily in the classroom. Teachers are just supposed to revel in the intrinsic rewards of their private successes. This lack of positive feedback from any adult peer can wear down even the most robust of spirits. And when the silence is compounded by other kinds of ego assaults (infantilizing inservice workshops or top-down mandates for reform), it is no wonder that so many teachers become cynical. When administrators teach, they remember to *think* about teaching; they remember how hard it is; they remember to value it.

Schools don't need large ranks of exceptional teachers, and it is unrealistic to expect they will ever attract so many. What they do need is a critical mass of impassioned, intellectual individuals—enough to influence the tone and character of the institution. By improving the morale of even a handful of a school's faculty, these "teacher-centered" reforms cannot help but benefit students. From any perspective, it just seems so obvious: if we can create the schools our *teachers* deserve, we will have created the schools our *children* deserve—and desperately need.

Notes

1. Alfie Kohn, *The Schools Our Children Deserve* (Boston: Houghton Mifflin, 1999).
2. Martin Gross, *The Conspiracy of Ignorance: The Failure of American Public Education* (New York: HarperCollins, 1999); and Theodore Sizer and Nancy Faust Sizer, *The Students Are Watching: Schools and the Moral Contract* (Boston: Beacon Press, 1999).
3. Dan Lortie, *Schoolteacher: A Sociological Study* (Chicago: University of Chicago Press, 1975).
4. Sara Lawrence Lightfoot, *The Good High School: Portraits of Character and Culture* (Boston: Basic Books, 1983).
5. Jeffrey Pfeffer, *Competitive Advantage Through People: Unleashing the Power of the Workforce* (Boston: Harvard Business School Press, 1994). See also Natalie J. Allen and John Meyer, *Commitment in the Workplace: Theory, Research, and Application* (Thousand Oaks, Calif.: Sage, 1997); and Oliver E. Williamson, *Organization Theory* (New York: Oxford University Press, 1995).

Postnote

A good general always keeps in touch with his troops. He realizes that his foot soldiers have more knowledge about what is going on in the trenches than he and his headquarters staff. This may also be the case with educational "generals." The author makes a strong plea for giving greater attention to teachers and the wisdom they possess about the real world of schools.

One telling point is that teachers in elite private schools are honored to a greater degree than those in public schools. Although they typically receive lower salaries, their role and position are given prominence. Private school boards and administrators, whose schools cater to the rich and powerful, appreciate that the quality of their schools is directly related to the quality of their teachers. Typically, private school teachers are respected. They are listened to. As more Americans make the connection that our nation's future is tied to the quality of our children's education, the author's ideas for enhancing the status of classroom teachers should take hold. Until this connection is made, real educational reform will be elusive.

Discussion Questions

1. In the schools you attended, were teachers respected? Specifically, how?
2. Do you agree with the author's view that schools need to become more "teacher-centered" rather than "student-centered"? Why or why not?
3. Which of the author's several reform suggestions do you think is most valuable? Why?

Remaking High School

KATHLEEN VAIL

FOCUS Question

The American comprehensive high school was once the envy of the world. What happened?

Fifty years ago, the American high school was doing fine. Most students weren't headed for college. If they earned a high school diploma, they could land a well-paying job. If they didn't graduate, they could still find good work.

"But today it's a disaster," says Tom Vander Ark, director of education for the Bill and Melinda Gates Foundation. "A third of American students drop out, half of Hispanic and African Americans drop out. That's a civic, social, and economic disaster."

Vander Ark, whose foundation has spent millions to reconfigure comprehensive high schools across the nation, is not alone in his assessment. Educators have spent much of the past two decades focusing on reform at the preschool and elementary school levels and not paying as much attention to high schools. Recent studies, however, have revealed soaring dropout rates, even more appallingly high for minorities. The higher education and business communities are speaking out about the huge numbers of high school graduates not prepared for work or college.

The resulting hue and cry, which has been gaining in intensity, has pushed high school reform to the forefront. In his bid for reelection, President Bush has proposed spending $300 million to bring all incoming high school students up to grade level in reading and math.

While different in philosophy and approach, reform models all seek to change the basic building blocks of high schools: their size and how and what they offer. The Gates Foundation and other private groups, as well as the U.S. Department of Education, are pouring millions of dollars in research and technical assistance into districts willing to change how they run high schools.

This influx of cash and aid is propelling school districts around the country—from New York City to San Diego, Minneapolis to Baltimore, and Boston to Mapleton, a suburb of Denver—to radically transform one of the most firmly entrenched icons in American education.

"The work on high school reform is crucial to the lives of young people and the future of public education and to our country," says

---

Kathleen Vail is a senior editor of *American School Board Journal.* "Remaking High School," by Kathleen Vail. Reprinted with permission from American School Board Journal, November 2004.

Michele Cahill, who is in charge of New York City's massive high school reform. "Unless we really face that we need to retool our system of public education, then we will have an increasingly divided society where a large group of youths are prepared only for the low-wage sector of the labor market."

Dropout Factories

The graduation rate for U.S. schools in 2000 was 85.7 percent, with a 14.3 percent dropout rate, according to the National Center for Education Statistics (NCES). However, several recent high-profile studies refute those numbers, showing that the dropout problem in our country is, indeed, a crisis.

For example, Jay Greene at the Manhattan Institute for Policy Research found that high school graduation rates in 1998 were only 70 percent. A study by the Business Roundtable in 2003 came to a similar conclusion, saying about 30 percent of students are not graduating with a high school diploma.

Why are these statistics so different from the NCES data? The Manhattan Institute's report looked at eighth-grade enrollment in 1993 and compared that with the number of students earning diplomas in 1998. The Roundtable report compared the number of diplomas earned with the number of 17- and 18-year-olds in the country.

According to the Roundtable report, students who complete GEDs frequently are not counted among dropouts in national data even though they did not receive high school diplomas. Also, students who are jailed are not counted as dropouts.

At least 14 states do not report dropout data in a uniform way, and reporting at the district level in all states is not uniform either. Some schools count only students who drop out in the 12th grade; others count only students who sign papers officially dropping out. In some cases, students who say they are transferring from one school to another, but never show up at the second school, are not counted among district dropouts.

The dropout rate is much worse for minority students. Gary Orfield of the Civil Rights Project at Harvard University and Christopher Swanson of the Urban Institute found that about 50 percent of black, Hispanic, and Native American students fail to earn high school diplomas.

Smaller schools with more personalization and high expectations are not new ideas, of course. The roots of much of this reform are 20 years old or more, researched and put forward by Theodore Sizer and his colleagues at the Coalition of Essential Schools and the Annenberg Institute for School Reform, two organizations that advocate for more personalized schools. However, many of the changes we're seeing now did not become mainstream until 1996, when the National Association of Secondary School Principals released Breaking Ranks, a reform blueprint containing many of the Annenberg ideas. (NASSP has subsequently published Breaking Ranks II, which gives more explicit examples of how to make these reforms work.)

While some believe that No Child Left Behind and high-stakes high school exit exams could exacerbate dropout rates, others say NCLB and the tests actually help put a spotlight on high schools by recording and reporting how students are performing.

Reform advocates say that for reform to really work, it must occur at the district and state level as well. The Department of Education's Office of Vocational and Adult Education has held regional meetings on reform with state and local education officials. The object is to align state and local law and policy with reforms. "If we are serious about saying all high school students will earn a diploma," says Susan Sclafani, assistant secretary for Adult and Vocational Education, "why have a law that allows students to drop out at 16?"

One thing is clear: Reform is happening, and the rate is accelerating. "There always is confusion before there is equilibrium," says Sizer. "We are in the middle of the confusing stage."

Barriers to Change

Reform models that transform high schools also seek to transform teaching and instruction. And as with any reform effort, if the teachers don't buy into it, it's not going to work.

High school teachers often aren't prepared to teach in teams, act as advisers, or teach across subjects. "We're asking people who work in high schools to do something they haven't signed up for. They say, 'Dropouts aren't my fault. Kids have issues at home.' Now we are asking teachers to be responsible for it. The nature of the job is different," says Joseph DiMartino of the Education Alliance at Brown University.

Union rules about seniority and other work-related issues can be a barrier, unless the union decides to work with the district on reform, as has happened in San Diego and the Mapleton School District, near Denver.

Nostalgia can also be an obstacle. Parents and community members who fondly remember their high school days often protest when changes are proposed. It can be especially hard to reform old, historic high schools. Some districts solve this by allowing a revered old school to maintain its name, mascot, sports teams, and colors while breaking it into smaller learning communities.

Sometimes, too, the doubt that students can perform to rigorous standards will impede change. "The biggest resistance to improving high schools is a deep-seated belief that many of our students cannot learn much. We've created a system that allows them to validate that," says Gene Bottoms, executive director of High Schools That Work, a reform effort now in about 1,000 schools in 30 states. "When adults decide to change that, wonderful things happen."

Making It Work

The mantra of high school reform is rigor, relationships, and relevance. The ultimate goal is to have all students prepared for college and the workplace when they graduate. Reformers also seek to make high schools places where students, and adults, want to be.

New York City opened 40 new small high schools last year and 60 more this fall. Cahill, who was in charge of urban school reform at the Carnegie Foundation, came to the nation's largest school district last year to oversee a total revamping of its high school program. "Fifty percent of our students graduate in four years," Cahill says. "There's an urgency to change."

A sense of urgency can also be seen in the 138,000-student San Diego Unified School District. "We can't put Band-Aids on sucking chest wounds," says Matthew Malone, the district's chief of secondary reform. "What about the 25 percent who drop out and don't do anything? That piece of the pie is too big, too much."

Malone is no stranger to controversial reform movements. In Massachusetts, he was the principal at a South Boston high school that was broken down into smaller schools. Now, in San Diego, he's overseeing high school reform on a larger scale. Funded in part by the Gates Foundation, three high schools—Crawford, Kearny, and 100-year-old San Diego High—closed over the summer and reopened this fall with redesigned, small, separate schools within their buildings.

Within San Diego High, for instance, are the School of International Studies, the School of Business, the School of Science and Technology, and the School of Media, Visual, and Performing Arts, among others. To maintain their traditions and sense of history, the three high schools have kept their own sports teams and mascots, though the learning communities within the schools have their own colors, as well.

From the start, a plus for the San Diego reform effort has been buy-in by the teachers union. "This had been teacher-led from the beginning," Malone says. "Teachers have dreams to do something new because it wasn't working for them. Who wants to work in a place where the dropout rates are higher? No one."

In addition to the small learning communities, San Diego is also using other reform models, all with the intent of breaking down the larger comprehensive high school and ultimately offering students a choice among many different kinds of schools that would suit their needs.

Small learning communities are the focus of the Minneapolis high school reform, as well. Bob McCauley, secondary school superintendent, says a data collection company helped the 43,000-student district assess its graduation rates in 2001. The number was 47 percent, and the dropout rate in ninth grade was even worse.

"We disaggregated data and faced the brutal facts. We cannot tolerate this any longer. We have to have a high school transformation process," says McCauley, noting the district set a goal of an 80 percent graduation rate by 2010 for its 12,000 high school students.

"We wanted an aggressive, accelerated high school reform program. We couldn't wait on any high school, so rather than phase in one school at a time, we'd try reform for all seven of the comprehensive high schools," he says.

With grants from the McKnight Foundation and the U.S. Department of Education, the district opened 34 small learning communities in 2002 in existing high school buildings. Students apply to the programs in eighth grade. If enough students don't enroll, the school will close.

"We are trying to create choice but not tracks," says McCauley, noting that some programs even compete with each other for students.

Colorado's Mapleton School District looked at its graduation rate and made a similar decision to reform. About 400 students showed up at the high school for their freshman year. Four years later, that number had dwindled to 200. So the 5,000-student district—which is 49 percent Hispanic and 44 percent white, with about 25 percent qualifying for free or reduced-price lunch—decided to radically alter its high school.

It formed a partnership with the Denver-based Coalition of Small Schools, which provided Gates funding as well as help with research and design. This year, the district opened a Big Picture high school and an expeditionary learning high school. Next year, a Coalition for Essential Schools high school will open, along with an Expeditionary Learning through the Arts school, and a technology school.

"The reason we are moving as quickly as we are," says Superintendent Charlotte Scarpella, "is that it's unethical not to do it, if you know there's a better way."

Postnote

Clearly the American high school is in trouble. Clearly, too, it is in the cross-hairs of reformers, from governors to industry to private foundations. While this article vividly lays out many of the problems with our high schools, one problem is not mentioned, the students.

Take a fantasy trip to three high schools: one in New Delhi, India; one in Singapore; and one in Averagetown, USA. Let's *not* look at the top 15 percent of the students, but the bottom 85 percent. Let's look at how these students approach their schoolwork, how much time they spend in and out of class, how much time they spend on homework, and how they respect their teachers. What our trip will show is that, compared to high school students in many, many parts of the world, American students, again the bottom 85 percent, do not study very hard or very long. Instead, huge numbers of students spend a great deal of time outside school at jobs, earning money to support cars and other luxuries. In America, high school is not the high priority and high demand factor it is for the students in many other countries.

The unpleasant fact is that if there is to be real reform of our high schools, educators and parents will have to make much greater demands on the time, energies, and attention of American adolescents.

Discussion Questions

1. What are the primary criticisms of the American high school in this article?
2. In what ways is the picture of the American high school presented here similar to or different from the high school you attended?
3. Why shouldn't the high school years, the time between childhood and the serious work of college or the work world, be more relaxed and enjoyable? Why don't we take the pressure off high school students, give them an opportunity to discover who they are and what they want out of life, instead of imposing all the rigor and demands suggested in this article? Why or why not?

23

Small Classes, Small Schools: The Time Is Now

PATRICIA A. WASLEY

FOCUS Question

What does the research tell us about the value of small classes and small schools?

Terms to Note

High-stakes tests

School-within-a-school

Standards

For many years, educators have debated the effects of class size and school size on student learning. The class size debate centers on the number of students a teacher can work with effectively in any given class period. The school size issue focuses on whether smaller schools encourage optimal student learning and development—and how small a "small school" must be to produce such effects.

This [article] examines the issues surrounding class size and school size to determine what the research says and what experts recommend. To frame these issues, I want to pose a series of questions:

- Why have issues of class and school size gained prominence?
- What does the research say?
- What does my experience lead me to believe about the impact of class and school size on teaching and learning?

Why Are Class and School Size Important?

Issues of class size and school size have resurfaced as important school improvement ideas for a variety of reasons. First, the standards movement has encouraged the resurgence of the class size and school size debates. All U.S. states but one have academic standards in place. Of those states with standards, 36 use or plan to use test results to make high-stakes decisions about students. Standards enable educators and the public to clarify what they believe students should know and be able to do before the students leave school.

The standards movement has highlighted the fact that schools are largely inequitable places. Students in schools with large populations of disadvantaged students perform least well on standardized assessments. Evidence also suggests that these schools often have the least-experienced teachers (NCTAF, 1996; Roza, 2001). In effect, having standards in place emphasizes that standards are necessary but insufficient in themselves

Patricia A. Wasley is dean of the College of Education at the University of Washington, Seattle; email: pwasley@u.washington.edu. From Patricia A. Wasley, "Small Classes, Small Schools," *Educational Leadership,* February 2002, pp. 6–10. Reprinted with permission of Patricia A. Wasley.

to improve student performance. Unless we change students' learning opportunities, especially for students who are ill-served by their schools, standards alone are unlikely to influence student learning. Educators and policymakers are looking for strategies that will enable students to succeed on the new assessments (thereby supporting the standards movement) and, more important, that will enhance students' learning opportunities. Small classes and small schools may be two such strategies.

Second, class size and school size issues have resurfaced because of the increasing consensus among educators and the public that all students can learn. When I began teaching in the early 1970s, teachers generally accepted the notion that some students had an exceptional aptitude for learning and others did not. At that time, my colleagues and I believed that as long as one-fourth of the students in a class performed exceptionally well and another half of the class did reasonably well, we were fulfilling our responsibilities as educators—even if one-fourth of the students in a class failed to learn at an acceptable level. We had been taught that the normal distribution of scores (the "bell curve") was what teachers should aim for and what we should accept as reasonable evidence of accomplishment. In the ensuing years, cognitive scientists, neurological biologists, and educators determined that all students have the capacity to learn. This new, convincing research means that no student should be left behind in the learning process. Educators need to examine all approaches to schooling to determine which strategies are most likely to return gains for students who typically have not done well in schools. Proponents of reduced class size and school size suggest that these factors contribute to the success of a broader swath of learners.

Third, following the events of September 11, educators have a renewed appreciation for the importance of the basic freedoms we enjoy and the advantages that a democracy provides its citizens. We know that a democratic citizenry must value differences among its participants. Schools should strive to develop in students the skills that they need to examine their differences productively and to coexist peacefully while protecting basic freedoms for all (Goodlad, Soder, & Sirotnik, 1990). Schools also have a central responsibility for helping students learn the basic skills of productive citizenry. Both class size and school size influence whether teachers are able to engage students in meaningful discussions of these issues and to help them build these crucial citizenship skills.

Renewed interest in class size and school size is broad-based and nationwide. The Bill & Melinda Gates Foundation has dedicated more than $250 million to reducing the size of U.S. high schools. The U.S. Department of Education has committed $125 million to fund small-school initiatives. In Boston, Chicago, and New York, small-school initiatives are under way. Small-school collaboratives, designed to support the change from comprehensive high schools to smaller learning communities, are springing up everywhere and include New Visions for Learning in New York, the Small Schools Workshop in Chicago (Illinois), the Small Schools Project in Seattle (Washington), and the Bay Area Coalition of Essential Schools in Oakland (California).

Lawmakers in Kentucky, California, Georgia, and Washington have passed legislation to reduce class sizes, believing that teachers will be better able to help all students meet the standards when the teacher-student ratio is substantially reduced.

What Does Research Tell Us?

The United States has had large schools for a relatively short period of time. Until the middle of the 20th century, most U.S. schools were small. In 1930, 262,000 U.S. public schools served 26 million students; by 1999, approximately 90,000 U.S. public schools served about 47 million students (National Center for Education Statistics, 1999). (Editor's note: By 2006, it was estimated that there were over 48.5 million students in public schools [*Projections of Education Statistics to 2014,* Washington, DC: NCES, U.S. Department of Education, 2005].) Responding to the recommendations of the Committee of Ten in 1894 and the authors of the Conant Report in 1959, proponents of the school consolidation movement suggested that schools would be more efficient and effective if they were larger. Single plants housing 500–2,000 students presumably could offer greater variety in subject matter, would provide teachers with the opportunity to track their students according to ability, and might put less strain on community resources (Wasley & Fine, 2000).

Research conducted on the validity of the assertions favoring large schools has suggested that less-advantaged students end up in the largest classes, with the least-experienced teachers and the least-engaging curriculum and instructional strategies (Oakes, 1987; Wheelock, 1992). Further research suggests that schools are organized more for purposes of maintaining control than for promoting learning (McNeil, 1988).

Powell (1996) examined independent schools in the United States and learned that private preparatory schools value both small school and small class size as necessary conditions for student success. In 1998, the average private school class size was 16.6 at the elementary level and 11.6 at the high school level. By contrast, the average class size was 18.6 in public elementary schools and 14.2 in public high schools (National Center for Education Statistics, 1999).[1]

Powell also determined that independent elementary schools tend to be small and independent high schools tend to be even smaller—in contrast to public schools, which tend to increase in size as the students they serve get older. In *The Power of Their Ideas,* Meier (1995) suggests that we abandon adolescents just at the time when they most often need to be in the company of trusted adults. . . .

What Has My Experience Taught Me?

Over the years, I have taught students at nearly every level, from 3rd grade through graduate school. As a researcher, I have spent time gathering data on students at every level from preschool through 12th grade. My teaching and research experiences have provided me with data that convince me that both small classes and small schools are crucial to a teacher's ability to succeed with students.

One of my earliest teaching experiences was in a large comprehensive high school in Australia that included grades 7–10. I had more than 40 students in each of seven classes each day. During my second year, I taught Ray Campano. He was a quiet 10th grader who wasn't doing well in English. His parents, aware of his academic weaknesses, came to see me early in the first term. They asked that I keep them informed of the homework required and let them know if Ray was in danger of failing. They wanted to help and were supportive of my efforts on their son's behalf. In the ensuing weeks, I kept track of Ray's progress, but I gradually paid less attention to him. He was pleasant and quiet and well behaved, but there were other students in the class who were not. Other students demanded that I give them individual attention because they wanted to excel. These two groups of students—the rebellious and the demanding—absorbed most of my time, while Ray quietly slipped out of my attention. To be sure, I saw him each day and recorded whether his work was coming in, but I neglected to examine his performance in the midst of competing demands to plan, grade papers, and work with the needier or more demanding students.

When midterm reports came due, I was horrified to realize that I had neglected to keep my eye on Ray's performance, which was less than satisfactory. I met with his parents and explained that I had not kept my end of our bargain. They were angry—and rightly so—but they were fair. Ray's mother asked to come to class for a week to see what was going on. At the end of that week, she said that she thought the work I asked the students to do was appropriate and that I was relatively well organized and focused. Nevertheless, she couldn't imagine how a teacher could manage anything more than a cursory relationship with any given student in so large a classroom. Mrs. Campano confirmed my own

[1]The low average class size of public high schools obscures the fact that upper division courses in math and science and Advanced Placement courses are typically smaller, whereas many lower-track courses have more than 30 students.

experience, which suggested that really knowing all 40 students in each of seven classes was impossible. Despite parental involvement and teachers' good intentions, it is easy for students to get lost in large classes and in large schools.

As Dean of Bank Street College of Education in New York City several years ago, I team-taught 5th and 6th graders in the College's School for Children. We were looking for a course of study that would engage the students in making some contribution to the local community while simultaneously building their reading, computer, writing, and observation skills. After long deliberation and engagement in a number of exploratory activities, our 5th and 6th graders decided that they would tutor younger students in a neighborhood public school. One of the students cried, "How are we supposed to teach reading? We're only kids. We just learned to read ourselves a few years ago!" A heated discussion ensued, during which one of the girls ran up to the chalkboard and said, "I know. Let's map how each of us learned to read."

The students made a chart of how old they were, where they were (home or school), with whom they were engaged in a reading activity, and what activity they were engaged in at the precise moment that they understood that they could read. Seventeen students in the classroom generated 14 different approaches to learning to read. I suggested that the students pick several of the most commonly used approaches and organize a seminar on each approach so that they could learn several methods for working with their reading buddies. They looked at me as if either I had lost my mind or I hadn't been listening. "We can't learn just three approaches, or we'll never learn to help all these kids learn to read! If we needed a bunch of different approaches to learn to read, why wouldn't they?"

This experience reinforced my belief that different students learn differently and that teachers need to build a repertoire of instructional strategies to reach individual students. Small class size is integral to this individualization: Teachers should be responsible for a smaller number of students so that they can get to know each student and his or her learning preferences. It takes time to get to know one's students and to individualize the learning experience, and doing so requires concentration. In a classroom with a large number of students, such attention simply isn't an option.

Colleagues and I recently conducted a study of small schools in Chicago. Part of our time was spent in a small school-within-a-school with eight teachers. Because they were few, they could meet together every day for an hour, work toward common agreements and understandings, and accept shared responsibility for their students. They discussed the curriculum in all subjects, agreed on instructional approaches, and tried to build as much coherence in the curriculum as they could manage. In the larger school, which had some 70 faculty members, a common agenda simply wasn't possible.

The school-within-a-school teachers spent an enormous amount of time talking about their 300 students. They argued about students, challenged one another to see individual students differently, and agreed to work together to communicate to students that math or English or science was important for everyone. By the end of the first year, students in the smaller school-within-a-school had outperformed their peers on a number of measures: More of the smaller-school students had stayed in school, completed their courses, and received higher grades than had students in the host school. For example, between September 1998 and September 1999, approximately 11.1 percent of school-within-a-school students dropped out of school. By contrast, about 19.8 percent of their host-school peers dropped out during the same period (Wasley et al., 2000).

When we asked the school-within-a-school students why they thought they had achieved such results, they said that their teachers "dog us every day. They're relentless. They call our parents. They really care whether we get our work done. There's no hiding in this school!"

The time is ripe for educators to make the case for what research suggests and what our own experience has been telling us for years: Students do best in places where they can't slip through the cracks, where they are known by their teachers, and where their improved learning becomes the collective mission of a number of trusted adults. We have the resources to ensure that every student gets a good education, and we know what conditions best support their success. It is time to do what is right.

References

Goodlad, J. I., Soder, R., & Sirotnik, K. A. (Eds.). (1990). *The moral dimensions of teaching.* San Francisco: Jossey-Bass.

McNeil, L. M. (1988). *Contradictions of control: School structure and school knowledge.* New York: Routledge.

Meier, D. (1995). *The power of their ideas: Lessons for America from a small school in Harlem.* Boston: Beacon Press.

National Commission on Teaching and America's Future. (1996). *What matters most: Teaching for America's future.* New York: NCTAF.

Oakes, J. (1987). *Improving inner-city schools. Current directions in urban district reform.* Santa Monica, CA: RAND.

Powell, A. G. (1996). *Lessons from privilege: The American prep school tradition.* Cambridge, MA: Harvard University Press.

Roza, M. (2001). The challenge for Title I. *Education Week, 20*(29), 38, 56.

Snyder, T. D. (2000). *Digest of education statistics, 1999.* Washington, DC: U.S. Department of Education, National Center for Education Statistics.

Wasley, P. A., & Fine, M. (2000). *Small schools and the issue of scale.* New York: Bank Street College of Education.

Wasley, P. A., Fine, M., Gladden, M., Holland, N. E., King, S. P., Mosak, E., & Powell, L. C. (2000). *Small schools: Great strides.* New York: Bank Street College of Education.

Wheelock, A. (1992). *Crossing the tracks: How untracking can save America's schools.* New York: The New Press.

Postnote

The focus of this article on the values of small classes and small schools is appropriately on students. The many benefits that accrue to students are persuasive, especially the effects of small classes in the early grades and small schools for high school students. Not fully articulated are the effects of small classes and schools on teachers, especially those in middle and high schools. While the many and varied courses, extracurricular clubs, sports, and other activities in large schools appeal to certain types of teachers, most people who select education as a life's work have chosen it because of their deep interest in young people. They want to help students make the transition into adulthood. They want to be a positive influence in their students' lives. For them, the impersonality that is a by-product of large schools often creates frustration with teaching. It limits their opportunity to forge significant relationships with the students who quickly pass through their classes and go on to other teachers. And as the author concludes, "Students do best in places where they can't slip through the cracks, where they are known by their teachers, and where their improved learning becomes the collective mission of a number of trusted adults." These are the conditions that appeal to most teachers.

Discussion Questions

1. What do you see as the primary gains from large schools?
2. What do you see as the major gains from small schools?
3. If the positive effects of small class size for the early grades are so compelling, why do you suppose more states haven't reduced class size in grades K–3?

Why Some Parents Don't Come to School

MARGARET FINDERS AND CYNTHIA LEWIS

FOCUS Question

Why is it that some parents just won't come to their children's schools?

TERMS TO NOTE

Institutional perspective

Parental involvement

In our roles as teachers and as parents, we have been privy to the conversations of both teachers and parents. Until recently, however, we did not acknowledge that our view of parental involvement conflicts with the views of many parents. It was not until we began talking with parents in different communities that we were forced to examine our own deeply seated assumptions about parental involvement.

From talking with Latino parents and parents in two low-income Anglo neighborhoods, we have gained insights about why they feel disenfranchised from school settings. In order to include such parents in the educational conversation, we need to understand the barriers to their involvement from their vantage point, as that of outsiders. When asked, these parents had many suggestions that may help educators re-envision family involvement in the schools.

The Institutional Perspective

The institutional perspective holds that children who do not succeed in school have parents who do not get involved in school activities or support school goals at home. Recent research emphasizes the importance of parent involvement in promoting school success (Comer 1984, Lareau 1987). At the same time, lack of participation among parents of socially and culturally diverse students is also well documented (Clark 1983, Delgado-Gaitan 1991).

The model for family involvement, despite enormous changes in the reality of family structures, is that of a two-parent, economically self-sufficient nuclear family, with a working father and homemaker mother (David 1989). As educators, we talk about "the changing family," but

At the time this article was written, **Margaret Finders** was an assistant professor of English education at Purdue University, West Lafayette, Indiana. **Cynthia Lewis** was on the faculty at Grinnell College, Grinnell, Iowa. From Margaret Finders and Cynthia Lewis, "Why Some Parents Don't Come to School," *Educational Leadership,* May 1994, pp. 50–54. Reprinted by permission. The Association for Supervision and Curriculum Development is a worldwide community of educators advocating sound policies and sharing best practices to achieve the success of each learner. To learn more, visit ASCD at **www.ascd.org.**

the language we use has changed little. The institutional view of nonparticipating parents remains based on a deficit model. "Those who *need* to come, don't come," a teacher explains, revealing an assumption that one of the main reasons for involving parents is to remediate them. It is assumed that involved parents bring a body of knowledge about the purposes of schooling to match institutional knowledge. Unless they bring such knowledge to the school, they themselves are thought to need education in becoming legitimate participants.

Administrators, too, frustrated by lack of parental involvement, express their concern in terms of a deficit model. An administrator expresses his bewilderment:

> Our parent-teacher group is the foundation of our school programs. . . . This group (gestures to the all-Anglo, all-women group seated in the library) is the most important organization in the school. You know, I just don't understand why *those other parents* won't even show up.

Discussions about family involvement often center on what families lack and how educators can best teach parents to support instructional agendas at home (Mansbach 1993). To revise this limited model for interaction between home and school, we must look outside of the institutional perspective.

The Voices of "Those Other Parents"

We asked some of "those other parents" what they think about building positive home/school relations. In what follows, parents whose voices are rarely heard at school explain how the diverse contexts of their lives create tensions that interfere with positive home/school relations. For them, school experiences, economic and time constraints, and linguistic and cultural practices have produced a body of knowledge about school settings that frequently goes unacknowledged.

Diverse School Experiences Among Parents

Educators often don't take into account how a parent's own school experiences may influence school relationships. Listen in as one father describes his son's school progress:

> They expect me to go to school so they can tell me my kid is stupid or crazy. They've been telling me that for three years, so why should I go and hear it again? They don't do anything. They just tell me my kid is bad.
>
> See, I've been there. I know. And it scares me. They called me a boy in trouble but I was a troubled boy. Nobody helped me because they liked it when I didn't show up. If I was gone for the semester, fine with them. I dropped out nine times. They wanted me gone.

This father's experiences created mistrust and prevent him from participating more fully in his son's education. Yet, we cannot say that he doesn't care about his son. On the contrary, his message is urgent.

For many parents, their own personal school experiences create obstacles to involvement. Parents who have dropped out of school do not feel confident in school settings. Needed to help support their families or care for siblings at home, these individuals' limited schooling makes it difficult for them to help their children with homework beyond the early primary level. For some, this situation is compounded by language barriers and lack of written literacy skills. One mother who attended school through 6th grade in Mexico, and whose first language is Spanish, comments about homework that "sometimes we can't help because it's too hard." Yet the norm in most schools is to send home schoolwork with little information for parents about how it should be completed.

Diverse Economic and Time Constraints

Time constraints are a primary obstacle for parents whose work doesn't allow them the autonomy and flexibility characteristic of professional positions. Here, a mother expresses her frustrations:

> Teachers just don't understand that I can't come to school at just any old time. I think Judy told you that we don't have a car right now. . . . Andrew catches a different bus than Dawn. He gets here a half an hour before her, and then I have to make sure Judy is home

> because I got three kids in three different schools. And I feel like the teachers are under pressure, and they're turning it around and putting the pressure on me cause they want me to check up on Judy and I really can't.

Often, parents work at physically demanding jobs, with mothers expected to take care of child-care responsibilities as well as school-related issues. In one mother's words:

> What most people don't understand about the Hispanic community is that you come home and you take care of your husband and your family first. Then if there's time you can go out to your meetings.

Other parents work nights, making it impossible to attend evening programs and difficult to appear at daytime meetings that interfere with family obligations and sleep.

At times, parents' financial concerns present a major obstacle to participation in their child's school activities. One mother expresses frustration that she cannot send eight dollars to school so her daughter can have a yearbook to sign like the other girls.

> I do not understand why they assume that everybody has tons of money, and every time I turn around it's more money for this and more money for that. Where do they get the idea that we've got all this money?

This mother is torn between the pressures of stretching a tight budget and wanting her daughter to belong. As is the case for others, economic constraints prevent her child from full participation in the culture of the school. This lack of a sense of belonging creates many barriers for parents.

Diverse Linguistic and Cultural Practices

Parents who don't speak fluent English often feel inadequate in school contexts. One parent explains that "an extreme language barrier" prevented her own mother from ever going to anything at the school. Cultural mismatches can occur as often as linguistic conflicts. One Latino educator explained that asking young children to translate for their parents during conferences grates against a cultural norm. Placing children in a position of equal status with adults creates dysfunction within the family hierarchy.

One mother poignantly expresses the cultural discomfort she feels when communicating with Anglo teachers and parents:

> [In] the Hispanic culture and the Anglo culture things are done different and you really don't know—am I doing the right thing? When they call me and say, "You bring the plates" [for class parties], do they think I can't do the cookies, too? You really don't know.

Voicing a set of values that conflicts with institutional constructions of the parent's role, a mother gives this culturally-based explanation for not attending her 12-year-old's school functions:

> It's her education, not mine. I've had to teach her to take care of herself. I work nights, so she's had to get up and get herself ready for school. I'm not going to be there all the time. She's gotta do it. She's a tough cookie. . . . She's almost an adult, and I get the impression that they want me to walk her through her work. And it's not that I don't care either. I really do. I think it's important, but I don't think it's my place.

This mother does not lack concern for her child. In her view, independence is essential for her daughter's success.

Whether it is for social, cultural, linguistic, or economic reasons, these parents' voices are rarely heard at school. Perhaps, as educators, we too readily categorize them as "those other parents" and fail to hear the concern that permeates such conversations. Because the experiences of these families vary greatly from our own, we operate on assumptions that interfere with our best intentions. What can be done to address the widening gap between parents who participate and those who don't?

Getting Involved: Suggestions from Parents

Parents have many suggestions for teachers and administrators about ways to promote active involvement. Their views, however, do not always match the role envisioned by educators. Possessing fewer economic resources and educational skills to participate in traditional ways (Lareau 1987), these parents operate at a disadvantage until they understand how schools are organized and how they can promote systemic change (Delgado-Gaitan 1991).

If we're truly interested in establishing a dialogue with the parents of all of our nation's students, however, we need to understand what parents think can be done. Here are some of their suggestions.

Clarify How Parents Can Help

Parents need to know exactly how they can help. Some are active in church and other community groups, but lack information about how to become more involved in their children's schooling. One Latina mother explains that most of the parents she knows think that school involvement means attending school parties.

As Concha Delgado-Gaitan (1991) points out ". . . the difference between parents who participate and those who do not is that those who do have recognized that they are a critical part of their children's education." Many of the parents we spoke to don't see themselves in this capacity.

Encourage Parents to Be Assertive

Parents who do see themselves as needed participants feel strongly that they must provide their children with a positive view of their history and culture not usually presented at school.

Some emphasize the importance of speaking up for their children. Several, for instance, have argued for or against special education placement or retention for their children; others have discussed with teachers what they saw as inappropriate disciplinary procedures. In one parent's words:

> Sometimes kids are taken advantage of because their parents don't fight for them. I say to parents, if you don't fight for your child, no one's going to fight for them.

Although it may sound as if these parents are advocating adversarial positions, they are simply pleading for inclusion. Having spent much time on the teacher side of these conversations, we realize that teachers might see such talk as challenging their positions as professional decision makers. Yet, it is crucial that we expand the dialogue to include parent knowledge about school settings, even when that knowledge conflicts with our own.

Develop Trust

Parents affirm the importance of establishing trust. One mother attributes a particular teacher's good turnout for parent/teacher conferences to her ability to establish a "personal relationship" with parents. Another comments on her need to be reassured that the school is open, that it's OK to drop by "anytime you can."

In the opportunities we provide for involvement, we must regularly ask ourselves what messages we convey through our dress, gestures, and talk. In one study, for example, a teacher described her school's open house in a middle-class neighborhood as "a cocktail party without cocktails" (Lareau 1987). This is the sort of "party" that many parents wouldn't feel comfortable attending.

Fear was a recurrent theme among the parents we interviewed: fear of appearing foolish or being misunderstood, fear about their children's academic standing. One mother explained:

> Parents feel like the teachers are looking at you, and I know how they feel, because I feel like that here. There are certain things and places where I still feel uncomfortable, so I won't go, and I feel bad, and I think maybe it's just me.

This mother is relaying how it feels to be culturally, linguistically, and ethnically different. Her body of knowledge does not match the institutional knowledge of the school and she is therefore excluded from home/school conversations.

Build on Home Experiences

Our assumptions about the home environments of our students can either build or serve as links between home and school. An assumption that "these kids don't live in good environments" can destroy the very network we are trying to create. Too often we tell parents what we want them to do at home with no understanding of the rich social interaction that already occurs there (Keenan et al. 1993). One mother expresses her frustrations:

> Whenever I go to school, they want to tell me what to do at home. They want to tell me how to raise my kid. They never ask me what I think. They never ask me anything.

When we asked parents general questions about their home activities and how these activities might build on what happens at school, most thought there was no connection. They claimed not to engage in much reading and writing at home, although their specific answers to questions contradicted this belief. One mother talks about her time at home with her teenage daughter:

> My husband works nights and sometimes she sleeps with me. . . . We would lay down in bed and discuss the books she reads.

Many of the parents we spoke to mentioned Bible reading as a regular family event, yet they did not see this reading in relation to schoolwork. In one mother's words:

> I read the Bible to the children in Spanish, but when I see they're not understanding me, I stop (laughing). Then they go and look in the English Bible to find out what I said.

Although the Bible is not a text read at public schools, we can build on the literacy practices and social interactions that surround it. For instance, we can draw upon a student's ability to compare multiple versions of a text. We also can include among the texts we read legends, folktales, and mythology—literature that, like the Bible, is meant to teach us about our strengths and weaknesses as we strive to make our lives meaningful.

As teachers, of course, we marvel at the way in which such home interactions do, indeed, support our goals for learning at school; but we won't know about these practices unless we begin to form relationships with parents that allow them to share such knowledge.

Use Parent Expertise

Moll (1992) underscores the importance of empowering parents to contribute *"intellectually* to the development of lessons." He recommends assessing the "funds of knowledge" in the community, citing a teacher who discovered that many parents in the Latino community where she taught had expertise in the field of construction. Consequently, the class developed a unit on construction, which included reading, writing, speaking, and building, all with the help of responsive community experts—the children's parents.

Parents made similar suggestions—for example, cooking ethnic foods with students, sharing information about multicultural heritage, and bringing in role models from the community. Latino parents repeatedly emphasized that the presence of more teachers from their culture would benefit their children as role models and would help them in home/school interactions.

Parents also suggested extending literacy by writing pen pal letters with students or involving their older children in tutoring and letter writing with younger students. To help break down the barriers that language differences create, one parent suggested that bilingual and monolingual parents form partnerships to participate in school functions together.

An Invitation for Involvement

Too often, the social, economic, linguistic, and cultural practices of parents are represented as serious problems rather than valued knowledge. When we reexamine our assumptions about parental absence, we may find that our interpretations of parents who care may simply be parents who are like us, parents who feel comfortable in the teacher's domain.

Instead of operating on the assumption that absence translates into noncaring, we need to focus on ways to draw parents into the schools. If we make explicit the multiple ways we value the language, culture, and knowledge of the parents in our communities, parents may more readily accept our invitations.

References

Clark, R. M. (1983). *Family Life and School Achievement: Why Poor Black Children Succeed or Fail.* Chicago: University of Chicago Press.

Comer, J. P. (1984). "Homeschool Relationships as They Affect the Academic Success of Children." *Education and Urban Society* 16: 323–337.

David, M. E. (1989). "Schooling and the Family." In *Critical Pedagogy, the State, and Cultural Struggle,* edited by H. Giroux and P. McLaren. Albany, N.Y.: State University of New York Press.

Delgado-Gaitan, C. (1991). "Involving Parents in the Schools: A Process of Empowerment." *American Journal of Education* 100: 20–46.

Keenan, J. W., J. Willett, and J. Solsken. (1993). "Constructing an Urban Village: School/Home Collaboration in a Multicultural Classroom." *Language Arts* 70: 204–214.

Lareau, A. (1987). "Social Class Differences in Family-School Relationships: The Importance of Cultural Capital." *Sociology of Education* 60: 73–85.

Mansbach, S. C. (February/March 1993). "We Must Put Family Literacy on the National Agenda." *Reading Today:* 37.

Moll, L. (1992). "Bilingual Classroom Studies and Community Analysis: Some Recent Trends." *Educational Researcher* 21: 20–24.

Postnote

Much research supports the principle that children whose parents are active in their schools are more likely to succeed in school, whereas children whose parents are not involved are more apt to do poorly. Some parents are eager to work as partners with schools to be certain that their children are well prepared for the life and career choices they will make. Other parents are almost never involved with the school.

This article is useful to educators working at schools where parental involvement is less than what they hoped for. By understanding why some parents never show up at schools, educators can take steps to help overcome the parents' reluctance. Remember, teachers need parents to help them succeed.

Discussion Questions

1. List some of the main reasons Finders and Lewis give for parents not coming to school. Which of these reasons do you find compelling? Do any of the reasons surprise you?
2. Can you identify any additional reasons for parents to stay away from school, besides those given by the authors?
3. What strategies for involving parents in school have you seen employed, and how successful were they?

Life After School

SANDRA L. HOFFERTH AND ZITA JANKUNIENE

FOCUS Question

After-school programs are one of the fastest-growing segments of the education world. What do we really know about what children—those enrolled in after-school programs as well as those who are not—do after school?

How students spend their nonschool hours is important to their social development and academic achievement. Today, about 30 percent of a student's week is discretionary or free time (Hofferth & Sandberg, 200lb). What students do during that time—whether they play, read, watch television, play video games, or hang out with friends—will affect their long-term achievement and social adjustment (Eccles & Barber, 1999).

We wanted to find out how preadolescent students spend their time from the end of the school day until they go to sleep at night. In particular, we wondered

- Where do students go after school?
- What do students do?
- Whom do students spend time with?
- How does location affect disadvantaged students' involvement in activities?

Although many researchers have studied students' use of time (Asmussen & Larson, 1991; Bianchi & Robinson, 1997; Hofferth & Sandberg, 2001a; Hofferth & Sandberg, 2001b; Timmer, Eccles, & O'Brien, 1985), few studies have focused on what students do after school (Eccles & Barber, 1999; Medrich, Roizen, Rubin, & Buckley, 1982; Miller, O'Connor, Sirignano, & Joshi, 1996). Fewer still have explored supervision after school among elementary school students. Our study attempted to fill that gap.

Background

Research suggests that what students do after school depends on where they go, what their own and their families' characteristics are,

---

Sandra L. Hofferth is a professor in the Department of Family Studies, University of Maryland, College Park, Maryland. At the time this article was written, **Zita Jankuniene** was a Database Marketing Analyst with Time Inc. From Sandra L. Hofferth and Zita Jankuniene, "Life After School," *Educational Leadership,* April 2001, pp. 19–23. Reprinted by permission. The Association for Supervision and Curriculum Development is a worldwide community of educators advocating sound policies and sharing best practices to achieve the success of each learner. To learn more, visit ASCD at **www.ascd.org.**

and with whom they spend time when they get there. When we began our study, we wanted to examine the following factors:

Location Physical context is an important determinant of what students do. One study (Medrich, Roizen, Rubin, & Buckley, 1982) found that nearly three-quarters of the students in the sample went straight home from school, regardless of whether an adult was home to greet them.

Students' Characteristics What students do and the amount of time they spend doing it are likely to be affected by the students' characteristics, such as age and gender. As students mature, the range of activities that they want and are allowed to do broadens. In addition, gender differences exist, particularly in such activities as household work, personal care, and participation in household conversations. Gender differences show up more clearly in older students.

Family Economics What students do also depends on their parents' education levels and income. Well-educated parents often encourage students to participate in educational activities, such as reading and studying. Higher-income families typically can afford more expensive sports clubs and lessons for their children than lower-income families can.

Supervision and Companionship The type of activity, the location, and the kind and amount of supervision are closely linked. In this study, we examined whether location is linked to supervision and the involvement of adults and peers.

Our Study

For our study, we classified the primary activities of students grades K–7 into 20 major categories. We used 18 categories from another study (Timmer, Eccles, & O'Brien, 1985), such as personal care, eating, sleeping, household work, school, studying, and reading, plus participation in day care and youth organizations.

Data

The data come from the 1997 Child Development Supplement to the Panel Study of Income Dynamics (Hofferth, Davis-Kean, Davis, & Finkelstein, 1999), an annual 30-year longitudinal survey of a representative sample of U.S. men, women, children, and the families with whom they reside. In spring and fall 1997, data were collected on randomly selected 0- to 12-year-olds, both from the primary caregivers and from the students themselves. We looked at a sample of 1,484 students grades K–7 who went to school on a sample day. Because we were interested in students' time during after-school waking hours, we studied only those activities that they participated in after the school day ended until they went to bed, a six-hour period.

We based the study on 24-hour time diaries during one weekday. An interviewer asked either the parent or the parent and the student questions about the student's flow of activities during the 24-hour period beginning at midnight. The interviewer asked about the primary activity that the child was doing, when the activity began and ended, and whether any other activity took place concurrently. The interviewer also asked where the child was during the activity, who participated with the child, and whether anyone else was with the child but was not directly involved in the activity.

Student Characteristics Because a major transition in child care occurs at about age 9 or 10 (Hofferth, Brayfield, Deich, & Holcomb, 1991), we divided the students into three age groups: kindergarten (age 5), grades 1–3 (ages 6–8), and grades 4–7 (ages 9–12). In our sample, 12 percent of the students were in kindergarten, 39 percent in grades 1–3, and 48 percent in grades 4–7. The sample contained an equal proportion of boys and girls.

Family Characteristics We categorized the mothers' education levels: 18 percent of the mothers had less than a high school education, 33 percent had a high school diploma, 27 percent had some college education, 14 percent had a college degree, and 8 percent had some graduate school experience. We also compared the income of students' families to the poverty line that was calculated by the U.S. Bureau of the Census and identified those families who were under 100 percent of the poverty line, between 100 and 200 percent, and 200 percent and over.

Results

Where Do Students Go First? At the end of the school day, 73 percent of the students went directly home, 8 percent stayed at school, 11 percent went to a day-care center or a family day-care home, and 8 percent went somewhere else, such as a parent's workplace, indoor or outdoor recreation centers, stores or shopping centers, restaurants, nonretail businesses, or churches. Where students went varied, first of all, by their grade level. More students in grades 4–7 went directly home and fewer were in day care, which makes sense: Older students are more often able to care for themselves. The number of students who stayed at school did not vary by age.

Participation in After-School Activities All students spent some time at home, and most spent some time elsewhere. One-quarter spent time in day care or at someone else's home, and 13 percent spent some time at school during the after-school hours.

Home At home, television viewing topped the list of activities. Seventy-six percent of students of all ages watched television. Playing and studying were also common; half the students played and half studied. A surprising one-third did household chores. One-quarter spent some time reading for pleasure. About 15 percent engaged in sports activities or household conversations. Ten percent engaged in "passive leisure," which involved such activities as listening to music or just sitting around.

School Students who stayed at school participated in sports (24 percent) and art activities (11 percent). They also studied (8 percent), visited with others (8 percent), and played (9 percent). Eleven percent were involved in youth organizations. About 10 percent engaged in passive leisure, and about 1 percent watched television at school.

Elsewhere Of students who went to other locations after school, half played sports and one-quarter went shopping. Fourteen percent visited other people and 12 percent played. Fifteen percent engaged in educational activities, such as religious education or tutoring. Twelve percent reported that they did nothing or they just "hung out." Again, about 1 percent reported watching television.

Interpretation of Findings

Location and Activity

Students played in all locations, most commonly at home (54 percent) and in day care (43 percent), and less frequently at school (9 percent) and in other locations (12 percent). Students played sports at school (24 percent) and elsewhere (46 percent). They read for pleasure primarily at home, where 25 percent of students read for about half an hour.

Students watched television mainly in the home, though a small proportion watched television in day-care centers or in a caregiver's home. They spent about 1 hour and 40 minutes watching television at home after school and about one hour watching in a child care setting.

About 20 percent of the students attended a youth organization meeting, mostly at school or elsewhere. Although this is a lower rate than the total number of students enrolled in those organizations, it gives an accurate picture of the involvement of youth in organizations on any given day. They spent between 30 minutes to 1 hour and 20 minutes at youth organizations.

Students did schoolwork in a variety of settings. Although some studied in child care and after-school programs, most studied at home. About half the students spent some time studying at home; however, they only studied for 45 minutes in the early primary grades and for one hour in grades 4–7.

Gender Differences

Gender differences were reflected only in certain activities. At home, boys in grades 4–7 tended to do more studying, sports, and playing, and less visiting, art, reading, and other passive leisure activities than girls did. At school, twice as many boys played sports. Girls did more tidying up, visiting, art, and passive leisure activities. But girls studied more at school than boys did. In other locations, boys were twice as likely to play sports, and girls were more likely to do household work, visit, and participate in art activities.

Supervision

Adult supervision varied by location. Although students were highly supervised for most of the time in all settings, adult supervision was greatest in day care and at school and was least available at home and in other settings. At school and day care, students were almost never unsupervised. At home, students spent more time unsupervised, but only a fraction—3 percent—were alone. Students spent the largest proportion of time (10 percent) with peers or siblings only in other locations and at home. The older the students, the less adult supervision they had and the more time they spent with peers or alone. Students in grades 4–7 spent almost 6 percent of their home time alone and 10 percent of home time with peers only, compared with kindergartners, who spent 1 percent alone and 6 percent with peers.

Family Income and Education

As we might expect, family income and maternal education related to the amount of time that students spent in activities after school. One of the best examples of income differences was participation in sports activities. Better-educated parents and those with higher incomes were able to afford more opportunities for their children. Schools equalized many of these opportunities, however. Although students from low-income families were no more or less likely to be enrolled in sports activities outside of school, they were more likely to be enrolled in school settings.

What Educators Need to Know

Although 73 percent of elementary school students go home right after school, the proportion increases—from two-thirds of kindergartners to three-fourths of students grades 4–7—as students become more responsible for their own care. Students' activities vary substantially, depending on where they go after school. At school and day-care programs after school, students watch little television and do little studying or reading. They participate in structured activities, such as sports and youth organizations. Students do the majority of studying, playing, television watching, and reading at home.

What are the implications? With both parents more likely to work outside the home in recent decades, students spend less time at home. Although students study and play in several contexts, our findings showed that their reading time takes place primarily at home. As their time at home declines, so too will their time spent reading for pleasure. Because reading is the activity most strongly and consistently associated with student achievement (Hofferth & Sandberg, 2001b), this finding is worrisome.

Our findings also suggest that schools can play an equalizing role in providing access to certain activities after school for less-privileged students. Low-income students and students whose mothers have little education are less likely to play sports in indoor or outdoor recreation centers than at school or home, but they are more likely to play sports at school. Program planners in schools must take this fact into account.

School-based programs provide supervision and a safe environment. As students mature, however, they often prefer to spend time after school at home, even if unsupervised, because they can relax, read, and watch television. To appeal to the 10- to 12-year-old group, after-school programs need to take into account the need for independence and self-determination as well as the need for supervision and help with homework. Serving this in-between age of students is a challenge for educators. Information on what students choose to do at home and in other locations may help educators plan attractive after-school activities for this group.

References

Asmussen, L., & Larson, R. (1991). The quality of family time among young adolescents in single-parent and married-parent families. *Journal of Marriage and the Family, 53,* 1021–1030.

Bianchi, S., & Robinson, J. (1997). What did you do today? Children's use of time, family composition, and the acquisition of social capital. *Journal of Marriage and the Family, 59,* 332–344.

Eccles, J., & Barber, B. (1999). Student council, volunteering, basketball, or marching band: What kind of extracurricular involvement matters? *Journal of Adolescent Research, 14,* 10–43.

Hofferth, S. L., Brayfield, A., Deich, S., & Holcomb, P. (1991). *National child care survey, 1990.* Washington, DC: The Urban Institute.

Hofferth, S. L., Davis-Kean, P., Davis, J., & Finkelstein, J. (1999). *1997 user guide: The child development supplement to the Panel Study of Income Dynamics.* Ann Arbor, MI: Institute for Social Research.

Hofferth, S. L., & Sandberg, J. F. (2001a). Changes in American children's time, 1981–1997. In T. Owens & S. L. Hofferth (Eds.), *Children at the millennium: Where have we come from, where are we going?* New York: Elsevier Science.

Hofferth, S. L., & Sandberg, J. F. (2001b, forthcoming). How American children use their time. *Journal of Marriage and the Family, 63*(3).

Medrich, E., Roizen, J., Rubin, V., & Buckley, S. (1982). *The serious business of growing up: A study of children's lives outside school.* Berkeley: University of California Press.

Miller, B., O'Connor, S., Sirignano, S., & Joshi, P. (1996). *I wish the kids didn't watch so much TV: Out-of-school time in three low-income communities* [School-age child care project]. Wellesley, MA: Center for Research on Women.

Timmer, S. G., Eccles, J., & O'Brien, K. (1985). How children use time. In F. S. Juster (Ed.), *Time, goods, and well-being* (pp. 353–382). Ann Arbor, MI: Institute for Social Research.

Authors' note: The National Institute of Child Health and Human Development funded this research under grant U01-HD37563, the Family and Child Well-Being Research Network.

Postnote

Once upon a time, American students left school at three o'clock, went home to Mom, had milk and cookies, went out to play with the neighborhood kids, had supper with the family at six, and spent the rest of the evening with a little television and a solid period of homework. For most American children, that world is past. Most dramatically, with some 80 percent of mothers in the work force, there is no one home to serve up the milk and cookies. Plus, many of our neighborhoods are hardly as safe as they once were.

While many parents try to provide for their children's after-school supervision by rearranging their work schedules or providing after-school programs for them, many leave their children unsupervised. This "leaving children unsupervised" is part of a large social movement, which has been described as the uncoupling or disengagement of the adult world from the close supervision of children. Many families today provide less guidance and have weaker authority over their children. Children fend for themselves at an earlier age and make their own choices, choices such as whether or not to do homework and how much and what television to watch. Of course, many young people rise to the challenge and take constructive control of their lives. But then there are the others who become addicted to television, Internet pornography, early sexuality, and that great American pastime: cruising the mall.

Discussion Questions

1. When you were in elementary and secondary schools, what kind of after-school experiences did you have?
2. Do you believe the school has the right and the responsibility to provide guidance to parents about what kinds of structured environment their children should have when they leave school for the day?
3. What do you think of our society's early disengagement of adults from children? What has been your own experience?

Home Schooling Comes of Age

PATRICIA M. LINES

FOCUS Question

What is home schooling, and how can we explain its tremendous growth in recent years?

TERMS TO NOTE

Home schooling

Home-school liaison

Individuals with Disabilities Education Act (IDEA)

This fall, when school bells summoned school-aged children, some did not respond. These children turned, instead, to home schooling, learning primarily at home or in the nearby community. Not so long ago, the families of these children might have gone underground, hiding from public view. Now they feel that they are simply exercising a valid educational option.

Home schooling has come of age. On any given day, more than a half million children are home schooled—perhaps little more than 1 percent of all school-aged children and about 10 percent of those who are privately schooled. This rough estimate assumes modest growth since 1990–1991, when I collected data from three independent sources—state education agencies, distributors of popular curricular packages, and state and local home-school associations. Knowing that all these figures represented the tip of the iceberg, I also used surveys of home-schoolers to estimate how many remained submerged (Lines 1991).

My current estimate rests in part on evidence of growth since then together with a rough assessment of the Census Bureau's 1994 Current Population Survey. Assuming the average home-schooling experience lasts only two years, as many as 6 percent of all families with children could have some home-schooling experience.

Making It Legal

A more favorable legal climate also signals the coming of age of home schooling. Twenty years ago, many states did not allow it. Constitutional protection for parents has always been ambiguous. The U.S. Supreme Court has never explicitly ruled on home schooling, although in 1972, in *Wisconsin* v. *Yoder,* the Court did restrict compulsory school requirements in a limited ruling involving the right of Amish students

---

Patricia M. Lines (JD, University of Minnesota; PhD, Catholic University of America) is Discovery Institute's senior fellow specializing in education issues. From Patricia M. Lines, "Home Schooling Comes of Age," *Educational Leadership,* October 1996, pp. 63–67. Reprinted by permission. The Association for Supervision and Curriculum Development is a worldwide community of educators advocating sound policies and sharing best practices to achieve the success of each learner. To learn more, visit ASCD at **www.ascd.org.**

not to attend high school. Nearly a half century earlier, in a case involving a Catholic private school (*Pierce* v. *Society of Sisters,* 1925), the high court upheld, in more general terms, the right of parents to direct the education of their children.

Home-schoolers have argued that these cases protect them. But public officials have often disagreed, charging parents with violating compulsory education laws. In most cases, the courts have avoided the heart of the matter and—as is traditional in the American judicial system—ruled on narrow legal grounds. For example, some courts have struck down compulsory education laws as too vague, or found that restrictive school board regulations exceeded the board's statutory authority. Yet some courts have upheld states' legal requirements and found that parents met or did not meet them. A few parents have gone to jail for the cause.

State legislatures have responded more vigorously than the courts. Where many states once forbade home schooling, all states now allow it. At the same time, all states do expect the home-schooling family to file basic information with either the state or local education agency. And some states have additional requirements, such as the submission of a curriculum plan; the testing of students; or, in a few cases, education requirements or testing for parents.

Bending Stereotypes

What do today's home-schoolers look like? The stereotypical view is that they are loners who do not care about the opinions of others. But in at least one survey of home-schooling parents, 95 percent of respondents said the single most important thing that they wanted was support and encouragement from family, friends, church, and community (Mayberry et al. 1995).

Certainly the image of the isolated family does not fit any home-schooling family that I have met. On the contrary, these families seem highly connected to other families and other institutions. Indeed, the most universal resource that home-schooling families draw upon are like-minded families. Wherever there is more than a handful of home-schooling families in an area, they tend to form at least one home-schooling association.

Though home-schoolers look to one another, they hardly look *like* one another. One family may start the day with prayer or a flag salute, followed by a traditional, scheduled curriculum. Another may throw out the schedule and opt for child-led learning, providing help as the child expresses interest in a topic. In either type of family, the children are likely to take increasing responsibility for choosing and carrying out projects as they mature. And either type of family is likely to collaborate with other families.

Some home-schooled children will spend part of their time—with or without parents—at a local public or private school or at a nearby college. Substantial numbers of home-schoolers have invaded the electronic world, using it heavily for educational materials and networking. Families also draw upon resources at libraries, museums, parks departments, churches, and local businesses and organizations, and take advantage of extension courses and various mentors. In addition, they use the curriculum packages, books, and other materials that many private schools offer for use in home schooling.

Courting Public Opinion

Now that all states have adopted more flexible legislation, the most important factor contributing to the growth of home schooling may be the increased receptivity of the general public. In the 1980s, few Americans gave home-schoolers much support or encouragement. In 1985, for example, only 16 percent of respondents to the annual *Phi Delta Kappan* Gallup poll thought that home schooling was a "good thing." By 1988, 28 percent thought so. That same year, Gallup asked whether parents should or should not have the legal right to home-school. Fifty-three percent said "should" and 39 percent said "should not" (Gallup and Elam 1988; Gallup 1984).

Because the *Kappan* Gallup poll has not asked these questions again, one must turn to other sources to gauge changing attitudes. Increasingly favorable media reports are one indicator. Mayberry and her colleagues have observed that media in the 1970s reported "the most divisive and extreme home education court cases and their outcomes" and tended to show home-schooling parents "as neglectful and irresponsible" (Mayberry et al. 1995). They note that recent news stories not only portray home-schoolers in a more positive light, but sometimes as folk heroes.

In a similar vein, Pat Farenga, a home-schooling leader employed by Holt publishers, told me that 10 years ago, *Good Housekeeping* and *Publisher's Weekly* would never run stories suggesting home schooling as an option for their readers, but both now do. (Based in Cambridge, Massachusetts, Holt Associates Inc. publishes *Growing Without Schooling,* a bimonthly newsletter designed to give practical advice to home-schooling parents.)

Last April, participants in a Home-School Association online discussion group (AHAonline @aol.com) reported how dramatically things have changed over the last decade. One home-schooler recalled that 10 years ago, if she told someone what she was doing, the first response would be "Is that legal?" Often this would be followed by strong disapproval. Another participant, Ann Lahrson (author of *Home Schooling in Oregon: The Handbook*), told how some friends, neighbors, and family members "rejected us, ignored us, clucked at us." She added that "professionally, I was shunned by colleagues at the public school where I had previously taught." Today, these home-schoolers said, they mostly hear remarks like, "Oh, do you enjoy it?" or "Oh, yeah, my brother/neighbor/cousin/fellow employee does that!"

Partnering Public Schools

Professional educators, on the other hand, remain wary. In 1988, the National Educational Association adopted a resolution calling for more rigorous regulation of home schooling. In March 1993, the National Association of Elementary School Principals adopted a resolution declaring that education is "most effectively done through cohesive organizations in formal settings" and specifically criticized home schooling. Even the national Parent-Teachers Association has passed a resolution opposing home schooling.

Other public educators have decided to work with home-schoolers. Most state education agencies have a home-schooling liaison, who at minimum will help a family understand state requirements. A small but growing number of school districts are offering home-schoolers access to schools on a part-time basis and, in some cases, special programs for home-schoolers.

In fact, the most exciting development in the home-schooling world is the emergence of partnerships between public schools and home schools, an arrangement that educators in Alaska pioneered. Teachers in Juneau work with students all over the state, staying in touch by mail and telephone and through occasional visits. Although the program was designed for students in remote areas, Alaska has never denied access to it because a child was near a school. The majority of the students now live in the Anchorage area.

Similar partnerships have emerged at the district level in other states. In California, for example, a child may enroll in an independent study program in a public school and base his or her studies in the home. Washington public schools must enroll children part-time if their families request it. The Des Moines (Iowa) School District, as well as several dozen in Washington, California, and other states, offer special programs for home-schooled children. Usually a child may enroll in such programs anywhere in the state. In a preview of education in the 21st century, these fledgling programs often rely heavily on electronic communications programs and software.

A few educators actually urge collaboration with home-schoolers, in the belief that they provide good models in exploring ways to involve parents and to individualize instruction and assessment (Weston 1996). For example, Dan Endsley, one of the founders of the Home Education League of Parents (HELP) in Toledo, Ohio, observes that

> As we helped more and more families learn about the home-school option, we found that school administrators also became

more tolerant of home schooling. In several cases, public school administrators even recommended that families get in touch with HELP and gave them our address and phone numbers.

Remaining Vigilant

Given the more favorable legal climate for home schooling, families are now freer to concentrate on access to public resources and scholastic and athletic competitions. Still, home-schoolers remain watchful. There are several national organizations and at least one statewide organization in every state. Some states also have a dozen or more regional associations. All these groups monitor issues that might affect home schoolers, and they can mobilize large numbers of constituents where their interests are at stake.

The Home-School Legal Defense Association, based in Paeonian Springs, Virginia, and headed by Michael P. Farris, maintains a staff of about seven lawyers specializing in home-schooling law. The organization routinely monitors developments in every state, and keeps its national membership informed of potential problems. The group is also ready to negotiate or sue where it believes a policy might threaten its members' interests. An affiliated organization, the National Center for Home Education, runs an aggressive congressional action program with a facsimile alert system (Mayberry et al. 1995). State associations provide the same services for their constituencies. So, too, do other organizations, such as Clonlara Home-Based Education, an Ann Arbor, Michigan–based group that offers support nationwide.

As a result of these interest groups, efforts to pass stricter home-schooling laws or to seek enforcement that exceeds statutory authorization are likely to face organized and informed opposition and legal challenges. Clonlara, for example, argued successfully that the Michigan Board of Education exceeded its statutory authority to regulate (*Clonlara* v. *State Board* 1993).

In an interview with me, an experienced staff member of the Congressional Research Service compared the activity of the home-schooling lobby to that of the lobby for the Individuals with Disabilities Education Act. He noted, though, that unlike disability law backers, home-schoolers are merely reactive, rarely taking the offensive.

Pointing the Way for Reform?

Does home schooling help children academically? There is considerable disagreement on this question. No one has undertaken research involving controls that indicates whether the *same* children would do better or worse in home schooling than in a public or private school classroom. States that require testing, however, have analyzed test scores, and home-schooling associations have a multitude of data from these states. Yet information from both these sources may reflect only a select group of home-schoolers, as not all families cooperate with state testing requirements, and private efforts rely on voluntary information. These caveats notwithstanding, virtually all the available data show that scores of the tested home-schooled children are above average, and comparable to the higher achievement pattern of private school students (Ray and Wartes 1991).

People also disagree on whether home schooling helps or hinders children's social development. Children engaged in home schooling spend less time with their peer group and more time with people of different ages. Most spend time with other children through support and networking groups, scouting, churches, and other associations. Many spend time with adults other than their parents through activities such as community volunteer work, home-based businesses, and tutoring or mentoring. No conclusive research suggests that time spent with same-aged peers is preferable to time spent with people of varying ages.

That said, limited testing of a self-selected group of home-schooled children suggests that these children are above average in their social and psychological development (Sheirs 1992, Delahooke 1986). At the very least, anyone who has observed home-schoolers will notice a high level of sharing, networking, collaboration, and cooperative learning.

Clearly, home schooling offers the potential for a very different educational environment for children. As such, it could be an important resource for studying how children learn, and whether and when formal or informal learning environments are superior. To the extent that home-schoolers are willing to cooperate, they could provide an opportunity to study the effects of one-on-one lay tutoring, child-led learning, and distance learning.

Although the percentage of children in home schooling on any one day is small, the number of adults in the home-schooling movement is much larger. Growth in numbers, increased acceptance by the public, and opportunities for engaging in the policy arena mean that home-schoolers could be an important part of a coalition seeking education reform at the state or national level.

References

Delahooke, M. M. (1986). "Home Educated Children's Social/Emotional Adjustment and Academic Achievement: A Comparison Study." Doctoral diss. Los Angeles: California School of Professional Psychology.

Gallup, A. M. (1984). "The Gallup Poll of the Public's Attitudes Toward the Public Schools." *Phi Delta Kappan* 66, 1: 23–28.

Gallup, A. M., and S. M. Elam. (September 1988). "The 20th Annual Gallup Poll of the Public's Attitudes Toward the Public Schools." *Phi Delta Kappan* 70, 1: 33–46.

Lines, P. (October 1991). "Estimating the Home-Schooled Population," U.S. Department of Education, Office of Research Working Paper.

Mayberry, M., J. G. Knowles, B. Ray, and S. Marlow. (1995). *Home Schooling: Parents as Educators.* Thousand Oaks, Calif.: Corwin Press.

Pierce v. *Society of Sisters.* (1925). 268 U.S. 510.

Ray, B. D., and J. Wartes. (1991). "The Academic Achievement and Affective Development of Home-Schooled Children." In *Home Schooling: Political, Historical and Pedagogical Perspectives,* edited by J. Van Galen and M. A. Pitman. Norwood, N.J.: Ablex Publishing Corporation.

Sheirs, L. E. (1992). "Comparison of Social Adjustment Between Home- and Traditionally-Schooled Students." Doctoral diss., University of Florida.

Weston, M. (April 3, 1996). "Reformers Should Take a Look at Home Schools." *Education Week:* 34.

Wisconsin v. *Yoder.* (1972). 406 U.S. 205.

Author's note: For an expanded version of this article, see P. Lines (in press). "Home Schooling," in *Private Education and Educational Choice,* edited by J. G. Cibulka (Westport, Conn.: Greenwood Press).

Postnote

Widespread criticism of our schools, along with the growing realization of education's importance, has set off an educational growth phase in the United States. As a historically innovative and experimental country, the United States is responding true to form, by striking out in new directions. The home-schooling movement is one such effort, as are charter schools, voucher experiments, and educational networks like the Coalition of Essential Schools.

Educational critics used to complain that our schools were captured by the "one right way" mentality. No longer. Home schooling is a case in point. It appears to be the right way for some, but for others it can be a disaster. To home-school well takes a special set of resources, among them a parent (or two) with the willingness and ability to teach. As this article suggests, however, home schooling seems to be satisfying the educational needs of hundreds of thousands of children and parents.

Discussion Questions

1. What do you believe are the greatest potential advantages and disadvantages of home schooling?
2. Why do you suppose there has been such strong opposition to home schooling in the United States?
3. List what you think are the resources needed by someone to be a successful home-school teacher.

4
Part Four

Curriculum and Standards

The bedrock question of education is this: What knowledge is most worth knowing? This question goes right to the heart of individual and social priorities. As our world has become more and more drenched with information—information pouring out at us from many different media—the question of what is worth our limited time and attention has increased in importance. It is the quintessential curriculum question.

In recent years, however, policymakers and educators have attempted to improve our schools by establishing what should be learned through state-mandated curriculum standards and by enforcing those standards through regular testing. The federal No Child Left Behind Act of 2001 requires states to test students in reading and mathematics each year in grades 3–8. This effort has dramatically affected what is going on in today's classrooms.

The question of what is most worth knowing, however, begets others. What is the purpose of knowledge? To make a great deal of money? To become a wise person? To prepare oneself for important work? To contribute to the general good of society?

This difficult question becomes more and more complex, and swiftly takes us into the realm of values. Nevertheless, it is a question communities must regularly address in our decentralized education system. In struggling with curriculum issues, a community is really making a bet on the future needs of society and of the young people who will have to live in that society. Behind the choice of a new emphasis on foreign language instruction or on computer literacy is a social gamble, and the stakes are high. Offering students an inadequate curriculum is like sending troops into battle with popguns.

Curriculum Matters

W. JAMES POPHAM

FOCUSQuestion

In what ways has the No Child Left Behind Act affected the way state standards are taught in schools and the way assessments are employed?

TERMS TO NOTE

Assessment
Coalesced content standard
Content standards
Curriculum
Derivative assessment framework

American educators use the word *curriculum* almost every day—and why not, since it describes the stuff we want our students to learn. What a curriculum contains, however, has historically had far less impact on instructional practice than is widely thought. But curriculum's modest influence on instruction has been dramatically transformed in the past few years, especially with respect to state-sanctioned curricula. These days, a state's curricular aims can have a decisive impact—either positive or negative—on the way students are taught.

Note that I am using the term *curriculum* in its traditional sense, namely, to describe the knowledge, skills, and (sometimes) feelings that educators want their students to acquire. In this time-honored definition, a curriculum represents educational *ends*. Educators hope, of course, that such ends will be attained as a consequence of instructional activities, which serve as the *means* of promoting the curricular ends.

In the past, the curricular things we wanted our students to learn were typically described as *goals* or *objectives*. These days, however, most educators tend to use the term *content standards* instead. But regardless of the label that's used, what's in a curriculum is supposed to describe the intended impact of an educational enterprise on the students being taught.

A Personal Perspective

My first serious brush with curriculum occurred some five decades ago, when I began teaching in eastern Oregon. Even way back then, Oregon had a state-approved curriculum syllabus, and I was given a copy of that thick text for my bookshelf. And that's where it stayed—right on that shelf. Other than glancing at the syllabus for an hour or so before the school year began to find out what goals the state decreed for the courses I was scheduled to teach, I never looked at it again.

W. James Popham is professor emeritus in the UCLA Graduate School of Education and Information Studies. "Curriculum Matters," by W. James Popham. Reprinted with permission from *American School Board Journal,* November 2004.

What actually determined the content I taught in my classes was, almost totally, the textbooks I used. As a first-year teacher in a small high school, I had five different preparations. Accordingly, my frantic instructional planning revolved completely around the textbooks I'd been told to use for those five courses. To illustrate, I was required, by a principal who had never heard of "highly qualified teachers," to teach a course in geography even though I had never in my entire life taken a course in geography. Given my lack of geographic expertise, I truly cherished the large red geography text without which I could not have survived a class of 30 sophomores, most of whom did not truly care about the location of Khartoum or the subtleties of a Mercator map projection.

But I was not alone. All of the other teachers in my school paid little, if any, attention to the state curriculum syllabus. My faculty colleagues, too, decided on what they should teach according to what was treated in their textbooks. In retrospect, "alignment" in those days might have referred to whether a teacher's lesson plan meshed suitably with the textbook's upcoming chapter.

No Clarity, No Consequences

The trifling impact that official curriculum documents have on teachers' instructional practices can probably be attributed, at least in part, to the documents' excessive generality. If, for example, social studies teachers discover that their students are supposed to acquire "a meaningful understanding of how our nation's government functions," there is obviously so much latitude in this curricular aim that a wide range of instructional activities legitimately could be regarded as germane. The mushiness of many curricular aims certainly plays a role in reducing the impact of those aims on classroom instruction.

However, a more fundamental reason that our nation's curricula have had so little influence on instructional practice is that what was in a curriculum, even a state-sanctioned or district-sanctioned curriculum, rarely made any sort of difference to anyone.

Oh, certainly, there have been occasional instances when a particular body of content was thought to be appropriate or inappropriate for a state curriculum. You might recall, for instance, the recent flap in Kansas about the inclusion of evolution content in the state's science curriculum. And, when a state's textbooks are under consideration for adoption, those doing the adopting surely pay some attention to what's in the state's curriculum when they review contending textbooks. But, considering the full-blown panorama of American public education, what has been identified in official curriculum documents has typically had only a slight impact on what actually goes on in classrooms.

Then Came NCLB

But that situation came to a screeching halt on Jan. 8, 2002, when President Bush affixed his signature to the No Child Left Behind Act. This important reauthorization of a federal law, first enacted in 1965, substantially altered the relationship between curriculum and instruction in America.

That's because NCLB first tied *assessments* to a state's curriculum, then tied important decisions to students' performances on those curriculum-based assessments. If students failed to make sufficient progress in their *assessed* mastery of a state's curricular aims, then all sorts of sanctions and public embarrassment would follow for educators who were running the schools and districts where insufficient progress had been seen. Because NCLB required a state's annual assessments to be based on the state's official curriculum, and because those annual assessments could cause plenty of trouble, what was in the curriculum suddenly mattered.

Educators, of course, were eager to avoid NCLB sanctions (or NCLB-induced embarrassment) by having been identified as failing to make adequate yearly progress in students' test performances. Accordingly, educators became far more attentive to what would be covered in their state's NCLB tests. But a state's NCLB tests, as required by law, must be based on the state's official curriculum, as represented by a state's "challenging" content standards.

Let me quickly tie a ribbon around this logic chain:

1. A state's schools and districts can get battered by NCLB sanctions and/or public embarrassment if students don't score well enough on the state's annual NCLB tests;
2. But what's measured on those annual NCLB tests must be based on a state's official curriculum; and, therefore,
3. Teachers will be certain to try to boost NCLB test scores by devoting substantial instructional time to what's likely to be assessed by their state's curriculum-based NCLB tests.

So, for the first time in the history of American public schooling, a potent federal law has made curriculum truly count—big time.

The problem is that most state curricula, against a backdrop of these significant NCLB pressures to improve test scores, are actually *lowering* the quality of education in a state's schools. We need to understand why that is so. And we need to do something about it.

Too Many Targets

Here, in a nutshell, is what currently constitutes an NCLB-triggered, curriculum-caused calamity. The content standards now found in almost all of our states originally were devised by competent, well-intentioned individuals—but at a time when a state-approved curriculum was merely supposed to reflect worthwhile educational aspirations for a state's students.

Unfortunately, in most states' current collections of content standards, there are far too many curriculum aims to teach or to test in the time available for teaching or testing. Almost all states' content standards reflect a "wish-list" mentality; that is, the determiners of a state's content standards in, say, mathematics, have listed all the nifty mathematical skills and knowledge they *wish* the state's students would be able to master. But the result of these cover-the-waterfront curriculum exercises—carried out before NCLB's arrival made curriculum a potent factor in a state's accountability game—was invariably to lay out way too many curricular targets.

A state's educators, therefore, have been forced to deal with—or try to deal with—an excessive number of curricular targets. Too many curricular aims must be assessed by a given year's NCLB tests, so teachers are obliged to guess which ones actually will be tested in a given year. On probability grounds alone, of course, many teachers guess wrong and end up teaching things that aren't on the NCLB tests or not teaching things that are on the tests.

A related problem arises because teachers are unable to learn from the results of NCLB tests which of their instructional activities have or haven't worked. Because there are so many curricular aims, the ones that actually are measured on a given year's test can't be assessed with enough test items to supply any sort of sensible estimate about which curricular aims were or weren't well taught. A collection of too-general score reports simply doesn't provide teachers with the information they need to improve their instruction, for those reports do not let teachers know *which* curricular aims have or haven't been mastered by their students. And, lurking as the culprit in this instructionally meaningless score reporting is a state curriculum containing too many curricular aims in the first place.

Given this regrettable situation, it is any wonder that some NCLB-pressured teachers engage in rampant curricular reductionism, excising any content—even important content—if it seems unlikely to be tested. Is it any wonder that some teachers oblige their students to take part in endless, mind-numbing test-preparation sessions? Is it any wonder that some engage in such dishonest practices as supplying their students with advance copies of covertly copied items from the actual tests?

All of these bad outcomes could be reduced or eliminated if only more sensible NCLB tests were employed. But, as you have now seen, first we must grapple with the inappropriate curricular targets found in so many states. Unless a state's decision makers figure out a way to have their state's NCLB tests function as a force for instructional improvement, not instructional decline, too many students will suffer. That suffering can be traced directly to curricular aims that, though perhaps serviceable in a former time, just don't work today.

These days, because of NCLB, curriculum *does* make a difference. And these days, because of NCLB, we need to rethink whether our state curricula are suitable.

Three Options

The task before education policy makers is to reduce the number of eligible-to-be-assessed curricular aims so that (1) teachers are not overwhelmed by too many instructional targets and (2) a student's mastery of each curricular aim that's assessed can be determined with reasonable accuracy.

Teachers who can focus their instructional attention on a modest number of truly significant skills usually can get their students to master those skills—even if the skills are genuinely challenging. Accurate reports of students' mastery of each skill will let the students and their parents know which curricular aims have or haven't been mastered—and let teachers know which ones have or haven't been well taught.

Here are three potential ways of coping with this curricular crisis:

Brand New Content Standards. The first option involves a start-from-scratch approach to identifying a state's curricular aims. Given a clean slate, and the recognition that a subject matter's most important curricular aims must be assessed by NCLB tests, a state's curriculum makers could attempt to come up with a markedly winnowed, more instructionally beneficial set of unarguably significant curricular aims.

Coalesced Content Standards. A second alternative would be for a state's curriculum officials to rework existing curricular aims so that the most important of them were subsumed under a smaller number of reconceptualized and measurable targets. Although, in many ways, this approach is similar to the first option, it might represent a modest repackaging of a state's extant curricular aims without a complete start-again approach to curriculum building.

Derivative Assessment Frameworks. The final option is to leave the state's current content standards untouched but derive from them a framework for NCLB assessment that focuses on a small number of reconceptualized, eligible-to-be-taught curricular targets. That way the state's curriculum-based NCLB tests would be likely to have a beneficial rather than a harmful impact on education. The skills and bodies of knowledge identified in an NCLB assessment framework would, of course, influence instructional practices and would need to be chosen with consummate care.

Proceeding Sensibly

Because the first two options are both likely to involve substantial time-consuming and resource-consuming activities, I believe option three is the most sensible way to proceed. Indeed, in many states the existing content standards have already been approved by a state school board or, sometimes, by the legislature itself—usually after substantial input from the state's educators and citizens. I prefer to leave those extant content standards as they are—untouched. If the content standards truly exert much of a positive influence on schooling (which I doubt), then that positive influence should continue. But if the content standards really aren't a positive factor (which I suspect), then letting them languish will be just fine.

However, because the law requires that a state's NCLB tests be clearly based on the state's content standards, it would be imperative to build a defensible case for federal officials that describes both the framework-derivation process and the relevant stakeholders involved. It is important that the state's NCLB assessment targets be *demonstrably* derivative from a state's existing curricular aims.

Let me illustrate, in the field of reading, how a defensible NCLB assessment framework might be derived from a state's existing curricular aims.

Most states' content standards in reading contain a dozen or more specific reading skills, such as identifying a selection's main idea, isolating key details in a reading passage, and using context clues to infer the meaning of unfamiliar words. A markedly more comprehensive curricular aim in reading has recently been devised by Indiana University's Roger Farr. It is a sort of "super-skill" that effectively subsumes a great many more specific skills such as those just mentioned. Farr's super-skill requires students to be able to read different kinds of reading materials in order to accomplish any of the most common real-world purposes for which people read such materials.

Described as *purposeful reading,* this super-skill can be assessed via constructed-response items (for example, essay or short answer) or selected-response items (for example, multiple choice). From an instructional perspective, delightfully, a student's responses to such items are always evaluated by using a scoring guide whose key evaluative criteria can be taught directly to students. The criteria, always based on the reader's purpose as well as the type of material being read, focus on the *relevance, accuracy,* and *sufficiency* of a student's response. Thus, a powerful and teachable curricular aim can be derived from a flock of more specific skills that, therefore, can be regarded as "en route" or "enabling" skills for the more comprehensive super-skill that would be assessed via a state's NCLB tests.

Farr's *purposeful reading* is clearly analogous to the kinds of composition skills we routinely assess when we measure students' ability to write via writing-sample tests. In these tests, which have been in widespread use for over two decades in the United States, we call on students to display a super-skill, namely, being able to write an original composition (for example, a persuasive or narrative essay). Based on the student's essay, we are then able to gauge the student's ability to organize content, to use appropriate mechanics, and to display a number of other more specific subskills relevant to composition.

To derive an appropriate assessment framework from a state's collection of numerous existing curricular aims requires more than modest instructional and assessment acumen. The trick is to isolate a small number of aims that can be described to teachers, are genuinely teachable, and coalesce the most important of the state's existing curricular aims. That sort of activity, of course, demands loads of curricular artistry from those who are deriving the assessment framework. But this approach seems to be the most sensible way of dealing with our current NCLB-induced curricular crisis.

A Final Plea

The need to deal with our current state-approved curricular aims is, in my view, imperative. The longer we delay in coming up with educationally sound, curriculum-derived NCLB tests, the more children there will be who receive a less-than-lustrous education because their teachers are being driven by ill-conceived, curriculum-based NCLB assessments into shabby instructional practices.

Sure, I know many states have invested dollars galore in the creation of customized state-based tests that are supposedly "aligned" to their states' official curriculum. And, of course, it would be costly to move toward different tests. But those existing tests were developed at a time when a state's curriculum exercised little or no impact on classroom instruction. Those times have changed. And that's because, unless NCLB is seriously altered or disappears altogether, today's state curricula do make a difference. It's time to fix them.

Postnote

W. James Popham sees a dysfunctional relationship between the No Child Left Behind (NCLB) Act and state standards and assessments. He argues that most state content standards are too encyclopedic. That is, they try to cover too much material, so much so that teachers have to guess which standards are likely to be tested and have to focus their instruction only on those standards, often eliminating instruction on other important content. He is also critical because teachers are unable to learn from the results of their assessments and cannot tell which of their instructional activities have or haven't worked.

Popham's proposed solution is for states to choose from their content standards a modest number to be tested for purposes of the NCLB Act, and to alert educators and students as to those selected. In this manner, educators could focus on a reasonable number of content standards for assessment.

His solution is, we suspect, a compromise. He, and others, would probably prefer that the high-stakes testing imposed by the NCLB legislation be abandoned because it creates more problems than it purports to solve.

Discussion Questions

1. Do you agree with Popham's analysis of the misfit between state content standards and the requirements of NCLB? Why or why not?
2. What do you think should be done with students who fail the assessments of state standards? Should they be eligible to move on to the next grade or graduate from high school? Why or why not?
3. What is the strongest argument you can make in favor of high-stakes testing? What is the strongest argument you can make against it?

CLASSIC

The Saber-Tooth Curriculum

J. ABNER PEDDIWELL

FOCUS Question

As you read this article think of what subjects, if any, in the current school curriculum you believe are outmoded and should be replaced.

The first great educational theorist and practitioner of whom my imagination has any record (began Dr. Peddiwell in his best professional tone) was a man of Chellean times whose full name was *New-Fist-Hammer-Maker* but whom, for convenience, I shall hereafter call *New-Fist*.

New-Fist was a doer, in spite of the fact that there was little in his environment with which to do anything very complex. You have undoubtedly heard of the pear-shaped, chipped-stone tool which archaeologists call the *coup-de-poing* or fist hammer. New-Fist gained his name and a considerable local prestige by producing one of these artifacts in less rough and more useful form than any previously known to his tribe. His hunting clubs were generally superior weapons, moreover, and his fire-using techniques were patterns of simplicity and precision. He knew how to do things his community needed to have done, and he had the energy and will to go ahead and do them. By virtue of these characteristics he was an educated man.

New-Fist was also a thinker. Then, as now, there were few lengths to which men would not go to avoid the labor and pain of thought. More readily than his fellows, New-Fist pushed himself beyond those lengths to the point where cerebration was inevitable. The same quality of intelligence which led him into the socially approved activity of producing a superior artifact also led him to engage in the socially disapproved practice of thinking. When other men gorged themselves on the proceeds of a successful hunt and vegetated in dull stupor for many hours thereafter, New-Fist ate a little less heartily, slept a little less stupidly, and arose a little earlier than his comrades to sit by the fire and think. He would stare moodily at the flickering flames and wonder about various parts of his environment until he finally got to the point where he became strongly dissatisfied with the accustomed ways of his tribe. He began to catch glimpses of ways in which life might be made better for himself, his family, and his group. By virtue of this development, he became a dangerous man.

J. Abner Peddiwell is the pseudonym for Harold W. Benjamin, a professor of education who died in 1969. From *The Saber-Tooth Curriculum* by J. Abner Peddiwell.

This was the background that made this doer and thinker hit upon the concept of a conscious, systematic education. The immediate stimulus which put him directly into the practice of education came from watching his children at play. He saw these children at the cave entrance before the fire engaged in activity with bones and sticks and brightly colored pebbles. He noted that they seemed to have no purpose in their play beyond immediate pleasure in the activity itself. He compared their activity with that of the grown-up members of the tribe. The children played for fun; the adults worked for security and enrichment of their lives. The children dealt with bones, sticks, and pebbles; the adults dealt with food, shelter, and clothing. The children protected themselves from boredom; the adults protected themselves from danger.

"If I could only get these children to do the things that will give more and better food, shelter, clothing, and security," thought New-Fist, "I would be helping this tribe to have a better life. When the children became grown, they would have more meat to eat, more skins to keep them warm, better caves in which to sleep, and less danger from the striped death with the curving teeth that walks these trails at night."

Having set up an educational goal, New-Fist proceeded to construct a curriculum for reaching that goal. "What things must we tribesmen know how to do in order to live with full bellies, warm backs, and minds free from fear?" he asked himself.

To answer this question, he ran various activities over in his mind. "We have to catch fish with our bare hands in the pool far up the creek beyond that big bend," he said to himself. "We have to catch fish with our bare hands in the pool right at the bend. We have to catch them in the same way in the pool just this side of the bend. And so we catch them in the next pool and the next and the next. And we catch them with our bare hands."

Thus New-Fist discovered the first subject of the first curriculum—fish-grabbing-with-the-bare-hands.

"Also we club the little woolly horses," he continued with his analysis. "We club them along the bank of the creek where they come down to drink. We club them in the thickets where they lie down to sleep. We club them in the upland meadow where they graze. Wherever we find them we club them."

So woolly-horse-clubbing was seen to be the second main subject of the curriculum.

"And finally, we drive away the saber-tooth tigers with fire," New-Fist went on in his thinking. "We drive them from the mouth of our caves with fire. We drive them from our trail with burning branches. We wave firebrands to drive them from our drinking hole. Always we have to drive them away, and always we drive them with fire."

Thus was discovered the third subject—saber-tooth-tiger-scaring-with-fire.

Having developed a curriculum, New-Fist took his children with him as he went about his activities. He gave them an opportunity to practice these three subjects. The children liked to learn. It was more fun for them to engage in these purposeful activities than to play with colored stones just for the fun of it. They learned the new activities well, and so the educational system was a success.

As New-Fist's children grew older, it was plain to see that they had an advantage in good and safe living over other children who had never been educated systematically. Some of the more intelligent members of the tribe began to do as New-Fist had done, and the teaching of fish-grabbing, horse-clubbing, and tiger-scaring came more and more to be accepted as the heart of real education.

For a long time, however, there were certain more conservative members of the tribe who resisted the new, formal educational system on religious grounds. "The Great Mystery who speaks in thunder and moves in lightning," they announced impressively, "the Great Mystery who gives men life and takes it from them as he wills—if that Great Mystery had wanted children to practice fish-grabbing, horse-clubbing, and tiger-scaring before they were grown up, he would have taught them these activities himself by implanting in their natures instincts for fish-grabbing, horse-clubbing, and tiger-scaring. New-Fist is not only impious to attempt something the Great Mystery never intended to have done; he is also a damned fool for trying to change human nature."

Whereupon approximately half of these critics took up the solemn chant, "If you oppose the will of the Great Mystery, you must die," and the remainder sang derisively in unison, "You can't change human nature."

Being an educational statesman as well as an educational administrator and theorist, New-Fist replied politely to both arguments. To the more theologically minded, he said that, as a matter of fact, the Great Mystery had ordered this new work done, that he even did the work himself by causing children to want to learn, that children could not learn by themselves without divine aid, that they could not learn at all except through the power of the Great Mystery, and that nobody could really understand the will of the Great Mystery concerning fish, horses, and saber-tooth tigers unless he had been well grounded in three fundamental subjects of the New-Fist school. To the human-nature-cannot-be-changed shouters, New-Fist pointed out the fact that paleolithic culture had attained its high level by changes in human nature and that it seemed almost unpatriotic to deny the very process which had made the community great.

"I know you, my fellow tribesmen," the pioneer educator ended his argument gravely, "I know you as the humble and devoted servants of the Great Mystery. I know that you would not for one moment consciously oppose yourselves to his will. I know you as intelligent and loyal citizens of the great cave-realm, and I know that your pure and noble patriotism will not permit you to do anything which will block the development of that most cave-realmish of all our institutions—the paleolithic educational system. Now that you understand the true nature and purpose of this institution, I am serenely confident that there are no reasonable lengths to which you will not go in its defense and its support."

By this appeal the forces of conservatism were won over to the side of the new school, and in due time everybody who was anybody in the community knew that the heart of good education lay in the three subjects of fish-grabbing, horse-clubbing, and tiger-scaring. New-Fist and his contemporaries grew older and were gathered by the Great Mystery to the Land of the Sunset far down the creek. Other men followed their educational ways more and more, until at last all the children of the tribe were practiced systematically in the three fundamentals. Thus the tribe prospered and was happy in the possession of adequate meat, skins, and security.

It is to be supposed that all would have gone well forever with this good educational system if conditions of life in that community had remained forever the same. But conditions changed, and life which had once been so safe and happy in the cave-realm valley became insecure and disturbing.

A new ice age was approaching in that part of the world. A great glacier came down from the neighboring mountain range to the north. Year after year it crept closer and closer to the headwaters of the creek which ran through the tribe's valley, until at length it reached the stream and began to melt into the water. Dirt and gravel which the glacier had collected on its long journey were dropped into the creek. The water grew muddy. What had once been a crystal-clear stream in which one could see easily to the bottom was now a milky stream into which one could not see at all.

At once the life of the community was changed in one very important respect. It was no longer possible to catch fish with the bare hands. The fish could not be seen in the muddy water. For some years, moreover, the fish in the creek had been getting more timid, agile, and intelligent. The stupid, clumsy, brave fish, of which originally there had been a great many, had been caught with the bare hands for fish generation after fish generation, until only fish of superior intelligence and agility were left. These smart fish, hiding in the muddy water under the newly deposited glacial boulders, eluded the hands of the most expertly trained fish-grabbers. Those tribesmen who had studied advanced fish-grabbing in the secondary school could do no better than their less well-educated fellows who had taken only an elementary course in the subject, and even the university graduates with majors in ichthyology were baffled by the problem. No matter how good a man's fish-grabbing education had been, he could not grab fish when he could not find fish to grab.

The melting waters of the approaching ice sheet also made the country wetter. The ground became marshy far back from the banks of the creek. The stupid woolly horses, standing only five or six hands high and running on four-toed front feet and three-toed hind feet, although admirable objects for clubbing, had one dangerous characteristic. They were ambitious. They all wanted to learn to run on their middle toes. They all had visions of becoming powerful and aggressive animals instead of little and timid ones. They dreamed of a far-distant day when some of their descendants would be sixteen hands high, weigh more than half a ton, and be able to pitch their would-be riders into the dirt. They knew they could never attain these goals in a wet, marshy country, so they all went east to the dry, open plains, far from the paleolithic hunting grounds. Their places were taken by little antelopes who came down with the ice sheet and were so shy and speedy and had so keen a scent for danger that no one could approach them closely enough to club them.

The best trained horse-clubbers of the tribe went out day after day and employed the most efficient techniques taught in the schools, but day after day they returned empty-handed. A horse-clubbing education of the highest type could get no results when there were no horses to club.

Finally, to complete the disruption of paleolithic life and education, the new dampness in the air gave the saber-tooth tigers pneumonia, a disease to which these animals were peculiarly susceptible and to which most of them succumbed. A few moth-eaten specimens crept south to the desert, it is true, but they were pitifully few and weak representatives of a once numerous and powerful race.

So there were no more tigers to scare in the paleolithic community, and the best tiger-scaring techniques became only academic exercises, good in themselves, perhaps, but not necessary for tribal security. Yet this danger to the people was lost only to be replaced by another and even greater danger, for with the advancing ice sheet came ferocious glacial bears which were not afraid of fire, which walked the trails by day as well as by night, and which could not be driven away by the most advanced methods developed in the tiger-scaring course of the schools.

The community was now in a very difficult situation. There was no fish or meat for food, no hides for clothing, and no security from the hairy death that walked the trails day and night. Adjustment to this difficulty had to be made at once if the tribe was not to become extinct.

Fortunately for the tribe, however, there were men in it of the old New-Fist breed, men who had the ability to do and the daring to think. One of them stood by the muddy stream, his stomach contracting with hunger pains, longing for some way to get a fish to eat. Again and again he had tried the old fish-grabbing technique that day, hoping desperately that at last it might work, but now in black despair he finally rejected all that he had learned in the schools and looked about him for some new way to get fish from that stream. There were stout but slender vines hanging from trees along the bank. He pulled them down and began to fasten them together more or less aimlessly. As he worked, the vision of what he might do to satisfy his hunger and that of his crying children back in the cave grew clearer. His black despair lightened a little. He worked more rapidly and intelligently. At last he had it—a net, a crude seine. He called a companion and explained the device. The two men took the net into the water, into pool after pool, and in one hour they caught more fish—intelligent fish in muddy water—than the whole tribe could have caught in a day under the best fish-grabbing conditions.

Another intelligent member of the tribe wandered hungrily through the woods where once the stupid little horses had abounded but where now only the elusive antelope could be seen. He had tried the horse-clubbing technique on the antelope until he was fully convinced of its futility. He knew that one would starve who relied on school learning to get him meat in those woods. Thus it was that he too, like the fish-net inventor, was finally impelled by hunger to new ways. He bent a strong, springy young tree over an antelope trail, hung a noosed vine therefrom, and fastened the whole device in so ingenious a fashion that the passing animal would release a trigger and be snared neatly when the tree jerked upright. By setting a line of these snares, he was able in one night to secure more meat and skins than a dozen horse-clubbers in the old days had secured in a week.

A third tribesman, determined to meet the problem of the ferocious bears, also forgot what he had been taught in school and began to think in direct and radical fashion. Finally, as a result of this thinking, he dug a deep pit in a bear trail, covered it with branches in such a way that a bear would walk on it unsuspectingly, fall through to the bottom, and remain trapped until the tribesmen could come up and despatch him with sticks and stones at their leisure. The inventor showed his friends how to dig and camouflage other pits until all the trails around the community were furnished with them. Thus the tribe had even more security than before and in addition had the great additional store of meat and skins which they secured from the captured bears.

As the knowledge of these new inventions spread, all the members of the tribe were engaged in familiarizing themselves with the new ways of living. Men worked hard at making fish nets, setting antelope snares, and digging bear pits. The tribe was busy and prosperous.

There were a few thoughtful men who asked questions as they worked. Some of them even criticized the schools.

"These new activities of net-making and operating, snare-setting, and pit-digging are indispensable to modern existence," they said. "Why can't they be taught in school?"

The safe and sober majority had a quick reply to this naive question. "School!" they snorted derisively. "You aren't in school now. You are out here in the dirt working to preserve the life and happiness of the tribe. What have these practical activities got to do with schools? You're not saying lessons now. You'd better forget your lessons and your academic ideals of fish-grabbing, horse-clubbing, and tiger-scaring if you want to eat, keep warm, and have some measure of security from sudden death."

The radicals persisted a little in their questioning. "Fishnet-making and using, antelope-snare construction and operation, and bear-catching and killing," they pointed out, "require intelligence and skills—things we claim to develop in schools. They are also activities we need to know. Why can't the schools teach them?"

But most of the tribe, and particularly the wise old men who controlled the school, smiled indulgently at this suggestion. "That wouldn't be *education*," they said gently.

"But why wouldn't it be?" asked the radicals.

"Because it would be mere training," explained the old men patiently. "With all the intricate details of fish-grabbing, horse-clubbing, and tiger-scaring—the standard cultural subjects—the school curriculum is too crowded now. We can't add these fads and frills of net-making, antelope-snaring, and—of all things—bear-killing. Why, at the very thought, the body of the great New-Fist, founder of our paleolithic educational system, would turn over in its burial cairn. What we need to do is to give our young people a more thorough grounding in the fundamentals. Even the graduates of the secondary schools don't know the art of fish-grabbing in any complete sense nowadays, they swing their horse clubs awkwardly too, and as for the old science of tiger-scaring—well, even the teachers seem to lack the real flair for the subject which we oldsters got in our teens and never forgot."

"But, damn it," exploded one of the radicals, "how can any person with good sense be interested in such useless activities? What is the point of trying to catch fish with the bare hands when it just can't be done any more? How can a boy learn to club horses when there are no horses left to club? And why in hell should children try to scare tigers with fire when the tigers are dead and gone?"

"Don't be foolish," said the wise old men, smiling most kindly smiles. "We don't teach fish-grabbing to grab fish; we teach it to develop a generalized agility which can never be developed by mere training. We don't teach horse-clubbing to club horses; we teach it to develop a generalized strength in the learner which he can never get from so prosaic and specialized a thing as antelope-snare-setting. We don't teach tiger-scaring to scare tigers; we teach it for the purpose of giving that noble courage which carries over into all the affairs of life and which can never come from so base an activity as bear-killing."

All the radicals were silenced by this statement, all except the one who was most radical of all. He felt abashed, it is true, but he was so radical that he made one last protest.

"But—but anyway," he suggested, "you will have to admit that times have changed. Couldn't you please *try* these other, more up-to-date activities? Maybe they have *some* educational value after all?"

Even the man's fellow radicals felt that this was going a little too far.

The wise old men were indignant. Their kindly smiles faded. "If you had any education yourself," they said severely, "you would know that the essence of true education is timelessness. It is something that endures through changing conditions like a solid rock standing squarely and firmly in the middle of a raging torrent. You must know that there are some eternal verities, and the saber-tooth curriculum is one of them!"

Postnote

The Saber-Tooth Curriculum is one of the greatest Classic curriculum articles ever written; its message is timeless. One might think that it had been written by a modern-day critic of the public school curriculum instead of someone writing in 1939. It is virtually impossible to read this selection without drawing parallels to courses and curricula that we have experienced. Fish-grabbing-with-the-bare-hands has not disappeared. It still exists today in many American schools, but it is called by a different name. And the same arguments used by the elders to defend the saber-tooth curriculum are used today to defend subjects that many say have outlived their right to remain in the curriculum. Why do they remain?

Discussion Questions

1. What is the main message of this excerpt from *The Saber-Tooth Curriculum?*
2. What subjects, if any, in the current school curriculum would you equate with fish-grabbing-with-the-bare-hands? Why?
3. What new subjects would you suggest adding to the school curriculum to avoid creating our own saber-tooth curriculum? Why?

29

The Authentic Standards Movement and Its Evil Twin

SCOTT THOMPSON

FOCUS Question

What are the advantages and disadvantages of primarily using high-stakes testing to assess student learning on content standards?

TERMS TO NOTE

Assessment
Charter school
High-stakes tests
Home schooling
Privatization
Professional development
Standardized tests
Standards-based reform
Standards movement
Tracking
Voucher programs

One thing the standards movement will never be accused of is a lack of critical opposition. But for all the fiery rhetoric that critics direct against this powerful, nationwide movement, there is perhaps no greater threat to standards-based reform than much of what is being perpetrated in the name of standards-based reform. The so-called movement—so-called, because it is not truly a single movement but twin movements bearing the same name—has become its own worst enemy.

If giving twins the same name is a recipe for confusion, consider the havoc that gets unleashed when one of them proves to be an "evil twin."[1] In the case of the standards movement, the evil twin is the more visible and powerful of the siblings, and so its authentic namesake is in an increasingly perilous situation. In fact, the problem is even worse: the two are essentially joined at the hip.

So what are these twin movements? First, let's distinguish them by name. I would rename the evil twin "test-based reform" or more specifically "high-stakes, standardized, test-based reform." The sibling, then, is "authentic, standards-based reform." The defining distinction between them is their respective influence on the instructional core of schooling and on equity issues.

When academic progress is judged by a single indicator and when high stakes—such as whether a student is promoted from one grade to the next or is eligible for a diploma—are attached to that single indicator, the common effect is to narrow curriculum and reduce instruction to test "prepping." What gets lost when teachers and students are pressured to make students better test-takers is precisely the rich, high-level teaching and learning that authentic, standards-based reform aims to promote in all classrooms and for all students.

Scott Thompson is assistant director of the Panasonic Foundation, Secaucus, N.J.
Scott Thompson, "The Authentic Standards Movement and Its Evil Twin," January 2001, *Phi Delta Kappan*. Originally appeared in *Improving Schools for African American Students: A Reader for Educational Leaders,* edited by Sheryl Denbo and Lynson Moore Beaulieu, September 2002, Charles C. Thomas Publishers. Reprinted with permission of Charles C. Thomas and the author.

Authentic, standards-based reform is fundamentally concerned with equity. It departs radically from the tracking and sorting carried out by the factory-style school of yore. Instead, it aims to hold high expectations and *provide high levels of support* for all students, teachers, and educational leaders. Under the evil twin's (per)version of standards and accountability, we see students retained in grade because of a single test score, and we typically see a corresponding increase in dropout rates where such *worst* practice is in place.[2] Equity then becomes the casualty rather than the fruit of reform. And as Sandra Feldman, president of the American Federation of Teachers, recently observed, "When tests are allowed to become the be-all and end-all, they deform, not reform, education."[3]

In its influence on both the instructional core of schooling and on equity, the evil twin constitutes an inversion of the "real thing." It is a politically warped variation on what is arguably among this nation's most powerful and promising education reforms. Although the evil twin purports to be standards-based, it actually flies in the face of research-based standards on the appropriate use of testing. Consider, for example, the conclusions of the National Research Council's Committee on Appropriate Test Use, which are being systematically, if not willfully, ignored by many education policy makers, especially at the state level: "An educational decision that will have a major impact on a test taker should not be made solely or automatically on the basis of a single test score."[4]

There are many reasons not to use any single assessment as the basis for assignment high-stakes consequences. Not only does such a practice tend to diminish curriculum and instruction, but most psychometricians will tell you that the assessment has yet to be created with a high enough level of validity and reliability to justify its use as the sole basis for making consequential decisions about the test-taker. This problem is not unique to education. Consider the words of Lt. Gen. Roland Kadish, director of the Ballistic Missile Defense Organization: "I don't think we should draw conclusions from any one test that are irrevocable. No one test tells you everything you need to know."[5]

Another problem is that tests are frequently misused. Standardized tests designed for national comparisons between students, without reference to a particular school's curriculum or content standards, are, for example, too often used to evaluate teachers and schools. As I have noted elsewhere, that's a bit like trying to use a jigsaw and screw driver to eat a plate of angel hair pasta. The tools are not necessarily bad in themselves, but they are certainly ill-suited to the task.[6]

High-stakes, test-based reform is an approach that is most often driven by state-level mandate, and it suits the political appetite for rapid, quantifiable (hence readily digestible by the public) results.[7] Test-based reform represents a potentially lethal threat to its authentic twin. Whether by design or happenstance, it is effectively sabotaging the authentic standards movement. And not surprisingly, it is unleashing a swelling and intensifying backlash against standards and testing that is taking form legally and politically, as well as through mobilized grassroots opposition.[8]

It is the combination of test-based reform, in the name of standards, and the wholesale backlash that such practice provokes that is placing the authentic standards movement in peril. Not only in the general media, but also in specialized education media, one can see that the war between proponents and opponents of high-stakes testing tends to define the entire standards movement in such a way that its actual nature and potential, which some school districts are beginning to demonstrate, gets buried under an avalanche of rhetoric.

A Rationale for Authentic, Standards-Based Reform

Too few children in many of our public schools are receiving the quality of education needed for successful life and work in a rapidly changing world. The imperative to provide them with a high-quality education is not so much economic as moral. Given what we know of the lifelong consequences for individuals of educational deprivation—not to mention the broader consequences for society and democracy—providing a high-quality education for all children is quite simply the right thing to do.

We know that some good schools have succeeded in providing a high-quality education to students deemed least likely to succeed: students of color and students in poverty.[9] But in a nation of 50 million schoolchildren, we face an enormous, yet-to-be-met challenge: namely, taking such success to scale. There are various theories of change that aim to address this challenge. The theory of change behind authentic, standards-based reform (again, I'm not talking about test-based reform) is that, if you want to improve student learning across the board, then you need to improve the quality of instructional content and practice across the board. In order to do that, you must fundamentally transform schools and school systems so that their focus, energy, and resources are wholly aimed at the primary goal of improving instruction in order to improve learning and thus to improve student performance as measured by a variety of assessments. In short, it is all about quality.

We know that bureaucratic school systems that focus on monitoring mandated inputs for compliance hold little, if any, promise of creating and sustaining good schools for children across the socioeconomic spectrum. An authentic, standards-based system departs radically from this model. It shifts from a focus on inputs to a focus on outcomes or performance. It shifts from a focus on quantity to a focus on quality. It shifts from a concern with organizational doings to a singular, systemwide focus on improving the performance of every student. It shifts from what Richard Elmore calls the "loose coupling" approach to educational governance to a system of governance that is structured around public accountability for educational results.[10]

Loose coupling is an arrangement in which governing authorities in public schools—from school boards down to principals—essentially run political interference so that classroom teachers are shielded from public scrutiny and can pursue their idiosyncratic pedagogical approaches. Under this governing structure, which is pervasive in public schools at this time, you can easily find that second-grade teachers in neighboring classrooms are doing completely different things with their students—in terms of content, instructional practice, and even basic objectives.

A standards-based approach departs from this model in two ways. First, it breaks down teacher isolation and calls for collaboration around a common set of standards so that students, parents, and teachers have a widely shared understanding of common educational goals at various levels of schooling. Second, it responds to the demands for public accountability by assuming a results orientation and making those results public.

These shifts mean that structures, roles, responsibilities, and budgets must be rethought and redesigned to dramatically increase the system's investment in high-quality learning for teachers, for school leaders, and for those in the central office whose job it is to support teachers and school leaders. A school system that is not accountable for providing continuous, high-quality, standards-based professional development for teachers and leaders has no business holding students and their teachers accountable for performance against student learning standards.

The urgency of the need for systematic improvement of public education would be difficult to overstate. Any observer of public education whose eyes are even partially open has discerned various currents that represent a potential threat to our public schools. The number of parents who are home schooling their children is growing significantly, as are the number of states that are fostering charter schools, some of which are operated by for-profit firms. Meanwhile, efforts to secure vouchers—including both private and public schools—are not going away.

Over the next decade or two, it is not difficult to imagine a scenario unfolding in which home-schoolers begin forming cooperatives and the number of students participating in them greatly expands.[11] In this scenario, publicly funded vouchers also take off, and the charter school movement increasingly caters to groups of families with specialized interests. We might then find textbook publishers customizing their wares for the narrow interests of parents whose children are being educated in cooperatives or in independent schools organized around parochial values. Meanwhile, the remaining public school systems would find themselves increasingly segregated and educationally crippled. The common school—as a meeting ground for students from diverse economic, cultural, and racial backgrounds—would be lost, as society itself became ever more fragmented. Such a scenario would represent a serious threat to the health of our democracy.

The real potential of authentic, standards-based reform can be seen most clearly against this disturbing backdrop. We live in a time when both politicians and the general public are demanding educational accountability. Public opinion research shows that, while the public favors public schools over publicly funded vouchers, patience is wearing thin.[12] Public schools must demonstrate their ability to help students across the socioeconomic spectrum achieve high-quality educational results. Majorities of the public and of teachers support the movement toward high standards. But, according to poll results recently released by the American Association of School Administrators, a majority of voters reject the idea that a single test can accurately measure students' educational growth.[13]

Authentic, standards-based reform holds the potential for improving the quality of student performance to meet systemwide standards. It is an approach that is designed to make schools accountable to the communities they are meant to serve and to do so by focusing on high-quality teaching and learning, not on test scores. It is an approach that could stand up to the threat of privatization. It is an approach that aspires to reach a goal this nation has never achieved through its systems of public education: a high-quality education for all students, regardless of socioeconomic background. But authentic, standards-based reform—and arguably public education itself—is seriously threatened when high standards get confused with high-stakes, standardized tests.

A 180-Degree Inversion

Identical twins can be difficult to distinguish solely by surface characteristics. But if one is evil and the other virtuous, their character traits or essential natures will stand in stark contrast. So it is with test-based reform and standards-based reform. On the face of it, they are both about moving from an approach to education that values inputs to an approach that values outputs or results. But a deeper look into the essential natures of these twins reveals that test-based reform is nothing less than a 180-degree inversion of its authentic counterpart. This, I believe, becomes readily apparent when their essential characteristics are considered side by side.

- Authentic, standards-based reform involves teachers, parents, and others as active participants in developing and refining common learning standards. Test-based reform uses high-stakes tests, written in secret by expert psychometricians, as single indicators for deciding whether students are promoted or graduate, thereby making the tests the *real* standards.
- Authentic standards describe what *all* students should be learning at each level (not necessarily at each grade level). Test-based reform makes the scores on standardized tests for students at specific grade levels, in effect, the only meaningful standards.
- Under a system of authentic standards, the school system invests heavily in high-quality professional development for teachers and administrators in an effort to support their work in teaching to the standards. Under a system of test-based reform, teachers and principals are pressured in a variety of ways to raise test scores, and students are drilled accordingly.
- Under a system of authentic reform, student assessments are aligned with the standards,

and students have numerous opportunities to demonstrate that they have met the standards. No single test is used to determine whether a standard has been met. Under test-based reform, a single state or national test is used to determine whether students are promoted to the next grade or are allowed to receive a diploma.

- High-quality, individualized support for students is a hallmark of authentic, standards-based reform. Such support is rare in test-based reform efforts. When it is present, it tends to focus on test-taking techniques rather than on teaching and learning.
- Authentic, standards-based reform has implications for every person, policy, and practice in a school system because it involves a complete abandonment of the bureaucratic, "seat time" approach to education and replaces it with a system of learning communities dedicated to helping all students reach their intellectual, social, and personal potential. By contrast, test-based reform, through its focus on high-stakes tests, narrows the curriculum to what is included on the tests and reduces instructional practice to test preparation.

A still more profound point of contrast between the two movements emerges when we consider what educational *purpose* is implicit in each kind of reform. In the case of test-based reform, the purpose of education is raising test scores. In the case of authentic, standards-based reform, the purpose is enabling all students to achieve as much of their creative, intellectual, and social potential as possible. Thus the goal of authentic, standards-based reform is to prepare students to live successfully and contribute actively in their communities.

The Wrong Question

As opposition to high-stakes testing mounts and as negative consequences pile up, observers and policy makers are beginning to ask, "Are we moving too quickly?"[14] But this is the wrong question, and it represents an extreme misreading of the problem at hand. The problem is not one of pacing, quantity, or timing. It is a problem of replacing a reform aimed at systematically enriching and deepening teaching and learning with a reform aimed at raising test scores, regardless of the impact on the quality of instruction or on the number of students being pushed out of schools and onto the streets. At *whatever* point a high-stakes, standardized test is imposed as the sole basis for determining student success, that test will replace whatever content and performance standards were previously in place. It's something like a computer virus that erases and replaces everything that was stored on one's hard drive.

We could realize significant progress in public education if the proponents of standards-based reform joined hands with the critics of high-stakes testing and effectively outlawed the use of high-stakes tests as sole indicators of student success. Moreover, such a move need not lead to toothless standards. It is possible to require all students to meet a set of rigorous standards in order to graduate from high school without using a single test as the means of determining whether those standards have been met. We should be interested in students who can produce high-quality work rather than students who have mastered the ability to take standardized tests. It is the former who will be rewarded in their personal and professional lives after graduation, when test-taking skills will no longer be relevant.

A Personal Note

I hope my use of the "evil twin" metaphor helps bring some clarity to this time of rampant educational confusion. But I want to be clear about what I don't mean, as well as what I do mean, in using this metaphor. I do not intend to call any individuals "evil." I believe that the tendency to demonize people who hold opposing points of view has a coarsening influence on civil discourse and so is bad for democracy itself. What I refer to as the "evil twin" is a set of actions and the consequences I believe these actions can have and are having on children and on schools. Determining whether such consequences are intended or unintended requires discerning what is at work in the hearts and minds of many people who are crafting and enacting such policies. The human hearts and minds of others, I believe, are simply too complex and too inaccessible to read as a book.

But I see the metaphor as useful in bringing out how sharp the contrast actually is between the two movements. At the same time, it's important to acknowledge the complexity of the relationship between the authentic, standards-based reform and test-based reform. As I noted above, these twins are often essentially joined at the hip. What I mean by that is that most of the districts that I would point to as exemplars of authentic, standards-based reform are operating within state systems that more or less exemplify test-based reform.

The Theory in Action

The task of sorting through the complexities of conflicting policy contexts is daunting, but when it is done, what emerges is evidence of what the authentic twin is already beginning to accomplish in a number of school districts. I would point, for example, to District 2 in New York City, which has posted some exemplary early results in its efforts to institute best practices. This story has been extensively documented by Richard Elmore, Deanna Burney, and others, and I recommend that readers explore their work.[15] Anthony Alvarado, who was the chief architect of the reform effort in District 2, has since become the chancellor of instruction in San Diego. That district is now moving forward rapidly along the same lines and has developed a unique "blueprint" for intervention and for support of students who are failing to meet standards.

As uneven as some of the early results may be at this stage, I would point to a number of other districts whose experience suggests the potential of standards-based reform: Aurora, Colorado; Clovis, California; Edmonds, Washington; Minneapolis; and the three districts constituting the El Paso Collaborative for Academic Excellence, as well as the Houston Independent School District.[16] And there are certainly others.[17]

For an example of a state accountability system that balances the public's need for individual student and school-level results against the school's need for support and for a genuine measure of autonomy in achieving those results, I would point readers to Rhode Island's SALT (School Accountability for Learning and Teaching), an accountability program that gathers extensive qualitative as well as quantitative data on school quality for the purpose of supporting continuous, standards-based school improvement.[18] Each school in the state engages in self-study and develops a school improvement plan. Periodically, a team of teachers, parents, and administrators from outside the district spends a full week in the school, reviewing the self-study and other data, shadowing students, visiting classes, and interviewing teachers, parents, and administrators. The results of this external review are written up as a report containing conclusions, recommendations, and commendations. The full report is read to the entire faculty by the chair of the visit on the Monday following the visit.

School districts that are working to fulfill the original promise of standards-based reform can play a vital role in the future of public education. They will be more likely to succeed in this critical task if increasing numbers of states adopt approaches to standards and accountability that look more like Rhode Island's SALT and less like a brawny and aggressive twin—wielding a high-stakes weapon.

Notes

1. Richard Elmore has observed, "We will get standards-based reform. But what kind is in doubt. Will it be the version that proponents envision or a corrupted and poorly-thought-out evil twin?" See Richard F. Elmore, "Building a New Structure for School Leadership," *American Educator,* Winter 1999–2000, p. 8.
2. See, for example, Maureen Kelleher, "Dropout Rate Climbs as Schools Dump Truants,"

Catalyst, June 1999; and Walter M. Haney, *Supplementary Report on Texas Assessment of Academic Skills Exit Test (TAAS-X)* (Los Angeles: Mexican American Legal Defense and Education Fund, 30 July 1999).

3. Sandra Feldman, "Where We Stand," *Education Week,* 12 July 2000, p. 17.
4. Jay P. Heubert and Robert M. Hauser, eds., *High Stakes: Testing for Tracking, Promotion, and Graduation* (Washington, D.C.: National Academy Press, 1999), p. 15.
5. Quoted in Elaine Sciolino, "Key Missile Parts Are Left Untested as Booster Fails," *New York Times,* 9 July 2000.
6. Scott Thompson, "Shared Accountability—Shifting from Heavy-Handed to Helping Hands," *Strategies,* May 2000, p. 1.
7. Donald B. Gratz, "High Standards for Whom?," *Phi Delta Kappan,* May 2000, p. 684.
8. See, for example, Lynn Olson, "Worries of a Standards 'Backlash' Grow," *Education Week,* 5 April 2000, p. 1; and Drew Lindsay, "Contest," *Education Week,* 5 April 2000, p. 30. For more information on the growing opposition to test-based reform, see Alfie Kohn, "Fighting the Tests: A Practical Guide to Rescuing Our Schools," *Phi Delta Kappan,* January 2001, pp. 348–57.
9. The evidence along these lines is enormous. One good example is a study conducted by the Center for Performance Assessment on what it calls the "90/90/90 Schools." These are schools in which more than 90% of students qualify for a subsidized lunch, more than 90% of students are ethnic minorities, and more than 90% of students still achieved "high academic standards, according to independently conducted tests of academic achievement." The results of this study appear in Douglas B. Reeves, *Accountability in Action* (Denver, Colo.: Advanced Learning Press, 1999), Chapter 19. See also "Doing What Works: Improving Big City School Districts," AFT Educational Issues Policy Brief No. 12, Washington, D.C., October 2000, pp. 1–12; and Scott Justus et al., *Student Achievement and Reform Trends in 13 Urban Districts* (Washington, D.C.: The McKenzie Group, May 2000).
10. Richard F. Elmore, "Building a New Structure for School Leadership," *American Educator,* Winter 1999–2000, p. 8.
11. I credit the observations in this paragraph to Phillip Schlechty, who outlined a similar scenario in a keynote speech he delivered to the Panasonic Foundation's Leadership Associates Program in October 1999. He has since written up this scenario in the epilogue to his new book, *Shaking Up the Schoolhouse* (San Francisco: Jossey-Bass, 2001).
12. Jean Johnson, *Assignment Incomplete: The Unfinished Business of Education Reform* (New York: Public Agenda, 1995).
13. Lynn Olson, "Poll Shows Public Concern over Emphasis on Standardized Tests," *Education Week,* 12 July 2000, p. 9.
14. "High-Stakes Testing: Too Much? Too Soon?," *State Education Leader,* Winter 2000, p. 1. See also Chris Pipho, "The Sting of High-Stakes Testing and Accountability," *Phi Delta Kappan,* May 2000, pp. 645–46.
15. Richard F. Elmore with Deanna Burney, *Investing in Teacher Learning: Staff Development and Instructional Improvement in Community School District #2, New York City* (New York: National Commission on Teaching and America's Future and the Consortium for Policy Research in Education, 1997); Richard F. Elmore and Deanna Burney, "School Variation and Systemic Instructional Improvement in Community School District #2, New York City," unpublished paper prepared for High Performance Learning Communities Project, Learning Research and Development Center, University of Pittsburgh, October 1997; idem, "Continuous Improvement in Community District #2, New York City," unpublished paper prepared for High Performance

Learning Communities Project, Learning Research and Development Center, University of Pittsburgh, December 1998; "District 2, NYC: Teacher Learning Comes First," *Strategies,* August 1998, pp. 11–13; and Liz Gewirtzman and Elaine Fink, *Realignment of Policies & Resources* (Chicago: Cross City Campaign for Urban School Reform, 2000).

16. "Aurora, CO: A Long, Bumpy Road," *Strategies,* August 1998, pp. 4–10; "Clovis, CA: Thirty Years and Counting—Sustaining Continuous Improvement," *Strategies,* July 1999, pp. 4–7; "Minneapolis: Aligning Assessments," *Strategies,* August 1998, pp. 13–14; Stephen Fink and Scott Thompson, "Standards and Whole System Change," unpublished paper on standards-based reform in Edmonds, Washington, prepared for Panasonic Foundation, December 1998; M. Susanna Navarro and Diana S. Natalicio, "Closing the Achievement Gap in El Paso: A Collaboration for K–16 Renewal," *Phi Delta Kappan,* April 1999, pp. 597–601; "Houston, TX: Aiming High," *Strategies,* May 2000, pp. 3–6; and Rod Paige, "No Simple Answer," *Education Week,* 8 November 2000, p. 48. (*Strategies* can be accessed at **http:www.aasa.org/publications/strategies/index.htm.**)
17. See, for example, "Doing What Works."
18. "Rhode Island: Accountability = School Improvement," *Strategies,* May 2000, pp. 3–6; and "Coming to Judgment," *Strategies,* May 2000, pp. 7–8.

Postnote

Scott Thompson makes a very important distinction between content standards and how they are being assessed through high-stakes, standardized tests. He takes strong issue with the latter. The problem with high-stakes tests, as he points out, is that they narrow the curriculum and reduce instruction to test prepping. In our conversations with teachers, they too echo this concern. Some teachers report to us that rather than spending time on enrichment topics, they feel pressure to cover over and over again the content on which the students will be tested. Furthermore, many of these teachers also report that considerable time is given to teaching students how to take the tests. The result is that the tail wags the dog, certainly an unintended consequence of the standards movement. In addition to these arguments, high-stakes testing has led to teachers and students cheating to improve results.

Many people point to elite private schools as the kind of schooling that public schools should emulate. However, elite private schools typically don't have a set of uniform standards to which all students are held accountable. Nor do they place such strong emphasis on a single standardized test to assess student learning. In these private schools, teachers are given much more freedom in curriculum choice than are public school teachers. If these elite private schools are to be emulated, why are states implementing policies for public schools that are so contrary to what is going on in the private schools?

Discussion Questions

1. Why do you think many states use only one high-stakes test to assess student achievement on content standards?
2. Should teachers be held accountable for their students' mastery of course content according to some expected standard? List reasons why teachers should or should not be held accountable for their students' test results.
3. In what ways should teachers be held accountable? Parents?

CLASSIC

The Paideia Proposal: Rediscovering the Essence of Education

MORTIMER J. ADLER

FOCUSQuestion

Should the objectives and curriculum of basic schooling be the same for the whole school population, as Adler asserts? Why or why not?

Term to Note

Paideia

In the first 80 years of this century, we have met the obligation imposed on us by the principle of equal educational opportunity, but only in a quantitative sense. Now, as we approach the end of the century, we must achieve equality in qualitative terms.

This means a completely one-track system of schooling. It means, at the basic level, giving all the young the same kind of schooling, whether or not they are college bound.

We are aware that children, although equal in their common humanity and fundamental human rights, are unequal as individuals, differing in their capacity to learn. In addition, the homes and environments from which they come to school are unequal—either predisposing the child for schooling or doing the opposite.

Consequently, the Paideia Proposal, faithful to the principle of equal educational opportunity, includes the suggestion that inequalities due to environmental factors must be overcome by some form of preschool preparation—at least one year for all and two or even three for some. We know that to make such preschool tutelage compulsory at the public expense would be tantamount to increasing the duration of compulsory schooling from 12 years to 13, 14, or 15 years. Nevertheless, we think that this preschool adjunct to the 12 years of compulsory basic schooling is so important that some way must be found to make it available for all and to see that all use it to advantage.

The Essentials of Basic Schooling

The objectives of basic schooling should be the same for the whole school population. In our current two-track or multitrack system, the learning objectives are not the same for all. And even when the objectives aimed at those on the upper track are correct, the course of study now provided does not adequately realize these correct objectives. On all

---

At the time this article was written, **Mortimer J. Adler** was chairman of the board of editors of *Encyclopaedia Britannica* and director of the Institute of Philosophical Research in Chicago, Illinois. Adler died in 2001. From "The Paideia Proposal: Rediscovering the Essence of Education" by Mortimer J. Adler. Reprinted with permission from *The American School Board Journal,* July 1982.

tracks in our current system, we fail to cultivate proficiency in the common tasks of learning, and we especially fail to develop sufficiently the indispensable skills of learning.

The uniform objectives of basic schooling should be threefold. They should correspond to three aspects of the common future to which all the children are destined: (1) Our society provides all children ample opportunity for personal development. Given such opportunity, each individual is under a moral obligation to make the most of himself and his life. Basic schooling must facilitate this accomplishment. (2) All the children will become, when of age, full-fledged citizens with suffrage and other political responsibilities. Basic schooling must do everything it can to make them good citizens, able to perform the duties of citizenship with all the trained intelligence that each is able to achieve. (3) When they are grown, all (or certainly most) of the children will engage in some form of work to earn a living. Basic schooling must prepare them for earning a living, but not by training them for this or that specific job while they are still in school.

To achieve these three objectives, the character of basic schooling must be general and liberal. It should have a single, required, 12-year course of study for all, with no electives except one—an elective choice with regard to a second language, to be selected from such modern languages as French, German, Italian, Spanish, Russian, and Chinese. The elimination of all electives, with this one exception, excludes what *should* be excluded—all forms of specialization, including particularized job training.

In its final form, the Paideia Proposal will detail this required course of study, but I will summarize the curriculum here in its bare outline. It consists of three main columns of teaching and learning, running through the 12 years and progressing, of course, from the simple to the more complex, from the less difficult to the more difficult, as the students grow older. Understand: The three columns (see table on page 165) represent three distinct modes of teaching and learning. They do not represent a series of courses. A specific course or a class may employ more than one mode of teaching and learning, but all three modes are essential to the overall course of study.

The three columns do not correspond to separate courses, nor is one kind of teaching and learning necessarily confined to any one class.

The first column is devoted to acquiring knowledge in three subject areas: (A) language, literature, and the fine arts; (B) mathematics and natural science; (C) history, geography, and social studies.

The second column is devoted to developing the intellectual skills of learning. These include all the language skills necessary for thought and communication—the skills of reading, writing, speaking, listening. They also include mathematical and scientific skills; the skills of observing, measuring, estimating, and calculating; and skills in the use of the computer and of other scientific instruments. Together, these skills make it possible to think clearly and critically. They once were called the liberal arts—the intellectual skills indispensable to being competent as a learner.

The third column is devoted to enlarging the understanding of ideas and values. The materials of the third column are books (*not* textbooks), and other products of human artistry. These materials include books of every variety—historical, scientific, and philosophical as well as poems, stories, and essays—and also individual pieces of music, visual art, dramatic productions, dance productions, film or television productions. Music and works of visual art can be used in seminars in which ideas are discussed; but as with poetry and fiction, they also are to be experienced aesthetically, to be enjoyed and admired for their excellence. In this connection, exercises in the composition of poetry, music, and visual works and in the production of dramatic works should be used to develop the appreciation of excellence.

The three columns represent three different kinds of learning on the part of the student and three different kinds of instruction on the part of teachers.

In the first column, the students are engaged in acquiring information and organized knowledge about nature, man, and human society. The method of instruction here, using textbooks and manuals, is didactic. The teacher lectures, invites

The Paideia Curriculum

	COLUMN ONE	COLUMN TWO	COLUMN THREE
Goals	Acquisition of Organized Knowledge	Development of Intellectual Skills and Skills of Learning	Improved Understanding of Ideas and Values
	by means of	by means of	by means of
Means	Didactic Instruction, Lecturing, and Textbooks	Coaching, Exercises, and Supervised Practice	Maieutic or Socratic Questioning and Active Participation
	in these three subject areas	in these operations	in these activities
Subject Areas, Operations, and Activities	Language, Literature, and Fine Arts Mathematics and Natural Science History, Geography, and Social Studies	Reading, Writing, Speaking, Listening, Calculating, Problem Solving, Observing, Measuring, Estimating, Exercising Critical Judgment	Discussion of Books (Not Textbooks) and Other Works of Art Involvement in Music, Drama, and Visual Arts

responses from the students, monitors the acquisition of knowledge, and tests that acquisition in various ways.

In the second column, the students are engaged in developing habits of performance, which is all that is involved in the development of an art or skill. Art, skill, or technique is nothing more than a cultivated, habitual ability to do a certain kind of thing well, whether that is swimming and dancing or reading and writing. Here, students are acquiring linguistic, mathematical, scientific, and historical *know-how* in contrast to what they acquire in the first column, which is *know-that* with respect to language, literature, and the fine arts, mathematics and science, history, geography, and social studies. Here, the method of instruction cannot be didactic or monitorial; it cannot be dependent on textbooks. It must be coaching, the same kind used in the gym to develop bodily skills; only here it is used by a different kind of coach in the classroom to develop intellectual skills.

In the third column, students are engaged in a process of enlightenment, the process whereby they develop their understanding of the basic and controlling ideas in all fields of subject matter and come to appreciate better all the human values embodied in works of art. Here, students move progressively from understanding less to understanding more—understanding better what they already know and appreciating more what they already have experienced. Here, the method of instruction cannot be either didactic or coaching. It must be the Socratic, or maieutic, method of questioning and discussing. It should not occur in an ordinary classroom with the students sitting in rows and the teacher in front of the class, but in a seminar room, with the students sitting around a table and the teacher sitting with them as an equal, even though a little older and wiser.

Of these three main elements in the required curriculum, the third column is completely innovative. Nothing like this is done in our schools, and because it is completely absent from the ordinary curriculum of basic schooling, the students never have the experience of having their minds addressed in a challenging way or of being asked to think about important ideas, to express their thoughts, to defend their opinions in a reasonable fashion.

The only thing that is innovative about the second column is the insistence that the method of instruction here must be coaching carried on either with one student at a time or with very small groups of students. Nothing else can be effective in the development of a skill, be it bodily or intellectual. The absence of such individualized coaching in our schools explains why most of the students cannot read well, write well, speak well, listen well, or perform well any of the other basic intellectual operations.

The three columns are closely interconnected and integrated, but the middle column—the one concerned with linguistic, mathematical, and scientific skills—is central. It both supports and is supported by the other two columns. All the intellectual skills with which it is concerned must be exercised in the study of the three basic subject-matters and in acquiring knowledge about them, and these intellectual skills must be exercised in the seminars devoted to the discussion of books and other things.

In addition to the three main columns in the curriculum, ascending through the 12 years of basic schooling, there are three adjuncts: One is 12 years of physical training, accompanied by instruction in bodily care and hygiene. The second, running through something less than 12 years, is the development of basic manual skills, such as cooking, sewing, carpentry, and the operation of all kinds of machines. The third, reserved for the last year or two, is an introduction to the whole world of work—the range of occupations in which human beings earn their livings. This is not particularized job training. It is the very opposite. It aims at a broad understanding of what is involved in working for a living and of the various ways in which that can be done. If, at the end of 12 years, students wish training for specific jobs, they should get that in two-year or in technical institutes of one sort or another.

Everything that has not been specifically mentioned as occupying the time of the school day should be reserved for after-hours and have the status of extracurricular activities.

Please note: The required course of study just described is as important for what it *displaces* as for what it introduces. It displaces a multitude of elective courses, especially those offered in our secondary schools, most of which make little or no contribution to general, liberal education. It eliminates all narrowly specialized job training, which now abounds in our schools. It throws out of the curriculum and into the category of optional extracurricular activities a variety of things that have little or no educational value.

If it did not call for all these displacements, there would not be enough time in the school day or year to accomplish everything that is essential to the general, liberal learning that must be the content of basic schooling.

The Quintessential Element

So far, I have set forth the bare essentials of the Paideia Proposal with regard to basic schooling. I have not yet mentioned the quintessential element—the *sine qua non*—without which nothing else can possibly come to fruition, no matter how sound it might be in principle. The heart of the matter is the quality of learning and the quality of teaching that occupies the school day, not to mention the quality of the homework after school.

First, the learning must be active. It must use the whole mind, not just the memory. It must be learning by discovery, in which the student, never the teacher, is the primary agent. Learning by discovery, which is the only genuine learning, may be either unaided or aided. It is unaided only for geniuses. For most students, discovery must be aided.

Here is where teachers come in—as aids in the process of learning by discovery, not as knowers who attempt to put the knowledge they have into the minds of their students. The quality of the teaching, in short, depends crucially upon how the teacher conceives his role in the process of learning, and that must be as an aid to the student's process of discovery.

I am prepared for the questions that must be agitating you by now: How and where will we get the teachers who can perform as teachers should? How will we be able to staff the program with teachers so trained that they will be competent to provide the quality of instruction required for the quality of learning desired?

The first part of our answer to these questions is negative: We *cannot* get the teachers we need for the Paideia program from schools of education *as they are now constituted.* As teachers are now trained for teaching, they simply will not do. The ideal—an impracticable ideal—would be to ask for teachers who are, themselves, truly educated human beings. But truly educated human beings are too rare. Even if we could draft all who are now alive, there still would be far too few to staff our schools.

Well, then, what can we look for? Look for teachers who are actively engaged in the process of *becoming* educated human beings, who are themselves deeply motivated to develop their own minds. Assuming this is not too much to ask for the present, how should teachers be schooled and trained in the future? First, they should have the same kind of basic schooling that is recommended in the Paideia Proposal. Second, they should have additional schooling, at the college and even the university level, in which the same kind of general, liberal learning is carried on at advanced levels—more deeply, broadly, and intensively than it can be done in the first 12 years of schooling. Third, they must be given something analogous to the clinical experience in the training of physicians. They must engage in practice-teaching under supervision, which is another way of saying that they must be *coached* in the arts of teaching, not just given didactic instruction in educational psychology and in pedagogy. Finally, and most important of all, they must learn how to teach well by being exposed to the performances of those who are masters of the arts involved in teaching.

It is by watching a good teacher at work that they will be able to perceive what is involved in the process of assisting others to learn by discovery. Perceiving it, they must then try to emulate what they observe, and through this process, they slowly will become good teachers themselves.

The Paideia Proposal recognizes the need for three different kinds of institutions at the collegiate level: The two-year community or junior college should offer a wide choice of electives that give students some training in one or another specialized field, mainly those fields of study that have something to do with earning a living. The four-year college also should offer a wide variety of electives, to be chosen by students who aim at the various professional or technical occupations that require advanced study. Those elective majors chosen by students should be accompanied, for all students, by one required minor, in which the kind of general and liberal learning that was begun at the level of basic schooling is continued at a higher level in the four years of college. And we should have still a third type of collegiate institution—a four-year college in which general, liberal learning at a higher level constitutes a required course of study that is to be taken by all students. *It is this third type of college, by the way, that should be attended by all who plan to become teachers in our basic schools.*

At the university level, there should be a continuation of general, liberal learning at a still higher level to accompany intensive specialization in this or that field of science or scholarship, this or that learned profession. Our insistence on the continuation of general, liberal learning at all the higher levels of schooling stems from our concern with the worst cultural disease that is rampant in our society—*the barbarism of specialization.*

There is no question that our technologically advanced industrial society needs specialists of all sorts. There is no question that the advancement of knowledge in all fields of science and scholarship, and in all the learned professions, needs intense specialization. But for the sake of preserving and enhancing our cultural traditions, as well as for the health of science and scholarship, we need specialists who also are generalists—generally cultivated human beings, not just good plumbers. We need truly educated human beings who can perform their special tasks better precisely because they have general cultivation as well as intensely specialized training.

Changes indeed are needed in higher education, but those improvements cannot reasonably be expected unless improvement in basic schooling makes that possible.

The Future of Our Free Institutions

I already have declared as emphatically as I know how that the quality of human life in our society depends on the quality of the schooling we give our young people, both basic and advanced. But a marked elevation in the quality of human life is not the only reason improving the quality of schooling is so necessary—not the only reason we must move heaven and earth to stop the deterioration of our schools and turn them in the opposite direction. The other reason is to safeguard the future of our free institutions.

They cannot prosper, they may not even survive, unless we do something to rescue our schools from their current deplorable deterioration. Democracy, in the full sense of the term, came into existence only in this century and only in a few countries on earth, among which the United States is an outstanding example. But democracy came into existence in this century only in its initial conditions, all of which hold out promises for the future that remain to be fulfilled. Unless we do something about improving the quality of basic schooling for all and the quality of advanced schooling for some, there is little chance that those promises ever will be fulfilled. And if they are not, our free institutions are doomed to decay and wither away.

We face many insistently urgent problems. Our prosperity and even our survival depend on the solution of those problems—the threat of nuclear war, the exhaustion of essential resources and of supplies of energy, the pollution or spoilage of the environment, the spiraling of inflation accompanied by the spread of unemployment.

To solve these problems, we need resourceful and innovative leadership. For that to arise and be effective, an educated populace is needed. Trained intelligence—not only on the part of leaders, but also on the part of followers—holds the key to the solution of the problems our society faces. Achieving peace, prosperity, and plenty could put us on the threshold of an early paradise. But a much better educational system than now exists is needed, for that alone can carry us across the threshold. Without it, a poorly schooled population will not be able to put to good use the opportunities afforded by the achievement of the general welfare. Those who are not schooled to enjoy society can only despoil its institutions and corrupt themselves.

Postnote

This article by Mortimer J. Adler is representative of a *perennialist* philosophy. Perennialists believe that truth is best revealed in the enduring classics of Western culture and that the schools' curriculum should consist of the traditional subjects—history, language, mathematics, science, and the arts.

The late Mortimer Adler was an erudite, multifaceted scholar whose contributions to education through his work with the *Encyclopaedia Britannica,* the Great Books program, and the Paideia Program have earned him a spot among our Classic selections. Derived from the Greek word, *paideia* signifies the general level of personal excellence that should be the possession of all human beings.

By eliminating a differentiated curriculum from elementary and secondary schools and requiring all students to take a common curriculum, Adler believed that we can give all students the quality education currently available only to those on a high track. Adler and many of his supporters established a network of individuals who are implementing these ideas in a variety of public and private schools around the country.

Discussion Questions

1. What do you see as the merits of Adler's proposal? The drawbacks? Why?
2. What kinds of individuals or groups are likely to support a curriculum structured according to Adler's "three columns"? Who is apt to oppose this type of curriculum? Why?
3. Should vocational education be eliminated from K–12 schooling? Why or why not?

CLASSIC

The Quality School Curriculum

WILLIAM GLASSER

FOCUS Question

As you read this article, think about what elements you believe constitute a quality school curriculum.

Recently I had a chance to talk to the staff members of a high school who had been hard at work for six months trying to change their school into a Quality School. They believed that they were much less coercive than in the past, but they complained that many of their students were still not working hard and that a few continued to be disruptive. They admitted that things were better but asked me if maybe they should reinject a little coercion back into their classroom management in order to "stimulate" the students to work harder.

I assured them that the answer to their complaints was to use less, not more, coercion. At the same time, I realized that in their teaching they had not yet addressed a vital component of the Quality School, the curriculum. To complete the move from coercive boss-managing to noncoercive lead-managing,[1] they had to change the curriculum they were teaching.

This was made ever clearer to me during the break when I talked to a few teachers individually. They told me that they had already made many of the changes that I suggest below and that they were not having the problems with students that most of the staff members were having. Until almost all the teachers change their curriculum, I strongly believe that they will be unable to rid their classrooms of the coercion that causes too many of their students to continue to be their adversaries.

In Chapter 1 of *The Quality School*, I briefly cited the research of Linda McNeil of Rice University to support my claim that boss-management is destructive to the quality of the curriculum.[2] From feedback I have been receiving, it seems that the schools that are trying to become Quality Schools have not paid enough attention to this important point. I am partly at fault. When I wrote *The Quality School*, I did not realize how vital it is for teachers to make sure that they teach quality, and I did not

William Glasser, M.D., is a board-certified psychiatrist and founder and president of the William Glasser Institute, an international training organization devoted to teaching his ideas in countries across the world. Glasser, William, "The Quality School Curriculum," *Phi Delta Kappan,* May 1992.

explain sufficiently what this means. To correct this shortcoming, I want to expand on what I wrote in the book, and I strongly encourage staff members of all the schools that seek to move to quality to spend a great deal of time discussing this matter.

We must face the fact that a majority of students, even good ones, believe that much of the present academic curriculum is not worth the effort it takes to learn it. No matter how well the teachers manage them, if students do not find quality in what they are asked to do in their classes, they will not work hard enough to learn the material. The answer is not to try to make them work harder; the answer is to increase the quality of what we ask them to learn.

Faced with students who refuse to make much effort, even teachers who are trying to become lead-managers give a lot of low grades—a practice so traditional that they fail to perceive it as coercive. Then the students deal with their low grades by rebelling and working even less than before. The teachers, in turn, resent this attitude. They believe that, because they are making the effort to be less coercive, the students should be appreciative and work harder. The teachers fail to see that the students are not rebelling against them and their efforts to become lead-managers; they are rebelling against a curriculum that lacks quality. Therefore, if we want to create Quality Schools, we must stop *all* coercion, not just some, and one way to do this is to create a quality curriculum.

Before I describe a quality curriculum, let me use a simple nonschool example to try to explain what it is about the curriculum we have now that lacks quality. Suppose you get a job in a factory making both black shoes and brown shoes. You are well-managed and do quality work. But soon you become aware that all the brown shoes you make are sold for scrap; only the black shoes are going into retail stores. How long would you continue to work hard on the brown shoes? As you slack off, however, you are told that this is not acceptable and that you will lose pay or be fired if you don't buckle down and do just as good a job on the brown as on the black. You are told that what happens to the brown shoes is none of your business. Your job is to work hard. Wouldn't it be almost impossible to do as you are told?

As silly as the preceding example may seem, students in schools, even students in colleges and graduate schools, are asked to learn well enough to remember for important tests innumerable facts that both they and their teachers know are of no use except to pass the tests. I call this throwaway information because, after they do the work to learn it, that is just what students do with it. Dates and places in history, the names of parts of organisms and organs in biology, and formulas in mathematics and science are all examples of throwaway information.

Newspapers sometimes publish accounts of widespread cheating in schools and label it a symptom of the moral disintegration of our society. But what they call "cheating" turns out to be the ways that students have devised to avoid the work of memorizing throwaway knowledge. The honest students who are penalized are not pleased, but many students and faculty members and most of the informed public do not seem unduly upset about the "cheating." They are aware that there is no value to much of what students are asked to remember. I certainly do not condone cheating, but I must stress that, as long as we have a curriculum that holds students responsible for throwaway information, there will be cheating—and few people will care.

Elsewhere I have suggested that this throwaway knowledge could also be called "nonsense."[3] While it is not nonsense to ask students to be aware of formulas, dates, and places and to know how to use them and where to find them if they need them, it becomes nonsense when we ask students to memorize this information and when we lower their grades if they fail to do so. Whether called throwaway knowledge or nonsense, this kind of memorized information can never be a part of the curriculum of a Quality School.

This means that in a Quality School there should never be test questions that call for the mere regurgitation of bare facts, such as those written in a book or stored in the memory of a computer. Students should never be asked to commit this portion of the curriculum to memory. All available information on what is being studied should always be on hand, not only during class but during all tests. No student should ever suffer academically because he or she forgot some fact or formula. The only useful way to test students' knowledge of facts, formulas, and other information is to ask not what the information is, but where, when, why, and how it is of use in the real world.

While a complete definition of quality is elusive, it certainly would include usefulness in the real world. And useful need not be restricted to practical or utilitarian. That which is useful can be aesthetically or spiritually useful or useful in some other way that is meaningful to the student—but it can never be nonsense.

In a Quality School, when questions of where, why, when, and how are asked on a test, they are never part of what is called an "objective" test, such as a multiple-choice, true/false, or short answer test. For example, if a multiple-choice test is used to ask where, why, when, and how, the student in a Quality School should not be restricted to a list of predetermined choices. There should always be a place for a student to write out a better answer if he or she believes that the available choices are less accurate than another alternative. For example, a multiple-choice test question in history might be: "George Washington is called 'the father of his country' for the following reasons: [four reasons would then be listed]. Which do you think is the best reason?" The student could choose one of the listed answers or write in another and explain why he or she thought it better than those listed.

In a Quality School questions as narrow as the preceding example would be rare, simply because of the constant effort to relate all that is taught to the lives of the students. Therefore, if a question asking where, when, why, and how certain information could be used were asked, it would always be followed by the further question: "How can you use this information in your life, now or in the future?"

However, such a follow-up question would never come out of the blue. The real-world value of the material to be learned would have been emphasized in lectures, in class discussions, in cooperative learning groups, and even in homework assignments that ask students to discuss with parents or other adults how what they learn in school might be useful outside of school. The purpose of such follow-up questions is to stress that the curriculum in a Quality School focuses on useful skills, not on information that has no use in the lives of those who are taught it. I define a *skill* as the ability to use knowledge. If we emphasized such skills in every academic subject, there would be no rebellion on the part of students. Students could earn equal credit on a test for explaining why what was taught was or was not of use to them. This would encourage them to think, not to parrot the ideas of others.

Continuing with the George Washington question, if a student in a Quality School said that Washington's refusal to be crowned king makes him a good candidate to be considered father of this republic, a teacher could ask that student how he or she could use this information in life now or later. The student might respond that he or she prefers to live in a republic and would not like to live in a country where a king made all the laws. A student's answer could be more complicated than this brief example, but what the student would have thought over would be how Washington's decision affects his or her life today.

Without memorizing any facts, students taught in this way could learn more history in a few weeks than they now learn in years. More important, they would learn to *like* history. Too many students tell me that they hate history, and I find this to be an educational disaster. I hope that what they are really saying is that they hate the history curriculum, not history.

Another important element in the curriculum of a Quality School is that the students be able to *demonstrate* how what they have learned can be used in their lives now or later. Almost all students would have no difficulty accepting that reading, writing, and arithmetic are useful skills, but in a Quality School they would be asked to demonstrate that they can use them. For example, students would not be asked to learn the multiplication tables as if this knowledge were separate from being able to use the tables in their lives.

To demonstrate the usefulness of knowing how to multiply, students would be given problems to solve and asked to show how multiplication helped in solving them. These problems might require the use of several different mathematical processes, and students could show how each process was used. Students would learn not only how to multiply but also when, where, and why to do so. Once students have demonstrated that they know *how* to multiply, the actual multiplication could be done on a small calculator or by referring to tables.

In a Quality School, once students have mastered a mathematical process they would be encouraged to use a calculator. To do math processes involving large numbers over and over is boring and nonessential. Today, most students spend a lot of time memorizing the times tables. They learn how to multiply, but fail to demonstrate when, where, and why to multiply. I will admit that the tables and the calculators do not teach students *how* to multiply, but they are what people in the real world use to find answers—a fact finally recognized by the Educational Testing Service, which now allows the use of calculators on the Scholastic Aptitude Test.

Teachers in a Quality School would teach the "how" by asking students to demonstrate that they can do calculations without a calculator. Students would be told that, as soon as they can demonstrate this ability by hand, they will be allowed to use a calculator. For most students, knowing that they will never be stuck working one long, boring problem after another would be more than enough incentive to get them to learn to calculate.

In a Quality School there would be a great deal of emphasis on the skill of writing and much less on the skill of reading. The reason for this is that anyone who can write well can read well, but many people who can read well can hardly write at all. From grade 1 on, students would be asked to write: first, words; then, sentences and paragraphs; and finally, articles, stories, and letters. An extremely good project is to have each middle school student write a book or keep a journal. Students who do so will leave middle school with an education—even if that is all that they have done.

To write a great deal by hand can be onerous, but using a computer makes the same process highly enjoyable. In a Quality School, all teachers would be encouraged to learn word-processing skills and to teach them to their students. Moreover, these skills should be used in all classes. Computers are more readily available in schools today than would seem to be the case, judging from their actual use. If they are not readily available, funds can be raised to buy the few that would be needed. If students were encouraged to write, we would see fewer students diagnosed as having language learning disabilities.

At Apollo High School,[4] where I consult, the seniors were asked if they would accept writing a good letter on a computer as a necessary requirement for graduation. They agreed, and almost all of them learned to do it. One way they demonstrated that their letters were good was by mailing them and receiving responses. They were thrilled by the answers, which we used as one criterion for satisfying the requirement. Clearly, demonstrating the use of what is learned in a real-life situation is one of the best ways to teach.

While demonstrating is the best way to show that something worthwhile has been learned, it is not always easy or even possible to do so. Thus there must be some tests. But, as I stated above, the tests in a Quality School would always show the acquisition of skills, never the acquisition of facts or information alone.

Let me use an example from science to explain what would be considered a good way to test in a Quality School. Science is mostly the discovery of how and why things work. But where and when they work can also be important. Too much science is taught as a simple listing of what works—e.g., these are the parts of a cell. Students all over America are busy memorizing the parts of a cell, usually by copying and then labeling a cell drawn in a textbook. The students are then tested to see if they can do this from memory—a wonderful example of throwaway information, taught by coercion. Teaching and testing in this way is worse than teaching no science at all, because many students learn to hate science as a result. Hating something as valuable as science is worse than simply not knowing it.

The students in a Quality School would be taught some basics about how a cell works, and they would be told that all living organisms are made up of cells. To show them that this is useful knowledge, the teacher might bring up the subject of cancer, explaining how a cancer cell fails to behave as normal cells do and so can kill the host in which it grows. All students know something about cancer, and all would consider this useful knowledge.

The subsequent test in a Quality School might ask students to describe the workings of a cell (or of some part of a cell) with their books open and available. They would then be asked how they could use this information in their lives and would be encouraged to describe the differences between a normal cell and a cancer cell. They would be taught that one way to use this information might be to avoid exposure to too much sunlight because excessive sunlight can turn normal skin cells into cancer cells. For most students, this information would be of use because all students have some fear of cancer.

Readers might feel some concern that what I am suggesting would not prepare students for standardized tests that mostly ask for throwaway information, such as the identification of the parts of a cell. My answer is that students would be better prepared—because, by learning to *explain* how and why something works, they are more likely to remember what they have learned. Even if less ground is covered, as is likely to be the case when we move from facts to skills, a little ground covered well is better preparation, even for nonsense tests, than a lot of ground covered poorly.

We should never forget that people, not curriculum, are the desired outcomes of schooling. What we want to develop are students who have the skills to become active contributors to society, who are enthusiastic about what they have learned, and who are aware of how learning can be of use to them in the future. The curriculum changes I have suggested above will certainly produce more students who fit this profile.

Will the students agree that these outcomes are desirable? If we accept control theory, the answer is obvious. When the outcomes the teachers want are in the quality worlds of their students, the students will accept them. In my experience skills will be accepted as quality in almost all cases; facts and information will rarely be accepted.

Assuming that skills are taught, the teacher must still explain clearly what will be asked on tests. Sample questions should be given to the students, and the use of all books, notes, and materials should be permitted. Even if a student copies the workings of a cell from a book at the time of the test, the student will still have to explain how this information can be used in life. If students can answer such questions, they can be said to know the material—whether or not they copied some of it.

Tests—especially optional retests for students who wish to improve their grades—can be taken at home and can include such items as, "Explain the workings of a cell to an adult at home, write down at least one question that was asked by that person, and explain how you answered it." All the facts would be available in the test; it is the skill to use them that would be tested. The main thing to understand here is that, after a school stops testing for facts and begins to test for skills, it will not be long before it is clear to everyone that skills are the outcomes that have value; facts and information have none.

In most schools, the teacher covers a body of material, and the students must guess what is going to appear on the test. Some teachers even test for material that they have not covered. In a Quality School this would not happen. There would be no limitation on input, and the teacher would not ask students to figure out which parts of this input will be on the test. There would be no hands raised asking the age-old question, Is this going to be on the test?

Since it is always skills that are tested for in a Quality School, it is very likely that the teacher would make the test available to the students before teaching the unit so that, as they went through the material in class, they would know that these are the skills that need to be learned. Students could also be asked to describe any other skill that they have learned from the study of the material. This is an example of the open-endedness that is always a part of testing and discussion in a Quality School. A number of questions would be implicit in all tests: What can you contribute? What is your opinion? What might I (the teacher) have missed? Can you give a better use or explanation?

Keep in mind that, in a Quality School, students and teachers would evaluate tests. Students who are dissatisfied with either their own or the teacher's evaluation could continue to work on the test and improve. Building on the thinking of W. Edwards Deming, the idea is to constantly improve usable skills. In a Quality School, this opportunity is always open.

As I look over what I have written, I see nothing that requires any teacher to change anything that he or she does. If what I suggest appeals to you, implement it at your own pace. Those of us in the Quality School movement believe in lead-management, so there is no coercion—no pressure on you to hurry. You might wish to begin by discussing any of these ideas with your students. In a Quality School students should be aware of everything that the teachers are trying to do. If it makes sense to them, as I think it will, they will help you to put it into practice.

Notes

1. For a definition of boss-management and lead-management, see William Glasser, "The Quality School," *Phi Delta Kappan,* February 1990, p. 428.
2. William Glasser, *The Quality School: Managing Students Without Coercion* (New York: Harper & Row, 1990), Ch. 1.
3. See Supplementary Information Bulletin No. 5 of the Quality School Training Program. All of these bulletins are available from the Institute for Reality Therapy, 7301 Medical Center Dr., Suite 104, Canoga Park, CA 91307.
4. Apollo High School is a school for students who refuse to work in a regular high school. It enrolls about 240 students (9–12) and is part of the Simi Valley (Calif.) Unified School District.

Postnote

William Glasser's training as a psychiatrist has enabled him to examine schools and their effects on children in ways that are unique and important, earning his article a place among our Classic selections. His *choice theory* represents an attempt to base schooling on different principles that satisfy students' needs for friendship, freedom, fun, and power. Glasser's philosophy has been implemented by many educators for whom his humanistic approach has great appeal.

Glasser asserts that a majority of students believe that much of the present academic curriculum is not worth the effort needed to learn it. To overcome this problem, Glasser suggests that the quality of what we ask students to learn must be increased. Some guiding principles of this quality curriculum include reducing the quantity of what students are asked to memorize, emphasizing the usefulness of knowledge and the development of useful skills (including writing skills), covering less material, and assessing performance.

Many of Glasser's ideas are compatible with the curriculum reform movement occurring in such fields as mathematics, science, and history. Asking students to construct their own knowledge, rather than memorize packaged knowledge, is clearly the direction in which these curriculum efforts are headed. However, many of the content standards being implemented by states, along with their associated assessments, seem to be emphasizing memorization of facts.

Discussion Questions

1. Do Glasser's ideas appeal to you? Why or why not? What problems, if any, do you see in implementing them?
2. What do you think about Glasser's notion of allowing open-book tests? Explain your position.
3. Glasser states that in looking over his ideas, he sees nothing that requires teachers to change what they do. Do you agree or disagree with his statement? Why?

Teaching What We Hold to Be Sacred

JOHN I. GOODLAD

FOCUS Question

As you read this article, try to think of the various ways that schools can address social inequality to promote social justice.

TERMS TO NOTE

Moral ecology

Social justice

On February 1, 1994, the U.S. Postal Service added a new postage stamp honoring Allison Davis to its Black Heritage Series. An important figure in psychology, social anthropology, and education for more than 40 years, Davis was the first person from the field of education to be elected to the American Academy of Arts and Sciences (Unicover, 2003).

In the 1940s, Davis became the first African American ever appointed to a tenured position at a major "white" university, the University of Chicago. His appointment was controversial. Ralph Tyler, chairman of the department of education, and Robert M. Hutchins, president of the university, overcame the opposition's pretext of lack of funds for hiring Davis by securing private funding to underwrite Davis's salary and related expenses for the first three years.

Even so, Davis did not gain access to the amenities that his colleagues took for granted. He unsuccessfully sought housing in the surrounding Hyde Park neighborhood. He was ineligible for membership in the university's Quadrangle Club until women, too, finally gained admittance in 1948. And he could not find living quarters and mixed-race meeting places when conducting field research in the South and the Southwest (Finder, in press).

Much of Davis's research centered on the effects of the color-caste system in U.S. society, particularly on the ways in which biases in standardized intelligence tests unfairly stigmatized poor and minority students. With colleague Robert Havighurst, Davis produced a series of papers arguing that the American social class system actually prevents the vast majority of children of the working classes, or of the slums,

---

John I. Goodlad is President of the Institute for Educational Inquiry and a founder of the Center for Educational Renewal at the University of Washington. "Teaching What We Hold to Be Sacred," by John I. Goodlad, *Educational Leadership,* December 2004, pp. 18–21. Reprinted by permission. The Association for Supervision and Curriculum Development is a worldwide community of educators advocating sound policies and sharing best practices to achieve the success of each learner. To learn more, visit ASCD at **www.ascd.org.**

from learning any culture but that of their own groups (cited in University of Chicago, 2003).

Davis and Havighurst challenged the conventional wisdom of their day that claimed that social inequalities resulted from racial biological inferiority. They envisioned a day in which this misconception would be replaced by the knowledge that inequalities in achievement stemmed from environmental factors, such as widespread denial of educational and economic opportunities to people of color.

In the ensuing years, innumerable researchers and thinkers have confirmed Davis's message, including James B. Conant (1961), who documented the shameful differences between the relatively lavish provisions for schooling in the suburbs and the shamefully shabby provisions in the inner cities.

Unfortunately, the biological causation thesis as an explanation of social inequality has had a stubborn longevity. As Stephen J. Gould tells us in *The Mismeasure of Man* (1981), researchers (of a sort) have extended this thesis beyond race. Gould's account of the efforts to assign lower levels of intelligence to women because of their generally smaller craniums is eerily hilarious. He cites the French anthropologist Hervé, who savaged women and black men with one stroke in 1881: "Men of the black races have a brain scarcely heavier than that of white women" (p. 3). As Gould points out, attempts to rank people—whether by brain size or by an IQ test score—have consistently recorded "little more than social prejudice" (p. 28).

History demonstrates that people will find ingenious ways and develop elaborate constructs to create and harden categories of status and privilege among the diverse groups that constitute humankind. And they will produce a litany of justifications to convince the populace that these inequalities are natural and right.

One might argue that a more enlightened era has, in part, arrived. The end of legal racial segregation, improved access to higher education for minorities, and increased economic opportunities have improved individual lives. But the caste system is still entrenched in society; social prejudices and injustices remain.

Our Moral Ecology

Will humankind ever manage—or want—to do away with social inequality? The apparent inevitability and tenacity of caste as a way of life may make us feel hopeless about trying to eliminate this system. Why try to reform what exists? To quote the 19th century British politician, Lord Thomas Macaulay, "Reform, reform, don't speak to me of reform. We have enough problems already."

Nonetheless, the history of civilization reveals that in every era, some people, somewhere, have envisioned gaining freedom from the caste system. The themes of enlightenment have been argued from both the rational and the divine perspectives. The two perspectives have come together to form a central core of common principles. This evolving center, never static, takes on a kind of cultural sacredness, an abstract moral ecology. It provides, in Seymour Sarason's words, a "sense of interconnections among the individual, the collectivity, and ultimate purpose and meaning of human existence" (1986, p. 899).

In societies seeking to balance the private and public good, we might well consider what we commonly hold sacred. If our moral ecology encompasses equality and social justice, and if we want that moral ecology to guide our society, then equality and social justice must be taught—carefully taught.

Many people assign to our schools the task of nurturing these values in the populace. In its much lauded experiment, universal schooling, the United States set as a major purpose the enculturation of the young—specifically the children of immigrants—into a social and political democracy.

But when we place this responsibility entirely on schools, we forget that between the years of 6 and 18, young people spend approximately 55 percent of their time in activities other than school and sleep. We give little critical thought to the cacophony of teaching that now surrounds our young throughout the day, and nearly all of which is driven by economic ends rather than by the ideals of education that we espouse in the rhetoric of school and college graduation ceremonies.

Political scientist Benjamin Barber brings our attention sharply to the daunting task that schools undertake when they attempt to develop students' democratic character amid the ubiquitous culture that surrounds young people throughout the day:

> We honor ambition, we reward greed, we celebrate materialism, we worship acquisitiveness, we cherish success, and we commercialize the classroom—and then we bark at the young about the gentle art of the spirit. (1993, p. 42)

The Role of Schools

In spite of the obstacles, it would be the height of folly for our schools not to have as their central mission educating the young in the democratic ideals of humankind, the freedoms and responsibilities of a democratic society, and the civil and civic understandings and dispositions necessary to democratic citizenship. And yet here we are, hardening into place the caste categories linked to test scores, a practice that directly impedes such a mission. When polls ask people what they want of their schools, the people say over and over that the personal and social development of their children is just as important to them as vocational and academic development. As the accumulating body of knowledge about cognition clearly reveals, test scores do not correlate at all with the other attributes that people believe their schools should develop in students.

But not to worry. High test scores will get your offspring into a college or university if the money is available from family resources or scholarships. Forget those who dominate among the low scorers, such as low-income children whose late-in-the-year birthdays kept them out of kindergarten for most of an additional year, during which their families had no resources to send them to preschool. Funding for Head Start did not quite embrace their neighborhoods. And, oh yes, those children in the inner cities who had substitute teachers for every year of their schooling did not reach the upper levels of test scores, either. But let us keep the system, anyway—it offers special rewards for those who succeed and who then join the upper levels of the layers of power.

We need to pay increased attention to the commonalities that bind humankind. Our schools are not lacking in the rhetoric of "respecting diversity" and social studies texts extolling "understanding other people." What *other* people?

We all belong to one species—humankind. There is only one ongoing conversation—the human conversation, consisting of the work, play, parenting, conversing, and imagining in which we all engage and of the beliefs, hopes, and aspirations that we hold. To be sure, within those commonalities there is rich diversity—not only in the rainbow of colors to which the Reverend Jesse Jackson refers, but also in all human characteristics. The diversity in color, language, song, ceremony, religion, games, flora, and fauna that exists among us adds to the miracle of life. Why else do we travel to other parts of the world?

But if we begin with the concept of one humankind and then add the concept of diversity in addressing such democratic essentials as liberty and justice for all, we embark on a slippery slope. Some years ago, a critic attacked the late Ernest Boyer's book, *High School* (1983), and my book, *A Place Called School* (1984), on the grounds that we did not address special education. A specialist in the field defended us by pointing out that we *had* addressed special education—by advocating individualized education for all students.

A few years later, Thomas Lovitt and I were gently taken to task for our advocacy of integrating general and special education (Goodlad & Lovitt, 1993). Critics argued that the road to bringing attention—some of it now required by federal law—to students who require substantial deviations from the norms of schooling had been a rocky one. Many of the hard-won gains could be wiped out if schools eliminated special education as a separate service, even with the best intentions of providing for the individual differences and education needs of all children. We agreed with their assessment. Our agreement did not change our basic argument for the benefits of bringing general and special education together in classrooms, but it did caution us to emphasize that exceptional provisions are sometimes necessary to provide equal opportunity in education. The same perspective applies to our efforts to provide equal education opportunities to diverse students, no matter what type of diversity we mean.

Beyond Social Caste

The struggle for justice, equity, respect, and appreciation for human diversity has been long and often troubled. It continues to be so. The human race's proclivity for arranging its members in hierarchies of strongly maintained status and privilege is likely to continue as a malaise that can become cancerous.

The answer, we know, is education. But education, despite our honoring the concept, is not in itself good. We must intentionally and even passionately inject morality into education (Goodlad, 1999).

Winston Churchill said, "Democracy is the worst form of government except for all those others that have been tried." If we agree, we must do more than teach students only about the political structures of democracy. We must teach students the ideals of democracy and social equality and give our young people opportunities to practice those ideals in their daily lives, both in and out of school.

Unless we work simultaneously as a society to eliminate in our schools and society a caste system harboring and even fostering beliefs and practices that contradict these ideals, our hypocrisy will become transparent. We are all participants in the informal education that goes on outside of schools. The larger community must ensure a democracy that protects and supports the democratic education that needs to go on inside of schools. The clear purpose of schooling, then, becomes attending to all those educational matters that the larger communsity does not address, especially enculturating the young into satisfying, responsible citizens in a social and political democracy.

Once formal education inside of schools and informal education outside of schools, working together, make morally grounded democratic behavior routine—as John Dewey said it must become—such principles as justice, equity, and freedom for everyone will need no special advocacy. But when we parcel them out into the tiers of caste privilege, as we often do today, we endanger these precious principles.

References

Barber, B. R. (1993, November). America skips school. *Harper's Magazine, 286,* 42.

Boyer, E. L. (1983). *High school.* New York: Harper & Row.

Conant, J. B. (1961). *Slums and suburbs: A commentary on schools in metropolitan areas.* New York: McGraw-Hill.

Finder, M. (in press). *Educating America: The extraordinary career of Ralph W. Tyler.* New York: Praeger.

Goodlad, J. I. (1984). *A place called school.* New York: McGraw-Hill.

Goodlad, J. I. (1999). Convergence. In R. Soder, J. I. Goodlad, & T. J. McMannon (Eds.), *Developing Democratic Character in the Young* (pp. 1–25). San Francisco: Jossey-Bass.

Goodlad, J. I., & Lovitt, T. C. (Eds.). (1993). *Integrating general and special education.* New York: Merrill.

Gould, S. J. (1981). *The mismeasure of man.* New York: W. W. Norton.

Sarason, S. B. (1986, August). And what is the public interest? *American Psychologist, 41,* 899.

Unicover. (2003). *U.S. proofcard: 29¢ Dr. Allison Davis: Black heritage series* [Online]. Available: **www.unicover.com/EA4PAD1J.htm**

University of Chicago. (2003). *The University of Chicago faculty: A centennial view—Allison Davis/Education* [Online]. Available: **www.lib.uchicago.edu/projects/centcat/centcats/fac/facch25_01.html**

Postnote

John Goodlad is one of the elder statesmen of education. He has written on many different topics throughout his career, such as teacher education, curriculum, and instruction. On all of these topics, he focuses on the important, salient features and never becomes bogged down in details. In this article, he addresses one of the ultimate purposes of public schooling in a democratic society, ensuring that principles of equality and social justice are carefully taught.

With our current focus on content standards, high-stakes testing, and other accountability features, Goodlad reminds us that most parents want more from our schools than this emphasis on acquiring knowledge. They want their children to learn the freedoms and responsibilities of living in a democracy. Sometimes, we lose sight of this most important goal of schooling. As Socrates said, education has a dual responsibility: to make people smart and to make people good.

Discussion Questions

1. In your own schooling, did you receive specific instruction or lessons on social justice or civic responsibility? If so, can you describe them?
2. Can you think of any events that you observed in school that violated the concept of social justice and equality? Was anything done about them? If so, what?
3. If you were to design a school that focused strongly on civic responsibility, social justice, and equality, what would be some of its practices?

33

The Relevance of Religion to the Curriculum

WARREN A. NORD

FOCUS Question

What, if anything, should public schools teach about religion?

For some time now, public school administrators have been on the front lines of our culture wars over religion and education—and I expect it would be music to their ears to hear that peace accords have been signed.

Unfortunately, the causes of war are deep-seated. Peace is not around the corner.

At the same time, however, it is also easy to overstate the extent of the hostilities. At least at the national level—but also in many communities across America—a large measure of common ground has been found. The leaders of most major national educational, religious and civil liberties organizations agree about the basic principles that should govern the role of religion and public schools. No doubt we don't agree about everything, but we agree about a lot.

For example, in 1988, a group of 17 major religious and educational organizations—the American Jewish Congress and the Islamic Society of North America, the National Association of Evangelicals and the National Council of Churches, the National Education Association and American Federation of Teachers, the National School Boards Association and AASA among them—endorsed a statement of principles that describes the importance of religion in the public school curriculum.

The statement, in part, says this: "Because religion plays significant roles in history and society, study about religion is essential to understanding both the nation and the world. Omission of facts about religion can give students the false impression that the religious life of humankind is insignificant or unimportant. Failure to understand even the basic symbols, practices and concepts of the various religions makes much of history, literature, art and contemporary life unintelligible."

Warren A. Nord works in the philosophy of the humanities, the philosophy of religion, the philosophy of education (especially moral education), and the relationship of religion and education. He is the author of two books: *Religion and American Education: Rethinking a National Dilemma* (1995); and, with Charles C. Haynes, *Taking Religion Seriously Across the Curriculum* (1998). Reprinted with permission from the January 1999 issue of *The School Administrator* magazine.

A Profound Problem

As a result of this (and other "common ground" statements) it is no longer controversial to assert that the study of religion has a legitimate and important place in the public school curriculum.

Where in the curriculum? In practice, the study of religion has been relegated almost entirely to history texts and courses, for it is widely assumed that religion is irrelevant to every other subject in the curriculum—that is, to understanding the world here and now.

This is a deeply controversial assumption, however. A profoundly important educational problem lingers here, one that is almost completely ignored by educators.

Let me put it this way. Several ways exist for making sense of the world here and now. Many Americans accept one or another religious interpretation of reality; others accept one or another secular interpretation. We don't agree—and the differences among us often cut deeply.

Yet public schools systematically teach students to think about the world in secular ways only. They don't even bother to inform them about religious alternatives—apart from distant history. That is, public schooling discriminates against religious ways of making sense of the world. This is no minor problem.

An Economic Argument

To get some sense of what's at issue, let's consider economics.

One can think about the economic domain of life in various ways. Scriptural texts in all religious traditions address questions of justice and morality, poverty and wealth, work and stewardship, for example. A vast body of 20th century literature in moral theology deals with economic issues. Indeed most mainline denominations and ecumenical agencies have official statements on justice and economics. What's common to all of this literature is the claim that the economic domain of life cannot be understood apart from religion.

Needless to say, this claim is not to be found in economics textbooks. Indeed, if we put end to end all the references to religion in the 10 high school economics texts I've reviewed in the past few years, they would add up to about two pages—out of 4,400 pages combined (and all of the references are to premodern times). There is but a single reference to religion—a passing mention in a section on taxation and nonprofit organizations—in the 47 pages of the new national content standards in economics. Moreover, the textbooks and the standards say virtually nothing about the problems that are the major concern of theologians—problems relating to poverty, justice, our consumer culture, the Third World, human dignity and the meaningfulness of work.

The problem isn't just that the texts ignore religion and those economic problems of most concern to theologians. A part of the problem is what the texts do teach—that is, neoclassical economic theory. According to the texts, economics is a science, people are essentially self-interested utility-maximizers, the economic realm is one of competition for scarce resources, values are personal preferences and value judgments are matters of cost-benefit analysis. Of course, no religious tradition accepts this understanding of human nature, society, economics and values.

That is, the texts and standards demoralize and secularize economics.

An Appalling Claim

To be sure, they aren't explicitly hostile to religion; rather they ignore it. But in some ways this is worse than explicit hostility, for students remain unaware of the fact that there are tensions and conflicts between their religious traditions and what they are taught about economics.

In fact, the texts and the standards give students no sense that what they are learning is controversial. Indeed, the national economics standards make it a matter of principle that students be kept in the dark about alternatives to neoclassical theory. As the editors put it in their introduction, the standards were developed to convey a single conception of economics, the "majority paradigm" or neoclassical model of economic behavior. For, they argue, to include "strongly held minority views of economic processes [would only risk] confusing and frustrating teachers and students who are then left with the responsibility of sorting the qualifications and alternatives without a sufficient foundation to do so."

This is an appalling statement. It means, in effect, that students should be indoctrinated; they should be given no critical perspective on neoclassical economic theory.

The problem with the economics texts and standards is but one aspect of the much larger problem that cuts across the curriculum, for in every course students are taught to think in secular ways that often (though certainly not always) conflict with religious alternatives. And this is always done uncritically.

Even in history courses, students learn to think about historical meaning and causation in exclusively secular ways in spite of the fact that Judaism, Christianity and Islam all hold that God acts in history, that there is a religious meaning to history. True, they learn a few facts about religion, but they learn to think about history in secular categories.

Nurturing Secularity

Outside of history courses and literature courses that use historical literature, religion is rarely even mentioned, but even on those rare occasions when it is, the intellectual context is secular. As a result, public education nurtures a secular mentality. This marginalizes religion from our cultural and intellectual life and contributes powerfully to the secularization of our culture.

Ignoring religious ways of thinking about the world is a problem for three important reasons.

- *It is profoundly illiberal.*

Here, of course, I'm not using the term "liberal" to refer to the left wing of the Democratic Party. A liberal education is a broad education, one that provides students with the perspective to think critically about the world and their lives. A good liberal education should introduce students—at least older students—to the major ways humankind has developed for making sense of the world and their lives. Some of those ways of thinking and living are religious and it is illiberal to leave them out of the discussion. Indeed, it may well constitute indoctrination—secular indoctrination.

We indoctrinate students when we uncritically initiate them into one way of thinking and systematically ignore the alternatives. Indeed, if students are to be able to think critically about the secular ways of understanding the world that pervade the curriculum, they must understand something about the religious alternatives.

- *It is politically unjust.*

Public schools must take the public seriously. But religious parents are now, in effect, educationally disenfranchised. Their ways of thinking and living aren't taken seriously.

Consider an analogy. A generation ago textbooks and curricula said virtually nothing about women, blacks and members of minority subcultures. Hardly anyone would now say that that was fair or just. We now—most of us—realize this was a form of discrimination, of educational disenfranchisement. And so it is with religious subcultures (though, ironically, the multicultural movement has been almost entirely silent about religion).

- *It is unconstitutional.*

It is, of course, uncontroversial that it is constitutionally permissible to teach about religion in public schools when done properly. No Supreme Court justice has ever held otherwise. But I want to make a stronger argument.

The court has been clear that public schools must be neutral in matters of religion—in two senses. Schools must be neutral among religions (they can't favor Protestants over Catholics or Christians over Jews), and they must be neutral between religion and nonreligion. Schools can't promote religion. They can't proselytize. They can't conduct religious exercises.

Of course, neutrality is a two-edged sword. Just as schools can't favor religion over nonreligion, neither can they favor nonreligion over religion. As Justice Hugo Black put it in the seminal

1947 *Everson* ruling, "State power is no more to be used so as to handicap religions than it is to favor them."

Similarly, in his majority opinion in *Abington v. Schempp* in 1963, Justice Tom Clark wrote that schools can't favor "those who believe in no religion over those who do believe." And in a concurring opinion, Justice Arthur Goldberg warned that an "untutored devotion to the concept of neutrality [can lead to a] pervasive devotion to the secular and a passive, or even active, hostility to the religious."

Of course this is just what has happened. An untutored, naïve conception of neutrality has led educators to look for a smoking gun, an explicit hostility to religion, when the hostility has been philosophically rather more subtle—though no less substantial for that.

The only way to be neutral when all ground is contested ground is to be fair to the alternative. That is, given the Supreme Court's longstanding interpretation of the Establishment Clause, public schools must require the study of religion if they require the study of disciplines that cumulatively lead to a pervasive devotion to the secular—as they do.

Classroom Practices

So how can we be fair? What would a good education look like? Here I can only skim the surface—and refer readers to *Taking Religion Seriously Across the Curriculum,* in which Charles Haynes and I chart what needs to be done in some detail.

Obviously a great deal depends on the age of students. In elementary schools students should learn something of the relatively uncontroversial aspects of different religions—their traditions, holidays, symbols and a little about religious histories, for example. As students mature, they should be initiated into the conversation about truth and goodness that constitutes a good liberal education. Here a two-prong approach is required.

First, students should learn something about religious ways of thinking about any subject that is religiously controversial in the relevant courses. So, for example, a biology text should include a chapter in which scientific ways of understanding nature are contrasted with religious alternatives. Students should learn that the relationship of religion and science is controversial, and that while they will learn what most biologists believe to be the truth about nature, not everyone agrees.

Indeed, every text and course should provide students with historical and philosophical perspective on the subject at hand, establishing connections and tensions with other disciplines and domains of the culture, including religion.

This is not a balanced-treatment or equal-time requirement. Biology courses should continue to be biology courses and economics courses should continue to be economics courses. In any case, given their competence and training, biology and economics teachers are not likely to be prepared to deal with a variety of religious ways of approaching their subject. At most, they can provide a minimal fairness.

A robust fairness is possible only if students are required to study religious as well as secular ways of making sense of the world in some depth, in courses devoted to the study of religion.

A good liberal education should require at least one year-long high school course in religious studies (with other courses, I would hope, available as electives). The primary goal of such a course should be to provide students with a sufficiently intensive exposure to religious ways of thinking and living to enable them to actually understand religion (rather than simply know a few facts about religion). It should expose students to scriptural texts, but it also should use more recent primary sources that enable students to understand how contemporary theologians and writers within different traditions think about those subjects in the curriculum—morality, sexuality, history, nature, psychology and the economic world—that they will be taught to interpret in secular categories in their other courses.

Of course, if religion courses are to be offered, there must be teachers competent to teach them. Religious studies must become a certifiable field in public education, and new courses must not be offered or required until competent teachers are available.

Indeed, all teachers must have a much clearer sense of how religion relates to the curriculum and, more particularly, to their respective subjects. Major reforms in teacher education are necessary—as is a new generation of textbooks sensitive to religion.

Some educators will find it unrealistic to expect such reforms. Of course several decades ago textbooks and curricula said little about women and minority cultures. Several decades ago, few universities had departments of religious studies. Now multicultural education is commonplace and most universities have departments of religious studies. Things change.

Stemming an Exodus

No doubt some educators will find these proposals controversial, but they will be shortsighted if they do. Leaving religion out of the curriculum is also controversial. Indeed, because public schools don't take religion seriously many religious parents have deserted them and, if the Supreme Court upholds the legality of vouchers, as they may well do, the exodus will be much greater.

In the long run, the least controversial position is the one that takes everyone seriously. If public schools are to survive our culture wars, they must be built on common ground. But there can be no common ground when religious voices are left out of the curricular conversation.

It is religious conservatives, of course, who are most critical of public schooling—and the most likely to leave. But my argument is that public schooling doesn't take any religion seriously. It marginalizes all religion—liberal as well as conservative, Catholic as well as Protestant, Jewish, Muslim and Buddhist as well as Christian. Indeed, it contributes a great deal to the secularization of American culture—and this should concern any religious person.

But, in the end, this shouldn't concern religious people only. Religion should be included in the curriculum for three very powerful secular reasons. The lack of serious study of religion in public education is illiberal, unjust and unconstitutional.

Postnote

Parents rightfully want to pass on to their children their most deeply held beliefs. Many of these beliefs about what constitutes a good life, and what is a person's true nature, are theological questions that are embedded in their religious convictions. For a variety of reasons, many of which are touched on in this article, the public schools have ignored and marginalized religion. Besides the educational implications of this policy, the impact on the public support of public schools is beginning to show. America is a religious nation, founded on religious principles ("In God we trust" and "All men are created equal"). Also, about 80 percent of American adults describe themselves as belonging to some religion. It would seem, then, that the current condition of the two powerful educational influences on children, the media and the public school system, being areligious or antireligious is bound to have political consequences. Since parents can do little to punish Hollywood, the temptation to take out their resentments on the local, tax-supported schools is strong.

Discussion Questions

1. Professor Nord ends his essay with the words, "The lack of serious study of religion in public education is illiberal, unjust and unconstitutional." What is your reaction to this statement?
2. Has your previous school experience strengthened, undermined, or had no effect on your religious convictions?
3. What solutions to the problem he has outlined does Nord offer? Do you agree with them? Why? Why not?

Teaching Themes of Care

NEL NODDINGS

FOCUS Question

As you read this article, ask yourself whether our schools need to give more attention to caring as part of the curriculum and, if so, how such themes of caring could be implemented.

Some educators today—and I include myself among them—would like to see a complete reorganization of the school curriculum. We would like to give a central place to the questions and issues that lie at the core of human existence. One possibility would be to organize the curriculum around themes of care—caring for self, for intimate others, for strangers and global others, for the natural world and its nonhuman creatures, for the human-made world, and for ideas.[1]

A realistic assessment of schooling in the present political climate makes it clear that such a plan is not likely to be implemented. However, we can use the rich vocabulary of care in educational planning and introduce themes of care into regular subject-matter classes. In this article, I will first give a brief rationale for teaching themes of care; second, I will suggest ways of choosing and organizing such themes; and, finally, I'll say a bit about the structures required to support such teaching.

Why Teach Caring?

In an age when violence among schoolchildren is at an unprecedented level, when children are bearing children with little knowledge of how to care for them, when the society and even the schools often concentrate on materialistic messages, it may be unnecessary to argue that we should care more genuinely for our children and teach them to care. However, many otherwise reasonable people seem to believe that our educational problems consist largely of low scores on achievement tests. My contention is, first, that we should want more from our educational efforts than adequate academic achievement and, second, that we will not achieve even that meager success unless our children believe that they themselves are cared for and learn to care for others.

There is much to be gained, both academically and humanly, by including themes of care in our curriculum. First, such inclusion may well

---

Nel Noddings is among the leading figures in the field of Educational Philosophy. She is Professor of Philosophy and Education at Teachers College, Columbia University, and Lee L. Jacks Professor of Child Education Emerita at Stanford University.

expand our students' cultural literacy. For example, as we discuss in math classes the attempts of great mathematicians to prove the existence of God or to reconcile a God who is all good with the reality of evil in the world, students will hear names, ideas, and words that are not part of the standard curriculum. Although such incidental learning cannot replace the systematic and sequential learning required by those who plan careers in mathematically oriented fields, it can be powerful in expanding students' cultural horizons and in inspiring further study.

Second, themes of care help us to connect the standard subjects. The use of literature in mathematics classes, of history in science classes, and of art and music in all classes can give students a feeling of the wholeness in their education. After all, why should they seriously study five different subjects if their teachers, who are educated people, only seem to know and appreciate one?

Third, themes of care connect our students and our subjects to great existential questions. What is the meaning of life? Are there gods? How should I live?

Fourth, sharing such themes can connect us person-to-person. When teachers discuss themes of care, they may become real persons to their students and so enable them to construct new knowledge. Martin Buber put it this way:

> Trust, trust in the world, because this human being exists—that is the most inward achievement of the relation in education. Because this human being exists, meaninglessness, however hard pressed you are by it, cannot be the real truth. Because this human being exists, in the darkness the light lies hidden, in fear salvation, and in the callousness of one's fellow-man the great love.[2]

Finally, I should emphasize that caring is not just a warm, fuzzy feeling that makes people kind and likable. Caring implies a continuous search for competence. When we care, we want to do our very best for the objects of our care. To have as our educational goal the production of caring, competent, loving, and lovable people is not anti-intellectual. Rather, it demonstrates respect for the full range of human talents. Not all human beings are good at or interested in mathematics, science, or British literature. But all humans can be helped to lead lives of deep concern for others, for the natural world and its creatures, and for the preservation of the human-made world. They can be led to develop the skills and knowledge necessary to make positive contributions, regardless of the occupation they may choose.

Choosing and Organizing Themes of Care

Care is conveyed in many ways. At the institutional level, schools can be organized to provide continuity and support for relationships of care and trust.[3] At the individual level, parents and teachers show their caring through characteristic forms of attention: by cooperating in children's activities, by sharing their own dreams and doubts, and by providing carefully for the steady growth to the children in their charge. Personal manifestations of care are probably more important in children's lives than any particular curriculum or pattern of pedagogy.

However, curriculum can be selected with caring in mind. That is, educators can manifest their care in the choice of curriculum, and appropriately chosen curriculum can contribute to the growth of children as carers. Within each large domain of care, many topics are suitable for thematic units: in the domain of "caring for self," for example, we might consider life stages, spiritual growth, and what it means to develop an admirable character; in exploring the topic of caring for intimate others, we might include units on love, friendship, and parenting; under the theme of caring for strangers and global others, we might study war, poverty, and tolerance; in addressing the idea of caring for the human-made world, we might encourage competence with the machines that surround us and a real appreciation for the marvels of technology. Many other examples exist. Furthermore, there are at least two different ways to approach the development of such themes: units can be constructed by interdisciplinary teams, or themes can be identified by individual teachers and addressed periodically throughout a year's or semester's work.

The interdisciplinary approach is familiar in core programs, and such programs are becoming more and more popular at the middle school level. One key to a successful interdisciplinary unit is the degree of genuinely enthusiastic support it receives from the teachers involved. Too often, arbitrary or artificial groupings are formed, and teachers are forced to make contributions that they themselves do not value highly. For example, math and science teachers are sometimes automatically lumped together, and rich humanistic possibilities may be lost. If I, as a math teacher, want to include historical, biographical, and literary topics in my math lessons, I might prefer to work with English and social studies teachers. Thus it is important to involve teachers in the initial selection of broad areas for themes, as well as in their implementation.

Such interdisciplinary arrangements also work well at the college level. I recently received a copy of the syllabus for a college course titled "The Search for Meaning," which was co-taught by an economist, a university chaplain, and a psychiatrist.[4] The course is interdisciplinary, intellectually rich, and aimed squarely at the central questions of life.

At the high school level, where students desperately need to engage in the study and practice of caring, it is harder to form interdisciplinary teams. A conflict arises as teachers acknowledge the intensity of the subject-matter preparation their students need for further education. Good teachers often wish there were time in the day to co-teach unconventional topics of great importance, and they even admit that their students are not getting what they need for full personal development. But they feel constrained by the requirements of a highly competitive world and the structures of schooling established by that world.

Is there a way out of this conflict? Imaginative, like-minded teachers might agree to emphasize a particular theme in their separate classes. Such themes as war, poverty, crime, racism, or sexism can be addressed in almost every subject area. The teachers should agree on some core ideas related to caring that will be discussed in all classes, but beyond the central commitment to address themes of care, the topics can be handled in whatever way seems suitable in a given subject.

Consider, for example, what a mathematics class might contribute to a unit on crime. Statistical information might be gathered on the location and number of crimes, on rates for various kinds of crime, on the ages of offenders, and on the cost to society; graphs and charts could be constructed. Data on changes in crime rates could be assembled. Intriguing questions could be asked: Were property crime rates lower when penalties were more severe—when, for example, even children were hanged as thieves? What does an average criminal case cost by way of lawyers' fees, police investigation, and court processing? Does it cost more to house a youth in a detention center or in an elite private school?

None of this would have to occupy a full period every day. The regular sequential work of the math class could go on at a slightly reduced rate (e.g., fewer textbook exercises as homework), and the work on crime could proceed in the form of interdisciplinary projects over a considerable period of time. Most important would be the continual reminder in all classes that the topic is part of a larger theme of caring for strangers and fellow citizens. It takes only a few minutes to talk about what it means to live in safety, to trust one's neighbors, to feel secure in greeting strangers. Students should be told that metal detectors and security guards were not part of their parents' school lives, and they should be encouraged to hope for a safer and more open future. Notice the words I've used in this paragraph: caring, trust, safety, strangers, hope. Each could be used as an organizing theme for another unit of study.

English and social studies teachers would obviously have much to contribute to a unit on crime. For example, students might read *Oliver*

Twist, and they might also study and discuss the social conditions that seemed to promote crime in 19th-century England. Do similar conditions exist in our country today? The selection of materials could include both classic works and modern stories and films. Students might even be introduced to some of the mystery stories that adults read so avidly on airplanes and beaches, and teachers should be engaged in lively discussion about the comparative value of the various stories.

Science teachers might find that a unit on crime would enrich their teaching of evolution. They could bring up the topic of social Darwinism, which played such a strong role in social policy during the late 19th and early 20th centuries. To what degree are criminal tendencies inherited? Should children be tested for the genetic defects that are suspected of predisposing some people to crime? Are females less competent than males in moral reasoning? (Why did some scientists and philosophers think this was true?) Why do males commit so many more violent acts than females?

Teachers of the arts can also be involved. A unit on crime might provide a wonderful opportunity to critique "gangsta rap" and other currently popular forms of music. Students might profitably learn how the control of art contributed to national criminality during the Nazi era. These are ideas that pop into my mind. Far more various and far richer ideas will come from teachers who specialize in these subjects.

There are risks, of course, in undertaking any unit of study that focuses on matters of controversy or deep existential concern, and teachers should anticipate these risks. What if students want to compare the incomes of teachers and cocaine dealers? What if they point to contemporary personalities from politics, entertainment, business, or sports who seem to escape the law and profit from what seems to be criminal behavior? My own inclination would be to allow free discussion of these cases and to be prepared to counteract them with powerful stories of honesty, compassion, moderation, and charity.

An even more difficult problem may arise. Suppose a student discloses his or her own criminal activities? Fear of this sort of occurrence may send teachers scurrying for safer topics. But, in fact, any instructional method that uses narrative forms or encourages personal expression runs this risk. For example, students of English as a second language who write proudly about their own hard lives and new hopes may disclose that their parents are illegal immigrants. A girl may write passages that lead her teacher to suspect sexual abuse. A boy may brag about objects that he has "ripped off." Clearly, as we use these powerful methods that encourage students to initiate discussion and share their experiences, we must reflect on the ethical issues involved, consider appropriate responses to such issues, and prepare teachers to handle them responsibly.

Caring teachers must help students make wise decisions about what information they will share about themselves. On the one hand, teachers want their students to express themselves, and they want their students to trust in and consult them. On the other hand, teachers have an obligation to protect immature students from making disclosures that they might later regret. There is a deep ethical problem here. Too often educators assume that only religious fundamentalists and right-wing extremists object to the discussion of emotionally and morally charged issues. In reality, there is a real danger of intrusiveness and lack of respect in methods that fail to recognize the vulnerability of students. Therefore, as teachers plan units and lessons on moral issues, they should anticipate the tough problems that may arise. I am arguing here that it is morally irresponsible to simply ignore existential questions and themes of care; we must attend to them. But it is equally irresponsible to approach these deep concerns without caution and careful preparation.

So far I have discussed two ways of organizing interdisciplinary units on themes of care. In one, teachers actually teach together in teams; in the other, teachers agree on a theme and a central focus on care, but they do what they can, when they can, in their own classrooms. A variation on this second way—which is also open to teachers who have to work alone—is to choose several themes and weave them into regular course material over an entire semester or year. The particular themes will depend on the interests and preparation of each teacher.

For example, if I were teaching high school mathematics today, I would use religious/existential questions as a pervasive theme because the biographies of mathematicians are filled with accounts of their speculations on matters of God, other dimensions, and the infinite—and because these topics fascinate me. There are so many wonderful stories to be told: Descartes's proof of the existence of God, Pascal's famous wager, Plato's world of forms, Newton's attempt to verify Biblical chronology, Leibnitz' detailed theodicy, current attempts to describe a divine domain in terms of metasystems, and mystical speculations on the infinite.[5] Some of these stories can be told as rich "asides" in five minutes or less. Others might occupy the better part of several class periods.

Other mathematics teachers might use an interest in architecture and design, art, music, or machinery as continuing themes in the domain of "caring for the human-made world." Still others might introduce the mathematics of living things. The possibilities are endless. In choosing and pursuing these themes, teachers should be aware that they are both helping their students learn to care and demonstrating their own caring by sharing interests that go well beyond the demands of textbook pedagogy.

Still another way to introduce themes of care into regular classrooms is to be prepared to respond spontaneously to events that occur in the school or in the neighborhood. Older teachers have one advantage in this area: they probably have a greater store of experience and stories on which to draw. However, younger teachers have the advantage of being closer to their students' lives and experiences; they are more likely to be familiar with the music, films, and sports figures that interest their students.

All teachers should be prepared to respond to the needs of students who are suffering from the death of friends, conflicts between groups of students, pressure to use drugs or to engage in sex, and other troubles so rampant in the lives of today's children. Too often schools rely on experts—"grief counselors" and the like—when what children really need is the continuing compassion and presence of adults who represent constancy and care in their lives. Artificially separating the emotional, academic, and moral care of children into tasks for specially designated experts contributes to the fragmentation of life in schools.

Of course, I do not mean to imply that experts are unnecessary, nor do I mean to suggest that some matters should not be reserved for parents or psychologists. But our society has gone too far in compartmentalizing the care of its children. When we ask whose job it is to teach children how to care, an appropriate initial response is "Everyone's." Having accepted universal responsibility, we can then ask about the special contributions and limitations of various individuals and groups.

Supporting Structures

What kinds of schools and teacher preparation are required, if themes of care are to be taught effectively? First, and most important, care must be taken seriously as a major purpose of our schools; that is, educators must recognize that caring for students is fundamental in teaching and that developing people with a strong capacity for care is a major objective of responsible education. Schools properly pursue many other objectives—developing artistic talent, promoting multicultural understanding, diversifying curriculum to meet the academic and vocational needs of all students, forging connections with community agencies and parents, and so on. Schools cannot be single-purpose institutions. Indeed, many of us would argue that it is logically and practically impossible to achieve that single academic purpose if other purposes are not recognized and accepted. This contention is confirmed in the success stories of several inner-city schools.[6]

Once it is recognized that school is a place in which students are cared for and learn to care, that recognition should be powerful in guiding policy. In the late 1950s, schools in the U.S., under the guidance of James Conant and others, placed the curriculum at the top of the educational priority list. Because the nation's leaders wanted schools to provide high-powered courses in mathematics and science, it was recommended that small high schools be replaced by efficient larger structures complete with sophisticated laboratories and specialist teachers. Economies of scale were anticipated, but the main argument for consolidation and regionalization centered on the curriculum. All over the country, small schools were closed, and students were herded into larger facilities with "more offerings." We did not think carefully about schools as communities and about what might be lost as we pursued a curriculum-driven ideal.

Today many educators are calling for smaller schools and more family-like groupings. These are good proposals, but teachers, parents, and students should be engaged in continuing discussion about what they are trying to achieve through the new arrangements. For example, if test scores do not immediately rise, participants should be courageous in explaining that test scores were not the main object of the changes. Most of us who argue for caring in schools are intuitively quite sure that children in such settings will in fact become more competent learners. But, if they cannot prove their academic competence in a prescribed period of time, should we give up on caring and on teaching them to care? That would be foolish. There is more to life and learning than the academic proficiency demonstrated by test scores.

In addition to steadfastness of purpose, schools must consider continuity of people and place. If we are concerned with caring and community, then we must make it possible for students and teachers to stay together for several years so that mutual trust can develop and students can feel a sense of belonging in their "school-home."[7]

More than one scheme of organization can satisfy the need for continuity. Elementary school children can stay with the same teacher for several years, or they can work with a stable team of specialist teachers for several years. In the latter arrangement, there may be program advantages; that is, children taught by subject-matter experts who get to know them well over an extended period of time may learn more about the particular subjects. At the high school level, the same specialist teaching might work with students throughout their years in high school. Or, as Theodore Sizer has suggested, one teacher might teach two subjects to a group of 30 students rather than one subject to 60 students, thereby reducing the number of different adults with whom students interact each day.[8] In all the suggested arrangements, placements should be made by mutual consent whenever possible. Teachers and students who hate or distrust one another should not be forced to stay together.

A policy of keeping students and teachers together for several years supports caring in two essential ways: it provides time for the development of caring relations, and it makes teaching themes of care more feasible. When trust has been established, teachers and students can discuss matters that would be hard for a group of strangers to approach, and classmates learn to support one another in sensitive situations.

The structural changes suggested here are not expensive. If a high school teacher must teach five classes a day, it costs no more for three of these classes to be composed of continuing students than for all five classes to comprise new students—i.e., strangers. The recommended changes come directly out of a clear-headed assessment of our major aims and purposes. We failed to suggest them earlier because we had other, too limited, goals in mind.

I have made one set of structural changes sound easy, and I do believe that they are easily made. But the curricular and pedagogical changes that are required may be more difficult. High school textbooks rarely contain the kinds of supplementary material I have described, and teachers are not formally prepared to incorporate such material. Too often, even the people we regard as strongly prepared in a liberal arts major are unprepared to discuss the history of their subject, its relation to other subjects, the biographies of its great figures, its connections to the great existential questions, and the ethical responsibilities of those who work in that discipline. To teach themes of care in an academically effective way, teachers will have to engage in projects of self-education.

At present, neither liberal arts departments nor schools of education pay much attention to connecting academic subjects with themes of care. For example, biology students may learn something of the anatomy and physiology of mammals but nothing at all about the care of living animals; they may never be asked to consider the moral issues involved in the annual euthanasia of millions of pets. Mathematics students may learn to solve quadratic equations but never study what it means to live in a mathematicized world. In enlightened history classes, students may learn something about the problems of racism and colonialism but never hear anything about the evolution of childhood, the contributions of women in both domestic and public caregiving, or the connection between the feminization of caregiving and public policy. A liberal education that neglects matters that are central to a fully human life hardly warrants the name,[9] and a professional education that confines itself to technique does nothing to close the gaps in liberal education.

The greatest structural obstacle, however, may simply be legitimizing the inclusion of themes of care in the curriculum. Teachers in the early grades have long included such themes as a regular part of their work, and middle school educators are becoming more sensitive to developmental needs involving care. But secondary schools—where violence, apathy, and alienation are most evident—do little to develop the capacity to care. Today, even elementary teachers complain that the pressure to produce high test scores inhibits the work they regard as central to their mission: the development of caring and competent people. Therefore, it would seem that the most fundamental change required is one of attitude. Teachers can be very special people in the lives of children, and it should be legitimate for them to spend time developing relations of trust, talking with students about problems that are central to their lives, and guiding them toward greater sensitivity and competence across all the domains of care.

Notes

1. For the theoretical argument, see Nel Noddings, *The Challenge to Care in Schools* (New York: Teachers College Press, 1992); for a practical example and rich documentation, see Sharon Quint, *Schooling Homeless Children* (New York: Teachers College Press, 1994).
2. Martin Buber, *Between Man and Man* (New York: Macmillan, 1965), p. 98.
3. Noddings, chap. 12.
4. See Thomas H. Naylor, William H. Willimon, and Magdalena R. Naylor, *The Search for Meaning* (Nashville, Tenn.: Abingdon Press, 1994).
5. For many more examples, see Nel Noddings, *Educating for Intelligent Belief and Unbelief* (New York: Teachers College Press, 1993).
6. See Deborah Meier, "How Our Schools Could Be," *Phi Delta Kappan*, January 1995, pp. 369–73; and Quint, op. cit.
7. See Jane Roland Martin, *The Schoolhome: Rethinking Schools for Changing Families* (Cambridge, Mass.: Harvard University Press, 1992).
8. Theodore Sizer, *Horace's Compromise: The Dilemma of the American High School* (Boston: Houghton Mifflin, 1984).
9. See Bruce Wilshire, *The Moral Collapse of the University* (Albany: State University of New York Press, 1990).

Postnote

Getting over selfishness and self-preoccupation is a major task of one's early years. As Nel Noddings demonstrates in this article, schools have a responsibility to help children develop the habit of caring for others. She makes a strong case for giving this task a more prominent place in our educational planning.

As children grow older, however, they need to develop some sterner virtues to complement caring. They need to acquire self-discipline and self-control. They need to acquire the habit of persistence at hard tasks. They need, too, to learn how to strive for individual excellence and to compete against others without hostility. We could argue that both a strong individual and a strong nation need a balance of strengths. To pursue one strength, such as caring, without developing the full spectrum of human virtues, leaves both the individual and the nation incomplete.

Discussion Questions

1. Do you agree with the primacy given to caring by the author? Why or why not?
2. What obstacles does the author identify and what additional ones can you name that would stand in the way of implementing themes of care in the school curriculum?
3. What practical classroom suggestions to advance caring have you gleaned from this article?

Mining the Values in the Curriculum

KEVIN RYAN

FOCUS Question

Schools have recently witnessed a resurgence in attention given to character education. As you read this article, think about reasons for why character education is seeing this renewal of interest.

TERMS TO NOTE

Formal curriculum

Hidden curriculum

Tao

While the development of a child's character is clearly not the sole responsibility of the school, historically and legally schools have been major players in this arena. Young people spend much of their lives within school walls. There they will learn, either by chance or design, moral lessons about how people behave.

In helping students develop good character—the capacity to know the good, love the good, and do the good—schools should above all be contributing to a child's knowing what is good. But what is most worth knowing? And for what purpose? How do educators decide what to teach? Pressing concerns for ancient philosophers, these questions are even more demanding today as we struggle to make order out of our information-saturated lives. New dilemmas brought on by such developments as computers, doomsday weaponry, and lethal viruses challenge us daily.

What Is a Good Person?

Before curriculum builders can answer "What's most worth knowing?" we have to know "For what?" To be well adjusted to the world around us? To become wealthy and self-sufficient? To be an artist? With a little reflection, most of us would come to similar conclusions as our great philosophers and spiritual leaders: education should help us become wise and good people.

What constitutes a "good person" has paralyzed many sincere educators and noneducators. Because the United States is a multiracial, multiethnic nation, many educators despair of coming up with a shared vision of the good person to guide curriculum builders. Our founders and early educational pioneers saw in the very diverse, multicultural

Kevin Ryan is founder and director emeritus of the Center for the Advancement of Ethics and Character, School of Education, Boston University, Massachusetts. From Kevin Ryan, "Mining the Values in the Curriculum," *Educational Leadership,* November 1993, pp. 16–18. Reprinted with permission. The Association for Supervision and Curriculum Development is a worldwide community of educators advocating sound policies and sharing best practices to achieve the success of each learner. To learn more, visit ASCD at **www.ascd.org.**

American scene of the late 18th and early 19th centuries the clear need for a school system that would teach the civic virtues necessary to maintain our novel political and social experiment. They saw the school's role not only as contributing to a person's understanding of what it is to be good, but also as teaching the enduring habits required of a democratic citizen.

Yet the school's curriculum must educate more than just the citizen. Conway Dorsett recently suggested that a good curriculum respects and balances the need "to educate the 'three people' in each individual: the worker, the citizen, and the private person" (1993). Our schools must provide opportunities for students to discover what is most worth knowing, as they prepare, not only to be citizens, but also good workers and good private individuals.

The work of C. S. Lewis may provide us with the multicultural model of a good person that we are seeking. Lewis discovered that certain ideas about how one becomes a good person recur in the writing of ancient Egyptians, Babylonians, Hebrews, Chinese, Norse, Indians, and Greeks, and in Anglo-Saxon and American writings as well. Common values included kindness; honesty; loyalty to parents, spouses, and family members; an obligation to help the poor, the sick, and the less fortunate; and the right to private property. Some evils, such as treachery, torture, and murder, were considered worse than one's own death (1947).

Lewis called this universal path to becoming a good person by the Chinese name, "the Tao." Combining the wisdom of many cultures, this Tao could be our multicultural answer for how to live our lives, the basis for what is most worth knowing.

Over the years, teachers, curriculum specialists, and school officials have used the Tao, albeit unconsciously, to guide the work of schools. Translated into curriculum, the Tao guides schools to educate children to be concerned about the weak and those in need; to help others; to work hard and complete their tasks well and promptly, even when they do not want to; to control their tempers; to work cooperatively with others and practice good manners; to respect authority and other people's rights; to help resolve conflicts; to understand honesty, responsibility, and friendship; to balance pleasures with responsibilities; and to ask themselves and decide "What is the right thing to do?"

Most educators agree that our schools should teach these attitudes both in the formal and in the hidden curriculum.

The Formal Curriculum

The formal curriculum is usually thought of as the school's planned educational experiences—the selection and organization of knowledge and skills from the universe of possible choices. Of course, not all knowledge nor every skill contributes directly to knowing the good, but much of the subject matter of English and social studies is intimately connected to the Tao. Stories, historical figures, and events are included in the formal curriculum to illuminate the human condition. From them we can learn how to be a positive force in the lives of others, and we can also see the effects of a poorly lived life.

The men and women, real or fictitious, who we learn about in school are instruments for understanding what it is to be (or not to be) a good person. One of the strengths and attractions of good literature is its complexity. As students read, they learn about themselves and the world. For example, students come face-to-face with raw courage in the exploits of Harriet Tubman and further understand the danger of hate and racism through *The Diary of Anne Frank*. They glimpse in Edward Arlington Robinson's poem "Miniver Cheevy" the folly of storing up earthly treasures. They see in Toni Cade Bambera's "Your Blues Ain't Like Mine" the intrinsic dignity of each human being. They gain insight into the heart of a truly noble man, Atticus Finch, in *To Kill a Mockingbird*. They perceive the thorny relationships between the leader and the led by following the well-intended but failed efforts of Brutus in Shakespeare's *Julius Caesar*.

Our formal curriculum is a vehicle to teach the Tao, to help young people to come to know the good. But simply selecting the curriculum is not enough; like a vein of precious metal, the teacher and students must mine it together. To engage students in the lessons in human character and ethics contained in our history and literature without resorting to empty preaching and crude didacticism is the great skill of teaching.

The Hidden Curriculum

In addition to the formal curriculum, students learn from a hidden curriculum—all the personal and social instruction that they acquire from their day-to-day schooling. Much of what has been written about the hidden curriculum in recent decades has stressed that these school experiences often lead to students' loss of self-esteem, unswerving obedience to silly rules, and the suppression of their individuality. While true of some students and some schools, the hidden curriculum can lead either to negative or positive education.

Many of education's most profound and positive teachings can be conveyed in the hidden curriculum. If a spirit of fairness penetrates every corner of the school, children will learn to be fair. Through the service of teachers, administrators, and older students, students learn to be of service to others. By creating an atmosphere of high standards, the hidden curriculum can teach habits of accuracy and precision. Many aspects of school life, ranging from homework assignments to sporting events, can teach self-control and self-discipline.

While unseen, the hidden curriculum must be considered with the same seriousness as the written, formal curriculum. The everyday behavior of the faculty, staff, and other students cannot fail to have an impact on a student.

One school concerned with the hidden curriculum is Roxbury Latin, a fine academic high school in Boston. In the spring of 1992, an accredited team interviewed 27 students, ranging from 7th to 12th grade, asking them the same question, "What do you think is Roxbury Latin's philosophy of education?" Every one of the students came back with the same answer: "This school is most concerned about what kind of people we are becoming." What the review team did not know was that every September, the school's headmaster, Anthony Jarvis, assembles all the new students and delivers a short message:

> We want you to excel in academics and sports and the arts while you are here. But, remember this: we care much more about your characters, what kind of people you are becoming.

End of message. End of assembly. All indications are that the message is getting through.

Policies and Practices

A school that makes a positive impact on the character of young people helps children to know the Tao and make it part of their lives. Such a school has in place the following policies and practices.

- The school has a mission statement widely known by students, teachers, administrators, parents, and the entire school community.
- The school has a comprehensive program of service activities, starting in the early grades and requiring more significant contributions of time and energy in the later years of high school.
- School life is characterized by a high level of school spirit and healthy intergroup competition.
- The school has an external charity or cause (a local home for the elderly or educational fundraising for a Third World community) to which all members of the community contribute.
- The school has a grading and award system that does more than give lip service to character formation and ethics, but recognizes academic effort, good discipline, contributions to the life of the classroom, service to the school and the community, respect for others, and good sportsmanship.
- The school expects not only teachers but also the older students to be exemplars of high ethical standards.

- The school's classrooms and public areas display mottoes and the pictures of exemplary historical figures.
- The school has regular ceremonies and rituals that bring the community together to celebrate achievements of excellence in all realms: academic, athletic, artistic and ethical.[1]

Our students have a major task in life: to become individuals of character. Character education, then, is the central curriculum issue confronting educators. Rather than the latest fad, it is a school's oldest mission. Nothing is better for the human soul than to discuss excellence every day. The curriculum of our elementary and secondary schools should be the delivery system for this encounter with excellence.

Note

1. Several of these policies and procedures are elaborated in *Reclaiming Our Schools: A Handbook for Teaching Character, Academics, and Discipline*, by E. A. Wynne and K. Ryan (Columbus, Ohio: Merrill, 1992).

References

Dorsett, C. (March 1993). "Multicultural Education: Why We Need It and Why We Worry About It." *Network News and Views* 12, 3:31.

Lewis, C. S. (1947). *The Abolition of Man*. New York: Macmillan.

Author's note: I wish to acknowledge Catherine Kinsella Stutz of Boston University for her contributions to this article.

Postnote

C. S. Lewis, the late English scholar and writer of children's stories (e.g., *The Chronicles of Narnia* and others), used to tell a modern fable about a country that decided to abandon teaching mathematics because the curriculum was too crowded and no one was exactly sure of what to teach. Dropping mathematics from the school curriculum pleased students and teachers, as well as parents who were no longer embarrassed each night, struggling over their children's homework. All went well for several years, until shopkeepers began to complain that their clerks couldn't "do sums" and kept billing customers incorrectly. Passengers on trains and buses were furious because they were continually getting shortchanged by ticket collectors. And worst of all, politicians became frenzied because people could not fill out their tax forms properly. But still, no one thought to consider that mathematics was no longer in the curriculum. Lewis intended the fable as a parable about the failure to teach religion. Today, we might see parallels between the imaginary country's abandonment of mathematics and America's recent failure to consciously and directly teach character and ethical values.

Discussion Questions

1. What is the Tao? Should it be taught in American public schools? Why or why not?
2. Review Headmaster Anthony Jarvis's message to new students. Do you agree or disagree with it as the major purpose of schooling?
3. Some educators argue that schools can't help but teach character and ethical values. The question is whether they do it consciously and deliberately. What are the strongest arguments for and against character education in U.S. schools?

Part Five 5

Instruction

What should we teach? is the fundamental question. But next in importance is: How do we teach it? Instructional questions range from the very nature of students as learners to how to organize a third-grade classroom.

In this section, we present a palette of new and old ideas about how to organize classrooms and schools to meet the needs of new students and a new society. A number of the most high-profile topics in education—such as cooperative learning, classroom management, assessment, constructivism, and differentiated instruction are presented. It is important to realize, however, as you read about an instructional methodology or set of procedures, that each represents a view of what the teaching-learning process is and what students are like. So, as you read these articles, we urge you to probe for their foundational ideas.

Closing the Achievement Gap

KATI HAYCOCK

FOCUS Question

As you read this article, try to determine if the achievement gap between low-income students and middle-class students is due primarily to deficiencies in our educational system, or to socioeconomic factors beyond the school's control.

Terms to Note

Achievement gap

National Assessment of Educational Progress (NAEP)

There's been a lot of talk lately about the achievement gap that separates low-income and minority youngsters from other young Americans. For more than a generation, we focused on improving the education of poor and minority students. Not surprisingly, we made real gains. Between 1970 and 1988, the achievement gap between African American and white students was cut in half, and the gap separating Latinos and whites declined by one-third. That progress came to a halt around 1988, however, and since that time, the gaps have widened.

Although everybody wanted to take credit for narrowing the gap, nobody wanted to take responsibility for widening it. So, for a while, there was mostly silence.

But that is changing. Good. Because if we don't get the numbers out on the table and talk about them, we're never going to close the gap once and for all. I worry, though, about how many people head into discussions without accurate data. And I worry even more about how many education leaders have antiquated—and downright wrong—notions about the whys beneath the achievement gap.

I want to respond to both these worries by putting some crucial data on the table and by sharing what both research and experience teach us about how schools can close the gaps between groups of students. Most of the data are from standard national sources, including the National Center for Education Statistics (NCES) and the National Assessment of Educational Progress (NAEP), as well as from states and local school districts that have been unusually successful at educating poor and minority students.[1]

Kati Haycock is director of The Education Trust, 1725 K St. NW, Ste. 200, Washington, DC 20006. From Kati Haycock, "Closing the Achievement Gap," *Educational Leadership,* March 2001. Reprinted by permission. The Association for Supervision and Curriculum Development is a worldwide community of educators advocating sound policies and sharing best practices to achieve the success of each learner. To learn more, visit **www.ascd.org.**

Understanding Achievement Patterns

The performance of African American and Latino youngsters improved dramatically during the 1970s and 1980s. The 1990s, however, were another matter. In some subjects and at some grade levels, the gaps started growing; in others, they were stagnant (National Center for Education Statistics, 2001).

- Reading achievement among 17-year-old African Americans and Latinos climbed substantially through the 1970s and 1980s, but gaps separating them from other students widened somewhat during the 1990s.
- The patterns in mathematics achievement look similar for 13-year-olds, with the African American and white gap reaching its narrowest in 1990 and the Latino and white gap narrowing until 1992, and the gaps widening thereafter.

In 1999, by the end of high school

- Only 1 in 50 Latinos and 1 in 100 African American 17-year-olds can read and gain information from specialized text—such as the science section in the newspaper (compared to about 1 in 12 whites), and
- Fewer than one-quarter of Latinos and one-fifth of African Americans can read the complicated but less specialized text that more than half of white students can read.

The same patterns hold in math.

- About 1 in 30 Latinos and 1 in 100 African Americans can comfortably do multistep problem solving and elementary algebra, compared to about 1 in 10 white students.
- Only 3 in 10 African American and 4 in 10 Latino 17-year-olds have mastered the usage and computation of fractions, commonly used percents, and averages, compared to 7 in 10 white students.

By the end of high school, in fact, African American and Latino students have skills in both reading and mathematics that are the same as those of white students in 8th grade. Significant differences also persist in the rates at which different groups of students complete high school and in their postsecondary education experiences.

- In the 18- to 24-year-old group, about 90 percent of whites and 94 percent of Asians have either completed high school or earned a GED. Among African Americans, the rate drops to 81 percent; among Latinos, 63 percent.
- Approximately 76 percent of white graduates and 86 percent of Asian graduates go directly to college, compared to 71 percent of African American and 71 percent of Latino graduates.
- Young African Americans are only about half as likely as white students to earn a bachelor's degree by age 29; young Latinos are only one-third as likely as whites to earn a college degree (see Table 1).

What's Going On?

Over the past five years, staff members at the Education Trust have shared these and related data on the achievement gap with hundreds of audiences all over the United States. During that time, we've learned a lot about what people think is going on.

When we speak with adults, no matter where we are in the country, they make the same comments. "They're too poor." "Their parents don't care." "They come to school without an adequate breakfast." "They don't have enough books in the home." "Indeed, there aren't enough parents in the home." Their reasons, in other words, are always about the children and their families.

Young people, however, have different answers. They talk about teachers who often do not know the subjects that they are teaching. They talk about counselors who consistently underestimate their potential and place them in lower-level courses. They talk about principals who dismiss their concerns. And they talk about a curriculum and a set of expectations that feel so miserably low-level that they literally bore the students right out the school door.

TABLE 1

Highest Educational Attainment for Every 100 Kindergartners

AGES 15 TO 29	AFRICAN AMERICANS	ASIANS	LATINOS	WHITES
Graduate from high school	88	90	63	88
Complete at least some college	50	74	33	59
Obtain at least a bachelor's degree	16	51	10	28

Source: U.S. Census Bureau. (1998). Educational Attainment Detailed Tables, October CPS.

When we ask, "What about the things that the adults are always talking about—neighborhood violence, single-parent homes, and so on?"—the young people's responses are fascinating. "Sure, those things matter," they say. "But what hurts us more is that you teach us less."

The truth is that the data bear out what the young people are saying. It's not that issues like poverty and parental education don't matter. Clearly they do. But we take the students who have less to begin with and then systematically give them less in school. In fact, we give these students less of everything that we believe makes a difference. We do this in hundreds of different ways.

Let me be clear. It would help if changes were made outside of schools, too: if parents spent more time with their children, if poverty didn't crush so many spirits, and if the broader culture didn't bombard young people with so many destructive messages. But because both research and experience show that what schools do matters greatly, I'll concentrate on what works in education.

Lesson 1: Standards Are Key

Historically, we have not agreed on what U.S. students should learn at each grade level—or on what kind of work is good enough. These decisions have been left to individual schools and teachers. The result is a system that, by and large, doesn't ask much of most of its students. And we don't have to go far to find that out: Ask the nearest teenager. In survey after survey, young people tell us that they are not challenged in school.

The situation is worse in high-poverty and high-minority schools. For the past six years, our staff at the Education Trust has worked with teachers who are trying to improve the achievement levels of their students. But while we've been observing these high-poverty classrooms, we've also looked carefully at what happens there—what kinds of assignments teachers give, for example—compared to what happens in other classrooms.

We have come away stunned. Stunned, first, by how little is expected of students in high-poverty schools—how few assignments they get in a given school week or month. Stunned, second, by the low level of the few assignments that they do get. In high-poverty urban middle schools, for example, we see a lot of coloring assignments, rather than writing or mathematics assignments. Even at the high school level, we found coloring assignments. "Read *To Kill a Mockingbird,*" says the 11th grade English teacher, "and when you're finished, color a poster about it." Indeed, national data make it clear that we expect so little of students in high-poverty schools that we give them *A*s for work that would earn a *C* or *D* anywhere else.

Clear and public standards for what students should learn at benchmark grade levels are a crucial part of solving the problem. They are a guide—for teachers, administrators, parents, and students themselves—to what knowledge and skills students must master.

Kentucky was the first state to embrace standards-based reform. Ten years ago, the Kentucky legislature put out an ambitious set of learning goals and had the audacity to declare that all of its children—even the poorest—would meet those goals. Leaders in Kentucky are the first to acknowledge that they are not there yet. But their progress is clear and compelling. And poor children are, in fact, learning in all subjects. For example, in reading, 7 of the 20 top-performing elementary schools are high-poverty; in math, 8 of the top 20 are high-poverty; in writing, 13 of the top 20 are high-poverty.

Lesson 2: All Students Must Have a Challenging Curriculum

Standards won't make much of a difference, though, if they are not accompanied by a rigorous curriculum that is aligned with those standards. Yet in too many schools, some students are taught a high-level curriculum, whereas other students continue to be taught a low-level curriculum that is aligned with jobs that no longer exist.

Current patterns are clearest in high schools, where students who take more rigorous coursework learn more and perform better on tests. Indeed, the more rigorous courses they take, the better they do.

- In mathematics, students who complete the full college preparatory sequence perform much higher on the National Assessment of Educational Progress (NAEP) than those who complete only one or two courses.
- The reverse is true of watered-down, traditional "vocational" courses. The more vocational education courses students take, the lower their performance on the NAEP.
- Although some of these differences are clearly attributable to the fact that higher-scoring students are often assigned to tougher classes, careful research shows the positive impact of more-rigorous coursework even on formerly low-achieving students.

Since 1983, we've made progress in increasing the number of students who take a rigorous, college-preparatory curriculum. But the pace is not fast enough.

- Almost three-quarters of high school graduates go on to higher education, but only about half of them complete even a mid-level college-preparatory curriculum (four years of English and three years each of math, science, and social studies). If we also include two years of a foreign language and a semester of computer science, the numbers drop to about 12 percent. The numbers are worse for African Americans, Latinos, and low-income students.

These patterns are disturbing because the quality and intensity of high school coursework are the most important determinants of success in college—more important than class rank or scores on college admissions tests (Adelman, 1998). Curriculum rigor is also important for work-bound students (Bottoms, 1998).

A few years ago, the chancellor of the New York City schools required all 9th graders to take the Regents math and science exams. Though many people were worried that failure rates would be astronomical, in one year the number of Latinos in New York City who passed the Regents science exam tripled, and the number of African Americans who passed doubled. Other groups also had gains in science and mathematics. Did they *all* pass? No, they didn't. But as a principal friend of mine used to say, "At least they failed something worthwhile." And remember, these youngsters previously would never even have been given a chance to learn higher-order content.

Lesson 3: Students Need Extra Help

Ample evidence shows that almost all students can achieve at high levels if they are taught at high levels. But equally clear is that some students require more time and more instruction. It won't do, in other words, just to throw students into a high-level course if they can't even read the textbook.

One of the most frequent questions we are asked by stressed-out middle and high school teachers is "How am I supposed to get my students ready to pass the (fill-in-the-blank) grade test when they enter with 3rd grade reading skills and I have only my 35-minute period each day?"

The answer, of course, is "You can't." Especially when students are behind in foundational skills like reading and mathematics, we need to double or even triple the amount and quality of instruction that they get.

Around the United States, states and communities are wrestling with how best to provide those extras. Kentucky gives high-poverty schools extra funds every year to extend instruction in whatever way works best for their community: before school, after school, weekends, or summers. Maryland provides a wide range of assistance to students who are not on track to pass its new high school graduation test. And San Diego created more time, mostly within the regular school day, by doubling—even tripling—the amount of instructional time devoted to literacy and mathematics for low-performing students and by training *all* of its teachers.

Lesson 4: Teachers Matter a Lot

If students are going to be held to high standards, they need teachers who know the subjects and know how to teach the subjects. Yet large numbers of students, especially those who are poor or are members of minority groups, are taught by teachers who do not have strong backgrounds in the subjects they teach.

- In every subject area, students in high-poverty schools are more likely than other students to be taught by teachers without even a minor in the subjects they teach (see Figure 1).
- The differences are often greater in predominantly minority high schools. In math and science, for example, only about half the teachers in schools with 90 percent or greater minority enrollments meet even their states' minimum requirements to teach those subjects—far fewer than in predominantly white schools.
- The patterns are similar regardless of the measure of teacher qualifications—experience, certification, academic preparation, or performance on licensure tests. We take the students who most depend on their teachers for subject-matter learning and assign them teachers with the weakest academic foundations.

FIGURE 1

Percentage of Underqualified* Teachers in High School Classrooms

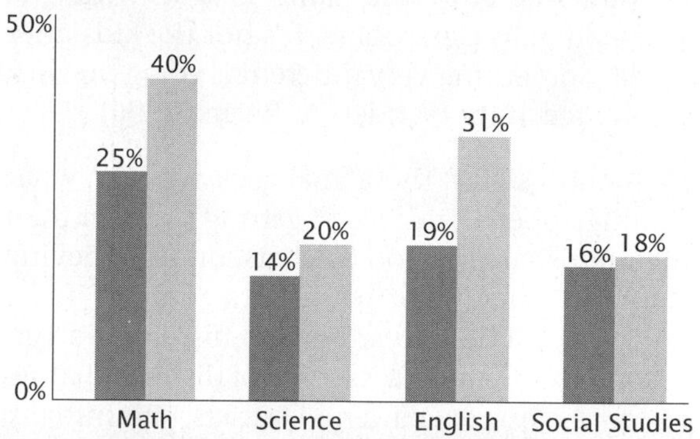

*Teachers who lack a major or minor in this field

Source: National Commission on Teaching and America's Future. (1996). *What matters most: Teaching for America's future.* New York: Author, p. 16.

A decade ago, we might have said that we didn't know how much this mattered. We believed that what students learned was largely a factor of their family income or parental education, not of what schools did. But recent research has turned these assumptions upside down. What schools do matters enormously. And what matters most is good teaching.

- Results from a recent Boston study of the effects teachers have on learning are fairly typical (Boston Public Schools, 1998). In just one academic year, the top third of teachers produced as much as six times the learning growth as the bottom third of teachers. In fact, 10th graders taught by the least effective teachers made nearly no gains in reading and even lost ground in math.
- Groundbreaking research in Tennessee and Texas shows that these effects are cumulative and hold up regardless of race, class, or prior

achievement levels. Some of the classrooms showing the greatest gains are filled with low-income students, some with well-to-do students. And the same is true with the small-gain classrooms. It's not the kids after all: Something very different is going on with the teaching (Sanders & Rivers, 1996).

Findings like these make us wonder what would happen if, instead of getting far fewer than their fair share of good teachers, underachieving students actually got more. In a study of Texas school districts, Harvard economist Ronald Ferguson (1998) found a handful of districts that reversed the normal pattern: Districts with initially high-performing (presumably relatively affluent) 1st graders hired from the bottom of the teacher pool, and districts with initially low-performing (presumably low-income) 1st graders hired from the upper tiers of the teacher pool. By the time their students reached high school, these districts swapped places in student achievement.

El Paso, Texas, is a community that has taken such research seriously. Eight years ago, despite the extraordinarily high poverty of their city, local education leaders set some very high standards for what their students should know and be able to do. Unlike other communities, though, they didn't stop there. At the University of Texas, El Paso, the faculty revamped how it prepared teachers. New elementary teachers, for example, take more than twice as much math and science as their predecessors. More to the point, though, the teachers of these courses are math and science professors who themselves participated in the standard-setting process and who know, at a much deeper level, what kinds of mathematical understanding the teachers need.

The community also organized a structure—the El Paso Collaborative—to provide support to existing teachers and to help them teach to the new standards. The collaborative sponsored intensive summer workshops, monthly meetings for teachers within content areas, and work sessions in schools to analyze student assignments against the standards. The three school districts also released 60 teachers to coach their peers.

The results are clear: no more low performing schools and increased achievement for *all groups of students,* with bigger increases among the groups that have historically been behind.

An Academic Core

El Paso and the other successful communities and states have a lot to teach us about how to raise overall achievement and close gaps. Each community, of course, does things a little bit differently. What we learn is the value of a relentless focus on the academic core. Clear and high standards. Assessments aligned with those standards. Accountability systems that demand results for all kinds of students. Intensive efforts to assist teachers in improving their practice. And extra instruction for students who need it.

Note

1. For state and national data on student achievement, visit the Education Trust Web site at **www.edtrust.org** and click the data icon.

References

Adelman, C. (1998). *Answers in the toolbox.* Washington, DC: U.S. Department of Education.

Boston Public Schools. (1998, March 9). High school restructuring. Boston: Author.

Bottoms, G. (1998). *High schools that work.* Atlanta, GA: Southern Regional Education Board.

Ferguson, R. (1998). Can schools narrow the black-white test score gap? In C. Jencks & M. Phillips (Eds.), *The black-white test score gap* (pp. 318–374). Washington, DC: The Brookings Institute.

National Center for Education Statistics. (2001). *NAEP summary data tables* [Online]. Washington, DC: U.S. Department of Education. Available: **http://nces.ed.gov/nationsreportcard**

Sanders, W., & Rivers, J. (1996). *Cumulative and residual effects of teachers on future student academic achievement.* Knoxville, TN: University of Tennessee Value-Added Research and Assessment Center.

Postnote

As Kati Haycock points out, many people see the academic achievement problem of students from urban poverty schools as being intractable. Poverty is too great . . . parents don't care . . . drugs and violence take a toll. Haycock shows that with high standards, a challenging curriculum, and good teachers, children from poverty schools can learn, and at surprisingly high levels. As Jaime Escalante demonstrated at Garfield High School in East Los Angeles, poor Latino youths could learn calculus well enough to score at high levels on AP exams. He set high standards and made serious demands on students. His success is celebrated in the Academy Award–nominated movie *Stand and Deliver.* Marva Collins, in Chicago, also demonstrated that poor African American children could learn a classical curriculum at high levels.

Discussion Questions

1. Was there anything in this article that surprised you? If so, what?

2. What does the author believe can be done to ensure that children in poverty have schools with highly qualified teachers?

3. In addition to the author's suggestions, what do you believe can be done to improve the quality of schools serving the urban poor?

The Key to Classroom Management

ROBERT J. MARZANO AND JANA S. MARZANO

FOCUS Question

As you read this article, note the teacher behaviors that establish effective teacher-student relationships—a key for effective classroom management and student achievement.

TERMS TO NOTE

Assertive behavior

Dominance

Today, we know more about teaching than we ever have before. Research has shown us that teachers' actions in their classrooms have twice the impact on student achievement as do school policies regarding curriculum, assessment, staff collegiality, and community involvement (Marzano, 2003a). We also know that one of the classroom teacher's most important jobs is managing the classroom effectively.

A comprehensive literature review by Wang, Haertel, and Walberg (1993) amply demonstrates the importance of effective classroom management. These researchers analyzed 86 chapters from annual research reviews, 44 handbook chapters, 20 government and commissioned reports, and 11 journal articles to produce a list of 228 variables affecting student achievement. They combined the results of these analyses with the findings from 134 separate meta-analyses. Of all the variables, classroom management had the largest effect on student achievement. This makes intuitive sense—students cannot learn in a chaotic, poorly managed classroom.

Research not only supports the importance of classroom management, but it also sheds light on the dynamics of classroom management. Stage and Quiroz's meta-analysis (1997) shows the importance of there being a balance between teacher actions that provide clear consequences for unacceptable behavior and teacher actions that recognize and reward acceptable behavior. Other researchers (Emmer, Evertson, & Worsham, 2003; Evertson, Emmer, & Worsham, 2003) have identified important components of classroom management, including beginning the school year with a positive emphasis on management; arranging the room in

Robert J. Marzano is a senior scholar at Mid-continent Research for Education and Learning in Aurora, Colorado, and an associate professor at Cardinal Stritch University in Milwaukee, Wisconsin. **Jana S. Marzano** is a licensed professional counselor in private practice in Centennial, Colorado. "The Key to Classroom Management," by Robert J. Marzano and Jana S. Marzano, *Educational Leadership,* September 2001, pp. 6–13. Reprinted by permission. The Association for Supervision and Curriculum Development is a worldwide community of educators advocating sound policies and sharing best practices to achieve the success of each learner. To learn more, visit ASCD at **www.ascd.org.**

a way conducive to effective management; and identifying and implementing rules and operating procedures.

In a recent meta-analysis of more than 100 studies (Marzano, 2003b), we found that the quality of teacher-student relationships is the keystone for all other aspects of classroom management. In fact, our meta-analysis indicates that on average, teachers who had high-quality relationships with their students had 31 percent fewer discipline problems, rule violations, and related problems over a year's time than did teachers who did not have high-quality relationships with their students.

What are the characteristics of effective teacher-student relationships? Let's first consider what they are not. Effective teacher-student relationships have nothing to do with the teacher's personality or even with whether the students view the teacher as a friend. Rather, the most effective teacher-student relationships are characterized by specific teacher behaviors: exhibiting appropriate levels of dominance; exhibiting appropriate levels of cooperation; and being aware of high-needs students.

Appropriate Levels of Dominance

Wubbels and his colleagues (Wubbels, Brekelmans, van Tartwijk, & Admiral, 1999; Wubbels & Levy, 1993) identify appropriate dominance as an important characteristic of effective teacher-student relationships. In contrast to the more negative connotation of the term *dominance* as forceful control or command over others, they define dominance as the teacher's ability to provide clear purpose and strong guidance regarding both academics and student behavior. Studies indicate that when asked about their preferences for teacher behavior, students typically express a desire for this type of teacher-student interaction. For example, in a study that involved interviews with more than 700 students in grades 4–7, students articulated a clear preference for strong teacher guidance and control rather than more permissive types of teacher behavior (Chiu & Tulley, 1997). Teachers can exhibit appropriate dominance by establishing clear behavior expectations and learning goals and by exhibiting assertive behavior.

Establish Clear Expectations and Consequences

Teachers can establish clear expectations for behavior in two ways: by establishing clear rules and procedures, and by providing consequences for student behavior.

The seminal research of the 1980s (Emmer, 1984; Emmer, Sanford, Evertson, Clements, & Martin, 1981; Evertson & Emmer, 1982) points to the importance of establishing rules and procedures for general classroom behavior, group work, seat work, transitions and interruptions, use of materials and equipment, and beginning and ending the period or the day. Ideally, the class should establish these rules and procedures through discussion and mutual consent by teacher and students (Glasser, 1969, 1990).

Along with well-designed and clearly communicated rules and procedures, the teacher must acknowledge students' behavior, reinforcing acceptable behavior and providing negative consequences for unacceptable behavior. Stage and Quiroz's research (1997) is instructive. They found that teachers build effective relationships through such strategies as the following:

- Using a wide variety of verbal and physical reactions to students' misbehavior, such as moving closer to offending students and using a physical cue, such as a finger to the lips, to point out inappropriate behavior.
- Cuing the class about expected behaviors through prearranged signals, such as raising a hand to indicate that all students should take their seats.
- Providing tangible recognition of appropriate behavior—with tokens or chits, for example.
- Employing group contingency policies that hold the entire group responsible for behavioral expectations.
- Employing home contingency techniques that involve rewards and sanctions at home.

Establish Clear Learning Goals

Teachers can also exhibit appropriate levels of dominance by providing clarity about the content and expectations of an upcoming instructional unit. Important teacher actions to achieve this end include

- Establishing and communicating learning goals at the beginning of a unit of instruction.
- Providing feedback on those goals.
- Continually and systematically revisiting the goals.
- Providing summative feedback regarding the goals.

The use of rubrics can help teachers establish clear goals. To illustrate, assume that a teacher has identified the learning goal "understanding and using fractions" as important for a given unit. That teacher might present students with the following rubric:

> 4 points. You understand the characteristics of fractions along with the different types. You can accurately describe how fractions are related to decimals and percentages. You can convert fractions to decimals and can explain how and why the process works. You can use fractions to understand and solve different types of problems.
>
> 3 points. You understand the basic characteristics of fractions. You know how fractions are related to decimals and percentages. You can convert fractions to decimals.
>
> 2 points. You have a basic understanding of the following, but have some small misunderstandings about one or more: the characteristics of fractions; the relationships among fractions, decimals, and percentages; how to convert fractions to decimals.
>
> 1 point. You have some major problems or misunderstandings with one or more of the following: the characteristics of fractions; the relationships among fractions, decimals, and percentages; how to convert fractions to decimals.
>
> 0 points. You may have heard of the following before, but you do not understand what they mean: the characteristics of fractions; the relationships among fractions, decimals, and percentages; how to convert fractions to decimals.

The clarity of purpose provided by this rubric communicates to students that their teacher can provide proper guidance and direction in academic content.

Exhibit Assertive Behavior

Teachers can also communicate appropriate levels of dominance by exhibiting assertive behavior. According to Emmer and colleagues, assertive behavior is

> the ability to stand up for one's legitimate rights in ways that make it less likely that others will ignore or circumvent them. (2003, p. 146)

Assertive behavior differs significantly from both passive behavior and aggressive behavior. These researchers explain that teachers display assertive behavior in the classroom when they

- Use assertive body language by maintaining an erect posture, facing the offending student but keeping enough distance so as not to appear threatening and matching the facial expression with the content of the message being presented to students.
- Use an appropriate tone of voice, speaking clearly and deliberately in a pitch that is slightly but not greatly elevated from normal classroom speech, avoiding any display of emotions in the voice.
- Persist until students respond with the appropriate behavior. Do not ignore an inappropriate behavior; do not be diverted by a student denying, arguing, or blaming, but listen to legitimate explanations.

Appropriate Levels of Cooperation

Cooperation is characterized by a concern for the needs and opinions of others. Although not the antithesis of dominance, cooperation certainly occupies a different realm. Whereas dominance focuses on the teacher as the driving force in the classroom, cooperation focuses on the students and teacher functioning as a team. The interaction of these two dynamics—dominance and cooperation—is a central force in effective teacher-student relationships. Several strategies can foster appropriate levels of cooperation.

Provide Flexible Learning Goals

Just as teachers can communicate appropriate levels of dominance by providing clear learning goals, they can also convey appropriate levels of cooperation by providing flexible learning goals. Giving students the opportunity to set their own objectives at the beginning of a unit or asking students what they would like to learn conveys a sense of cooperation. Assume, for example, that a teacher has identified the topic of fractions as the focus of a unit of instruction and has provided students with a rubric. The teacher could then ask students to identify some aspect of fractions or a related topic that they would particularly like to study. Giving students this kind of choicc, in addition to increasing their understanding of the topic, conveys the message that the teacher cares about and tries to accommodate students' interests.

Take a Personal Interest in Students

Probably the most obvious way to communicate appropriate levels of cooperation is to take a personal interest in each student in the class. As McCombs and Whisler (1997) note, all students appreciate personal attention from the teacher. Although busy teachers—particularly those at the secondary level—do not have the time for extensive interaction with all students, some teacher actions can communicate personal interest and concern without taking up much time. Teachers can

- Talk informally with students before, during, and after class about their interests.
- Greet students outside of school—for instance, at extracurricular events or at the store.
- Single out a few students each day in the lunchroom and talk with them.
- Be aware of and comment on important events in students' lives, such as participation in sports, drama, or other extracurricular activities.
- Compliment students on important achievements in and outside of school.
- Meet students at the door as they come into class; greet each one by name.

Use Equitable and Positive Classroom Behaviors

Programs like Teacher Expectations and Student Achievement emphasize the importance of the subtle ways in which teachers can communicate their interest in students (Kerman, Kimball, & Martin, 1980). This program recommends many practical strategies that emphasize equitable and positive classroom interactions with all students. Teachers should, for example,

- Make eye contact with each student. Teachers can make eye contact by scanning the entire room as they speak and by freely moving about all sections of the room.
- Deliberately move toward and stand close to each student during the class period. Make sure that the seating arrangement allows the teacher and students clear and easy ways to move around the room.
- Attribute the ownership of ideas to the students who initiated them. For instance, in a discussion a teacher might say, "Cecilia just added to Aida's idea by saying that. . . ."
- Allow and encourage all students to participate in class discussions and interactions. Make sure to call on students who do not commonly participate, not just those who respond most frequently.
- Provide appropriate wait time for all students to respond to questions, regardless of their past performance or your perception of their abilities.

Awareness of High-Needs Students

Classroom teachers meet daily with a broad cross-section of students. In general, 12–22 percent of all students in school suffer from mental, emotional, or behavioral disorders, and relatively few receive mental health services (Adelman & Taylor, 2002). The Association of School Counselors notes that 18 percent of students have special needs and require extraordinary interventions and treatments that go beyond the typical resources available to the classroom (Dunn & Baker, 2002).

Although the classroom teacher is certainly not in a position to directly address such severe problems, teachers with effective classroom management skills are aware of high-needs students and have a repertoire of specific techniques for meeting some of their needs (Marzano, 2003b). Table 1 summarizes five categories of high-needs students and suggests classroom strategies for each category and subcategory.

- *Passive* students fall into two subcategories: those who fear *relationships* and those who fear *failure.* Teachers can build strong relationships with these students by refraining from criticism, rewarding small successes, and creating a classroom climate in which students feel safe from aggressive people.
- The category of *aggressive* students comprises three subcategories: *hostile, oppositional,* and *covert.* Hostile students often have poor anger control, low capacity for empathy, and an

TABLE 1

Categories of High-Needs Students

CATEGORY	DEFINITIONS & SOURCE	CHARACTERISTICS	SUGGESTIONS
Passive	Behavior that avoids the domination of others or the pain of negative experiences. The child attempts to protect self from criticism, ridicule, or rejection, possibly reacting to abuse and neglect. Can have a biochemical basis, such as anxiety.	**Fear of relationships:** Avoids connection with others, is shy, doesn't initiate conversations, attempts to be invisible. **Fear of failure:** Gives up easily, is convinced he or she can't succeed, is easily frustrated, uses negative self-talk.	Provide safe adult and peer interactions and protection from aggressive people. Provide assertiveness and positive self-talk training. Reward small successes quickly. Withhold criticism.
Aggressive	Behavior that overpowers, dominates, harms, or controls others without regard for their well-being. The child has often taken aggressive people as role models. Has had minimal or ineffective limits set on behavior. Is possibly reacting to abuse and neglect. Condition may have a biochemical basis, such as depression.	**Hostile:** Rages, threatens, or intimidates others. Can be verbally or physically abusive to people, animals, or objects. **Oppositional:** Does opposite of what is asked. Demands that others agree or give in. Resists verbally or nonverbally. **Covert:** Appears to agree but then does the opposite of what is asked. Often acts innocent while setting up problems for others.	Describe the student's behavior clearly. Contract with the student to reward corrected behavior and set up consequences for uncorrected behavior. Be consistent and provide immediate rewards and consequences. Encourage and acknowledge extracurricular activities in and out of school. Give student responsibilities to help teacher or other students to foster successful experiences.

inability to see the consequences of their actions. Oppositional students exhibit milder forms of behavior problems, but they consistently resist following rules, argue with adults, use harsh language, and tend to annoy others. Students in the covert subcategory may be quite pleasant at times, but they are often nearby when trouble starts and they never quite do what authority figures ask of them. Strategies for helping aggressive students include creating behavior contracts and providing immediate rewards and consequences. Most of all, teachers must keep in mind that aggressive students, although they may appear highly resistant to behavior change, are still children who are experiencing a significant amount of fear and pain.

TABLE 1 (CONTINUED)

CATEGORY	DEFINITIONS & SOURCE	CHARACTERISTICS	SUGGESTIONS
Attention problems	Behavior that demonstrates either motor or attentional difficulties resulting from a neurological disorder. The child's symptoms may be exacerbated by family or social stressors or biochemical conditions, such as anxiety, depression, or bipolar disorders.	**Hyperactive:** Has difficulty with motor control, both physically and verbally. Fidgets, leaves seat frequently, interrupts, talks excessively. **Inattentive:** Has difficulty staying focused and following through on projects. Has difficulty with listening, remembering, and organizing.	Contract with the student to manage behaviors. Teach basic concentration, study, and thinking skills. Separate student in a quiet work area. Help the student list each step of a task. Reward successes; assign a peer tutor.
Perfectionist	Behavior that is geared toward avoiding the embarrassment and assumed shame of making mistakes. The child fears what will happen if errors are discovered. Has unrealistically high expectations of self. Has possibly received criticism or lack of acceptance while making mistakes during the process of learning.	Tends to focus too much on the small details of projects. Will avoid projects if unsure of outcome. Focuses on results and not relationships. Is self-critical.	Ask the student to make mistakes on purpose, then show acceptance. Have the student tutor other students.
Socially inept	Behavior that is based on the misinterpretation of nonverbal signals of others. The child misunderstands facial expressions and body language. Hasn't received adequate training in these areas and has poor role modeling.	Attempts to make friends but is inept and unsuccessful. Is forced to be alone. Is often teased for unusual behavior, appearance, or lack of social skills.	Teach the student to keep the appropriate physical distance from others. Teach the meaning of facial expressions, such as anger and hurt. Make suggestions regarding hygiene, dress, mannerisms, and posture.

Source: Marzano, R. J. (2003). *What works in schools: Translating research into action* (pp. 104–105). Alexandria, VA: ASCD.

- Students with *attention* problems fall into two categories: *hyperactive* and *inattentive.* These students may respond well when teachers contract with them to manage behaviors; teach them basic concentration, study, and thinking skills; help them divide tasks into manageable parts; reward their successes; and assign them a peer tutor.
- Students in the *perfectionist* category are driven to succeed at unattainable levels. They are self-critical, have low self-esteem, and feel inferior. Teachers can often help these students by encouraging them to develop more realistic standards, helping them to accept mistakes, and giving them opportunities to tutor other students.
- *Socially inept* students have difficulty making and keeping friends. They may stand too close and touch others in annoying ways, talk too much, and misread others' comments. Teachers can help these students by counseling them about social behaviors.

School may be the only place where many students who face extreme challenges can get their needs addressed. The reality of today's schools often demands that classroom teachers address these severe issues, even though this task is not always considered a part of their regular job.

In a study of classroom strategies (see Brophy, 1996; Brophy & McCaslin, 1992), researchers examined how effective classroom teachers interacted with specific types of students. The study found that the most effective classroom managers did not treat all students the same; they tended to employ different strategies with different types of students. In contrast, ineffective classroom managers did not appear sensitive to the diverse needs of students. Although Brophy did not couch his findings in terms of teacher-student relationships, the link is clear. An awareness of the five general categories of high-needs students and appropriate actions for each can help teachers build strong relationships with diverse students.

Don't Leave Relationships to Chance

Teacher-student relationships provide an essential foundation for effective classroom management—and classroom management is a key to high student achievement. Teacher-student relationships should not be left to chance or dictated by the personalities of those involved. Instead, by using strategies supported by research, teachers can influence the dynamics of their classrooms and build strong teacher-student relationships that will support student learning.

References

Adelman, H. S., & Taylor, L. (2002). School counselors and school reform: New directions. *Professional School Counseling, 5*(4), 235–248.

Brophy, J. E. (1996). *Teaching problem students.* New York: Guilford.

Brophy, J. E., & McCaslin, N. (1992). Teachers' reports of how they perceive and cope with problem students. *Elementary School Journal, 93,* 3–68.

Chiu, L. H. & Tulley, M. (1997). Student preferences of teacher discipline styles. *Journal of Instructional Psychology, 24*(3), 168–175.

Dunn, N. A., & Baker, S. B. (2002). Readiness to serve students with disabilities: A survey of elementary school counselors. *Professional School Counselors, 5*(4), 277–284.

Emmer, E. T. (1984). *Classroom management: Research and implications.* (R & D Report No. 6178). Austin, TX: Research and Development Center for Teacher Education, University of Texas. (ERIC Document Reproduction Service No. ED251448)

Emmer, E. T., Evertson, C. M., & Worsham, M. E. (2003). *Classroom management for secondary teachers* (6th ed.). Boston: Allyn and Bacon.

Emmer, E. T., Sanford, J. P., Evertson, C. M., Clements, B. S., & Martin, J. (1981). *The classroom management improvement study: An experiment in elementary school classrooms.* (R & D Report No. 6050). Austin, TX: Research and

Development Center for Teacher Education, University of Texas. (ERIC Document Reproduction Service No. ED226452)

Evertson, C. M., & Emmer, E. T. (1982). Preventive classroom management. In D. Duke (Ed.), *Helping teachers manage classrooms* (pp. 2–31). Alexandria, VA: ASCD.

Evertson, C. M., Emmer, E. T., & Worsham, M. E. (2003). *Classroom management for elementary teachers* (6th ed.). Boston: Allyn and Bacon.

Glasser, W. (1969). *Schools without failure.* New York: Harper and Row.

Glasser, W. (1990). *The quality school: Managing students without coercion.* New York: Harper and Row.

Kerman, S., Kimball, T., & Martin, M. (1980). *Teacher expectations and student achievement.* Bloomington, IN: Phi Delta Kappa.

Marzano, R. J. (2003a). *What works in schools.* Alexandria, VA: ASCD.

Marzano, R. J. (with Marzano, J. S., & Pickering, D. J.). (2003b). *Classroom management that works.* Alexandria, VA: ASCD.

McCombs, B. L., & Whisler, J. S. (1997). *The learner-centered classroom and school.* San Francisco: Jossey-Bass.

Stage, S. A., & Quiroz, D. R. (1997). A meta-analysis of interventions to decrease disruptive classroom behavior in public education settings. *School Psychology Review, 26*(3), 333–368.

Wang, M. C., Haertel, G. D., & Walberg, H. J. (1993). Toward a knowledge base for school learning. *Review of Educational Research, 63*(3), 249–294.

Wubbels, T., Brekelmans, M., van Tartwijk, J., & Admiral, W. (1999). Interpersonal relationships between teachers and students in the classroom. In H. C. Waxman & H. J. Walberg (Eds.), *New directions for teaching practice and research* (pp. 151–170). Berkeley, CA: McCutchan.

Wubbels, T., & Levy, J. (1993). *Do you know what you look like? Interpersonal relationships in education.* London: Falmer Press.

Postnote

No issue is of greater concern to beginning teachers than classroom management. New teachers worry that they may not be effective because of their inability to maintain discipline. The authors point out that being an effective teacher is not a function of your personality or being a friend to students. Rather, establishing effective teacher-student relationships is the key to effective management and instruction, and the authors identify specific teacher behaviors that characterize effective relationships: appropriate levels of dominance, appropriate levels of cooperation, and awareness of high-needs students. Work on developing these behaviors, and you will experience greater success and fewer discipline problems. There are a number of excellent books, based on research, to guide you in becoming a good classroom manager, some of which are mentioned in the references of this article.

Discussion Questions

1. Think of some teachers you have had who could not maintain discipline in their classrooms. What made them ineffective in managing the classroom?
2. Conversely, think of some teachers who were very effective in maintaining order and had good relations with students. What made them so effective?
3. Are there any points in the article with which you disagree? Are there other aspects to effective classroom management that you think should have been discussed? If so, what are they?

Engaging Students: What I Learned Along the Way

ANNE WESCOTT DODD

FOCUS Question

As you read this article, try to envision other ways that you can personalize instruction and engage students.

TERMS TO NOTE

Extrinsic motivation

Intrinsic motivation

When I was a first-year teacher, I was concerned with survival. My attempts to control students led to many power struggles from which both the students and I emerged discouraged or defeated. These feelings were not conducive to teaching or learning.

I wish someone had told me then that knowing my students was as important as knowing my subject. I didn't realize until much later that to motivate and engage students, teachers must create a classroom environment in which every student comes to believe, "I count, I care, and I can."

The best advice I could give to beginning teachers now is the secret of the fox in Antoine de Saint-Exupéry's *The Little Prince* (1943): "What is essential is invisible to the eye." What teachers need most to know about students is hidden; unless they develop a trusting relationship with their students, teachers will not have access to the knowledge they need either to solve classroom problems or to motivate students.

I Wish I Had Known . . .

As a novice teacher, I didn't realize that a seemingly logical response to tardiness—detention—did not take into account students' reasons for being late, some of which were valid. If I had allowed students to explain why they were late before telling them to stay after school, I might have prevented hurt feelings and hostility. A 6th grader who hides from an 8th grade bully in the bathroom until the coast is clear shouldn't be treated the same as someone who chats too long with a friend in the hall.

I wish I had found out sooner that simply asking students to tell me their side of the story could make such a positive difference in their

---

A former secondary school teacher and principal, **Anne Wescott Dodd** is chair of the department of education at Bates College, Lewiston, Maine. From Anne Wescott Dodd, "Engaging Students: What I Learned Along the Way," *Educational Leadership,* September 1995, pp. 65–67. Reprinted by permission. The Association for Supervision and Curriculum Development is a worldwide community of educators advocating sound policies and sharing best practices to achieve the success of each learner. To learn more, visit ASCD at **www.ascd.org.**

attitudes. When I tried to understand situations from their points of view, students were willing to consider them from my vantage point. These conversations opened the way for us to jointly resolve problems and did a great deal to build trust.

But, most of all, I wish someone had told me that understanding students' perspectives was the best way to foster engagement and learning. Like other novice teachers, I wasted a great deal of time searching for recipes to make learning more fun. Only much later did I find out that the most effective veteran teachers reflect on their classroom experience (Dodd 1994). Instead of thinking in terms of making learning *fun* (extrinsic motivation), they look for ways to make assignments and activities *engaging* (intrinsic motivation). Although they may express these ideas differently, effective teachers know that to become engaged, students must have some feelings of *ownership*—of the class or the task—and *personal power*—a belief that what they do will make a difference.

From the Student's Perspective

Because beginning teachers often focus on what they will do or require students to do, they often overlook some important principles about learning.

First, learning is personal and idiosyncratic. Thus, it helps to view students as individuals (Marina, Hector, and Scott) rather than as groups (Period 1 Class, Sophomore English). Consider that even when there is only *one* right answer, there are *many* ways students can misunderstand. Thus, teachers need to find out how students individually make sense of any lesson or explanation.

Second, every student behavior—from the most outrageous classroom outburst to the more common failure to do homework—is a way of trying to communicate something the student cannot express any other way or doesn't consciously understand. Punishing the behavior without learning its possible cause does nothing to solve a problem and, in fact, may intensify it. Because the student may interpret detention or a zero in the gradebook as additional evidence that the teacher is uncaring, he or she may become less inclined to do future assignments.

Third, teachers should never assume, because too often they can be wrong. Low grades on tests do not necessarily mean that students haven't studied. Some students may have been confused when the material was covered in class. Incomplete homework isn't always a sign that students don't care. A student may be too busy helping care for younger siblings to finish assignments. The student who sleeps in class or responds angrily to a teacher's question may be exhausted, ill, or unable to cope with personal difficulties.

By inviting students to share their feelings and perceptions, teachers can establish positive relationships with them and thus minimize classroom problems. But even more important, they will discover how to modify their teaching methods and personalize assignments in ways that engage students in learning.

Getting Students to Open Up

There are many ways that teachers can get to know their students. Here are a few useful strategies.

- *On the first day of class, give students a questionnaire to complete, or invite them to write you a letter about themselves*. The sooner you learn something about your students, the better equipped you will be to build personal relationships and address their concerns. By knowing which students consider themselves math phobics, poor writers, or reluctant readers, you can find ways to make sure they have a chance to feel good about a small success right away.
- *Ask students who have not done the homework or who have come late to class to write a note explaining why.* Establish this requirement on the first day of class, but don't present it as a punishment. Students should see these notes as an opportunity to communicate privately with the teacher. As trust is established, students will feel freer about sharing personal

concerns that affect their classroom performance. Even if you can do nothing to solve a problem a student has at home, you may be able to suggest better ways to deal with it.

- *Ask students to write learning logs from time to time. Logs are especially useful at the end of a class in which new material has been introduced.* For example, "Briefly summarize what you learned today, and note any questions you have." Don't grade the logs; just read them quickly to note common problems to address in the next class, and list names of students who may need extra help. Taking the time to write a short comment or just draw a smiley face on each student's log before returning them also shows students that you care about them as people and want them to learn.

  The same kind of assignment can be added to a homework paper or as the last question on a test: "What did you find confusing about this assignment?" or "How do you feel you did on this test? What would have helped you do even better?"

- *Invite students to help you solve classroom problems, such as a lack of classroom participation or students' constantly interrupting one another.* Even if you wish to discuss the issue with the students, having them write their ideas down first will make the discussion more productive. Although students may not suggest any workable solutions to the problem, their comments can often lead to a strategy for solving the problem. Perhaps even more important, students will feel empowered.

Writing works because every student gets to share what he or she thinks, misunderstands, or needs to know. Teachers who depend on students to say aloud what they don't understand may be fooled into thinking that everything is okay when there are no questions. Many students, however, are reluctant to speak up in front of their peers for fear of looking foolish. Unfortunately, teachers don't have time for individual conversations with each student, but writing can be an invaluable substitute.

How to Personalize Assignments

All of the information teachers gather from students will be of little use if students do not have any opportunity to personalize their learning. While the idea of having students doing a variety of things at the same time may appear chaotic, there are some easy ways to try out this approach to see how it works.

- Give students some choice of topics for research, books for reading, and planning methods for projects or papers (outlining, webbing, or focused free writing).
- Let students prepare a lesson and teach their classmates. (If teachers want students to be exposed to several aspects of the Civil War or three different novels, small groups of students learn about one aspect of the war or one of the novels in depth and the others in less detail. This approach is one way of solving the depth versus coverage dilemma all teachers wrestle with.)
- Encourage students who understand a concept to help those who don't understand. This is a productive way of channeling students' desire to be social.
- Allow students to choose how to demonstrate their understanding. (One student might draw the solution to a math problem or the plot in a novel; another might write about it; someone else might videotape a real-life connection for it.)
- Give students permission occasionally to work on homework or routine assignments together. They can learn from one another, and a test will show what each has learned.

Reflection Is the Key

Trying out a practice offers fertile ground for reflection even if the trial fails. As teachers look for new ways to engage students in learning, they are likely to find that the search itself will re-energize their teaching.

Recipes are useful for beginners who haven't yet had time to analyze how and why students engage in learning, but reflection is the key to understanding why some recipes work better than others. That understanding depends on knowing more about students' perceptions. As teachers learn more about how students think and feel, they will be able to create classes where students have fun *because* they are engaged in learning in diverse, purposeful, and meaningful ways.

References

de Saint-Exupéry, A. (1943). *The Little Prince.* New York: Harcourt Brace.

Dodd, A. W. (1994). "Learning to Read the Classroom: The Stages Leading to Teacher Self-Actualization." *Northwords* 4: 13–26.

Postnote

This article is based on a fundamental principle of good teaching: engaging the student in his or her own learning. Along with the principle, the author offers several practical suggestions and adds to our large literature on the subject of good teaching—a literature that has been evolving for centuries. But why, if the principle is so fundamental, do so few teachers follow it?

One possible explanation is that beginning teachers quite naturally lack confidence. They are on the defensive and, as a result, are "self-focused": "Will I survive?" "Will they accept me as a teacher, or are they seeing through this teacher-act I am performing?" "Will they like me?" "Can they tell how little I really know about what I'm doing?" The great majority of teachers pass out of this phase, but some survive by imposing their will, their lesson plans, their expectations (or some downsized version of their original expectations) on the class. And that habit of mind, focusing on *their* plans, takes over and becomes for them "teaching." To put it another way, "engaging" students involves risks, and many new teachers are not ready to take risks.

Discussion Questions

1. Can you recall teachers who engaged you in your own learning? How did they do it?
2. The article's author, Anne Wescott Dodd, offers four suggestions for "getting students to open up." What are they? What suggestions can you add?
3. What are some of the problems and risks in this approach?

Students Need Challenge, Not Easy Success

MARGARET M. CLIFFORD

FOCUS Question

What are the psychological principles advocated by the author that enhance the likelihood of motivating students to succeed?

TERMS TO NOTE

Formative evaluation
Intrinsic motivation
Summative evaluation

Hundreds of thousands of apathetic students abandon their schools each year to begin lives of unemployment, poverty, crime, and psychological distress. According to Hahn (1987), "Dropout rates ranging from 40 to 60 percent in Boston, Chicago, Los Angeles, Detroit, and other major cities point to a situation of crisis proportions." The term *dropout* may not be adequate to convey the disastrous consequences of the abandonment of school by children and adolescents; *educational suicide* may be a far more appropriate label.

School abandonment is not confined to a small percentage of minority students, or low ability children, or mentally lazy kids. It is a systemic failure affecting the most gifted and knowledgeable as well as the disadvantaged, and it is threatening the social, economic, intellectual, industrial, cultural, moral, and psychological well-being of our country. Equally disturbing are students who sever themselves from the flow of knowledge while they occupy desks, like mummies.

Student apathy, indifference, and under-achievement are typical precursors of school abandonment. But what causes these symptoms? Is there a remedy? What will it take to stop the waste of our intellectual and creative resources?

To address these questions, we must acknowledge that educational suicide is primarily a motivational problem—not a physical, intellectual, financial, technological, cultural, or staffing problem. Thus, we must turn to motivational theories and research as a foundation for examining this problem and for identifying solutions.

Curiously enough, modern theoretical principles of motivation do not support certain widespread practices in education. I will discuss four such discrepancies and offer suggestions for resolving them.

At the time this article was written, **Margaret M. Clifford** was professor emeritus of educational psychology, College of Education, University of Iowa, Iowa City. "Students Need Challenge, Not Easy Success" by Margaret M. Clifford, *Educational Leadership,* 48, 1:32–36. Reprinted with permission of the Association for Supervision and Curriculum Development and the author. The Association for Supervision and Curriculum Development is a worldwide community of educators advocating sound policies and sharing best practices to achieve the success of each learner. To learn more, visit ASCD at **www.ascd.org.**

Moderate Success Probability Is Essential to Motivation

The maxim, "Nothing succeeds like success," has driven educational practice for several decades. Absolute success for students has become the means *and* the end of education: It has been given higher priority than learning, and it has obstructed learning.

A major principle of current motivation theory is that tasks associated with a moderate probability of success (50 percent) provide maximum satisfaction (Atkinson 1964). Moderate probability of success is also an essential ingredient of intrinsic motivation (Lepper and Greene 1978, Csikszentmihalyi 1975, 1978). We attribute the success we experience on easy tasks to task ease; we attribute the success we experience on extremely difficult tasks to luck. Neither type of success does much to enhance self-image. It is only success at moderately difficult or truly challenging tasks that we explain in terms of personal effort, well-chosen strategies, and ability; and these explanations give rise to feelings of pride, competence, determination, satisfaction, persistence, and personal control. Even very young children show a preference for tasks that are just a bit beyond their ability (Danner and Lonky 1981).

Consistent with these motivational findings, learning theorists have repeatedly demonstrated that moderately difficult tasks are a prerequisite for maximizing intellectual development (Fischer 1980). But despite the fact that moderate challenge (implying considerable error-making) is essential for maximizing learning and optimizing motivation, many educators attempt to create error-proof learning environments. They set minimum criteria and standards in hopes of ensuring success for all students. They often reduce task difficulty, overlook errors, de-emphasize failed attempts, ignore faulty performances, display "perfect papers," minimize testing, and reward error-free performance.

It is time for educators to replace easy success with challenge. We must encourage students to reach beyond their intellectual grasp and allow them the privilege of learning from mistakes. There must be a tolerance for error-making in every classroom, and gradual success rather than continual success must become the yardstick by which learning is judged. Such transformations in educational practices will not guarantee the elimination of educational suicide, but they are sure to be one giant step in that direction.

External Constraints Erode Motivation and Performance

Intrinsic motivation and performance deteriorate when external constraints such as surveillance, evaluation by others, deadlines, threats, bribes, and rewards are accentuated. Yes, even rewards are a form of constraint! The reward giver is the General who dictates rules and issues orders; rewards are used to keep the troops in line.

Means-end contingencies, as exemplified in the statement, "If you complete your homework, you may watch TV" (with homework being the means and TV the end), are another form of external constraint. Such contingencies decrease interest in the first task (homework, the means) and increase interest in the second task (TV, the end) (Boggiano and Main 1986).

Externally imposed constraints, including material rewards, decrease task interest, reduce creativity, hinder performance, and encourage passivity on the part of students—even preschoolers (Lepper and Hodell 1989)! Imposed constraints also prompt individuals to use the "minimax strategy"—to exert the minimum amount of effort needed to obtain the maximum amount of reward (Kruglanski et al. 1977). Supportive of these findings are studies showing that autonomous behavior—that which is self-determined, freely chosen, and personally controlled—elicits high task interest, creativity, cognitive flexibility, positive emotion, and persistence (Deci and Ryan 1987).

Unfortunately, constraint and lack of student autonomy are trademarks of most schools. Federal and local governments, as well as teachers, legislate academic requirements; impose guidelines; create rewards systems; mandate behavioral contracts; serve warnings of expulsion; and use rules, threats, and punishments as routine problem-solving strategies. We can legislate school attendance and the conditions for obtaining a diploma, but we cannot legislate the development of intelligence, talent, creativity, and intrinsic motivation—resources this country desperately needs.

It is time for educators to replace coercive, constraint-laden techniques with autonomy-supportive techniques. We must redesign instructional and evaluation materials and procedures so that every assignment, quiz, text, project, and discussion activity not only allows for, but routinely *requires,* carefully calculated decision making on the part of students. Instead of minimum criteria, we must define multiple criteria (levels of minimum, marginal, average, good, superior, and excellent achievement), and we must free students to choose criteria that provide optimum challenge. Constraint gives a person the desire to escape; freedom gives a person the desire to explore, expand, and create.

Prompt, Specific Feedback Enhances Learning

A third psychological principle is that specific and prompt feedback enhances learning, performance, and motivation (Ilgen et al. 1979, Larson 1984). Informational feedback (that which reveals correct responses) increases learning (Ilgen and Moore 1987) and also promotes a feeling of increased competency (Sansone 1986). Feedback that can be used to improve future performance has powerful motivational value.

Sadly, however, the proportion of student assignments or activities that are promptly returned with informational feedback tends to be low. Students typically complete an assignment and then wait one, two, or three days (sometimes weeks) for its return. The feedback they do get often consists of a number or letter grade accompanied by ambiguous comments such as "Is this your best?" or "Keep up the good work." Precisely what is good or what needs improving is seldom communicated.

But, even if we could convince teachers of the value of giving students immediate, specific, informational feedback, our feedback problem would still be far from solved. How can one teacher provide 25 or more students immediate feedback on their tasks? Some educators argue that the solution to the feedback problem lies in having a tutor or teacher aide for every couple of students. Others argue that adequate student feedback will require an increased use of computer technology. However, there are less expensive alternatives. First, answer keys for students should be more plentiful. Resource books containing review and study activities should be available in every subject area, and each should be accompanied by a key that is available to students.

Second, quizzes and other instructional activities, especially those that supplement basic textbooks, should be prepared with "latent image" processing. With latent image paper and pens, a student who marks a response to an item can watch a hidden symbol emerge. The symbol signals either a correct or incorrect response, and in some instances a clue or explanation for the response is revealed. Trivia and puzzle books equipped with this latent image, immediate feedback process are currently being marketed at the price of comic books.

Of course, immediate informational feedback is more difficult to provide for composition work, long-term projects, and field assignments. But this does not justify the absence of immediate feedback on the learning activities and practice exercises that are aimed at teaching concepts, relationships, and basic skills. The mere availability of answer keys and latent image materials would probably elicit an amazing amount of self-regulated learning on the part of many students.

Moderate Risk Taking Is a Tonic for Achievement

A fourth motivational research finding is that moderate risk taking increases performance, persistence, perceived competence, self-knowledge, pride, and satisfaction (Deci and Porac 1978,

Harter 1978, Trope 1979). Moderate risk taking implies a well-considered choice of an optimally challenging task, willingness to accept a moderate probability of success, and the anticipation of an outcome. It is this combination of events (which includes moderate success, self-regulated learning, and feedback) that captivates the attention, interest, and energy of card players, athletes, financial investors, lottery players, and even juvenile video arcade addicts.

Risk takers continually and freely face the probability of failing to attain the pleasure of succeeding under specified odds. From every risk-taking endeavor—whether it ends in failure or success—risk takers learn something about their skill and choice of strategy, and what they learn usually prompts them to seek another risk-taking opportunity. Risk taking—especially moderate risk taking—is a mind-engaging activity that simultaneously consumes and generates energy. It is a habit that feeds itself and thus requires an unlimited supply of risk-taking opportunities.

Moderate risk taking is likely to occur under the following conditions.

- The success probability for each alternative is clear and unambiguous.
- Imposed external constraints are minimized.
- Variable payoff (the value of success increases as risk increases) in contrast to fixed payoff is available.
- The benefits of risk taking can be anticipated.

My own recent research on academic risk taking with grade school, high school, and college students generally supports these conclusions. Students do, in fact, freely choose more difficult problems (a) when the number of points offered increases with the difficulty level of problems, (b) when the risk-taking task is presented within a game or practice situation (i.e., imposed constraint or threat is minimized), and (c) when additional opportunities for risk taking are anticipated (relatively high risk taking will occur on a practice exercise when students know they will be able to apply the information learned to an upcoming test). In the absence of these conditions we have seen students choose tasks that are as much as one-and-a-half years below their achievement level (Clifford 1988). Finally, students who take moderately high risks express high task interest even though they experience considerable error making.

In summary, risk-taking opportunities for students should be (a) plentiful, (b) readily available, (c) accompanied by explicit information about success probabilities, (d) accompanied by immediate feedback that communicates competency and error information, (e) associated with payoffs that vary with task difficulty, (f) relatively free from externally imposed evaluation, and (g) presented in relaxing and nonthreatening environments.

In today's educational world, however, there are few opportunities for students to engage in academic risk taking and no incentives to do so. Choices are seldom provided within tests or assignments, and rarely are variable payoffs made available. Once again, motivational theory, which identifies risk taking as a powerful source of knowledge, motivation, and skill development, conflicts with educational practice, which seeks to minimize academic risk at all costs.

We must restructure materials and procedures to encourage moderate academic risk taking on the part of students. I predict that if we fill our classrooms with optional academic risk-taking materials and opportunities so that all students have access to moderate risks, we will not only lower our educational suicide rate, but we will raise our level of academic achievement. If we give students the license to take risks and make errors, they will likely experience genuine success and the satisfaction that accompanies it.

Using Risk Can Ensure Success

Both theory and research evidence lead to the prediction that academic risk-taking activities are a powerful means of increasing the success of our educational efforts. But how do we get students to take risks on school-related activities? Students will choose risk over certainty when the consequences of the former are more satisfying and informative. Three basic conditions are needed to ensure such outcomes.

- First, students must be allowed to freely select from materials and activities that vary in difficulty and probability of success.
- Second, as task difficulty increases, so too must the payoffs for success.
- Third, an environment tolerant of error making and supportive of error correction must be guaranteed.

The first two conditions can be met rather easily. For example, on a 10-point quiz, composed of six 1-point items and four 2-point items, students might be asked to select and work only 6 items. The highest possible score for such quizzes is 10 and can be obtained only by correctly answering the four 2-point items and any two 1-point items. Choice and variable payoff are easily built into quizzes and many instructional and evaluation activities.

The third condition, creating an environment tolerant of error making and supportive of error correction, is more difficult to ensure. But here are six specific suggestions.

First, teachers must make a clear distinction between formative evaluation activities (tasks that guide instruction during the learning process) and summative evaluation activities (tasks used to judge one's level of achievement and to determine one's grade at the completion of the learning activity). Practice exercises, quizzes, and skill-building activities aimed at acquiring and strengthening knowledge and skills exemplify formative evaluation. These activities promote learning and skill development. They should be scored in a manner that excludes ability judgments, emphasizes error detection and correction, and encourages a search for better learning strategies. Formative evaluation activities should generally provide immediate feedback and be scored by students. It is on these activities that moderate risk taking is to be encouraged and is likely to prove beneficial.

Major examinations (unit exams and comprehensive final exams) exemplify summative evaluation; these activities are used to determine course grades. Relatively low risk taking is to be expected on such tasks, and immediate feedback may or may not be desirable.

Second, formative evaluation activities should be far more plentiful than summative. If, in fact, learning rather than grading is the primary object of the school, the percentage of time spent on summative evaluation should be small in comparison to that spent on formative evaluation (perhaps about 1:4). There should be enough formative evaluation activities presented as risk-taking opportunities to satisfy the most enthusiastic and adventuresome learner. The more plentiful these activities are, the less anxiety-producing and aversive summative activities are likely to be.

Third, formative evaluation activities should be presented as optional; students should be enticed, not mandated, to complete these activities. Enticement might be achieved by (a) ensuring that these activities are course-relevant and varied (e.g., scrambled outlines, incomplete matrices and graphs, exercises that require error detection and correction, quizzes); (b) giving students the option of working together; (c) presenting risk-taking activities in the context of games to be played individually, with competitors, or with partners; (d) providing immediate, informational, nonthreatening feedback; and (e) defining success primarily in terms of improvement over previous performance or the amount of learning that occurs during the risk-taking activity.

Fourth, for every instructional and evaluation activity there should be at least a modest percentage of content (10 percent to 20 percent) that poses a challenge to even the best students completing the activity. Maximum development of a country's talent requires that *all* individuals (a) find challenge in tasks they attempt, (b) develop tolerance for error making, and (c) learn to adjust strategies when faced with failure. To deprive the most talented students of these opportunities is perhaps the greatest resource-development crime a country can commit.

Fifth, summative evaluation procedures should include "retake exams." Second chances will not only encourage risk taking but will provide good reasons for students to study their incorrect responses made on previous risk-taking tasks. Every error made on an initial exam and subsequently corrected on a second chance represents real learning.

Sixth, we must reinforce moderate academic risk taking instead of error-free performance or excessively high or low risk taking. Improvement scores, voluntary correction of errors, completion of optional risk-taking activities—these are behaviors that teachers should recognize and encourage.

Toward a New Definition of Success

We face the grim reality that our extraordinary efforts to produce "schools without failure" have not yielded the well-adjusted, enthusiastic, self-confident scholars we anticipated. Our efforts to mass-produce success for every individual in every educational situation have left us with cheap reproductions of success that do not even faintly represent the real thing. This overdose of synthetic success is a primary cause of the student apathy and school abandonment plaguing our country.

To turn the trend around, we must emphasize error tolerance, not error-free learning; reward error correction, not error avoidance; ensure challenge, not easy success. Eventual success on challenging tasks, tolerance for error making, and constructive responses to failure are motivational fare that school systems should be serving up to all students. I suggest that we engage the skills of researchers, textbook authors, publishers, and educators across the country to ensure the development and marketing of attractive and effective academic risk-taking materials and procedures. If we convince these experts of the need to employ their creative efforts toward this end, we will not only stem the tide of educational suicide, but we will enhance the quality of educational success. We will witness self-regulated student success and satisfaction that will ensure the intellectual, creative, and motivational well-being of our country.

References

Atkinson, J. W. (1964). *An Introduction to Motivation.* Princeton, N.J.: Van Nostrand.

Boggiano, A. K., and D. S. Main. (1986). "Enhancing Children's Interest in Activities Used as Rewards: The Bonus Effect." *Journal of Personality and Social Psychology* 51: 1116–1126.

Clifford, M. M. (1988). "Failure Tolerance and Academic Risk Taking in Ten- to Twelve-Year-Old Students." *British Journal of Educational Psychology* 58: 15–27.

Csikszentmihalyi, M. (1975). *Beyond Boredom and Anxiety.* San Francisco: Jossey-Bass.

Csikszentmihalyi, M. (1978). "Intrinsic Rewards and Emergent Motivation." In *The Hidden Costs of Reward,* edited by M. R. Lepper and D. Greene. Hillsdale, N.J.: Lawrence Erlbaum Associates.

Danner, F. W., and D. Lonky. (1981). "A Cognitive-Developmental Approach to the Effects of Rewards on Intrinsic Motivation." *Child Development* 52: 1043–1052.

Deci, E. L., and J. Porac. (1978). "Cognitive Evaluation Theory and the Study of Human Motivation." In *The Hidden Costs of Reward,* edited by M. R. Lepper and D. Greene. Hillsdale, N.J.: Lawrence Erlbaum Associates.

Deci, E. L., and R. M. Ryan. (1987). "The Support of Autonomy and the Control of Behavior." *Journal of Personality and Social Psychology* 53: 1024–1037.

Fischer, K. W. (1980). "Learning as the Development of Organized Behavior." *Journal of Structural Learning* 3: 253–267.

Hahn, A. (1987). "Reaching Out to America's Dropouts: What to Do?" *Phi Delta Kappan* 69: 256–263.

Harter, S. (1978). "Effective Motivation Reconsidered: Toward a Developmental Model." *Human Development* 1: 34–64.

Ilgen, D. R., and C. F. Moore. (1987). "Types and Choices of Performance Feedback." *Journal of Applied Psychology* 72: 401–406.

Ilgen, D. R., C. D. Fischer, and M. S. Taylor. (1979). "Consequences of Individual Feedback on Behavior in Organizations." *Journal of Applied Psychology* 64: 349–371.

Kruglanski, A., C. Stein, and A. Riter. (1977). "Contingencies of Exogenous Reward and Task Performance: On the 'Minimax' Strategy in Instrumental Behavior." *Journal of Applied Social Psychology* 2: 141–148.

Larson, J. R., Jr. (1984). "The Performance Feedback Process: A Preliminary Model." *Organizational Behavior and Human Performance* 33: 42–76.

Lepper, M. R., and D. Greene. (1978). *The Hidden Costs of Reward.* Hillsdale, N.J.: Lawrence Erlbaum Associates.

Lepper, M. R., and M. Hodell. (1989). "Intrinsic Motivation in the Classroom." In *Motivation in Education, Vol. 3,* edited by C. Ames and R. Ames. New York: Academic Press.

Sansone, C. (1986). "A Question of Competence: The Effects of Competence and Task Feedback on Intrinsic Motivation." *Journal of Personality and Social Psychology* 51: 918–931.

Trope, Y. (1979). "Uncertainty Reducing Properties of Achievement Tasks." *Journal of Personality and Social Psychology* 37: 1505–1518.

Postnote

In the 1980s, educators and their many critics recognized that our schools were failing many of our students and that our students were failing many of our schools. An avalanche of reports, books, television specials, and columns lambasted the schools' performance. In response, standards have been raised, graduation requirements increased, and more rigorous courses of study implemented.

However, as an old adage says, "You can lead a horse to water, but you can't make it drink." Vast numbers of students still commit "educational suicide," and student apathy, indifference, and underachievement are widespread. Margaret Clifford's remedy first takes a realistic look at the mismatch between the student and the school and then suggests quite tangible modifications to match the student's motivational system with the goals of schooling.

Discussion Questions

1. This article pinpoints student motivation as a major source of school problems. Do you agree with this assessment? Why or why not?
2. What are the most important remedies Clifford offers for our schools' ills? In your judgment, will these remedies solve the problem?
3. What is the author's new definition of *success*? Do you agree with it? Why or why not?

You *Can* Teach for Meaning

JAY McTIGHE, ELLIOTT SEIF, AND GRANT WIGGINS

FOCUSQuestion

As you read this article, think of how teaching "for meaning" differs from "covering content."

TERMS TO NOTE

Content standards
Rubric
Teaching for meaning
TIMSS

Teaching is more than covering content, learning is more than merely taking in, and assessment is more than accurate recall. Meaning must be made, and understanding must be earned. Students are more likely to make meaning and gain understanding when they link new information to prior knowledge, relate facts to "big ideas," explore essential questions, and apply their learning in new contexts.

Consider the following classroom scenarios (Tharp, Estrada, & Yamauchi, 2000). A 6th grade teacher asks students to collect data from home on the height and weight of various family members. Students discuss the following questions in groups: How could we represent these data? What is the most effective way? Students decide on specific approaches and share them with the class. A spirited discussion takes place on the best approach.

A 4th grade teacher asks students to explore the Eskimo culture through research and discussion. Using the textbook and multiple resources, the class tackles the following question: What makes Eskimo life similar to and different from your life? Students define and describe ideas about Eskimo life, using a graphic organizer to make connections between concepts and facts. In small groups, they develop a project on an aspect of Eskimo life, conduct research, organize data, and draw conclusions that compare Eskimo life with their own lives. The teacher has shared a rubric identifying the key features of successful project work. She regularly collects samples of student work to provide feedback and offer suggestions for improvement.

Jay McTighe is director of the Maryland Assessment Consortium, a statewide collaborative of school districts. **Elliott Seif** is an educational consultant from Philadelphia, Pennsylvania. **Grant Wiggins** is President of Authentic Education, located in Hopewell, New Jersey. "You Can Teach for Meaning," by Jay McTighe, Elliott Seif, and Grant Wiggins, *Educational Leadership,* September 2004, pp. 26–30. Reprinted by permission. The Association for Supervision and Curriculum Development is a worldwide community of educators advocating sound policies and sharing best practices to achieve the success of each learner. To learn more, visit ASCD at **www.ascd.org.**

These two examples illustrate a curricular and instructional approach that we call *teaching for meaning and understanding*. This approach embodies five key principles:

- Understanding big ideas in content is central to the work of students.
- Students can only find and make meaning when they are asked to inquire, think at high levels, and solve problems.
- Students should be expected to apply knowledge and skills in meaningful tasks within authentic contexts.
- Teachers should regularly use thought-provoking, engaging, and interactive instructional strategies.
- Students need opportunities to revise their assignments using clear examples of successful work, known criteria, and timely feedback.

Teachers who regularly use this approach center their planning on three recurring questions that should be at the heart of any serious education reform: What are the big ideas and core processes that students should come to understand? What will teachers look for as evidence that students truly understand the big ideas and can apply their knowledge and skills in meaningful and effective ways? What teaching strategies will help students make meaning of curriculum content while avoiding the problems of aimless coverage and activity-oriented instruction?

Such an approach to teaching and learning is more apt to engage the learner and yield meaningful, lasting learning than traditional fact-based and procedure-based lecture, recitation, or textbook instruction. Yet when well-intentioned teachers and administrators are asked to put these ideas into practice, it is not uncommon to hear a chorus of *Yes, but*'s. The message? Teaching for meaning is fine in the abstract, but such ideas are impractical in the real world of content standards and high-stakes testing. The current focus on state and local content standards, related testing programs, No Child Left Behind, and accountability have strengthened the view that we must use more traditional teaching approaches to produce high levels of achievement.

Ironically, a key lever in the standards-based reform strategy—the use of high-stakes external tests—has unwittingly provided teachers with a rationalization for avoiding or minimizing the need to teach for meaning and in-depth understanding. Teachers are more likely to spend time practicing for the test, covering many facts and procedures and using traditional lecture and recitation methods in the hope that more students will become proficient.

Two key *Yes, but*'s interfere with the promise of teaching for meaning: Yes, but . . . we have to teach to the state or national test. Yes, but . . . we have too much content to cover. Both are misconceptions.

Misconception Number 1: We Have to Teach to the Test.

Many educators believe that instructing and assessing for understanding are incompatible with state mandates and standardized tests. Although they rarely offer research to support this claim, these educators imply that teachers are stuck teaching to the test against their will. They would teach for meaning, if they could. The implicit assumption is that teachers can only safeguard or raise test scores by covering tested items and practicing the test format. By implication, there is no time for the kind of in-depth and engaging instruction that helps students make meaning and deepens their understanding of big ideas.

We contend that teachers can best raise test scores over the long haul by teaching the key ideas and processes contained in content standards in rich and engaging ways: by collecting evidence of student understanding of that content through robust local assessments rather than one-shot standardized testing; and by using engaging and effective instructional strategies that help students explore core concepts through inquiry and problem solving.

What evidence supports these contentions? A summary of the last 30 years of research on learning and cognition shows that learning for meaning leads to greater retention and use of information and ideas (Bransford, Brown, & Cocking, 2000). One avenue of this research explored the differences between novices and experts in various fields. Psychologists learned that experts have more than just a lot of facts in their heads: They actually *think* differently than novices do. According to the researchers, "expertise requires something else: a well-organized knowledge of concepts, principles, and procedures of inquiry" (p. 239). This finding suggests that students, to become knowledgeable and competent in a field of study, should develop not only a solid foundation of factual knowledge but also a conceptual framework that facilitates meaningful learning.

Data from the Trends in International Mathematics and Science Study (TIMSS) also challenge the premise that teaching to the test is the best way to achieve higher scores. TIMSS tested the mathematics and science achievement of students in 42 countries at three grade levels (4, 8, and 12). Although the outcomes of TIMSS are well known—U.S. students do not perform as well as students in most other industrialized countries (Martin, Mullis, Gregory, Hoyle, & Shen, 2000)—the results of its less publicized teaching studies offer additional insights. In an exhaustive analysis of mathematics instruction in Japan, Germany, and the United States, Stigler and Hiebert (1999) present striking evidence of the benefits of teaching for meaning and understanding. In Japan, a high-achieving country, mathematics teachers state that their primary aim is to develop conceptual understanding in their students. Compared with teachers in the United States, they cover less ground in terms of discrete topics, skills, or pages in a textbook, but they emphasize problem-based learning in which students derive and explain rules and theorems, thus leading to deeper understanding. A recent TIMSS analysis of data from seven countries indicates that all high-achieving countries use a percentage of their mathematics problems to help students explore concepts and make connections, whereas U.S. teachers tend to emphasize algorithmic plug-in of procedures instead of genuine reasoning and problem solving (Hiebert et al., 2003; Stigler & Hiebert, 2004).

Compatible findings emerged in an ambitious study of 24 restructured schools—eight elementary, eight middle, and eight high schools—in 16 states (Newmann & Associates, 1996). The research showed that students improved their performance in mathematics and social studies and that inequalities among high- and low-performing students diminished when the curriculum included sustained examination of a few important topics rather than superficial coverage of many topics; when teachers framed instruction around challenging and relevant questions; and when students were required to provide oral and written explanations for their responses.

Two additional studies of factors influencing student achievement were conducted in Chicago Public Schools. Smith, Lee, and Newmann (2001) examined test scores from more than 100,000 students in grades 2–8 and surveys from more than 5,000 teachers in 384 Chicago elementary schools. The study compared teachers who used interactive teaching methods with those who used noninteractive teaching methods. The researchers then looked at subsequent achievement in reading and mathematics.

The researchers described interactive instruction methods as follows:

> Teachers . . . create situations in which students . . . ask questions, develop strategies for solving problems, and communicate with one another. Students are often expected to explain their answers and discuss how they arrived at their conclusions. These teachers usually assess students' mastery of knowledge through discussions, projects, or tests that demand explanation and extended writing. Students work on applications or interpretations of the material to develop new or deeper understandings of a given topic. Such assignments may take several days to complete. Students in interactive classrooms are often encouraged to choose the questions or topics they wish to study within an instructional unit designed by the teacher. Different students may be working on different tasks during the same class period. (p. 12)

The study found clear and consistent correlations between interactive teaching methods and higher levels of learning and achievement.

In a related study (Newmann, Bryk, & Nagaoka, 2001), researchers in Chicago systematically collected and analyzed classroom writing and mathematics assignments given in grades 3, 6, and 8 by randomly selected schools and control schools for a three-year period. Researchers rated assignments according to the degree to which the work required authentic intellectual activity, which the researchers defined as "construction of knowledge, through the use of disciplined inquiry, to produce discourse, products, or performances that have value beyond school" (pp. 14–15). The study concluded that students who received assignments requiring more challenging intellectual work also achieved greater-than-average gains on the Iowa Tests of Basic Skills in reading and mathematics and demonstrated higher performance in reading, mathematics, and writing on the Illinois Goals Assessment Program.

Misconception Number 2: We Have Too Much Content to Cover.

Teachers from kindergarten to graduate school wrestle with the realities of the information age and the knowledge explosion: There is simply too much information to cover. In theory, the standards movement promised a solution to the problem of information overload by identifying curricular priorities. Content standards were intended to specify what is most important for students to know and be able to do, thus providing a much-needed focus and set of priorities for curriculum, instruction, and assessment. In practice, however, content standards committees at the national, state, and district levels often worked in isolation to produce overly ambitious lists of "essentials" for their disciplines. Rather than streamlining the curriculum, the plethora of standards added to the coverage problem, especially at the elementary level, where teachers must teach standards and benchmarks in multiple subjects (Marzano & Kendall, 1998). The matter is further complicated by teachers' propensity to focus on overloaded textbooks as the primary resource for addressing their obligations to the content standards. U.S. textbook publishers try to cover the waterfront to appease state textbook adoption committees, national subject-area organizations, and various special-interest groups. Project 2061's study of mathematics and science textbooks (Kesidou & Roseman, 2002; Kulm, 1999) found few commercial texts that were not "a mile wide and an inch deep."

Teachers confronted with thick textbooks and long lists of content standards may understandably come to the erroneous conclusion that they must cover huge amounts of content. They feel that "if it is in my book, it has to be taught." The perceived need to "cover" is typically based on two implicit assumptions that we think are unfounded. The first assumption is that if a teacher covers specific material—that is, talks about it and assigns some work—students will adequately learn it for tests. The second is that teachers should typically address standards one at a time in lesson planning.

We know of no research that supports the idea that a coverage mode of instruction increases achievement on external tests. In fact, current research suggests that "uncoverage"—focusing on fewer topics and core understandings—is more likely to increase student achievement. The TIMSS research that demonstrated lower achievement scores for U.S. students found that U.S. mathematics and science curriculums were unfocused and included too many topics (Schmidt, McKnight, & Raizen, 1997). In contrast, high-achieving countries offered fewer topics at each level, coupled with more coherent and focused content. This concentrated focus enabled teachers and students to gradually build more complex understandings in mathematics, to delve deeply into subject matter, and to attain higher levels of achievement (Schmidt, 2004; Schmidt, Houang, & Cogan, 2002).

Recent studies on mathematics reform curriculums described by Senk and Thompson (2003) also support using an "uncoverage" approach to improve student achievement. All the mathematics reform curriculums that Senk and Thompson studied were designed to help students understand fundamental mathematical concepts and ideas. Longitudinal data from middle schools show that students using understanding-based mathematics curriculums demonstrated superior performance in both nonroutine problem solving and mathematical skills. Other studies on high school mathematics reform programs showed that students in these programs developed additional skills and understandings while not falling behind on traditional content.

The second misconception—that content standards and benchmarks should be addressed one at a time through targeted lessons—is often reinforced by state and national standardized tests that typically sample the standards and benchmarks one at a time through decontextualized items. Thus, the presentation of both tests and standards documents often misleadingly suggests that teachers should teach to standards one bit at a time. From this point of view, teachers certainly do not have enough time to address all standards.

We suggest clustering discrete standards under an umbrella of big ideas. This approach renders teaching more efficient while applying a principle of effective learning derived from research. Bransford and colleagues suggest that

> Experts' knowledge is not simply a list of facts and formulas that are relevant to the domain; instead, their knowledge is organized around core concepts or "big ideas" that guide their thinking about the domain. (2000, p. 24)

Similarly, the use of complex performance assessments enables students to apply facts, concepts, and skills contained in multiple standards in a more meaningful way while enabling educators to assess for true understanding, not just for recall or recognition.

Implications

Teaching for meaning and understanding leads to more lasting and significant student learning. Although we have made a strong case against two widely held objections to this approach, we realize that educators must test, debate, and explore these claims in their respective settings.

We therefore encourage you to conduct ongoing action research at the school and district levels that compares the kind of curriculum, assessment, and instruction described here with teaching that focuses on covering content or practicing for standardized accountability tests. Are students more engaged when you frame content in provocative essential questions? Do students show increased understanding when they have some choice in the manner in which they demonstrate their knowledge? Is performance on traditional assessments compromised when learners have the opportunity to apply their knowledge in authentic situations? Do inquiry-based and problem-based instruction energize teachers?

Let the results speak for themselves. We hope that by "uncovering" some of these unfounded claims, we will encourage educators and district leaders to take a more proactive stance and focus on what they *can* do to improve learning in today's standards-based world.

References

Bransford, J., Brown, A., & Cocking, R. (Eds.). (2000). *How people learn: Brain, mind, experience, and school.* Washington, DC: National Research Council.

Hiebert, J., Gallimore, R., Garnier, H., Givvin, K. B., Hollingsworth, H., Jacobs, J., et al. (2003). *Teaching mathematics in seven countries: Results from the TIMSS 1999 video study* (NCES 2003–013). Washington, DC: U.S. Department of Education.

Kesidou, S., & Roseman, J. E. (2002). How well do middle school science programs measure up? *Journal of Research in Science Teaching, 39*(6), 522–549.

Kulm, G. (1999). Evaluating mathematics textbooks. *Basic Education, 43*(9), 6–8.

Martin, M., Mullis, I., Gregory, K., Hoyle, C., & Shen, C. (2000). *Effective schools in science and mathematics: IEA's Third International*

Mathematics and Science Study. Boston: International Study Center, Lynch School of Education, Boston College.

Marzano, R. J., & Kendell, J. S. (1998). *Awash in a sea of standards*. Aurora, CO: Mid-continent Research for Education and Learning.

Newmann, F., & Associates. (1996). *Authentic achievement: Restructuring schools for intellectual quality*. San Francisco: Jossey-Bass.

Newmann, F., Bryk, A., & Nagaoka, J. (2001). *Authentic intellectual work and standardized tests: Conflict or coexistence?* Chicago: Consortium on Chicago School Research.

Schmidt, W. (2004). A vision for mathematics. *Educational Leadership, 61*(5), 6–11.

Schmidt, W., Houang, R., & Cogan, L. (2002). A coherent curriculum: The case for mathematics. *American Educator, 26*(2), 10–26, 47–48.

Schmidt, W., McKnight, C., & Raizen, S. (1997). *A splintered vision: An investigation of U.S. science and mathematics education*. Norwell, MA: Kluwer Academic Publishers.

Senk, S., & Thompson, D. (2003). *Standards-based school mathematics curricula: What are they? What do students learn?* Mahwah, NJ: Erlbaum.

Smith, J., Lee, V., & Newmann, F. (2001). *Instruction and achievement in Chicago elementary schools*. Chicago: Consortium on Chicago School Research.

Stigler, J., & Hiebert, J. (1999). *The teaching gap*. New York: Free Press.

Stigler, J., & Hiebert, J. (2004). Improving mathematics teaching. *Educational Leadership, 61*(5), 12–16.

Tharp, R., Estrada, S., & Yamauchi, I. (2000). *Teaching transformed: Achieving excellence, fairness, inclusion, and harmony*. Boulder, CO: Westview Press.

Postnote

Teaching for meaning and understanding is a popular topic at educational meetings and conventions. Many educators believe that our accountability system of high-stakes tests works against teaching for meaning because teachers try to cover content and focus on facts. The authors of this article argue that these excuses for not emphasizing teaching for meaning are bogus. Rather, by focusing on meaning and understanding, student performance on state assessments is likely to improve.

Another characteristic of American education that many other countries, including Japan, want to emulate relates to creativity. Americans hold more patents than citizens of any other country, and no Japanese individual has ever won a Nobel Prize. Many Japanese educators want to develop an educational system that will unleash creativity and entrepreneurial efforts, while the United States is trying to emulate aspects of the Japanese educational system. Obviously, both educational systems do some things well and others not so well. We should be able to provide students with deep understanding of subjects, as well as ample opportunity to be creative.

Discussion Questions

1. Have you had teachers who taught for "meaning and understanding"? If so, how did their teaching differ from the teaching of your other teachers?
2. Why do you suppose that the majority of "high-stakes" tests emphasize recall of information rather than deeper meaning and understanding?
3. Are there aspects of the typical classroom that would need to change to focus on teaching for meaning? If so, what might they be?

CLASSIC

The Many Faces of Constructivism

DAVID PERKINS

FOCUS Question

Do the benefits of constructivist techniques outweigh their drawbacks? Why or why not?

TERM TO NOTE

Constructivism

Betty Fable's first day as a student at Constructivist High School was interesting but puzzling. In European history, the teacher challenged each student to write a letter from a French aristocrat to an Italian one, describing a key event of the French Revolution. In physics, the teacher asked students to predict whether heavy objects would fall faster than light ones, how much faster, and why. Then small groups of students designed their own experiments to test their theories. In algebra, where the class was learning the basic skill of simplifying algebraic expressions, the teacher insisted on conducting a discussion about what it means to simplify. Were simplified expressions the same as simplified equations? In English, after the class read Robert Frost's "Acquainted with the Night," the teacher asked students to relate the poem to an episode in their own lives.

Betty Fable expected all the teachers at Constructivist High to teach in a constructivist way—whatever that was. But what was it? Role playing, experimenting, analyzing, making connections to one's life? To her, each teacher seemed to be doing something different.

Many talented, dedicated, and experienced teachers find constructivist ideologies and practices just as bewildering, and for reasons not unlike Betty's. Constructivism does not seem to be one thing. And whatever constructivism is, its advocates sometimes have championed it to the point of overkill. Here and there, mentioning the C word is almost bad manners.

Perhaps it's possible to make better sense of the vexed and messy landscape of constructivism by asking appropriate questions.

What Is Constructivism in Its Variety?

No one can live in the world of education long without becoming aware that constructivism is more than one thing. But what accounts for the

---

David Perkins was Co-Director of Project Zero at Harvard University for more than twenty-five years and is now a member of the steering committee. He has conducted long-term programs of research and development in the areas of teaching and learning for understanding, creativity, problem solving, and reasoning in the arts, sciences, and everyday life. From David Perkins, "The Many Faces of Constructivism," *Educational Leadership,* November 1999, pp. 6–11. Reprinted with permission of the author.

variety? Philosopher D. C. Phillips (1995) identifies three distinct roles in constructivism. We'll call them the *active learner,* the *social learner,* and the *creative learner.*

The active learner: Knowledge and understanding as actively acquired. Constructivism generally casts learners in an active role. Instead of just listening, reading, and working through routine exercises, they discuss, debate, hypothesize, investigate, and take viewpoints—a common thread in Betty Fable's first day at Constructivist High.

The social learner: Knowledge and understanding as socially constructed. Constructivists often emphasize that knowledge and understanding are highly social. We do not construct them individually; we coconstruct them in dialogue with others. The teaching of history should make students aware of how historical "truth" varies with the interest groups—hence in Betty's history class, the letters from the aristocratic perspective. The teaching of science should lead students to recognize that scientific truths are arrived at by a social critical process that shapes their supposedly objective reality—thus, the group work in Betty's science class.

The creative learner: Knowledge and understanding as created or recreated. Often, constructivists hold that learners need to create or recreate knowledge for themselves. It is not enough that they assume an active stance. Teachers should guide them to rediscover scientific theories, historical perspectives, and so on. Betty's history teacher hopes that the letter exercise will help students reconstruct the aristocratic perspective, and her science teacher hopes that the students' theories and experiments will build a strong understanding of why objects fall as they do.

It is natural to ask how the three constructivist roles relate to one another. An active role for the learner is basic; in practice, social and creative aspects often accompany this role. However, an active learner does not logically require the other two. Teachers can organize learning experiences in active ways that do not require learners to engage in testing and building knowledge in a social manner or to invent or reinvent theories or viewpoints.

Why—and Why Not—Constructivism?

Why has constructivism enjoyed such advocacy for several decades? One reason is simply the search for better ways to teach and learn. With traditional methods, researchers and teachers have noted persistent shortfalls in students' understanding and a great deal of passive knowledge across all ages and grades, including the university (Gardner, 1991).

A philosophical argument also supports constructivist educational practices. The stimuli that we encounter, including messages from others, are never logically sufficient to convey meaning. To some extent, the individual always has to construct or reconstruct what things mean. It thus makes sense to organize learning to reflect this reality.

Another kind of argument looks to psychological sources (Perkins, 1992a; Duffy & Jonassen, 1992; Reigeluth, 1999; Wilson, 1996; Wiske, 1998). Considerable research shows that active engagement in learning may lead to better retention, understanding, and active use of knowledge. A social dimension to learning—what is sometimes called *collaborative* or *cooperative learning*—often, although not always, fosters learning. Sometimes, engaging students in discovery or rediscovery processes energizes them and yields deeper understanding.

Such arguments certainly encourage constructivist teaching practices. However, complications arise. Constructivist techniques often require more time than do traditional educational practices—a cost worth paying, enthusiasts say, but many teachers feel the pressures and conclude that they need to make compromises. Asking learners to discover or rediscover principles can foster understanding, but learners sometimes persist in discovering the wrong principles—for instance, an idiosyncratic scientific theory. Although ardent constructivists may argue that process is all, others believe that one way or another, students need to arrive at an understanding of the best theories propounded by the disciplines.

Also, constructivist learning experiences can exert high cognitive demands on learners, and not all learners respond well to the challenge (Perkins, 1992b). Constructivist techniques can even seem deceptive and manipulative. "Why don't you just tell me what you want me to know instead of making a big secret of it?" is not always an unreasonable question.

What Kind of Constructivism Makes Sense When?

The complications make it important to deploy constructivist techniques wisely, in the right place for the right purpose. How can a teacher create appropriate, targeted constructivist responses to learners' difficulties? One approach to the challenge recognizes that different kinds of knowledge—inert, ritual, conceptually difficult, and foreign—are likely to prove troublesome for learners in different ways.

Inert Knowledge

Inert knowledge sits in the mind's attic, unpacked only when specifically called for by a quiz or a direct prompt but otherwise gathering dust (Bransford, Franks, Vye, & Sherwood, 1989; Bereiter & Scardamalia, 1985). A familiar and relatively benign example is passive vocabulary—words that we understand but do not use actively. Unfortunately, considerable knowledge that we would like to see used actively proves to be inert. Students commonly learn ideas about society and self in history and social studies but make no connections to today's events or family life. Students learn concepts in science but make little connection to the world around them. Students learn techniques in math but fail to connect them to everyday applications or to their science studies.

What is the constructivist response when teaching knowledge that is likely to become inert? One strategy is to engage learners in active problem solving with knowledge that makes connections to their world. Betty Fable's English teacher asked her students to make connections between Frost's "Acquainted with the Night" and episodes in their own lives. For another example, science students studying basic machines (levers, pulleys, and so on) might find and analyze examples around their homes.

Another approach is to engage students in problem-based learning, where they acquire the target concepts while addressing some medium-scale problem or project (Boud & Feletti, 1991; Savery & Duffy, 1996). The English students might search out varied poems for a project on the theme "poems of the nights of our lives." The science students might build a Rube Goldberg apparatus or construct useful gadgets that use basic machines.

Ritual Knowledge

Ritual knowledge has a routine and rather meaningless character. It feels like part of a social or an individual ritual: how we answer when asked such-and-such, the routine that we execute to get a particular result. Names and dates often are little more than ritual knowledge. So are routines in arithmetic—an analogue of misconceptions in science (Gardner, 1991)—such as the notorious "invert and multiply" to divide fractions. Whereas inert knowledge needs more active use, ritual knowledge needs more meaningfulness (of course, knowledge can be both inert and ritualized).

A constructivist response to knowledge likely to become ritualized strives to make it more meaningful. For example, a teacher can wrap such knowledge in authentic problem-solving activities, another opportunity for problem-based learning. Students can explore its rationale and utility through discussion, as in the discussion of simplification in Betty Fable's algebra class. A teacher can sometimes involve students in surveying a large-scale story or historical episode or controversy that lends meaning to a piece of ritual knowledge. If Columbus "discovered" America in 1492, what else was going on in the world at about that time? How did Columbus's activities interact in the following decades with those other circumstances?

Conceptually Difficult Knowledge

Before students reach the university level, they meet conceptually difficult knowledge most commonly in mathematics and science, although it can occur in any discipline.

Understanding objects in motion is a good example (McCloskey, 1983). Learners find it hard to accept that objects in motion will continue at the same rate in the same direction unless some force, such as friction or gravity, impedes them. They find it hard to believe that heavier objects fall at the same rate as lighter ones, air resistance aside.

A mix of misimpressions from everyday experience (objects slow down automatically), reasonable but mistaken expectations (heavier objects fall faster), and the strangeness and complexity of scientists' views of matter (Newton's laws; such concepts as velocity as a vector, momentum, and so on) stand in the way. The result is often a mix of misunderstandings and ritual knowledge: Students learn the ritual responses to definitional questions and quantitative problems, but their intuitive beliefs and interpretations resurface on qualitative problems and in outside-of-classroom contexts.

What are reasonable constructivist responses to conceptually difficult knowledge? Perhaps the most common is to arrange inquiry processes that confront students with discrepancies in their initial theories—either discrepancies between theory and observations (as in Betty Fable's experiments with falling objects) or logical discrepancies.

For example, students commonly believe that a fly on a table pushes down but that the table does not push up on the fly. But they believe that the same table *does* push up on a bowling ball sitting on it. Imagine the bowling ball shrinking down to fly size. Where, all of a sudden, does the table stop pushing? Discussing such cases provides "anchoring intuitions" that make the principle clear and provoke students to extend it (Clement, 1993).

As with the bowling ball example, it often helps to introduce learners to imagistic mental models or to invite them to invent their own (Gentner & Stevens, 1983). It also often helps to engage learners with qualitative problems rather than with the solely quantitative ones that dominate some textbooks. Qualitative problems lead students to confront the character of the phenomenon rather than just to master computational routines. Such strategies may involve asking learners to "rediscover" the principle in some sense. But not necessarily. The teacher can instead introduce the principles directly and ask learners to test them and to use them to interpret phenomena in an active, exploratory way.

Foreign Knowledge

Foreign knowledge comes from a perspective that conflicts with our own. Sometimes the learner does not even recognize the knowledge as foreign. An example is "presentism" in historical understanding: Students tend to view past events through present knowledge and values (Carretero & Voss, 1994). Harry Truman's decision to drop the atomic bomb on Hiroshima may seem foolish to today's students. Perhaps it was vexed, but viewed through the knowledge and cultural mindsets of the era, it was hardly foolish.

Other examples include value systems carried by different nationalities, faiths, and ethnic groups. How indeed did the French aristocracy view the Revolution, the question that Betty Fable encountered in her history class? To pose such a puzzle is not, of course, to recommend the aristocratic view. But it *is* to recognize that many situations in history, contemporary society, literature, and current science and technology allow multiple serious, sincere, and well-elaborated perspectives that deserve understanding.

What then are constructivist responses to foreign knowledge? We can engage learners in recognizing that there *are* alternative perspectives by asking them to identify and elaborate on them. We can provoke compare-and-contrast discussions that map the perspectives in relation to one another. This method may sometimes involve extensive investigation as students set out to research what other perspectives have to say. Still another approach is to foster role-playing activities that ask students to get inside mindsets different from their own.

Of course, these are neither the only ways that knowledge can be troublesome nor the only constructivist responses possible. For instance, knowledge can be hard to remember—complex, with many pieces of information. Surprisingly, even this difficulty invites a constructivist response. Research shows that the best way to remember a body of information is to organize it actively, looking for internal patterns and relating it to what you already know. Simple repetition is much less effective. Or knowledge can be full of seeming inconsistencies and paradoxes, as when art critics or scientists disagree. Or knowledge can be full of subtle distinctions, such as that between weight and mass. Add your own categories and your own constructivist responses, by all means.

Pragmatic Constructivism

Often, the case made for constructivism seems resoundingly ideological. If learners do not rediscover Greek philosophy or Newton's laws for themselves, they will never truly understand them. To arrive at meaningful knowledge, they must learn through deep inquiry. As the unexamined life is not worth living, so the unexamined fact is not worth believing. And so on.

But the constructivist ideas assembled here are anything but ideological. They make up what we might call pragmatic constructivism. Their message asks us to view constructivism as a toolbox for problems of learning. Troublesome knowledge of various kinds invites constructivist responses to fit the difficulties—not one standard constructivist fix. If a particular approach does not solve the problem, try another—more structured, less structured, more discovery oriented, less discovery oriented, whatever works. And when knowledge is not particularly troublesome for the learners in question, well, forget about active, social, creative learners. Teaching by telling may serve just fine.

In keeping with this flexibility, active, social, and creative learning can play out in rather different ways, depending on the circumstances. Active learning is the common denominator. However, some examples more than others tapped the social dimension of constructivism. For instance, foreign knowledge intrinsically demands that we recognize differently constructed social perspectives. In contrast, inert or ritual knowledge may not call much upon the social dimension of constructivism, unless it happens to concern the social domain. Some constructivist responses to conceptually difficult knowledge ask learners to create and investigate their own theories. But responses to potentially inert and ritual knowledge may well simply foreground the wide and meaningful application of knowledge.

We began with Betty Fable's bewilderment about Constructivist High. In part, her confusion reflected the disparate constructivist moves in different classes. However, we see now that it also reflected a tension between ideological constructivism and pragmatic constructivism. The term *constructivism,* with its ideological overtones, suggests a single philosophy and a uniquely potent method—like one of those miracle knives advertised on late-night TV that will cut anything, even tin cans. But we could look at constructivism in another way, more like a Swiss army knife with various blades for various needs. Indeed, the miracle-knife version of constructivism has become as tired over the years as those TV commercials. At Constructivist High and elsewhere, it's high time we got pragmatic about constructivism.

References

Bereiter, C., & Scardamalia, M. (1985). Cognitive coping strategies and the problem of inert knowledge. In S. S. Chipman, J. W. Segal, & R. Glaser (Eds.), *Thinking and learning skills, Vol. 2: Current research and open questions* (pp. 65–80). Hillsdale, NJ: Erlbaum.

Boud, D., & Feletti, G. (Eds.). (1991). *The challenge of problem-based learning.* New York: St. Martin's Press.

Bransford, J. D., Franks, J. J., Vye, N. J., & Sherwood, R. D. (1989). New approaches to instruction: Because wisdom can't be told. In S. Vosniadou & A. Ortony (Eds.), *Similarity and analogical reasoning* (pp. 470–497). New York: Cambridge University Press.

Carretero, M., & Voss., J. F. (Eds.). (1994). *Cognitive and instructional processes in history and the social sciences.* Hillsdale, NJ: Erlbaum.

Clement, J. (1993). Using bridging analogies and anchoring intuitions to deal with students' preconceptions in physics. *Journal of Research in Science Teaching, 30*(10), 1241–1257.

Duffy, T. M., & Jonassen, D. H. (Eds.). (1992). *Constructivism and the technology of instruction: A conversation.* Hillsdale, NJ: Erlbaum.

Gardner, H. (1991). *The unschooled mind: How children think and how schools should teach.* New York: Basic Books.

Gentner, D., & Stevens, A. L. (Eds.). (1983). *Mental models.* Hillsdale, NJ: Erlbaum.

McCloskey, M. (1983). Naive theories of motion. In D. Gentner & A. L. Stevens (Eds.), *Mental models* (pp. 299–324). Hillsdale, NJ: Erlbaum.

Perkins, D. N. (1992a). *Smart schools: From training memories to educating minds.* New York: Free Press.

Perkins, D. N. (1992b). What constructivism demands of the learner. In T. M. Duffy & D. H. Jonassen (Eds.), *Constructivism and the technology of instruction: A conversation* (pp. 161–165). Hillsdale, NJ: Erlbaum.

Phillips, D. C. (1995). The good, the bad, and the ugly: The many faces of constructivism. *Educational Researcher, 24*(7), 5–12.

Reigeluth, C. (Ed.). (1999). *Instructional design theories and models: Vol. II.* Mahwah, NJ: Erlbaum.

Savery, J. R., & Duffy, T. M. (1996). Problem-based learning: An instructional model and its constructivist framework. In B. G. Wilson (Ed.), *Constructivist learning environments: Case studies in instructional design* (pp. 130–143). Englewood Cliffs, NJ: Educational Technology Publications.

Wilson, B. G. (Ed.). (1996). *Constructivist learning environments: Case studies in instructional design.* Englewood Cliffs, NJ: Educational Technology Publications.

Wiske, M. S. (Ed.). (1998). *Teaching for understanding: Linking research with practice.* San Francisco: Jossey-Bass.

Author's note: Some of the ideas presented here were developed as part of the Understandings of Consequence Project, which is supported by the National Science Foundation, Grant No. REC-9725502 to Tina Grotzer and David Perkins, coprincipal investigators. Any opinions, conclusions, or recommendations expressed here are those of the author and do not necessarily reflect the views of the National Science Foundation.

Postnote

This article was chosen as a Classic because the topic of constructivism has become such a dominant instructional philosophy in American education. Research from cognitive scientists has taught us that when confronted with new learning, human beings "construct" new understandings of relationships and phenomena, rather than simply receiving others' understandings. Learners are always fitting new information into the schemas they carry in their heads, or else they adjust or change the schema to fit the new information. As the author of this article states, knowledge is not passively received, but actively constructed by learners on a base of prior knowledge, attitudes, and values.

The implications for teachers are enormous. Constructivism suggests that educators should invite students to explore the world's complexity, proposing situations for students to think about and observing how the students use their prior knowledge to confront the problems. When students make errors, teachers can analyze the errors to understand better just how the students are approaching the matter. Throughout the process, teachers must accept that there is no single "right" way to solve a problem.

Discussion Questions

1. In what ways does constructivism challenge your ideas about how people learn?
2. How do you think constructivism will affect what goes on in classrooms? Describe a scenario in which a teacher conducts a lesson, using constructivist principles similar to those the author presents at the beginning of the article. Choose any subject or grade level you wish.
3. How does constructivism dispute the notion of a fixed world that students need to understand?

42

Making the Grade: What Benefits Students?

THOMAS R. GUSKEY

FOCUS Question

What are the attributes of a good grading system?

TERMS TO NOTE

Median
Process criteria
Product criteria
Progress criteria

Charged with leading a committee that would revise his school's grading and reporting system Warren Middleton described his work this way:

> The Committee on Grading was called upon to study grading procedures. At first, the task of investigating the literature seemed to be a rather hopeless one. What a mass and a mess it all was! Could order be brought out of such chaos? Could points of agreement among American educators concerning the perplexing grading problem actually be discovered? It was with considerable misgiving and trepidation that the work was finally begun.

Few educators today would consider the difficulties encountered by Middleton and his colleagues to be particularly surprising. In fact, most probably would sympathize with his lament. What they might find surprising, however, is that this report from the Committee on Grading was published in 1933!

The issues of grading and reporting on student learning have perplexed educators for the better part of this century. Yet despite all the debate and the multitude of studies, coming up with prescriptions for best practice seems as challenging today as it was for Middleton and his colleagues more than 60 years ago.

Points of Agreement

Although the debate over grading and reporting continues, today we know better which practices benefit students and encourage learning. Given the multitude of studies—and their often incongruous results—researchers do appear to agree on the following points:

1. ***Grading and reporting aren't essential to instruction.*** Teachers don't need grades or reporting forms to teach well. Further, students don't need them to learn (Frisbie and Waltman 1992).

Thomas R. Guskey is professor of education policy studies and evaluation, College of Education, University of Kentucky, Lexington, Kentucky. From Thomas R. Guskey, "Making the Grade: What Benefits Students?" *Educational Leadership,* October 1994, pp. 14–20. Reprinted by permission. The Association for Supervision and Curriculum Development is a worldwide community of educators advocating sound policies and sharing best practices to achieve the success of each learner. To learn more, visit ASCD at **www.ascd.org.**

Teachers do need to check regularly on how students are doing, what they've learned, and what problems or difficulties they've experienced. But grading and reporting are different from checking; they involve judging the adequacy of students' performance at a specific time. Typically, teachers use checking to diagnose and prescribe and use grading to evaluate and describe (Bloom et al. 1981).

When teachers do both checking and grading, they become advocates as well as judges—roles that aren't necessarily compatible (Bishop 1992). Finding a meaningful compromise between these dual roles makes many teachers uncomfortable, especially those with a child-centered orientation (Barnes 1985).

2. *No one method of grading and reporting serves all purposes well.* Grading enables teachers to communicate the achievements of students to parents and others, provides incentives to learn, and provides information that students can use for self-evaluation. In addition, schools use grades to identify or group students for particular educational paths or programs and to evaluate a program's effectiveness (Feldmesser 1971, Frisbie and Waltman 1992). Unfortunately, many schools attempt to address all of these purposes with a single method and end up achieving none very well (Austin and McCann 1992).

Letter grades, for example, briefly describe learning progress and give some idea of its adequacy (Payne 1974). Their use, however, requires abstracting a great deal of information into a single symbol (Stiggins 1994). In addition, the cut-off between grade categories is always arbitrary and difficult to justify. If scores for a grade of *B* range from 80 to 89, students at both ends of that range receive the same grade, even though their scores differ by nine points. But the student with a score of 79—a one-point difference—receives a grade of *C*.

The more detailed methods also have their drawbacks. Narratives and checklists of learning outcomes offer specific information for documenting progress, but good narratives take time to prepare, and—not surprisingly—as teachers complete more narratives, their comments become increasingly standardized. From the parents' standpoint, checklists of learning outcomes often appear too complicated to understand. In addition, checklists seldom communicate the appropriateness of students' progress in relation to expectations for their level (Afflerbach and Sammons 1991).

Because one method won't adequately serve all purposes, schools must identify their primary purpose for grading and select or develop the most appropriate approach (Cangelosi 1990). This process often involves the difficult task of seeking consensus among several constituencies.

3. *Regardless of the method used, grading and reporting remain inherently subjective.* In fact, the more detailed the reporting method and the more analytic the process, the more likely subjectivity will influence results (Ornstein 1994). That's why, for example, holistic scoring procedures tend to have greater reliability than analytic procedures.

Subjectivity in this process, however, isn't always bad. Because teachers know their students, understand various dimensions of students' work, and have clear notions of the progress made, their subjective perceptions may yield very accurate descriptions of what students have learned (Brookhart 1993, O'Donnell and Woolfolk 1991).

When subjectivity translates into bias, however, negative consequences can result. Teachers' perceptions of students' behavior can significantly influence their judgments of scholastic performance (Hills 1991). Students with behavior problems often have no chance to receive a high grade because their infractions overshadow their performance. These effects are especially pronounced in judgments of boys (Bennett et al. 1993). Even the neatness of students' handwriting can significantly affect a teacher's judgment (Sweedler-Brown 1992).

Training programs can help teachers identify and reduce these negative effects and lead to greater consistency in judgments (Afflerbach and Sammons 1991). Unfortunately, few teachers receive adequate training in grading or reporting as part of their preservice experiences (Boothroyd and McMorris 1992). Also, few school districts provide adequate guidance to ensure consistency in teachers' grading or reporting practices (Austin and McCann 1992).

4. *Grades have some value as rewards, but no value as punishments.* Although educators would undoubtedly prefer that motivation to learn be entirely intrinsic, the existence of grades and other reporting methods are important factors in determining how much effort students put forth (Chastain 1990, Ebel 1979). Most students view high grades as positive recognition of their success, and some work hard to avoid the consequences of low grades (Feldmesser 1971).

At the same time, no studies support the use of low grades as punishments. Instead of prompting greater effort, low grades usually cause students to withdraw from learning. To protect their self-image, many students regard the low grade as irrelevant and meaningless. Other students may blame themselves for the low mark, but feel helpless to improve (Selby and Murphy 1992).

Sadly, some teachers consider grades or reporting forms their "weapon of last resort." In their view, students who don't comply with requests suffer the consequences of the greatest punishment a teacher can bestow: a failing grade. Such practices have no educational value and, in the long run, adversely affect students, teachers, and the relationship they share. Rather than attempting to punish students with a low mark, teachers can better motivate students by regarding their work as incomplete and requiring additional effort.

5. *Grading and reporting should always be done in reference to learning criteria, never on the curve.* Using the normal probability curve as a basis for assigning grades typically yields greater consistency in grade distributions from one teacher to the next. The practice, however, is detrimental to teaching and learning.

Grading on the curve pits students against one another in a competition for the few rewards (high grades) distributed by the teacher. Under these conditions, students readily see that helping others will threaten their own chances for success (Johnson et al. 1979, Johnson et al. 1980). Learning becomes a game of winners and losers—with the most students falling into the latter category (Johnson and Johnson 1989). In addition, modern research has shown that the seemingly direct relationship between aptitude or intelligence and school achievement depends upon instructional conditions, not a probability curve.

When the instructional quality is high and well matched to students' learning needs, the magnitude of this relationship diminishes drastically and approaches zero (Bloom 1976). Moreover, the fairness and equity of grading on the curve is a myth.

Learning Criteria

When grading and reporting relate to learning criteria, teachers have a clearer picture of what students have learned. Students and teachers alike generally prefer this approach because it seems fairer (Kovas 1993). The types of learning criteria usually used for grading and reporting fall into three categories:

- *Product criteria* are favored by advocates of performance-based approaches to teaching and learning. These educators believe grading and reporting should communicate a summative evaluation of student achievement (Cangelosi 1990). In other words, they focus on what students know and are able to do at that time. Teachers who use product criteria often base their grades or reports exclusively on final examination scores, overall assessments, or other culminating demonstrations of learning.
- *Process criteria* are emphasized by educators who believe product criteria don't provide a complete picture of student learning. From their perspective, grading and reporting should reflect not just the final results but also *how* students got there. Teachers who consider effort or work habits when reporting on student learning are using process criteria. So are teachers who take into consideration classroom quizzes, homework, class participation, or attendance.

- *Progress criteria,* often referred to as "improvement scoring" and "learning gain," consider how much students have gained from their learning experiences. Teachers who use progress criteria look at *how far* students have come rather than where they are. As a result, scoring criteria may become highly individualized.

Teachers who base their grading and reporting procedures on learning criteria typically use some combination of the three types (Frary et al. 1993; Nava and Loyd 1992; Stiggins et al. 1989). Most researchers and measurement specialists, on the other hand, recommend using product criteria exclusively. They point out that the more process and progress criteria come into play, the more subjective and biased grades become (Ornstein 1994). How can a teacher know, for example, how difficult a task was for students or how hard they worked to complete it? If these criteria are included at all, most experts recommend they be reported separately (Stiggins 1994).

Practical Guidelines

Despite years of research, there's no evidence to indicate that one grading or reporting method works best under all conditions, in all circumstances. But in developing practices that seek to be fair, equitable, and useful to students, parents, and teachers, educators can rely on two guidelines:

- *Provide accurate and understandable descriptions of learning.* Regardless of the method or form used, grading and reporting should communicate effectively what students have learned, what they can do, and whether their learning status is in line with expectations for that level. More than an exercise in quantifying achievement, grading and reporting must be seen as a challenge in clear thinking and effective communication (Stiggins 1994).
- *Use grading and reporting methods to enhance, not hinder, teaching and learning.* A clear, easily understood reporting form facilitates communication between teachers and parents. When both parties speak the same language, joint efforts to help students are likely to succeed. But developing such an equitable and understandable system will require the elimination of long-time practices such as averaging and assigning a zero to work that's late, missed, or neglected.
- *Averaging* falls far short of providing an accurate description of what students have learned. For example, students often say, "I have to get a *B* on the final to pass this course." Such a comment illustrates the inappropriateness of averaging. If a final examination is truly comprehensive and students' scores accurately reflect what they've learned, why should a *B* level of performance translate to a *D* for the course grade?

Any single measure of learning can be unreliable. Consequently, most researchers recommend using several indicators in determining students' grades or marks—and most teachers concur (Natriello 1987). Nevertheless, the key question remains, "What information provides the most accurate depiction of students' learning at this time?" In nearly all cases, the answer is "the most current information." If students demonstrate that past assessment information doesn't accurately reflect their learning, new information must take its place. By continuing to rely on past assessment data, the grades can be misleading about a student's learning (Stiggins 1994).

Similarly, assigning a score of zero to work that is late, missed, or neglected doesn't accurately depict learning. Is the teacher certain the student has learned absolutely nothing, or is the zero assigned to punish students for not displaying appropriate responsibility (Canady and Hotchkiss 1989, Stiggins and Duke 1991)?

Further, a zero has a profound effect when combined with the practice of averaging. Students who receive a single zero have little chance of success because such an extreme score skews the average. That is why, for example, Olympic events such as gymnastics and ice skating eliminate the highest and lowest scores; otherwise, one judge could control the entire competition simply by giving extreme scores. An alternative is to use the median score rather than the average (Wright 1994) but use of the most current information remains the most defensible option.

Meeting the Challenge

The issues of grading and reporting on student learning continue to challenge educators today, just as they challenged Middleton and his colleagues in 1933. But today we know more than ever before about the complexities involved and how certain practices can influence teaching and learning.

What do educators need to develop grading and reporting practices that provide quality information about student learning? Nothing less than clear thinking, careful planning, excellent communication skills, and an overriding concern for the well-being of students. Combining these skills with our current knowledge on effective practice will surely result in more efficient and more effective reporting.

A Look Back at Grading Practices

Although student assessment has been a part of teaching and learning for centuries, grading is a relatively recent phenomenon. The ancient Greeks used assessments as formative, not evaluative, tools. Students demonstrated, usually orally, what they had learned, giving teachers a clear indication of which topics required more work or instruction.

In the United States, grading and reporting were virtually unknown before 1850. Back then, most schools grouped students of all ages and backgrounds together with one teacher. Few students went beyond the elementary education offered in these one-room schoolhouses. As the country grew—and as legislators passed compulsory attendance laws—the number and diversity of students increased. Schools began to group students in grades according to their age, and to try new ideas about curriculum and teaching methods. Here's a brief timeline of significant dates in the history of grading:

Late 1800s: Schools begin to issue progress evaluations. Teachers simply write down the skills that students have mastered; once students complete the requirements for one level, they can move to the next level.

Early 1900s: The number of public high schools in the United States increases dramatically. While elementary teachers continue using written descriptions to document student learning, high school teachers introduce percentages as a way to certify students' accomplishments in specific subject areas. Few educators question the gradual shift to percentage grading, which seems a natural by-product of the increased demands on high school teachers.

1912: Starch and Elliott publish a study that challenges percentage grades as reliable measures of student achievement. They base their findings on grades assigned to two papers written for a first-year English class in high school. Of the 142 teachers grading on a 0 to 100 scale, 15 percent give one paper a failing mark; 12 percent give the same paper a score of 90 or more. The other paper receives scores ranging from 50 to 97. Neatness, spelling, and punctuation influenced the scoring of many teachers, while others considered how well the paper communicated its message.

1913: Responding to critics—who argue that good writing is, by nature, a highly subjective judgment—Starch and Elliott repeat their study but use geometry papers. Even greater variations occur, with scores on one paper ranging from 28 to 95. Some teachers deducted points only for wrong answers, but others took neatness, form, and spelling into account.

1918: Teachers turn to grading scales with fewer and larger categories. One three-point scale, for example, uses the categories of Excellent, Average, and Poor. Another has five categories (Excellent, Good, Average, Poor, and Failing) with the corresponding letters of *A, B, C, D,* and *F* (Johnson 1918, Rugg 1918).

(continued)

1930s: Grading on the curve becomes increasingly popular as educators seek to minimize the subjective nature of scoring. This method ranks students according to some measure of their performance or proficiency. The top percentage receives an *A*, the next percentage receives a *B*, and so on (Corey 1930). Some advocates (Davis 1930) even specify the precise percentage of students to be assigned each grade, such as 6–22–44–22–6.

Grading on the curve seems fair and equitable, given research suggesting that students' scores on tests of innate intelligence approximate a normal probability curve (Middleton 1933).

As the debate over grading and reporting intensifies, a number of schools abolish formal grades altogether (Chapman and Ashbaugh 1925) and return to using verbal descriptions of student achievement. Others advocate pass-fail systems that distinguish only between acceptable and failing work (Good 1937). Still others advocate a "mastery approach": Once students have mastered a skill or content, they move to other areas of study (Heck 1938, Hill 1935).

1958: Ellis Page investigates how student learning is affected by grades and teachers' comments. In a now classic study, 74 secondary school teachers administer a test, and assign a numerical score and letter grade of *A, B, C, D,* or *F* to each student's paper. Next, teachers randomly divide the tests into three groups. Papers in the first group receive only the numerical score and letter grade. The second group, in addition to the score and grade, receive these standard comments: *A—Excellent! B—Good work. Keep at it. C—Perhaps try to do still better? D—Let's bring this up. F—Let's raise this grade!* For the third group, teachers mark the score and letter grade, and write individualized comments.

Page evaluates the effects of the comments by considering students' scores on the next test they take. Results show that students in the second group achieved significantly higher scores than those who received only a score and grade. The students who received individualized comments did even better. Page concludes that grades can have a beneficial effect on student learning, but only when accompanied by specific or individualized comments from the teacher.

Source: H. Kirschenbaum, S. B. Simon, and R. W. Napier (1971), *Wad-ja-get? The Grading Game in American Education* (New York: Hart).

References

Afflerbach, P., and R. B. Sammons. (1991). "Report Cards in Literacy Evaluation: Teachers' Training, Practices, and Values." Paper presented at the annual meeting of the National Reading Conference, Palm Springs, Calif.

Austin, S., and R. McCann. (1992). "'Here's Another Arbitrary Grade for Your Collection': A Statewide Study of Grading Policies." Paper presented at the annual meeting of the American Educational Research Association, San Francisco.

Barnes, S. (1985). "A Study of Classroom Pupil Evaluation: The Missing Link in Teacher Education." *Journal of Teacher Education* 36, 4: 46–49.

Bennett, R. E., R. L. Gottesman, D. A. Rock, and F. Cerullo. (1993). "Influence of Behavior Perceptions and Gender on Teachers' Judgments of Students' Academic Skill." *Journal of Educational Psychology,* 85: 347–356.

Bishop, J. H. (1992). "Why U.S. Students Need Incentives to Learn." *Educational Leadership* 49, 6: 15–18.

Bloom, B. S. (1976). *Human Characteristics and School Learning.* New York: McGraw-Hill.

Bloom, B. S., G. F. Madaus, and J. T. Hastings (1981). *Evaluation to Improve Learning.* New York: McGraw-Hill.

Boothroyd, R. A., and R. F. McMorris. (1992). "What Do Teachers Know About Testing and How Did They Find Out?" Paper presented at the annual meeting of the National Council on Measurements in Education, San Francisco.

Brookhart, S. M. (1993). "Teachers' Grading Practices: Meaning and Values." *Journal of Educational Measurement* 30, 2: 123–142.

Canady, R. L., and P. R. Hotchkiss. (1989). "It's a Good Score! Just a Bad Grade." *Phi Delta Kappan* 71: 68–71.

Cangelosi, J. S. (1990). "Grading and Reporting Student Achievement." In *Designing Tests for Evaluating Student Achievement,* pp. 196–213. New York: Longman.

Chapman, H. B., and E. J. Ashbaugh. (October 7, 1925). "Report Cards in American Cities." *Educational Research Bulletin* 4: 289–310.

Chastain, K. (1990). Characteristics of Graded and Ungraded Compositions." *Modern Language Journal,* 74, 1: 10–14.

Corey, S. M. (1930). "Use of the Normal Curve as a Basis for Assigning Grades in Small Classes." *School and Society* 31: 514–516.

Davis, J. D. W. (1930). "Effect of the 6–22–44–22–6 Normal Curve System on Failures and Grade Values." *Journal of Educational Psychology* 22: 636–640.

Ebel, R. L. (1979). *Essentials of Educational Measurement* (3rd ed.). Englewood Cliffs, N.J.: Prentice-Hall.

Feldmesser, R. A. (1971). "The Positive Functions of Grades." Paper presented at the annual meeting of the American Educational Research Association, New York.

Frary, R. B., L. H. Cross, and L. J. Weber. (1993). "Testing and Grading Practices and Opinions of Secondary Teachers of Academic Subjects: Implications for Instruction in Measurement." *Educational Measurement: Issues and Practices* 12, 3: 23–30.

Frisbie, D. A., and K. K. Waltman. (1992). "Developing a Personal Grading Plan." *Educational Measurement: Issues and Practices* 11, 3: 35–42.

Good, W. (1937). "Should Grades Be Abolished?" *Education Digest* 2, 4: 7–9.

Heck, A. O. (1938). "Contributions of Research to Classification, Promotion, Marking and Certification." Reported in *The Science Movement in Education (Part II), Twenty-Seventh Yearbook of the National Society for the Study of Education.* Chicago: University of Chicago Press.

Hill, G. E. (1935). "The Report Card in Present Practice." *Education Methods* 15, 3: 115–131.

Hills, J. R. (1991). "Apathy Concerning Grading and Testing." *Phi Delta Kappan* 72, 2: 540–545.

Johnson, D. W., and R. T. Johnson. (1989). *Cooperation and Competition: Theory and Research.* Endina, Minn.: Interaction.

Johnson, D. W., L. Skon, and R. T. Johnson. (1980). "Effects of Cooperative, Competitive, and Individualistic Conditions on Children's Problem-Solving Performance." *American Educational Research Journal* 17, 1: 83–93.

Johnson, R. H. (1918). "Educational Research and Statistics: The Coefficient Marking System." *School and Society* 7, 181: 714–716.

Johnson, R. T., D. W. Johnson, and M. Tauer. (1979). "The Effects of Cooperative, Competitive, and Individualistic Goal Structures on Students' Attitudes and Achievement." *Journal of Psychology* 102: 191–198.

Kovas, M. A. (1993). "Making Your Grading Motivating: Keys to Performance-Based Evaluation." *Quill and Scroll* 68, 1: 10–11.

Middleton, W. (1933). "Some General Trends in Grading Procedure." *Education* 54, 1: 5–10.

Natriello, G. (1987). "The Impact of Evaluation Processes on Students." *Educational Psychologists* 22: 155–175.

Nava, F. J. G., and B. H. Loyd. (1992). "An Investigation of Achievement and Nonachievement Criteria in Elementary and Secondary School Grading." Paper presented at the annual meeting of the American Educational Research Association, San Francisco.

O'Donnell, A., and A. E. Woolfolk. (1991). "Elementary and Secondary Teachers' Beliefs About Testing and Grading." Paper presented at the annual meeting of the American Psychological Association, San Francisco.

Ornstein, A. C. (1994). "Grading Practices and Policies: An Overview and Some Suggestions." *NASSP Bulletin* 78, 559: 55–64.

Page, E. B. (1958). "Teacher Comments and Student Performance: A Seventy-Four Classroom Experiment in School Motivation." *Journal of Educational Psychology* 49: 173–181.

Payne, D. A. (1974). *The Assessment of Learning.* Lexington, Mass.: Heath.

Rugg, H. O. (1918). "Teachers' Marks and the Reconstruction of the Marking System." *Elementary School Journal* 18, 9: 701–719.

Selby, D., and S. Murphy. (1992). "Graded or Degraded: Perceptions of Letter-Grading for Mainstreamed Learning-Disabled Students." *British Columbia Journal of Special Education* 16, 1: 92–104.

Starch, D., and E. C. Elliott. (1912). "Reliability of the Grading of High School Work in English." *School Review* 20: 442–457.

Starch, D., and E. C. Elliott. (1913). "Reliability of the Grading of High School Work in Mathematics." *School Review* 21: 254–259.

Stewart, L. G., and M. A. White. (1976). "Teacher Comments, Letter Grades, and Student Performance." *Journal of Educational Psychology* 68, 4: 488–500.

Stiggins, R. J. (1994). "Communicating with Report Card Grades." In *Student-Centered Classroom Assessment,* pp. 363–396. New York: Macmillan.

Stiggins, R. J., and D. L. Duke. (1991). "District Grading Policies and Their Potential Impact on At-risk Students." Paper presented at the annual meeting of the American Educational Research Association, Chicago.

Stiggins, R. J., D. A. Frisbie, and P. A. Griswold. (1989). "Inside High School Grading Practices: Building a Research Agenda." *Educational Measurement: Issues and Practice* 8, 2: 5–14.

Sweedler-Brown, C. O. (1992). "The Effect of Training on the Appearance Bias of Holistic Essay Graders." *Journal of Research and Development in Education* 26, 1: 24–29.

Wright, R. G. (1994). "Success for All: The Median Is the Key." *Phi Delta Kappan* 75, 9: 723–725.

Postnote

Grading students is one of the most troubling tasks that beginning teachers face. While working with students to help them learn and develop is a source of great pleasure for teachers, grading students provokes anxiety and avoidance. Unfortunately, grading is a part of almost all schooling and is not likely to go away anytime soon. Therefore, teachers need to learn how to grade in the fairest way possible.

To do this may require you to unlearn many aspects of grading that you have experienced as a student. For example, consider using the median instead of the mean when averaging a student's grades. Statistically, it is a more fair measure. In general, take time to learn effective and fair evaluation procedures.

Discussion Questions

1. Did any of the author's recommendations surprise you? If so, which ones and why?
2. Can you think of any time when you thought you didn't get the grade you deserved? What were the circumstances? In what way do you think you were treated unfairly?
3. How would a zero score count differently in averaging scores if you used the median instead of the mean as the measure of central tendency?

CLASSIC

Making Cooperative Learning Work

DAVID W. JOHNSON AND ROGER T. JOHNSON

FOCUS Question

What are the benefits of employing cooperative learning strategies in classrooms?

TERM TO NOTE

Cooperative learning

Sandy Koufax was one of the greatest pitchers in the history of baseball. Although he was naturally talented, he was also unusually well trained and disciplined. He was perhaps the only major-league pitcher whose fastball could be heard to hum. Opposing batters, instead of talking and joking around in the dugout, would sit quietly and listen for Koufax's fastball to hum. When it was their turn to bat, they were already intimidated.

There was, however, a simple way for Koufax's genius to have been negated: by making the first author of this article his catcher. To be great, a pitcher needs an outstanding catcher (his great partner was Johnny Roseboro). David is such an unskilled catcher that Koufax would have had to throw the ball much slower in order for David to catch it. This would have deprived Koufax of his greatest weapon.

Placing Roger at key defensive positions in the infield or outfield, furthermore, would have seriously affected Koufax's success. Sandy Koufax was not a great pitcher on his own. Only as part of a team could Koufax achieve greatness. In baseball and in the classroom, it takes a cooperative effort. Extraordinary achievement comes from a cooperative group, not from the individualistic or competitive efforts of an isolated individual.

In 1966 David began training teachers at the University of Minnesota in how to use small groups for instructional purposes. In 1969 Roger joined David at Minnesota, and the training of teachers in how to use cooperative learning groups was extended into teaching methods courses in science education. The formation of the Cooperative Learning Center soon followed to focus on five areas:

1. Summarizing and extending the theory on cooperation and competition.
2. Reviewing the existing research in order to validate or disconfirm the theory and establish what is known and unknown.

David W. Johnson and **Roger T. Johnson** are professors of education and codirectors of the Cooperative Learning Center at the University of Minnesota. "Making Cooperative Learning Work" by David W. Johnson and Roger T. Johnson, *Theory into Practice,* Volume 38, Number 2 (Spring 1999) is reprinted by permission.

3. Conducting a long-term program of research to validate and extend the theory and to identify (a) the conditions under which cooperative, competitive, and individualistic efforts are effective and (b) the basic elements that make cooperation work.
4. Operationalizing the validated theory into a set of procedures for teachers and administrators to use.
5. Implementing the procedures in classes, schools, school districts, colleges, and training programs.

These five activities result in an understanding of what is and is not a cooperative effort, the different types of cooperative learning, the five basic elements that make cooperation work, and the outcomes that result when cooperation is carefully structured.

What Is and Is Not a Cooperative Effort

Not all groups are cooperative. There is nothing magical about working in a group. Some kinds of learning groups facilitate student learning and increase the quality of life in the classroom. Other types of learning groups hinder student learning and create disharmony and dissatisfaction. To use cooperative learning effectively, one must know what is and is not a cooperative group (Johnson, Johnson, & Holubec, 1998b).

1. *Pseudo learning group:* Students are assigned to work together but they have no interest in doing so and believe they will be evaluated by being ranked from the highest to the lowest performer. Students hide information from each other, attempt to mislead and confuse each other, and distrust each other. The result is that the sum of the whole is less than the potential of the individual members. Students would achieve more if they were working alone.
2. *Traditional classroom learning group:* Students are assigned to work together and accept that they have to do so. Assignments are structured so that students are evaluated and rewarded as individuals, not as members of the group. They seek each other's information but have no motivation to teach what they know to group-mates. Some students seek a free ride on the efforts of group-mates, who feel exploited and do less. The result is that the sum of the whole is more than the potential of some of the members, but the more hard working and conscientious students would perform higher if they worked alone.
3. *Cooperative learning group:* Students work together to accomplish shared goals. Students seek outcomes that are beneficial to all. Students discuss material with each other, help one another understand it, and encourage each other to work hard. Individual performance is checked regularly to ensure that all students are contributing and learning. The result is that the group is more than a sum of its parts, and all students perform higher academically than they would if they worked alone.
4. *High-performance cooperative learning group:* This is a group that meets all the criteria for being a cooperative learning group and outperforms all reasonable expectations, given its membership. The level of commitment members have to each other and the group's success is beyond that of most cooperative groups. Few groups ever achieve this level of development.

How well any small group performs depends on how it is structured. Seating people together and calling them a cooperative group does not make them one. Study groups, project groups, lab groups, homerooms, and reading groups are groups, but they are not necessarily cooperative. Even with the best of intentions, teachers may be using traditional classroom learning groups rather than cooperative learning groups. To ensure that a group is cooperative, educators must understand the different ways cooperative learning may be used and the basic elements that need to be carefully structured within every cooperative activity.

Types of Cooperative Learning

> Two are better than one, because they have a good reward for toil. For if they fall, one will lift up his fellow; but woe to him who is alone when he falls and has not another to lift him up. . . . And though a man might prevail against one who is alone, two will withstand him. A threefold cord is not quickly broken. (Ecclesiastes 4:9–12)

Cooperative learning is a versatile procedure and can be used for a variety of purposes. Cooperative learning groups may be used to teach specific content (formal cooperative learning groups), to ensure active cognitive processing of information during a lecture or demonstration (informal cooperative learning groups), and to provide long-term support and assistance for academic progress (cooperative base groups) (Johnson, Johnson, & Holubec, 1998a, 1998b).

Formal cooperative learning consists of students working together, for one class period or several weeks, to achieve shared learning goals and complete specific tasks and assignments (e.g., problem solving, writing a report, conducting a survey or experiment, learning vocabulary, or answering questions at the end of the chapter) (Johnson, Johnson, & Holubec, 1998b). Any course requirement or assignment may be structured cooperatively. In formal cooperative learning groups, teachers:

1. Make a number of *preinstructional decisions.* Teachers specify the objectives for the lesson (both academic and social skills) and decide on the size of groups, the method of assigning students to groups, the roles students will be assigned, the materials needed to conduct the lesson, and the way the room will be arranged.
2. *Explain* the task and the positive interdependence. A teacher clearly defines the assignment, teaches the required concepts and strategies, specifies the positive interdependence and individual accountability, gives the criteria for success, and explains the social skills to be used.
3. *Monitor* students' learning and *intervene* within the groups to provide task assistance or to increase students' interpersonal and group skills. A teacher systematically observes and collects data on each group as it works. When needed, the teacher intervenes to assist students in completing the task accurately and in working together effectively.
4. *Assess* students' learning and help students process how well their groups functioned. Students' learning is carefully assessed and their performances evaluated. Members of the learning groups then discuss how effectively they worked together and how they can improve in the future.

Informal cooperative learning consists of having students work together to achieve a joint learning goal in temporary, ad-hoc groups that last from a few minutes to one class period (Johnson, Johnson, & Holubec, 1998a; Johnson, Johnson, & Smith, 1998). During a lecture, demonstration, or film, informal cooperative learning can be used to (a) focus student attention on the material to be learned, (b) set a mood conducive to learning, (c) help set expectations as to what will be covered in a class session, (d) ensure that students cognitively process the material being taught, and (e) provide closure to an instructional session.

During direct teaching the instructional challenge for the teacher is to ensure that students do the intellectual work of organizing material, explaining it, summarizing it, and integrating it into existing conceptual structures. Informal cooperative learning groups are often organized so that students engage in 3–5 minute focused discussions before and after a lecture and 2–3 minute turn-to-your-partner discussions interspersed throughout a lecture.

Cooperative base groups are long-term, heterogeneous cooperative learning groups of 3–4 members with stable membership (Johnson, Johnson, & Holubec, 1998a; Johnson, Johnson, & Smith, 1998). Base groups give the support, help, encouragement, and assistance each member needs to make academic progress (attend class, complete all assignments, learn) and develop cognitively and socially in healthy ways.

Base groups meet daily in elementary school and twice a week in secondary school (or whenever the class meets). They are permanent (lasting from one to several years) and provide the long-term caring peer relationships necessary to influence members consistently to work hard in school.

The use of base groups tends to improve attendance, personalize the work required and the school experience, and improve the quality and quantity of learning. School and classroom management is enhanced when base groups are given the responsibility for conducting a yearlong service project to improve the school. The larger the class or school and the more complex and difficult the subject matter, the more important it is to have base groups. Base groups are also helpful in structuring homerooms and when a teacher meets with a number of advisees.

Example of Integrated Use of Cooperative Learning

An example of the integrated use of the cooperative learning procedures is as follows. Students arrive at class and meet in their base groups to welcome each other, check each student's homework to make sure all members understand the academic material and are prepared for the class session, and tell each other to have a great day.

The teacher then begins a lesson on the limitations of being human (Billion-Dollar Being, 1974). To help students cognitively organize in advance what they know about the advantages and disadvantages of being human, the teacher uses informal cooperative learning. The teacher asks students to form a triad and ponder, "What are five things you cannot do with your human limitations that a billion-dollar being might be designed to do?" Students have 4 minutes to do so. In the next 10 minutes, the teacher explains that while the human body is a marvelous system, we (like other organisms) have very specific limitations. We cannot see bacteria in a drop of water or the rings of Saturn unaided. We cannot hear as well as a deer or fly like an eagle. Humans have never been satisfied being so limited and, therefore, we have invented microscopes, telescopes, and our own wings. The teacher then instructs students to turn to the person next to them and answer the questions, "What are three limitations of humans, what have we invented to overcome them, and what other human limitations might we be able to overcome?"

Formal cooperative learning is now used in the lesson. The teacher has the 32 students count off from 1 to 8 to form groups of four randomly. Group members sit in a semicircle so they can face each other and still be facing the teacher. Each member is assigned a role: researcher/runner, summarizer/timekeeper, collector/recorder, and technical adviser (role interdependence). Every group gets one large (2 × 3-feet) piece of paper, a marking pen, a rough draft sheet for designing the being, an assignment sheet explaining the task and cooperative goal structure, and four student self-evaluation checklists (resource interdependence). The task is to design a billion-dollar being that overcomes the human limitations thought of by the class and the group. The group members are to draw a diagram of the being on the scratch paper and, when they have something they like, transfer it to the larger paper.

The teacher establishes positive goal interdependence by asking for one drawing from the group that all group members contribute to and can explain. The criterion for success is to complete the diagram in the 30-minute time limit. The teacher observes each group to ensure that members are fulfilling their roles and that any one member can explain any part of the being at any time. The teacher informs students that the expected social skills to be used by all students are encouraging each other's participation, contributing ideas, and summarizing. She defines the skill of encouraging participation and has each student practice it twice before the lesson begins.

While students work in their groups, the teacher monitors by systematically observing each group and intervening to provide academic assistance and help in using the interpersonal and small group skills required to work together effectively. At the end of the lesson, the groups hand in their diagrams of the billion-dollar being to be assessed and evaluated. Group members then process how well they worked together by identifying actions each member engaged in that helped the group succeed and one thing that could be added to improve their group next time.

The teacher uses informal cooperative learning to provide closure to the lesson by asking students to meet in new triads and write out six conclusions about the limitations of human beings and what we have done to overcome them. At the end of the class session, the cooperative base groups meet to review what students believe is the most important thing they have learned during the day, what homework has been assigned, what help each member needs to complete the homework, and to tell each other to have a fun afternoon and evening.

The Cooperative School

Teachers are not the only ones who need to carefully structure cooperation. Administrators need to create a learning community by structuring cooperation at the school level (Johnson & Johnson, 1994, 1999). In addition, they have to attend to the cooperation among faculty, between the school and parents, and between the school and the community.

Administrators, for example, may structure three types of cooperative faculty teams. Collegial teaching teams are formed to increase teachers' instructional expertise and success. They consist of 2–5 teachers who meet weekly and discuss how to better implement cooperative learning within their classrooms. Teachers are assigned to task forces to plan and implement solutions to school-wide issues and problems such as curriculum adoptions and lunchroom behavior. Ad hoc decision-making groups are used during faculty meetings to involve all staff members in important school decisions.

The use of cooperative teams at the building level ensures that there is a congruent cooperative team-based organizational structure within both classrooms and the school. Finally, the superintendent uses the same types of cooperative teams to maximize the productivity of district administrators.

Basic Elements of Cooperation

In order for an activity to be cooperative, five basic elements are essential and need to be included (Johnson & Johnson, 1989; Johnson, Johnson, & Holubec, 1998a). The five essential elements are as follows.

1. *Positive interdependence:* Positive interdependence is the perception that we are linked with others in a way so that we cannot succeed unless they do. Their work benefits us and our work benefits them. Within every cooperative lesson, positive goal interdependence must be established through mutual learning goals (learn the assigned material and make sure that all members of your group learn the assigned material). In order to strengthen positive interdependence, joint rewards (if all members of your group score 90 percent correct or better on the test, each will receive 5 bonus points), divided resources (giving each group member a part of the total information required to complete an assignment), and complementary roles (reader, checker, encourager, elaborator) may also be used.

2. *Individual accountability:* Individual accountability exists when the performance of each individual student is assessed and the results are given back to the group and the individual. The purpose of cooperative learning groups is to make each member a stronger individual. Students learn together so that they can subsequently perform higher as individuals. To ensure that each member is strengthened, students are held individually accountable to do their share of the work. Common ways to structure individual accountability include (a) giving an individual test to each student, (b) randomly selecting one student's product to represent the entire

group, or (c) having each student explain what they have learned to a classmate.

3. *Face-to-face promotive interaction:* Individuals promote each other's success by helping, assisting, supporting, encouraging, and praising each other's efforts to achieve. Certain cognitive activities and interpersonal dynamics only occur when students get involved in promoting each other's learning. These include orally explaining how to solve problems, discussing the nature of the concepts being learned, teaching one's knowledge to classmates, and connecting present with past learning. Accountability to peers, ability to influence each other's reasoning and conclusions, social modeling, social support, and interpersonal rewards all increase as the face-to-face interactions among group members increase.

   In addition, the verbal and nonverbal responses of other group members provide important information concerning a student's performance. Silent students are uninvolved students who are not contributing to the learning of others as well as themselves. To obtain meaningful face-to-face interaction, the size of groups needs to be small (2–4 members).

4. *Social skills:* Contributing to the success of a cooperative effort requires interpersonal and small group skills. Placing socially unskilled individuals in a group and telling them to cooperate does not guarantee that they will be able to do so effectively. Persons must be taught the leadership, decision-making, trust-building, communication, and conflict-management skills just as purposefully and precisely as academic skills. Procedures and strategies for teaching students social skills may be found in Johnson (1997) and Johnson and F. Johnson (1997).

5. *Group processing:* Group processing exists when group members discuss how well they are achieving their goals and maintaining effective working relationships. Groups need to describe what member actions are helpful and unhelpful and make decisions about what behaviors to continue or change. When difficulties in relating to each other arise, students must engage in group processing and identify, define, and solve the problems they are having working together effectively.

Understanding these five basic elements and developing skills in structuring them allows teachers to (a) adapt cooperative learning to their unique circumstances, needs, and students, (b) fine tune their use of cooperative learning, and (c) prevent and solve problems students have in working together.

What Do We Know About Cooperative Efforts?

> Everyone has to work together; if we can't get everybody working toward common goals, nothing is going to happen. (Harold K. Sperlich, president, Chrysler Corporation)

A great deal of research has been conducted comparing the relative effects of cooperative, competitive, and individualistic efforts on instructional outcomes. During the past 100 years, over 550 experimental and 100 correlational studies have been conducted by a wide variety of researchers in different decades with different age subjects, in different subject areas, and in different settings (see Johnson & Johnson, 1989, for a complete listing and review of these studies).

The type of interdependence structured among students determines how they interact with each other, which, in turn, largely determines instructional outcomes. Structuring situations cooperatively results in students interacting in ways that promote each other's success, structuring situations competitively results in students interacting in ways that oppose each other's success, and structuring situations individualistically results in no interaction among students. These interaction patterns affect numerous instructional outcomes, which may be subsumed within the three broad and interrelated categories of effort exerted to achieve, quality of relationships among participants, and participants' psychological adjustment and social competence (see Figure 1) (Johnson & Johnson, 1989).

FIGURE 1
Outcomes of Cooperative Learning

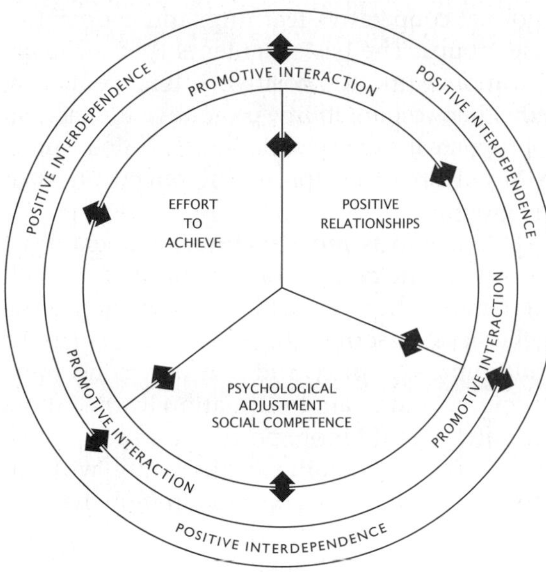

Source: Johnson & Johnson, 1989.

Achievement

> Achievement is a we thing, not a me thing, always the product of many hands and heads. (John Atkinson)

Regarding the question of how successful competitive, individualistic, and cooperative efforts are in promoting productivity and achievement, over 375 studies have been conducted in the past 100 years (Johnson & Johnson, 1989). Working together to achieve a common goal produces higher achievement and greater productivity than does working alone. This is so well confirmed by so much research that it stands as one of the strongest principles of social and organizational psychology.

Cooperative learning, furthermore, results in process gain (i.e., more higher-level reasoning, more frequent generation of new ideas and solutions), greater transfer of what is learned within one situation to another (i.e., group to individual transfer), and more time on task than does competitive or individualistic learning. The more conceptual the task, the more problem solving required; the more higher-level reasoning and critical thinking, the more creativity required; and the greater the application required of what is being learned to the real world, the greater the superiority of cooperative over competitive and individualistic efforts.

Cooperative learning ensures that all students are meaningfully and actively involved in learning. Active, involved students do not tend to engage in disruptive, off-task behavior. Cooperative learning also ensures that students are achieving up to their potential and are experiencing psychological success, so they are motivated to continue to invest energy and effort in learning. Those who experience academic failure are at risk for tuning out and acting up, which often leads to physical or verbal aggression.

Interpersonal Relationships

> A faithful friend is a strong defense, and he that hath found him, hath found a treasure. (Ecclesiastes 6:14)

Over 180 studies have been conducted since the 1940s on the relative impact of cooperative, competitive, and individualistic experiences on interpersonal attraction (Johnson & Johnson, 1989). The data indicate that cooperative experiences promote greater interpersonal attraction than do competitive or individualistic ones. Cooperative learning promotes the development of caring and committed relationships for every student. Even when individuals initially dislike each other or are obviously different from each other, cooperative experiences have been found to promote greater liking than is found in competitive and individualistic situations.

Cooperative groups help students establish and maintain friendships with peers. As relationships become more positive, there are corresponding improvements in productivity, morale, feelings of personal commitment and responsibility to do the assigned work, willingness to take on and persist in completing difficult tasks, and commitment to peers' success and growth. Absenteeism and turnover of membership decreases. Students who are isolated or alienated from their peers and who do not have friends are more likely to be at risk for violent and destructive behavior than students who experience social support and a sense of belonging.

Psychological Health and Social Competence

Working cooperatively with peers, and valuing cooperation, results in greater psychological health, higher self-esteem, and greater social competencies than does competing with peers or working independently. When individuals work together to complete assignments, they interact (improving social skills and competencies), promote each other's success (gaining self-worth), and form personal as well as professional relationships (creating the basis for healthy social development).

Cooperative efforts with caring people tend to increase personal ego-strength, self-confidence, independence, and autonomy. They provide the opportunity to share and solve personal problems, which increases an individual's resilience and ability to cope with adversity and stress. The more individuals work cooperatively, the more they see themselves as worthwhile and as having value and the more autonomous and independent they tend to be.

Cooperative groups provide an arena in which individuals develop the interpersonal and small group skills needed to work effectively with diverse schoolmates. Students learn how to communicate effectively, provide leadership, help the group make good decisions, build trust, repair hurt feelings, and understand others' perspectives. Even kindergartners can practice social skills each day in cooperative activities. Cooperative experiences are not a luxury. They are a necessity for the healthy social and psychological development of individuals who can function independently.

Conclusion

Cooperative learning is the instructional use of small groups in which students work together to maximize their own and each other's learning. Cooperative learning may be differentiated from pseudo groups and traditional classroom learning groups. There are three types of cooperative learning: formal cooperative learning, informal cooperative learning, and cooperative base groups. The basic elements that make cooperation work are positive interdependence, individual accountability, promotive interaction, appropriate use of social skills, and periodic processing of how to improve the effectiveness of the group.

When efforts are structured cooperatively, there is considerable evidence that students will exert more effort to achieve (learn more, use higher-level reasoning strategies more frequently, build more complete and complex conceptual structures, and retain information learned more accurately), build more positive and supportive relationships (including relationships with diverse individuals), and develop in more healthy ways (psychological health, self-esteem, ability to manage stress and adversity).

References

Billion-Dollar Being. (1974). *Topics in applied science.* Golden, CO: Jefferson County Schools.

Johnson, D. W. (1997). *Reaching out: Interpersonal effectiveness and self-actualization* (6th ed.). Boston: Allyn & Bacon.

Johnson, D. W., & Johnson, F. (1997). *Joining together: Group theory and group skills* (6th ed.). Boston: Allyn & Bacon.

Johnson, D. W., & Johnson, R. (1989). *Cooperation and competition: Theory and research.* Edina, MN: Interaction Book Co.

Johnson, D. W., & Johnson, R. (1994). *Leading the cooperative school* (2nd ed.). Edina, MN: Interaction Book Co.

Johnson, D. W., & Johnson, R. (1999). The three Cs of classroom and school management. In H. Freiberg (Ed.), *Beyond behaviorism: Changing the classroom management paradigm.* Boston: Allyn & Bacon.

Johnson, D. W., Johnson, R., & Holubec, E. (1998a). *Advanced cooperative learning* (3rd ed.). Edina, MN: Interaction Book Co.

Johnson, D. W., Johnson, R., & Holubec, E. (1998b). *Cooperation in the classroom* (7th ed.). Edina, MN: Interaction Book Co.

Johnson, D. W., Johnson, R., & Smith, K. (1998). *Active learning: Cooperation in the college classroom* (2nd ed.). Edina, MN: Interaction Book Co.

Postnote

The authors have been researching and championing cooperative learning for many years, and their efforts have made a major contribution to American education. Cooperative learning has become a staple in both pre-service and in-service teacher education. David and Roger Johnson's contributions in developing and researching cooperative learning strategies have placed them among our Classic selections.

Although most educators applaud the idea of cooperative learning, few use it on a regular basis. Many young teachers read about cooperative learning, become advocates, try it a few times with few of the positive results discussed in this article, then put it away in a mental closet (labeled "Great Ideas from the Ivory Tower That Don't Work in the Trenches") and go on to more traditional "sage on the stage" instructional approaches. The key to a more widespread use of cooperative learning may be captured by the well-known story of the tourist in New York City who stops a native and asks: "Sir, how do I get to Carnegie Hall?" The New Yorker doesn't stop, but yells over his shoulder, "Practice! Practice! Practice!" From personal experiences, we know that becoming skillful at cooperative learning takes more than just knowledge of it. Like Sandy Koufax, knowing the mechanics of throwing a fastball is hardly enough. Our advice: Practice! Practice! Practice!

Discussion Questions

1. Describe the experiences you, as a student, have had with cooperative learning.
2. Do you agree or disagree with the common criticism that cooperative learning is unfair because it slows down the progress of the academically gifted?
3. Which aspects of cooperative learning are most appealing? Which are least appealing?

Mapping a Route Toward Differentiated Instruction

CAROL ANN TOMLINSON

FOCUS Question

How does differentiated instruction address the needs of individual learners?

TERMS TO NOTE

Differentiation

Readiness

Developing academically responsive classrooms is important for a country built on the twin values of equality and excellence. Our schools can achieve both of these competing values only to the degree that they can establish heterogeneous communities of learning (attending to issues of equity) built solidly on high-quality curriculum and instruction that strive to maximize the capacity of each learner (attending to issues of excellence).

A serious pursuit of differentiation, or personalized instruction, causes us to grapple with many of our traditional—if questionable—ways of "doing school." Is it reasonable to expect all 2nd graders to learn the same thing, in the same ways, over the same time span? Do single-textbook adoptions send inaccurate messages about the sameness of all learners? Can students learn to take more responsibility for their own learning? Do report cards drive our instruction? Should the classroom teacher be a solitary specialist on all learner needs, or could we support genuinely effective generalist-specialist teams? Can we reconcile learning standards with learner variance?

The questions resist comfortable answers—and are powerfully important. En route to answering them, we try various roads to differentiation. The concreteness of having something ready to do Monday morning is satisfying—and inescapable. After all, the students will arrive and the day must be planned. So we talk about using reading buddies in varied ways to support a range of readers or perhaps developing a learning contract with several options for practicing math skills. Maybe we could try a tiered lesson or interest centers. Three students who clearly understand the chapter need an independent study project. Perhaps we should begin with a differentiated project assignment, allowing

Carol Ann Tomlinson is professor of educational leadership, foundations, and policy at the Curry School of Education, University of Virginia, Charlottesville, Virginia. She is the author of *How To Differentiate Instruction in Mixed-Ability Classrooms* (ASCD, 2001). From Carol Ann Tomlinson, "Mapping a Route Toward Differentiated Instruction," *Educational Leadership,* September 1999, pp. 12–16. Reprinted by permission. The Association for Supervision and Curriculum Development is a worldwide community of educators advocating sound policies and sharing best practices to achieve the success of each learner. To learn more, visit ASCD at **www.ascd.org.**

students to choose a project about the Middle Ages. That's often how our journey toward differentiation begins.

The nature of teaching requires doing. There's not much time to sit and ponder the imponderables. To a point, that's fine—and, in any case, inevitable. A reflective teacher can test many principles from everyday interactions in the classroom. In other words, philosophy can derive from action.

We can't skip one step, however. The first step in making differentiation work is the hardest. In fact, the same first step is required to make all teaching and learning effective: We have to know where we want to end up before we start out—and plan to get there. That is, we must have solid curriculum and instruction in place before we differentiate them. That's harder than it seems.

Looking Inside Two Classrooms

Mr. Appleton is teaching about ancient Rome. His students are reading the textbook in class today. He suggests that they take notes of important details as they read. When they finish, they answer the questions at the end of the chapter. Students who don't finish must do so at home. Tomorrow, they will answer the questions together in class. Mr. Appleton likes to lecture and works hard to prepare his lectures. He expects students to take notes. Later, he will give a quiz on both the notes and the text. He will give students a study sheet before the test, clearly spelling out what will be on the test.

Mrs. Baker is also teaching about ancient Rome. She gives her students graphic organizers to use as they read the textbook chapter and goes over the organizers with the class so that anyone who missed details can fill them in. She brings in pictures of the art and the architecture of the period and tells how important the Romans were in shaping our architecture, language, and laws. When she invites some students to dress in togas for a future class, someone suggests bringing in food so that they can have a Roman banquet—and they do. One day, students do a word-search puzzle of vocabulary words about Rome. On another day, they watch a movie clip that shows gladiators and the Colosseum and talk about the favored "entertainment" of the period. Later, Mrs. Baker reads aloud several myths, and students talk about the myths that they remember from 6th grade. When it's time to study for the test, the teacher lets students go over the chapter together, which they like much better than working at home alone, she says.

She also wants students to like studying about Rome, so she offers a choice of 10 projects. Among the options are creating a poster listing important Roman gods and goddesses, their roles, and their symbols; developing a travel brochure for ancient Rome that a Roman of the day might have used; writing a poem about life in Rome; dressing dolls like citizens of Rome or drawing the fashions of the time; building a model of an important ancient Roman building or a Roman villa; and making a map of the Holy Roman Empire. Students can also propose their own topic.

Thinking About the Two Classrooms

Mr. Appleton's class is not differentiated. He does not appear to notice or respond to student differences. Mrs. Baker's is differentiated—at least by some definitions. Each class has serious flaws in its foundations, however, and for that reason, Mrs. Baker's class may not be any more successful than Mr. Appleton's—and perhaps less so.

Successful teaching requires two elements: student understanding and student engagement. In other words, students must really understand, or make sense of, what they have studied. They should also feel engaged in or "hooked by" the ways that they have learned. The latter can greatly enhance the former and can help young people realize that learning is satisfying.

Mr. Appleton's class appears to lack engagement. There's nothing much to make learning appealing. He may be satisfied by his lecture, but it's doubtful that many of the students are impressed. It is also doubtful that much real student understanding will come from the teaching-learning scenario. Rather, the goal seems to be memorizing data for a test.

Memorizing and understanding are very different. The first has a short life span and little potential to transfer into a broader world. However, at least Mr. Appleton appears clear about what the students should memorize for the test. Mrs. Baker's class lacks even that clarity.

Students in Mrs. Baker's classroom are likely engaged. It is a lively, learner-friendly place with opportunity for student movement, student choice, and peer work. Further, Mrs. Baker's list of project options draws on different student interests or talents—and she is even open to their suggestions.

Although Mrs. Baker succeeds to some degree with engagement, a clear sense of what students should understand as a result of their study is almost totally missing. Thus her careful work to provide choice and to build a comfortable environment for her learners may not net meaningful, long-term learning. Her students are studying "something about ancient Rome." Nothing focuses or ties together the ideas and information that they encounter. Activities are more about being happy than about making meaning. No set of common information, ideas, or skills will stem from completing the various projects. In essence, she has accomplished little for the long haul. Her "differentiation" provides varied avenues to "mush"—multiple versions of fog. Her students work with different tasks, not differentiated ones.

Mr. Appleton's class provides little engagement, little understanding, and scant opportunity for attending to student differences. Mrs. Baker's class provides some engagement, little understanding, and no meaningful differentiation.

An Alternative Approach

To make differentiation work—in fact, to make teaching and learning work—teachers must develop an alternative approach to instructional planning beyond "covering the text" or "creating activities that students will like."

Ms. Cassell has planned her year around a few key concepts that will help students relate to, organize, and retain what they study in history. She has also developed principles or generalizations that govern or uncover how the concepts work. Further, for each unit, she has established a defined set of facts and terms that are essential for students to know to be literate and informed about the topic. She has listed skills for which she and the students are responsible as the year progresses. Finally, she has developed essential questions to intrigue her students and to cause them to engage with her in a quest for understanding.

Ms. Cassell's master list of facts, terms, concepts, principles, and skills stems from her understanding of the discipline of history as well as from the district's learning standards. As the year evolves, Ms. Cassell continually assesses the readiness, interests, and learning profiles of her students and involves them in goal setting and decision making about their learning. As she comes to understand her students and their needs more fully, she modifies her instructional framework and her instruction.

Ms. Cassell is also teaching about ancient Rome. Among the key concepts in this unit, as in many others throughout the year, are culture, change, and interdependence. Students will be responsible for important terms, such as *republic, patrician, plebeian, veto, villa,* and *Romance language;* names of key individuals, for example, Julius Caesar, Cicero, and Virgil; and names of important places, for instance, the Pantheon and the Colosseum.

For this unit, students explore key generalizations or principles: Varied cultures share common elements. Cultures are shaped by beliefs and values, customs, geography, and resources. People are shaped by and shape their cultures. Societies and cultures change for both internal and external reasons. Elements of a society and its cultures are interdependent.

Among important skills that students apply are using resources on history effectively, interpreting information from resources, blending data from several resources, and organizing effective paragraphs. The essential question that Ms. Cassell often poses to her students is, How would your life and culture be different if you lived in a different time and place?

Looking Inside the Third Classroom

Early in the unit, Ms. Cassell's students begin work, both at home and in class, on two sequential tasks that will extend throughout the unit as part of their larger study of ancient Rome. Both tasks are differentiated.

For the first task, students assume the role of someone from ancient Rome, such as a soldier, a teacher, a healer, a farmer, a slave, or a farmer's wife. Students base their choice solely on their own interests. They work both alone and with others who select the same topic and use a wide variety of print, video, computer, and human resources to understand what their life in ancient Rome would have been like.

Ultimately, students create a first-person data sheet that their classmates can use as a resource for their second task. The data sheet calls for the person in the role to provide accurate, interesting, and detailed information about what his or her daily schedule would be like, what he or she would eat and wear, where he or she would live, how he or she would be treated by the law, what sorts of problems or challenges he or she would face, the current events of the time, and so on.

Ms. Cassell works with both the whole class and small groups on evaluating the availability and appropriate use of data sources, writing effective paragraphs, and blending information from several sources into a coherent whole. Students use these skills as they develop the first-person data sheets. The teacher's goal is for each student to increase his or her skill level in each area.

The second task calls on students to compare and contrast their own lives with the lives of children of similar age in ancient Rome. Unlike the first task, which was based on student interest, this one is differentiated primarily on the basis of student readiness. The teacher assigns each student a scenario establishing his or her family context for the task: "You are the eldest son of a lawmaker living during the later years of the period known as Pax Romana," for example. Ms. Cassell bases the complexity of the scenario on the student's skill with researching and thinking about history. Most students work with families unlike those in their first task. Students who need continuity between the tasks, however, can continue in a role familiar from their first investigation.

All students use the previously developed first-person data sheets as well as a range of other resources to gather background information. They must address a common set of specified questions: How is what you eat shaped by the economics of your family and by your location? What is your level of education and how is that affected by your status in society? How is your life interdependent with the lives of others in ancient Rome? How will Rome change during your lifetime? How will those changes affect your life? All students must also meet certain research and writing criteria.

Despite the common elements, the task is differentiated in several ways. It is differentiated by interest because each student adds questions that are directed by personal interests: What games did children play? What was the practice of science like then? What was the purpose and style of art?

Readiness differentiation occurs because each student adds personal research and writing goals, often with the teacher's help, to his or her criteria for success. A wide range of research resources is available, including books with varied readability levels, video and audiotapes, models, and access to informed people. The teacher also addresses readiness through small-group sessions in which she provides different sorts of teacher and peer support, different kinds of modeling, and different kinds of coaching for success, depending on the readiness levels of students.

Finally, the teacher adds to each student's investigation one specific question whose degree of difficulty is based on her most recent assessments of student knowledge, facility with research, and thinking about history. An example of a more complex question is, How will your life differ from that of the previous generation in your family, and how will your grandchildren's lives compare with yours? A less complex, but still challenging question is, How will language change from the generation before you to two generations after you, and why will those changes take place?

Learning-profile differentiation is reflected in the different media that students use to express their findings: journal entries, an oral monologue, or a videotape presentation. Guidelines for each type of product ensure quality and focus on essential understandings and skills established for the unit. Students may work alone or with a "parallel partner" who is working with the same role, although each student must ultimately produce his or her own product.

At other points in the study of ancient Rome, Ms. Cassell differentiates instruction. Sometimes she varies the sorts of graphic organizers that students use when they read, do research, or take notes in class. She may use review groups of mixed readiness and then conduct review games with students of like readiness working together. She works hard to ask a range of questions that move from concrete and familiar to abstract and unfamiliar in all class discussions. She sometimes provides homework options in which students select the tasks that they believe will help them understand important ideas or use important skills best. Of course, the class also plans, works, reviews, and debates as a whole group.

Students find Ms. Cassell's class engaging—and not just because it's fun. It's engaging because it shows the connection between their own lives and life long ago. It helps them see the interconnectedness among times in history and make links with other subjects. It tickles their curiosity. And it provides a challenge that pushes each learner a bit further than is comfortable—and then supports success. Sometimes those things are fun. Often they are knotty and hard. Always they dignify the learner and the subject.

Mr. Cassell's class is highly likely to be effective for her varied learners, in part because she continually attempts to reach her students where they are and move them on—she differentiates instruction. The success of the differentiation, however, is not a stand-alone matter. It is successful because it is squarely rooted in student engagement plus student understanding.

This teacher knows where she wants her students to arrive at the end of their shared learning journey and where her students are along that journey at a given time. Because she is clear about the destination and the path of the travelers, she can effectively guide them, and she varies or differentiates her instruction to accomplish this goal. Further, her destination is not merely the amassing of data but rather the constructing of understanding. Her class provides a good example of the close and necessary relationship between effective curriculum and instruction and effective differentiation.

The First Step Is the Compass

Mr. Appleton may have a sense of what he wants his students to know at the end of the road, but not about what his students should understand and be able to do. He teaches facts, but no key concepts, guiding principles, or essential questions. With a fact-based curriculum, differentiating instruction is difficult. Perhaps some students could learn more facts and some, fewer. Perhaps some students could have more time to drill the facts, and some, less. It's difficult to envision a defensible way to differentiate a fact-driven curriculum, probably because the curriculum itself is difficult to defend.

Mrs. Baker also appears to lack a clear vision of the meaning of her subject, of the nature of her discipline and what it adds to human understanding, and of why it should matter to a young learner to study old times. There is little clarity about facts—let alone concepts, guiding principles, or essential questions. Further, she confuses folly with engagement. She thinks that she is differentiating instruction, but without instructional clarity, her activities and projects are merely different—not differentiated. Because there is no instructional clarity, there is no basis for defensible differentiation.

Ms. Cassell plans for what students should know, understand, and be able to do at the end of a sequence of learning. She dignifies each learner by planning tasks that are interesting, relevant, and powerful. She invites each student to wonder. She determines where each student is in knowledge, skill, and understanding and where he or she needs to move. She differentiates instruction to facilitate that goal. For her, differentiation is one piece of the mosaic of professional expertise. It is not a strategy to be plugged in occasionally or often, but is a way of thinking about the classroom. In her class, there is a platform for differentiation.

Ms. Cassell helps us see that differentiated instruction must dignify each learner with learning that is "whole," important, and meaning making. The core of *what* the students learn remains relatively steady. *How* the student learns—including degree of difficulty, working arrangements, modes of expression, and sorts of scaffolding—may vary considerably. Differentiation is not so much the "stuff" as the "how." If the "stuff" is ill conceived, the "how" is doomed.

The old saw is correct: Every journey *does* begin with a single step. The journey to successfully differentiated or personalized classrooms will succeed only if we carefully take the first step—ensuring a foundation of best-practice curriculum and instruction.

Postnote

The term *differentiated instruction* is relatively new in education circles, but its practice is as old as teachers and classrooms. Teachers know that their classrooms contain students with tremendous diversity—ethnic, cultural, racial, academic, learning styles, to name but a few of the diverse characteristics. How can teachers plan and deliver instruction and assessment that will respond to these forms of diversity to help students learn better? Differentiated instruction is teaching with student variance in mind and using practical ways to respond to learner needs. Instead of presuming that all of your students are essentially alike, differentiated instruction means starting where the students are and planning varied approaches to what individual students need to learn, how they will learn it, and how they can express what they have learned. The idea of differentiated or personalized instruction has great appeal to teachers and teacher educators, but its implementation may seem overwhelming, particularly for new teachers.

In other writings, Carol Ann Tomlinson advises that teachers start the process slowly and gradually expand differentiation as they feel comfortable and have the time. Most important is making a commitment to the process of responding to student differences.

Discussion Questions

1. As you read the three vignettes involving Mr. Appleton, Mrs. Baker, and Ms. Cassell, which approach was more indicative of your elementary and secondary schooling? Which approach did you find more appealing? Why?
2. What concerns or questions do you have regarding differentiated instruction?
3. Did you have a teacher who used differentiated instruction particularly successfully? Describe what he or she did that made the instruction successful.

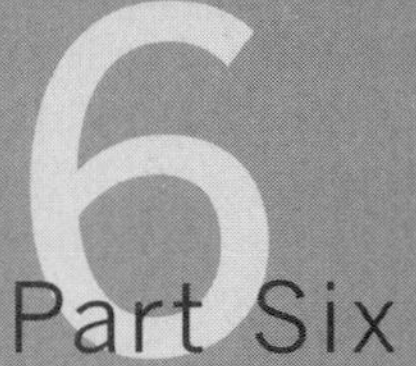

Part Six

Foundations

As a career, education is a practical field like medicine or criminal justice. It is not a discipline or content area, such as anthropology, physics, or English literature. However, education draws on these various disciplines and fields of knowledge to guide teachers in their work.

The term *foundations* refers to the particular group of academic disciplines from which the practice of education draws quite heavily, including philosophy, history, psychology, and sociology. It is often said that a house is as good as the foundation upon which it rests. In our view, likewise, the most effective teaching is firmly grounded on these educational foundations.

CLASSIC

My Pedagogic Creed

JOHN DEWEY

FOCUS Question

What did the Father of Progressive Education actually believe?

TERM TO NOTE

Education

Article I—What Education Is

I BELIEVE THAT

- all education proceeds by the participation of the individual in the social consciousness of the race. This process begins unconsciously almost at birth, and is continually shaping the individual's powers, saturating his consciousness, forming his habits, training his ideas, and arousing his feelings and emotions. Through this unconscious education the individual gradually comes to share in the intellectual and moral resources which humanity has succeeded in getting together. He becomes an inheritor of the funded capital of civilization. The most formal and technical education in the world cannot safely depart from this general process. It can only organize it or differentiate it in some particular direction.
- the only true education comes through the stimulation of the child's powers by the demands of the social situations in which he finds himself. Through these demands he is stimulated to act as a member of a unity, to emerge from his original narrowness of action and feeling, and to conceive of himself from the standpoint of the welfare of the group to which he belongs. Through the responses which others make to his own activities he comes to know what these mean in social terms. The value which they have is reflected back into them. For instance, through the response which is made to the child's instinctive babblings the child comes to know what those babblings mean; they are transformed into articulate language, and thus the child is introduced into the consolidated wealth of ideas and emotions which are now summed up in language.
- this educational process has two sides—one psychological and one sociological—and that neither can be subordinated to the other, or neglected, without evil results following. Of these two sides, the psychological is the basis. The child's own instincts and powers furnish

John Dewey was a philosopher and educator; he founded the progressive education movement. This article was published originally as a pamphlet by E. L. Kellogg and Co., 1897.

the material and give the starting-point for all education. Save as the efforts of the educator connect with some activity which the child is carrying on of his own initiative independent of the educator, education becomes reduced to a pressure from without. It may, indeed, give certain external results, but cannot truly be called educative. Without insight into the psychological structure and activities of the individual the educative process will, therefore, be haphazard and arbitrary. If it chances to coincide with the child's activity it will get a leverage; if it does not, it will result in friction, or disintegration, or arrest of the child-nature.

- knowledge of social conditions, of the present state of civilization, is necessary in order properly to interpret the child's powers. The child has his own instincts and tendencies, but we do not know what these mean until we can translate them into their social equivalents. We must be able to carry them back into a social past and see them as the inheritance of previous race activities. We must also be able to project them into the future to see what their outcome and end will be. In the illustration just used, it is the ability to see in the child's babblings the promise and potency of a future social intercourse and conversation which enables one to deal in the proper way with that instinct.
- the psychological and social sides are organically related, and that education cannot be regarded as a compromise between the two, or a superimposition of one upon the other. We are told that the psychological definition of education is barren and formal—that it gives us only the idea of a development of all the mental powers without giving us any idea of the use to which these powers are put. On the other hand, it is urged that the social definition of education, as getting adjusted to civilization, makes of it a forced and external process, and results in subordinating the freedom of the individual to a preconceived social and political status.
- each of these objections is true when urged against one side isolated from the other. In order to know what a power really is we must know what its end, use, or function is, and this we cannot know save as we conceive of the individual as active in social relationships. But, on the other hand, the only possible adjustment which we can give to the child under existing conditions is that which arises through putting him in complete possession of all his powers. With the advent of democracy and modern industrial conditions, it is impossible to foretell definitely just what civilization will be twenty years from now. Hence it is impossible to prepare the child for any precise set of conditions. To prepare him for the future life means to give him command of himself; it means so to train him that he will have the full and ready use of all his capacities; that his eye and ear and hand may be tools ready to command, that his judgment may be capable of grasping the conditions under which it has to work, and the executive forces be trained to act economically and efficiently. It is impossible to reach this sort of adjustment save as constant regard is had to the individual's own powers, tastes, and interests—that is, as education is continually converted into psychological terms.

In sum, I believe that the individual who is to be educated is a social individual, and that society is an organic union of individuals. If we eliminate the social factor from the child we are left only with an abstraction; if we eliminate the individual factor from society, we are left only with an inert and lifeless mass. Education, therefore, must begin with a psychological insight into the child's capacities, interests, and habits. It must be controlled at every point by reference to these same considerations. These powers, interests, and habits must be continually interpreted—we must know what they mean. They must be translated into terms of their social equivalents—into terms of what they are capable of in the way of social service.

Article II—What the School Is

I BELIEVE THAT

- the school is primarily a social institution. Education being a social process, the school is simply that form of community life in which all those agencies are concentrated that will be most effective in bringing the child to share in the inherited resources of the race, and to use his own powers for social ends.
- education, therefore, is a process of living and not a preparation for future living.
- the school must represent present life—life as real and vital to the child as that which he carries on in the home, in the neighborhood, or on the playground.
- that education which does not occur through forms of life, forms that are worth living for their own sake, is always a poor substitute for the genuine reality, and tends to cramp and to deaden.
- the school, as an institution, should simplify existing social life; should reduce it, as it were, to an embryonic form. Existing life is so complex that the child cannot be brought into contact with it without either confusion or distraction; he is either overwhelmed by the multiplicity of activities which are going on, so that he loses his own power of orderly reaction, or he is so stimulated by these various activities that his powers are prematurely called into play and he becomes either unduly specialized or else disintegrated.
- as such simplified social life, the school life should grow gradually out of the home life; that it should take up and continue the activities with which the child is already familiar in the home.
- it should exhibit these activities to the child, and reproduce them in such ways that the child will gradually learn the meaning of them, and be capable of playing his own part in relation to them.
- this is a psychological necessity, because it is the only way of securing continuity in the child's growth, the only way of giving a background of past experience to the new ideas given in school.
- it is also a social necessity because the home is the form of social life in which the child has been nurtured and in connection with which he has had his moral training. It is the business of the school to deepen and extend his sense of the values bound up in his home life.
- much of the present education fails because it neglects this fundamental principle of the school as a form of community life. It conceives the school as a place where certain information is to be given, where certain lessons are to be learned, or where certain habits are to be formed. The value of these is conceived as lying largely in the remote future; the child must do these things for the sake of something else he is to do; they are mere preparations. As a result they do not become a part of the life experience of the child and so are not truly educative.
- the moral education centers upon this conception of the school as a mode of social life, that the best and deepest moral training is precisely that which one gets through having to enter into proper relations with others in a unity of work and thought. The present educational systems, so far as they destroy or neglect this unity, render it difficult or impossible to get any genuine, regular moral training.
- the child should be stimulated and controlled in his work through the life of the community.
- under existing conditions far too much of the stimulus and control proceeds from the teacher, because of neglect of the idea of the school as a form of social life.
- the teacher's place and work in the school is to be interpreted from this same basis. The teacher is not in the school to impose certain ideas or to form certain habits in the child, but is there as a member of the community to select the influences which shall affect the

child and to assist him in properly responding to these influences.

- the discipline of the school should proceed from the life of the school as a whole and not directly from the teacher.
- the teacher's business is simply to determine, on the basis of larger experience and riper wisdom, how the discipline of life shall come to the child.
- all questions of the grading of the child and his promotion should be determined by reference to the same standard. Examinations are of use only so far as they test the child's fitness for social life and reveal the place in which he can be of the most service and where he can receive the most help.

Article III—The Subject-Matter of Education

I BELIEVE THAT

- the social life of the child is the basis of concentration, or correlation, in all his training or growth. The social life gives the unconscious the unity and the background of all his efforts and of all his attainments.
- the subject-matter of the school curriculum should mark a gradual differentiation out of the primitive unconscious unity of social life.
- we violate the child's nature and render difficult the best ethical results by introducing the child too abruptly to a number of special studies, of reading, writing, geography, etc., out of relation to this social life.
- the true center of correlation on the school subjects is not science, nor literature, nor history, nor geography, but the child's own social activities.
- education cannot be unified in the study of science, or so-called nature study, because apart from human activity, nature itself is not a unity; nature in itself is a number of diverse objects in space and time, and to attempt to make it the center of work by itself is to introduce a principle of radiation rather than one of concentration.
- literature is the reflex expression and interpretation of social experience; that hence it must follow upon and not precede such experience. It, therefore, cannot be made the basis, although it may be made the summary of unification.
- history is of educative value in so far as it presents phases of social life and growth. It must be controlled by reference to social life. When taken simply as history it is thrown into the distant past and becomes dead and inert. Taken as the record of man's social life and progress it becomes full of meaning. I believe, however, that it cannot be so taken excepting as the child is also introduced directly into social life.
- the primary basis of education is in the child's powers at work along the same general constructive lines as those which have brought civilization into being.
- the only way to make the child conscious of his social heritage is to enable him to perform those fundamental types of activity which make civilization what it is.
- the so-called expressive or constructive activities are the center of correlation.
- this gives the standard for the place of cooking, sewing, manual training, etc., in the school.
- they are not special studies which are to be introduced over and above a lot of others in the way of relaxation or relief, or as additional accomplishments. I believe rather that they represent, as types, fundamental forms of social activity, and that it is possible and desirable that the child's introduction into the more formal subjects of the curriculum be through the medium of these activities.
- the study of science is educational in so far as it brings out the materials and processes which make social life what it is.
- one of the greatest difficulties in the present teaching of science is that the material is

presented in purely objective form, or is treated as a new peculiar kind of experience which the child can add to that which he has already had. In reality, science is of value because it gives the ability to interpret and control the experience already had. It should be introduced, not as so much new subject-matter, but as showing the factors already involved in previous experience and as furnishing tools by which that experience can be more easily and effectively regulated.

- at present we lose much of the value of literature and language studies because of our elimination of the social element. Language is almost always treated in the books of pedagogy simply as the expression of thought. It is true that language is a logical instrument, but it is fundamentally and primarily a social instrument. Language is the device for communication; it is the tool through which one individual comes to share the ideas and feelings of others. When treated simply as a way of getting individual information, or as a means of showing off what one had learned, it loses its social motive and end.
- there is, therefore, no succession of studies in the ideal school curriculum. If education is life, all life has, from the outset, a scientific aspect, an aspect of art and culture, and an aspect of communication. It cannot, therefore, be true that the proper studies for one grade are mere reading and writing, and that at a later grade, reading, or literature, or science, may be introduced. The progress is not in the succession of studies, but in the development of new attitudes towards, and new interests in, experience.
- education must be conceived as a continuing reconstruction of experience; that the process and the goal of education are one and the same thing.
- to set up any end outside of education, as furnishing its goal and standard, is to deprive the educational process of much of its meaning, and tends to make us rely upon false and external stimuli in dealing with the child.

Article IV—The Nature of Method

I BELIEVE THAT

- the question of method is ultimately reducible to the question of the order of development of the child's powers and interests. The law for presenting and treating material is the law implicit within the child's own nature. Because this is so I believe the following statements are of supreme importance as determining the spirit in which education is carried on:
- the active side precedes the passive in the development of the child-nature; that expression comes before conscious impression; that the muscular development precedes the sensory; that movements come before conscious sensation; I believe that consciousness is essentially motor or impulsive; that conscious states tend to project themselves in action.
- the neglect of this principle is the cause of a large part of the waste of time and strength in school work. The child is thrown into a passive, receptive, or absorbing attitude. The conditions are such that he is not permitted to follow the law of nature; the result is friction and waste.
- ideas (intellectual and rational processes) also result from action and devolve for the sake of the better control of action. What we term reason is primarily the law of orderly and effective action. To attempt to develop the reasoning powers, the powers of judgment, without reference to the selection and arrangement of means in action, is the fundamental fallacy in our present methods of dealing with this matter. As a result we present the child with arbitrary symbols. Symbols are a necessity in mental development, but they have their place as tools for economizing effort; presented by themselves they are a mass of meaningless and arbitrary ideas imposed from without.
- the image is the great instrument of instruction. What a child gets out of any subject presented to him is simply the images which he himself forms with regard to it.

- if nine-tenths of the energy at present directed towards making the child learn certain things were spent in seeing to it that the child was forming proper images, the work of instruction would be indefinitely facilitated.
- much of the time and attention now given to the preparation and presentation of lessons might be more wisely and profitably expended in training the child's power of imagery and in seeing to it that he was continually forming definite, vivid, and growing images of the various subjects with which he comes in contact in his experience.
- interests are the signs and symptoms of growing power. I believe that they represent dawning capacities. Accordingly the constant and careful observation of interests is of the utmost importance for the educator.
- these interests are to be observed as showing the state of development which the child has reached.
- they prophesy the stage upon which he is about to enter.
- only through the continual and sympathetic observation of childhood's interests can the adult enter into the child's life and see what it is ready for, and upon what material it could work most readily and fruitfully.
- these interests are neither to be humored nor repressed. To repress interest is to substitute the adult for the child, and so to weaken intellectual curiosity and alertness, to suppress initiative, and to deaden interest. To humor the interests is to substitute the transient for the permanent. The interest is always the sign of some power below; the important thing is to discover this power. To humor the interest is to fail to penetrate below the surface, and its sure result is to substitute caprice and whim for genuine interest.
- the emotions are the reflex of actions.
- to endeavor to stimulate or arouse the emotions apart from their corresponding activities is to introduce an unhealthy and morbid state of mind.
- if we can only secure right habits of action and thought, with reference to the good, the true, and the beautiful, the emotions will for the most part take care of themselves.
- next to deadness and dullness, formalism and routine, our education is threatened with no greater evil than sentimentalism.
- this sentimentalism is the necessary result of the attempt to divorce feeling from action.

Article V—The School and Social Progress

I BELIEVE THAT

- education is the fundamental method of social progress and reform.
- all reforms which rest simply upon enactment of law, or the threatening of certain penalties, or upon changes in mechanical or outward arrangements, are transitory and futile.
- education is a regulation of the process of coming to share in the social consciousness; and that the adjustment of individual activity on the basis of this social consciousness is the only sure method of social reconstruction.
- this conception has due regard for both the individualistic and socialistic ideals. It is duly individual because it recognizes the formation of a certain character as the only genuine basis of right living. It is socialistic because it recognizes that this right character is not to be formed by merely individual precept, example, or exhortation, but rather by the influence of a certain form of institutional or community life upon the individual, and that the social organism through the school, as its organ, may determine ethical results.
- in the ideal school we have the reconciliation of the individualistic and the institutional ideals.
- the community's duty to education is, therefore, its paramount moral duty. By law and punishment, by social agitation and discussion, society can regulate and form itself in

a more or less haphazard and chance way. But through education society can formulate its own purposes, can organize its own means and resources, and thus shape itself with definiteness and economy in the direction in which it wishes to move.

- when society once recognizes the possibilities in this direction, and the obligations which these possibilities impose, it is impossible to conceive of the resources of time, attention, and money which will be put at the disposal of the educator.
- it is the business of every one interested in education to insist upon the school as the primary and most effective interest of social progress and reform in order that society may be awakened to realize what the school stands for, and aroused to the necessity of endowing the educator with sufficient equipment properly to perform his task.
- education thus conceived marks the most perfect and intimate union of science and art conceivable in human experience.
- the art of thus giving shape to human powers and adapting them to social service is the supreme art; one calling into its service the best of artists; that no insight, sympathy, tact, executive power, is too great for such service.
- with the growth of psychological service, giving added insight into individual structure and laws of growth; and with growth of social science, adding to our knowledge of the right organization of individuals, all scientific resources can be utilized for the purpose of education.
- when science and art thus join hands the most commanding motive for human action will be reached, the most genuine springs of human conduct aroused, and the best service that human nature is capable of guaranteed.
- the teacher is engaged, not simply in the training of individuals, but in the formation of the proper social life.
- every teacher should realize the dignity of his calling; that he is a social servant set apart for the maintenance of proper social order and the securing of the right social growth.
- in this way the teacher always is the prophet of the true God and the usherer in of the true kingdom of God.

Postnote

This article is a Classic because it outlines the core beliefs of the American who has had the most powerful impact on our schools—John Dewey. Dewey, the father of progressivism, was the most influential educational thinker of the last 100-plus years. Many of the beliefs expressed in this article (originally published in 1897) have greatly affected educational practice in America. What we find most curious is how current some of these statements still are. On the other hand, many seem dated and clearly from another era. Those that appeal to altruism and idealism have a particularly old-fashioned ring to them. The question remains, however: Which is "out of sync"—the times or the appeals to idealism and altruism?

Discussion Questions

1. How relevant do you believe Dewey's statements are today? Why?
2. Which of Dewey's beliefs do you personally agree or disagree with? Why?
3. How does Dewey's famous statement that "education . . . is a process of living and not a preparation for future living" square with what your parents, guidance counselors, and teachers have told you over the years? If different, how do you explain this?

CLASSIC

46 Personal Thoughts on Teaching and Learning

CARL ROGERS

FOCUS Question

One of the twentieth century's most influential psychologists asks the question, "What can teachers really teach us?"

Terms to Note

Inconsequential learning

Self-discovered learning

I wish to present some very brief remarks, in the hope that if they bring forth any reaction from you, I may get some new light on my own ideas.

I find it a very troubling thing to *think*, particularly when I think about my own experiences and try to extract from those experiences the meaning that seems genuinely inherent in them. At first such thinking is very satisfying, because it seems to discover sense and pattern in a whole host of discrete events. But then it very often becomes dismaying, because I realize how ridiculous these thoughts, which have much value to me, would seem to most people. My impression is that if I try to find the meaning of my own experience it leads me, nearly always, in directions regarded as absurd.

So in the next three or four minutes, I will try to digest some of the meanings which have come to me from my classroom experience and the experience I have had in individual and group therapy. They are in no way intended as conclusions for someone else, or a guide to what others should do or be. They are the very tentative meanings, as of April 1952, which my experience has had for me, and some of the bothersome questions which their absurdity raises. I will put each idea or meaning in a separate lettered paragraph, not because they are in any particular logical order, but because each meaning is separately important to me.

a. I may as well start with this one in view of the purposes of this conference. *My experience has been that I cannot teach another person how to teach.* To attempt it is for me, in the long run, futile.

b. *It seems to me that anything that can be taught to another is relatively inconsequential, and has little or no significant influence on behavior.*

Carl Rogers, now deceased, was the most noted leader of the nondirective, client-centered theory of psychotherapy. He was president of the American Psychological Association and the American Academy of Psychotherapists. "Personal Thoughts on Teaching and Learning" by Carl Rogers, from *On Becoming a Person* (Boston: Houghton Mifflin, 1961), pp. 275–278.

That sounds so ridiculous I can't help but question it at the same time that I present it.

c. *I realize increasingly that I am only interested in learnings which significantly influence behavior.* Quite possibly this is simply a personal idiosyncrasy.

d. *I have come to feel that the only learning which significantly influences behavior is self-discovered, self-appropriated learning.*

e. *Such self-discovered learning, truth that has been personally appropriated and assimilated in experience, cannot be directly communicated to another.* As soon as an individual tries to communicate such experience directly, often with a quite natural enthusiasm, it becomes teaching, and its results are inconsequential. It was some relief recently to discover that Søren Kierkegaard, the Danish philosopher, had found this too, in his own experience, and stated it very clearly a century ago. It made it seem less absurd.

f. As a consequence of the above, *I realize that I have lost interest in being a teacher.*

g. When I try to teach, as I do sometimes, I am appalled by the results, which seem a little more than inconsequential, because sometimes the teaching appears to succeed. When this happens I find that the results are damaging. It seems to cause the individual to distrust his own experience, and to stifle significant learning. *Hence I have come to feel that the outcomes of teaching are either unimportant or hurtful.*

h. When I look back at the results of my past teaching, the real results seem the same—either damage was done, or nothing significant occurred. This is frankly troubling.

i. As a consequence, *I realize that I am only interested in being a learner, preferably learning things that matter, that have some significant influence on my own behavior.*

j. *I find it very rewarding to learn,* in groups, in relationship with one person as in therapy, or by myself.

k. *I find that one of the best, but most difficult ways for me to learn is to drop my own defensiveness, at least temporarily, and try to understand the way in which his experience seems and feels to the other person.*

l. *I find that another way of learning for me is to state my own uncertainties, to try to clarify my puzzlements, and thus get closer to the meaning that my experience actually seems to have.*

m. This whole train of experiencing, and the meanings that I have thus far discovered in it, seem to have launched me on a process which is both fascinating and at times a little frightening. *It seems to mean letting my experience carry me on, in a direction which appears to be forward, toward goals that I can but dimly define, as I try to understand at least the current meaning of that experience.* The sensation is that of floating with a complex stream of experience, with the fascinating possibility of trying to comprehend its ever changing complexity.

I am almost afraid I may seem to have gotten away from any discussion of learning, as well as teaching. Let me again introduce a practical note by saying that by themselves these interpretations of my own experience may sound queer and aberrant, but not particularly shocking. It is when I realize the *implications* that I shudder a bit at the distance I have come from the commonsense world that everyone knows is right. I can best illustrate that by saying that if the experiences of others had been the same as mine, and if they had discovered similar meanings in it, many consequences would be implied.

a. Such experience would imply that we would do away with teaching. People would get together if they wished to learn.

b. We would do away with examinations. They measure only the inconsequential type of learning.

c. The implication would be that we would do away with grades and credits for the same reason.

d. We would do away with degrees as a measure of competence partly for the same reason. Another reason is that a degree marks an end or a conclusion of something, and a learner is only interested in the continuing process of learning.

e. It would imply doing away with the exposition of conclusions, for we would realize that no one learns significantly from conclusions.

I think I had better stop there. I do not want to become too fantastic. I want to know primarily whether anything in my inward thinking as I have tried to describe it, speaks to anything in your experience of the classroom as you have lived it, and if so, what the meanings are that exist for you in *your* experience.

Postnote

This article is a Classic because it had a significant influence on educational practice during the 1960s and 1970s, and some of its effects are still with us. Rogers's personal philosophy of teaching and learning, so well expressed in this selection, is of course quite controversial. Give it a little test for yourself. Think of a couple of the most significant things you have learned as a human being. Now think of how you learned them. Did someone teach them to you, or did you discover them yourself through experience? Try a different approach and ask yourself what of significance you have ever been taught. Be specific. How do you feel about Rogers's statements now?

Discussion Questions

1. Do you agree or disagree with Rogers's ideas on teaching and learning? Why?
2. Do Rogers's statements have any implications for you as a teacher? Explain your answer.
3. Identify three points in the article with which you agree and three with which you disagree.

CLASSIC

The Educated Person

ERNEST L. BOYER

FOCUS Question

There is no more important question than the one answered here: "What is most worth knowing?"

TERMS TO NOTE

Carnegie unit

Educated person

As we anticipate a new century, I am drawn back to questions that have, for generations, perplexed educators and philosophers and parents. What *is* an educated person? What *should* schools be teaching to students?

In searching for answers to these questions, we must consider first not the curriculum, but the human condition. And we must reflect especially on two essential realities of life. First, each person is unique. In defining goals, it is crucial for educators to affirm the special characteristics of each student. We must create in schools a climate in which students are empowered, and we must find ways in the nation's classrooms to celebrate the potential of each child. But beyond the diversity of individuals, educators also must acknowledge a second reality: the deeply rooted characteristics that bind together the human community. We must show students that people around the world share a great many experiences. Attention to both these aspects of our existence is critical to any discussion of what all children should learn.

What, then, does it mean to be an educated person? It means developing one's own aptitudes and interests and discovering the diversity that makes us each unique. And it means becoming permanently empowered with language proficiency, general knowledge, social confidence, and moral awareness in order to be economically and civically successful. But becoming well educated also means discovering the connectedness of things. Educators must help students see relationships across the disciplines and learn that education is a communal act, one that affirms not only individualism, but community. And for these

---

Ernest L. Boyer was, until his death in 1996, one of the key figures in American education. He held numerous positions in education from classroom teacher to president of the Carnegie Foundation for the Advancement of Teaching, and throughout his career he was widely respected for his sound, balanced views. "The Educated Person," by Ernest L. Boyer, from *Toward a Coherent Curriculum* by James A. Beane, pp. 16–25.

goals to be accomplished, we need a new curriculum framework that is both comprehensive and coherent, one that can encompass existing subjects and integrate fragmented content while relating the curriculum to the realities of life. This curriculum must address the uniqueness of students' histories and experiences, but it also must guide them to understand the many ways that humans are connected.

Some schools and teachers are aiming to fully educate students, but most of us have a very long way to go in reaching this goal. Today, almost all students in U.S. schools still complete Carnegie units in exchange for a diploma. The time has come to bury the old Carnegie unit; since the Foundation I now head created this unit of academic measure nearly a century ago, I feel authorized to declare it obsolete. Why? Because it has helped turn schooling into an exercise in trivial pursuit. Students get academic "credit," but they fail to gain a coherent view of what they study. Education is measured by seat time, not time for learning. While curious young children still ask why things are, many older children ask only, "Will this be on the test?" All students should be encouraged to ask "Why?" because "Why?" is the question that leads students to connections.

In abandoning the Carnegie unit, I do not endorse the immediate adoption of national assessment programs; indeed, I think we must postpone such programs until we are much clearer about what students should be learning. The goal, again, is not only to help students become well informed and prepared for lifelong learning, but also to help them put learning into the larger context of discovering the connectedness of things. Barbara McClintock, the 1983 winner of the Nobel Prize for Physiology–Medicine, asserts: "Everything is one. There is no way to draw a line between things." Contrary to McClintock's vision, the average school or college catalog dramatizes the separate academic boxes.

Frank Press, president of the National Academy of Sciences, compares scientists to artists, evoking the magnificent double helix, which broke the genetic code. He said the double helix is not only rational, but beautiful. Similarly, when scientists and technicians watch the countdown to a space launch, they don't say, "Our formulas worked again." They respond, "Beautiful!" instinctively reaching for the aesthetic term to praise a technological achievement. When physicist Victor Weisskopf was asked, "What gives you hope in troubled times?" he replied, "Mozart and quantum mechanics." Most schools, however, separate science and art, discouraging students from seeing the connections between them.

How, then, can we help students see relationships and patterns and gain understanding beyond the separate academic subjects? How can we rethink the curriculum and use the disciplines to illuminate larger, more integrated ends?

Human Commonalities

In the 1981 book *A Quest for Common Learning*, I suggested that we might organize the curriculum not on the basis of disciplines or departments, but on the basis of "core commonalities." By core commonalities, I mean universal experiences that make us human, experiences shared by all cultures on the planet. During the past decade and a half, my thinking about this thematic structure has continued to evolve. I now envision eight commonalities that bind us to one another:

I. The Life Cycle

As life's most fundamental truth, we share, first, the experience that connects birth, growth, and death. This life cycle binds each of us to others, and I find it sad that so many students go through life without reflecting on the mystery of their own existence. Many complete twelve or sixteen years of formal schooling not considering the sacredness of their own bodies, not learning to sustain wellness, not pondering the imperative of death.

In reshaping the curriculum to help students see connections, I would position study of "The Life Cycle" at the core of common learning. Attention would go to nutrition, health, and all aspects of wellness. For a project, each student would undertake the care of some life form.

My wife is a certified nurse-midwife who delivers babies, including seven grandchildren of our own. Kay feels special pain when delivering the baby of a teenage girl because she knows that she is delivering one child into the arms of another, and that both have all too often lived for nine months on soda and potato chips. Some young mothers first learn about the birth process between the sharp pains of labor.

Too many young women and young men pass through our process of education without learning about their own bodies. Out of ignorance, they suffer poor nutrition, addiction, and violence. "Maintaining children's good health is a shared responsibility of parents, schools, and the community at large," according to former Secretary of Education William Bennett (1986, p. 37). He urges elementary schools "to provide children with the knowledge, habits, and attitudes that will equip them for a fit and healthy life."

Study of the Life Cycle would encourage students to reflect sensitively on the mystery of birth and growth and death, to learn about body functions and thus understand the role of choice in wellness, to carry some of their emotional and intellectual learning into their relations with others, and to observe, understand, and respect a variety of life forms.

II. Language

Each life on the planet turns to symbols to express feelings and ideas. After a first breath, we make sounds as a way of reaching out to others, connecting with them. We develop a variety of languages: the language of words (written and spoken), the language of symbols (mathematics, codes, sign systems), and the language of the arts (aesthetic expressions in language, music, painting, sculpture, dance, theater, craft, and so on). A quality education develops proficiency in the written and the spoken word, as well as a useful knowledge of mathematical symbol systems and an understanding that the arts provide countless ways to express ourselves.

Our sophisticated use of language sets human beings apart from all other forms of life. Through the created words and symbols and arts, we connect to one another. Consider the miracle of any moment. One person vibrates his or her vocal cords. Molecules shoot in the direction of listeners. They hit the tympanic membrane; signals go scurrying up the eighth cranial nerve. From that series of events, the listener feels a response deep in the cerebrum that approximates the images in the mind of the speaker. Because of its power and scope, language is the means by which all other subjects are pursued.

The responsible use of language demands both *accuracy* and *honesty*, so students studying "Language" must also learn to consider the ethics of communication. Students live in a world where obscenities abound. They live in a world where politicians use sixty-second sound bites to destroy integrity. They live in a world where clichés substitute for reason. To make their way in this world, students must learn to distinguish between deceit and authenticity in language.

Writers and mathematicians have left a long and distinguished legacy for students to learn from. Through words, each child can express something personal. Through symbols, each child can increase the capacity to calculate and reason. Through the arts, each child can express a thought or a feeling. People need to write with clarity, read with comprehension, speak effectively, listen with understanding, compute accurately, and understand the communicative capabilities of the arts. Education for the next century means helping students understand that language in all its forms is a powerful and sacred trust.

III. The Arts

All people on the planet respond to the aesthetic. Dance, music, painting, sculpture, and architecture are languages understood around the world. "Art represents a social necessity that no nation can neglect without endangering its intellectual existence," said John Ruskin (Rand 1993). We all know how art can affect us. Salvador Dali's painting *The Persistence of Memory* communicates its meaning to anyone ever haunted by time passing. The gospel song "Amazing Grace" stirs people from both Appalachia and Manhattan. "We Shall Overcome," sung in slow and solemn cadence, invokes powerful feelings regardless of the race or economic status of singer or audience.

Archaeologists examine the artifacts of ancient civilization—pottery, cave paintings, and musical instruments—to determine the attainments and quality of a culture. As J. Carter Brown (1986) observes, "The texts of man's achievements are not written exclusively in words. They are written, as well, in architecture, paintings, sculpture, drawing, photography, and in urban, graphic, landscape, and industrial design."

Young children understand that the arts are language. Before they learn to speak, they respond intuitively to dance, music, and color. The arts also help children who are disabled. I once taught deaf children, who couldn't speak because they couldn't hear. But through painting, sculpture, and rhythm, they found new ways to communicate.

Every child has the urge and capacity to be expressive. It is tragic that for most children the universal language of the arts is suppressed, then destroyed, in the early years of learning, because traditional teaching does not favor self-expression and school boards consider art a frill. This is an ironic deprivation when the role of art in developing critical thinking is becoming more widely recognized.

Jacques d'Amboise, former principal dancer with the New York City Ballet, movie star, and founder of the National Dance Institute, offers his view on how art fits into education: "I would take the arts, science and sports, or play, and make all education involve all of them. It would be similar to what kindergarten does, only more sophisticated, right through life. All of the disciplines would be interrelated. You dance to a poem: poetry is meter, meter is time, time is science" (Ames and Peyser 1990).

For our most moving experiences, we turn to the arts to express feelings and ideas that words cannot convey. The arts are, as one poet has put it, "the language of the angels." To be truly educated means being sensitively responsive to the universal language of art.

IV. Time and Space

While we are all nonuniform and often seem dramatically different from one another, all of us have the capacity to place ourselves in time and space. We explore our place through geography and astronomy. We explore our sense of time through history.

And yet, how often we squander this truly awesome capacity for exploration, neglecting even our personal roots. Looking back in my own life, my most important mentor was Grandpa Boyer, who lived to be one hundred. Sixty years before that, Grandpa moved his little family into the slums of Dayton, Ohio. He then spent the next forty years running a city mission, working for the poor, teaching me more by deed than by word that to be truly human, one must serve. For far too many children, the influence of such intergenerational models has diminished or totally disappeared.

Margaret Mead said that the health of any culture is sustained when three generations are vitally interacting with one another—a "vertical culture" in which the different age groups are connected. Yet in America today we've created a "horizontal culture," with each generation living alone. Infants are in nurseries, toddlers are in day care, older children are in schools organized by age. College students are isolated on campuses. Adults are in the workplace. And older citizens are in retirement villages, living and dying all alone.

For several years, my own parents chose to live in a retirement village where the average age was eighty. But this village had a day-care center, too, and all the three- and four-year-olds had adopted grandparents to meet with every day. The two generations quickly became friends. When I called my father, he didn't talk about his aches and pains, he talked about his little friend. And when I visited, I saw that my father, like any proud grandparent, had the child's drawings taped to the wall. As I watched the two of them together, I was struck by the idea that there is something really special about a four-year-old seeing the difficulty and courage of growing old. And I was struck, too, by watching an eighty-year-old being informed and inspired by the energy and innocence of a child. Exposure to such an age difference surely increases the understanding of time and personal history.

The time has come to break up the age ghettos. It is time to build intergenerational institutions that bring together the old and young. I'm impressed by the "grandteacher" programs in the schools, for example. In the new core curriculum, with a strand called "Time and Space," students should discover their own roots and complete an oral history. But beyond their own extended family, all students should also become well informed about the influence of the culture that surrounds them and learn about the traditions of other cultures.

A truly educated person will see connections by placing his or her life in time and space. In the days ahead, students should study *Western* civilization to understand our past, but they should study *non-Western* cultures to understand our present and our future.

V. Groups and Institutions

All people on the planet belong to groups and institutions that shape their lives. Nearly 150 years ago, Ralph Waldo Emerson observed, "We do not make a world of our own, but rather fall into institutions already made and have to accommodate ourselves to them." Every society organizes itself and carries on its work through social interaction that varies from one culture to another.

Students must be asked to think about the groups of which they are members, how they are shaped by those groups, and how they help to shape them. Students need to learn about the social web of our existence, about family life, about how governments function, about the informal social structures that surround us. They also must discover how life in groups varies from one culture to another.

Civic responsibility also must be taught. The school itself can be the starting point for this education, serving as a "working model" of a healthy society in microcosm that bears witness to the ideals of community. Within the school, students should feel "enfranchised." Teachers, administrators, and staff should meet often to find their *own* relationship to the institution of the school. And students should study groups in their own community, finding out about local government.

One of my sons lives in a Mayan village in the jungle of Belize. When my wife and I visit Craig each year, I'm impressed that Mayans and Americans live and work in very similar ways. The jungle of Manhattan and the one of Belize are separated by a thousand miles and a thousand years, and yet the Mayans, just like us, have their family units. They have elected leaders, village councils, law enforcement officers, jails, schools, and places to worship. Life there is both different and very much the same. Students in the United States should be introduced to institutions in our own culture and in other cultures, so they might study, for example, both Santa Cruz, California, and Santa Cruz, Belize.

We all belong to many groups. Exploring their history and functions helps students understand the privileges and the responsibilities that belong to each of us.

VI. Work

We all participate, for much of our lives, in the commonality of work. As Thoreau reminds us, we both "live" and "get a living." Regardless of differences, all people on the planet produce and consume. A quality education will help students understand and prepare for the world of work. Unfortunately, our own culture has become too preoccupied with *consuming*, too little with the tools for *producing*. Children may see their parents leave the house carrying briefcases or lunch pails in the morning and see them come home again in the evening, but do they know what parents actually do during the day?

Jerome Bruner (1971) asks: "Could it be that in our stratified and segmented society, our students simply do not know about local grocers and their styles, local doctors and their styles, local taxi drivers and theirs, local political activists and theirs? . . . I would urge that we find some way of connecting the diversity of the society to the phenomenon of school" (p. 7). A new, integrative curriculum for the schools needs to give attention to "Producing and Consuming," with each student studying simple economics, different money systems, vocational studies, career planning, how work varies from one culture to another, and with each completing a work project to gain a respect for craftsmanship.

Several years ago when Kay and I were in China, we were told about a student who had defaced the surface of his desk. As punishment, he spent three days in the factory where desks were made, helping the woodworkers, observing the effort involved. Not surprisingly, the student never defaced another desk.

When I was Chancellor of the State University of New York, I took my youngest son, then eight, to a cabin in the Berkshires for the weekend. My goal: to build a dock. All day, instead of playing, Stephen sat by the lake, watching me work. As we drove home, he looked pensive. After several miles, he said, "Daddy, I wish you'd grown up to be a carpenter—instead of you-know-what!"

VII. Natural World

Though all people are different, we are all connected to the earth in many ways. David, my grandson in Belize, lives these connections as he chases birds, bathes in the river, and watches corn being picked, pounded into tortillas, and heated outdoors. But David's cousins in Boston and Princeton spend more time with appliances, asphalt roadways, and precooked food. For them, discovering connectedness to nature does not come so naturally.

When I was United States Commissioner of Education, Joan Cooney, the brilliant creator of *Sesame Street*, told me that she and her colleagues at Children's Television Workshop wanted to start a new program on science and technology for junior high school kids. They wanted young people to learn a little more about their world and what they must understand as part of living. Funds were raised, and *3–2–1 Contact* went on the air. To prepare scripts, staff surveyed junior high school kids in New York City, asking questions such as "Where does water come from?"—which brought from some students the disturbing reply, "The faucet." They asked, "Where does light come from?" and heard, "The switch." And they asked, "Where does garbage go?" "Down the chute." These students' sense of connectedness stopped at the VCR or refrigerator door.

Canadian geneticist David Suzuki, host of *The Nature of Things*, says: "We ought to be greening the school yard, breaking up the asphalt and concrete. . . . We have to give children hand-held lenses, classroom aquariums and terrariums, lots of field trips, organic garden plots on the school grounds, butterfly gardens, trees. Then insects, squirrels—maybe even raccoons and rabbits—will show up, even in the city. We've got to reconnect those kids, and we've got to do it very early. . . . Our challenge is to reconnect children to their natural curiosity" (Baron Estes 1993).

With all our differences, each of us is inextricably connected to the natural world. During their days of formal learning, students should explore this commonality by studying the principles of science, by discovering the shaping power of technology, and, above all, by learning that survival on this planet means respecting and preserving the earth we share.

VIII. Search for Meaning

Regardless of heritage or tradition, each person searches for some larger purpose. We all seek to give special meaning to our lives. Reinhold Niebuhr said, "Man cannot be whole unless he be committed, he cannot find himself, unless he find a purpose beyond himself." We all need to examine values and beliefs, and develop convictions.

During my study of the American high school, I became convinced ours is less a school problem and more a youth problem. Far too many teenagers feel unwanted, unneeded, and unconnected. Without guidance and direction, they soon lose their sense of purpose—even their sense of wanting purpose.

Great teachers allow their lives to express their values. They are matchless guides as they give the gift of opening truths about themselves to their students. I often think of three or four teachers, out of the many I have worked with, who changed my life. What made them truly great? They were well informed. They could relate their knowledge to students. They created an active, not passive, climate for learning. More than that, they were authentic human beings who taught their subjects and were open enough to teach about themselves.

Service projects instill values. All students should complete a community service project, working in day-care centers and retirement villages or tutoring other students at school. The North Carolina School of Science and Math develops an ethos of responsible citizenship. To be admitted, a child must commit to sixty hours of community service per summer and three hours per week during the school year (Beach 1992, p. 56).

Martin Luther King, Jr., preached: "Everyone can be great because everyone can serve." I'm convinced the young people of this country want inspiration from this kind of larger vision, whether they come across it in a book or in person, or whether they find it inside themselves.

Values, Beliefs, and Connections

What, then, does it mean to be an educated person? It means respecting the miracle of life, being empowered in the use of language, and responding sensitively to the aesthetic. Being truly educated means putting learning in historical perspective, understanding groups and institutions, having reverence for the natural world, and affirming the dignity of work. And, above all, being an educated person means being guided by values and beliefs and connecting the lessons of the classroom to the realities of life. These are the core competencies that I believe replace the old Carnegie units.

And all of this can be accomplished as schools focus not on seat time, but on students involved in true communities of learning. I realize that remarkable changes must occur for this shift in goals to take place, but I hope deeply that in the century ahead students will be judged not by their performance on a single test but by the quality of their lives. It is my hope that students in the classrooms of tomorrow will be encouraged to create more than conform, and to cooperate more than compete. Each student deserves to see the world clearly and in its entirety and to be inspired by both the beauty and the challenges that surround us all.

Above all, I pray that Julie and David, my granddaughter in Princeton and my grandson in Belize, along with all other children on the planet, will grow to understand that they belong to the same human family, the family that connects us all.

Fifty years ago, Mark Van Doren wrote, "The connectedness of things is what the educator contemplates to the limit of his capacity." The student, he says, who can begin early in life to see things as connected has begun the life of learning. This, it seems to me, is what it means to be an educated person.

References

Ames, Katrine, and Marc Peyser. (Fall/Winter 1990). "Why Jane Can't Draw (or Sing, or Dance . . .)." *Newsweek* Special Edition: 40–49.

Baron Estes, Yvonne. (May 1993). "Environmental Education: Bringing Children and Nature Together." *Phi Delta Kappan* 74, 9: K2.

Beach, Waldo. (1992). *Ethical Education in American Public Schools*. Washington, D.C.: National Education Association.

Bennett, William J. (1986). *First Lessons*. Washington, D.C.: U.S. Department of Education.

Boyer, Ernest L. (1981). *A Quest for Common Learning: The Aims of General Education*. Washington, D.C.: Carnegie Foundation for the Advancement of Teaching.

Brown, J. Carter. (November/December 1983). "Excellence and the Problem of Visual Literacy." *Design for Arts in Education* 84, 3.

Bruner, Jerome. (November 1971). "Process of Education Reconsidered." An address presented before the 16th Annual Conference of the Association for Supervision and Curriculum Development.

Rand, Paul. (May 2, 1993). "Failure by Design," *The New York Times*, p. E19.

Postnote

In this Classic article, the late Ernest Boyer demonstrates his power as a profound educational thinker. Boyer was widely acknowledged during the last two decades of the twentieth century as America's leading practitioner of education. There is no more important or fundamental question in education than "What is most worth knowing?" Schools have a mission, derived from the society at large, to prepare children to become fully developed people, to prepare them for the demands of adult life in an unknown future. As educators, our mission is to identify what our students need today and will need in the future. But the universe of knowledge, which once inched along at a snail's pace, is currently racing ahead like a sprinter. The child's future, which once we could say would be much like his or her parents' life, now is impossible to predict.

In this essay, Ernest Boyer lays out his answer to the question of what an educated person most needs to know. Though there is great merit in his educational vision, a question arises: How many of us as teachers have a clear sense of goals, guided by a similar vision of what a person really is and what a person ought to become?

Discussion Questions

1. What feature of Boyer's "educated person" do you believe currently receives the greatest attention in our schools?
2. What feature of his vision do you believe receives the least attention today? Why?
3. Why do you think there is so little discussion of the question, "What is most worth knowing?"

48

A Reader's Guide to Scientifically Based Research

ROBERT E. SLAVIN

FOCUS Question

As education becomes increasingly important, research studies on various instructional programs and strategies proliferate. How can a classroom teacher separate the wheat from the chaff, the solid research from the dubious?

TERMS TO NOTE

Bottom fishing
Cherry picking
Evidence-based research
Matched group experiment
Pre–post studies
Randomized experiment
Scientifically based research
Valid research

In every successful, dynamic part of our economy, evidence is the force that drives change. In medicine, researchers continually develop medications and procedures, compare them with current drugs and practices, and if they produce greater benefits, disseminate them widely. In agriculture, researchers develop and test better seeds, equipment, and farming methods. In technology, in engineering, in field after field, progress comes from research and development. Physicians, farmers, consumers, and government officials base key decisions on the results of rigorous research.

In education reform, on the other hand, research has played a relatively minor role. Untested innovations appear, are widely embraced, and then disappear as their unrealistic claims fail to materialize. We then replace them with equally untested innovations diametrically opposed in philosophy, in endless swings of the reform pendulum. Far more testing goes into our students' hair gel and acne cream than into most of the curriculums or instructional methods teachers use. Yet which of these is more important to our students' future?

Evidence-Based Reform

At long last, education reform may be entering an era of well-researched programs and practices (Slavin, 2002). The U.S. government is now interested in the research base for programs that schools adopt. The Comprehensive School Reform Demonstration legislation of 1997 gives grants to schools to adopt "proven, comprehensive" reform designs. Ideally, "proven" means that programs have been evaluated in "scientifically based research," which is defined as "rigorous, systematic, and objective procedures to obtain valid knowledge" (U.S. Department of

---

Robert E. Slavin is the codirector of the Center for Research on the Education of Students Placed At Risk at Johns Hopkins University and the chairman of the Success for All Foundation. "A Reader's Guide to Scientifically Based Research," by Robert E. Slavin, *Educational Leadership,* February 2003, pp. 12–16. Reprinted by permission. The Association for Supervision and Curriculum Development is a worldwide community of educators advocating sound policies and sharing best practices to achieve the success of each learner. To learn more, visit ASCD at **www.ascd.org.**

Education, 1998). The emphasis is on evaluations that use experimental or quasi-experimental designs, preferably with random assignment. The Bush administration's No Child Left Behind Act mentions "scientifically based research" 110 times in references to Reading First programs for grades K–3, Early Reading First for preK, Title I school improvement programs, and many more. In each case, schools, districts, and states must justify the programs that they expect to implement under federal funding.

Judging the Validity of Education Research

The new policies that base education funding and practice on scientifically based, rigorous research have important consequences for educators. Research matters. Educators have long given lip service to research as a guide to practice. But increasingly, they are being asked to justify their choices of programs and practices using the findings of rigorous, experimental research.

Why is one study valid whereas another is not? There are many valid forms of research conducted for many reasons, but for evaluating the achievement outcomes of education programs, judging research quality is relatively straightforward. Valid research for this purpose uses meaningful measures of achievement to compare several schools that used a given program with several carefully matched control schools that did not. It's that simple.

Control Groups

A hallmark of valid, scientifically based research on education programs is the use of control groups. In a good study, researchers compare several schools using a given program with several schools not using the program but sharing similar demographics and prior performance, preferably in the same school district. Having at least five schools in each group is desirable; circumstances unique to a given school can bias studies with just one or two schools in each group.

A control group provides an estimate of what students in the experimental program would have achieved if they had been left alone. That's why the control schools must be as similar as possible to the program schools at the outset.

Randomized and Matched Experiments

The most convincing form of a control group comparison is a randomized experiment in which students, teachers, or schools are assigned by chance to a group. For example, the principals and staffs at ten schools might express interest in using a given program. The schools might be paired up and then assigned by a coin flip to the experimental or control group.

Randomized experiments are very rare in education, but they can be very influential. Perhaps the best known example in recent years is the Tennessee class size study (Achilles, Finn, & Bain, 1997/1998) in which researchers assigned students at random to small classes (15 students), regular classes (20–25 students), or regular classes with an aide. The famous Perry Preschool Program (Berrueta-Clement, Schweinhart, Barnett, Epstein, & Weikart, 1984) assigned four-year-olds at random to attend an enriched preschool program or to stay at home. Two recent studies of James Corner's School Development Project randomly assigned schools to use the School Development Project or keep using their current program (Cook et al., 1999; Cook, Murphy, & Hunt, 2000). In each of these studies, random assignment made it very likely that the experimental and control groups were identical at the outset, so any differences at the end were sure to have resulted from the program.

Matched studies are far more common than randomized ones. In a matched program evaluation, researchers compare students in a given program with those in a control group that is similar in prior achievement, poverty level, demographics, and so on. Matched studies can be valid if the experimental and control groups are very similar. Often, researchers use statistical methods to "control for" pretest differences between experimental and control groups. This can work if the differences are small, but if there are large differences at pretest, statistical controls or use of test-gain scores (calculated by subtracting pretest scores from posttest scores) are generally not adequate.

The potential problem with even the best matched studies is the possibility that the schools that chose a given program have (unmeasured) characteristics that are different from those that did not choose it. For example, imagine that a researcher asked 10 schools to implement a new program. Five enthusiastically take it on and five refuse. Using the refusal group as a control group, even if it is similar in other ways, can introduce something called selection bias. In this example, selection bias would work in favor of finding a positive treatment effect because the volunteer schools are more likely to have enthusiastic, energetic teachers willing to try new methods than are the control schools. In other cases, however, the most desperate or dysfunctional schools may have chosen or been assigned to a given program, giving an advantage to the control schools.

Is Random Assignment Essential?

Random assignment to experimental and control groups is the gold standard of research. It virtually eliminates selection bias because students, classes, or schools were assigned to treatments not by their own choice but by the flip of a coin or another random process.

Because randomized studies can rule out selection bias, the U.S. Department of Education and many researchers and policymakers have recently been arguing for a substantial increase in the use of randomized designs in evaluations of education programs. Already, more randomized studies are under way in education than at any other point in history.

The only problem with random assignment is that it is very difficult and expensive to do, especially for schoolwide programs that necessitate random assignment of whole schools. No one likes to be assigned at random, so such studies often have to provide substantial incentives to get educators to participate. Still, such studies are possible; we have such a study under way to evaluate our Success for All comprehensive reform model, and, as noted earlier, Comer's School Development Program has been evaluated in two randomized studies.

At present, with the movement toward greater use of randomized experiments in education in its infancy, educators evaluating the research base for various programs must look carefully at well-matched experiments, valuing those that try to minimize bias by using closely matched experimental and control groups, having adequate numbers of schools, avoiding comparing volunteers with nonvolunteers, and so on.

Statistical and Educational Significance and Sample Size

Reports of education experiments always indicate whether a statistically significant difference exists between the achievement of students in the experimental group and those in the control group, usually controlling for pretests and other factors. A usual criterion is "$p < 0.05$," which means that the probability is less than 5 percent that an observed difference might have happened by chance.

The proportion of students within a program getting "significantly higher" scores than those in a control group is important, but it may not be important enough. In a large study, a small difference could be significant. A typical measure of the size of a program effect is "effect size," the experimental-control difference divided by the control group's standard deviation (a measure of the dispersion of scores). In education experiments, an effect size of +0.20 (20 percent of a standard deviation) is often considered a minimum for significance; effect sizes above +0.50 would be considered very strong.

But student groupings can have a profound impact on student outcomes. Often, an experiment will compare one school using Program *X* with one matched control school. If 500 students are in each school, this is a very large experiment. Yet the difference between the Program *X* school and the control school could be due to any number of factors that have nothing to do with Program *X*. Perhaps the Program *X* school has a better principal or a cohesive group of teachers or has been redistricted to include a higher-performing group of students. Perhaps one of the schools experienced a disaster of some sort—in an early study of our Success for All program, Hurricane Hugo blew the roof off of the Success for All school but did not affect the one control school.

Because of the possibility that something unusual that applies to an entire school could affect scores for all students in that school, statisticians insist on using the *school's* means, not individual student scores, in their analyses. In this way, individual school factors are likely to balance out. Statistical requirements would force a researcher to have at least 20–25 *schools* in each condition. Very few education experiments are this large, however, so the vast majority of experiments analyze at the student level.

Readers of research must apply a reasonable approach to this problem. We should view studies that observe a single school or class for each condition with great caution. However, a study with as many as five program schools and five control schools probably has enough schools to ensure that a single unusual school will not skew the results. Such a study would still use individual scores, not school means, but it would be far preferable to a comparison between only two schools.

A single study involving a small number of schools or classes may not be conclusive in itself, but many such studies, preferably done by many researchers in a variety of locations, can add confidence that a program's effects are valid. In fact, experimental research in education usually develops in this way. Rather than evaluate one large, definitive study, researchers must usually look at many small studies that may be flawed in various (unbiased) ways. But if these studies tend to find consistent effects, the entire set of studies may produce a meaningful conclusion.

Research to Avoid

All too often, program developers or advocates cite evidence that is of little value or that is downright misleading. A rogue's gallery of such research follows.

Cherry Picking

Frequently, program developers or marketers report on a single school or a small set of schools that made remarkable gains in a given year. Open any education magazine and you'll see an ad like this: "Twelfth Street Elementary went from the 20th percentile to the 60th in only one year!" Such claims have no more validity than advertisements for weight loss programs that tell the story of one person who lost 200 pounds (forgetting to mention the hundreds who did not lose weight on the diet). This kind of "cherry picking" is easy to do in a program that serves many schools; there are always individual schools that make large gains in a given year, and the marketer can pick them after the fact just by looking down a column of numbers to find a big gainer. (Critics of the program can use the same technique to find a big loser.) Such reports are pure puffery, not to be confused with science.

Bottom Fishing

A variant of cherry picking is "bottom fishing," using an after-the-fact comparison in which an evaluator compares schools using a given program with matched "similar schools" known to have made poor gains in a given year. Researchers can legitimately compare gains made in program schools and gains made in the entire district or state because the large comparison group makes "bottom fishing" impossible. However, readers should interpret with caution after-the-fact studies purporting to compare groups selected by the evaluator.

Pre–Post Studies

Another common but misleading design is the pre–post comparison, lacking a control group. Typically, the designer cites standardized test data, with the rationale that the expected year-to-year gain in percentiles, normal curve equivalents, or percent passing is zero, so any school that gained more than zero has made good progress.

The problem with this logic is that many states and districts make substantial gains in a given year, so the program schools may be doing no better than other schools. In particular, states usually make rapid gains in the years after they adopt a new test. At a minimum, studies should compare gains made in program schools in a given district or state with the gains made in the entire district or state.

Scientifically Based Versus Rigorously Evaluated

A key issue in the recent No Child Left Behind legislation is the distinction between programs that are "based on scientifically based research" and those that have been evaluated in valid scientific experiments. A program can be "based on scientifically based research" if it incorporates the findings of rigorous experimental research. For example, reading programs are eligible for funding under the federal Reading First initiative if states determine that they incorporate a focus on five elements of effective reading instruction: phonemic awareness, phonics, fluency, vocabulary, and comprehension. The National Reading Panel (1999) identified these elements as having been established in rigorous research, especially in randomized experiments. Yet there is a big difference between a program *based* on such elements and a program that has itself been compared with matched or randomly assigned control groups. We can easily imagine a reading program that would incorporate the five elements but whose training was so minimal that teachers did not implement these elements well, or whose materials were so boring that students were not motivated to study them.

The No Child Left Behind guidance (U.S. Department of Education, 2002) recognizes this distinction and notes a preference for programs that have been rigorously evaluated, but also recognizes that requiring such evaluations would screen out many new reading programs that have not been out long enough to have been evaluated, and so allows for their use. This approach may make sense from a pragmatic or political perspective, but from a research perspective, a program that is unevaluated is unevaluated, whether or not it is "based on" scientifically based research. A basis in scientifically based research makes a program promising, but not proven.

Research Reviews

In order to judge the research base for a given program, it is not necessary that every teacher, principal, or superintendent carry out his or her own review of the literature. Several reviews applying standards have summarized evidence on various programs.

For comprehensive school reform models, for example, the American Institutes for Research published a review of 24 programs (Herman, 1999). The Thomas Fordham Foundation (Traub, 1999) commissioned an evaluation of 10 popular comprehensive school reform models. And Borman, Hewes, Rachuba, and Brown (2002) carried out a meta-analysis (or quantitative synthesis) of research on 29 comprehensive school reform models.

Research reviews facilitate the process of evaluating the evidence behind a broad range of programs, but it's still a good idea to look for a few published studies on a program to get a sense of the nature and quality of the evidence supporting a given model. Also, we should look at multiple reviews because researchers differ in their review criteria, conclusions, and recommendations. Adopting a program for a single subject, much less for an entire school, requires a great deal of time, money, and work—and can have a profound impact on a school for a long time. Taking time to look at the research evidence with some care before making such an important decision is well worth the effort. Accepting the developer's word for a program's research base is not a responsible strategy.

How Evidence-Based Reform Will Transform Our Schools

The movement to ask schools to adopt programs that have been rigorously researched could have a profound impact on the practice of education and on the outcomes of education for students. If this movement prevails, educators will increasingly be able to choose from among a variety of models known to be effective if well implemented, rather than reinventing (or misinventing) the wheel in every school. There will never be a guarantee that a given program will work in a given school, just as no physician can guarantee that a given treatment will work in every case. A focus on rigorously evaluated programs, however, can at least give school staffs confidence that their efforts to implement a new program will pay off in higher student achievement.

In an environment of evidence-based reform, developers and researchers will continually work to create new models and improve existing ones. Today's substantial improvement will soon be replaced by something even more effective. Rigorous evaluations will be common, both to replicate evaluations of various models and to discover the conditions necessary to make programs work. Reform organizations will build capacity to serve thousands of schools. Education leaders will become increasingly sophisticated in judging the adequacy of research, and, as a result, the quality and usefulness of research will grow. In programs such as Title I, government support will focus on helping schools adopt proven programs, and schools making little progress toward state goals may be required to choose from among a set of proven programs.

Evidence-based reform could finally bring education to the point reached early in the 20th century by medicine, agriculture, and technology, fields in which evidence is the lifeblood of progress. No Child Left Behind, Reading First, Comprehensive School Reform, and related initiatives have created the possibility that evidence-based reform can be sustained and can become fundamental to the practice of education. Informed education leaders can contribute to this effort. It is ironic that the field of education has embraced ideology rather than knowledge in its own reform process. Evidence-based reform honors the best traditions of our profession and promises to transform schooling for all students.

References

Achilles, C. M., Finn, J. D., & Bain, H. P. (1997/1998). Using class size to reduce the equity gap. *Educational Leadership, 55*(4), 40–43.

Berrueta-Clement, J. R., Schweinhart, L. J., Barnett, W. S., Epstein, A. S., & Weikart, D. P. (1984). *Changed lives.* Ypsilanti, MI: High/Scope.

Borman, G. D., Hewes, G. M., Rachuba, L. T., & Brown, S. (2002). *Comprehensive school reform and student achievement: A meta-analysis.* Submitted for publication. (Available from the author at **gborman@education.wisc.edu**)

Cook, T. D., Habib, F., Phillips, M., Settersten, R. A., Shagle, S., & Degirmencioglu, M. (1999). Comer's school development program in Prince George's County, Maryland: A theory-based evaluation. *American Educational Research Journal, 36*(3), 543–597.

Cook, T., Murphy, R. F., & Hunt, H. D. (2000). Comer's school development program in Chicago: A theory-based evaluation. *American Educational Research Journal, 37*(2), 543–597.

Herman, R. (1999). *An educator's guide to schoolwide reform.* Arlington, VA: Educational Research Service.

National Reading Panel. (1999). *Teaching children to read.* Washington, DC: U.S. Department of Education.

Slavin, R. E. (2002). Evidence-based education policies: Transforming educational practice and research. *Educational Researcher, 31*(7), 15–21.

Traub, J. (1999). *Better by design? A consumer's guide to schoolwide reform.* Washington, DC: Thomas Fordham Foundation.

U.S. Department of Education. (1998). *Guidance on the comprehensive school reform demonstration program.* Washington, DC: Author.

U.S. Department of Education. (2002). *Draft guidance on the comprehensive school reform program* (June 14, 2002 update). Washington, DC: Author.

Postnote

The world is awash with claims that this soap cleans stains or that drug brings happiness. Many of these claims are backed up by "research." Increasingly, the field of education—a vast market for products and programs—has been encouraged to ensure that its expenditures and programs are also supported by research. As Robert E. Slavin, one of education's most distinguished scientists, makes clear in this article, however, "there is research and there is research." Educators need to be vigilant about the claims of promoters and be ready to look below a program's or product's "research" label.

This article also demonstrates how difficult it is to do truly scientific (or to use Slavin's term, "evidence-based") research. Educational researchers are rarely in a position to control for all the variables that may affect the outcome of a particular innovation or program. Still, the perspectives offered here can shield us from erroneous claims made by educational promoters and salespeople. As a bonus, perhaps we will also be protected from the tall tales of soap sellers and drug manufacturers.

Discussion Questions

1. What are the major obstacles to conducting evidence-based research?
2. What is the relationship between evidence-based research and true educational reform?
3. This article focuses on the limitations frequently found in educational research, but what applications of this information do you see to areas of life other than education?

The Changing Landscape of U.S. Education

JAMES C. CARPER

FOCUS Question

Education, like other social institutions, is changing. But in what directions are our schools moving?

TERMS TO NOTE

Academies
Accountability
Charter schools
Dame schools
Home schooling
Magnet schools
Old Deluder Act
Oldfield schools
Private-venture schools
Voucher programs

Since the 1960s, the educational landscape of the United States has been swept by the winds of change. Old educational forms have been reformed and new ones created. For example, the public sector now includes magnet and charter schools, while the private sector has further diversified the development of various kinds of independent Christian schools, Muslim schools, and a revival of the virtually extinct practice of home schooling. Despite standardizing pressures driven largely by recent accountability reforms, alternative forms of schooling are increasing in number and popularity. Other innovations, such as experimental voucher programs in Milwaukee and Cleveland and various kinds of tax credits for educational expenses and donations, suggest that the trend toward institutional diversity is being paralleled by a blurring of the line between the state and private sectors. If these two trends continue, the educational landscape of the future may bear a resemblance to that of the distant past.

Colonial Educational Pluralism

Prior to the advent of modern public education in the mid-19th century, institutional diversity dominated U.S. education, and the line between "public" and "private" schools was often blurred. Colonial education consisted of an incredible variety of institutions, including a significant amount of home education. From the town schools of various types, dame schools—where women taught reading skills in their homes for a small fee—and private-venture schools of New England; to the various denominational, charity, and pay schools of the Middle Colonies; to the oldfield schools and Society for the Propagation of the Gospel in Foreign Parts missionary efforts in the South; to academies that appeared throughout the provinces in the 1700s, the colonial educational

---

James C. Carper is a Professor of Social Foundations of Education and Chairman Department of Educational Studies at the University of South Carolina. From James C. Carper, "The Changing Landscape of U.S. Education," *Kappa Delta Pi Record,* Spring 2001.

landscape was dotted with many kinds of institutions. Classifying schools as purely public or private is problematic from a historical perspective. To most colonials, a school was public if it served a public purpose, such as promoting civic responsibility. Public education, therefore, did not necessarily require public support and control (Bailyn 1960; Carper 2000).

Indeed, colonial institutions were supported from various sources, including taxation, land grants by the colony to a town for school purposes, private subscriptions, bequests and donations, endowments, tuition, lotteries, rents, and income from public utilities, such as fisheries. It was not unusual for educational institutions to depend on support from a variety of public and private sources. Often, schools administered by public officials charged tuition to students able to pay, while institutions under the control of boards of trustees or religious bodies received public funds or land grants, frequently for providing charity education for the poor, and were often perceived as public schools.

For example, "public" town schools in Massachusetts, mandated by the famous 1647 "Old Deluder" school law, were often funded by tuition charges to parents of school children as well as by taxes. Entrance fees and firewood charges were also levied occasionally. On the other hand, schools not under town control and heavily dependent on tuition charges received local and colonial land grants and appropriations as well as a share of town taxes. In 1660, for example, the privately endowed Roxbury Grammar School received 500 acres of land from the General Court. Dame schools likewise often received public aid. This pattern of mixed support of schools was common in New Hampshire, Connecticut, Rhode Island, and Massachusetts. Although schooling opportunities in Virginia, the Carolinas, and Georgia were fewer than in New England, patterns of school finance were similar. In Virginia, for instance, schools considered orthodox (Anglican) could obtain public funds to defray the costs of educating children too poor to pay tuition charges (Carper 1991; Gabel 1937).

Reflecting the religious diversity of the region, denominational schooling was prevalent in the Middle Colonies. Dutch Reformed, Lutherans, Mennonites, Amish, Moravians, Quakers, Baptists, Episcopalians, Presbyterians, and Catholics established schools throughout the region for members of their respective congregations and occasionally opened them to all children in a given locality. For instance, the Quakers opened the William Penn Charter School in 1689; the school was chartered in 1697 as a *public* grammar school to instruct the rich at "reasonable rates, and the poor . . . for nothing." With the exception of the Dutch Reformed schools in New Netherlands, these denominational institutions apparently received little tax support during the colonial period (Carper 1991).

This broad concept of education persisted without major modification throughout the Early National Period (circa 1780s to 1820s). Almost every state provided land grants or financial aid to academies. Primary religious and private schools also received public support in many states, including Pennsylvania, Georgia, Connecticut, Ohio, Tennessee, Virginia, South Carolina, Indiana, New York, Illinois, and Maryland. Usually tax support was conditional upon providing charity education for poor students. Even privately organized Sunday schools received public funds from at least three states—Delaware, Virginia, and Maryland (Carper 1991; Gabel 1937).

By the 1820s, private and quasi-public schooling was widely available to children of European-American citizens in most settled parts of the country, though less so in the South. This was due primarily to the efforts of parents, churches, voluntary associations, entrepreneurs, and local communities rather than state mandates. In some areas, school attendance was nearly universal, though often irregular. Despite some references to common pay schools as private and charity school systems as public, these terms still lacked their modern connotations. Public funding of privately controlled institutions was a common practice. During the next three decades, however, this multifaceted educational arrangement inherited from the Colonial Era would be significantly altered (Cremin 1977; Kaestle 1983; Reese 1995).

Common School Reform

The middle decades of the 19th century marked a period of intense debate and reform focusing on issues of control, finance, and curriculum that led to major changes in educational beliefs and practices. The modern concept and practice of public schooling was gradually emerging in the United States. Distressed by the social and cultural tensions wrought by mid-19th-century urbanization, industrialization, and immigration—that included many Roman Catholics—and energized by the values and beliefs of republicanism, Protestantism, and capitalism, educational reformers like Horace Mann touted the messianic power of tax-supported, universal common schooling. Common schools, proponents argued, would create a moral, disciplined, and unified population prepared to participate in U.S. political, social, and economic life. Private schools, which reformers believed would sabotage the goals of common schooling, were often cast as divisive, undemocratic, and inimical to the public interest (Glenn 1988; Kaestle 1983; Reese 1995).

With the exception of a few groups, such as Lutheran and Calvinist bodies that designed schools to preserve cultural or confessional purity, Protestants generally supported the common school movement. Indeed, many were in the vanguard of the reform effort. Rather than sharing public funds with Roman Catholic schools, as Bishop John Hughes proposed in the early 1840s in New York City, they united behind the "non-sectarian" (in reality, pan-Protestant) common school as the sole recipient of government funds for education. Catholic schools and those of other dissenters from the common school movement were thus denied tax dollars as well as legitimacy (Carper 2000; Curran 1954; Jorgenson 1987).

Reformers' efforts in the antebellum North were generally successful. By 1860, state legislatures had created common school systems. Common school reform led to a clear line of demarcation between private education and public schooling as states eliminated tax support for private schools, increased expenditures for public schools, and experienced a marked expansion of enrollment in the public sector.

As noted earlier, the distinction between public and private was still fuzzy in the early 19th century. By the 1860s, however, the label "public" became increasingly associated with free, tax-supported schools under government control. Driven to some degree by anti-Catholicism, Michigan (1835), New Hampshire (1848), Ohio (1851), Massachusetts (1855), Illinois (1855), California (1855), and New Jersey (1866) eliminated government funding of private schools by either statute or constitutional provision. Though these restrictions were neither ironclad nor consistently enforced, particularly as applied to secondary schools, tax subsidies for private schools dropped precipitously after the Civil War as expenditures for public education increased markedly. In 1850, for example, only 47 percent of the \$16.1 million spent on schools and colleges came from the public purse. By 1870, however, expenditures for schooling at all levels surged to \$95.4 million, with 65 percent coming from public sources and more than 90 percent of the public school funds derived from public sources (Carper 1991, 1998; Cremin 1980).

Paralleling the sharpening distinction between public and private education, and a growing commitment to public funding, was a shift in enrollment from more or less private schools to public schools as free common schooling became more accessible and acceptable and charity schools came under the public aegis. This trend accelerated in the late 1800s as the modern definition of public was extended to secondary education and many academies were incorporated into expanding public systems. Academies that were not transformed into public high schools or state normal schools either went defunct or redefined themselves as colleges or elite boarding schools (Cremin 1980; Kaestle 1983; Reese 1995).

By 1890, then, there was far less institutional diversity in U.S. education than 100 years earlier.

Ninety-two percent of school children in the country were enrolled in state school systems; 65 percent of the remainder attended the burgeoning Roman Catholic schools, with most of the rest in Lutheran, Reformed, Episcopal, or independent institutions (Carper 1991).

As had been the case with the common school movement, protean educational reform in the Progressive Era impacted private as well as public schools. Although pedagogical progressives stimulated the creation of independent schools devoted to active, child-centered learning, such as Marietta Johnson's School of Organic Education (1907) and Carolina Pratt's Play School (1914), administrative progressives influenced efforts to regulate alternatives to the public schools or simply to abolish them. Roman Catholic and Lutheran schools bore the brunt of these initiatives during the late 19th and the first quarter of the 20th centuries. Restrictions on foreign-language instruction were the most common form of state regulation of nonpublic schools, but several states attempted to go much further. In 1922, for example, Oregon required that, with few exceptions, all children between the ages of eight and 16 attend public schools. Drawing upon *Meyer* v. *Nebraska* (1923), which overturned restrictions on foreign-language instruction in nonpublic schools, the U.S. Supreme Court in *Pierce* v. *Society of Sisters* (1925) declared Oregon's law unconstitutional. In this case, the court asserted the right of private schools to exist, affirmed the fundamental right of parents to direct the "education and upbringing" of their children, and maintained that the state could "reasonably" regulate nonpublic schools (Cremin 1988; Randall 1994; Ross 1994).

After the passions of World War I and the "Red Scare" subsided and immigration rates fell precipitously, major private school groups became more accepting of the public school model and associated accreditation and certification standards. As a consequence, disputes between the state and private schools in general and religious schools in particular declined markedly after 1930. For nearly four decades, guidelines for state regulation of private schools laid down in *Meyer* and *Pierce* were widely accepted, and, at least in the realm of state regulation, peaceful coexistence was the rule.

Diversity Redivivus

Private as well as public institutions have been affected by both the tumultuous, two-decade-long period of reform that commenced in the late 1950s and the era of reform that began in the mid-1980s (Tyack and Cuban 1995). Equality concerns of the earlier period certainly have impacted alternatives to the state system. While the federal government provided funds for services for disadvantaged students in private schools, it also threatened some of them. In particular, the "segregation academies" founded in the South between the mid-1960s and early '70s—in response to court-ordered integration of public schools—lost their tax-exempt status for failure to abide by civil rights regulations (Nevin and Bills 1976; Skerry 1980). At the same time, however, many private schools voluntarily opened their doors to minorities who sought alternatives to public schools. As early as 1982, James Coleman (1982) had asserted that the private sector was more racially integrated than the public sector.

Besides the increase in minority enrollments, the nonpublic sector has been shaped by three additional trends since the 1960s. First, though enrollment in the private sector has fallen from about 15 percent of the elementary and secondary student population in the mid-1960s to around 11 percent currently, enrollment patterns within the sector have shifted markedly. Although Catholic school enrollment has increased slightly since the mid-1990s to approximately 2.5 million, it is down considerably from the high watermark of 5.6 million students in 1965. On the other hand, enrollment in other religious and nonreligious school groups has increased significantly, to 35 and 15 percent, respectively, in 1995 (Carper 1991; National Center for Education Statistics 1998, 2000).

Second, since the mid-1960s, many evangelical Protestants and their churches have forsaken their longstanding commitment to public education and founded at least 10,000 independent Christian day schools, including a small growing number established by and for African Americans. In the 1970s and '80s, these Christian schools were occasionally embroiled in legal battles over the extent to which religious educational institutions must abide by rules and regulations applied to public schools (Carper 1983, 1985, 1997). In the mid-1990s, enrollment in these schools had topped one million.

Finally, adding further to the diversity of educational institutions in the United States, a growing number of middle-class parents, a majority of whom would be classified as conservative Christians, have chosen to teach their children at home since the 1970s. Their decision to revert to a practice common 300 years ago has been influenced by the same factors that contributed to the growth of the 1960s and '70s alternative school movement—objections to the rigidity of public school pedagogy and structure—and the aforementioned Christian day school movement—objections to the religious, moral, and academic climate of public education. Like other patrons of private schools, home school parents have often clashed with government officials regarding regulation of home education. Such conflict has not slowed the growth of this alternative to public and private schooling that now embraces more than 1 million children as compared to a mere 10,000–15,000 in the late 1970s (Carper 2000; Ray 1997).

Counting children taught by their parents, enrollment in the private sector, including at least 30 different groups of religious and nonaffiliated schools, now exceeds the 1965 level. Alternatives to the traditional school are also thriving in the public sector. For example, since the first charter school was founded in 1991, the number of these quasi-independent public schools has increased to more than 1,700, with an enrollment of about 400,000 students (Center for Education Reform 2000).

Accompanying the increasing diversity in both public and private sectors, experimental voucher programs and tax credits for educational expenses and donations suggest the line between the two sectors is becoming more blurred. With its 2000 decision in *Mitchell* v. *Helms* upholding government provision of computer resources to students in nonpublic schools, the U.S. Supreme Court appears to have adopted a strong position that government aid may be directed toward the education of children regardless of their enrollment status. Some observers of the court believe that this decision suggests that it would uphold a carefully crafted voucher program. Such a reform would certainly further blur the line between the nongovernment and public sectors (Bork, Smolin, Kmiec, George, Uhlmann, and McConnell 2000).

Often, the future is merely the past in different garb. If the aforementioned trends continue, perhaps the educational landscape of the United States will come to resemble that of the Colonial Era, with a variety of educational institutions sharing equally in public resources and contributing in different ways to the accomplishment of public purposes. Education of the public, rather than public education, might become the primary concern of the state. The winds of change continue to blow.

References

Bailyn, B. 1960. *Education in the forming of American society*. New York: Norton.

Bork, R. H., D. M. Smolin, D. W. Kmiec, R. P. George, M. M. Uhlmann, and M. W. McConnell, 2000. The Supreme Court: A symposium. *First Things: A Journal of Religion and Public Life* 106 (October): 25–38.

Carper, J. C. 1982. The *Whisner* decision: A case study in state regulation of Christian day schools. *Journal of Church and State* 24(2): 281–302.

Carper, J. C. 1983. The Christian day school movement. *Educational Forum* 47(2): 135–49.

Carper, J. C. 1991. An historical view of private schooling in the United States. Paper presented at the Dollars and Cents of Private Schools Conference, 9–10 May, Washington, D.C.

Carper, J. C. 1998a. History, religion, and schooling: A context for conversation. In *Curriculum, religion, and public education: Conversations for an enlarging public square*, ed. J. T. Sears with J. C. Carper, 11–24. New York: Teachers College Press.

Carper, J. C. 1998b. William Morgan Beckner: The Horace Mann of Kentucky. *Register of the Kentucky Historical Society* 96(1): 29–60.

Carper, J. C. 2000. Pluralism to establishment to dissent. The religious and educational context of home schooling. *Peabody Journal of Education* 75(1/2): 8–19.

Carper, J. C., and N. E. Devins. 1985. The state and the Christian day school. In *Religion and the state: Essays in honor of Leo Pfeffer*, ed. J. E. Wood Jr., 211–32. Waco, Tex.: Baylor University Press.

Carper, J. C., and J. Layman. 1995. Independent Christian day schools: Past, present, and prognosis. *Journal of Research on Christian Education* 4(1): 7–19.

Carper, J. C., and J. Layman. 1997. Blackflight academies: The new Christian day schools. *The Educational Forum* 61(2): 114–21.

Center for Education Reform. 2000. *National charter school directory 2000*. Washington, D.C.: CER.

Coleman, J. S., T. Hoffer, and S. Kilgore. 1982. *High school achievement: Public, Catholic, and private schools compared*. New York: Basic Books.

Cremin, L. A. 1980. *American education: The democratic experience, 1783–1876*. New York: Harper & Row.

Cremin, L. A. 1988. *American education: The metropolitan experience, 1876–1980*. New York: Harper & Row.

Cremin, L. A. 1997. *Traditions of American education*. New York: Basic Books.

Curran, F. X. 1954. *The churches and the schools: American Protestantism and popular elementary education*. Chicago: Loyola University Press.

Gabel, R. J. 1937. Public funds for church and private schools. Ph.D. diss., The Catholic University of America.

Glenn, C. L. 1988. *The myth of the common school*. Amherst: University of Massachusetts Press.

Jorgenson, L. P. 1987. *The state and the non-public school, 1825–1925*. Columbia: University of Missouri Press.

Kaestle, C. F. 1983. *Pillars of the republic: Common schools in American society*, 1780–1860. New York: Hill & Wang.

Nevin, D., and R. E. Bills. 1976. *The schools that fear built: Segregation academies in the South*. Washington, D.C.: Acropolis Books.

National Center for Education Statistics. 1998. Private school universe survey, 1995–96. Washington, D.C.: U.S. Department of Education.

National Center for Education Statistics. 2000. *Mini-digest of education statistics*. 1999. Washington, D.C.: U.S. Department of Education.

Randall, E. V. 1994. *Private schools and public power. A case for pluralism*. New York: Teachers College Press.

Ray, B. D. 1997. *Strengths of their own—Home schoolers across America: Academic achievement, family characteristics, and longitudinal traits*. Salem, Ore.: National Home Education Research Institute.

Reese, W. F. 1995. *Origins of the American high school*. New Haven, Conn.: Yale University Press.

Ross, W. G. 1994. *Forging new freedoms: Nativism, education, and the Constitution, 1917–1927*. Lincoln: University of Nebraska Press.

Skerry, P. 1980. Christian schools versus the I.R.S. *Public Interest* 61 (October): 18–41.

Tyack, D. and L. Cuban. 1995. *Tinkering toward utopia: A century of public school reform*. Cambridge, Mass.: Harvard University Press.

Postnote

This article shows that American schools have not been static institutions. They have evolved to meet the needs and values of society as our country has developed. During the course of our history, schools have been the battleground for competing groups, interests, and philosophies.

Writing in the spring of 2001, Carper accurately predicted the 2002 Supreme Court decision upholding the use of "carefully crafted" vouchers, which enable parents in certain circumstances to use public tax money to purchase private, even religious, education for their children. Whether vouchers will be limited to students in failing public schools or will be offered to all parents, independent of income, appears to be the next educational policy battle.

Discussion Questions

1. Which of the many revealing facts about the history of our schools was most surprising to you?
2. What does Carper's second-to-last sentence mean—"Education of the public, rather than public education, might become the primary concern of the state"?
3. Are you in favor of choice within the public schools or a more radical choice plan, such as giving parents an educational check or voucher that allows them to buy the schooling they desire for their children? What are your reasons?

The Ethics of Teaching

KENNETH A. STRIKE

FOCUS Question

What are the ethical principles that underlie teaching?

TERMS TO NOTE

Benefit maximization
Equal respect
Ethics
Values

Mrs. Porter and Mr. Kennedy have divided their third-grade classes into reading groups. In her class, Mrs. Porter tends to spend the most time with students in the slowest reading group because they need the most help. Mr. Kennedy claims that such behavior is unethical. He maintains that each reading group should receive equal time.

Miss Andrews has had several thefts of lunch money in her class. She has been unable to catch the thief, although she is certain that some students in the class know who the culprit is. She decides to keep the entire class inside for recess, until someone tells her who stole the money. Is it unethical to punish the entire class for the acts of a few?

Ms. Phillips grades her fifth-grade students largely on the basis of effort. As a result, less able students who try hard often get better grades than students who are abler but less industrious. Several parents have accused Ms. Phillips of unethical behavior, claiming that their children are not getting what they deserve. These parents also fear that teachers in the middle school won't understand Ms. Phillips' grading practices and will place their children in inappropriate tracks.

The Nature of Ethical Issues

The cases described above are typical of the ethical issues that teachers face. What makes these issues ethical?

First, ethical issues concern questions of right and wrong—our duties and obligations, our rights and responsibilities. Ethical discourse is characterized by a unique vocabulary that commonly includes such words as *ought* and *should, fair* and *unfair*.

Second, ethical questions cannot be settled by an appeal to facts alone. In each of the preceding cases, knowing the consequences of our

---

Kenneth A. Strike is an emeritus professor of philosophy of education at Cornell University, Ithaca, New York. Strike, Kenneth A., "The Ethics of Teaching," *Phi Delta Kappan,* October 1988.

actions is not sufficient for determining the right thing to do. Perhaps, because Mrs. Porter spends more time with the slow reading group, the reading scores in her class will be more evenly distributed than the scores in Mr. Kennedy's class. But even knowing this does not tell us if it is fair to spend a disproportionate amount of time with the slow readers. Likewise, if Miss Andrews punishes her entire class, she may catch the thief, but this does not tell us whether punishing the entire group was the right thing to do. In ethical reasoning, facts are relevant in deciding what to do. But by themselves they are not enough. We also require ethical principles by which to judge the facts.

Third, ethical questions should be distinguished from values. Our values concern what we like or what we believe to be good. If one enjoys Bach or likes skiing, that says something about one's values. Often there is nothing right or wrong about values, and our values are a matter of our free choice. For example, it would be difficult to argue that someone who preferred canoeing to skiing had done something wrong or had made a mistake. Even if we believe that Bach is better than rock, that is not a reason to make people who prefer rock listen to Bach. Generally, questions of values turn on our choices: what we like, what we deem worth liking. But there is nothing obligatory about values.

On the other hand, because ethics concern what we ought to do, our ethical obligations are often independent of what we want or choose. The fact that we want something that belongs to someone else does not entitle us to take it. Nor does a choice to steal make stealing right or even "right for us." Our ethical obligations continue to be obligations, regardless of what we want or choose.

Ethical Reasoning

The cases sketched above involve ethical dilemmas: situations in which it seems possible to give a reasonable argument for more than one course of action. We must think about our choices, and we must engage in moral reasoning. Teaching is full of such dilemmas. Thus teachers need to know something about ethical reasoning.

Ethical reasoning involves two stages: applying principles to cases and judging the adequacy or applicability of the principles. In the first stage, we are usually called upon to determine the relevant ethical principle or principles that apply to a case, to ascertain the relevant facts of the case, and to judge the facts by the principles.

Consider, for example, the case of Miss Andrews and the stolen lunch money. Some ethical principles concerning punishment seem to apply directly to the case. Generally, we believe that we should punish the guilty, not the innocent; that people should be presumed innocent until proven guilty; and that the punishment should fit the crime. If Miss Andrews punishes her entire class for the behavior of an unknown few, she will violate these common ethical principles about punishment.

Ethical principles are also involved in the other two cases. The first case involves principles of equity and fairness. We need to know what counts as fair or equal treatment for students of different abilities. The third case requires some principles of due process. We need to know what are fair procedures for assigning grades to students.

However, merely identifying applicable principles isn't enough. Since the cases described above involve ethical dilemmas, it should be possible to argue plausibly for more than one course of action.

For example, suppose Miss Andrews decides to punish the entire class. It could be argued that she had behaved unethically because she has punished innocent people. She might defend herself, however, by holding that she had reasons for violating ethical principles that we normally apply to punishment. She might argue that it was important to catch the thief or that it was even more important to impress on her entire class that stealing is wrong. She could not make these points by ignoring the matter. By keeping the entire class inside for recess, Miss Andrews could maintain, she was able to catch the thief and to teach her class a lesson about the importance of honesty. Even if she had to punish some innocent people, everyone was better off as a result. Can't she justify her action by the fact that everyone benefits?

Two General Principles

When we confront genuine ethical dilemmas such as this, we need some general ethical concepts in order to think our way through them. I suggest two: the principle of benefit maximization and the principle of equal respect for persons.

The principle of benefit maximization holds that we should take that course of actions which will maximize the benefit sought. More generally, it requires us to do that which will make everyone, on the average, as well off as possible. One of the traditional formulations of this principle is the social philosophy known as utilitarianism, which holds that our most general moral obligation is to act in a manner that produces the greatest happiness for the greatest number.

We might use the principle of benefit maximization to think about each of these cases. The principle requires that in each case we ask which of the possible courses of action makes people generally better off. Miss Andrews has appealed to the principle of benefit maximization in justifying her punishment of the entire class. Ms. Phillips might likewise appeal to it in justifying her grading system. Perhaps by using grades to reward effort rather than successful performance, the overall achievement of the class will be enhanced. Is that not what is important?

It is particularly interesting to see how the principle of benefit maximization might be applied to the question of apportioning teacher time between groups with different levels of ability. Assuming for the moment that we wish to maximize the overall achievement of the class, the principle of benefit maximization dictates that we allocate time in a manner that will produce the greatest overall learning.

Suppose, however, we discover that the way to produce the greatest overall learning in a given class is for a teacher to spend the most time with the *brightest* children. These are the children who provide the greatest return on our investment of time. Even though the least able children learn less than they would with an equal division of time, the overall learning that takes place in the class is maximized when we concentrate on the ablest.

Here the principle of benefit maximization seems to lead to an undesirable result. Perhaps we should consider other principles as well.

The principle of equal respect requires that our actions respect the equal worth of moral agents. We must regard human beings as intrinsically worthwhile and treat them accordingly. The essence of this idea is perhaps best expressed in the Golden Rule. We have a duty to accord others the same kind of treatment that we expect them to accord us.

The principle of equal respect can be seen as involving three subsidiary ideas. First, it requires us to treat people as ends in themselves, rather than as means to further our own goals. We must respect their goals as well.

Second, when we are considering what it means to treat people as ends rather than as means, we must regard as central the fact that people are free and rational moral agents. This means that, above all, we must respect their freedom of choice. And we must respect the choices that people make even when we do not agree.

Third, no matter how people differ, they are of equal value as moral agents. This does not mean that we must see people as equal in abilities or capacities. Nor does it mean that we cannot take relevant differences between people into account when deciding how to treat them. It is not, for example, a violation of equal respect to give one student a higher grade than another because that student works harder and does better.

That people are of equal value as moral agents does mean, however, that they are entitled to the same basic rights and that their interests are of equal value. Everyone, regardless of native ability, is entitled to equal opportunity. No one is entitled to act as though his or her happiness counted for more than the happiness of others. As persons, everyone has equal worth.

Notice three things about these two moral principles. First, both principles (in some form) are part of the moral concepts of almost everyone who is reading this article. These are the sorts of moral principles that everyone cites in making moral arguments. Even if my formulation is new, the ideas themselves should be familiar. They are part of our common ethical understandings.

Second, both principles seem necessary for moral reflection. Neither is sufficient by itself. For example, the principle of equal respect requires us to value the well-being of others as we value our own well-being. But to value the welfare of ourselves *and* others is to be concerned with maximizing benefits; we want all people to be as well-off as possible.

Conversely, the principle of benefit maximization seems to presuppose the principle of equal respect. Why, after all, must we value the welfare of others? Why not insist that only our own happiness counts or that our happiness is more important than the happiness of others? Answering these questions will quickly lead us to affirm that people are of equal worth and that, as a consequence, everyone's happiness is to be valued equally. Thus our two principles are intertwined.

Third, the principles may nevertheless conflict with one another. One difference between the principle of benefit maximization and the principle of equal respect is their regard for consequences. For the principle of benefit maximization, only consequences matter. The sole relevant factor in choosing between courses of action is which action has the best overall results. But consequences are not decisive in the principle of equal respect; our actions must respect the dignity and worth of the individuals involved, even if we choose a course of action that produces less benefit than some other possible action.

The crucial question that characterizes a conflict between the principle of benefit maximization and the principle of equal respect is this:

When is it permissible to violate a person's rights in order to produce a better outcome? For example, this seems the best way to describe the issue that arises when a teacher decides to punish an entire class for the acts of a few. Students' rights are violated when they are punished for something they haven't done, but the overall consequence of the teacher's action may be desirable. Is it morally permissible, then, to punish everyone?

We can think about the issue of fair allocation of teacher time in the same way. Spending more time with the brightest students may enhance the average learning of the class. But we have, in effect, traded the welfare of the least able students for the welfare of the ablest. Is that not failing to respect the equal worth of the least able students? Is that not treating them as though they were means, not ends?

The principle of equal respect suggests that we should give the least able students at least an equal share of time, even if the average achievement of the class declines. Indeed, we might use the principle of equal respect to argue that we should allocate our time in a manner that produces more equal results—or a more equal share of the benefits of education.

I cannot take the discussion of these issues any further in this short space. But I do want to suggest some conclusions about ethics and teaching.

First, teaching is full of ethical issues. It is the responsibility of teachers, individually and collectively, to consider these issues and to have informed and intelligent opinions about them.

Second, despite the fact that ethical issues are sometimes thorny, they can be thought about. Ethical reflection can help us to understand what is at stake in our choices, to make more responsible choices, and sometimes to make the right choices.

Finally, to a surprising extent, many ethical dilemmas, including those that are common to teaching, can be illuminated by the principles of benefit maximization and equal respect for persons. Understanding these general ethical principles and their implications is crucial for thinking about ethical issues.

Postnote

Ethics seems to be making a comeback. We may not be behaving better, but we are talking about it more. Street crime and white-collar crime, drugs and violence, our inability to keep promises in our personal and professional lives—all these suggest a renewed need for ethics.

Kenneth Strike points out that teaching is full of ethical issues, and it is true that teachers make promises to perform certain duties and that they have real power over the lives of children. This article, however, speaks to only one end of the spectrum of ethical issues faced by the teacher: what we call "hard-case" ethics, complex problems, often dilemmas. Certainly, these are important, but there are also everyday teaching ethics—the issues that fill a teacher's day: Should I correct this stack of papers or watch *The Simpsons?* Should I "hear" that vulgar comment or stroll right by? Should I read this story again this year before I teach it tomorrow or spend some time with my colleagues in the teachers' lounge? Should I bend down and pick up yet another piece of paper in the hall or figure I've done my share for the day?

Like hard-case ethical issues, these questions, in essence, ask, What's the right thing to do? Our answers to these everyday questions often become our habits, good and bad. These, in turn, define much of our ethical behavior as teachers.

Discussion Questions

1. What three factors or qualities make an issue an ethical one?
2. What two ethical principles are mentioned in the article? Give your own examples of classroom situations that reflect these principles.
3. Do you believe that all there is to being a moral teacher is making ethical decisions? Why or why not?

The Teacher's Ten Commandments: School Law in the Classroom

THOMAS R. McDANIEL

FOCUSQuestion

What are the overarching legal principles that can guide the work of a teacher?

TERMS TO NOTE

Academic freedom

Due process

In recent years public school teachers have been made painfully aware that the law defines, limits, and prescribes many aspects of a teacher's daily life. Schools are no longer protected domains where teachers rule with impunity; ours is an age of litigation. Not only are parents and students ready to use the courts for all manner of grievances against school and teacher, the growing legislation itself regulates more and more of school life. In addition to an unprecedented number of laws at all levels of government, the mind-boggling array of complex case law principles (often vague and contradictory) adds to the confusion for the educator.

The Ten Commandments of School Law described below are designed to provide the concerned and bewildered teacher with some significant general guidelines in the classroom. While statutes and case law principles may vary from state to state or judicial circuit to judicial circuit, these school law principles have wide applicability in the United States today.

Commandment I: Thou Shalt Not Worship in the Classroom

This may seem something of a parody of the Biblical First Commandment—and many teachers hold that indeed their religious freedom and that of the majority of students has been limited by the court cases prohibiting prayer and Bible reading—but the case law principles here have been designed to keep public schools *neutral* in religious matters. The First Amendment to the Constitution, made applicable by the Fourteenth Amendment to state government (and hence to public schools, which are agencies of state government), requires that there be no law "respecting the establishment of religion or prohibiting the free exercise thereof." As the Supreme Court declared in the *Everson* decision of 1947, "Neither [a state nor the federal government] can pass laws that aid one religion, aid all religions, or prefer one religion

Thomas R. McDaniel is Senior Vice President and Professor of Education at Converse College in Spartanburg, South Carolina. "The Teacher's Ten Commandments: School Law in the Classroom" by Thomas R. McDaniel. Revised and updated from *Phi Delta Kappan,* June 1979. Reprinted by permission from Thomas R. McDaniel.

over another." Such rules, said the Court, would violate the separation of church and state principle of the First Amendment.

In 1971 the Supreme Court ruled in *Lemon* v. *Kurtzman* that separation of church and state required that government action or legislation in education must clear a three-pronged test. It must: 1) not have a religious purpose, 2) not have the primary effect of either enhancing or inhibiting religion, and 3) not create "excessive entanglement" between church and state. This Lemon Test has been attacked by Justice Anton Scalia and others in recent years but continues to be used (at least as a guideline) in court rulings. In a 1992 case, *Lee* v. *Wiseman*, the Supreme Court ruled that an invocation and benediction at commencement by a clergyman was unconstitutional—perhaps because the school principal chose the clergyman and gave him directions for the content of the prayer. In another 1992 case a circuit court of appeals upheld a policy that permitted high school seniors to choose student volunteers to deliver nonsectarian, nonproselytizing invocations at graduation ceremonies. Courts continue to wrestle with questions about "establishment" and "freedom" of religion. However, acts of worship in public schools usually violate the neutrality principle—especially when they appear to be planned and promoted by school officials.

On the other hand, public schools may offer courses in comparative religion, history of religion, or the Bible as literature, because these would be academic experiences rather than religious ones. "Released-time" programs during school hours for outside-of-school religious instruction have been held to be constitutional by the Supreme Court (*Zorach* v. *Clauson*, 1952). Other religious practices that have been struck down by the Supreme Court include a Kentucky statute requiring that the Ten Commandments be posted in every public school classroom, a Michigan high school's 30-year practice of displaying a 2-foot by 3-foot portrait of Jesus in the hallways, laws in Arkansas and Louisiana requiring that "scientific creationism" (based on Genesis) be taught in science classes to "balance" the teaching of evolution, the Gideons' distribution of Bibles in the public schools of Indiana. Other courts have questioned (or struck down) certain practices such as invocations at football games, nativity scenes and other religious displays, and laws requiring a "moment of silence" when the purpose is to promote prayer. Finding the line that separates church and state has not been easy. The "wall of separation" has often seemed more like a semi-permeable membrane.

In 1984, Congress passed the Equal Access Act. This statute made it unlawful for any public secondary school receiving federal funds to discriminate against any students who wanted to conduct a meeting on school premises during "non-instructional time" (before and after regular school hours) if other student groups (such as clubs) were allowed to use school facilities during these times. Religious groups that are voluntary and student initiated (not officially sponsored or led by school personnel) may, under the EAA, meet on school premises. Such meetings may not be conducted or controlled by others not associated with the school nor may they interfere with educational activities of the school. In a 1990 case (*Westside Community Schools* v. *Mergens*) the Supreme Court upheld the constitutionality of the EAA and declared this federal statute did not violate the First Amendment or any of the three prongs of the Lemon Test. However, a 1993 case (*Sease* v. *School District of Philadelphia*) in Pennsylvania disallowed a gospel choir that advertised itself as sponsored by the school district, was directed by the school secretary, had another school employee attending all practices, and had non-school persons regularly attending meetings of the choir. There were several violations of the EAA in this case.

The application of the neutrality principle to education has resulted in some of the following guidelines for public schools:

1. Students may not be required to salute the flag nor to stand for the flag salute, if this conflicts with their religious beliefs.

2. Bible reading, even without comment, may not be practiced in a public school when the intent is to promote worship.

3. Prayer is an act of worship and as such cannot be a regular part of opening exercises or other aspects of the regular school day (including grace at lunch).
4. Worship services (e.g., prayer and Bible reading) are not constitutional even if voluntary rather than compulsory. Not consensus, not majority vote, nor excusing objectors from class or participation makes these practices legal.
5. Prayer and other acts of worship (benedictions, hymns, invocations, etc.) at school-related or school-sponsored events are increasingly under scrutiny by courts and may be disallowed when found to be initiated or controlled by school officials.

Commandment II: Thou Shalt Not Abuse Academic Freedom

Under First Amendment protection, teachers are given the necessary freedom and security to use the classroom as a forum for the examination and discussion of ideas. Freedom of expression is a prerequisite for education in a democracy—and the schools, among other responsibilities, are agents of democracy. Students are citizens too, and they are also entitled to freedom of speech. As Justice Abe Fortas, who delivered the Supreme Court's majority opinion in the famous *Tinker* decision (1969), put it:

> It can hardly be argued that either students or teachers shed their constitutional rights at the schoolhouse gate. . . . In our system state-operated schools may not be enclaves of totalitarianism . . . [and] students may not be regarded as closed-circuit recipients of only that which the state chooses to communicate.

Case law has developed over the years to define the parameters of free expression for both teachers and students:

1. Teachers may discuss controversial issues in the classroom if they are relevant to the curriculum, although good judgment is required. Issues that disrupt the educational process, are demonstrably inappropriate to the legitimate objectives of the curriculum, or are unreasonable for the age and maturity of the students may be prohibited by school officials. The routine use of profanity by teachers is not a protected First Amendment right (*Martin* v. *Parrish*, 1986, Fifth Circuit Court).
2. Teachers may discuss current events, political issues, and candidates so long as neutrality and balanced consideration prevail. When teachers become advocates and partisans, supporters of a single position rather than examiners of all positions, they run the risk of censure.
3. A teacher may use controversial literature containing "rough" language but must "take care not to transcend his legitimate professional purpose" (*Mailoux* v. *Kiley*, 1971, U.S. District Court, Massachusetts). Again, courts will attempt to determine curriculum relevance, disruption of the educational process, and appropriateness to the age and maturity of the students.
4. Teachers and students are increasingly (but not yet universally) guaranteed symbolic free speech, including hair length and beards, armbands, and buttons. Courts generally determine such issues in terms of the "substantial disruption" that occurs or is clearly threatened. Dress codes for students are generally allowable when they are intended to provide for health, safety, and "decency." When they exist merely to promote the "tastes" of the teacher or administration, they have usually been struck down by the courts.
5. Teachers have some control over school-sponsored publications and plays. In *Hazelwood School District* v. *Kuhlmeier* (1988) the Supreme Court held that "educators do not offend the First Amendment by exercising editorial control over the style and content of student speech in school-sponsored expressive activities so long as their actions are reasonably related to legitimate pedagogical concerns." This authority, however, does not extend to censorship of student expression. It does not appear to extend to a school board's

banning and regulating textbooks and other "learning materials" (*Virgil* v. *School Board of Columbia County*, 1989, Eleventh Circuit).

6. Teachers do not have a constitutional right to use any teaching method they want. School district officials and boards may establish course content and teaching methods as matters of policy. Courts will support such policies but will examine the reasonableness of sanctions against teachers. For example, a California court ruled that firing a teacher for unwittingly permitting students to read obscene poetry was too severe (*De Groat* v. *Newark*, 1976) while a nine-month suspension of a West Virginia teacher showing cartoons of "Fritz the Cat" undressing was judged appropriate (*DeVito* v. *Board of Education*, 1984).

Teachers in short are free to deal with controversial issues (including politics and sex) and to use controversial methods and materials if these are educationally defensible, appropriate to the students, and not "materially and substantially" disruptive. But school boards also have authority to maintain curricular policies governing what (and even how) teachers should teach. Courts use a balancing test to determine when students' and teachers' rights to academic freedom must give way to the competing need of society to have reasonable school discipline.

Commandment III: Thou Shalt Not Engage in Private Activities That Impair Teaching Effectiveness

Of all the principles of school law, this commandment is probably the most difficult to delineate with precision. The private and professional areas of a teacher's life have been, for the most part, separated by recent court decisions. A mere 75 years ago teachers signed contracts with provisions prohibiting marriage, falling in love, leaving town without permission of the school board, smoking cigarettes, loitering in ice-cream stores, and wearing lipstick. But now a teacher's private life is considered his or her own business. Thus, for example, many court cases have established that teachers have the same citizenship rights outside the classroom that any other person has.

Teachers, however, have always been expected by society to abide by high standards of personal conduct. Whenever a teacher's private life undermines effective instruction in the class, there is a possibility that the courts will uphold his or her dismissal. To guard against this possibility, the teacher should consider some of the following principles:

1. Teachers may belong to any organization or association—but if they participate in illegal activities of that organization they may be dismissed from their job.

2. A teacher may write letters to newspapers criticizing school policies—unless it can be shown that such criticism impairs morale or working relationships. In the landmark *Pickering* decision (1968), the Supreme Court upheld a teacher who had written such a letter but pointed out that there was in this case "no question of maintaining either discipline by immediate supervisors or harmony among co-workers. . . ."

3. Teachers do not have a right to air private grievances or personnel judgments publicly. Free speech on public issues should not lead teachers to criticize superiors or other school employees in public settings. In a 1983 case, *Connick* v. *Myers*, the Supreme Court ruled against a discharged public employee, saying that he spoke out "not as a citizen upon matters of public concern but instead as an employee on matters of personal interest." A judge in Florida, applying *Connick* to a history teacher discharged for outspoken criticism of his administrators, ruled that the teacher's speech was "nothing more than a set of grievances with school administrators over internal school policies" (*Ferrara* v. *Mills*, 1984). Teachers should distinguish between *public* citizenship issues and *private* personnel issues before making controversial and critical public comments about their schools.

4. A teacher's private affairs do not normally disqualify him or her from teaching except to the

extent that it can be shown that such affairs undermine teaching effectiveness. Teachers who are immoral in public, or who voluntarily (or through indiscretion) make known in public private acts of immorality, may indeed be dismissed. Courts are still debating the rights of homosexual teachers, with decisions falling on both sides of this issue.

5. Laws which say that teachers may be dismissed for "unprofessional conduct" or "moral turpitude" are interpreted narrowly, with the burden of proof on the employer to show that the particular circumstances in a case constitute "unfitness to teach." Dismissal must be based on fact, not mere rumor.
6. Whenever a teacher's private affairs include sexual involvement with students, it may be presumed that courts will declare that such conduct constitutes immorality indicating unfitness to teach.

Commandment IV: Thou Shalt Not Deny Students Due Process

The Fourteenth Amendment guarantees citizens "due process of law" whenever the loss of a right is at stake. Because education has come to be considered such a right (a "property" right), and because students are considered to be citizens, case law in recent years has defined certain procedures to be necessary in providing due process in particular situations:

1. A rule that is patently or demonstrably unfair or a punishment that is excessive may be found by a court to violate the "substantive" due process of a student (see, for example, the Supreme Court's 1969 *Tinker* decision). At the heart of due process is the concept of fair play, and teachers should examine the substance of their rules and the procedures for enforcing them to see if both are reasonable, nonarbitrary, and equitable.
2. The extent to which due process rights should be observed depends on the gravity of the offense and the severity of punishment that follows. The Supreme Court's *Goss* v. *Lopez* decision (1975) established minimal due process for suspensions of 10 days or less, including oral or written notice of charges and an opportunity for the student to present his or her side of the story.
3. When students are expelled from school, they should be given a statement of the specific charges and the grounds for expulsion, a formal hearing, names of witnesses, and a report of the facts to which each witness testifies (see the leading case, *Dixon* v. *Alabama State Board of Education*, 1961). Furthermore, it is probable that procedural due process for expelled students gives them the right to challenge the evidence, cross-examine witnesses, and be represented by counsel. (See, for example, the New York Supreme Court's 1967 *Goldwyn* v. *Allen* decision.) Finally, such students may appeal the decision to an impartial body for review.
4. Special education students have an added measure of due process protection. In 1990 Congress consolidated earlier special education federal statutes—including the 1975 Education of All Handicapped Children Act (Public Law 94-142) and section 504 of the Rehabilitation Act of 1973—into the Individuals with Disabilities Education Act (IDEA). These laws stipulate extensive due process rights for *all* children with disabilities (whether or not they have "the ability to benefit") to ensure a free, "appropriate" education. These provisions include prior written notice before any proposed change in a child's educational program; testing that is non-discriminatory in language, race, or culture; parental access to records; fair and impartial hearing by the State Education Agency or local district; and a student's right to remain in a current placement until due process proceedings are completed. These due process guarantees supersede district level policies relating to placement, suspension, or expulsion of students. As the Supreme Court ruled in *Honig* v. *Doe* (1988), the IDEA does not allow even for a "dangerous exception" to the "stay put" provision.

It is advisable for schools to develop written regulations governing procedures for such areas as suspension, expulsion, discipline, publications, and placement of the disabled. The teacher should be aware of these regulations and should provide his or her administration with specific, factual evidence whenever a student faces a serious disciplinary decision. The teacher is also advised to be guided by the spirit of due process—fairness and evenhanded justice—when dealing with less serious incidents in the classroom.

Commandment V: Thou Shalt Not Punish Behavior Through Academic Penalties

It is easy for teachers to lose sight of the distinction between punishing and rewarding academic performance, on the one hand, and disciplinary conduct on the other. Grades, for example, are frequently employed as motivation for both study behavior and paying-attention behavior. There is a great temptation for teachers to use one of the few weapons still in their arsenal (i.e., grades) as an instrument of justice for social infractions in the classroom. While it may indeed be the case that students who misbehave will not perform well academically because of their conduct, courts are requiring schools and teachers to keep those two domains separate.

In particular, teachers are advised to heed the following general applications of this principle:

1. Denial of a diploma to a student who has met all the academic requirements for it but who has broken a rule of discipline is not permitted. Several cases (going back at least as far as the 1921 Iowa *Valentine* case) are on record to support this guideline. It is also probable that exclusion from a graduation ceremony as a punishment for behavior will not be allowed by the courts.
2. Grades should not be reduced to serve disciplinary purposes. In the *Wermuth* case (1965) in New Jersey, the ruling against such practice included this observation by the state's commissioner of education: "Whatever system of marks and grades a school may devise will have serious inherent limitations at best, and it must not be further handicapped by attempting to serve disciplinary purposes too." In a 1984 case in Pennsylvania (*Katzman* v. *Cumberland Valley School District*) the court struck down a policy requiring a reduction in grades by two percentage points for each day of suspension.
3. Lowering grades—or awarding zeros—for absences is a questionable legal practice. In the Kentucky case of *Dorsey* v. *Bale* (1975), a student had his grades reduced for unexcused absences, and under the school's regulation, was not allowed to make up the work; five points were deducted from his nine-weeks' grade for each unexcused absence. A state circuit court and the Kentucky Court of Appeals declared the regulation to be invalid. The courts are particularly likely to invalidate regulations that constitute "double jeopardy"—e.g., suspending students for disciplinary reasons and giving them zeros while suspended.

In general, teachers who base academic evaluation on academic performance have little to fear in this area. Courts do not presume to challenge a teacher's grades *per se* when the consideration rests only on the teacher's right or ability to make valid academic judgments.

Commandment VI: Thou Shalt Not Misuse Corporal Punishment

Corporal punishment is a controversial method of establishing discipline. The Supreme Court refused to disqualify the practice under a suit (*Ingraham* v. *Wright*, 1977) in which it was argued that corporal punishment was "cruel and unusual punishment" and thus a violation of the Constitution's Eighth Amendment. An increasing number of states—up from only two in 1979 to 27 in 1996—ban corporal punishment in public schools.

In those states not prohibiting corporal punishment, teachers may—as an extension of their *in loco parentis* authority—use "moderate" corporal punishment to establish discipline. There are, however, many potential legal dangers in the practice. *In loco parentis* is a limited, perhaps even a vanishing, concept, and teachers must be careful to avoid these misuses of corporal punishment if they want to stay out of the courtroom:

1. The punishment must never lead to permanent injury. No court will support as "reasonable" or "moderate" that physical punishment which permanently disables or disfigures a student. Many an assault and battery judgment has been handed down in such cases. Unfortunately for teachers, "accidents" that occur during corporal punishment and ignorance of a child's health problems (brittle bones, hemophilia, etc.) do not always excuse a teacher from liability.

2. The punishment must not be unreasonable in terms of the offense, nor may it be used to enforce an unreasonable rule. The court examines all the circumstances in a given case to determine what was or was not "reasonable" or "excessive." In 1980 the Fourth Circuit Court of Appeals ruled that "excessive" corporal punishment might well violate Fourteenth Amendment rights. In 1987 the Tenth Circuit Court of Appeals reached a similar conclusion.

3. The punishment must not be motivated by spite, malice, or revenge. Whenever teachers administer corporal punishment in a state of anger, they run a high risk of losing an assault and battery suit in court. Since corporal punishment is practiced as a method of correcting student behavior, any evidence that physical force resulted from a teacher's bad temper or quest for revenge is damning. On the other hand, in an explosive situation (e.g., a fight) teachers may protect themselves and use that force necessary to restrain a student from harming the teacher, others, or himself.

4. The punishment must not ignore such variables as the student's age, sex, size, and physical condition.

5. The punishment must not be administered with inappropriate instruments or to parts of the body where risk of injury is great. For example, a Texas case ruled that it is not reasonable for a teacher to use his fists in administering punishment. Another teacher lost a suit when he struck a child on the ear, breaking an eardrum. The judge noted, "Nature has provided a part of the anatomy for chastisement, and tradition holds that such chastisement should there be applied." It should be noted that creating mental anguish and emotional stress by demeaning, harassing, or humiliating a child may be construed as illegal punishment too.

6. Teachers must not only take care not to harm children by way of corporal punishment; they also have a responsibility to report suspected child abuse by parents or others. Congress passed the National Child Abuse Prevention and Treatment Act in 1974 and followed with stronger laws in 1988 and 1992. Child abuse is a state (not federal) crime with many variations in definition and reporting procedure. But *all* states require reporting if the neglect or abuse results in physical injury. Teachers need not be absolutely certain of abuse but must act "in good faith" if they have "reason to believe" a child is being subjected to abuse or neglect. Every state also provides legal protection from suit for such reporting. In most states, failure to report is a misdemeanor.

Courts must exercise a good deal of judgment in corporal punishment cases to determine what is "moderate," "excessive," "reasonable," "cruel," "unusual," "malicious," or "capricious." Suffice it to say that educators should exercise great care in the use of corporal punishment.

Commandment VII: Thou Shalt Not Neglect Students' Safety

One of the major responsibilities of teachers is to keep their students safe from unreasonable risk of harm or danger. The major cases involving teachers grow out of negligence charges relating to the teacher's failure to supervise properly in accordance with *in loco parentis* obligations (to act "in place of the parents"), contractual obligations, and professional responsibility. While the courts do not expect teachers to protect children from "unforeseeable accidents" and "acts of God," they do require teachers to act as a reasonably prudent teacher should in protecting students from possible harm or injury.

Negligence is a tort ("wrong") that exists only when the elements of *duty*, *violation*, *cause*, and *injury* are present. Teachers are generally responsible for using good judgment in determining what steps are necessary to provide for adequate supervision of the particular students in their charge, and the given circumstances dictate what is reasonably prudent in each case. A teacher who has a duty to his or her students but who fails to fulfill this duty because of carelessness, lack of discretion, or lack of diligence may violate this duty with a resultant injury to a student. In this instance the teacher may be held liable for negligence as the cause of the injury to the student.

Several guidelines can help teachers avoid this all-too-common and serious lawsuit:

1. Establish and enforce rules of safety in school activities. This is particularly important for the elementary teacher, since many injuries to elementary students occur on playgrounds, in hallways, and in classroom activity sessions. The prudent teacher anticipates such problems and establishes rules to protect students from such injuries. Generally, rules should be written, posted, and taught.
2. Be aware of school, district, and state rules and regulations as they pertain to student safety. One teacher was held negligent when a child was injured because the teacher did not know that there was a state law requiring safety glasses in a shop activity. It is also important that a teacher's own rules not conflict with regulations at higher levels. *Warn* students of any hazard in a room or in an instructional activity.
3. Enforce safety rules when violations are observed. In countless cases teachers have been found negligent when students repeatedly broke important safety rules, eventually injuring themselves or others, or when a teacher should have foreseen danger but did not act as a "reasonably prudent" teacher would have in the same situation to correct the behavior. One teacher observing a mumblety-peg game at recess was held negligent for not stopping it before the knife bounced up and put out an eye of one of the players.
4. Provide a higher standard of supervision when students are younger, disabled, and/or in a potentially dangerous activity. Playgrounds, physical education classes, science labs, and shop classes require particular care and supervision. Instruction must be provided to insure safety in accordance with the children's maturity, competence, and skill.
5. Learn first aid, because teachers may be liable for negligence if they do not get or give prompt, appropriate medical assistance when necessary. While teachers should not give children medicine, even aspirin, they should, of course, allow any legitimate prescriptions to be taken as prescribed. There should be school policy governing such procedures.
6. Advise substitute teachers (and student teachers) about any unusual medical, psychological, handicapping, or behavioral problem in your class. If there are physical hazards in your class—bare light cords, sharp edges, loose boards, insecure window frames, etc.—warn everyone about these too. Be sure to report such hazards to your administration and janitorial staff—as a "prudent" teacher would do.
7. Be where you are assigned to be. If you have playground, hall, cafeteria, or bus duty, be there. An accident that occurs when you are someplace other than your assigned station may be blamed on your negligence, whereas if you had been there it would not be so charged. Your responsibility for safety is the same for extracurricular activities you are monitoring as it is for classes.

8. If you have to leave a classroom (particularly a rowdy one), stipulate the kind of conduct you expect and make appropriate arrangements—such as asking another teacher to check in. Even this may not be adequate precaution in terms of your duty to supervise if the students are known to be troublemakers, are quite immature, or are mentally retarded or emotionally disabled. You run a greater risk leaving a science class or a gym class than you do a social studies class.
9. Plan field trips with great care and provide for adequate supervision. Many teachers fail to realize that permission notes from home—no matter how much they disclaim teacher liability for injury—do not excuse a teacher from providing proper supervision. A parent cannot sign away this right of his or her child. Warn children of dangers on the trip and instruct them in rules of conduct and safety.
10. Do not send students on errands off school grounds, because they then become your agents. If they are injured or if they injure someone else, you may well be held liable. Again, the younger and less responsible the child, the greater the danger of a teacher negligence charge. To state the obvious, some children require more supervision than others.

Much of the advice is common sense, but the "reasonably prudent" teacher needs to be alert to the many requirements of "due care" and "proper supervision." The teacher who anticipates potentially dangerous conditions and actions and takes reasonable precautions—through rules, instruction, warnings, communications to superiors, and presence in assigned stations—will do a great deal in minimizing the chances of pupil injury and teacher negligence.

Commandment VIII: Thou Shalt Not Slander or Libel Your Students

This tort is much less common than negligence, but it is an area of school law that can be troublesome. One of the primary reasons for the Family Educational Rights and Privacy Act (1974) was that school records contain so much misinformation and hearsay and so many untrue (or, at least, questionable) statements about children's character, conduct, and morality that access to these records by students or their parents, in order to correct false information, seemed warranted. A teacher's right to write anything about a student under the protection of confidential files no longer exists. Defamation of character through written communication is "libel" while such defamation in oral communication is "slander." There are ample opportunities for teachers to commit both offenses.

Teachers are advised to be careful about what they say about students (let alone other teachers!) to employers, colleges, parents, and other personnel at the school. Adhere to the following guidelines:

1. Avoid vague, derogatory terms on permanent records and recommendations. Even if you do not intend to be derogatory, value judgments about a student's character, life-style, or home life may be found defamatory in court. In one case, a North Carolina teacher was found guilty of libel when she said on a permanent record card that a student was "ruined by tobacco and whiskey." Avoid characterizing students as "crazy," "immoral," or "delinquent."
2. Say or write only what you know to be true about a student. It is safer to be an objective describer of what you have observed than to draw possibly unwarranted and untrue conclusions and judgments. The truth of a statement is strong evidence that character has not been defamed, but in some cases where the intent has been to malign and destroy the person, truth is not an adequate defense.
3. Communicate judgments of character only to those who have a right to the information. Teachers have "qualified privileged communication," which means that so long as they communicate in good faith information that they believe to be true to a person who has reason to have this information,

they are protected. However, the slandering of pupils in a teachers' lounge bull session is another thing altogether.

4. If a student confides a problem to you in confidence, keep that communication confidential. A student who is on drugs, let us say, may bring you to court for defamation of character and/or invasion of privacy if you spread such information about indiscriminately. On the other hand, if a student confides that he or she has participated in a felonious crime or gives you information that makes you aware of a "clear and present" danger, you are obligated to bring such information to the appropriate authorities. Find out the proper limits of communication and the authorized channels in your school and state.

5. As a related issue, be careful about "search and seizure" procedures too. Generally, school lockers are school property and may be searched by school officials if they have reasonable grounds to suspect that the locker has something dangerous or illegal in it. In its landmark 1985 decision in *New Jersey* v. *T.L.O.*, the Supreme Court rejected the notion that school officials had to have the police standard of "probable cause" before conducting a search; the court approved the lower standard of "reasonable suspicion." So long as both the grounds (i.e., reason) and scope are reasonable, school personnel can search student suspects. The growing concern in society about drugs and weapons in school has led courts to support school officials conducting searches for dangerous or illegal items. Strip searches, however, are often deemed to be too intrusive.

Teachers need to remember that students are citizens and as such enjoy at least a limited degree of the constitutional rights that adult citizens enjoy. Not only "due process," "equal protection," and "freedom of religion" but also protection from teacher torts such as "negligence" and "defamation of character" is provided to students through our system of law. These concepts apply to all students, including those in elementary grades.

Commandment IX: Thou Shalt Not Photocopy in Violation of Copyright Law

In January, 1978, the revised copyright law went into effect and with it strict limitations on what may be photocopied by teachers for their own or classroom use under the broad concept of "fair use." The "fair use" of copyrighted material means that the use should not impair the value of the owner's copyright by diminishing the demand for that work, thereby reducing potential income for the owner.

In general, educators are given greater latitude than most other users. "Spontaneous" copying is more permissible than "systematic" copying. Students have greater latitude than teachers in copying materials.

Teachers may:

1. Make a single copy for their own research or class preparation of a chapter from a book; an article from a periodical or newspaper; a short story, poem, or essay; a chart, graph, diagram, cartoon, or picture from a book, periodical, or newspaper.
2. Make multiple copies for classroom use only (but not to exceed one copy per student) of a complete poem, if it is fewer than 250 words and printed on not more than two pages; an excerpt from a longer poem, if it is fewer than 250 words; a complete article, story, or essay, if it is fewer than 2,500 words; an excerpt from a prose work, if it is fewer than 1,000 words or 10% of the work, whichever is less; one chart, graph, diagram, drawing, cartoon, or picture per book or periodical.

However, teachers may not:

1. Make multiple copies of work for classroom use if another teacher has already copied the work for use in another class in the same school.
2. Make copies of a short poem, article, story, or essay from the same author more than once in the same term.
3. Make multiple copies from the same collective work or periodical issue more than three

times a term. (The limitations in Items 1–3 do not apply to current news periodicals or newspapers.)

4. Make a copy of works to take the place of anthologies.
5. Make copies of "consumable" materials such as workbooks, exercises, answer sheets to standardized tests, and the like.

More recent technologies have led to extended applications of the "fair use" doctrine:

1. The "fair use" doctrine does not apply to copyrighted computer software programs; however, teachers may load a copyrighted program onto a classroom terminal or make a "backup" copy for archival purposes. Teachers may not make copies of such programs for student use. In 1991 the Department of Justice and Department of Education called on schools to teach the ethical use of computers to counteract illegal copying of software.
2. Schools may videotape copyrighted television programs but may keep the tape no longer than 45 days without a license. Teachers may use the tapes for instruction during the first 10 consecutive days after taping but may repeat such use only once. Commercial videotapes may not be rented to be played for instruction (or entertainment) in classrooms.
3. Scanning copyrighted material into a computer and distributing it via the Internet is a violation of copyright law. The Internet should be viewed as a giant photocopying machine. Bills are now in Congress to restrict and punish those who misuse the Internet. We may expect to see other legal complications from this emerging technology: defamation, obscenity, threats of violence, disruption of the academic environment, and sexual harassment—to list but a few.

When teachers make brief, spontaneous, and limited copies of copyrighted materials other than consumables, they are likely to be operating within the bounds of fair use. Whenever multiple copies of copyrighted materials are made (within the guidelines above), each copy should include a notice of the copyright. Teachers should consult media specialists and others in their school about questions relating to "fair use"—whether for print, videotape, or computer materials.

Commandment X: Thou Shalt Not Be Ignorant of the Law

The axiom, "Ignorance of the law is no excuse," holds as true for teachers as anyone else. Indeed, courts are increasingly holding teachers to higher standards of competence and knowledge commensurate with their higher status as professionals. Since education is now considered a right—guaranteed to black and white, rich and poor, "normal" and disabled—the legal parameters have become ever more important to teachers in this litigious era.

How, then, can the teacher become aware of the law and its implications for the classroom? Consider the following possibilities:

1. Sign up for a course in school law. If the local college or university does not offer such a course, attempt to have one developed.
2. Ask your school system administration to focus on this topic in inservice programs.
3. Tap the resources of the local, state, and national professional organizations for pertinent speakers, programs, and materials.
4. Explore state department of education sources, since most states will have personnel and publications that deal with educational statutes and case law in your particular state.
5. Establish school (if not personal) subscriptions to professional journals. *Phi Delta Kappan*, *Journal of Law and Education*, and *Mental Disability Law Reporter* are only a few of the journals that regularly have columns and/or articles to keep the teacher aware of new developments in school law.
6. Make sure that your school or personal library includes such books as *Teachers and the Law* (Louis Fischer et al., 4th edition, Longman, 1995); *The Law of Schools, Students, and Teachers* (Kern and David Alexander, 2nd

edition, West, 1995); *Special Education Law* (Laura Rothstein, 2nd edition, Longman, 1995); and *Deskbook Encyclopedia of American School Law* (Data Research, Rosemount, Minnesota, 1996). Monthly newsletters can keep schools up-to-date in the school law area. Consider a subscription to *School Law Bulletin* (Quinlan Publishing Company, Boston) or *Legal Notes for Educators* (Data Research, Rosemount, Minnesota).

The better informed teachers are about their legal rights and responsibilities, the more likely they are to avoid the courtroom—and there are many ways to keep informed.

My Teacher's Ten Commandments are not exhaustive, nor are they etched in stone. School law, like all other law, is constantly evolving and changing so as to reflect the thinking of the times; and decisions by courts are made in the context of particular events and circumstances that are never exactly the same. But prudent professionals will be well served by these commandments if they internalize the spirit of the law as a guide to actions as teachers—in the classroom, the school, and the community.

Postnote

The United States is an increasingly litigious society. Rather than settle disagreements and disputes face to face, we quickly turn over our problems to lawyers. In recent years, business owners and managers, doctors, and even lawyers have been held liable for various consequences of their work. Such situations were almost unknown to their colleagues in an earlier age.

Although relatively few teachers have been prosecuted successfully in the courts, the number of cases has dramatically increased. Therefore, it is important for teachers—both in training and in service—to be aware of areas of legal vulnerability. McDaniel, himself a former teacher, has presented an outstanding summary of the law as it affects teachers.

Discussion Questions

1. Before reading this article, were you aware that school law governed teachers' behavior as much as it does? In which of the areas described by McDaniel do you, personally, feel most vulnerable? Why?
2. What steps can you take to protect yourself as a teacher from legal liability?
3. Which of these "commandments" has the most negative impact on the effectiveness of the average teacher? Why?

CLASSIC

The Return of Character Education

THOMAS LICKONA

FOCUS Question

By the very nature of schooling, the characters of children are affected. But what is character education, and what can teachers and schools do to develop the character of students?

TERMS TO NOTE

Character education
Moral leadership
Personalism
Positivism
Secularism
Values
Values clarification

To educate a person in mind and not in morals is to educate a menace to society.

—Theodore Roosevelt

Increasing numbers of people across the ideological spectrum believe that our society is in deep moral trouble. The disheartening signs are everywhere: the breakdown of the family; the deterioration of civility in everyday life; rampant greed at a time when one in five children is poor; an omnipresent sexual culture that fills our television and movie screens with sleaze, beckoning the young toward sexual activity at ever earlier ages; the enormous betrayal of children through sexual abuse; and the 1992 report of the National Research Council that says the United States is now *the* most violent of all industrialized nations.

As we become more aware of this societal crisis, the feeling grows that schools cannot be ethical bystanders. As a result, character education is making a comeback in American schools.

Early Character Education

Character education is as old as education itself. Down through history, education has had two great goals: to help people become smart and to help them become good.

Acting on that belief, schools in the earliest days of our republic tackled character education head on—through discipline, the teacher's example, and the daily school curriculum. The Bible was the public school's sourcebook for both moral and religious instruction. When struggles eventually arose over whose Bible to use and which doctrines to teach, William McGuffey stepped onto the stage in 1836 to offer his McGuffey Readers, ultimately to sell more than 100 million copies.

Thomas Lickona is a developmental psychologist at the State University of New York at Cortland and one of the leading experts in character education. From Thomas R. Lickona, "The Return of Character Education," *Educational Leadership,* November 1993, pp. 6–11.

McGuffey retained many favorite Biblical stories but added poems, exhortations, and heroic tales. While children practiced their reading or arithmetic, they also learned lessons about honesty, love of neighbor, kindness to animals, hard work, thriftiness, patriotism, and courage.

Why Character Education Declined

In the 20th century, the consensus supporting character education began to crumble under the blows of several powerful forces.

Darwinism introduced a new metaphor—evolution—that led people to see all things, including morality, as being in flux.

The philosophy of logical positivism, arriving at American universities from Europe, asserted a radical distinction between *facts* (which could be scientifically proven) and *values* (which positivism held were mere expressions of feeling, not objective truth). As a result of positivism, morality was relativized and privatized—made to seem a matter of personal "value judgment," not a subject for public debate and transmission through the schools.

In the 1960s, a worldwide rise in personalism celebrated the worth, autonomy, and subjectivity of the person, emphasizing individual rights and freedom over responsibility. Personalism rightly protested societal oppression and injustice, but it also delegitimized moral authority, eroded belief in objective moral norms, turned people inward toward self-fulfillment, weakened social commitments (for example, to marriage and parenting), and fueled the socially destabilizing sexual revolution.

Finally, the rapidly intensifying pluralism of American society (Whose values should we teach?) and the increasing secularization of the public arena (Won't moral education violate the separation of church and state?) became two more barriers to achieving the moral consensus indispensable for character education in the public schools. Public schools retreated from their once central role as moral and character educators.

The 1970s saw a return of values education, but in new forms: values clarification and Kohlberg's moral dilemma discussions. In different ways, both expressed the individualist spirit of the age. Values clarification said, don't impose values; help students choose their values freely. Kohlberg said, develop students' powers of moral reasoning so they can judge which values are better than others.

Each approach made contributions, but each had problems. Values clarification, though rich in methodology, failed to distinguish between personal preferences (truly a matter of free choice) and moral values (a matter of obligation). Kohlberg focused on moral reasoning, which is necessary but not sufficient for good character, and underestimated the school's role as a moral socializer.

The New Character Education

In the 1990s we are seeing the beginnings of a new character education movement, one which restores "good character" to its historical place as the central desirable outcome of the school's moral enterprise. No one knows yet how broad or deep this movement is; we have no studies to tell us what percentage of schools are making what kind of effort. But something significant is afoot.

In July 1992, the Josephson Institute of Ethics called together more than 30 educational leaders representing state school boards, teachers' unions, universities, ethics centers, youth organizations, and religious groups. This diverse assemblage drafted the Aspen Declaration on Character Education, setting forth eight principles of character education.[1]

The Character Education Partnership was launched in March 1993, as a national coalition committed to putting character development at the top of the nation's educational agenda. Members include representatives from business, labor, government, youth, parents, faith communities, and the media.

The last two years have seen the publication of a spate of books—such as *Moral, Character, and Civic Education in the Elementary School, Why Johnny Can't Tell Right from Wrong*, and *Reclaiming Our Schools: A Handbook on Teaching Character,*

Academics, and Discipline—that make the case for character education and describe promising programs around the country. A new periodical, the *Journal of Character Education*, is devoted entirely to covering the field.[2]

Why Character Education Now?

Why this groundswell of interest in character education? There are at least three causes:

1. The decline of the family. The family, traditionally a child's primary moral teacher, is for vast numbers of children today failing to perform that role, thus creating a moral vacuum. In her recent book *When the Bough Breaks: The Cost of Neglecting Our Children*, economist Sylvia Hewlett documents that American children, rich and poor, suffer a level of neglect unique among developed nations (1991). Overall, child well-being has declined despite a decrease in the number of children per family, an increase in the educational level of parents, and historically high levels of public spending in education.

In "Dan Quayle Was Right" (April 1993) Barbara Dafoe Whitehead synthesizes the social science research on the decline of the two biological-parent family in America:

> If current trends continue, less than half of children born today will live continuously with their own mother and father throughout childhood. . . . An increasing number of children will experience family break-up two or even three times during childhood.

Children of marriages that end in divorce and children of single mothers are more likely to be poor, have emotional and behavioral problems, fail to achieve academically, get pregnant, abuse drugs and alcohol, get in trouble with the law, and be sexually and physically abused. Children in stepfamilies are generally worse off (more likely to be sexually abused, for example) than children in single-parent homes.

No one has felt the impact of family disruption more than schools. Whitehead writes:

> Across the nation, principals report a dramatic rise in the aggressive, acting-out behavior characteristic of children, especially boys, who are living in single-parent families. Moreover, teachers find that many children are so upset and preoccupied by the explosive drama of their own family lives that they are unable to concentrate on such mundane matters as multiplication tables.

Family disintegration, then, drives the character education movement in two ways: schools have to teach the values kids aren't learning at home; and schools, in order to conduct teaching and learning, must become caring moral communities that help children from unhappy homes focus on their work, control their anger, feel cared about, and become responsible students.

2. Troubling trends in youth character. A second impetus for renewed character education is the sense that young people in general, not just those from fractured families, have been adversely affected by poor parenting (in intact as well as broken families); the wrong kind of adult role models; the sex, violence, and materialism portrayed in the mass media; and the pressures of the peer group. Evidence that this hostile moral environment is taking a toll on youth character can be found in 10 troubling trends: rising youth violence; increasing dishonesty (lying, cheating, and stealing); growing disrespect for authority; peer cruelty; a resurgence of bigotry on school campuses, from preschool through higher education; a decline in the work ethic; sexual precocity; a growing self-centeredness and declining civil responsibility; an increase in self-destructive behavior; and ethical illiteracy.

The statistics supporting these trends are overwhelming.[3] For example, the U.S. homicide rate for 15- to 24-year-old males is 7 times higher than Canada's and 40 times higher than Japan's. The U.S. has one of the highest teenage pregnancy rates, the highest teen abortion rate, and the highest level of drug use among young people in the developed world. Youth suicide has tripled in the past 25 years, and a survey of more than 2,000 Rhode Island students, grades six through nine, found that two out of three boys and one of two girls thought it "acceptable for a man to force sex on a woman" if they had been dating for six months or more (Kikuchi 1988).

3. A recovery of shared, objectively important ethical values. Moral decline in society has gotten bad enough to jolt us out of the privatism and relativism dominant in recent decades. We are recovering the wisdom that we do share a basic morality, essential for our survival; that adults must promote this morality by teaching the young, directly and indirectly, such values as respect, responsibility, trustworthiness, fairness, caring, and civil virtue; and that these values are not merely subjective preferences but that they have objective worth and a claim on our collective conscience.

Such values affirm our human dignity, promote the good of the individual and the common good, and protect our human rights. They meet the classic ethical tests of reversibility (Would you want to be treated this way?) and universalizability (Would you want all persons to act this way in a similar situation?). They define our responsibilities in a democracy, and they are recognized by all civilized people and taught by all enlightened creeds. *Not* to teach children these core ethical values is grave moral failure.

What Character Education Must Do

In the face of a deteriorating social fabric, what must character education do to develop good character in the young?

First, it must have an adequate theory of what good character is, one which gives schools a clear idea of their goals. Character must be broadly conceived to encompass cognitive, affective, and behavioral aspects of morality. Good character consists of knowing the good, desiring the good, and doing the good. Schools must help children *understand* the core values, *adopt* or commit to them, and then *act upon* them in their own lives.

The cognitive side of character includes at least six specific moral qualities: awareness of the moral dimensions of the situation at hand, knowing moral values and what they require of us in concrete cases, perspective-taking, moral reasoning, thoughtful decision making, and moral self-knowledge. All these powers of rational moral thought are required for full moral maturity and citizenship in a democratic society.

People can be very smart about matters of right and wrong, however, and still choose the wrong. Moral education that is merely intellectual misses the crucial emotional side of character, which serves as the bridge between judgment and action. The emotional side includes at least the following qualities: conscience (the felt obligation to do what one judges to be right), self-respect, empathy, loving the good, self-control, and humility (a willingness to both recognize and correct our moral failings).

At times, we know what we should do, feel strongly that we should do it, yet still fail to translate moral judgment and feeling into effective moral behavior. Moral action, the third part of character, draws upon three additional moral qualities: competence (skills such as listening, communicating, and cooperating), will (which mobilizes our judgment and energy), and moral habit (a reliable inner disposition to respond to situations in a morally good way).

Developing Character

Once we have a comprehensive concept of character, we need a comprehensive approach to developing it. This approach tells schools to look at themselves through a moral lens and consider how virtually everything that goes on there affects the values and character of students. Then, plan how to use all phases of classroom and school life as deliberate tools of character development.

If schools wish to maximize their moral clout, make a lasting difference in students' character, and engage and develop all three parts of character (knowing, feeling, and behavior), they need a comprehensive, holistic approach. Having a comprehensive approach includes asking, Do present school practices support, neglect, or contradict the school's professed values and character education aims?

In classroom practice, a comprehensive approach to character education calls upon the individual teacher to:

- *Act as caregiver, model, and mentor,* treating students with love and respect, setting a good example, supporting positive social behavior, and correcting hurtful actions through one-on-one guidance and whole-class discussions;

- *Create a moral community,* helping students know one another as persons, respect and care about one another, and feel valued membership in, and responsibility to, the group;
- *Practice moral discipline,* using the creation and enforcement of rules as opportunities to foster moral reasoning, voluntary compliance with rules, and respect for others;
- *Create a democratic classroom environment,* involving students in decision making and the responsibility for making the classroom a good place to be and learn;
- *Teach values through the curriculum,* using the ethically rich content of academic subjects (such as literature, history, and science), as well as outstanding programs (such as *Facing History and Ourselves*[4] and *The Heartwood Ethics Curriculum for Children*[5]), as vehicles for teaching values and examining moral questions;
- *Use cooperative learning* to develop students' appreciation of others, perspective taking, and ability to work with others toward common goals;
- *Develop the "conscience of craft"* by fostering students' appreciation of learning, capacity for hard work, commitment to excellence, and sense of work as affecting the lives of others;
- *Encourage moral reflection* through reading, research, essay writing, journal keeping, discussion, and debate;
- *Teach conflict resolution,* so that students acquire the essential moral skills of solving conflicts fairly and without force.

Besides making full use of the moral life of classrooms, a comprehensive approach calls upon the school *as a whole* to:

- *Foster caring beyond the classroom,* using positive role models to inspire altruistic behavior and providing opportunities at every grade level to perform school and community service;
- *Create a positive moral culture in the school,* developing a schoolwide ethos (through the leadership of the principal, discipline, a schoolwide sense of community, meaningful student government, a moral community among adults, and making time for moral concerns) that supports and amplifies the values taught in the classrooms;
- *Recruit parents and the community as partners in character education,* letting parents know that the school considers them their child's first and most important moral teacher, giving parents specific ways they can reinforce the values the school is trying to teach, and seeking the help of the community, churches, businesses, local government, and the media in promoting the core ethical values.

The Challenges Ahead

Whether character education will take hold in American schools remains to be seen. Among the factors that will determine the movement's long-range success are:

- *Support for schools.* Can schools recruit the help they need from the other key formative institutions that shape the values of the young—including families, faith communities, and the media? Will public policy act to strengthen and support families, and will parents make the stability of their families and the needs of their children their highest priority?
- *The role of religion.* Both liberal and conservative groups are asking, How can students be sensitively engaged in considering the role of religion in the origins and moral development of our nation? How can students be encouraged to use their intellectual and moral resources, including their faith traditions, when confronting social issues (for example, what is my obligation to the poor?) and making personal moral decisions (for example, should I have sex before marriage?)?
- *Moral leadership.* Many schools lack a positive, cohesive moral culture. Especially at the building level, it is absolutely essential to have

moral leadership that sets, models, and consistently enforces high standards of respect and responsibility. Without a positive schoolwide ethos, teachers will feel demoralized in their individual efforts to teach good values.

- *Teacher education*. Character education is far more complex than teaching math or reading; it requires personal growth as well as skills development. Yet teachers typically receive almost no preservice or inservice training in the moral aspects of their craft. Many teachers do not feel comfortable or competent in the values domain. How will teacher education colleges and school staff development programs meet this need?

"Character is destiny," wrote the ancient Greek philosopher Heraclitus. As we confront the causes of our deepest societal problems, whether in our intimate relationships or public institutions, questions of character loom large. As we close out a turbulent century and ready our schools for the next, educating for character is a moral imperative if we care about the future of our society and our children.

Notes

1. For a copy of the Aspen Declaration and the issue of *Ethics* magazine reporting on the conference, write the Josephson Institute of Ethics, 310 Washington Blvd., Suite 104, Marina del Rey, CA 90292.
2. For information write Mark Kann, Editor, *The Journal of Character Education*, Jefferson Center for Character Education, 202 S. Lake Ave., Suite 240, Pasadena, CA 91101.
3. For documentation of these youth trends, see T. Lickona, (1991), *Educating for Character: How Our Schools Can Teach Respect and Responsibility* (New York: Bantam Books).
4. *Facing History and Ourselves* is an 8-week Holocaust curriculum for 8th graders. Write Facing History and Ourselves National Foundation, 25 Kennard Rd., Brookline, MA 02146.
5. *The Heartwood Ethics Curriculum for Children* uses multicultural children's literature to teach universal values. Write The Heartwood Institute, 12300 Perry Highway, Wexford, PA 15090.

References

Benninga, J. S., ed. (1991). *Moral, Character, and Civic Education in the Elementary School*. New York: Teachers College Press.

Hewlett, S. (1991). *When the Bough Breaks: The Cost of Neglecting Our Children*. New York: Basic Books.

Kikuchi, J. (Fall 1988). "Rhode Island Develops Successful Intervention Program for Adolescents." *National Coalition Against Sexual Assault Newsletter*.

National Research Council. (1992). *Understanding and Preventing Violence*. Washington, D.C.: National Research Council.

Whitehead, B. D. (April 1993). "Dan Quayle Was Right." *The Atlantic* 271: 47–84.

Wynne, E. A., and K. Ryan. (1992). *Reclaiming Our Schools: A Handbook on Teaching Character, Academics, and Discipline*. New York: Merrill.

Postnote

The force and clarity of this article in calling educators to recapture the school's moral mission earn it a place among our Classics. Education for good character is one of our schools' latest fads—and also one of their oldest missions. This article by the nation's leading proponent of character education lays out the case for our schools' involvement in teaching core moral values and helping children acquire good habits, such as respect and responsibility.

But despite the call for character education from our parents, pulpits, and politicians, schools and teachers are often unsure of what to do. Because character education has been absent from the great majority of our schools for fully three decades, few educators know how to translate their good intentions into practice. Many schools are having one or two in-service days, buying boxes of character-oriented banners to put up on their walls, and purchasing "Character Counts!" coffee cups for the teachers' lounge.

Developing in our young the strong moral habits that constitute good character needs to be a central priority for a school community. What Lickona calls a "comprehensive approach" will take time, energy, and deep commitment to achieve. But, curiously, schools that take on this mission wholeheartedly find that many of their other goals—academic, athletic, and social—are achieved in the process.

Discussion Questions

1. What is your personal experience with character education in the schools?
2. Do you agree with the thrust of this article, that schools have a major role in the fostering of good character? Why or why not?
3. From your perspective, what are the hard questions that schools must grapple with if they are to engage in character education responsibly?

Educational Reform

Part Seven

7

Since the publication of *A Nation at Risk* in 1983 (a report of President Reagan's National Commission on Excellence in Education), American schools have been in what is referred to as an "era of school reform." Both educators and private citizens are worried about our schools' ability to supply an adequately educated workforce. New jobs in the information age require a worker to solve problems, often as a member of a team, write and speak proficiently, and carry out higher levels of mathematical computations. Dismal research reports on the academic achievement of American students—particularly when compared with students from other countries—have sent a clear message: Something must be done.

In recent years, the primary response has been at the state level, where governors and legislatures across the country have passed laws requiring higher standards for students and teachers alike. Recently their efforts have been reinforced and financially supported by the federal No Child Left Behind Act. In addition, ways of more effectively and efficiently organizing schools have surfaced—some borrowed from industry, some from schools in other nations. Increasingly, too, parents, politicians, and policymakers are examining and experimenting with ways to offer students greater educational choice. This section presents an overview of some of the most important developments in reforming education.

What Matters Most: A Competent Teacher for Every Child

LINDA DARLING-HAMMOND

FOCUS Question

How can we fulfill the promise of a competent teacher for every child?

TERMS TO NOTE

Interstate New Teacher Assessment and Support Consortium (INTASC)

National Board for Professional Teaching Standards (NBPTS)

National Commission on Teaching and America's Future

National Council for Accreditation of Teacher Education (NCATE)

Professional development

Professional development school

Standard

> We propose an audacious goal . . . by the year 2006, America will provide all students with what should be their educational birthright: access to competent, caring, and qualified teachers.[1]

With these words, the National Commission on Teaching and America's Future summarized its challenge to the American public. After two years of intense study and discussion, the commission—a 26-member bipartisan blue-ribbon panel supported by the Rockefeller Foundation and the Carnegie Corporation of New York—concluded that the reform of elementary and secondary education depends first and foremost on restructuring its foundation, the teaching profession. The restructuring, the commission made clear, must go in two directions: toward increasing teachers' knowledge to meet the demands they face and toward redesigning schools to support high-quality teaching and learning.

The commission found a profession that has suffered from decades of neglect. By the standards of other professions and other countries, U.S. teacher education has historically been thin, uneven, and poorly financed. Teacher recruitment is distressingly ad hoc, and teacher salaries lag significantly behind those of other professions. This produces chronic shortages of qualified teachers in fields like mathematics and science and the continual hiring of large numbers of "teachers" who are unprepared for their jobs.

Furthermore, in contrast to other countries that invest most of their education dollars in well-prepared and well-supported teachers, half of the education dollars in the United States are spent on personnel and activities outside the classroom. A lack of standards for students and teachers, coupled with schools that are organized for 19th-century learning, leaves educators without an adequate foundation for constructing good teaching. Under these conditions, excellence is hard to achieve.

Linda Darling-Hammond is professor of education at Stanford University. Darling-Hammond, Linda, "What Matters Most: A Competent Teacher for Every Child," *Phi Delta Kappan,* November 1996.

The commission is clear about what needs to change. No more hiring unqualified teachers on the sly. No more nods and winks at teacher education programs that fail to prepare teachers properly. No more tolerance for incompetence in the classroom. Children are compelled to attend school. Every state guarantees them equal protection under the law, and most promise them a sound education. In the face of these obligations, students have a right to competent, caring teachers who work in schools organized for success.

The commission is also clear about what needs to be done. Like the Flexner report that led to the transformation of the medical profession in 1910, this report, *What Matters Most: Teaching for America's Future*, examines successful practices within and outside the United States to describe what works. The commission concludes that children can reap the benefits of current knowledge about teaching and learning only if schools and schools of education are dramatically redesigned.

The report offers a blueprint for recruiting, preparing, supporting, and rewarding excellent educators in all of America's schools. The plan is aimed at ensuring that all schools have teachers with the knowledge and skills they need to enable all children to learn. If a caring, qualified teacher for every child is the most important ingredient in education reform, then it should no longer be the factor most frequently overlooked.

At the same time, such teachers must have available to them schools and school systems that are well designed to achieve their key academic mission: they must be focused on clear, high standards for students; organized to provide a coherent, high-quality curriculum across the grades; and designed to support teachers' collective work and learning.

We note that this challenge is accompanied by an equally great opportunity: over the next decade we will recruit and hire more than two million teachers for America's schools. More than half of the teachers who will be teaching 10 years from now will be hired during the next decade. If we can focus our energies on providing this generation of teachers with the kinds of knowledge and skills they need to help students succeed, we will have made an enormous contribution to America's future.

The Nature of the Problem

The education challenge facing the U.S. is not that its schools are not as good as they once were. It is that schools must help the vast majority of young people reach levels of skill and competence that were once thought to be within the reach of only a few.

After more than a decade of school reform, America is still a very long way from achieving its educational goals. Instead of all children coming to school ready to learn, more are living in poverty and without health care than a decade ago.[2] Graduation rates and student achievement in most subjects have remained flat or have increased only slightly.[3] Fewer than 10% of high school students can read, write, compute, and manage scientific material at the high levels required for today's "knowledge work" jobs.[4]

This distance between our stated goals and current realities is not due to lack of effort. Many initiatives have been launched in local communities with positive effects. Nonetheless, we have reached an impasse in spreading these promising efforts to the system as a whole. It is now clear that most schools and teachers cannot produce the kind of learning demanded by the new reforms—not because they do not want to, but because they do not know how, and the systems they work in do not support their efforts to do so.

The Challenge for Teaching

A more complex, knowledge-based, and multicultural society creates new expectations for teaching. To help diverse learners master more challenging content, teachers must go far beyond dispensing information, giving a test, and giving a grade. They must themselves know their subject areas deeply, and they must understand how students think, if they are to create experiences that actually work to produce learning.

Developing the kind of teaching that is needed will require much greater clarity about what students need to learn in order to succeed in the world that awaits them and what teachers need to know and do in order to help students learn it. Standards that reflect these imperatives for student learning and for teaching are largely absent in our nation today. States are just now beginning to establish standards for student learning.

Standards for teaching are equally haphazard. Although most parents might assume that teachers, like other professionals, are educated in similar ways so that they acquire common knowledge before they are admitted to practice, this is not the case. Unlike doctors, lawyers, accountants, or architects, all teachers do not have the same training. Some teachers have very high levels of skills—particularly in states that require a bachelor's degree in the discipline to be taught—along with coursework in teaching, learning, curriculum, and child development; extensive practice teaching; and a master's degree in education. Others learn little about their subject matter or about teaching, learning, and child development—particularly in states that have low requirements for licensing.

And while states have recently begun to require some form of testing for a teaching license, most licensing exams are little more than multiple-choice tests of basic skills and general knowledge, widely criticized by educators and experts as woefully inadequate to measure teaching skill.[5] Furthermore, in many states the cutoff scores are so low that there is no effective standard for entry.

These difficulties are barely known to the public. The schools' most closely held secret amounts to a great national shame: roughly one-quarter of newly hired American teachers lack the qualifications for their jobs. More than 12% of new hires enter the classroom without any formal training at all, and another 14% arrive without fully meeting state standards.

Although no state will permit a person to write wills, practice medicine, fix plumbing, or style hair without completing training and passing an examination, more than 40 states allow districts to hire teachers who have not met basic requirements. States pay more attention to the qualifications of the veterinarians treating America's pets than to those of the people educating the nation's youngsters. Consider the following facts:

- In recent years, more than 50,000 people who lack the training required for their jobs have entered teaching annually on emergency or substandard licenses.[6]
- Nearly one-fourth (23%) of all secondary teachers do not have even a minor in their main teaching field. This is true for more than 30% of mathematics teachers.[7]
- Among teachers who teach a second subject, 36% are unlicensed in that field, and 50% lack a minor in it.[8]
- Fifty-six percent of high school students taking physical science are taught by out-of-field teachers, as are 27% of those taking mathematics and 21% of those taking English.[9] The proportions are much greater in high-poverty schools and lower-track classes.
- In schools with the highest minority enrollments, students have less than a 50% chance of getting a science or mathematics teacher who holds a license and a degree in the field in which he or she teaches.[10]

In the nation's poorest schools, where hiring is most lax and teacher turnover is constant, the results are disastrous. Thousands of children are taught throughout their school careers by a parade of teachers without preparation in the fields in which they teach, inexperienced beginners with little training and no mentoring, and short-term substitutes trying to cope with constant staff disruptions.[11] It is more surprising that some of these children manage to learn than that so many fail to do so.

Current Barriers

Unequal resources and inadequate investments in teacher recruitment are major problems. Other industrialized countries fund their schools equally and make sure there are qualified teachers for all of them by underwriting teacher preparation and salaries. However, teachers in the U.S. must go into substantial debt to become prepared for a field that in most states pays less than any other occupation requiring a college degree.

This situation is not necessary or inevitable. The hiring of unprepared teachers was almost eliminated during the 1970s with scholarships and loans for college students preparing to teach, Urban Teacher Corps initiatives, and master of arts in teaching (MAT) programs, coupled with wage increases. However, the cancellation of most of these recruitment incentives in the 1980s led to renewed shortages when student enrollments started to climb once again, especially in cities. Between 1987 and 1991, the proportion of well-qualified new teachers—those entering teaching with a college major or minor and a license in their fields—actually declined from about 74% to 67%.[12]

There is no real system for recruiting, preparing, and developing America's teachers. Major problems include:

Inadequate Teacher Education Because accreditation is not required of teacher education programs, their quality varies widely, with excellent programs standing alongside shoddy ones that are allowed to operate even when they do an utterly inadequate job. Too many American universities still treat their schools of education as "cash cows" whose excess revenues are spent on the training of doctors, lawyers, accountants, and almost any students other than prospective teachers themselves.

Slipshod Recruitment Although the share of academically able young people entering teaching has been increasing, there are still too few in some parts of the country and in critical subjects like mathematics and science. Federal incentives that once existed to induce talented people into high-need fields and locations have largely been eliminated.

Haphazard Hiring and Induction School districts often lose the best candidates because of inefficient and cumbersome hiring practices, barriers to teacher mobility, and inattention to teacher qualifications. Those who do get hired are typically given the most difficult assignments and left to sink or swim, without the kind of help provided by internships and residencies in other professions. Isolated behind classroom doors with little feedback or help, as many as 30% leave in the first few years, while others learn merely to cope rather than to teach well.

Lack of Professional Development and Rewards for Knowledge and Skill In addition to the lack of support for beginning teachers, most school districts invest little in ongoing professional development for experienced teachers and spend much of these limited resources on unproductive "hit-and-run" workshops. Furthermore, most U.S. teachers have only three to five hours each week for planning. This leaves them with almost no regular time to consult together or to learn about new teaching strategies, unlike their peers in many European and Asian countries who spend between 15 and 20 hours per week working jointly on refining lessons and learning about new methods.

The teaching career does not encourage teachers to develop or use growing expertise. Evaluation and tenure decisions often lack a tangible connection to a clear vision of high-quality teaching, important skills are rarely rewarded, and—when budgets must be cut—professional development is often the first item sacrificed. Historically, the only route to advancement in teaching has been to leave the classroom for administration.

In contrast, many European and Asian countries hire a greater number of better-paid teachers, provide them with more extensive preparation, give them time to work together, and structure schools so that teachers can focus on teaching and can come to know their students well. Teachers share decision making and take on a range of professional responsibilities without leaving teaching. This is possible because these other countries invest their resources in many more classroom teachers—typically constituting 60% to 80% of staff, as compared to only 43% in the United States—and many fewer nonteaching employees.[13]

Schools Structured for Failure Today's schools are organized in ways that support neither student learning nor teacher learning well. Teachers are isolated from one another so that they cannot share knowledge or take responsibility for overall student learning. Technologies that could enable alternative uses of personnel and time are not yet readily available in schools, and few staff members are prepared to use them. Moreover, too many people and resources are allocated to jobs and activities outside of classrooms, on the sidelines rather than at the front lines of teaching and learning.

High-performance businesses are abandoning the organizational assumptions that led to this way of managing work. They are flattening hierarchies, creating teams, and training employees to take on wider responsibilities using technologies that allow them to perform their work more efficiently. Schools that have restructured their work in these ways have been able to provide more time for teachers to work together and more time for students to work closely with teachers around more clearly defined standards for learning.[14]

Goals for the Nation

To address these problems, the commission challenges the nation to embrace a set of goals that will put us on the path to serious, long-term improvements in teaching and learning for America. The commission has six goals for the year 2006.

- All children will be taught by teachers who have the knowledge, skills, and commitment to teach children well.
- All teacher education programs will meet professional standards, or they will be closed.
- All teachers will have access to high-quality professional development, and they will have regularly scheduled time for collegial work and planning.
- Both teachers and principals will be hired and retained based on their ability to meet professional standards of practice.
- Teachers' salaries will be based on their knowledge and skills.
- High-quality teaching will be the central investment of schools. Most education dollars will be spent on classroom teaching.

The Commission's Recommendations

The commission's proposals provide a vision and a blueprint for the development of a 21st-century teaching profession that can make good on the nation's educational goals. The recommendations are systemic in scope—not a recipe for more short-lived pilot and demonstration projects. They describe a new infrastructure for professional learning and an accountability system that ensures attention to standards for educators as well as for students at every level: national, state, district, school, and classroom.

The commission urges a complete overhaul in the systems of teacher preparation and professional development to ensure that they reflect current knowledge and practice. This redesign should create a continuum of teacher learning based on compatible standards that operate from recruitment and preservice education through licensing, hiring, and induction into the profession, to advanced certification and ongoing professional development.

The commission also proposes a comprehensive set of changes in school organization and management. And finally, it recommends a set of measures for ensuring that only those who are competent to teach or to lead schools are allowed to enter or to continue in the profession—a starting point for creating professional accountability. The specific recommendations are enumerated below.

1. Get Serious About Standards for Both Students and Teachers

"The Commission recommends that we renew the national promise to bring every American child up to world-class standards in core academic areas and to develop and enforce rigorous standards for teacher preparation, initial licensing, and continuing development."

With respect to student standards, the commission believes that every state should work on incorporating challenging standards for learning—such as those developed by professional bodies like the National Council of Teachers of Mathematics—into curriculum frameworks and new assessments of student performance. Implementation must go beyond the tautology that "all children can learn" to examine what they should learn and how much they need to know.

Standards should be accompanied by benchmarks of performance—from "acceptable" to "highly accomplished"—so that students and teachers know how to direct their efforts toward greater excellence.

Clearly, if students are to achieve high standards, we can expect no less from teachers and other educators. Our highest priority must be to reach agreement on what teachers should know and be able to do in order to help students succeed. Unaddressed for decades, this task has recently been completed by three professional bodies: the National Council for Accreditation of Teacher Education (NCATE), the Interstate New Teacher Assessment and Support Consortium (INTASC), and the National Board for Professional Teaching Standards (the National Board). Their combined efforts to set standards for teacher education, beginning teacher licensing, and advanced certification outline a continuum of teacher development throughout the career and offer the most powerful tools we have for reaching and rejuvenating the soul of the profession.

These standards and the assessments that grow out of them identify what it takes to be an effective teacher: subject-matter expertise coupled with an understanding of how children learn and develop; skill in using a range of teaching strategies and technologies; sensitivity and effectiveness in working with students from diverse backgrounds; the ability to work well with parents and other teachers; and assessment expertise capable of discerning how well children are doing, what they are learning, and what needs to be done next to move them along.

The standards reflect a teaching role in which the teacher is an instructional leader who orchestrates learning experiences in response to curriculum goals and student needs and who coaches students to high levels of independent performance. To advance standards, the commission recommends that states:

- establish their own professional standards boards;
- insist on professional accreditation for all schools of education;
- close inadequate schools of education;
- license teachers based on demonstrated performance, including tests of subject-matter knowledge, teaching knowledge, and teaching skill; and
- use National Board standards as the benchmark for accomplished teaching.

2. Reinvent Teacher Preparation and Professional Development

"The Commission recommends that colleges and schools work with states to redesign teacher education so that the two million teachers to be hired in the next decade are adequately prepared and so that all teachers have access to high-quality learning opportunities."

For this to occur, states, school districts, and education schools should:

- organize teacher education and professional development around standards for students and teachers;
- institute extended, graduate-level teacher preparation programs that provide yearlong internships in a professional development school;
- create and fund mentoring programs for beginning teachers, along with evaluation of teaching skills;
- create stable, high-quality sources of professional development—and then allocate 1% of state and local spending to support them, along with additional matching funds to school districts;

- organize new sources of professional development, such as teacher academies, school/university partnerships, and learning networks that transcend school boundaries; and
- make professional development an ongoing part of teachers' daily work.

If teachers are to be ready to help their students meet the new standards that are now being set for them, teacher preparation and professional development programs must consciously examine the expectations embodied in new curriculum frameworks and assessments and understand what they imply for teaching and for learning to teach. Then they must develop effective strategies for preparing teachers to teach in these much more demanding ways.

Over the past decade, many schools of education have changed their programs to incorporate new knowledge. More than 300 have developed extended programs that add a fifth (and occasionally a sixth) year to undergraduate training. These programs allow beginning teachers to complete a degree in their subject area as well as to acquire a firmer ground in teaching skills. They allow coursework to be connected to extended practice teaching in schools—ideally, in professional development schools that, like teaching hospitals in medicine, have a special mission to support research and training. Recent studies show that graduates of extended programs are rated as better-prepared and more effective teachers and are far more likely to enter and remain in teaching than are their peers from traditional four-year programs.[15]

New teachers should have support from an expert mentor during the first year of teaching. Research shows that such support improves both teacher effectiveness and retention.[16] In the system we propose, teachers will have completed initial tests of subject-matter and basic teaching knowledge before entry and will be ready to undertake the second stage—a performance assessment of teaching skills—during this first year.

Throughout their careers, teachers should have ongoing opportunities to update their skills. In addition to time for joint planning and problem solving with in-school colleagues, teachers should have access to networks, school/university partnerships, and academies where they can connect with other educators to study subject-matter teaching, new pedagogies, and school change. The benefit of these opportunities is that they offer sustained work on problems of practice that are directly connected to teachers' work and student learning.

3. Overhaul Teacher Recruitment and Put Qualified Teachers in Every Classroom

"The Commission recommends that states and school districts pursue aggressive policies to put qualified teachers in every classroom by providing financial incentives to correct shortages, streamlining hiring procedures, and reducing barriers to teacher mobility."

Although each year the U.S. produces more new teachers than it needs, shortages of qualified candidates in particular fields (e.g., mathematics and science) and particular locations (primarily inner city and rural) are chronic.

In large districts, logistics can overwhelm everything else. It is sometimes the case that central offices cannot find out about classroom vacancies, principals are left in the dark about applicants, and candidates cannot get any information at all.

Finally, it should be stressed that large pools of potential mid-career teacher entrants—former employees of downsizing corporations, military and government retirees, and teacher aides already in the schools—are for the most part untapped.

To remedy these situations, the commission suggests the following actions:

- increase the ability of financially disadvantaged districts to pay for qualified teachers and insist that school districts hire only qualified teachers;
- redesign and streamline hiring at the district level—principally by creating a central "electronic hiring hall" for all qualified candidates and establishing cooperative relationships with universities to encourage early hiring of teachers;

- eliminate barriers to teacher mobility by promoting reciprocal interstate licensing and by working across states to develop portable pensions;
- provide incentives (including scholarships and premium pay) to recruit teachers for high-need subjects and locations; and
- develop high-quality pathways to teaching for recent graduates, mid-career changers, paraprofessionals already in the classroom, and military and government retirees.

4. Encourage and Reward Knowledge and Skill

"The Commission recommends that school districts, states, and professional associations cooperate to make teaching a true profession, with a career continuum that places teaching at the top and rewards teachers for their knowledge and skills."

Schools have few ways of encouraging outstanding teaching, supporting teachers who take on the most challenging work, or rewarding increases in knowledge and skill. Newcomers who enter teaching without adequate preparation are paid at the same levels as those who enter with highly developed skills. Novices take on exactly the same kind of work as 30-year veterans, with little differentiation based on expertise. Mediocre teachers receive the same rewards as outstanding ones. And unlicensed "teachers" are placed on the same salary schedule as licensed teachers in high-demand fields such as mathematics and science or as teachers licensed in two or more subjects.

One testament to the inability of the existing system to understand what it is doing is that it rewards experience with easier work instead of encouraging senior teachers to deal with difficult learning problems and tough learning situations. As teachers gain experience, they can look forward to teaching in more affluent schools, working with easier schedules, dealing with "better" classes, or moving out of the classroom into administration. Teachers are rarely rewarded for applying their expertise to the most challenging learning problems or major needs of the system.

To address these issues, the commission recommends that state and local education agencies:

- develop a career continuum linked to assessments and compensation systems that reward knowledge and skill (e.g., the ability to teach expertly in two or more subjects, as demonstrated by additional licenses, or the ability to pass examinations of teaching skill, such as those offered by INTASC and the National Board);
- remove incompetent teachers through peer review programs that provide necessary assistance and due process; and
- set goals and enact incentives for National Board certification in every district, with the aim of certifying 105,000 teachers during the next 10 years.

If teaching is organized as are other professions that have set consistent licensing requirements, standards of practice, and assessment methods, then advancement can be tied to professional growth and development. A career continuum that places teaching at the top and supports growing expertise should 1) recognize accomplishment, 2) anticipate that teachers will continue to teach while taking on other roles that allow them to share their knowledge, and 3) promote continued skill development related to clear standards.

Some districts, such as Cincinnati and Rochester, New York, have already begun to develop career pathways that tie evaluations to salary increments at key stages as teachers move from their *initial license* to *resident teacher* (under the supervision of a mentor) to the designation of *professional teacher*. The major decision to grant *tenure* is made after rigorous evaluation of performance (including both administrator and peer review) in the first several years of teaching. Advanced certification from the National Board for Professional Teaching Standards may qualify teachers for another salary step and/or for the position of lead teacher—a role that is awarded to those who have demonstrated high levels of competence and want to serve as mentors or consulting teachers.

One other feature of a new compensation system is key. The central importance of teaching to the mission of schools should be acknowledged by having the highest-paid professional in a school system be an experienced, National Board–certified teacher. As in other professions, roles should become less distinct. The jobs of teacher, consultant, supervisor, principal, curriculum developer, researcher, mentor, and professor should be hyphenated roles, allowing many ways for individuals to use their talents and expertise without abandoning the core work of the profession.

5. Create Schools That Are Organized for Student and Teacher Success

"The Commission recommends that schools be restructured to become genuine learning organizations for both students and teachers: organizations that respect learning, honor teaching, and teach for understanding."

Many experts have observed that the demands of serious teaching and learning bear little relationship to the organization of the typical American school. Nothing more clearly reveals this problem than how we allocate the principal resources of school—time, money, and people. Far too many people sit in offices on the sidelines of the school's core work, managing routines rather than improving learning. Our schools are bureaucratic inheritances from the 19th century, not the kinds of learning organizations required of the 21st century.

Across the United States, the ratio of school staff to students is 1 to 9 (with "staff" including district employees, school administrators, teachers, instructional aides, guidance counselors, librarians, and support staff). However, actual class size averages about 24 and reaches 35 or more in some cities. Teaching loads for high school teachers generally exceed 100 students per day. Yet many schools have proved that it is possible to restructure adults' use of time so that more teachers and administrators actually work in the classroom, face-to-face with students on a daily basis, thus reducing class sizes while creating more time for teacher collaboration. They do this by creating teams of teachers who share students; engaging almost all adults in the school in these teaching teams, where they can share expertise directly with one another; and reducing pullouts and nonteaching jobs.

Schools must be freed from the tyrannies of time and tradition to permit more powerful student and teacher learning. To accomplish this the commission recommends that state and local boards work to:

- flatten hierarchies and reallocate resources to invest more in teachers and technology and less in nonteaching personnel;
- provide venture capital in the form of challenge grants that will promote learning linked to school improvement and will reward effective team efforts; and
- select, prepare, and retain principals who understand teaching and learning and who can lead high-performing schools.

If students have an inalienable right to be taught by a qualified teacher, teachers have a right to be supervised by a highly qualified principal. The job began as that of a "principal teacher," and this conception is ever more relevant as the focus of the school recenters on academic achievement for students. Principals should teach at least part of the time (as do most European, Asian, and private school directors), and they should be well prepared as instructional leaders, with a solid understanding of teaching and learning.

Next Steps

Developing recommendations is easy. Implementing them is hard work. The first step is to recognize that these ideas must be pursued together—as an entire tapestry that is tightly interwoven.

The second step is to build on the substantial work of education reform undertaken in the last decade. All across the country, successful programs for recruiting, educating, and mentoring new teachers have sprung up. Professional networks and teacher academies have been launched, many teacher preparation programs have been redesigned, higher standards for licensing teachers and accrediting education schools have been developed, and, of course, the National Board for Professional Teaching Standards is now fully established and beginning to define and reward accomplished teaching.

While much of what the commission proposes can and should be accomplished by reallocating resources that are currently used unproductively, there will be new costs. The estimated additional annual costs of the commission's key recommendations are as follows: scholarships for teaching recruits, $500 million; teacher education reforms, $875 million; mentoring supports and new licensing assessments, $750 million; and state funds for professional development, $2.75 billion. The total is just under $5 billion annually—less than 1% of the amount spent on the federal savings-and-loan bailout. This is not too much, we believe, to bail out our schools and to secure our future.

A Call to Action

Setting the commission's agenda in motion and carrying it to completion will demand the best of us all. The commission calls on governors and legislators to create state professional boards to govern teacher licensing standards and to issue annual report cards on the status of teaching. It asks state legislators and governors to set aside at least 1% of funds for standards-based teacher training. It urges Congress to put money behind the professional development programs it has already approved but never funded.

Moreover, the commission asks the profession to take seriously its responsibilities to children and the American future. Among other measures, the commission insists that state educators close the loopholes that permit administrators to put unqualified "teachers" in the classroom. It calls on university officials to take up the hard work of improving the preparation and skills of new and practicing teachers. It asks administrators and teachers to take on the difficult task of guaranteeing teaching competence in the classroom. And it asks local school boards and superintendents to play their vital role by streamlining hiring procedures, upgrading quality, and putting more staff and resources into the front lines of teaching.

If all of these things are accomplished, the teaching profession of the 21st century will look much different from the one we have today. Indeed, someone entering the profession might expect to advance along a continuum that unfolds much like this:

> For as long as she could remember, Elena had wanted to teach. As a peer tutor in middle school, she loved the feeling she got whenever her partner learned something new. In high school, she served as a teacher's aide for her community service project. She linked up with other students through an Internet group started by Future Educators of America.
>
> When she arrived at college she knew she wanted to prepare to teach, so she began taking courses in developmental and cognitive psychology early in her sophomore year. She chose mathematics as a major and applied in her junior year for the university's five-year course of study leading to a master of arts in teaching. After a round of interviews and a review of her record thus far, Elena was admitted into the highly selective teacher education program.
>
> The theories Elena studied in her courses came to life before her eyes as she conducted a case study of John, a 7-year-old whom she tutored in a nearby school. She was struck by John's amazing ability to build things, in contrast with his struggles to learn to read. She carried these puzzles back to her seminar and on into her other courses as she tried to understand learning.
>
> Over time, she examined other cases, some of them available on a multimedia computer system that allowed her to see videotapes of children, samples of their work, and documentation from their teachers about their learning strategies, problems, and progress. From these data, Elena and her classmates developed a concrete sense of different learning approaches. She began to think about how she could use John's strengths to create productive pathways into other areas of learning.

Elena's teachers modeled the kinds of strategies she herself would be using as a teacher. Instead of lecturing from texts, they enabled students to develop and apply knowledge in the context of real teaching situations. These frequently occurred in the professional development school (PDS) where Elena was engaged in a yearlong internship, guided by a faculty of university- and school-based teacher educators.

In the PDS, Elena was placed with a team of student teachers who worked with a team of expert veteran teachers. Her team included teachers of art, language arts, and science, as well as mathematics. They discussed learning within and across these domains in many of their assignments and constructed interdisciplinary curricula together.

Most of the school- and university-based teacher educators who made up the PDS faculty had been certified as accomplished practitioners by the National Board for Professional Teaching Standards, having completed a portfolio of evidence about their teaching along with a set of rigorous performance assessments. The faculty members created courses, internship experiences, and seminars that allowed them to integrate theory and practice, pose fundamental dilemmas of teaching, and address specific aspects of learning to teach.

Elena's classroom work included observing and documenting the learning and behavior of specific children, evaluating lessons that illustrated important concepts and strategies, tutoring and working with small groups, sitting in on family conferences, engaging in school and team planning meetings, visiting homes and community agencies to learn about their resources, planning field trips and curriculum segments, teaching lessons and short units, and ultimately taking major responsibility for the class for a month at the end of the year. This work was supplemented by readings and discussions grounded in case studies of teaching.

A team of PDS teachers videotaped all their classes over the course of the year to serve as the basis for discussions of teaching decisions and outcomes. These teachers' lesson plans, student work, audiotaped planning journals, and reflections on lessons were also available in a multimedia database. This allowed student teachers to look at practice from many angles, examine how classroom situations arose from things that had happened in the past, see how various strategies turned out, and understand a teacher's thinking about students, subjects, and curriculum goals as he or she made decisions. Because the PDS was also wired for video and computer communication with the school of education, master teachers could hold conversations with student teachers by teleconference or e-mail when on-site visits were impossible.

When Elena finished her rich, exhausting internship year, she was ready to try her hand at what she knew would be a demanding first year of teaching. She submitted her portfolio for review by the state professional standards board and sat for the examination of subject-matter and teaching knowledge that was required for an initial teaching license. She was both exhilarated and anxious when she received a job offer, but she felt she was ready to try her hand at teaching.

Elena spent that summer eagerly developing curriculum ideas for her new class. She had the benefit of advice from the district mentor teacher already assigned to work with her in her first year of teaching, and she had access to an on-line database of teaching materials developed by teachers across the country and organized around the curriculum standards of the National Council of Teachers of Mathematics, of which she had become a member.

Elena's mentor teacher worked with her and several other new middle school mathematics and science teachers throughout the year, meeting with them individually and in groups to examine their teaching and provide support. The mentors and their first-year colleagues also met in groups once a month at the PDS to discuss specific problems of practice.

Elena met weekly with the other math and science teachers in the school to discuss curriculum plans and share demonstration lessons. This extended lunch meeting occurred while her students were in a Project Adventure/physical education course that taught them teamwork and cooperation skills. She also met with the four other members of her teaching team for three hours each week while their students were at community-service placements. The team used this time to discuss cross-disciplinary teaching plans and the progress of the 80 students they shared.

In addition to these built-in opportunities for daily learning, Elena and her colleagues benefited from the study groups they had developed at their school and the professional development offerings at the local university and the Teachers Academy.

At the Teachers Academy, school- and university-based faculty members taught extended courses in areas ranging from advances in learning theory to all kinds of teaching methods, from elementary science to advanced calculus. These courses usually featured case studies and teaching demonstrations as well as follow-up work in teachers' own classrooms. The academy provided the technologies needed for multimedia conferencing, which allowed teachers to "meet" with one another across their schools and to see one another's classroom work. They could also connect to courses and study groups at the university, including a popular master's degree program that helped teachers prepare for National Board certification.

With the strength of a preparation that had helped her put theory and practice together and with the support of so many colleagues, Elena felt confident that she could succeed at her life's goal: becoming—and, as she now understood, *always* becoming—a teacher.

Notes

1. *What Matters Most: Teaching for America's Future* (New York: National Commission on Teaching and America's Future, 1996). Copies of this report can be obtained from the National Commission on Teaching and America's Future, P.O. Box 5239, Woodbridge, VA 22194-5239. Prices, including postage and handling, are $18 for the full report, $5 for the summary report, and $20 for both reports. Orders must be prepaid.
2. *Income, Poverty, and Valuation of Non-Cash Benefits: 1993* (Washington, D.C.: U.S. Bureau of the Census, Current Population Reports, Series P-60, No. 188, 1995), Table D-5, p. D-17. See also *Current Population Survey: March 1988/March 1995* (Washington, D.C.: U.S. Bureau of the Census, 1995).
3. *National Education Goals Report: Executive Summary* (Washington, D.C.: National Education Goals Panel, 1995).
4. National Center for Education Statistics, *Report in Brief: National Assessment of Educational Progress (NAEP) 1992 Trends in Academic Progress* (Washington, D.C.: U.S. Department of Education, 1994).
5. For reviews of teacher licensing tests, see Linda Darling-Hammond, "Teaching Knowledge: How Do We Test It?," *American Educator*, Fall 1986, pp. 18–21, 46; Lee Shulman, "Knowledge and Teaching: Foundations of the New Reform," *Harvard Educational Review*, January 1987, pp. 1–22; C. J. MacMillan and Shirley Pendlebury, "The Florida Performance Measurement System: A Consideration," *Teachers College Record*, Fall 1985, pp. 67–78; Walter Haney, George Madaus, and Amelia Kreitzer, "Charms Talismanic: Testing Teachers for the Improvement of American Education," in Ernest Z. Rothkopf, ed., *Review of Research in Education, Vol. 14* (Washington, D.C.: American Educational Research Association, 1987), pp. 169–238; and Edward H. Haertel, "New Forms of Teacher Assessment," in Gerald Grant, ed., *Review of Research in Education, Vol. 17* (Washington, D.C.: American Educational Research Association, 1991), pp. 3–29.
6. C. Emily Feistritzer and David T. Chester, *Alternative Teacher Certification: A State-by-State Analysis* (Washington, D.C.: National Center for Education Information, 1996).
7. Marilyn M. McMillen, Sharon A. Bobbitt, and Hilda F. Lynch, "Teacher Training, Certification, and Assignment in Public

Schools: 1990–91," paper presented at the annual meeting of the American Educational Research Association, New Orleans, April 1994.

8. National Center for Education Statistics, *The Condition of Education 1995* (Washington, D.C.: U.S. Department of Education, 1995), p. x.
9. Richard M. Ingersoll, *Schools and Staffing Survey: Teacher Supply, Teacher Qualifications, and Teacher Turnover, 1990–1991* (Washington, D.C.: National Center for Education Statistics, 1995), p. 28.
10. Jeannie Oakes, *Multiplying Inequalities: The Effects of Race, Social Class, and Tracking on Opportunities to Learn Mathematics and Science* (Santa Monica, Calif.: RAND Corporation, 1990).
11. *Who Will Teach Our Children?* (Sacramento: California Commission on Teaching, 1985); and Linda Darling-Hammond, "Inequality and Access to Knowledge," in James Banks, ed., *Handbook of Research on Multicultural Education* (New York: Macmillan, 1995), pp. 465–83.
12. Mary Rollefson, *Teacher Supply in the United States: Sources of Newly Hired Teachers in Public and Private Schools* (Washington, D.C.: National Center for Education Statistics, 1993).
13. *Education Indicators at a Glance* (Paris: Organisation for Economic Cooperation and Development, 1995).
14. Linda Darling-Hammond, "Beyond Bureaucracy: Restructuring Schools for High Performance," in Susan Fuhrman and Jennifer O'Day, eds., *Rewards and Reform* (San Francisco: Jossey-Bass, 1996), pp. 144–94; Linda Darling-Hammond, Jacqueline Ancess, and Beverly Falk, *Authentic Assessment in Action: Studies of Schools and Students at Work* (New York: Teachers College Press, 1995); Fred Newman and Gary Wehlage, *Successful School Restructuring: A Report to the Public and Educators by the Center on Organization and Restructuring of Schools* (Madison: Board of Regents of the University of Wisconsin System, 1995); and Ann Lieberman, ed., *The Work of Restructuring Schools: Building from the Ground Up* (New York: Teachers College Press, 1995).
15. For data on effectiveness and retention, see Michael Andrew, "The Differences Between Graduates of Four-Year and Five-Year Teacher Preparation Programs," *Journal of Teacher Education*, vol. 41, 1990, pp. 45–51; Thomas Baker, "A Survey of Four-Year and Five-Year Program Graduates and Their Principals," *Southeastern Regional Association of Teacher Educators (SRATE) Journal*, Summer 1993, pp. 28–33; Michael Andrew and Richard L. Schwab, "Has Reform in Teacher Education Influenced Teacher Performance? An Outcome Assessment of Graduates of Eleven Teacher Education Programs," *Action in Teacher Education*, Fall 1995, pp. 43–53; Jon J. Denton and William H. Peters, "Program Assessment Report: Curriculum Evaluation of a Nontraditional Program for Certifying Teachers," unpublished report, Texas A & M University, College Station, 1988; and Hyun-Seok Shin, "Estimating Future Teacher Supply: An Application of Survival Analysis," paper presented at the annual meeting of the American Educational Research Association, New Orleans, April 1994.
16. Leslie Huling-Austin, ed., *Assisting the Beginning Teacher* (Reston, Va.: Association of Teacher Educators, 1989); Mark A. Smylie, "Redesigning Teachers' Work: Connections to the Classroom," in Linda Darling-Hammond, ed., *Review of Research in Education, Vol. 20* (Washington, D.C.: American Educational Research Association, 1994); and Linda Darling-Hammond, ed., *Professional Development Schools: Schools for Developing a Profession* (New York: Teachers College Press, 1994).

Postnote

The education of teachers has been a long-standing concern both inside and outside the profession. As Linda Darling-Hammond points out, many school reform efforts have been stymied because the teaching force was ill-equipped to put the reforms into effect. Two issues in particular have threatened efforts to reform teacher education. One is underfunding of the preparation of teachers. As a society, we spend few social resources on training teachers. While the preparation of most other professions has evolved out of the undergraduate years into concentrated graduate study and practical experience, most teachers still must skimp on their basic liberal education. Until we are ready to support the education of teachers at a much higher level, we will be sending teachers into schools with too much to learn on the job.

The second issue is related to the first: the underestimation of what it takes to be a teacher. If teaching is simply a matter of standing in front of students and transferring information, then perhaps limited teacher education programs are adequate. However, if we want our teachers to help children engage in their own discoveries and become self-starting inquirers, we need a larger vision of the teacher to guide teacher education. The report described by Darling-Hammond offers such a vision.

Linda Darling-Hammond has become the foremost spokesperson for teacher education and the professionalization of teaching in the United States. Her work with the National Commission on Teaching and America's Future places her article among our Classic selections.

Discussion Questions

1. What are some of the developments leading to the call for reform of teacher education?
2. According to Darling-Hammond, what workplace factors are currently affecting the education of teachers?
3. In your own view, what aspect of teacher education is most in need of reform? Why?

CLASSIC

The Kind of Schools We Need

ELLIOT W. EISNER

FOCUS Question

What kind of schools do we want . . . really?

TERMS TO NOTE

Accountability
Intrinsic motivation
Standards
Transfer of learning
Vouchers

As everyone knows, there is both great interest in and great concern about the quality of education in American schools. Solutions to our perceived educational ills are often not very deep. They include mandating uniforms for students to improve their behavior; using vouchers to create a competitive climate to motivate educators to try harder; testing students each year for purposes of accountability; retaining students whose test scores have not reached specified levels; paying teachers and school administrators bonuses in relation to the measured performance of their students; and defining standards for aims, for content, for evaluation practices, and, most important, for student and teacher performance.

Ironically, what seldom gets addressed in our efforts to reform schools is the vision of education that serves as the ideal for both the practice of schooling and its outcomes. We are not clear about what we are after. Aside from literacy and numeracy, what do we want to achieve? What are our aims? What is important? What kind of educational culture do we want our children to experience? In short, what kind of schools do we need?

What we do seem to care a great deal about are standards and monitoring procedures. We want a collection of so-called best methods that will guarantee success. We want a testing program that will display the results of our efforts, often in rank-ordered league standings. We want an assessment program that allows little space for personal judgment, at least when it comes to evaluation. Personal judgment is equated with subjectivity, and we want none of that. We want to boil down teaching and evaluation practices to a scientifically grounded technology.

Whether we can ever have a scientific technology of teaching practice, given the diversity of the students we teach, is problematic. Artistry and professional judgment will, in my opinion, always be required to teach well, to make intelligent education policy, to establish personal

---

Elliot W. Eisner is Lee Jacks Professor of Education and Art, Stanford University, Stanford, California. His latest book is *The Arts and the Creation of Mind*. From Elliot W. Eisner, "The Kind of Schools We Need," *Phi Delta Kappan,* April 2002. Published with the permission of Elliot W. Eisner, Lee Jacks Professor of Education and Professor of Art, Stanford University.

relationships with our students, and to appraise their growth. Those of us who work in the field of education are neither bank tellers who have little discretion nor assembly line workers whose actions are largely repetitive. Each child we teach is wonderfully unique, and each requires us to use in our work that most exquisite of human capacities, the ability to make judgments in the absence of rules. Although good teaching uses routines, it is seldom routine. Good teaching depends on sensibility and imagination. It courts surprise. It profits from caring. In short, good teaching is an artistic affair.

But even artistry can profit from a vision of the kind of education we want to provide. The reason I believe it is important to have a vision of education is because without one we have no compass, no way of knowing which way we are headed. As a result, we succumb to the pet ideas that capture the attention of policy makers and those with pseudo-solutions to supposed problems. Is it really the case that more testing will improve teaching and learning or that uniforms will improve student behavior and build character? I have my doubts. We need a conception of what good schools provide and what students and teachers do in them.

So let me share with you one man's vision of the kind of schools we need.

The kind of schools we need would provide time during the school day at least once a week for teachers to meet to discuss and share their work, their hopes, and their problems with their colleagues. It is the school, not the university, that is the real center of teacher education.

The idea that the school is the center of teacher education is built on the realization that whatever teachers become professionally, the process is not finished when they complete their teacher education program at age 21. Learning to teach well is a lifetime endeavor. The growth of understanding and skill in teaching terminates only when we do.

This fact means that we need to rethink whom the school serves. The school serves the teachers who work there as well as the students who learn there. The school needs to be designed in a way that affords opportunities to teachers to learn from one another. Such learning is so important that it should not be an addendum, relegated to an after-school time slot. Teachers, like others who do arduous work, are tired at the end of the day. Learning from our colleagues certainly deserves space and attention, and, even more important, it requires a reconceptualization of the sources of teacher development. One thing we can be sure of is that the school will be no better for the students who attend than it is for the teachers who teach there. What we do typically to improve teaching is to send teachers somewhere else to be "inserviced"—every 6,000 miles or so—usually by someone who has never seen them teach. The expectation is that what teachers are exposed to will somehow translate more or less automatically into their classrooms. Again, I have my doubts.

Teaching from a cognitive perspective requires a change in paradigm, what Thomas Kuhn once described as a "paradigm shift." Such shifts are changes in conception. From a behavioral perspective, change requires the development of those sensibilities and pedagogical techniques that make it possible to realize the conceptions and values that one defines for oneself educationally. Of course, the cognitive and the behavioral cannot truly be separated; I make the distinction here for purposes of clarity. What one conceptualizes as appropriate gives direction and guidance to what one does. And what one is able to do culminates in what one achieves. Schools ought to be places in which teachers have access to other teachers so that they have an opportunity to create the kind of supportive and educative community that culminates in higher-quality education than is currently provided.

The kind of schools we need would make teaching a professionally public process. By "professionally public" I mean that teachers would have opportunities to observe other teachers and provide feedback. No longer would isolated teachers be left to themselves to figure out what went on when they were teaching; secondary ignorance is too prevalent and too consequential to depend on one's personal reflection alone. I used the term "secondary ignorance," and I used it intentionally. I like to make a distinction between what I refer to as *primary* ignorance and *secondary* ignorance.

Primary ignorance refers to a condition in which an individual recognizes that he does not know something but also recognizes that, if he wanted to know it, he could find out. He could inquire of others, he could use the library, he could go to school. Primary ignorance is a condition that in some sense is correctable and often easily correctable.

Secondary ignorance, however, is another matter. When an individual suffers from secondary ignorance, not only does she not know something, but she does not know that she does not know. In such a situation, correcting the problem may not be possible. Secondary ignorance is as consequential for the process of parenting and for the sustenance of friendships as it is for the conduct of teaching. The way in which one remedies secondary ignorance is not through self-reflection, but through the assistance of others. Really good friends can help you understand aspects of your behavior that you might not have noticed. These observations need not be negative. It is as important to appreciate one's virtues as to become cognizant of one's weaknesses.

For this process to occur professionally, teachers need access to other teachers' classrooms. Teaching needs to be made a professionally public endeavor. The image of the teacher isolated in a classroom from 8 a.m. to 3 p.m. for five days a week, 44 weeks per year, is not the model of professional teaching practice that we need. If even world-class artists and athletes profit from feedback on their performance from those who know, so too do the rest of us. We need a conception of schooling that makes possible teachers' access to one another in helpful and constructive ways. This will require redefining what the job of teaching entails.

For most individuals who select teaching as a career, the expectation is that they will be with children exclusively, virtually all day long. But teachers also need to interact with other adults so that the secondary ignorance that I described can be ameliorated.

The model of professional life that I am suggesting will not be easy to attain. We are often quite sensitive about what we do in our own classrooms, and many of us value our privacy. Yet privacy ought not to be our highest priority. We ought to hold as our highest priority our students' well-being. And their well-being, in turn, depends on the quality of our pedagogical work. This work, I am arguing, can be enhanced with the assistance of other caring adults.

The kind of schools we need would provide opportunities for members of subject-matter departments to meet to share their work. It would recognize that different fields have different needs and that sharing within fields is a way to promote coherence for students.

Departmentalization in our schools has been a long-standing way of life. It usually begins at the middle school level and proceeds through secondary school. Teachers of mathematics have a field and a body of content that they want to help students understand; so too do teachers of the arts. These commonalities within subject-matter fields can promote a wonderful sense of esprit, a sense built on a common language to describe shared work. The strength of the educational programs in these fields can be promoted when teachers in departmentalized systems have opportunities to meet and share their work, to describe the problems they have encountered, and to discuss the achievements they have made. In short, different fields often have different needs, and these different needs can be met within the school through the colleagueship that teachers within a discipline share. The department in the middle school and in the high school provides a substantial structure for promoting the sense of community I have described.

The kind of schools we need would have principals who spend about a third of their time in classrooms, so that they know firsthand what is going on. We often conceive of the role of the school principal not only as that of a skilled administrator but also as that of an educational leader. At least one of the meanings of educational leadership is to work with a staff in a way that will make leadership unnecessary. The aim of leadership in an educational institution is to work itself out of a job.

What this approach requires, at a minimum, is an understanding of the conditions of the school and the characteristics of the classrooms in which teachers work. To understand the school and the classroom requires that school administrators leave their offices and spend at least a third of their time in teachers' classrooms. In the business community this is called "supervision by walking around."

The term supervision is a bit too supervisory for my taste. I am not sure that school administrators have "super" vision. But they should have a grasp of what happens in their schools—substantively, as well as administratively. Administrators can be in a position to recognize different kinds of talents among faculty members; they can help initiate activities and support the initiatives of teachers. They can develop an intimacy that will enable them to promote and develop the leadership potential of teachers. Thus, paradoxically, the principal as leader is most successful when he or she no longer leads but promotes the initiative and leadership of others.

The kind of schools we need would use videotaped teaching episodes to refine teachers' ability to take the practice of teaching apart—not in the negative sense, but as a way of enlarging our understanding of a complex and subtle process. No one denies that teaching is a subtle and complex art. At least it is an art when it is done well. To teach really well, it is necessary to reflect on the processes of one's own teaching and on the teaching practices of others. Our ability to perform is related, as I suggested above, to our understanding of the relationship between teaching and learning. This relationship can be illuminated through the analysis of videotaped episodes of teaching practices. Just what is a teacher up to when he or she teaches? What are the consequences? What are the compromises and trade-offs that exist in virtually any context? What institutional or organizational pressures in a school must teachers contend with? How does a teacher insert herself into her teaching? What does his body language express?

Questions such as these can be profitably addressed through the analysis of videotapes. Indeed, the collaborative analysis of a teaching episode can provide a very rich resource that can illuminate differences in perspective, in educational values, and in the meanings being conveyed. This is all to the good. Teaching is not reducible to a single frame. From my perspective, the use of such tapes not only can make our understanding of teaching more appropriately complex, but it can also refine our ability to see and interpret the process of teaching. And the more subtle perspective on teaching that such analysis creates can only enhance the quality of what we have to say to one another about the kind of work we do.

The kind of schools we need would be staffed by teachers who are interested in the questions students ask after a unit of study as they are in the answers students give. On the whole, schools are highly answer-oriented. Teachers have the questions, and students are to have the answers. Even with a problem-solving approach, the focus of attention is on the student's ability to solve a problem that someone else has posed. Yet the most intellectually demanding tasks lie not so much in solving problems as in posing questions. The framing of what we might oxymoronically call the "telling question" is what we ought to care much more about.

Once students come to deal with real situations in life, they will find that few of them provide defined problems. On the contrary, the primary task is often to define a problem so that one can get on with its solution. And to define a problem, one needs to be able to raise a question.

What would it mean to students if they were asked to raise questions coming out of a unit of study? What kinds of questions would they raise? How incisive and imaginative would these questions be? Would the students who do well in formulating questions be the same ones who do well when asked to converge upon a correct answer?

What I am getting at is the importance of developing an intellectual context designed to promote student growth. That context must surely give students an opportunity to pose questions and to entertain alternative perspectives on what they study. The last thing we want in an intellectually liberating environment is a closed set of attitudes and fealty to a single set of correct answers.

The kind of schools we need would not hold as an ideal that all students get to the same destinations at the same time. They would embrace the idea that good schools increase the variance in student performance and at the same time escalate the mean.

To talk about the idea that schools should increase individual differences rather than reduce them may at first seem counterintuitive and perhaps even antidemocratic. Don't we want all students to do the same? If we have a set of goals, don't we want all students to achieve them? To both of those questions I would give a qualified yes and no.

Individuals come into the world with different aptitudes, and, over the course of their lives, they develop different interests and proclivities. In an ideal approach to educational practice—say, one in which teaching practices were ideally designed to suit each youngster—each youngster would learn at an ideal rate. Students whose aptitudes were in math would travel farther and faster in that subject than students who had neither interest not aptitude in math but who, for example, might have greater aptitude in language or in the visual arts. In those two fields, students would travel faster and farther than those with math aptitudes but with low interests or proclivities in language or the arts. Over time, the cumulative gap between students would grow. Students would travel at their own optimal rates, and some would go faster than others in different areas of work.

What one would have at the end of the school year is wide differences in students' performance. At the same time, since each program is ideally suited to each youngster, the mean for all students in all of the areas in which they worked would be higher than it would be in a more typical program of instruction.

Such a conception of the aims of education would actually be instrumental to the creation of a rich culture. It is through our realized aptitudes that we can contribute to the lives of others and realize our own potential. It is in the symbiotic relationships among us that we come to nurture one another, to provide for others what they cannot provide—at least, not as well—for themselves, and to secure from others the gifts they have to offer that we cannot create—at least, not as well—for ourselves.

The idea that getting everyone to the same place is a virtue really represents a limitation on our aspirations. It does not serve democratic purposes to treat everybody identically or to expect everyone to arrive at the same destination at the same time. Some students need to go farther in one direction and others need to go farther in a different direction because that's where their aptitudes lie, that's where their interests are, and that's where their proclivities lead them.

The British philosopher and humanist Sir Herbert Read once said that there were two principles to guide education.[1] One was to help children become who they are not; the other was to help children become who they are. The former dominates in fascist countries, he believed, where the image defined by the state becomes the model to which children must adapt. The fascist view is to help children become who they are not. Read believed that education was a process of self-actualization and that in a truly educational environment children would come to realize their latent potentials. In this age of high technology and highly monitored systems and standards, I believe that Read's views bear reflection.

The kind of schools we need would take seriously the idea that a child's personal signature, his or her distinctive way of learning and creating, is something to be preserved and developed. We are not in the shoe manufacturing business. By saying that we are not in the shoe manufacturing business, I mean that we are not in the business of producing identical products. On an assembly line, one seeks predictability, even certainty, in the outcomes. What one wants on both assembly lines and airlines flights are uneventful events. No surprises.

In education, surprise ought to be seen not as a limitation but as the mark of creative work. Surprise breeds freshness and discovery. We ought to be creating conditions in school that enable students to pursue what is distinctive about themselves; we ought to want them to retain their personal signatures, their particular ways of seeing things.

Of course, their ways of seeing things need to be enhanced and enriched, and the task of teaching is, in part, to transmit the culture while simultaneously cultivating those forms of seeing, thinking, and feeling that make it possible for personal idiosyncrasies to be developed. In the process, we will discover both who children are and what their capabilities are.

The kind of schools we need would recognize that different forms of representation develop different forms of thinking, convey different kinds of meaning, and make possible different qualities of life. Literacy should not be restricted to decoding text and number.

Normally the term literacy refers to the ability to read, and numeracy, the ability to compute. However, I want to recast the meaning of literacy so that it refers to the process of encoding or decoding meaning in whatever forms are used in the culture to express or convey meaning. With this conception in mind and with the realization that humans throughout history have employed a variety of forms to express meaning, literacy becomes a process through which meanings are made. Meanings, of course, are made in the visual arts, in music, in dance, in poetry, in literature, as well as in physics, in mathematics, and in history. The best way to ensure that we will graduate semiliterate students from our schools is to make sure that they have few (or ineffective) opportunities to acquire the multiple forms of literacy that make multiple forms of meaning possible.

That meanings vary with the forms in which they are cast is apparent in the fact that, when we bury and when we marry, we appeal to poetry and music to express what we often cannot express literally. Humans have invented an array of means through which meaning is construed. I use the word *construe* because meaning making is a construal, both with respect to the perception of forms made by others and with respect to the forms that we make ourselves.

We tend to think that the act of reading a story or reading a poem is a process of decoding. And it is. But it is also a process of encoding. The individual reading a story must *make* sense of the story; he or she must produce meanings from the marks on the page. The mind must be constructive, it must be active, and the task of teaching is to facilitate effective mental action so that the work encountered becomes meaningful.

The kind of schools we need would recognize that the most important forms of learning are those that students know how to use outside of school, not just inside school. And the teachers in such schools would consistently try to help students see the connections between the two. The transfer of learning cannot be assumed; it needs to be taught.

The idea that transfer needs to be taught is not a new one. I reiterate an old idea here because it is absolutely fundamental to effective education. If all that students get out of what they learn in history or math or science are ideas they rapidly forget and cannot employ outside of the context of a classroom, then education is a casualty. The point of learning anything in school is not primarily to enable one to do well in school—although most parents and students believe this to be the case—it is to enable one to do well in life. The point of learning something in school is to enrich life outside of school and to acquire the skills and ideas that will enable one to produce the questions and perform the activities that one's outside life will require.

In the field of education, we have yet to begin to conceive of educational evaluation in these terms. But these are precisely the terms that we need to employ if what we do in school is to be more than mere jumping through hoops.

The kind of schools we need would take seriously the idea that, with regard to learning, the joy is in the journey. Intrinsic motivation counts the most because what students do when they can do what they want to do is what really matters. It is here that the educational process most closely exemplifies the lived experience found in the arts. We ought to stop reinforcing our students' lust for "point accumulation."

Point accumulation is *not* an educational aim. Educational aims have to do with matters of enlightenment, matters of developing abilities, matters of aesthetic experience. What we ought to be focusing our attention on is the creation of conditions in our classrooms and in our schools that make the process of education a process that students wish to pursue. The joy must be in the journey. It is the quality of the chase that matters most.

Alfred North Whitehead once commented that most people believe that a scientist inquires in order to know. Just the opposite is true, he said. Scientists know in order to inquire. What Whitehead was getting at was the idea that the vitality, challenge, and engagement that scientists find in their work is what matters most to them. At its best, this kind of satisfaction is an aesthetic experience.

We don't talk much about the aesthetic satisfactions of teaching and learning, but those of us who have taught for more than a few years know full well the feeling we experience when things go really well in our teaching. When things go really well for students, they experience similar feelings.

We ought not to marginalize the aesthetic in our understanding of what learning is about because, in the end, it is the only form of satisfaction that is likely to predict the uses of the knowledge, skills, and perspectives that students acquire in school. There is a huge difference between what a child *can* do and what a child *will* do. A child who learns to read but has no appetite for reading is not really succeeding in school. We want to promote that appetite for learning, and it ought to be built on the satisfactions that students receive in our classrooms. It is the aesthetic that represents the highest forms of intellectual achievement, and it is the aesthetic that provides the natural high and contributes the energy we need to want to pursue an activity again and again and again.

The kind of schools we need would encourage deep conversation in classrooms. They would help students learn how to participate in that complex and subtle art, an art that requires learning how to listen as well as how to speak. Good conversation is an activity for which our voyeuristic interest in talk shows offers no substitute.

It may seem odd recommending that deep conversation be promoted in our classrooms. Conversation has a kind of shallow ring, as if it were something you do when you don't have anything really important to do. Yet conversation, when it goes well, when the participants really listen to each other, is like an acquired taste, an acquired skill. It does not take much in the way of resources, but, ironically, it is among the rarest features of classroom life. It is also, I believe, among the rare features of our personal life, and that is why we often tune in to Oprah Winfrey, Larry King, and other talk show hosts to participate vicariously in conversation. Even when the conversations are not all that deep, they remain interesting.

How do we help students learn to become listeners? How do we enable them to understand that comments and questions need to flow from what preceded and not simply express whatever happens to be on one's mind at the time? How do we enable students to become more like the members of a jazz quartet, whose interplay good conversation sometimes seems to emulate? Conversation is akin to deliberation, a process that searches for possible answers and explores blind alleys as well as open freeways. How do we create in our classrooms a practice that, when done well, can be a model of intellectual activity?

Of course, all of us need to learn to engage in deep conversation. In many ways, we need to model what we expect our students to learn. But I am convinced that conversation about ideas that matter to students and teachers and that occupy a central place in our curriculum can be a powerful means of converting the academic institutions we call schools into intellectual institutions. Such a transformation would represent a paradigmatic shift in the culture of schooling.

The kind of schools we need would help students gradually assume increased responsibility for framing their own goals and learning how to achieve them. We want students eventually to become the architects of their own education. The long-term aim of teaching is to make itself unnecessary.

Saying that the long-term aim of teaching is to render itself unnecessary is simply to make explicit what I hope readers have gleaned from my arguments here. Helping students learn how to formulate their own goals is a way to enable them to secure their freedom. Helping them learn how to plan and execute their lives in relation to those goals is a way of developing their autonomy. Plato once defined a slave as someone who executes the purposes of another. Over the grade levels, we have conceived of teaching as setting problems that students solve. Only rarely have we created the conditions through which students set the problems that they wish to pursue. Yet this is precisely what they will need to be able to do once they leave the protected sphere of the school.

It is interesting to me that, in discourse about school reform and the relation of goals and standards to curriculum reform, the teacher is given the freedom to formulate means but not to decide upon ends. The prevailing view is that professional judgment pertains to matters of technique, rather than to matters of goals.

I believe this conception of school reform is shortsighted. If our students were simply inert entities, something like copper or plastic, it would be possible in principle to formulate methods of acting on them that would yield uniform responses. A thousand pounds of pressure by a punch press on a steel plate has a given effect. But our students are not uniform, they are not steel, and they do not respond in the same way to pressures of various kinds. Thus teachers will always need the discretionary space to determine not only matters of means but also matters of ends. And we want students, gradually to be sure, to have the opportunity to formulate ends as well. Withholding such opportunities is a form of de-skilling for both teachers and students.

The kind of schools we need would make it possible for students who have particular interests to pursue those interests in depth and, at the same time, to work on public service projects that contribute to something larger than their own immediate interests. This twofold aim—the ability to serve the self through intensive study and the desire and ability to provide a public service—is like the head and tail of a coin. Both elements need to be a part of our educational agenda.

The long-term aim of education may be said to be to learn how to engage in personally satisfying activities that are at the same time socially constructive. Students need to learn that there are people who need services and that they, the students themselves, can contribute to meeting these people's needs. Service learning is a move in the right direction. It affords adolescents an opportunity to do something whose scope is beyond themselves. The result, at least potentially, is the development of an attitude that schools would do well to foster. That, too, should be a part of our curricular agenda.

The kind of schools we need would treat the idea of "public education" as meaning not only the education of the public inside schools, but also the education of the public outside schools. The school's faculty will find it difficult to proceed farther or faster than the community will allow. Our task, in part, is to nurture public conversation in order to create a collective vision of education.

Realistically speaking, our responsibilities as educators extend beyond the confines of our classrooms and even beyond the walls of our schools. We also have responsibilities to our communities. We need desperately to create educational forums for members of the community in which the purposes and processes of education can be discussed, debated, and deliberated and from which consensus can be arrived at with regard to our broad mission as an educational institution. Parents need to know why, for example, inquiry-oriented methods matter, why rote learning may not be in the best long-term interest of their children, why problem-centered activities are important, and why the ability to frame telling questions is crucial.

Most parents and even many teachers have a yellow-school-bus image when it comes to conceiving what teaching, learning, and schooling should look like. The yellow school bus is a metaphor for the model of education that they encountered and that, all too often, they wish to replicate in the 21st century. Our schools, as they are now designed, often tacitly encourage the re-creation of such a model. Yet we know there is a better way. That better way ought to be a part of the agenda the community discusses with teachers and school administrators. Principals and school superintendents ought to perform a leadership role in deepening that community conversation. Without having such a conversation, it will be very difficult to create the kind of schools we need.

I acknowledge that the features of schooling that I have described will not be easy to attain, but they are important. We get so caught up in debating whether or not we should extend the school year that we seem to forget to consider what should go into that year. We seem to forget about our vision of education and the kind of educational practices that will move the school in the direction we value. Too often we find ourselves implementing policies that we do not value. Those of us in education need to take a stand and to serve as public advocates for our students. Who speaks for our students? We need to.

Some of the features I have described—perhaps all of them—may not be ones that you yourself cherish. Fine. That makes conversation possible. And so I invite you to begin that conversation in your school, so that out of the collective wisdom of each of our communities can come a vision of education that our children deserve and, through that vision, the creation of the kind of schools that our children need.

Note

1. Herbert Read, *Education Through Art* (New York: Pantheon Books, 1944).

Postnote

Elliot Eisner's contributions to education span many areas, including art education, curriculum development, qualitative research, and educational connoisseurship. His renaissance qualities earn him a place among our Classic authors.

As young graduate students, both editors of *Kaleidoscope* were privileged to have Elliot Eisner (at the time, a young professor) as a teacher. It was at the height of interest in B. F. Skinner's behaviorism and the applications of programmed instruction and behavioral objectives to American classrooms. There was a heady belief throughout the educational community that this new movement would soon transform our schools. Professor Eisner would have little of it. His was one of the few voices at that time to raise questions and urge caution.

Today we are in the midst of a new national movement that many believe will revolutionize our schools and lead to much higher levels of academic achievement among our students. As he has throughout his career, Eisner is again asking the hard questions, this time about standards and the effects of the tests we use to gauge our successes and failures to reach those standards. Here, he asks us to step back and think hard about what we really desire. "What kind of schools do we *really* need?"

Discussion Questions

1. In what specific ways has Eisner's article challenged you? Or do you agree with everything he seems to suggest?
2. What are the challenges and hurdles to overcome to achieve the kind of schools that Eisner suggests?
3. What are the most positive suggestions for school improvement that the author makes?

Class and the Classroom

RICHARD ROTHSTEIN

FOCUS Question

For over two decades, Americans from the White House to the teachers' lounge have been deeply committed to major improvements in how our schools serve the poor. What is it, then, that keeps real reform from taking place?

TERMS TO NOTE

Conversation gap

Health and housing gap

Reading gap

Role model gap

The achievement gap between poor and middle-class black and white children is widely recognized as our most important educational challenge. But we prevent ourselves from solving it because of a commonplace belief that poverty and race can't "cause" low achievement and that therefore schools must be failing to teach disadvantaged children adequately. After all, we see many highly successful students from lower-class backgrounds. Their success seems to prove that social class cannot be what impedes most disadvantaged students.

Yet the success of some lower-class students proves nothing about the power of schools to close the achievement gap. In every social group, there are low achievers and high achievers alike. On average, the achievement of low-income students is below the average achievement of middle-class students, but there are always some middle-class students who achieve below typical low-income levels. Similarly, some low-income students achieve above typical middle-class levels. Demography is not destiny, but students' family characteristics are a powerful influence on their relative average achievement.

Widely repeated accounts of schools that somehow elicit consistently high achievement from lower-class children almost always turn out, upon examination, to be flawed. In some cases, these "schools that beat the odds" are highly selective, enrolling only the most able or most motivated lower-class children. In other cases, they are not truly lower-class schools—for example, a school enrolling children who qualify for subsidized lunches because their parents are graduate students living on low stipends. In other cases, such schools define high achievement at such a low level that all students can reach it, despite big gaps that remain at more meaningful levels.

It seems plausible that if *some* children can defy the demographic odds, *all* children can, but that belief reflects a reasoning whose naiveté

Richard Rothstein is a research associate of the Economic Policy Institute and a visiting lecturer at Teachers College, Columbia University. From 1999 to 2002 he was the national education columnist of *The New York Times.* "Class and the Classroom," by Richard Rothstein. Reprinted with permission from American School Board Journal, October 2004.

we easily recognize in other policy areas. In human affairs where multiple causation is typical, causes are not disproved by exceptions. Tobacco firms once claimed that smoking does not cause cancer because some people smoke without getting cancer. We now consider such reasoning specious. We do not suggest that alcoholism does not cause child or spousal abuse because not all alcoholics are abusers. We understand that because no single cause is rigidly deterministic, some people can smoke or drink to excess without harm. But we also understand that, on average, these behaviors are dangerous. Yet despite such understanding, quite sophisticated people often proclaim that the success of some poor children proves that social disadvantage does not cause low achievement.

Partly, our confusion stems from failing to examine the concrete ways that social class actually affects learning. Describing these may help to make their influence more obvious—and may make it more obvious why the achievement gap can be substantially narrowed only when school improvement is combined with social and economic reform.

The Reading Gap

Consider how parents of different social classes tend to raise children. Young children of educated parents are read to more consistently and are encouraged to read more to themselves when they are older. Most children whose parents have college degrees are read to daily before they begin kindergarten, but few children whose parents have only a high school diploma or less benefit from daily reading. And, white children are more likely than black children to be read to in their prekindergarten years.

A 5-year-old who enters school recognizing some words and who has turned the pages of many stories will be easier to teach than one who has rarely held a book. The second child can be taught, but with equally high expectations and effective teaching, the first will be more likely to pass an age-appropriate reading test than the second. So the achievement gap begins.

If a society with such differences wants all children, irrespective of social class, to have the same chance to achieve academic goals, it should find ways to help lower-class children enter school having the same familiarity with books as middle-class children have. This requires rethinking the institutional settings in which we provide early childhood care, beginning in infancy.

Some people acknowledge the impact of such differences but find it hard to accept that good schools should have so difficult a time overcoming them. This would be easier to understand if Americans had a broader international perspective on education. Class backgrounds influence *relative* achievement everywhere. The inability of schools to overcome the disadvantage of less-literate homes is not a peculiar American failure but a universal reality. The number of books in students' homes, for example, consistently predicts their test scores in almost every country. Turkish immigrant students suffer from an achievement gap in Germany, as do Algerians in France, as do Caribbean, African, Pakistani, and Bangladeshi pupils in Great Britain, and as do Okinawans and low-caste Buraku in Japan.

An international reading survey of 15-year-olds, conducted in 2000, found a strong relationship in almost every nation between parental occupation and student literacy. The gap between the literacy of children of the highest-status workers (such as doctors, professors, and lawyers) and the lowest-status workers (such as waiters and waitresses, taxi drivers, and mechanics) was even greater in Germany and the United Kingdom than it was in the United States.

After reviewing these results, a U.S. Department of Education summary concluded that "most participating countries do not differ significantly from the United States in terms of the strength of the relationship between socioeconomic status and literacy in any subject." Remarkably, the department published this conclusion at the same time that it was guiding a bill through Congress—the No Child Left Behind Act—that demanded every school in the nation abolish social class differences in achievement within 12 years.

Urging less-educated parents to read to children can't fully compensate for differences in school readiness. Children who see parents read to solve their own problems or for entertainment are more likely to want to read themselves. Parents who bring reading material home from work demonstrate by example to children that reading is not a segmented burden but a seamless activity that bridges work and leisure. Parents who read to children but don't read for themselves send a different message.

How parents read to children is as important as whether they do, and an extensive literature confirms that more educated parents read aloud differently. When working-class parents read aloud, they are more likely to tell children to pay attention without interruptions or to sound out words or name letters. When they ask children about a story, the questions are more likely to be factual, asking for names of objects or memory of events.

Parents who are more literate are more likely to ask questions that are creative, interpretive, or connective, such as "What do you think will happen next?" "Does that remind you of what we did yesterday?" Middle-class parents are more likely to read aloud to have fun, to start conversations, or as an entree to the world outside. Their children learn that reading is enjoyable and are more motivated to read in school.

The Conversation Gap

There are stark class differences not only in how parents read but in how they converse. Explaining events in the broader world to children at the dinner table, for example, may have as much of an influence on test scores as early reading itself. Through such conversations, children develop vocabularies and become familiar with contexts for reading in school. Educated parents are more likely to engage in such talk and to begin it with infants and toddlers, conducting pretend conversations long before infants can understand the language.

Typically, middle-class parents ask infants about their needs, then provide answers for the children. ("Are you ready for a nap now? Yes, you are, aren't you?") Instructions are more likely to be given indirectly: "You don't want to make so much noise, do you?" This kind of instruction is really an invitation for a child to work through the reasoning behind an order and to internalize it. Middle-class parents implicitly begin academic instruction for infants with such indirect guidance.

Yet such instruction is quite different from what policy-makers nowadays consider "academic" for young children: explicit training in letter and number recognition, letter-sound correspondence, and so on. Such drill in basic skills can be helpful but is unlikely to close the social class gap in learning.

Soon after middle-class children become verbal, their parents typically draw them into adult conversations so the children can practice expressing their own opinions. Being included in adult conversations this early develops a sense of entitlement in children; they feel comfortable addressing adults as equals and without deference. Children who ask for reasons, rather than accepting assertions on adult authority, develop intellectual skills upon which later academic success in school will rely. Certainly, some lower-class children have such skills and some middle-class children lack them. But, on average, a sense of entitlement is based on one's social class.

Parents whose professional occupations entail authority and responsibility typically believe more strongly that they can affect their environments and solve problems. At work, they explore alternatives and negotiate compromises. They naturally express these personality traits at home when they design activities in which children figure out solutions for themselves. Even the youngest middle-class children practice traits that make academic success more likely when they negotiate what to wear or to eat. When middle-class parents give orders, the parents are more likely to explain why the rules are reasonable.

But parents whose jobs entail following orders or doing routine tasks show less sense of efficacy. They are less likely to encourage their children to negotiate over clothing or food and more likely to instruct them by giving directions without extended discussion. Following orders, after all, is how they themselves behave at work. Their children are also more likely to be fatalistic about obstacles they face, in and out of school.

Middle-class children's self-assurance is enhanced in after-school activities that sometimes require large fees for enrollment and almost always require parents to have enough free time and resources to provide transportation. Organized sports, music, drama, and dance programs build self-confidence and discipline in middle-class children. Lower-class parents find the fees for such activities more daunting, and transportation may also be more of a problem. Organized athletic and artistic activities may not be available in their neighborhoods, so lower-class children's sports are more informal and less confidence-building, with less opportunity to learn teamwork and self-discipline. For children with greater self-confidence, unfamiliar school challenges can be exciting. These children, who are more likely to be from middle-class homes, are more likely to succeed than those who are less self-confident.

Homework exacerbates academic differences between these two groups of children because middle-class parents are more likely to help with homework. Yet homework would increase the achievement gap even if all parents were able to assist. Parents from different social classes supervise homework differently. Consistent with overall patterns of language use, middle-class parents—especially those whose own occupational habits require problem solving—are more likely to assist by posing questions that break large problems down into smaller ones and that help children figure out correct answers. Lower-class parents are more likely to guide children with direct instructions. Children from both classes may go to school with completed homework, but middle-class children are more likely to gain in intellectual power from the exercise than lower-class children.

Twenty years ago, Betty Hart and Todd Risley, two researchers from the University of Kansas, visited families from different social classes to monitor the conversations between parents and toddlers. Hart and Risley found that, on average, professional parents spoke more than 2,000 words per hour to their children, working-class parents spoke about 1,300, and welfare mothers spoke about 600. So by age 3, the children of professionals had vocabularies that were nearly 50 percent greater than those of working-class children and twice as large as those of welfare children.

Deficits like these cannot be made up by schools alone, no matter how high the teachers' expectations. For all children to achieve the same goals, the less advantaged would have to enter school with verbal fluency that is similar to the fluency of middle-class children.

The Kansas researchers also tracked how often parents verbally encouraged children's behavior and how often they reprimanded their children. Toddlers of professionals got an average of six encouragements per reprimand. Working-class children had two. For welfare children, the ratio was reversed—an average of one encouragement for two reprimands. Children whose initiative was encouraged from a very early age are more likely, on average, to take responsibility for their own learning.

The Role Model Gap

Social class differences in role modeling also make an achievement gap almost inevitable. Not surprisingly, middle-class professional parents tend to associate with, and be friends with, similarly educated professionals. Working-class parents have fewer professional friends. If parents and their friends perform jobs requiring little academic skill, their children's images of their own futures are influenced. On average, these children must struggle harder to motivate themselves to achieve than children who assume, on the basis of their parents' social circle, that the only roles are doctor, lawyer, teacher, social worker, manager, administrator, or businessperson.

Even disadvantaged children usually say they plan to attend college. College has become such a broad rhetorical goal that black eighth-graders tell surveyors they expect to earn college degrees as often as white eighth-graders do. But despite these intentions, fewer black than white eighth-graders actually graduate from high school four years later; fewer enroll in college the following year; and fewer still persist to get bachelor's degrees.

This discrepancy is not due simply to the cost of college. A bigger reason is that while disadvantaged students *say* they plan to go to college, they don't feel as much parental, community, or peer pressure to take the courses or to get the grades they need to become more attractive to college admission offices. Lower-class parents say they expect children to get good grades, but they are less likely to enforce these expectations, for example with rewards or punishments. Teachers and counselors can stress doing well in school to lower-class children, but such lessons compete with children's own self-images, formed early in life and reinforced daily at home.

As John Ogbu and others have noted, a culture of underachievement may help explain why even middle-class black children often don't do as well in school as white children from seemingly similar socioeconomic backgrounds. On average, middle-class black students don't study as hard as white middle-class students and blacks are more disruptive in class than whites from similar income strata.

This culture of underachievement is easier to understand than to cure. Throughout American history, many black students who excelled in school were not rewarded for that effort in the labor market. Many black college graduates could find work only as servants or Pullman car porters or, in white-collar fields, as assistants to less-qualified whites. Many Americans believe that these practices have disappeared and that blacks and whites with similar test scores now have similar earnings and occupational status. But labor market discrimination continues to be a significant obstacle—especially for black males with high school educations.

Evidence for this comes from employment discrimination cases, such as the prominent 1996 case in which Texaco settled for a payment of $176 million to black employees after taped conversations of executives revealed pervasive racist attitudes, presumably not restricted to executives of this corporation alone. Other evidence comes from studies that find black workers with darker complexions have less success in the labor market than those with identical education, age, and criminal records but lighter complexions.

Still more evidence comes from studies in which blacks and whites with similar qualifications are sent to apply for job vacancies; the whites are typically more successful than the blacks. In one recent study where young, well-groomed, and articulate black and white college graduates, posing as high school graduates with identical qualifications, submitted applications for entry-level jobs, the applications of whites with criminal records got positive responses more often than the applications of blacks with no criminal records.

So the expectation of black students that their academic efforts will be less rewarded than the efforts of their white peers is rational for the majority of black students who do not expect to complete college. Some will reduce their academic efforts as a result. We can say that they should not do so and, instead, should redouble their efforts in response to the greater obstacles they face. But as long as racial discrimination persists, the average achievement of black students will be lower than the average achievement of whites, simply because many blacks (especially males) who see that academic effort has less of a payoff will respond rationally by reducing their effort.

The Health and Housing Gaps

Despite these big race and social class differences in child rearing, role modeling, labor market experiences, and cultural characteristics, the lower achievement of lower-class students is not caused by these differences alone. Just as important are differences in the actual social and economic conditions of children.

Overall, lower-income children are in poorer health. They have poorer vision, partly because of prenatal conditions and partly because, even as toddlers, they watch too much television, so their eyes are poorly trained. Trying to read, their eyes may wander or have difficulty tracking print or focusing. A good part of the over-identification of learning disabilities for lower-class children may well be attributable to undiagnosed vision problems that could be easily treated by optometrists and for which special education placement then should be unnecessary.

Lower-class children have poorer oral hygiene, more lead poisoning, more asthma, poorer nutrition, less-adequate pediatric care, more exposure to smoke, and a host of other health problems. Because of less-adequate dental care, for example, they are more likely to have toothaches and resulting discomfort that affects concentration.

Because low-income children live in communities where landlords use high-sulfur home heating oil and where diesel trucks frequently pass en route to industrial and commercial sites, they are more likely to suffer from asthma, leading to more absences from school and, when they do attend, drowsiness from lying awake at night, wheezing. Recent surveys in Chicago and in New York City's Harlem community found one of every four children suffering from asthma, a rate six times as great as that for all children.

In addition, there are fewer primary-care physicians in low-income communities, where the physician-to-population ratio is less than a third the rate in middle-class communities. For that reason, disadvantaged children—even those with health insurance—are more likely to miss school for relatively minor problems, such as common ear infections, for which middle-class children are treated promptly.

Each of these well-documented social class differences in health is likely to have a palpable effect on academic achievement; combined, their influence is probably huge.

The growing unaffordability of adequate housing for low-income families also affects achievement. Children whose families have difficulty finding stable housing are more likely to be mobile, and student mobility is an important cause of failing student performance. A 1994 government report found that 30 percent of the poorest children had attended at least three different schools by third grade, while only 10 percent of middle-class children had done so. Black children were more than twice as likely as white children to change schools this often. It is hard to imagine how teachers, no matter how well trained, can be as effective for children who move in and out of their classrooms as they can be for those who attend regularly.

Differences in wealth are also likely to be important determinants of achievement, but these are usually overlooked because most analysts focus only on annual family income to indicate disadvantage. This makes it hard to understand why black students, on average, score lower than whites whose family incomes are the same. It is easier to understand this pattern when we recognize that children can have similar family incomes but be of different economic classes. In any given year, black families with low income are likely to have been poor for longer than white families with similar income in that year.

White families are also likely to own far more assets that support their children's achievement than are black families at the same income level, partly because black middle-class parents are more likely to be the first generation in their families to have middle-class status. Although the median black family income is about two-thirds the median income of white families, the assets of black families are still only 12 percent those of whites. Among other things, this difference means that, among white and black families with the same middle-class incomes, the whites are more likely to have savings for college. This makes white children's college aspirations more practical, and therefore more commonplace.

Narrowing the Gaps

If we properly identify the actual social class characteristics that produce differences in average achievement, we should be able to design policies that narrow the achievement gap. Certainly, improvement of instructional practices is among these, but a focus on school reform alone is bound to be frustrating and ultimately unsuccessful. To work, school improvement must combine with policies that narrow the social and economic differences between children. Where these differences cannot easily be narrowed, school should be redefined to cover more of the early childhood, after-school, and summer times, when the disparate influences of families and communities are now most powerful.

Because the gap is already huge at age 3, the most important new investment should no doubt be in early childhood programs. Prekindergarten classes for 4-year-olds are needed, but they barely begin to address the problem. The quality of early childhood programs is as important as the existence of such programs themselves. Too many low-income children are parked before television sets in low-quality day-care settings. To narrow the gap, care for infants and toddlers should be provided by adults who can create the kind of intellectual environment that is typically experienced by middle-class infants and toddlers. This requires professional caregivers and low child-adult ratios.

After-school and summer experiences for lower-class children, similar to programs middle-class children take for granted, would also be needed to narrow the gap. This does not mean remedial programs where lower-class children get added drill in math and reading. Certainly, remediation should be part of an adequate after-school and summer program, but only a part. The advantage that middle-class children gain after school and in summer comes from the self-confidence they acquire and the awareness of the world outside that they develop through organized athletics, dance, drama, museum visits, recreational reading, and other activities that develop inquisitiveness, creativity, self-discipline, and organizational skills. After-school and summer programs can be expected to narrow the achievement gap only by attempting to duplicate such experiences.

Provision of health-care services to lower-class children and their families is also required to narrow the achievement gap. Some health services are relatively inexpensive, such as school vision and dental clinics. A full array of health services will cost more, but it cannot be avoided if we truly intend to raise the achievement of lower-class children.

The connection between social and economic disadvantage and an academic achievement gap has long been well known. Most educators, however, have avoided the obvious implication: Improving lower-class children's learning requires ameliorating the social and economic conditions of their lives. School board members—who are often the officials with the closest ties to public opinion—cannot afford to remain silent about the connection between school improvement and social reform. Calling attention to this link is not to make excuses for poor school performance. It is only to be honest about the social support schools require if they are to fulfill the public's expectation that the achievement gap will disappear.

Postnote

It is easy to be discouraged, reading hard-hitting articles such as this one. Richard Rothstein questions the belief of many that America has been a world leader in providing a "social escalator" out of poverty through our public school system. Although that may have been true in the past, the escalator is slowing down and is badly in need of repair.

The solutions offered here for fundamental social and economic change are indeed radical. They are also extraordinarily expensive and represent a quantum jump in educational expenditure. Tallying up the tax implications, public policy analysts will quickly start shaking their heads. Our priorities, such as the burgeoning population of elderly and their sky-rocketing health costs, are making more insistent demands. And, besides, in the real world of American politics, the poor have little political clout.

One answer to this argument is that uneducated and unskilled "graduates" of our schools are potential "social dynamite." The costs to the country of not educating them properly will be far greater than the price tag on the author's proposals. A sounder answer, though, is that we should make these investments in poor children because it is the right—the just—thing to do. If each of us thought about these individual children as our own children, our own flesh, blood and DNA, this problem would be solved, and we could move on to consider the issue of health care.

Discussion Questions

1. The author mentions several "gaps." What are they, and which one do you believe is most severe?
2. Restate in your own words the relationship between the social and economic disadvantages of poor children and the achievement gap.
3. What do you believe are the key reasons that keep Americans from fundamentally reforming the schools serving poor children?

The Case for Being Mean

FREDERICK M. HESS

FOCUS Question

The American public is demanding results, and they want to hold educators accountable for students' progress or lack of progress in school. Which of the two forms of accountability discussed here should be adopted by our schools?

TERMS TO NOTE

Coercive accountability

Suggestive accountability

The enactment of the federal No Child Left Behind Act in January 2002 made performance-based education accountability a federal mandate. The legislation followed a decade of concerted state activity across the states that produced an array of high-stakes accountability systems. Those state systems have already come under fire. In such places as Nevada, Florida, and Massachusetts, where thousands of high school seniors are at risk of being denied diplomas in 2004, angry parents are protesting, civil rights groups have threatened boycotts over the high rates of failing minority students, and educators worry that their schools will be targeted by state education agencies as low-performing or inadequate.

Performance-based accountability's allure is its promise to ensure that *all* students, even the most disadvantaged, will master crucial knowledge and skills. An overwhelming percentage of adults, often 90 percent or higher, support accountability in the abstract (Public Agenda, 2000), recognizing the appropriateness of holding public educators responsible for teaching essential material instead of permitting them to use public classrooms as personal forums. Aside from a few ideological critics, even most educators are sympathetic to the goals of performance-based accountability. The important split is not between ideological proponents and opponents of accountability, but between those who support tough-minded accountability, despite all its warts, and those who like the ideal of accountability but shrink from its reality.

Nice Versus Mean Accountability

Simply put, there are two kinds of accountability: suggestive and coercive, or, more plainly, "nice" and "mean."

Advocates of nice accountability presume that the key to school improvement is to provide educators with more resources, expertise,

---

Frederick M. Hess is a resident scholar at the American Enterprise Institute. "The Case for Being Mean," by Frederick M. Hess, *Educational Leadership,* November 2003, pp. 22–26. Reprinted by permission. The Association for Supervision and Curriculum Development is a worldwide community of educators advocating sound policies and sharing best practices to achieve the success of each learner. To learn more, visit ASCD at **www.ascd.org.**

training, support, and "capacity." They view accountability as a helpful tool that seeks to improve schooling by developing standards, applying informal social pressures, using tests as a diagnostic device, increasing coordination across schools and classrooms, and making more efficient use of school resources through standardization. The educational benefits produced by nice accountability depend on individual volition.

Mean accountability, on the other hand, uses coercive measures—incentives and sanctions—to ensure that educators teach and students master specified content. Students must demonstrate their mastery of essential knowledge and skills in the areas of math, writing, reading, and perhaps core disciplines at certain key points and before graduating from high school. Educators are expected to do what is necessary to ensure that they no longer pass on students unequipped for the most fundamental requirements of further education, work, or good citizenship.

In such a system, school performance no longer rests on fond wishes and good intentions. Instead, such levers as diplomas and job security are used to compel students and teachers to cooperate. Mean accountability seeks to harness the self-interest of students and educators to refocus schools and redefine the expectations of teachers and learners.

For educators, mean accountability offers many benefits that nice accountability does not. Unlike its nicer variant, mean accountability gives the school and district leadership personal incentives to seek out and cultivate excellence. It enables policymakers to roll back regulations designed to control quality by means of micromanaging procedures. It builds popular support for education by providing state officials and voters with hard evidence on school performance. And, in well-run schools and districts, mean accountability gives effective teachers new freedom to teach as they see fit and with the materials they deem appropriate, as long as their students master essential skills.

Advocates of mean accountability agree that nice accountability yields real benefits, but they point out that these benefits have been only modest and uneven. The 2002 National Assessment of Educational Progress reported that just 33 percent of U.S. 4th graders and 36 percent of 12th graders scored at least at the "proficient" level in reading; 36 percent of 4th graders and 26 percent of 12th graders scored "below basic." The results are far worse in urban communities, where two-thirds of 4th graders are routinely reading at a "below basic" level (National Center for Education Statistics, 2003).

The split between those who insist on mean accountability and the gentler souls comes down to whether one agrees with nice-accountability proponents that educators are doing all they can, that student failure is caused largely by factors outside the control of teachers or administrators, and that incentives will not productively alter educators' behavior.

Proponents of coercive accountability reject such claims. Common sense tells us that people work more effectively when we hold them accountable for performance, reward them for excellence, and give them opportunities to devise new paths to success. In any line of work, most employees will resist changes that require them to take on more responsibility, disrupt their routines, or threaten their jobs or wages. To overcome such resistance, we need to make inaction more painful than the proposed action. In education, this means making a lack of improvement so unpleasant for local officials and educators that they are willing to reconsider work rules, require teachers to change routines, assign teachers to classes and schools in more effective ways, increase required homework, fire ineffective teachers, and otherwise take those painful steps that are regarded as "unrealistic" most of the time.

The idea is not simply to lay more weight on the shoulders of teachers or principals. The challenge is more fundamental. In any line of work, decision makers want to avoid unpopular decisions. But sometimes school officials have to make painful choices: to drop a popular reading program that isn't working; to cut elective choices if students haven't mastered the basics; to fire a well-liked principal who isn't achieving results. In each case, the easiest course is not to act. The way to force people to make unpleasant choices is by pressing them to do so—even if it angers employees or constituents. Coercive accountability provides the best, most straightforward way to bring that pressure to bear in support of core academic subjects.

Rethinking Systems and Practices

For decades, U.S. schools have been constantly reforming without ever really changing. As long as we give veto power over change to those who will endure its costs, we will continue to shy away from reinventing schools as more efficient and effective organizations. We will not force painful improvement by convincing those who bear the costs of change that it really is a good idea. We must leave them no choice in the matter.

It's not just a question of making people work harder; it's about forcing managers and leaders to rethink systems and practices. Take the Detroit automakers who fell on hard times in the late 1970s. They were producing oversized and poorly designed cars, had gotten lazy about quality control, had permitted costs and union contracts to spiral out of hand, and had added layer upon layer of middle management. The emergence of fierce foreign competition and a dramatic loss of market share shocked these firms into action. Energetic new leadership rethought the product line, redesigned quality control, slashed middle management, renegotiated contracts, and cut costs. The transformation was not about berating workers: it was about forcing those in charge to focus on high performance and make painful decisions to achieve it.

Today, district and school leaders spend their time pleading with their subordinates to cooperate because they can imagine no other ways to drive change. They are mistaken. We can drive change by requiring educators to meet clear performance goals and attaching consequences to success or failure.

Ambivalence About Being Tough

Although public officials and educators are sympathetic to the notion of accountability, they are often squeamish about the demands of coercive accountability. The benefits of accountability—a more rigorous and focused school system—are broad and widely dispersed and often hard to isolate, whereas the costs are borne by visible students and teachers, many of whom can inevitably point to various extenuating circumstances. A Texas principal, after affirming that she believed in rigorous standards for student learning, expressed the ambivalence felt by many:

> Last year I had to tell a student that she didn't pass the "last chance" TAAS exam administered in May of her senior year. I do not even want to imagine the heartbreak that she and her family felt. I've only had to do this once, but it was one time too many, and I don't know that I have it in me to do it again. (cited in Holcombe, 2002, p. 20)

Accountability requires education officials to make five politically sensitive sets of decisions. First, they must designate a prescribed body of content and objectives to be tested. Such a course necessarily marginalizes some other goals, objectives, content, and skills. Second, officials must impose assessments that accurately measure whether or not students have mastered the requisite skills and content. Third, they must specify what constitutes mastery. Fourth, they need to decide what to do with students who fail to demonstrate mastery. Finally, for accountability to significantly alter education programs and practices, the system must reward or sanction educators on the basis of student performance.

Each decision tends to produce passionate opposition among those who bear the costs. Opponents of coercive accountability seize upon the arbitrary nature of many of these decisions, demanding modifications that will increase test validity and reduce any inequities or pernicious effects produced by misuse of assessments.

Proponents of coercive accountability often have trouble holding the line against the appeals of aggrieved constituencies. In the face of heated opposition, proponents often agree to a series of compromises on program design and implementation that eventually undercut the coercive promise of accountability.

For example, although most states have adopted mandatory graduation exams and about half offer school incentives linked to test scores, phase-in periods and implementation delays mean that graduation requirements and performance-based incentives for educators have taken effect in only a few states. Delays and adjustments may provide time to refine tests and curriculums and potential penalties, but they also conveniently push substantive challenges into the future.

To date, most states that have actually started to approach deadlines have blinked and delayed the implementation of sanctions. A 2000 analysis found that roughly one-third of the states that had adopted high-stakes accountability systems had slowed or scaled back their original efforts (Steinberg, 2000). In Arizona, for instance, when more than 80 percent of 10th graders failed the state math test in 1999 and 2000, the state board of education and the legislature scrambled to push back the graduation requirement from 2002 to 2006 (Bowman, 2001). In recent years, other states—including Alabama, Alaska, California, Delaware, Maryland, North Carolina, and Wyoming—scaled back testing programs or postponed their effects.

If policymakers don't delay implementation, they often soften accountability in various other ways. Although each accommodation can be justified on educational grounds, each of these common compromises also serves to dull the mean edge of accountability:

- *Lowering the stakes of the tests for students, for educators, or for both.* Weak or nonexistent sanctions offer little incentive for teachers, low-performing students, or anyone else to worry much about test results.

- *Making tests easier*—by lowering content standards, adopting easier questions, or reducing the cut-off scores for satisfactory performance.

- *Offering lots of second chances.* Giving students a number of retests or a teacher several years to boost his or her performance means that the law of averages will help a number of moderately low performers to clear the bar.

- *Permitting some students or educators to sidestep the required assessment*—for example, by issuing a "basic" diploma in lieu of a standard diploma or exempting teachers who teach specialized classes from evaluation.

The Temptations of Compromise

From the inception of high-stakes testing, proponents have tended to laud the requisite tests and accompanying systems as clear, scientifically defensible, manageable, and concise. Critics typically attack the tests and systems as unreliable, simplistic, overly focused on trivia, or lacking the necessary curricular and pedagogical support. They argue that linking teacher incentives or student advancement to anything so crude will pose inevitable perils. In truth, both sides are correct.

The details of accountability—the content to be tested, the assessments to use, the definition of minimum competency, and how to address the performance of educators or students—are inherently arbitrary. The closer one gets to crafting and enforcing standards, the less defensible specific program elements can appear.

Determining what students need to know, when they need to know it, and how well they need to know it is an ambiguous and value-laden exercise. Neither developmental psychologists nor psychometricians can "prove" the necessity to teach specified content at a particular grade level. Such decisions are imperfect judgments about students' needs and capacities.

Proponents have difficulty standing firm on program details precisely because decisions regarding what students need to know, when they need to know it, and how well they need to know it are only reasonable approximations. No amount of tweaking will yield a perfect instrument.

Loath to concede that graduation testing is inevitably flawed, proponents try to placate critics with one "refinement" after another. They soften sanctions, adjust passing scores, offer exemptions, fiddle with school performance targets, delay implementation, and take other similar steps as they seek to discover just the right balance. Unfortunately, the painless, happy medium is fundamentally at odds with the purpose of coercive accountability. This series of compromises may preserve the facade of accountability but will eventually strip accountability of its power.

The Importance of Being Mean

The challenge for proponents of coercive accountability is to acknowledge the localized pain and dislocation that they intend to visit upon some educators and students as the price of a system that will ensure that educators are serving all of our nation's students. The challenge for those enamored of nice accountability is to explain how they plan to ensure that schools prepare all students for their adult lives. Although their caveats about inequalities in home environments and natural student abilities have merit, surely it is not overly ambitious to demand that educators find a way to teach all students the essentials of reading, writing, math, and the rest of the key disciplines before sending them into the world.

Most accountability programs begin with at least a rhetorical commitment to the transformative ideal. Over time, critics weaken such systems, often while espousing their support for the principle of accountability. These critics trace their opposition to the specifics of existing arrangements, stating that they will support transformative accountability if only . . . it is stripped of its motivating power.

The choice is between an imperfect accountability system and none at all. In the absence of coercive accountability, we have seen how easy it is to graduate ill-equipped students and excuse inadequate school performance—especially among the most disadvantaged students.

In the end, standards are a useful and essential artifice. They and the accountability systems they support must be defended as such.

If accountability finally becomes part of the "grammar of schooling" for parents, voters, and educators, then its performance benchmarks for ensuring that students are learning, teachers are teaching, and schools are serving their public purpose will become accepted practice. State and federal officials now face the question, Will accountability fulfill this potential or become another hollow rite of spring?

References

Bowman, D. H. (2001, April 4). Turf war erupts in Arizona over delaying graduation test. *Education Week,* p. 21.

Holcombe, S. B. (2002). High stakes: School leaders weigh in on testing, reform, and the goal of educating every American child. *Ed. Magazine, 46*(1), 20.

National Center for Education Statistics. (2003). *The nation's report card: Reading 2002.* Washington, DC: Author.

Public Agenda. (2000). *Questionnaire and fall survey results: National poll of parents of public school students.* New York: Author.

Steinberg, J. (2000, Dec. 22). Student failure causes states to retool testing programs. *New York Times,* p. A1.

Author's note: Andrew Kelly and Brett Friedman contributed to this article.

Postnote

Critics of American education, and to some degree, American child-raising methods, claim that we have become "child-centered" to an extreme. They believe that we have gone to great efforts to relieve children of the serious work demands and stresses that historically have been a part of childhood. Beyond meeting their needs for food and shelter, we tend to lavish them with much free time and with many luxuries to fill that time. We are more concerned with their self-esteem than with their characters and good habits. These critics point, in particular, at our schools, which they believe are strikingly ineffective, compared with the schools of our international allies and trading partners. We have, in effect, a "soft" school system and we produce a rather "soft product."

The author of this article puts the blame on our schools' reward-and-punishment system, opining that we "suggest" reforms, and "suggest" changes in the behaviors of students and teachers, but that these suggestions are not backed up with real consequences. As a result (and in accord with human nature), reforms serve cosmetic purposes and very minimal real change takes place. The article suggests that, if this thesis is correct, our graduates are pouring out of our schools unprepared for the "mean, cruel world."

Discussion Questions

1. Do you think it is fair or reasonable to expect an educational system to have a coercive accountability system similar to the ones in the business world? Why or why not?
2. Do you believe the basic critique (that is, that schools operate according to suggestive accountability) is accurate? Why or why not?
3. If you were responsible for educational reform, which of these two accountability methods would you adopt? Why?

Accountability: What's Worth Measuring?

MARY ANNE RAYWID

FOCUSQuestion

In what ways has our focus on measurable outcomes and accountability had unanticipated consequences on the quality of education?

TERMS TO NOTE

Accountability

Hidden curriculum

School culture

Standards-based education

I wish the accountability movement that is now so strong had been launched for different reasons. It emerged, of course, from a growing mistrust of public schools and just how well they are serving us. Because that sentiment continues strong and is likely to be with us for some time to come, the press for accountability is likely to remain with us as well.

We can't beat the accountability movement, so we had better join it and try to shape it. Actually, there are things we can do that could turn it into a very positive force. After all, at root, accountability demands an openness on the part of the education system that we've not always seen and are all entitled to expect: information on just how well or how poorly each public school is doing. And what accountability then demands is that something be done about those schools that are failing.

I am very sympathetic to both these demands. Regarding the first, surely the public is entitled to know how the schools it pays for are faring. If they are *public* schools, surely information about them should be accessible to all. And regarding the second, there are schools in some places that have been failing for years, with little or nothing being done about it. In what was a new and very different kind of move in 1983, the chancellor of New York City's schools simply closed down a high school that was failing. Its numbers had been steadily worsening each year until finally it was failing, expelling, or otherwise pushing out 93% of its students. Only 7% of those enrolled were graduating. It is unforgivable to let things deteriorate to such a point.

Thus I am receptive to the idea of holding schools accountable and of forcing the failing ones to change. To my mind, accountability is a good thing. But the word is often used interchangeably with standards-based education, and they are not quite the same thing. For reasons

---

Mary Anne Raywid is professor emerita of educational administration and policy studies, Hofstra University, Hempstead, New York, and a member of the affiliate graduate faculty at the University of Hawaii, Manoa. This article is adapted from a speech to a conference on assessment, sponsored by the Hawaii Charter School Resources Center, May 2001. "Accountability: What's Worth Measuring?" by Mary Anne Raywid, *Phi Delta Kappan,* February 2002. Reprinted by permission.

that I hope will become clear, I think we ought to talk in terms of—and insist on—*accountability* rather than *standards-based education.* Doing so is by no means an abandonment of standards, but rather a broadening of concern.

The hard questions begin with "Accountable for what?" It seems reasonable to expect schools to do what they set out to do and thus to hold them accountable for fulfilling their own goals. This means that some school-to-school differences in accountability make sense, given the differences among us as to the goals to be sought in our schools. But there is also a great deal of commonality as to what we want schools to accomplish with our children. It is this that concerns me here: the goals and expectations for schools that I believe we share.

I've put the matter in the form of the question "What's worth measuring?" Of course, what's worth measuring depends on what's worth learning and acquiring and, hence, what's worth teaching and cultivating. What's worth measuring also depends on our expectations about the conditions and circumstances under which this teaching and cultivating ought to occur.

Our Goals for Children

There are really an awful lot of things we want our children to learn and our schools to teach them. We also have a number of different *kinds* of goals that we want to see fulfilled with and for our children, and we have some surrounding expectations that we want to see met. I'm going to present six rather different kinds of things that are worth learning—and thus worth measuring. I don't agree with the psychologist who launched the measurement movement in education by declaring that "whatever exists, exists in some amount and can be measured." He thought everything could be quantified, and I don't. But we can assess without quantifying, and, for me, if we have goals for children and expectations for schools, it's reasonable to try to find out whether they are being met. The short answer to my own question, then, is that whatever we're committed to accomplishing is worth measuring.

First, of course, are the things we call "basic skills"—the ability to read and report accurately on what one has read, to write, and to do elementary calculations. So important are these fundamental skills that they fill a lot of the time for the first three grades of a child's schooling. Much of the teaching that takes place in schools after the first three years calls for the application of these skills, so they really are essential groundwork. Thus it is important that we measure how well a child has learned them.

Second, there are all those pieces of information we want students to pick up: number facts, spelling facts, grammar facts, history facts, biology facts, geography facts, cultural facts, etc. There are lists and lists of these facts, without which you can't be an educated person. You can't even function very well in our society without many of them—like the number facts necessary to determine whether you are being given the right change. Teaching these facts is a perfectly reasonable expectation for schools, it seems to me, even though in some respects facts are really the lowest level of what we want youngsters to learn. They are necessary. But they are only a beginning.

Third, we want learners to be able to do something with all the facts they've learned. There's not much point in having learned the rules of grammar if you can't put together a grammatical sentence. Other applications are even more involved. We want learners to be able to select and retrieve from the information stored in their heads those facts relevant to a given situation, to be able to assemble them, and then to apply them so as to appropriately respond to a challenge or solve a problem.

Fourth, something else that's well worth measuring because it's so very much worth learning is the set of skills involved in using one's mind. We're not born knowing how to do that. And ironically, schools tend to give the most exercise—and hence developmental assistance—along these lines to the ablest students. The youngsters who need the most help in developing such intellectual skills and inclinations as weighing evidence, judging sources, making legitimate inferences, and distinguishing observations from assumptions are the very ones we tend not to bother with such matters. Instead, we focus on getting them to concentrate on those things that can be acquired by rote and drill—the fact-type learnings. But unless all youngsters are helped to acquire the habits of mind involved in sound judgment and good decision-making, they can never be aware of themselves as creatures of intellect, as beings with the ability to take control of their lives and to alter their circumstance if need be. They can thus never be the citizens we want them to be, with the power to realize their own goals while helping to shape society.

Then there's a whole different kind of learning, the fifth type I find to be important, that we want very much for children to acquire. One principal summed it up recently: "Schools are about all those things that make individuals good and bad." We want our children to grow up as caring, empathetic, compassionate human beings with a sense of stewardship for the land and for one another. We also want them to grow up with integrity, initiative, a sense of responsibility, and a sense of humor. Schools really are in the person-shaping business: they can operate in ways that encourage and reinforce the traits and dispositions just mentioned, or they can operate so as to discourage and squelch them. Since these are the attitudes and inclinations that distinguish a good citizen and a good neighbor from a parasite or an assassin, we certainly want schools to instill them and children to acquire them. So this is yet another sort of goal, and we ought to measure progress toward it.

The sixth goal covers a lot of territory: we expect a school to contribute to a child's individual development. It means, for instance, that we want to see school make a difference in a child's cognitive development. Learning those facts and learning what to do with them are important, but we want school to do more than that. We want school to stimulate young minds to grow and expand their capacity. A school that doesn't lead to such growth isn't fulfilling reasonable expectations, and we need a way to find out whether this is the case. In other words, a school loaded with high achievers has got to make them still better learners. If not, there's been no value added, and that's what individual development is about. It's also about helping youngsters to develop whatever may be their particular talents. Whether it's music or writing or leading others or gymnastics, school ought to be a place that helps young people develop their talents.

These, then, are six different goals for learners that I think most of us can agree are important for schools to work toward: learning basic skills, learning facts, learning how to use information, acquiring desirable habits of mind, developing character and other desirable traits, and developing individual talents. But this isn't all. In addition to these goals and expectations for learners, we have certain expectations that apply specifically to schools.

Reasonable Expectations of Schools

First, given that children are required to attend them, it seems reasonable to expect schools to be *effective* in teaching our children. This means we expect them to be successful with their students. We wouldn't accept a doctor's diagnosis of "incurable" without going elsewhere for another opinion, and we shouldn't settle for the diagnosis "uneducable" from a school. In other words, we don't expect schools to say, "Well, if you've got success in mind, you really should be sending us a different batch of kids."

On the contrary, we expect schools to be welcoming, user-friendly places, where all six of those different kinds of goals I named are pursued with all youngsters, where all are treated with respect and compassion, and where all can meet with some degree of success. This is a tall order.

But, as if this weren't enough, we also expect schools to carry out their functions in particular ways. For instance, we don't want any of those goals of ours to be pursued lackadaisically or perfunctorily. It's not enough merely to take a class to a concert; the teacher must demonstrate genuine engagement with the music. If instead, the teachers are grading papers or chatting together while the music plays, that's not modeling much by way of music appreciation.

Similarly in a classroom, if the teacher isn't fully engaged in listening and attending when children speak but is demonstrating what it is to half listen to another person, then it's anybody's guess whether children can take from these experiences the lessons we want them to learn. So just going through the motions in classrooms isn't enough. Activities must be conducted with a quality—an emotional tone—that can be as important as the content. Just how serious are teachers about what they are doing? We don't want them to appear to be in dead earnest all the time—in fact, that would be awful—but we do want them to be focused and trying all the time. This is certainly a central enough dimension of what we want school to be that it is worth measuring.

Another thing we expect from schools is that they teach in such a way that youngsters acquire positive attitudes toward what they are learning. If a teacher manages to convey the essentials of reading but strips all pleasure and delight from doing so, it's a questionable success. If a youngster manages to stumble his way through geometry but acquires a hatred for math in the process, that is also a questionable success. As a famous educational thinker put it many years ago, "It's not that children should do what they want, but it's important that they want what they do." And being able to generate this kind of positive receptivity with respect to learning is a legitimate expectation of schools and teachers. If learning new things is drudgery to be undergone only under duress, we haven't done much toward creating a lifelong learner. And since this is so widely voiced a concern, we surely ought to be making regular checks on how well teachers and schools are dealing with it.

These last several lessons are a part of the school's culture and hence of its "hidden curriculum." This curriculum consists of the messages typically delivered otherwise than directly in words and usually only as an accompaniment to announced purposes and content. Sometimes it is conveyed in the arrangements. For instance, one famous principal insists that sending children to schools that are too large for teachers and administrators to learn their names teaches students that who they are as individuals, what they are experiencing, and how they feel about it are things that don't matter. Sending them to schools where the toilets are broken or the doors to the stalls have been removed also conveys a message about what doesn't matter. In this case, their need for privacy has no importance. It seems reasonable to expect schools to treat both the children required to attend them and the teachers who teach in them with respect. And since this expectation is as reasonable as it is important, it's worth measuring.

So to our six goals we've added five expectations of schools: that they be successful, that they be welcoming and user-friendly places, that teachers be fully engaged in their teaching, that schools cultivate a receptivity to learning, and that the school's unspoken messages—its hidden curriculum—be positive and desirable ones.

Some Notes About Measuring

Just how do we measure success with these goals and expectations? That is a matter that must be left to another time. But I can underscore some things to be kept in mind in seeking an answer to the question. Several things need to be said about the six goals for learners and five expectations of schools stated here. First, all appear reasonable, widely shared, and well worth seeking. This means that all are worth measuring in order to determine whether students and schools are living up to what we want from them.

It is also worth noting that holding schools accountable for meeting our list of school expectations directly implicates a number of people beyond teachers: principals, in particular, and their office staffs, but also librarians and counselors and coaches and cafeteria workers and security guards and custodians. Moreover, another thing our two lists make clear is that the answer to how well students and schools are faring is not going to be accessible simply through a single observation of a school; it takes a lot more than that. This is why ongoing evaluation is absolutely necessary to school accountability. The public can't determine whether its goals and expectations are being met without real evaluation—which must rely not only on what is directly observable but also on a great deal of indirect observation.

Another thing that merits emphasis is that, of our 11 goals and expectations, the standards-based education that many states have embarked on addresses only the first two goals for learners that we identified as widely shared (basic skills and information). The best tests perhaps address a bit of the third goal (ability to use information). That's why I think we ought to talk about "accountability" in preference to "standards-based education." Many people talk as if the standards we've set are sufficient to render the schools accountable, but they certainly won't render them accountable for all our goals and expectations. It's going to take a lot more than a series of tests to do that.

It seems clear that paper-and-pencil tests aren't going to suffice. For half of our goals for students (the fourth through the sixth), we'll need some other measure, just as we will for all five of the expectations for schools. I have several suggestions in this regard. At the outset, we must recognize that there's not going to be any single test for any one of them. We can't afford the bad judgments that reductionist measures are sure to support. Many of us find it absurd to think you can determine how much a youngster knows from a single test score, and the same is true for each of these other goals and expectations. We'll need to have a lot of other data to consider, and we'll have to construct an answer to how well students and schools are faring from weighing a variety of evidence that must first be gathered and then assembled. So don't look for a single measure that will reveal all, and don't settle for any measure that purports to do so. There aren't any. But here are several things you might put together.

First, you might look to what are called "unobtrusive measures" for evidence that can be revealing about both goals and expectations. Such measures don't involve any special test or assignment or activity, but rather the devising of telling questions that can be answered from observations. Actually, a lot of the data we need to gather with respect to our school expectations will provide unobtrusive measures for everybody but the data collector. These measures make no demands on class time. They include such data as the attendance rates in schools and classrooms, the school dropout rate, the number of suspensions and expulsions, retention rates, the extent of teacher turnover. Each of these offers powerful testimony on whether schools are meeting our expectations.

But these are not what school evaluators usually have in mind when they speak of "unobtrusive measures." Here are a couple of the sorts of things they might be more likely to cite. John Goodlad used to say that one measure of how user-friendly first-grade classrooms are is the number of children who vomit before leaving home on school days. Another measure might be how quickly, and with what sorts of facial expressions, children *and* teachers leave school at the end of the day. Or we might look at the incidence of graffiti in and around the building. You can put together a set of such observations that should yield partial answers on some of the school expectations.

Student performance and behavior are other unobtrusive evaluation measures. Our fifth goal for learners, for instance—the development of character and other personal traits—could be measured by how youngsters carry out service-learning activities: how responsible they are, how sincere their efforts are, the degree of integrity and commitment and stewardship they display. The sixth goal for learners—individual development—may best be displayed through exhibitions in which the community is invited at intervals to observe students' artwork, dancing, singing, storytelling, or debating. In judging such performances, we need a set of carefully devised criteria for judging that are to be applied by a review panel consisting of parents and community members, some relevant experts, some teachers, and some fellow students.

Figuring out the measurements and doing the measuring will not be a simple task. But it is one that real accountability requires. If you agree that the goals and expectations I've stated here are both important and desirable, then we must try, despite the difficulty, to arrive at reliable and credible ways to check how well schools are succeeding at them. In this era of extreme accountability, it just might be our only way to keep test scores from deciding everything.

Postnote

The author's ideas of what schools should be about are certainly broader and more inclusive than simple standards-based reform. Besides learning content and how to use the content, she includes such learning goals as acquiring habits of mind—problem solving, making good decisions, judging sources; character development and good citizenship; and individual development of talent. She also expects schools to have certain characteristics, such as offering a welcoming atmosphere and effective teaching, modeling appropriate behavior, and sending good "hidden" messages.

The hidden curriculum mentioned by the author is an important concept. The hidden curriculum usually deals with attitudes, values, beliefs, and behavior—messages the school sends to students and teachers about what is valued. If a teacher consistently interrupts students when they are speaking, that teacher sends a message that students' ideas are not valued. If certain types of students receive favored treatment by teachers, other students receive the message that they are less valued. If a school building is always dirty, those who work and study in it receive the message that they are not valued. If athletes are feted, but scholars are not, messages are sent about what activities are valued. If you teach in or observe in a school, see if you pick up any aspects of its hidden curriculum.

Discussion Questions

1. Do you agree with the author's list of the six kinds of learning that are worth measuring and her five expectations of schools? Would you add any others to her list? What would they be?
2. Can you identify any hidden curriculum messages that your high school consistently sent? If so, what were they?
3. Which of the six learning goals mentioned by the author do you think would be the most difficult to measure? Which would be the easiest?

Putting Money Where It Matters

KAREN HAWLEY MILES

FOCUS Question

There are only so many dollars to spend on education. How should they be spent?

Terms to Note

Accountability

Professional development

Standards-based education

Title I

The focus in the United States on creating accountable, standards-based education is pushing districts and schools to more clearly define their goals and priorities for student learning. Districts and states make headlines with bold proclamations about the importance of academic achievement for all students. But the gap between rhetoric and reality threatens hopes for improvement. While teachers scramble to help students meet more ambitious academic targets, school and district spending patterns and organization structures have changed little in the past three decades (Miles, 1997a). No matter what school leaders and communities say is important, the way schools and districts use their dollars, organize their staff, and structure their time dictates the results.

As public institutions, schools and districts try to do everything for everyone—and do it all without making enemies. New dollars come to schools in small increments over time, usually tied to specific purposes. We add new priorities and programs on top of the old. Instead of restructuring and integrating school and district organizations, we create specialities and departments to meet newly defined needs. Schools and districts now spend significantly more to educate each pupil than ever before (Snyder & Hoffman, 1999). Taking advantage of these resources to meet higher academic standards requires a political will and singleness of purpose that is difficult to sustain in public schools. Such action also demands an attention to organizational and budget details that does not come naturally to many educators and policymakers.

If we hope to meet our seemingly unreachable goals, districts and schools must define priorities for student performance, make choices about how to organize to meet them, and then move the dollars and people to match those commitments. If school leaders give priority to

At the time this article was written, **Karen Hawley Miles** was president of Education Resource Management Strategies in Dallas, Texas. From Karen Hawley Miles, "Putting Money Where It Matters," *Educational Leadership,* September 2001, pp. 53–57. Reprinted by permission. The Association for Supervision and Curriculum Development is a worldwide community of educators advocating sound policies and sharing best practices to achieve the success of each learner. To learn more, visit ASCD at **www.ascd.org.**

improving academic achievement, for example, then the district staff and budget should shift to support that goal. If the district declares that all students will read by 3rd grade, then staff, dollars, and time should support more effective literacy teaching. Districts and schools should expect to give up some long-standing and useful programs to support these choices.

Matching Dollars to Priorities

For the past 10 years, I have helped districts and schools rethink their use of resources to support their reform efforts. In partnership with New American Schools and with support from Pew Charitable Trusts, I have worked with four large urban districts to analyze their district and school spending and then consider ways to reallocate dollars. My colleagues and I have discovered that, in many cases, the dollars needed for reform efforts are there, but they are tied up in existing staff, programs, and practices. We have found that schools need help shifting their use of resources to take advantage of what they already have and that districts often lag behind schools in changing their own spending and organization structures. To support schools in raising student performance, most districts need to realign spending and staffing in at least five ways.

Restructure Salaries to Attract and Retain High-Quality Teachers It is no secret that U.S. teaching salaries lag behind those of other professions. The discrepancy is especially great for two types of teachers needed in schools: high-performing students from top colleges who have many other career options and teachers trained in math and science (Mohrman, Mohrman, & Odden, 1995). The earnings gap grows wider over a teaching career (Conley & Odden, 1995). Maximum teaching salaries fall well below those in other professions, meaning that the most talented individuals sacrifice much higher potential earnings if they remain in teaching. Districts need to reconsider their practice of paying all teachers the same regardless of subject area. In addition, they must find ways to restructure teacher salaries and responsibilities to provide the most talented, productive teachers with the opportunity to earn more competitive salaries during their careers.

Increasing salaries significantly without bankrupting districts means taking a hard look at the way salary dollars are spent. Since the 1920s, virtually all districts have used a salary structure that applies to every teacher regardless of grade or subject. Teachers can move up the salary ladder either by logging more years of teaching or accumulating education credits. Most districts increase salaries far more for experience than they do for education (Miles, 1997b). Boston Public Schools, for example, spent 36 percent of its 1998–99 salary budget to buy years of experience (29 percent) and education credits (7 percent).

For this investment to make sense for students, both teaching experience and accumulated credits would have to be clearly linked to student achievement. But research shows that after the first five years, the quality of teaching does not automatically improve with either course credits or years of teaching (Hanushek, 1994; Murnane, 1996). Experience and coursework have value, but neither is a fail-safe investment without coaching, hard work, and systems that reward and encourage good teaching. Many districts are currently experimenting with increasing teacher salaries on the basis of more direct measures of teaching quality. Most of these plans give bonuses to teachers who meet certain criteria or student performance targets. These extra dollars are nice symbols, but the plans that have the most promise for significantly raising teacher salary levels redirect existing salary dollars even as they seek to add more.

Redirect District Staff and Spending from Compliance Efforts to Provide Schools with Integrated Support and Accountability Using standards to measure school performance changes the role of the district office. If schools do not have to report student performance, schools and districts are only held accountable for whether they do as they are told and keep children safe. As a result, curriculum offices issue guidebooks and sometimes check whether they are used, and districts create departments to monitor whether dollars from each funding source are spent as stipulated.

When schools become accountable for student learning, the district role must shift to helping schools measure student learning and supporting the changes in teaching and organization that best support improvement. Most districts need to focus more on four purposes: defining standards and targets, supporting schools and teachers, creating accountability, and restructuring school organizations.

Supporting these four goals is often possible by reallocating existing resources. In many large districts, the traditional compliance focus has resulted in a structure that spreads resources thinly across many schools and priorities. For example, one district was surprised to find that it devoted nine experts to supervising services across 30 schools. Each expert was responsible for making sure that schools met program requirements in one specific area, such as special education, Title I, bilingual education, literacy, or technology. Because these nine individuals focused on only one issue in multiple schools, they could conduct only superficial reviews of effectiveness, and they certainly couldn't provide support to underperforming schools. Even though the district devoted $24,000 in salaries and benefits to each school, the schools barely felt an impact. Instead, the schools needed deeper, integrated school support in specific areas where improvement was most needed.

Shift More Resources to Teaching Literacy in Grades K–3 Research consistently shows that smaller group sizes matter most in early grades when students learn to read (Wenglinsky, 2001). It also shows that when students don't learn to read by 3rd grade, they continue to fall farther behind in school and are more likely to be assigned to costly special education programs and to drop out of school. Research suggests concrete ways to improve reading achievement:

- Class size reduction in grades pre-K–2 can make an important, lasting difference in student achievement.
- Small reductions in class size make little difference; only when class sizes get down to 15–17 students does achievement increase predictably.
- Even smaller group sizes, including one-on-one instruction, are critical for developing readers, especially those from disadvantaged homes.
- If teachers don't change their classroom practice to take advantage of class size reductions, they can't expect improved student performance.

To incorporate these lessons, both districts and schools need to shift their use of existing resources. U.S. school districts average one teacher for every 17 students—with the ratio much higher in many urban districts—and one adult for every nine students. Yet, elementary school class size averages in the mid-20s (Miles, 1997a; Snyder & Hoffman, 1999). Most districts allocate more staff and dollars per pupil to high schools than to elementary schools.

To focus resources where they matter most, districts need to look first at how much they spend at the elementary school level compared to the high school level. Next, they need to invest to ensure that teachers have access to powerful professional development in teaching literacy. Third, they must actively support school-level changes that shift resources toward literacy instruction.

This active support of school-level changes in the use of resources creates special challenges for districts. For example, many schools have found ways to create small reading groups for part of the day by making group sizes larger at other times of the day. Others have reconsidered the role of each teacher, support person, and instructional aide to ensure that they support the focus on literacy. In some schools, this may mean changing the role of physical education, art, and music teachers or making these class sizes larger. It may mean hiring a highly trained literacy specialist instead of a traditional librarian. And redirecting resources toward literacy will mean integrating bilingual, Title I, and special education teachers more fully into a schoolwide literacy strategy. Schools need help making these shifts, which require changes in district policy, contract language, and staff allocation practices. Districts also need to be prepared to defend school leaders who abandon popular, but outmoded or less important, programs and staff positions to support literacy efforts.

Invest Strategically in Professional Development for Teachers To take advantage of smaller class sizes and to improve literacy instruction, districts need to offer teachers high-quality professional development. The assertion that districts invest only a small percentage of their budgets in professional development has become a cliché among education reformers. Although some districts may need to invest more money, the priority, for many, will be to refocus existing efforts to create more effective professional development and more useful teacher time. Research shows that professional development that responds to school-level student performance priorities, focuses on instruction, and provides coaching for individual teachers and teams over time can have a powerful impact on teacher practice. But professional development doesn't follow this model in most districts. And providing teachers with more professional time and intensive coaching support can seem expensive to districts that use a few traditional workshops as their "training."

In a detailed analysis of four large urban district budgets, we found that districts spend more than they think on professional development (Miles & Hornbeck, 2000). In these four districts, spending on professional development from all sources ranged 2–4 percent of the district budget. These figures are much larger than those districts traditionally report and manage. For example, one district reported $460,000 spent on strategic professional development, but the district actually spent nearly 20 times this amount when professional development efforts by all departments and sources were included. Worse, our analysis showed that professional development spending is often divided among many fragmented, sometimes conflicting, programs managed by different departments. Spending to support improved academic instruction represented only a fraction of total dollars in these districts, and the amount aimed at literacy instruction was even smaller. Harnessing these dollars requires district and school leaders to challenge the status quo and to abandon worthwhile initiatives in order to support more integrated models of professional development.

Reduce Spending on Nonacademic Teaching Staff in Secondary Schools The traditional comprehensive high school often employs more teaching staff in nonacademic subjects than it does in English, math, science, and history. Traditional high schools devote only about half of each student's school day to courses covering academic skills, resulting in more than half the high school resources being aimed at goals that are not measured by the state and district standards. This allocation of resources also means that class sizes for the core subjects are usually 30 students or more, with teachers responsible for a total of more than 125 students.

But changing the balance of staff to make a meaningful difference in student loads and academic time would require some high schools to double the number of academic staff. And shifting more resources toward academic subjects means reducing staff in other areas and challenging the structure—or even the existence—of such cherished programs as band and athletics. Given the number of the changes and their sometimes painful nature, it is unreasonable and impractical to expect principals or school-based decision-making groups to make them on their own. Until districts take steps to change the mix of staff, many high schools will make marginal improvements at best.

Making Choices

Organizing resources to act on urgent priorities, such as teaching all students to read in urban schools, requires leaders to take politically difficult stands. Union, district, and school board leaders need courage and strong community support to say:

- Even though all subjects are important, literacy is most important.
- Even though all teachers are important, those who bring deep subject knowledge and can integrate across disciplines or programs are worth more.
- Even though band, sports, and other electives can be a crucial part of a balanced education, the community must find new ways to pay for and provide them.
- Even though student readiness and social health provide a base for student learning, schools cannot be held accountable for providing all services to students, and they aren't staffed to do so.
- Even though investments in teacher professional development and technology may mean an extra student in your class, we can't build and sustain excellent schools without more of such investments.

Ensuring Adequate Funding

Regardless of overall spending levels, district and community leaders need to articulate priorities and direct spending to support them. But they must also ensure that schools have enough money to begin these tasks. There is no one way to define how much money is enough, but a few test questions can help put district spending in perspective: How does spending per pupil in your district compare to spending in other districts with similar student populations? How do teacher salary levels compare? How does the community's tax rate compare to the tax rates in similar districts?

If the community is underinvesting in education, leaders need to make the case for increased spending. But a community may be more likely to support increases in spending if citizens see that leaders have clear priorities and are willing to make difficult choices to ensure that new dollars get to the heart of improving student achievement.

References

Conley, S., & Odden, A. (1995). Linking teacher compensation to teacher career development: A strategic examination. *Educational Evaluation and Policy Analysis, 17,* 253–269.

Hanushek, E. A. (1994). *Making schools work: Improving performance and controlling costs.* Washington, DC: Brookings Institute.

Miles, K. H. (1997a). Finding the dollars to pay for 21st century schools: Taking advantage of the times. *School Business Affairs, 63*(6), 38–42.

Miles, K. H. (1997b). *Spending more on the edges: Public school spending from 1967 to 1991.* Ann Arbor, MI: UMI Press.

Miles, K. H., & Hornbeck, M. J. (2000). *Reinvesting in teaching: District spending on professional development.* Arlington, VA: New American Schools.

Mohrman, A., Mohrman, S. A., & Odden, A. (1995). Aligning teacher compensation with systemic school reform: Skill-based pay and group-based performance rewards. *Educational Evaluation and Policy Analysis, 18,* 51–71.

Murnane, R. J. (1996). Staffing the nation's schools with skilled teachers. In E. A. Hanushek & D. W. Jorgenson (Eds.), *Improving America's schools: The role of incentives* (pp. 243–260). Washington, DC: National Academy Press.

Snyder, T. D., & Hoffman, C. M. (1999). *Digest of education statistics 1999.* Washington, DC: National Center for Education Statistics, Office of Educational Research and Improvement, U.S. Department of Education.

Wenglinsky, H. (2001, June). The effect of class size on achievement [Memorandum]. Available: **www.ets.org/search97cgi/s97_cgi**

Postnote

Advocates of school choice, including school vouchers and charter schools, often point fingers at the educational bureaucracies in large school districts as a major culprits for student academic failures. These critics argue that these bureaucracies waste money, respond to problems too slowly, and lack accountability.

Rather than just criticizing large school districts, the author works actively with large school systems on how to get "more bang for the buck." The thrust of her recommendations is to invest money in good teachers and their continued professional development. More and more policymakers are coming to the conclusion that high-quality teachers are the essential key to successful educational reform, and school systems must be redesigned to provide the conditions and support that allow teachers to succeed. If school districts make student learning their top priority, then they must surely conclude that teachers need and deserve good working conditions to bring about student academic achievement. Only by investing in good teachers will we achieve the results with students that we seek.

Discussion Questions

1. The author argues that school districts need to reconsider the practice of paying all teachers the same regardless of subject matter. Do you agree with her argument that because highly qualified teachers in certain subject fields (mathematics, special education, for example) are in short supply, their salaries need to be increased in order to attract people to the positions? Why or why not?
2. Do you agree with the author's suggestion that school districts might have to reduce staff or even abandon programs such as band and athletics to focus more on academics? Why or why not?
3. What additional recommendations would you make to ensure that educational dollars are spent wisely by school districts on the most important programs?

Coming Around on School Choice

JOSEPH P. VITERITTI

FOCUS Question

Many of us have opinions about school choice. What evidence would it take to change your mind?

Terms to Note

Accountability
Charter schools
Competency-based testing
Magnet schools
School choice
Vouchers

Want to stir things up at your next meeting of professional educators? Just mention "school choice." Better yet, bring up the topic of vouchers, now referred to as the "V word" even among the most ardent advocates. It is difficult to have a reasoned discussion about vouchers (or choice) without setting off loud voices, angry accusations, and dreadful predictions from both sides. Opponents argue that vouchers will bring about an end to public schools; supporters contend that a lack of adequate choice might well do the same. Surely much is at stake—if not the end of public education, then at least a redefinition of what public education means to parents, students, and educators.

I first heard about vouchers 24 years ago. Fresh out of graduate school, I had taken a job as an aide to the incoming chancellor of the New York City public school system. The idea didn't pack much of a punch then. Our collective response at the time was one of suspicion and wonder. We knew that most of those who supported vouchers were down on public education and committed to an agenda that would divert resources from the public schools. We treated the voucher issue as a distraction from the more immediate problems we had to handle, like balancing a budget in the face of retrenchment, teaching basic skills to 1.1 million students, and dodging the political arrows that inevitably get aimed at school chiefs in large urban centers.

In 1978, the New York City school budget topped $3 billion, the state had just launched a new program of competency-based testing, and political minefields preceded every step the new school chief dared to take. Not much has changed since then except for the budget, which now, with the same number of students, exceeds $12 billion. The State

---

Joseph P. Viteritti holds the Blanche D. Blank Endowed Chair in Public Policy at Hunter College in New York City. He is the author of *Choosing Equality: School Choice, the Constitution, and Civil Society* (Brookings Institution Press, 1999). From Joseph Viteritti, "Coming Around on School Choice," *Educational Leadership,* April 2002, pp. 44–47. Reprinted by permission. The Association for Supervision and Curriculum Development is a worldwide community of educators advocating sound policies and sharing best practices to achieve the success of each learner. To learn more, visit ASCD at **www.ascd.org.**

Education Department is implementing a new competency-based testing program designed to raise academic standards, complemented by local initiatives. Student performance still lags abysmally. Only 22.8 percent of all 8th graders achieved passing grades on the most recent state test in math; in reading the pass rate was 33.1 percent (Goodnough, 2001).

Trying to make sense of the situation after several years of service in the chancellor's office, I wrote in 1983 that the fundamental political dilemma in urban education is a dichotomy between constituents and clients, each with different interests (Viteritti, 1983). On one side of the divide are those influential groups to whom school leaders are politically accountable; on the other are the parents of children whom schools are supposed to serve, who lack the clout to make the system respond to their needs. My initial observation was confirmed in later experiences that I had while working closely with school superintendents in Boston and San Francisco. It remains valid today in big-city school systems across the country. Proponents of school choice believe that it can alter the balance of power between those who govern public schools and those whose children attend them.

A Changing Dialogue

The conversation about choice is evolving. When economist Milton Friedman first proposed vouchers 50 years ago, he condemned public education in the United States as a failure. He argued that competition created by vouchers would force failing schools to close. He predicted that better-run private schools would replace public schools in a marketplace that would have little tolerance for academic failure.

Voucher opponents contended that vouchers would prompt an exodus from public schools, basing their thesis on several incriminating assumptions: that most parents are dissatisfied with public schools, that parents would prefer to send their children to private schools, and that parents send their children to public schools only for lack of a better choice.

Many opponents also predicted that a program of universal vouchers would have a disparate outcome, benefitting more aggressive and better-informed middle-class families who would take advantage of the opportunity, while leaving poor children behind in the worst public schools.

There is some evidence to support such claims, dating back to choice and magnet programs that were created to promote racial integration in the 1980s and 1990s (Fuller & Elmore, 1996). There is also a legal question as to whether providing students with public funding to attend religious schools violates the establishment clause of the First Amendment to the U.S. Constitution. This question should be resolved this spring when the U.S. Supreme Court rules on the constitutionality of the Ohio voucher program. Previous rulings by the Court suggest that it will approve the program, but whether it will do so remains to be seen (Viteritti, 1999).

The Ohio program, which began in 1995, and a similar initiative adopted in Wisconsin in 1990 signal how much the voucher debate has evolved. Rather than provide vouchers for all students, they target low-income students—serving 4,000 in Cleveland and 10,000 in Milwaukee. Another program in Florida targets students who attend chronically failing schools, but only a few dozen students are affected. Broad political coalitions composed of African American parents, white liberals, urban Democrats, and business leaders, as well as market-oriented conservatives and Republicans, supported the laws that brought about these programs.

For such advocates, a voucher is less an instrument for market discipline and more a means for enhancing education opportunity and equity (Viteritti, 1999). They see choice as a way for poor students to escape low-performing, inner-city schools. As they understand it, most middle-class parents in the United States already enjoy choice. Better-off families exercise choice by moving to high-priced communities that have good public schools or by using their own money to pay for tuition at private schools. Public voucher programs designed to aid economically and educationally disadvantaged students help level the playing field.

The Black Alliance for Educational Options, whose chairman of the board is former Milwaukee Superintendent of Schools Howard Fuller, demands choice in the name of social justice. Its logic is hard to refute. National test scores indicate that the average African American 12th grader is four years behind his or her white peer in academic achievement (National Center for Education Statistics, 2001). It is this stubborn learning gap—not public schools—that most contemporary choice advocates want to eliminate.

Most support charter schools—public schools that operate outside the legal jurisdiction of the local school district. Since 1991, 37 states and the District of Columbia have passed charter school laws. With 2,100 such schools in operation, public charter schools represent the bulk of opportunities advanced under the choice banner. When properly designed, charter laws grant school-based personnel the autonomy that they need to operate effectively, free from the usual bureaucratic constraints that hamper professional judgment. In a recent Public Agenda survey, 9 of 10 public school administrators reported that they lacked the managerial discretion to do their jobs properly. By devolving power to the school, charter laws enhance local authority (2001).

Beyond the public voucher and charter school initiatives now in existence, approximately 60,000 poor students around the country receive private tuition scholarships to attend nonpublic schools. Conceived as an abstract idea 50 years ago, choice is now a growing reality. The various programs implemented have provided researchers with a rich empirical base for assessing its merits. The evidence on these programs, although plentiful, remains inconclusive, however (Gill, Timpane, Ross, & Brewer, 2001; Peterson & Campbell, 2001).

Preliminary Evidence

So far, the harrowing predictions of mass evacuations and disparate impact have not materialized. Polls consistently show that parents across the United States have confidence in public schools, evidently much more than choice opponents surmise (Moe, 2001). The exception is found among minority parents living in urban communities, who consistently support choice and vouchers. This perspective puts a different face on the overall condition of U.S. education. Academic failure is not endemic to public education. It can be defined more specifically as an inadequate number of effective urban schools.

Even in urban settings, however, choice has not depleted public school enrollments. With 10,739 students receiving vouchers and 1,559 attending charter schools, Milwaukee offers a wide range of choices to parents; yet, because of a bulging school-age population, enrollment in regular public schools remains stable at 103,500 (Borsuk, 2001). Since 1997, private philanthropists have offered a full tuition scholarship to any student in the Edgewood, Texas, school district who wants to attend a private or parochial school. Yet only 11 percent of the students in this mostly Hispanic, low-performing district outside of San Antonio have taken advantage of the opportunity (McLemore, 2001).

By targeting disadvantaged students, public and private voucher programs have come a long way in assuring that choice is made available to those who need it most. Although charter schools enroll applicants on a first-come, first-served basis or by lottery, considerable evidence indicates that the profile of students attending charter schools is similar to those in nearby public schools (U.S. Department of Education, 2000). Many charter schools have a slight over-subscription of poor and minority students who are highly motivated to seek alternative providers of education services. Some evidence also shows that the poor students who take advantage of vouchers and charter schools have parents who are slightly better educated. But this is a far cry from the kind of middle-class "creaming" (a racially offensive term) predicted by choice opponents. The fact is that choice programs offer opportunities to disadvantaged students that were once available only to the middle class.

Most parents of students in public voucher, private scholarship, and charter school programs indicate that their students are better off for it. When asked, they point to more rigorous academic standards, higher expectations, safer environments, and a sense of community within their new schools as reasons for their satisfaction.

The evidence on academic performance is more mixed. Encouraging evidence suggests that African American students in voucher programs are registering higher gains than their public school peers. For example, research on inner-city Catholic high schools consistently shows that the low-income African American boys who attend them are more likely to graduate and attend college (Evans & Schwab, 1995). The data on Hispanic students are less positive, though.

Evidence on the academic performance of charter schools is also mixed, with some showing impressive results and others not doing as well as neighboring public schools. Some jurisdictions need to impose greater accountability standards on charter schools—and on many of their public schools as well. But if charter schools are to succeed as a viable alternative for under-served students, they must be adequately supported. The average charter school gets approximately 80 percent of the per-pupil funding received by regular public schools. Because of bargains struck between proponents and opponents in the legislative process, charter schools must function at a financial disadvantage.

In Cleveland, for example, per-pupil spending for regular public school students is $7,746, compared with $4,519 for students in charter schools. Each student who participates in the Cleveland voucher program receives $2,250 in public funding. In such cases, the home district of the student exercising choice gets to keep the portion of the funds that would have gone toward the student's education. Defenders of such practices claim that they protect school districts from financial hardship. If students are educated outside the district, however, the district has no justification for retaining the funds. The net result is to penalize the students. These are "opportunity costs" imposed on poor parents who seek to exercise education options similar to those enjoyed by their middle-class counterparts.

Proponents of the market model insist that the competition created by choice will provide underperforming public schools with an incentive to improve. That sounds reasonable enough, but again the evidence is inconclusive. Last year, after a decade of experimentation with choice, the Milwaukee school district failed to meet 14 of the 15 goals that it had set for itself. It is difficult to assess market effects when laws are written to curb competition. When the Wisconsin voucher plan was first enacted, participation was limited by statute to 1 percent of the student population. Most charter school laws impose strict caps on the number of schools allowed, regardless of demand. I believe that if unencumbered choice were allowed, inner-city schools would rise to the occasion and improve, which would be a good reason to support choice. But I could be wrong. Some urban school districts might still resist change and continue to fail. And that would be an even more compelling reason to support choice.

Plan for Success

School choice is not a panacea for the problems of urban schools. But to succeed on any level, school choice must be designed to succeed. It must be targeted to benefit those students with the greatest needs. Vouchers should be restricted to economically disadvantaged students who attend chronically failing schools. As long as the demand for seats in charter schools exceeds the supply, a certain percentage ought to be reserved for students from failing schools. No arbitrary cap should limit the number of students allowed to participate, and funding must be equitable.

Private schools that accept public vouchers should be held accountable to a public authority, just as charter schools are supposed to be. To qualify for public funding, private schools that accept students with vouchers should be required to demonstrate a level of academic proficiency comparable to those set by the states for regular public schools. Likewise, public schools that do not meet such standards should be reconstituted or closed. The real answer to the so-called "creaming" problem is a public policy that enforces a low tolerance for failing schools. That way no child gets left behind.

The fundamental injustice of urban education is that it consigns poor children to schools that most middle-class parents would not consider for their own children. The point was driven home in New York City last year during a hotly contested mayoral election between six major candidates. Despite their differences on issues, the candidates shared two things in common. All but one rejected school vouchers as a way to provide poor students with access to private schools, and all had sent their own children to private schools. This sounds incredible until you discover that the chancellor of schools and all but one member of the city's board of education also had sent their children to private schools. And one could add to the list of private school parents the mayor and the former mayor, the governor and the former governor, and the newly elected U.S. senator. Nearly every member of the political establishment in New York opposes private school vouchers for poor children while refusing to send their own children to public schools. As in other cities, the political and economic elite of New York views public schools as places for other people's children. The establishment provides the public school system with just enough support to keep it going but does not provide the commitment or determination to make it succeed.

Parents whose children get stuck in failing schools are told to be patient. Patience is an easy virtue when you do not need to live with the consequences of an inadequate education. But why is the public school system good enough for some kids and not for others? That position is no longer morally defensible. Indeed, it never was. That is why I have come around on school choice.

References

Borsuk, A. J. (2001, October 24). Choice program tops 10,000. *Milwaukee Sentinal Journal,* p. B1.

Evans, W. N., & Schwab, R. M. (1995). Finishing high school and starting college: Do Catholic schools make a difference? *Quarterly Journal of Economics, 110,* 941–974.

Fuller, B., & Elmore, R. F. (1996). *Who chooses? Who loses?* New York: Teachers College Press.

Gill, B. P., Timpane, P. M., Ross, K. E., & Brewer, D. J. (2001). *Rhetoric versus reality: What we know and what we need to know about vouchers and charter schools.* Santa Monica, CA: RAND.

Goodnough, A. (2001, October 24). Majority of eighth graders again fail statewide tests. *New York Times,* p. D5.

McLemore, D. (2001, November 11). Voucher program in its 4th year; school choice reviews mixed in San Antonio. *Dallas Morning News,* p. A45.

Moe, T. (2001). *Vouchers and the American public.* Washington, DC: Brookings Institution Press.

National Center for Education Statistics. (2001). *NAEP summary data tables.* Washington, DC: U.S. Department of Education.

Peterson, P. E., & Campbell, D. E. (2001). *Charters, vouchers, and public education.* Washington, DC: Brookings Institution Press.

Public Agenda. (2001). *Trying to stay ahead of the game: Superintendents and principals talk about school leadership.* Washington, DC: Author.

U.S. Department of Education. (2000, January). *The state of charter schools 2000: Fourth-year report.* Washington, DC: Author.

Viteritti, J. P. (1983). *Across the river: Politics and education in the city.* New York: Holmes & Meier.

Viteritti, J. P. (1999). *Choosing equality: School choice, the Constitution, and civil society.* Washington, DC: Brookings Institution Press.

Postnote

This thoughtful article examines various forms of school choice, along with the arguments for and against them. Few people object to choice within the public schools through such programs as magnet schools and intra-district enrollment plans. Charter schools, although more controversial, are generally supported by both Democrats and Republicans as a way to encourage school reform, respond to parental demand, and still stay within the public school domain. It is school voucher plans that generate the greatest controversy, primarily by allowing public money to be spent sending children to private and religious schools.

In summer 2002, shortly after this article was published, the U.S. Supreme Court ruled in a 5–4 decision that Cleveland's voucher plan, which empowers parents to redeem tuition vouchers at religious as well as nonreligious private schools, does not violate the constitutional prohibition of "establishment" of religion because government aid goes directly to parents who use it at their discretion. This decision is interpreted as giving a green light to states to implement school voucher plans to assist students attending "failing schools," and we are likely to see more school voucher plans being implemented.

Discussion Questions

1. Considering the various forms of school choice discussed in this article, and others that you may know of, which would you support? Why?
2. What concerns, if any, do you have regarding the issue of school choice?
3. Many other countries (Chile, the Netherlands, France, Australia, for example) already provide public money to send students to religious and private schools. Why do you think the issue is so controversial in the United States?

The False Promise of Vouchers

TIMOTHY McDONALD

FOCUS Question

What is the case against school vouchers?

TERMS TO NOTE

Accountability
Class size
School choice
Voucher

The book of Exodus tells the story of the Israelites who, losing hope as they waited for Moses to return from the mountaintop, began to worship the golden calf. For African Americans, this story provides an important context for one of our greatest challenges—the education of our children.

Too many African Americans live in communities where public schools have been struggling for a long time. Like the Israelites waiting for Moses's return, they fear that they have been abandoned. Now they are being asked to turn their backs on public schools and replace them with a golden calf called vouchers.

So far, the nationwide voucher movement has had little success. Voucher programs and tuition tax credit programs have been defeated in many states, including Maryland, California, Colorado, Washington, and Michigan (Walsh, 2000).

Both white Americans and people of color oppose vouchers. Election exit polls in Michigan and California, the two states that put voucher initiatives to a vote in 2000, found that African Americans and Hispanics had overwhelmingly voted no (People For the American Way Foundation, 2001). Results of a national poll released last fall found that when offered five options for improving education, only 5 percent of African Americans picked vouchers as the best approach. African Americans were much more likely to favor reducing class size (36 percent), improving teacher quality (23 percent), and increasing training for teachers and principals (26 percent) (Zogby International, 2001).

At the time this article was written, **Timothy McDonald** was the chair of the African American Ministers Leadership Council, a project of the People For the American Way Foundation, and pastor of the First Iconium Baptist Church of Atlanta, Georgia. From Timothy McDonald, "The False Promise of Vouchers," *Educational Leadership*, April 2002, pp. 33–37. Reprinted by permission. The Association for Supervision and Curriculum Development is a worldwide community of educators advocating sound policies and sharing best practices to achieve the success of each learner. To learn more, visit ASCD at **www.ascd.org.**

Vouchers Don't Improve Student Achievement

More than a decade after the first publicly funded voucher program began, we have no good evidence that vouchers do a better job of educating students than do public schools. The U.S. General Accounting Office (2001) found little or no difference between the academic achievement of voucher students and that of public school students in Cleveland, Ohio, and Milwaukee, Wisconsin, the two urban school systems with publicly funded voucher programs.

A report released last September compared groups of public school students and voucher students at the beginning of 1st grade and the end of 2nd grade. The public school students' average learning gains over those two years were greater than those of the voucher students in language, reading, and math (Metcalf, 2001).

In a 1998 report, Princeton University researcher Cecilia Rouse compared Milwaukee voucher schools with several of the city's public elementary schools that had reduced class size and provided additional resources in the early grades. The public school students performed as well as the voucher students in math; they significantly outperformed the voucher students in reading.

Vouchers Hurt Public Schools

Vouchers drain tax dollars from public schools and crowd out funding for crucial reforms that can improve public schools.

As much as $27.6 million that could have gone toward class size reduction, dropout prevention, or preschool programs was diverted to vouchers in the first five years of Cleveland's voucher program. Besides the funds for vouchers themselves (a maximum of $2,250 per child), tax dollars went to other expenses such as record keeping and transportation (Oplinger & Willard, 1998). During the voucher program's first year, budgetary pressures forced Cleveland officials to eliminate all-day kindergarten for nonmagnet schools (American Federation of Teachers, 1997).

Last year in Wisconsin, the governor's original budget proposal called for cutting money from the state's successful class size reduction program and spending a similar amount to increase funding for Milwaukee's voucher program (People For the American Way Foundation, 2001). Only a determined grassroots campaign by parents, teachers, and community leaders saved the state's commitment to the class size reduction program, which had demonstrated its effectiveness in narrowing the achievement gap between white and minority students (Molnar, Smith, & Zahorik, 1999, 2000).

Voucher proponents try to downplay public schools' loss of funding, claiming that any loss of per-pupil aid is offset by the money that public schools save because they no longer need to educate voucher students. But per-pupil aid does not only cover an individual student's desk, books, and instructional needs. It also covers the overhead and other fixed costs of operating a public school—teachers, counselors, and other staff; utility costs; maintenance and repairs; and more. Losing a handful of students to vouchers does nothing to change these fixed costs. A financial audit of the Cleveland public schools found that, several years into the voucher program, the public schools were "losing [state aid] without a change in their overall operating costs" (KPMG LLP, 1999, sec. 9, p. 5).

Vouchers Exclude Many Students

Private schools that participate in voucher programs frequently exclude students who have special education needs, disabilities, behavioral problems, poor academic performance, or the wrong religious affiliation. In other words, under voucher programs, the real "choice" belongs to the private schools, not the poor kids.

An investigation by the People For the American Way Foundation into the admissions practices of schools that participated in the Milwaukee voucher program in 1998–99 found that many voucher schools imposed unlawful admission requirements on voucher students, charged them unlawful fees, and discouraged parents of voucher students from exercising their statutory right to opt their children out of religious activities (NAACP-Milwaukee Branch & People For the American Way Foundation, 1999).

Besides the factors that prevent or discourage voucher students from entering many private schools, a considerable number of voucher students leave private schools before they graduate. In its fifth year, the Milwaukee voucher program had a student attrition rate of 28 percent (Wisconsin Department of Public Instruction, 2000; Witte, Sterr, & Thorn, 1995).

Voucher schools' inability or unwillingness to serve a variety of students is not exclusive to Milwaukee. In 1998, a federal survey of private schools in large inner cities found that between 70 and 85 percent of schools would "definitely or probably" *not* want to participate in a voucher program if they were required to accept "students with special needs, such as learning disabilities, limited English proficiency, or low achievement" (U.S. Department of Education, 1998, pp. xi, 51).

Vouchers Go to Many Students Who Don't Need Them

Voucher proponents emphasize the benefits of vouchers for poor families whose children attend public schools. In practice, however, voucher plans direct money to many students who aren't poor or haven't been attending public schools.

Florida's A+ voucher program sets no income caps for students to qualify for vouchers. A study in Ohio found that one in three students participating in the Cleveland program were *already* enrolled in a private school before receiving a voucher (Policy Matters Ohio, 2001). Although the Milwaukee program already serves families that are well above the poverty line, Wisconsin's pro-voucher governor has proposed raising the income caps even higher and permitting families to continue receiving vouchers once they are in the program no matter how high their incomes rise (Legislative Fiscal Bureau, 2001).

Voucher Programs Decrease Accountability

Over the years, public schools have rightly been urged to strengthen their accountability to the public, parents, and taxpayers. Yet, public schools are already much more accountable than the typical voucher school.

Decisions about the governance and operations of private schools eligible for voucher funds are typically made behind closed doors. Voucher schools aren't required to administer state achievement tests to their students. And it has been six years since the last comprehensive evaluation of Milwaukee's voucher schools (People For the American Way Foundation, 2001).

An independent auditor confirmed financial mismanagement of Cleveland's voucher schools and found nearly $2 million in questionable expenses in the first year alone (Petro, 1999). A Wisconsin state audit in 2000 revealed that about 10 percent of Milwaukee voucher schools "had no accreditation, were not seeking accreditation, and administered no standardized tests" (Wisconsin Legislative Audit Bureau, 2000).

Florida's A+ voucher program also fails to hold participating private schools accountable. Public schools receive a letter grade under the program, but private schools are not graded, making it impossible to know whether a student who leaves a "failing" public school is entering a better private school.

Florida's McKay Scholarships provide vouchers for students with disabilities, but state officials do not provide adequate oversight. In one instance, the state continued to send voucher payments to W. J. Redmond Academy even though the school had failed a health inspection, many students' records were incomplete, and Redmond officials had neglected to certify that all voucher students were eligible to receive funds (O'Connor, 2001).

When parents choose to pay to send their children to private schools, they do so knowing that these schools operate in a different way. But when the public is *required* to fund private schools, it's only fair to hold these schools accountable to the public for how they spend money, hire staff, and otherwise operate. Voucher supporters want to have it both ways—to operate with public funds but to ignore a variety of public laws and standards.

We Can Turn Public Schools Around

With nearly 90 percent of all school-age children in the United States attending public schools, we must focus our funding and energy on improving these schools. In the wake of September 11, we have gained a fresh appreciation for public schools and other institutions that instill common values and reflect the diversity and democratic heritage of the United States.

We *can* turn failing public schools around. Many public schools are already showing significant improvement. The Education Trust (2001) recently issued a report identifying 1,320 high-poverty, high-minority public schools in which students were high achievers, "often outperforming predominantly white schools in wealthy communities" (p. 1). Incidentally, more than a dozen high-poverty or high-minority Cleveland public schools were cited in this report. In other words, the public schools that children of color attend can be excellent schools.

Critics complain that turning around a troubled public school takes forever, but experience shows otherwise. The right resources and the right strategies can create positive changes within a matter of months. After-school tutoring and other reforms have been used with success at Rennert Elementary School in Robeson County, North Carolina, for example, where 94 percent of the students qualify for free or reduced-price lunch. Just one year after the school was assigned a state-mandated assistance team to help coordinate improvement strategies, Rennert students' scores in math and reading jumped 10 percent (National Education Association, 2001).

Reducing class size is one strategy that research has proven to make a difference for African American students (Krueger & Whitmore, 2001; Viadero, 1999). Tutorial and other programs that provide extra help are also effective. As Pedro Noguera, an education professor at Harvard, recently observed: "It's not rocket science. In many districts, we know what works and we know what schools need" (Chase, 2001).

So what's the problem? Very often, it's a lack of resources. Class size reduction, tutorial programs, and after-school programs cost money. States must do more to target funding to students who need the most help.

Ohio is one state that has failed to do its homework in this area. From 1991 through 1998, the state appropriated more money for its private schools ($1.1 billion) than it did to refurbish its public schools ($1 billion) (Hawthorne, 1998). Even as Ohio's leaders continue to support voucher funding, they have yet to comply with multiple state supreme court rulings that have struck down Ohio's school funding formula as unconstitutional (Archer, 2000; Sandham, 2002).

Public schools in every city *can* improve—many of them are already improving. Continued progress requires us to keep our eyes on the prize and make our voices and our votes count. We must not allow the false promise of vouchers to distract us from our rightful purpose.

References

American Federation of Teachers. (1997). *The Cleveland voucher program: Who chooses? Who gets chosen? Who pays?* Washington, DC: Author.

Archer, J. (2000, May 17). Ohio high court again overturns finance system. *Education Week*, p. 25.

Chase, R. (2001, November 11). *High hopes for low-performing schools.* Available: **www.nea.org/publiced/chase/bc011111.html**

Education Trust. (2001, December 12). *First-of-its-kind report identifies thousands of high-poverty and high-minority schools across U.S. performing among top schools in their states.* (News release). Washington, DC: Author. Available: **www.edtrust.org/news/12_12_01_dtm.asp**

Hawthorne, M. (1998, March 29). State aid to private schools up: Public districts feel slighted. *Cincinnati Enquirer*, p. A1.

KPMG LLP. (1999, September 9). *Cleveland Scholarship and Tutoring Program: Final management study*. Cleveland, OH: Cleveland Municipal School District.

Krueger, A. B., & Whitmore, D. M. (2001, March). *Would smaller classes help close the black-white achievement gap?* (Working Paper No. 451) Princeton, NJ: Princeton University. Available: **www.irs.princeton.edu/pubs/pdfs/451.pdf**

Legislative Fiscal Bureau. (2001, March). *2001–03 Wisconsin state budget summary of governor's budget recommendations*. Madison: Wisconsin Legislative Audit Bureau.

Metcalf, K. (2001, September). *Education of the Cleveland scholarship program, 1998–2000: Technical report*. Bloomington: Indiana Center for Evaluation, Indiana University.

Molnar, A., Smith, P., & Zahorik, J. (1999, December). *1998–1999 evaluation results of the Student Achievement Guarantee in Education (SAGE) program*. Milwaukee: University of Wisconsin-Milwaukee, Center for Education Research, Analysis, and Innovation.

Molnar, A., Smith, P., & Zahorik, J. (2000, December). *1999–2000 evaluation results of the Student Achievement Guarantee in Education (SAGE) program*. Milwaukee: University of Wisconsin-Milwaukee, Center for Education Research, Analysis, and Innovation.

NAACP-Milwaukee Branch, & People For the American Way Foundation. (1999, August 19). *Milwaukee parental choice program: Violations of statutory requirements*. (Legal complaint filed with Wisconsin Superintendent of Public Instruction).

National Education Association. (2001, January). *Priority schools resource guide*. Washington, DC: Author.

O'Connor, L. (2001, October 14). Control limited in state voucher program. *The South Florida Sun-Sentinel*, p. B1.

Oplinger, D., & Willard, D. J. (1998, March 27). Vouchers costing Ohio. *Akron Beacon Journal*, p. A1.

People For the American Way Foundation. (2000). *Voters affirm commitment to public schools and reject vouchers on November 7*. (Editorial memorandum). Washington, DC: Author. Available: **www.pfaw.org/issues/education/vouchers_lose.pdf**

People For the American Way Foundation. (2001, April). *Punishing success: The governor's proposed education budget in Wisconsin and the SAGE and voucher programs*. Washington, DC: Author.

Petro, J. (1999, January 5). *Petro issues special audit of Cleveland voucher program*. (Press release). Cleveland: Auditor of State, State of Ohio.

Policy Matters Ohio. (2001, September). *Cleveland school vouchers: Where the students come from*. Cleveland, OH: Author.

Rouse, C. E. (1998). Schools and student achievement: More evidence from the Milwaukee parental choice program. *Economic Policy Review*, 7(1): 61–76.

Sandham, J. (2002, January 23). Mediator has tough job in Ohio funding case. *Education Week*, pp. 14, 18.

U.S. Department of Education. (1998). *Barriers, benefits, and costs of using private schools to alleviate overcrowding in public schools*. Final report. Washington, DC: Author.

U.S. General Accounting Office. (2001, August). *School vouchers: Publicly funded programs in Cleveland and Milwaukee*. (GAO-01-914). Washington, DC: Author.

Viadero, D. (1999, May 5). Tenn. class-size study finds long-term benefits. *Education Week*, p. 5.

Walsh, M. (2000, November 15). Voucher initiatives defeated in Calif., Mich. *Education Week*, pp. 14, 18.

Wisconsin Department of Public-Instruction. (2000). *Milwaukee parental school choice program (MPSCP): MPSCP facts and figures for 1999–2000.* Madison: Author. Available: **www.dpi.state.wi.us/dpi/dfm/sms/mpcfnf99.html**

Wisconsin Legislative Audit Bureau. (2000, February). *Audit summary: Milwaukee Parental Choice program.* Madison: Author.

Witte, J. F., Steer, T. D., & Thorn, C. A. (1995). *Fifth-year report: Milwaukee parental choice program.* Madison: University of Wisconsin-Madison.

Zogby International. (2001, May 23–30). Telephone poll of 1,211 adults conducted for the National School Boards Association.

Postnote

This article was published just two months before a U.S. Supreme Court ruling was issued permitting school vouchers to be used for religious education by low-income parents. While this ruling will have a profound effect on the educational landscape, it signifies the end of the first real battle rather than the end of the war. Numerous groups of educators and citizens are gearing up for a long struggle against what they see as a violation of our traditional separation of church and state.

The author of this article, clearly a strong opponent of vouchers, marshals considerable evidence to cast doubt on the social and educational value of voucher programs. But consider two points: First, public tax monies going to religious schools is hardly new in this country. During the colonial era and the early years of this nation, taxes regularly went to support religious schools. Even in the nineteenth and early twentieth centuries, our public schools were, de facto, religious schools. There was regular prayer in school. The Christian Bible and the Ten Commandments were mainstays of a child's education. References to God permeated the school day and school functions, such as assemblies and graduation exercises. In addition, in recent years public tax monies, such as Pell Grants, regularly go to religious colleges and universities. There is nothing new here. Second, there are the real and legitimate desires of taxpaying parents. Consider the parents of a poor urban child who have seen firsthand the deadening effect of a failing public school on their child. While more financially advantaged Americans in this situation can move to communities with better public schools or purchase a private education for their children, these parents cannot. Nothing burns deeper in the heart of parents than to see their child falling behind, losing self-confidence, and facing a dismal future. There is educational policy, but there is also the issue of justice.

Discussion Questions

1. What do you believe are the author's strongest arguments against vouchers?
2. Do you believe the author's contention that more money and energy are needed to turn around failing public schools? Why or why not?
3. If you were the minority parents described in the postnote, what would you want for your child? Why?

Educational Technology

Part Eight

For much of the past decade, schools have emphasized the acquisition of technology hardware as a major objective. By 2005, it was estimated that there was one instructional computer for every 3.8 students in our public schools. Educators have now reached the point where their goal should not be just to acquire technology. Instead, they should ask how technologies should be used to help students reach the higher standards being developed by states and to prepare students for the world they will enter when they leave school.

Although most educators, policymakers, and business leaders believe that technology has the potential to alter dramatically how teachers teach and students learn, there are some who remain skeptical that technology will have a significant impact on education. These skeptics cite as historical evidence the "hype" that accompanied previous technologies, such as television, that failed to deliver on their promises.

It is clear that if computers and other related technologies are to transform educational practice, much time and effort must go into working with teachers. They need to understand the capabilities of technology and to develop the skills necessary to deliver those capabilities. They need to know how to integrate appropriate technologies into the content they teach. If this teacher development does not occur, then the latest educational technology, like some earlier ones, will prove to be a bust.

A Forecast for Schools

MARVIN CETRON AND KIMBERLEY CETRON

FOCUS Question

What role will technology play in educational reform in the years to come?

TERMS TO NOTE

International Baccalaureate program

Multiple intelligence theory

No Child Left Behind Act

Tracking

Education ranks high among the personal and political priorities of most people in the United States. Before considering our goals for education in the coming years, however, we must consider the environment in which schools will operate in the future.

For four decades, Forecasting International has conducted an ongoing study of the forces changing our world. As futurists, we collect all of our data and indicators from unclassified sources. Our computerized data bank, which we continually update, documents more than 3,500 events and trends. We use a variety of techniques, such as trend analysis, trend scanning, scenarios, stages of development, Delphi polls,[1] historic parallels, matrices, and visioning to discern what the future holds in store.

During the past decade, our expectations have proven to be consistently accurate. For instance, we predicted that the economy of the developed world would be more vibrant than most commentators imagined—and so it has been. We forecasted many of the political and social problems that resulted from a changing population. Ninety-five percent of our projections have proven correct.

Futurist research can yield an understanding of societal and economic trends to help schools implement reforms that prepare students

---

Marvin Cetron is founder and president of Forecasting International and serves as a consultant to government agencies, foreign governments, and industry. He is coauthor of *Probable Tomorrows: How Science and Technology Will Transform Our Lives in the Next 20 Years.* **Kimberley Cetron** teaches in the Fairfax County Public Schools. "A Forecast for Schools," by Marvin Cetron and Kimberley Cetron, *Educational Leadership,* December 2003/January 2004, pp. 22–29. Reprinted by permission. The Association for Supervision and Curriculum Development is a worldwide community of educators advocating sound policies and sharing best practices to achieve the success of each learner. To learn more, visit ASCD at **www.ascd.org.**

[1]In a Delphi poll, experts complete a questionnaire designed to elicit their views. The answers from this survey are circulated among the participants and the poll is reported. In the second round of questioning, participants reconsider their original views in light of the opinions of their peers. This typically results in a narrower range of replies and a more solid consensus. The Delphi technique has been used in several thousand studies and generally produces analyses and forecasts that are among the most reliable available.

more effectively for the changing world. Here we discuss four of the many trends that will have enormous impact on all schools. For each trend, we reflect on some of the education reforms that can help forward-thinking schools respond positively.

Trend: Funding Will Become More Limited

The economy of the developed world will continue to grow for at least the next three years. Many signs point to the continued recovery of the U.S. economy, including increases in the gross domestic product, consumer spending, real estate sales, and productivity.

For the longer run, however, the greatest economic threat is the projected deficit in the U.S. federal budget: at least $2 trillion, and up to $4 trillion by some estimates, over the next decade (Congressional Budget Office, 2003). Unless recent tax cuts are rescinded, the federal budget deficit will raise interest rates, slow economic growth, and further reduce federal assistance to state and cities. For public schools, these developments could have serious consequences. For example,

- Virtually all federal mandates in the foreseeable future will be unfunded. The underfunding of the No Child Left Behind Act demonstrates that the U.S. federal government will fail to supply sufficient resources to support even highly touted reforms. Additional unfunded mandates will also affect special education, an area in which change will continue to be regulated with insufficient supporting funds.
- Local taxpayers will have to absorb still more of the education budget as contributions from the state and federal levels continue to decline.
- Current school budget cuts are likely to be followed by further reductions. Already, the cash-strapped public education system is finding it increasingly difficult to maintain even its most important programs.
- The recent extension of performance deadlines under the No Child Left Behind program is only the first of many. Improved performance and smaller budgets are mutually exclusive.
- The pressures on state and local education budgets will make it extremely difficult to build and staff new schools.

How Schools Can Respond

The need to make more creative use of financial resources, combined with the availability of new technologies, makes this an optimal time to get rid of the "edifice complex" and shift as much teaching as possible to the Internet. Granted, different schools have differing available funds and allocate them in widely different ways, making it impossible to generalize. Even so, all schools and school systems can explore and expand on the use of available technology.

For example, students can "attend" some classes over the Internet and gather in a classroom only periodically for social interaction and other functions enhanced by meeting face-to-face. This innovation would dramatically reduce school costs while maintaining high educational performance. Most building budgets would be better invested in computer networks and hardware for students who do not already have their own computers than in new basal texts, which are often outdated by the time they are published.

The best schools are wired learning centers that can tap into information anywhere in the world. Teachers are becoming mentors and catalysts whose job is not to lecture but rather to help students learn to collect, evaluate, analyze, and synthesize information. For computer-literate teachers, much of this can be accomplished online.

Some schools (for example, in Fairfax County, Virginia) are piloting online summer school programs. In Blacksburg, Virginia, the public schools and Virginia Polytechnic Institute have been fully wired for almost 15 years, thereby enabling the town and university to integrate programs to make education and training available online (Cetron, Soriano, & Gayle, 1985).

The state of Maine has shown its commitment to educating students for the 21st century by issuing all middle school students laptop computers. The $37.2 million program, begun in 2002, has expanded this year in spite of the state's $1 billion budget deficit. As Seymour Papert, an expert in artificial intelligence, commented,

> As long as pencil and paper was the only medium, schooling was a static thing. . . . By giving all kids access to a computer, Maine is creating conditions for the development of a radically different way of thinking about education. (cited in Kleiner, 2003, p. 66)

Measures as simple as supporting classrooms from Web sites maintained by individual instructors or providing students with an online forum for writing revision provide excellent starting points for schools just beginning to explore the uses of technology for delivering instruction in the 21st century.

Trend: The Student Population Will Grow and Continue to Become More Diverse

Population projections show that the number of school-age children will be significantly higher than planners anticipated for much of the next two decades (U.S. Census Bureau, 2002). Between 1997 and 2007, at least 6,000 new schools and 190,000 new teachers will be needed in the United States (Jackson, 2002). This number could grow unexpectedly, just as the population is doing.

At the same time, the demographic makeup of the population is changing. Current minority groups will account for an ever larger part of the U.S. population.

Ten years from now, many school districts will have enrollments that are dramatically different from what they are now, with the largest growth occurring in the Hispanic population. Consider the following projections (Olson, 2000):

- Today, about 65 percent of school-age children are non-Hispanic whites. That figure is expected to drop to 56 percent by 2020 and to under 50 percent by 2040.
- Between 1999 and 2010, Hispanics will account for 43 percent of U.S. population growth. This Hispanic school-age population is predicted to increase by approximately 60 percent in the next 20 years. By 2025, nearly one in four school-age children will be Hispanic.
- The school-age Asian and Pacific Islander population is expected to increase from 4 percent in 2000 to 6.6 percent in 2025. African American and Native American school-age populations are predicted to remain relatively stable.

The growing racial and ethnic minority population will present continuing challenges for education. Schools will need to find new strategies to overcome longstanding achievement gaps and educate all students, including those in groups that have traditionally been considered difficult to educate. A continuing shortage of qualified teachers—particularly in special education and teaching English to speakers of other languages—will complicate this challenge.

How Schools Can Respond

To meet this challenge, educators need to focus on finding creative strategies to serve the learning needs of all students. Their task may be even more difficult because of the recent movement to reduce or eliminate tracking. Simply creating heterogeneous learning groups does not address the needs of individual learners. "One for all, all for one" learning and "teaching to the middle" create the risk that the fastest learners will be perpetually bored, while the slowest will continue to struggle. When teachers deliver instruction to one group, the other is inevitably lost.

Individualizing instruction is more sophisticated, more effective, and, with proper training and implementation, no more labor-intensive. All students learn the same material, but students arrive at the same goal by taking different routes. Student-centered instruction rooted in student choice and collaborative learning provides intrinsic motivation to learn and prepares students for the real-world application of their learning.

Elementary education allows for individualized instruction in ways that higher education rarely does. All content areas are taught by one teacher—ideally, in an interdisciplinary fashion—and the school day can be scheduled to best meet individual students' needs. With regular diagnostic assessments of student skills, teachers can provide instruction in fluid ability groups that they can adjust frequently during the grading period, semester, or school year. For example, teachers can individualize spelling instruction by noting student errors and then placing students in small groups on the basis of the specific needs that students' errors indicate.

Teachers can individualize mathematics instruction on the basis of aptitudes and learning styles. Students who work sequentially, employ linear reasoning, or grasp concepts in terms of numerals and symbols (through pencil-and-paper tasks) can work separately from those who employ more abstract, nonlinear, and kinesthetic reasoning and who tend to solve problems through concrete operations (manipulatives). Education centers in the classroom can provide both enrichment and remediation, with portions of the school day allocated to self-directed exploration of curricular content.

At the secondary level, the International Baccalaureate (IB) program does an exemplary job of offering students a voice in their own learning by embedding choice, collaboration, and performance assessment into each stage of a student's development. IB students spend 9th and 10th grade learning to become their own advocates, developing an appetite for intellectual inquiry and exchange and exploring the academic world in an interdisciplinary and global capacity. Students in 10th and 11th grade explore epistemology, ethics, issues in current affairs, and academic topics in ways that are alternately self-reflective and outward-focused while building knowledge and skills liberal enough to provide context and specific enough to provide ownership in their learning.

Educators at every age level can design alternative assessments (to objective or subjective testing instruments) that allow students to choose how to display their knowledge and skills in a highly personalized manner. Teachers often remark that they gain more insight into student learning from projects such as these than from traditional papers and tests. The best alternative assessments allow students to choose from among a variety of intelligences. Gardner's theory of multiple intelligences (2000) identifies nine ways in which we all make meaning and communicate our understanding to others: interpersonal, intrapersonal, linguistic, logical-mathematical, bodily-kinesthetic, musical, spatial, existentialist, and naturalist. Students can combine approaches to exhibit their evolving understanding of a particular subject.

Individualizing education also means providing the full range of resources to every student who needs the help of high-intensity summer classes, tutoring, remedial classes after hours, and English as a second language. This ideal has yet to be realized, but it remains an attainable goal during the early decades of the 21st century (Cetron & Cetron, 1999).

Trend: Technology Will Continue to Transform the Workplace

Advances in technology, especially computers and the Internet, are speeding up the pace of change. Half of the cutting-edge science and technology content that college students learn in their freshman year will be obsolete, revised, or taken for granted by their senior year. Roughly 80 percent of all scientists, engineers, and physicians who have ever lived are alive today—and are actively trading ideas in real time on the Internet (Cetron & Davies, 2003).

Technology will transform the future workplace of today's students. For a good career in almost any field, computer competence is becoming mandatory. Even entry-level jobs and formerly unskilled positions require a growing level of education.

In all fields, new technologies are replacing what was recently cutting-edge at an ever faster rate. New technologies often require more education and training. They also provide endless new opportunities to create new businesses and jobs. Corporations already recognize this need and have begun to provide time and compensation for training, considering it an investment rather than an expense.

How Schools Can Respond

The demand for computer and Internet training—especially at the middle school and high school levels—can only grow. Teachers who are still uncomfortable with computers and related technology can no longer do their jobs effectively. Even those teachers with a higher comfort level need ongoing training to upgrade their skills as technology rapidly advances. Schools need to provide time and money to enable faculties to upgrade their skills and knowledge. They should consider this training as an investment that helps recruit and retain the best educators.

Fortunately, the current generation of beginning teachers can cope with computers and related hardware with an ease and comfort level that their veteran colleagues can only envy. Their familiarity with technology should help reduce the problems of high-tech education in the years to come.

The transformation of the workplace also calls for a new kind of high-tech vocational education that can prepare tomorrow's medical technicians, computer programmers, and other technology specialists. Unfortunately, only about 30 percent of today's high school graduates go on to college (U.S. Census Bureau, 2002). Among the young people who enter the work force directly after high school graduation or who drop out before graduating, few have the skills to earn a good living in a high-tech economy.

The Fairfax County, Virginia, Academy program is a model for schools that wish to graduate students who are qualified to enter or apprentice in the specialized work force and maintain the infrastructure that business and service industries require. Through this program, students attend academic classes for part of the school day and travel to other county schools that specialize in a broad range of professional fields (computer science, communications, auto technology) to gain professional skills and often certification (Cetron & Cetron, 1999).

Unfortunately, in any shape or form, high-tech vocational education is another crucial educational resource that today's draconian budget cuts block or endanger.

Schools may need to form partnerships with industry leaders to establish high-tech vocational education programs at the local level—programs that would train students to meet these companies' professional standards for computer technicians and software specialists.

Trend: Tomorrow's Citizens Will Need and Expect to Engage in Lifelong Learning

A career used to last for life. Once a carpenter, always a carpenter; once a chemist, always a chemist. Today, new technology could redefine or replace almost anyone's job—even the industry in which they work. Today's students will pursue an average of five entirely different occupations during their working lives. Both management and employees must get used to the idea of lifelong learning, which is becoming a significant part of working life at all levels.

Automation, international competition, and other fundamental changes in the economy are destroying the few remaining well-paid jobs that do not require advanced training. The only way to survive in such an economy is through continual retraining. Public schools will need to provide some of this training after normal school hours. State, local, and private agencies are also likely to play a greater role in training by offering more internships, apprenticeships, pre-employment training, and adult education.

Lifelong learning is also becoming an expectation outside the workplace. Adult education is expanding—not only in response to adults' need to train for new careers, but also because healthy, energetic people need to keep active during retirement. And as current minority and low-income households buy computers and log on to the Internet, groups now disadvantaged will increasingly be able to engage in online education.

How Schools Can Respond

Ironically, as the need for lifelong learning, critical thinking skills, and creative problem solving in society increases, schools may be facing a new breed of student, born of a culture in which people begin building a résumé and working on college qualifications as early as 6th grade. In *Doing School,* Denise Clark Pope (2001) writes that these students often lack the intrinsic motivation to learn, bearing instead the enormous burden of part-time jobs, extracurricular activities, community service, and maintaining competitive test scores and grade point averages. High-stakes testing and similar offshoots of the standards and accountability movement add to the pressure, promoting rote learning of discrete pieces of knowledge instead of student engagement, initiative, and creativity.

To become lifelong learners, today's students will need educators who can skillfully weave choice and relevance into the curriculum so that students experience both pleasure and academic success during their schooling. To support this goal, policymakers should

- Encourage teachers to adopt lifelong learning, both in their subject specialties and in pedagogical practice. Science and technology in particular are experiencing rapid change, and teachers who rely on textbooks for their curriculum guarantee that their lessons will be obsolete.
- Envision schools, libraries, and community centers evolving into general-purpose facilities with Internet access, where students can gather to study online and adults can telecommute to remote jobs, reducing rush-hour traffic. This multifaceted approach would constitute a very efficient use of school facilities.
- Encourage high school seniors to engage in preprofessional, career preparation experiences (such as independent studies, international exchanges, apprenticeships, internships, or certification programs) rather than allowing them to waste valuable time between their acceptance into college and the start of their freshman year.

The demand for lifelong learning marks a sea change in U.S. education. Learning to learn must become the underpinning of all curriculums and must be a requirement of both students and their instructors in all content areas and grade levels.

This trend will also broaden the function of school systems, creating still more demands on their time and resources. Teens uncertain about going to college will train to earn a living. Adults will spend their evenings in class, preparing for their next careers. Teachers will study during nights and weekends to keep their subject knowledge and pedagogy current. Continual learning will become a way of life for all who wish to succeed. For 21st century schools, it will become a new mandate.

Cautious Optimism

These trends and other changes occurring in society and the work force place new demands on U.S. public schools at a time when budget cuts are making it difficult to meet today's basic needs. More challenging years lie ahead.

Yet we are cautiously optimistic about the future of education. In any poll, U.S. voters—the people who must pay for our schools—consistently cite education as the highest priority. Today's experiments in cut-rate, free-market education will not survive any longer than it takes to recognize their failure. If technology brings new challenges for our schools, it also provides a means to make schools more effective.

Ten years from now, teachers and administrators may look back on this decade as one of the most trying periods that U.S. schools have ever experienced. But if educators implement the reforms that the future demands, they will also remember this period as the time when they learned to give all their students an education suited to the modern, high-tech world.

References

Birkerts, S. (1995). *The Gutenberg elegies: The fate of reading in an electronic age.* Winchester, MA: Faber and Faber.

Cetron, M. J., & Cetron, K. (1999, December). An education renaissance. *The School Administrator,* 6–9.

Cetron, M. J., & Davies, O. (2003). *50 trends shaping the future* (special report). Bethesda, MD: World Future Society.

Cetron, M. J., Soriano, B., & Gayle, M. (1985). *Schools of the future: How American business and education can cooperate to save our schools.* New York: McGraw-Hill.

Congressional Budget Office. (2003, August). *The budget and economic outlook: An update.* Washington, DC: Author.

Gardner, H. (2000). *The disciplined mind: Beyond facts and standardized tests, the K–12 education that every child deserves.* New York: Penguin.

Jackson, R. (2002). *The global retirement crisis.* Washington, DC: Center for Strategic and International Studies.

Kleiner, C. (2003, Oct 20). Living in Tech State. *U.S. News and World Report,* 66.

Olson, L. (2000, Sept. 27). School-age "millenniboom" predicted for next 100 years. *Education Week,* 34–35.

Pope, D. C. (2001). *"Doing school": How we are creating a generation of stressed out, materialistic, and miseducated students.* New Haven, CT: Yale University Press.

U.S. Census Bureau. (2002). *Population projections* [Online]. Available: **www.census.gov/population/www/projections/popproj.html**

Postnote

Marvin Cetron is a well-known futurist; that is, someone who looks at current societal trends and makes predictions about the future based on those trends. What he and his coauthor see for education in the United States contains both optimistic and pessimistic elements. On the downside, they see more limited funding for education because of a rising federal budget deficit. To respond to this reduced funding, they believe education must make much greater and more creative use of technology, moving much teaching to the Internet.

What is missing in this analysis is a game plan for *how* to move education in the directions the authors suggest we need to go. Because education in the United States is so diverse, with each state government responsible for education in its state, coordinating and even agreeing on common directions is difficult to achieve. As two well-known educational historians have observed with respect to educational reform, the United States seems to "tinker toward utopia."

Discussion Questions

1. With which aspects of the authors' analyses of trends and school responses do you agree? With which do you disagree? Why?
2. What are the greatest obstacles that you can identify that would impede the educational reforms identified by the authors?
3. What additional societal trends can you identify that you believe will affect education in the future?

CLASSIC

The Mad Dash to Compute

JANE M. HEALY

FOCUS Question

Does technology hold the promise to transform teaching and learning processes, or are its benefits oversold to the general public and educators alike?

TERM TO NOTE

Simulation

"I feel as if we're being swept down this enormous river—we don't know where we're going or why, but we're caught in the current. I think we should stop and take a look before it's too late."

This comment about the use of technology in schools was voiced plaintively by an assistant superintendent from Long Island, N.Y. It was typical of many I collected recently in a three-year investigation of our heavily hyped technological revolution.

Having started this saga as a wide-eyed advocate for educational computing, I now must admit that the school official was right. New technologies hold enormous potential for education, but before any more money is wasted, we must pause and ask some pointed questions that have been bypassed in today's climate of competitive technophilia ("My district's hard drives are bigger than yours!").

Educators, who are seen as one of the ripest growth markets in hardware, software and Internet sales, have been carefully targeted by an industry that understandably wants to convince us that its products will solve all our problems. (Did you ever previously see multiple double-page ads in *Education Week* for any educational product? Have you been offered "free" equipment—that eventually demands as much upkeep and fiscal lifeblood as the man-eating plant in "Little Shop of Horrors"?) The advertising's thrust to both educators and parents is that you should invest in as much technology as early as possible or students will be left hopelessly behind. The parents, failing to appreciate the nonsense inherent in this assumption, in turn put additional pressure on schools to "get with the program."

As educators, we should have the wit to evaluate these pressures, resist public opinion and shun manipulative marketing. It also becomes our obligation to interpret to the public what we know is really good for kids. Yet three major issues are being largely overlooked as we rush to capture the trend. I will call them (1) trade-offs, (2) developmental questions and (3) winners in the long run.

Jane M. Healy is an educational psychologist and author of *Endangered Minds, Your Child's Growing Mind and Failure to Connect: How Computers Affect Our Children's Minds for Better and Worse.* Reprinted with permission from the April 1999 issue of *The School Administrator* magazine.

The Trade-Offs

During my recent research, which involved visits to dozens of elementary and secondary schools across the United States, I was invited to observe the flagship elementary school of a district that prides itself on the scope of its technology budget. Yet I had difficulty finding students using computers. Many expensive machines were sitting idle (and becoming increasingly obsolete) in classrooms where teachers have not learned to incorporate them into daily lessons. ("When they break, I just don't get them repaired," one 1st-grade teacher confided.)

Finally, in the computer lab, I found 32 5th-grade students lined up at two rows of machines and confronted the following scenario: The technology coordinator—technologically adept but with virtually no background in either teaching or curriculum development—explains that this group comes four times a week to practice reading and math skills. Many students are below grade level in basic skills.

I randomly select a position behind Raoul, who was using a math software program. The director, now occupied in fixing a computer that eager young fingers have crashed, hastily reminds the students to enter the program at the correct level for their ability, but I begin to suspect something is amiss when Raoul effortlessly solves a few simple addition problems and then happily accepts his reward—a series of smash-and-blast games in which he manages to demolish a sizeable number of aliens before he is electronically corralled into another series of computations. Groaning slightly, he quickly solves these problems and segues expertly into the next space battle.

By the time I move on, Raoul has spent many more minutes zapping aliens than he has in doing math. My teacher's soul cringes at the thought of important learning time squandered. I also wonder if what we are really teaching Raoul is that he should choose easy problems so he can play longer or that the only reason to use his brain even slightly is to be granted—by an automaton over which he has no personal control—some mindless fun as a reward. I wonder who selected this software or if any overall plan dictates the implementation of this expensive gadgetry.

Moreover, this computer lab, like so many others, has been morphed from a music room. In this school system, cutbacks in arts, physical education and even textbooks are used to beef up technology budgets.

The trade-offs inherent in this all-too-typical situation should be troubling to all of us:

- *Haste and pressure for electronic glitz.* These should not replace a carefully designed plan based on sound educational practice. Grafting technology onto schools without good curriculum or excellent teaching guarantees failure. First things first.
- *Money on hardware, software and networks instead of essential teacher education.* Informed estimates suggest it takes five years of ongoing in-service training before teachers can fully integrate computer uses into lesson plans. They must also have solid technical support so that instructional time is not spent repairing machines.
- *Technology coordinators without adequate preparation in education.* Rather, the key instructional decisions should be made by teachers who are adept in linking computer use to significant aspects of curriculum. "The 3rd-graders made T-shirts in computer lab today," one techie boasted during one of my school visits. "Why?" I asked. "Well, we can—and besides, the kids just loved it." If this sort of justification prevails in your schools, don't be surprised if your test scores start to drop!
- *Cuts in vital areas used to finance technology purchases.* Computers, which have as yet demonstrated questionable effects on student learning, must not be bought at the expense of proven staples of mental development, such as art, music, drama, debate, physical education, text literacy, manipulatives and hands-on learning aids. One teacher in a Western state told me her district "could be

IBM for all the technology we have," yet she was refused money to purchase a set of paperback literature books for her classroom. Why? "The money had all been spent on the machines," she sighed.

- *Pie-in-the-sky assumptions.* Don't be misled by claims that computers, instead of proven interventions, will remediate basic skills. Many of today's youngsters need solid, hands-on remediation in reading and math delivered by teachers trained in established programs such as Reading Recovery. Don't forget that those "proven studies" about the impact of electronic learning systems and their cost effectiveness were financed by people with products to sell.
- *Installing computers instead of reducing class size.* To my surprise, I found that good technology use is actually more teacher intensive than traditional instruction and works best with smaller classes! Research also is beginning to show the skill/drill software that manages learning for large groups actually may limit students' achievement once the novelty wears off. We need good, objective long-range data before committing money and growing minds to such programs.
- *Funding electronic glitz instead of quality early childhood programs.* Again, we must weigh a large expense of unproven value against proven upstream prevention of academic and social problems. Ironically, estimated costs for connecting all classrooms to the Internet also could provide every child with an adequate preschool program.
- *Time wasted vs. productive learning.* Without good planning and supervision, youngsters tend to use even the best educational programs for mindless fun rather than meaningful learning. Moreover, if you do not have a district policy on selecting software, implement one today. Poorly selected "edutainment" and drill-and-practice programs actually can depress academic gains, whereas well-implemented simulations and conceptually driven programs may improve learning—if a good teacher is in charge.

Engaged Learning

Consider a different scenario that I observed at a middle school in a suburban school district. A small group of 12-year-olds eagerly surround a computer terminal but don't complain about the slightly fuzzy image. They are too busy following the action on the screen where a disheveled-looking young man in bicycling clothes stands in a jungle talking earnestly with someone in a bush jacket who appears to be a scientist.

One of the students giggles, pokes another and attempts a whispered comment, but he is rapidly silenced. "Shush, Damon. Don't be such a jerk. We can't hear!" hisses his neighbor.

What has inspired such serious academic purpose among these kids? They and their teacher are involved in directing (along with others around the globe) a three-month bicycle expedition, manned by a team of cyclists and scientists, through the jungles of Central America in search of lost Mayan civilizations. At the moment, they are debating the possibility of sending the team through a difficult, untravelled jungle track to a special site. How fast can they ride? How far? What obstacles will they encounter? What are the odds of success? What plans must be made?

Like others in a new breed of simulations, this activity uses on-line and satellite phone communications to establish real-time links between students around the world and the adventurers. Because students' votes actually determine the course of the journey, they must problem-solve right along with the scientists. To acquire the necessary knowledge, the class also has plunged into a variety of real-life, hands-on learning: history, archaeology, visual arts, math (e.g., Mayans calculated in base 20), science of flora and fauna, Mayan poetry, building a miniature rain forest, reading the daily journals of the adventurers, researching, developing theories and debating about why the civilization collapsed.

This example is only one of many powerful supplements to a well-planned curriculum. New technologies can be used wisely—or they can be a costly impediment to educational quality. As you debate the trade-offs of your technology choices, you might keep these questions in mind:

1. What can this particular technology do that cannot be accomplished by other less expensive or more proven methods?
2. What will we gain—and what will we lose?
3. How can we sell wise educational decisions to a public foolishly buying thc message that computers are a magic bullet for education?

Developmental Questions

A question too rarely considered is what effect extended computer use will have on children's developing bodies and brains. Moreover, it is imperative to ask at what age this technology should really be introduced. My observations have convinced me that normally developing children under age seven are better off without today's computers and software. Technology funds should be first allocated to middle and high schools where computer-assisted learning is much more effective and age-appropriate.

- *Physical effects:* Too little is known about technology's physical effects on digitized youngsters, but troubling evidence of problems resulting from computer use include: vision (e.g., nearsightedness), postural and orthopedic complaints (e.g., neck and back problems; carpal tunnel syndrome), the controversial effects of electromagnetic radiation emitted from the backs and sides of machines and even the rare possibility of seizures triggered by some types of visual displays. Administrators should be on top of this.

  Nonetheless, I found a woeful disregard in schools of even the basic safety rules mandated for the adult workplace. Clear guidelines exist, and before you consign all your 3rd-graders to laptops you would be wise to check the suggestions out.

- *Brain effects:* In terms of what happens to children's cognitive, social and emotional development as a function of computer use, even less is known. The brain is significantly influenced by whatever media we choose for education, and poor choices now may well result in poor thinkers in the next generation.

In my book, *Failure to Connect,* I trace the course of brain development with technology use in mind, and one thing is clear. Computers can either help or hurt the process. For younger children, too much electronic stimulation can become addictive, replacing important experiences during critical periods of development: physical exploration, imaginative play, language, socialization and quiet time for developing attention and inner motivation. For children of any age, improper software choices can disrupt language development, attention, social skills and motivation to use the mind in effortful ways. (The next time you see a classroom of students motivated by computer use, be sure to question whether they are motivated to think and learn—or simply to play with the machines.)

By mid-elementary school, students can start to capitalize on the multimedia and abstract-symbolic capabilities of computers—if an effective teacher is present to guide the learning. For middle and high school students, new technologies can make difficult concepts (e.g., ratio, velocity) more accessible and provide new windows into visual reasoning, creativity and the challenges of research. Yet the first step must still be the filtering process: What is worthwhile in support of the curriculum, and what is merely flashy? Districts that take this job seriously and gear computer use to students' developmental needs are beginning to show real benefits from technology use.

Winners in the Long Run

"Kids need computers to prepare them for the future."

Like so many advertising slogans, this one bears closer examination. First, learning to use a computer today is a poor guarantee of a student's future, since workplace equipment will have changed dramatically for all but our oldest students. Moreover, because so much current use is harming rather than helping students' brain power and learning habits, the computer "have-nots" today actually may end up as the "haves" when future success is parcelled out.

But even more important is the question of what skills will really prepare today's students for the future. Surely the next decades will be ones of rapid change where old answers don't always work, where employers demand communication and human relations skills as well as the ability to think incisively and imagine creative solutions to unforeseen problems. Many of today's computer applications offer poor preparation for such abilities.

One skill of critical importance in a technological future is symbolic analysis, with reading and writing the common entry point. Yet while cyberspace may be filled with words, "a growing portion of the American population will not be able to use, understand or benefit from those words," contend Daniel Burstein and David Kline in their book, *Road Warriors*. "Some of these people may be digitally literate, in that they feel at home with joysticks and remote controls and are perfectly capable of absorbing the sights and sounds of multimedia entertainment. But if you are not functionally literate, your chances of getting a significant piece of the cyberspace pie are slim, even if you have access to it."

Our future workers also will need other abstract-symbolic skills. As the creation of wealth moves farther and farther away from raw materials and hands-on labor, successful workers will need to synthesize information, judge abstract numbers and acquire multiple-symbol systems in foreign languages, math or the arts; they will also need a familiarity with new digital languages and images. As software improves, computers will doubtless help with such preparation, but the key will continue to lie in the quality of the teachers who plan, mediate and interpret a thoughtful curriculum.

The future also will favor those who have learned how to learn, who can respond flexibly and creatively to challenges and master new skills. At the moment, the computer is a shallow and pedantic companion for such a journey. We should think long and carefully about whether our purpose is to be trendy or to prepare students to be intelligent, reasoning human beings whose skills extend far beyond droid-like button clicking.

If we ourselves cannot think critically about the hard sell vs. the real business of schooling, we can hardly expect our students to do so.

Postnote

Jane Healy is a deep thinker on the topic of educational technology and its effect on children's learning, earning her article a spot among our Classic selections. In this article, she raises a number of valuable points concerning education's embrace of technology. Two points seem particularly significant: teacher education and trade-offs. Citing research that indicates teachers need five years of in-service training before they can successfully integrate technology into the curriculum, Healy deplores the vast expenditure on hardware and software without concomitant spending on teacher training. The second important point revolves around the question of how else the money might be spent. What are schools not doing in order to buy technology? These are good issues worth thinking about.

Discussion Questions

1. What arguments would you state to counter Healy's concerns?
2. In your opinion, is the technology emphasis in schools here to stay or just a fad? Why do you think so?
3. Do you think there is an appropriate age at which to introduce children to computers? How would you address Healy's concern about the potential physical effects of using technology at too young an age?

Technology and the Culture of Learning

PAUL GOW

FOCUS Question

Do the benefits of technology outweigh the drawbacks in the educational process?

TERM TO NOTE

Acceptable use policy

Ruminating on recent conversations with leading technology developers, *M.I.T. Technology Review* editor Robert Buderi came to a stark conclusion: "[D]espite being at the forefront of technology, nobody cites technology as a tool for thinking better." Considering the source, this observation should have been enough to vaporize educational technology initiatives from Maine to Hawaii. Whatever else technology was supposed to do in schools, wasn't it supposed to make students think better?

Well, maybe.

Anyone who has followed educational technology knows that many educators, inventors, journalists, and even sci-fi writers have been touting the latest classroom gadget as the gateway to greater student knowledge and/or deeper understanding since at least the era of silent films. But as Larry Cuban has shown in *Teachers and Machines* (1986), educational history in the last hundred years is also littered with the wreckage of "cool tools" designed to make learning and teaching easier and better.

Indeed, it is not hard to find prominent voices expressing caution or even outright dismay about the impact of technology's latest evolution—the digital computer, the Internet, and a raft of chip-based gadgets for communicating, gathering and processing information more readily, and (it is supposed) increasing our output of work. The subtitles of two recent books tell all: Jane M. Healy's *Endangered Minds* (1999) informs us that technology is "Why Our Children Don't Think," and Todd Oppenheimer's *The Flickering Mind* (2003) reveals "The False Promise of Technology in the Classroom and How Learning Can Be Saved." William Pflaum in *The Technology Fix* (2004) and Larry Cuban in *Oversold and Underused* (2001) sum up the least aggressive of the critiques by suggesting that the problem with technology in schools is not that there is too

---

Paul Gow is the academic dean at Beaver Country Day School in Chestnut Hill, Massachusetts. "Technology and the Culture of Learning: How Our Digital Tools Change the Nature of School," by Peter Gow, *Independent School,* Summer 2004, pp. 18–26. Reprinted by permission.

much of it, but rather that students spend too little time using it.

The message from all these worriers is clear. Whatever is wrong with education technology, it is very wrong indeed. It comes down to deciding between extremes—demagoguery, or just negligence? Too much, or too little? And what, exactly, was the "promise" of technology in the first place?

Anecdotal evidence suggests that technology-heavy instruction can lead to important improvements in student performance and understanding. "Research" backs up these claims (although the Jeremiahs can cite anecdotes and studies that demonstrate the opposite). For their part, schools generally put faith in the promise of technology. Since the early 1980s, few schools have failed to sink vast quantities of capital into developing technological infrastructure and large amounts of staff time into technology training.

But the question remains: What has been the total impact of technology on the landscape of education and the culture of schools? The answer, it seems to me, flows from three premises. Each premise invites analysis not simply from a practical point of view but from a moral one as well. In all events, we can agree that technology has profoundly changed the way in which "school" happens.

Premise #1. In Spite of Our Best Efforts, Technology Has Succeeded in Breaching All Barriers Between Schools and the World.

Schools, especially independent schools, tend to see themselves as intentional communities, little utopias if you will, that thrive when they have a great amount of control over the influences on their members. The fewer the variables, the more limited the inputs, the more the school's intent can be realized. While this concept does not preclude a school from establishing rich and varied contacts with the world beyond, it does speak to the desirability of being able to manage their extent and nature.

For this reason, it has been a significant issue for schools in the past decade or so that the Internet, while a useful tool for research and learning, is also a playground for those who would exploit, distract, or even physically harm children and adolescents. These are facts of life, and so schools and the vendors who serve them—the educational defense industry—have developed many versions of Hadrian's Wall to keep the electronic barbarians at bay. Firewalls, air-tight acceptable use policies (AUPs), content filters, and a world of tracking and monitoring systems give schools the illusion that they have the capacity to exclude moral threats that travel by wire, or at least to track down and punish incursions.

But technology renders the supposedly secure world of the school simply one more dimension of the external environment, and the internal life of the institution is, regardless of AUPs or filters, open to forces without. We can prohibit instant messaging at school, but firestorms will still break out when malignant home IM-ing inflames the world of children, drawing parents, counselors, and teachers into the blaze. Blogging teenagers, or teachers, can find their anonymity blown and themselves held morally responsible not just for what they might have written but also for how others responded. And even the best filtering software, like the most iron-clad AUP, has loopholes. Risk management in such a world either demands the continual updating of Byzantine (or Machiavellian) preventive stratagems or simply invites schools to give up. The "prudent person" of legal mythology would unplug, turn off, and drop out, but schools cannot do this; instead, we become more vigilant, and more nervous.

In the same vein, 24/7 cell-phone contact between children and families penetrates a time-honored barrier between home and school. Despite the rules at most schools limiting such communication during school hours, students relay information on their school experience to parents in real time, and parents can respond—to the child or to the teacher—just as swiftly. Even as many independent schools are embracing the notion of parents as partners, instant communication based on immediate reaction, rather than dialogue, can stress that relationship. With some schools making assignments and even gradebooks available to parents online, the boundaries between the child working on independence and the parent or guardian learning to let go are at risk. In *Family Matters* (2004), Robert Evans describes a crisis of confidence in American families, and it is at least worth considering that technology might be furthering this crisis by giving insecure parents new and better means for playing out or fueling anxieties about their children's academic experience.

Last but not least, technology has made identity itself a variable rather than a constant. Chatrooms, blogs, and the instant message make it possible for anyone to hide behind an electronic curtain and to manufacture a persona, or personas, suited to the moment. Qualities once thought to be essential to one's being can now be elided, hidden, or changed; age, sex, race, class, ethnicity—all are in play when one chooses to become an e-person. For schools, this means that students—and it must be said, teachers—can experiment with different selves in environments beyond institutional control. Educators strive to develop students' capacities to consider issues from multiple perspectives, and the anonymity granted by technology can free students to find unusual and exciting vantage points. By the same token, however, the masking of identity can enable both the denial of responsibility and the abrogation of empathy.

Although this permeability of the membrane between school and the outside world seems to be all threat, it is not. The downsides discussed above are merely some unintended consequences of the expansion of opportunities for research, for students to connect with resources outside their school, for parents and teachers to engage in communication about children, or even for schools to seek—in a circumspect, protective manner—wider audiences for student work. That school cultures have been evolving in response to concerns does not minimize the degree to which they have also rightly embraced the phenomenal potential of technology.

Premise #2. By Making Many Tasks Much Easier, Technology Has Moved Us Toward Taking on More of Them.

Who among us would trade in our word processors and photocopiers for carbon paper, Corrasable bond, or a Selectric typewriter? Technology's greatest gift has been our enhanced ability to generate, process, and disseminate ideas swiftly and efficiently. Modern-day Luddites will say that more ideas don't necessarily make for better ideas, but fewer ideas don't either. The fact is that word processing, to take the most obvious example, allows students and teachers to produce and polish work with an ease that certainly invites continuous improvement, even if such improvement is not always made. In every aspect of school life, chip-based digital technology has transformed the way we work, and it has reduced many of our essential tasks to automatic functions. This, in turn, frees educators and students to think up more tasks for themselves—an effect that makes some people sputter but which actually results, often enough, in our raising the bar of learning and performance.

In the early 1970s, the digital calculator represented a quantum leap over the slide rule in generating precise numerical answers. In the past few years, Google has become to fact-gathering what the calculator is to arithmetic. PowerPoint, even if it has become the whipping boy of the moment, is a pretty good tool for organizing and displaying certain kinds of information. And no business officer reading this would really want to give up the spreadsheet, no development officer the database. Productivity software even more than operating systems has made Bill Gates the world's richest man.

Automation in schools has had truly amazing effects. As a teacher, I am enabled to write more detailed reports to parents than I could (or at least did) with a ballpoint pen and carbonless paper forms. Ten years ago, we mapped our curriculum using notecards pinned to a bulletin board; software now allows us to generate a comprehensive, linkable, searchable document. My ability to create and then improve teaching materials is a hundred times greater than when I had to rely on cleaning up after my own poor typing before cranking out copies on a spirit duplicator (although I miss the smell). Sitting at my desk, I can easily search out the title of that book that I vaguely remember, track my professional development budget, or paste my school's mission statement into a document for teaching candidates. I am able to communicate with colleagues, parents, and students quickly and reliably using voicemail or e-mail. If I used a Smartboard, or if I worked in an environment where all my students had laptop computers or PDAs (Palms and their ilk), my ability to get things done would be even greater, I am sure.

Some among you are now wondering whether all these things are "worth it." I sometimes wonder myself. As teachers, we have a long and proud tradition of making students perform tasks that we have deemed worthy of sweat, many of which are now (some would say, Alas!) history. Long division, spelling exercises past the fourth grade, drawing graphs, calculating chemical equilibria on paper, and writing high school English essays in longhand come to mind. While we may still make students learn to do these things "by hand," as soon as they have mastered the skill, or the basic idea, we permit them to use technology to apply these skills in the service of learning how to solve more complex problems. Any secondary science teacher will tell you that improved instruments of measurement and calculation allow the teaching of concepts that would not have been covered in the Eisenhower era. And anyone teaching in the humanities knows that the Internet and online subscription databases, even as a supplement to the printed works in the library, allow students to see, and force them to consider or reject, points of view that they might never have encountered in decades past. As teachers, we believe we know what are the fundamentals of our work, and we ought to trust ourselves to know when we are doing this work better with technology and when we are simply doing it, or doing more of it, because technology makes it possible to do so.

It is worth noting, however, that the automation of educational tasks, even when it leads clearly to better experiences for students and teachers, is in itself the most obvious and ubiquitous form of change that educators and schools have experienced in recent years. Elizabeth Sky-McIlvain makes this point emphatically in her online essay, "The Flickering Teacher" (2004), and she suggests that having to make technology-based changes in practice can be a primary factor in driving teachers toward feelings of disorientation and inadequacy—and, ultimately, burnout. Often enough, such changes are thrust upon teachers with little or no evidence that improvement will follow, and, as any number of commentators have pointed out, schools have a tendency to provide too little time or too little support and, in the end, too little follow-through to properly implement such changes. The road to hell, it seems, just may be paved with interesting technology initiatives. If my school decreed that each week I should turn in a spreadsheet of my grades, complete with distribution graphs, I would first wonder why and then I probably would say, like Melville's Bartleby (who was, after all, a human office machine, a copyist), that I would prefer not to. Most of us can identify a Bartleby or two in our schools, and it makes sense to consider the role technological change may have played in creating them. But if I could be shown some clear value in making this change, and if my experience were soon to confirm this, I could perhaps be convinced to comply.

In the end, one is forced to wonder whether the net effect of technology has been to relieve humankind of any burdens at all. But "labor saving devices" have always been about reducing one kind of labor to permit the performance of another that is deemed more valuable. As we gain more complex understandings of how children learn and of the subtleties of good teaching, it should not surprise us that that we respond by setting higher standards of productivity and quality in our students' work and in our own.

Premise #3. Technology Inevitably Carries Us Along Unseen Pathways, and Its Protean Nature Makes It Difficult to Predict or Control.

Thus far, I have considered mainly the uses of technology in school or in relation to schoolwork, but it is also entertaining and even a bit intoxicating to imagine how these things might change even more. Laptops will evolve to tablets, cell phones will turn to wrist or badge communicators (Dick Tracy or Star Trek; take your pick), textbooks will become e-books, and e-mail and Internet communication will take place in a totally wireless world. We can anticipate next year's fads by checking out *Wired* magazine's "Japanese Schoolgirl Watch"—a monthly feature on how technology is transforming teenage culture—and we can follow the serious science press as it considers the possibilities of nanotechnology, a field so new that its educational potential lies largely unconsidered. We need to consider that technologies far outside the realm of education have been known to intrude on the culture of learning, sometimes to a horrifying degree. At the same time that Walt Disney was producing "Our Friend the Atom," for instance, school buildings were being designed to serve as fallout shelters and classroom documentaries whirring on 16-millimeter projectors were showing us how to duck and cover.

More sobering is the thought that technology's next effects on the culture of schools may come as a result of the technological modification of children themselves. The first babies from the era of advertisements in Ivy League college papers calling for brainy, physically perfect egg donors should be entering kindergarten about now, and it is not unlikely that their affluent and ambitious families will consider independent schools. The next step may be genetically engineered superkids, whatever the legal and moral objections to the idea. If such children do appear, they will require, or at least their parents will think they require, some very special educational experiences. How will schools cope with a cohort of genetically modified "gifted" children? Who will teach them? Nancy Kress explores these questions in her dystopic short stories, but it is more than possible that our schools may have to respond in real life.

New technologies have seldom settled upon society in predictable ways, and the computer chip is no exception. As recently as 1978, the promise of technology involved programming classes and whiz kids performing wondrous mathematical feats. Few of us then would have predicted the prevalence of classroom word-processing or foreseen that translation sites in Denmark would facilitate cheating on Spanish homework. Fewer of us would have imagined the degree to which our worlds have been transformed by e-mail, mobile telephones, or the Internet, but we also have to consider the idea that our students can photograph tests with cell phones or hack into our school's administrative software. Our ability to create teaching materials and to give our students access to information is greater than it has ever been, and technology, though it has also led to a proliferation of standardized testing of uncertain value, can also be used to help us measure student learning.

Technology has changed, and will continue to change, the culture of our schools. By far the greatest lesson of the Digital Age so far has been its very unpredictability. Our attempts to control the direction of technological change, with the best will in the world, almost never succeed on our own terms. Equally unavailing are calls simply to declare the whole thing a bust; technology is with us even if we want it to go away. Whether, as M.I.T. author Robert Buderi suggested, technology fails at being "a tool for thinking better" may not actually matter. If it has not made us think better, it has surely done something else. That we do not yet know with clarity what it is does not diminish the effect.

Postnote

Paul Gow seems to be a realist in his thinking about the effects of technology on the culture of schools. Rather than arguing that technology is good or bad, he identifies some of the important ways that it has changed and affected schooling, including both benefits and drawbacks. There is no doubt, as the author states, that technology's greatest gift has been its ability to generate, process, and disseminate ideas quickly and efficiently. With this ability, however, comes the need or temptation to take on more and more tasks and responsibilities, which often complicate rather than simplify our lives.

One of Gow's most important observations is his third premise: "Technology inevitably carries us along unseen pathways, and its protean nature makes it difficult to predict or control." Ten years ago, who would have thought that one could have mobile telephones that would take and transmit pictures? And, who would have thought that this capability might be used to take and transmit compromising pictures of classmates as they dressed—and undressed—in locker rooms? And who would have anticipated the dangers of Internet predators? The unintended consequences of technological innovations force educators to respond and react to both the good and bad features of these outcomes, and it will forever do so.

Discussion Questions

1. What unanticipated consequences of technology development and use have you observed?
2. In what ways have schools yet to take advantage of some of the newer technologies with which you are familiar?
3. What technology skills do you possess that you think will be useful to you as a teacher? What skills do you need to develop?

Part Nine

Diversity and Social Issues

The United States is a nation of great diversity—in races, cultures, religions, languages, and lifestyles. Although these forms of diversity are part of what makes the United States strong, they nevertheless create challenges. The major challenge is how to recognize and respect these forms of diversity while still maintaining a common culture to which each subgroup can feel welcomed and valued. Early in the twentieth century, American schools tried to create a "melting pot," where group differences were boiled away so that only "Americans" survived. Today, the notion of cultural pluralism has replaced the assimilationist perspective, with the metaphor of a "mosaic" or "quilt" replacing that of the melting pot.

The readings in this section of the book address diversity issues such as multicultural education, immigration and languages, gender issues, and inclusion of children with disabilities. Many of these topics are controversial. The viewpoints of both strong proponents and opponents of the various positions are articulated in the articles. As you read the selections, try to sort out your own positions on the issues.

The New Diversity

LAWRENCE HARDY

FOCUS Question

As you read this article, think about what changes might occur in the United States as the Hispanic population of the country grows larger and larger. What are the implications for our educational system?

TERMS TO NOTE

Brown* v. *Board of Education of Topeka

Desegregation

White flight

Legal segregation might be dead, but many metropolitan schools remain overwhelmingly black and poor—a result of years of white flight from central cities and recent court decisions that have accelerated a return to neighborhood schools. At the same time, the burgeoning Hispanic population is finding itself in increasingly segregated schools across the country, particularly in the West.

How we respond to these trends—whether we bridge these divides or retreat into balkanized neighborhoods and schools separated by race, class, and wealth—will in large part determine what type of society we become in the 21st century.

One demographic change in our society is already clear. On June 18, 2003, the Census Bureau marked a milestone in U.S. history: Hispanics had become the largest minority group in this nation of immigrants, surpassing African Americans by some 500,000 people.

At more than 38.8 million, the Hispanic population is growing in states with well-established Hispanic communities—such as Texas, Arizona, and California—and in small towns and rural areas in the South and Midwest, where neighborhoods for years had been predominantly Anglo or a mix of Anglo and African American.

"If you consider that the black-white divide has been the basic social construct in American history for 300 years, this marks a change," Roberto Suro, director of the Pew Hispanic Center told the *Washington Post.* "This is the official reminder that we are moving into new territory."

Fifty years after *Brown,* the education of this growing Hispanic population is arguably the biggest challenge—and the biggest opportunity—facing the public schools. Like African Americans, Hispanics (who can be of any race) are more likely than Anglos to be poor, to live in substandard housing, or to be unemployed. While studies show that Hispanic parents place a high value on education, their children are three times more likely than non-Hispanic whites to drop out of school. The pressures on some of these students, especially the 40 percent who were born

---

Lawrence Hardy is an associate editor of *American School Board Journal.* "The New Diversity," by Lawrence Hardy. Reprinted with permission from American School Board Journal, May 1999.

outside the United States, can be tremendous. As their Anglo peers advance academically, many Hispanic students must struggle to learn English and resist the urge to drop out.

"Our Hispanic students, when they reach high school—it's [hard] getting them to stay," says Lois Hobbs, superintendent of the Indian River School District in Georgetown, Del., where hundreds of Hispanics have moved in recent years to work in the state's poultry industry. "They drop out and go to work and send money home to their families."

"Virtual Apartheid"

The surge in the Hispanic population may be the biggest story in minority education in the post-*Brown* years, but it is by no means the only one. Demographic trends have had a decided impact on African-American students as well, resulting in what many are calling the resegregation of U.S. schools.

After tremendous gains in integration since the 1960s, '70s, and '80s, African Americans' contact with white students has been declining, according to a recent report by the Civil Rights Project at Harvard University. In the South, for example, peak integration occurred in 1988, when 43.5 percent of black students attended majority white schools. By 2001, that number had dropped to 30.2 percent.

Gary Orfield, founding codirector of the Civil Rights Project, says two Supreme Court rulings in particular have helped reverse the gains made since *Brown:* the decision in *Milliken* v. *Bradley* (1974), which struck down a Detroit desegregation plan that involved the city and its largely white suburbs, and the decision in *Dowell* v. *Oklahoma City* (1991), which allowed courts to declare school districts "unitary" if they were deemed to have eliminated the vestiges of dual, and unequal, systems. This designation has enabled school systems to get out from under their court-ordered desegregation plans and return to neighborhood schools.

"The school desegregation orders were making schools substantially more integrated than the Southern neighborhoods," Orfield says. "Now we're reverting back to the neighborhood pattern. So if we don't do anything about the schools, and we don't do anything about the neighborhoods, we're going to have a substantially higher level of segregation than we had traditionally, or over the last 30 years, in the South.

"In the North, we never really desegregated the schools much," he adds. "So we basically have the neighborhood pattern there."

Absent any kind of desegregation remedy, those neighborhood patterns have resulted in "virtual apartheid" in some parts of the country, Orfield says. In the Northeast, for example, more than half of black students attend schools that are 90 to 100 percent nonwhite. In the South, almost one-third of black students go to these overwhelmingly minority schools.

The reverse is true for white students. "Nationally, the typical white student goes to a school that is 79 percent white," says researcher Chungmei Lee, who coauthored the Civil Rights Project report.

The report also noticed that Hispanics are increasingly segregated, particularly in the West, while Asian-Americans remain the most integrated minority.

Race, Poverty, and Housing

School integration is important to students living in an increasingly diverse society and a world that has grown smaller through globalization, Orfield says. Studies show, for example, that integrated schools have a positive impact on cross-racial friendships and the educational aspirations of both whites and African Americans.

On a more concrete level, highly racially identifiable schools and poverty go hand in hand for blacks and Hispanics alike. According to the Civil Rights Project report, "Only 15 percent of . . . intensely segregated white schools were schools of concentrated poverty, or schools with more than half of the students on free or reduced priced lunch. In contrast, 88 percent of the intensely segregated minority schools (or schools with less than 10 percent white) had concentrated poverty, with more than half of all students getting free lunches."

There is some good news. Because of the strong economy in the 1990s, the number of people living in high-poverty neighborhoods decreased by 24 percent, or 2.5 million, from 1990 to 2000, according to a Brookings Institution report. The number of African Americans living in such neighborhoods dropped from almost a third in 1990 to 19 percent in 2000.

"But the Brookings report clearly shows that the favorable trend of the 1990s may be temporary rather than long-term," Harvard professor William Julius Wilson wrote in the *New York Times*. "Unemployment and individual poverty rates are on the rise again; more than 2.4 million jobs have disappeared in the last two years. And given the continuing increase in the Hispanic population, the number of high-poverty barrios is likely to grow rapidly in a sluggish economy."

Indeed, despite the improved economic status of African Americans—and that of most Americans—in the 1990s, housing discrimination persists, says John R. Logan, director of the Lewis Mumford Center for Comparative Urban and Regional Research in Albany, N.Y. "Even middle-class African-American families tend to live in very different and much poorer communities than working-class white families," Logan says. ". . . There is separation based solely on race."

Certainly, choice plays a large part in where African Americans live, he says. But choice doesn't adequately explain these housing patterns. "Among Asians, we believe that choice is a stronger factor" than discrimination in neighborhood location, Logan says. "And among African Americans, it's very much outweighed by discrimination."

White Flight and City Schools

The 50 years since *Brown* have seen another population dynamic as well—the tremendous growth of largely white suburbs. ("Inner-ring" suburbs surrounding large cities have grown increasingly segregated, however.) Some observers contend that this trend has marginalized city residents, the vast majority of them minorities, who have less access to good jobs, adequate housing, and quality schools.

"One year after Rosa Parks made her stand against racial segregation in public transportation, the federal government elected to be the primary funder of a 41,000-mile interstate highway system, a system that would promote suburban expansion and contribute to the divestment of central cities," wrote John A. Powell, former executive director of the Institute on Race and Poverty at the University of Minnesota Law School and now in a similar position at Ohio State University.

Powell says that school desegregation plans "had just begun to prove themselves" when the courts began dismantling them, "declaring the power of local governments in metropolitan regions to be more sacred and important than racial justice in education."

"The blows to civil rights efforts of these and other governmental interventions—in shaping what today are racially and economically imbalanced and inequitable metropolitan regions—cannot be overstated," he wrote in the *Journal of Urban Ecology*.

As a result of white flight and depopulation, many urban districts are getting smaller, poorer, and more segregated. For example, the percentage of white students in the Chicago City Schools dropped from 37 percent in 1968 to less than 10 percent in 2000, according to Mumford Center statistics. In 1968, the St. Louis schools were 35 percent white; by 2000, the district was just 17 percent white, and overall enrollment had dropped by more than half. Similar transformations have occurred in cities like Indianapolis, Pittsburgh, and Philadelphia, to name just a few.

Despite these numbers, some observers are less pessimistic about the results of desegregation than either Orfield or Powell. While acknowledging the reality of segregation in many cities, Logan notes in a recent report that, on average, schools have desegregated substantially since 1968. For his Lewis Mumford Center analysis, Logan used an Index of Dissimilarity, which tells what share of black or white students would have to switch schools to achieve full racial balance.

The index goes from 0—totally integrated—to 100—completely segregated.

"By 1990, average within-district segregation had fallen to below 50" on this index, Logan writes. "Desegregation was widespread, and segregation scores dropped even more in districts without court-mandated plans than in those with plans."

But since 1990, the situation has changed. Although Logan disagrees with Orfield's contention that schools are substantially resegregating, he concludes that desegregation "has stopped in its tracks."

The Next 50 Years

What will the United States look like when we commemorate the 100th anniversary of *Brown?* It is difficult to predict the level of school or neighborhood integration, but demographers have a pretty good idea of what the nation as a whole will resemble. In fact, a model already exists on the border with Mexico.

"I tell people, if you want to see the America your kids or grandkids will live in—that is, about 2040 to '50—all you need to do is look at the demographics of Texas," says Steve Murdock, Texas' state demographer and a sociologist at Texas A&M. "The state of Texas is at about 53 percent non-Hispanic white, and that's what we're projecting for the United States at mid-century." As of the 2000 Census, the nation was 69 percent non-Hispanic white.

For Texas, giving these Hispanic students a sound education is not just important for the children and their families; it is essential to the state's economy as well, Murdock says. As long as Hispanic children are less likely than whites to complete high school or go to college, their earning power will be considerably less. And if lower-income residents are making up an increasingly larger share of the population, state tax revenues will suffer. This trend could be felt earliest, and most severely, in states with large immigrant populations, such as Texas, California, and New York. But eventually, it will affect the entire country, as the United States becomes a "majority minority" nation.

"I think the growth of non-Anglo children is so dominant in many parts of the country that that *is* the issue," Murdock says. "It's not the issue of what happens to these kids compared to other kids who aren't minority. They *are* the kids."

Where does this leave African Americans, the once dominant minority? It may be inevitable that there will be some degree of competition between minority groups for scarce economic—and educational—resources, says Jennifer Hochschild, a professor of government at Harvard.

"No group, historically, has moved over cheerfully for another group," Hochschild says.

On the other hand, to the extent that African Americans and Hispanics share similar problems, hopes, and aspirations, they could develop strong coalitions to support the education of all minority children.

Perhaps a more disturbing divide is one that could develop between a younger generation that is majority minority and an elderly one that is wealthier and largely white. In their recent book, *The American Dream and the Public Schools,* Hochschild and Nathan Scovronick, director of the undergraduate program at Princeton University's Woodrow Wilson School of Public and International Affairs, call this the "racial generation gap."

Competition for resources will grow as the "dependency ratio"—the ratio of the dependent young and old to those of working age—increases, the authors say. According to the U.S. Census, that ratio will rise from 63 dependents per 100 workers in 1992 to 83 per 100 in 2030.

Whether the nation can unite across these racial and generational divides will say a lot about the politics of the 21st century—about the kind of neighborhoods we choose to live in and the quality of education we offer our children in the public schools.

"Some people think that the demographics we will have in the future are unusual," Murdock says. "It may be that the demographics we have had in the past are unusual. In other words, we'll look a lot more like the world in 2050 than we do today."

Postnote

The recent wave of immigration to the United States has had tremendous consequences for our schools. Almost 4 million English language learners (also called limited English proficient [LEP] students) are enrolled in public elementary and secondary schools. They currently make up about 8.4 percent of the total enrollment, and the number has increased every year for the last decade. As these students enter school, most will need to make sense of a new language, a new culture, and possibly new ways of behaving.

The No Child Left Behind law requires that most of these English language learners (ELLs) take the state tests required by law, even though they may not speak English. Under the NCLB law, states are permitted to give the tests in the native language of the students. However, the costs involved in translating and reproducing the tests in the many languages spoken by various immigrant groups of students often prohibit doing so. As a result, most of these students take the tests in English, often with predictably poor results.

Discussion Questions

1. Would you like to work with English language learners? Why or why not? If so, what can you do to prepare yourself for success?
2. Are you concerned about the resegregation of American schools? Why or why not?
3. Why is it important economically and morally to educate children from all racial and ethnic groups?

CLASSIC

A Considered Opinion: Diversity, Tragedy, and the Schools

DIANE RAVITCH

FOCUS Question

What is the appropriate balance between teaching an American culture, on the one hand, and teaching about the contributions of various ethnic and racial minorities, on the other hand? Is it an either-or situation?

TERMS TO NOTE

Assimilation

Melting pot

Multicultural education

As U.S. immigration has surged over the past quarter-century, educators have been developing a new response to demographic diversity in the classroom. The public schools have turned away from their traditional emphasis on assimilating newcomers into the national "melting pot." Instead, they have put a new emphasis on multicultural education, deemphasizing the common American culture and teaching children to take pride in their racial, ethnic, and national origins. In the wake of the terrorist attacks on New York City and Washington last September 11, however, the tide may be turning away from multiculturalism. Americans' remarkable display of national unity in the aftermath of the attacks could change the climate in the nation's schools as much as it has the political climate in Washington.

Immigration is central to the American experience. Though it is on the rise today, immigration is proportionately smaller now than it was in the first three decades of the 20th century. The census of 2000 found that about 10 percent of the population was foreign-born. In the censuses of 1900, 1910, and 1920, that share was some 14 percent. (Then as now, the nation's black population was about 12 percent.) In those early years of the last century, American society was not certain of its ability to absorb millions of newcomers. The public schools took on the job of educating and preparing them for social, civic, and economic participation in the life of the nation.

What did the public schools in those early years do about their new clientele? First, they taught them to speak, read, and write English—a vital necessity for a successful transition into American society. Because many children served as translators for their parents, these skills were valuable to the entire family in negotiating with employers, shops, and government agencies. The schools also taught habits of good hygiene (a matter of public health), as well as appropriate self-discipline and behavior. More than the three "Rs," schools taught children how to speak correctly, how to behave in a group, how to meet deadlines, and how

---

Diane Ravitch is a nonresident senior fellow in the Brookings Governmental Studies program and research professor at New York University. From Diane Ravitch, "A Considered Opinion: Diversity, Tragedy, and the Schools," *Brookings Review,* Winter 2002. Reprinted with permission of The Brookings Institution.

to dress for different situations (skills needed as much by native-born rural youth as by immigrant children). Certainly, the schools taught foreign-born children about American history (especially about national holidays, the Constitution, the Revolutionary War, and the Civil War), with a strong emphasis on the positive aspects of the American drama.

They also taught children about the "American way of life," the habits, ideals, values, and attitudes (such as the American spirit of individualism) that made their new country special. If one could sum up this education policy, it was one that celebrated America and invited newcomers to become full members of American society.

During the late 1960s and early 1970s, assimilation came to be viewed as an illegitimate, coercive imposition of American ways on unwitting children, both foreign-born and nonwhite. With the rise of the black separatist movement in 1966, black nationalists such as Stokely Carmichael began inveighing against racial integration and advocating community control of public schools in black neighborhoods. In response, many black educators demanded African-American history, African-American heroes, African-American literature, and African-American celebrations in the public schools. In the 1970s, the white ethnic revival followed the black model, and soon government was funding celebrations of ethnic heritage in the schools. By the mid-1970s, just as immigration was beginning to increase rapidly, the public schools no longer focused on acculturating the children of newcomers to American society. Instead, they encouraged children to appreciate and retain their ethnic and racial origins.

The expectation that the public schools will teach children about their racial and ethnic heritage has created enormous practical problems. First, it has promoted the belief that what is taught in school will vary in response to the particular ethnic makeup of the school. Thus, a predominantly African-American school will learn one set of lessons, while a predominantly Hispanic school will learn yet another, and an ethnically mixed school will learn—what? Second, schools have begun to lose a sense of a distinctive American culture, a culture forged by people from many different backgrounds that is nonetheless a coherent national culture. No state in the nation requires students to read any particular book, poem, or play. Today schools are uncertain about how to teach American history, what to teach as "American" literature, and how to teach world history without omitting any corner of the world (many children learn no world history). Third, the teaching of racial and ethnic pride is itself problematic, as it appears to be a continuation in a new guise of one of the worst aspects of American history.

From our public schools' experiences over the past century, we have learned much about the relative advantages and disadvantages of assimilationism and multiculturalism in the public schools.

Assimilation surely has its strengths. A democratic society must seek to give every young person, whether native-born or newcomer, the knowledge and skills to succeed as an adult. In a political system that relies on the participation of informed citizens, everyone should, at a minimum, learn to speak, read, and write a common language. Those who would sustain our democratic life must understand its history. To maximize their ability to succeed in the future, young people must also learn mathematics and science. Tailoring children's education to the color of their skin, their national origins, or their presumed ethnicity is in some fundamental sense contrary to our nation's founding ideals of democracy, equality, and opportunity.

And yet we know that assimilationism by itself is an inadequate strategy for American public education, for two reasons. First, it ignores the strengths that immigrants have to offer; and second, it presumes that American culture is static, which is surely not true. When immigrants arrive in America, they tend to bring with them, often after an emotionally costly journey, a sense of optimism, a strong family and religious tradition, and a willingness to work hard—values and attitudes that our society respects, but that affluence and media cynicism have eroded among many of our own citizens.

But neither is "celebrating diversity" an adequate strategy for a multiracial, multi-ethnic society like ours. The public schools exist to build an American community, to help both newcomers and native-born children prepare for adulthood as fellow citizens. Strategies that divide children along racial and ethnic lines encourage resentment and alienation rather than mutual respect. The ultimate democratic lesson is human equality, and the schools must teach our children that we are all in the same boat, all members of one society, regardless of race, ethnicity, or place of origin.

We learned that lesson the hardest way possible on September 11, when thousands of people from many countries died together in a single tragedy.

How will America's schools respond in the days ahead? It seems clear that they must make a pact with the children in their care. They must honor the strong and positive values that the children's families bring to America, and in return they must be prepared to give the children access to the best of America's heritage.

America's newcomers did not come to our shores merely to become consumers. They came to share in our democratic heritage and to become possessors of the grand ideas that created and sustained the democratic experiment in this country for more than two centuries. They too have a contribution to make to the evolving story of our nation. Whether they do so will depend in large part on whether our educational system respects them enough to help them become Americans.

The terrible events of this past fall have shown that Americans of all races and ethnic groups share a tremendous sense of national spirit and civic unity. They recognize that, whatever their origins, they share a common destiny as Americans. America's schools should honor that reality.

Postnote

Diane Ravitch is one of the leading educational thinkers in the United States. Her training as a historian makes her a keen observer of educational trends and an advocate of strengthening student learning in core content subjects. As such, her article is one of our Classic picks.

The tensions Ravitch discusses, between multiculturalism and monoculturalism, between diversity and acculturation, are old and deep in the American schools. Emphasis has shifted back and forth toward one or the other extreme over the years, depending on historical events and, often, the energies of advocates. Currently, because of a huge influx of immigrants into the United States during the 1990s, and fueled by the 9/11 attacks on our country, the emphasis is shifting toward acculturation and a rebirth of patriotism. Nevertheless, this strikes us as an unnecessary distinction. Our national motto is "E pluribus unum," from the many comes the one. A good school can honor the varied backgrounds of its students and at the same time teach all the requirements and expectations of good citizens. To do less is to miseducate.

Discussion Questions

1. How was multiculturalism taught or exhibited in your schooling, and how did students respond to the school's efforts?
2. Have you seen a change in emphasis on either multiculturalism or national acculturation since 9/11?
3. What ideas do you have for dealing with these issues in your classroom?

Multicultural Illiteracy

SANDRA STOTSKY

FOCUS Question

Should schools try to develop students' self-esteem by including elements of their own cultures in the curriculum, or does student self-esteem develop as a result of solid, academic accomplishment?

TERM TO NOTE

National Assessment of Educational Progress (NAEP)

The meaning of the word "diversity" has been badly abused in recent decades. American educators have long honored diversity in the only educationally meaningful sense of the word—individual difference.

For generations teachers were trained to look at students as individuals. Each student was supposedly endowed with a different combination of talents, abilities, interests and opinions. There is no question that this way of understanding diversity created strong positive educational outcomes and could continue to do so. Intellectual or social conformity has never been an American trait.

But in an Orwellian transformation of the meaning of the word, diversity has come to mean looking at a student as a representative of a particular demographic category. It now conveys the erroneous notion that, for example, all girls think and learn in one way, all boys in another or that all black students think and learn in one way, all Asians in another, all white students in yet another. To see students as members of a particular racial category or "culture" (to use current educational jargon), rather than as unique individuals, makes all the difference in the world.

Few positive outcomes are possible in an educational system that slots all students into spurious racial categories and then attaches fictitious ways of thinking, learning and knowing to each. The result is not the elimination of stereotypes but the freezing of them.

Classified by Category

We always have had different races and ethnic groups in our schools, although not in the same numbers or kinds in all schools. I grew up in a small Massachusetts town in which the children or grandchildren of early 20th century immigrants were as numerous as the children of

---

Dr. Sandra Stotsky is the Assistant Commissioner for the Massachusetts Department of Education and a Visiting Principal Research Scholar in the School of Education and the College of Arts and Sciences, Northeastern University, as well as the director of two Harvard summer institutes on civic education. She is the author of *Losing Our Language: How Multicultural Classroom Instruction Is Undermining Our Children's Ability to Read, Write, and Reason*. Reprinted with permission from the May 1999 issue of *The School Administrator* magazine.

those whose families had lived in the town for several hundred years.

As children, we all knew each others' backgrounds. We knew who spoke Italian, Armenian, Greek, Portuguese, Lithuanian, Polish or French Canadian in their home. We knew which families attended the local Catholic church, one of the many Protestant churches in town or the synagogue in a neighboring city. But not one of my teachers, in my presence, ever denigrated our ethnic, linguistic or religious backgrounds. Indeed, what they emphasized was something all our parents wanted them to stress. All of us, we were told repeatedly, were American citizens. And we were individual American citizens, not Lithuanian Americans, Irish Americans and so on, even though our parents may have belonged to the local Lithuanian, Polish or Italian social club or read an Armenian or Polish newspaper. We were not classified into racial or ethnic categories for any purpose.

Yes, there was prejudice in America. Why should this country be different from the others? But we all knew from our families there was even more prejudice elsewhere in the world, especially in those countries from which our families had come. Furthermore, the prejudice here was not just in those families who had been here for generations, it was also in the newcomers.

Every group had its own prejudices toward outsiders, as we all learned through experience, and it didn't bother us much. It was just another one of life's many hurdles to surmount. What was more important was that we all lived under the same set of laws as American citizens. These were ideals, to be sure, not always realities, but they were official ideals with teeth behind them, and we learned that they could be appealed to or drawn on, as women found in the early part of the century in gaining the right to vote, or as court decisions and civil rights legislation showed us in the 1950s and 1960s.

Fortunately for us, our teachers didn't subject us to endless lessons on tolerance and on how to be respectful of each other's "culture." They simply modeled tolerance for us and dealt, briefly, with problematic incidents whenever they arose in school. We were thus able to spend most of our school time on academic matters. Our main responsibility was to go to school every day, to be respectful of our teachers and to do our homework.

It's true we didn't see our home cultures in what we read in school, but we identified with each other as American citizens, something we and our parents were proud to be, despite our country's flaws. We probably would have welcomed attempts at a realistic curriculum that included more information or literature on the many immigrant groups in this country, as well as on the African Americans and Native Americans, but only if it did not end up making it more difficult for us to learn how to read and write English or giving us a warped or dishonest view of our own country and the larger world within which we live.

Negative Connotations

It is highly ironic that multiculturalism has evolved as an educational philosophy from its original and positive meaning of inclusion to mean something very negative, especially for us. This was one of the major findings of my research on the contents of all the grade 4 and grade 6 readers in six leading basal reading series, published between 1993 and 1995, as reported in *Losing Our Language.*

Rather than broadening students' horizons about the ethnic diversity of this country, today's version of multiculturalism has led to the suppression of the stories of most immigrant groups to this country. Overall, the selections in these readers convey the picture of an almost monolithic white world, with none of the real ethnic diversity that can be seen in just the listing of restaurants in a telephone directory for any city in this country. Almost all of the various European ethnic groups I grew up with have been excluded. Instead of the real America, we find a highly shrunken mainstream culture in most series, surrounded by Native Americans, Asian Americans,

African Americans and Hispanics, none of whom seem to interact much with each other.

Nor do today's readers give children an informed understanding of the real world within which they live. Nowhere do children read about the first airplane flight, the first transatlantic flight, the first exploration of space, the discovery of penicillin or the polio vaccine or how such inventions as the light bulb, radio, telegraph, steamboat, telephone, sewing machine, phonograph or radar came about. Apparently, accounts of these significant discoveries or inventions have been banished from students' common knowledge because most portray the accomplishments of white males.

But without the stories about the pioneers in science and technology (a few of whom were females, like Marie Curie), both boys and girls are unlikely to acquire a historically accurate timeframe for sequencing the major discoveries that have shaped their life today. The greater loss is that of an educational role model. The current substitutes for these stories in the readers—stories about people who have overcome racism or sexism or physical disabilities—are unlikely to give children insights into the power of intellectual curiosity in sustaining perseverance or the role of intellectual gratification in rewarding this perseverance.

Wayward Literacy

The most visible problem I found in the readers is at the level of language itself. The kinds of selections now featured in the readers make it almost impossible for children to develop a rich, literate vocabulary in English over the grades. In some series, children must learn a dazzling array of proper nouns, words for the mundane features of daily life, words for ethnic foods in countries around the world and other non-English words, most of which contribute little if anything to the development of their competence in the English language.

For example, consider this paragraph near the end of a story in a grade 4 reader: "In the wee hours of the morning, the family made a circle around Grandma Ida, Beth and Chris. Grandma Ida gave the *tamshi la tutaonana:* 'In this new year let us continue to practice *umoja, kujichagulia, ujima, ujamaa, nia, kuumba* and *imani*. Let us strive to do something that will last as long as the earth turns and water flows.' "

Or consider this sentence in another grade 4 reader: "The whole family sat under wide trees and ate arroz con gandules, pernil, viandas and tostones, ensalada de chayotes y tomates and pasteles."

Or these sentences in a grade 6 reader: "On the *engawa* after dinner, Mr. Ono said to Mitsuo, 'Take Lincoln to the dojo. You are not too tired, are you, Lincoln-kun?'"

Not only are children in this country unlikely to see any of these Swahili, Spanish or Japanese words in any of their textbooks in science, mathematics or history, they are unlikely to see them in any other piece of literature as well. They have wasted their intellectual energy not only learning their meaning but also learning how to pronounce them. It is not clear why these academically useless words, some of which are italicized, some not, are judged to be of importance by contemporary teacher educators.

These educators also seem to think that children should spend a considerable amount of class time engaged in conversations with each other about each other's ethnic cultures and daily lives—in the name of building self-esteem and group identity. But using precious class time for frequent conversations about intellectually barren topics that draw on intellectually limited vocabularies deprives the very students who most need it of opportunities to practice using the lexical building blocks necessary for conceptual growth and analytical thinking.

The present version of multiculturalism may well be largely responsible, through its effects on classroom materials and instruction, for the growing gap between the scores of minority students and other students on the National Assessment of Educational Progress examinations in reading. We need public discussions of the goals that should dominate reading instruction. Do we want teachers absorbed with the development of their children's egos, intent on shaping their feelings about themselves and others in specific ways? Or do we want teachers to concentrate on developing their children's minds, helping them acquire the knowledge, vocabulary and analytical skills that enable them to think for themselves and to choose the kind of personal identity they find most meaningful?

Postnote

Raw perception of people and things can quickly overpower us and submerge us in a sea of confusion. The human mind fights back by organizing perceptions into categories and putting labels on those categories: boys, girls, friends, enemies, tall people, short people, conservatives, liberals. However, as soon as we have labeled someone, distortions and mischief tend to set in. Tim with his enormous array of talents is labeled "the ADD [attention deficit disorder] kid." Teresa with all her budding potentialities is "that Hispanic girl." Although we can't live without categories and a method of labeling, we must be constantly vigilant of their limitations and their dangers. Sandra Stotsky's essay points out how, in her lifetime, a system of labeling has changed. She raises serious questions about the education consequences of this change.

Discussion Questions

1. State three major points from this essay.
2. What is the difference between the meaning of "diversity" in today's schools and the schools of Stotsky's youth?
3. How do you believe the reality of multiculturalism should be dealt with in our schools?

The Importance of Multicultural Education

GENEVA GAY

67

FOCUSQuestion

What are the challenges educators face in trying to infuse multicultural perspectives into the curriculum and instruction of our elementary and secondary schools?

TERMS TO NOTE

Interdisciplinary (curriculum)

Multicultural education

Social justice

Multiculturalism in U.S. schools and society is taking on new dimensions of complexity and practicality as demographics, social conditions, and political circumstances change. Domestic diversity and unprecedented immigration have created a vibrant mixture of cultural, ethnic, linguistic, and experiential plurality.

Effectively managing such diversity in U.S. society and schools is at once a very old and a very new challenge. Benjamin Barber (1992) eloquently makes the point that

> America has always been a tale of peoples trying to be a People, a tale of diversity and plurality in search of unity. Cleavages among [diverse groups] . . . have irked and divided Americans from the start, making unity a civic imperative as well as an elusive challenge. (p. 41)

Accomplishing this end is becoming increasingly important as the 21st century unfolds. People coming from Asia, the Middle East, Latin America, Eastern Europe, and Africa differ greatly from earlier generations of immigrants who came primarily from western and northern Europe. These unfamiliar groups, cultures, traditions, and languages can produce anxieties, hostilities, prejudices, and racist behaviors among those who do not understand the newcomers or who perceive them as threats to their safety and security. These issues have profound implications for developing instructional programs and practices at all levels of education that respond positively and constructively to diversity.

A hundred years ago W. E. B. Du Bois (1994) proposed that the problem of the 20th century was conflict and controversy among racial groups, particularly between African and European Americans. He concluded that

> Between these two worlds [black and white], despite much physical contact and daily intermingling, there is almost no community of

---

Geneva Gay is a professor of education at the University of Washington, Seattle.
"The Importance of Multicultural Education," by Geneva Gay, *Educational Leadership,* December 2003/January 2004, pp. 30–35. Reprinted by permission. The Association for Supervision and Curriculum Development is a worldwide community of educators advocating sound policies and sharing best practices to achieve the success of each learner. To learn more, visit ASCD at **www.ascd.org.**

> intellectual life or point of transference where the thoughts and feelings of one race can come into direct contact and sympathy with the thoughts and feelings of the other.

Although much has changed since Du Bois's declarations, too much has not changed nearly enough. Of course, the color line has become more complex and diverse, and legal barriers against racial intermingling have been dismantled. People from different ethnic, racial, and cultural groups live in close physical proximity. But coexistence does not mean that people create genuine communities in which they know, relate to, and care deeply about one another. The lack of a genuine community of diversity is particularly evident in school curriculums that still do not regularly and systematically include important information and deep study about a wide range of diverse ethnic groups. As disparities in educational opportunities and outcomes among ethnic groups continue to grow, the resulting achievement gap has reached crisis proportions.

Multicultural education is integral to improving the academic success of students of color and preparing all youths for democratic citizenship in a pluralistic society. Students need to understand how multicultural issues shape the social, political, economic, and cultural fabric of the United States as well as how such issues fundamentally influence their personal lives.

Conceptions of Multicultural Education

Even though some theorists (Banks & Banks, 2002) have argued that multicultural education is a necessary ingredient of quality education, in actual practice, educators most often perceive it either as an addendum prompted by some crisis or as a luxury. Multicultural education has not yet become a central part of the curriculum regularly offered to all students; instead, educators have relegated it primarily to social studies, language arts, and the fine arts and have generally targeted instruction for students of color.

These attitudes distort multicultural education and make it susceptible to sporadic and superficial implementation, if any. Textbooks provide a compelling illustration of such an attitude: The little multicultural content that they offer is often presented in sidebars and special-events sections (Loewen, 1995).

Another obstacle to implementing multicultural education lies with teachers themselves. Many are unconvinced of its worth or its value in developing academic skills and building a unified national community. Even those teachers who are more accepting of multicultural education are nevertheless skeptical about the feasibility of its implementation. "I would do it if I could," they say, "but I don't know how." "Preparing students to meet standards takes up all my time," others point out. "School curriculums are already overburdened. What do I take out to make room for multicultural education?"

A fallacy underlies these conceptions and the instructional behaviors that they generate: the perception of multicultural education as separate content that educators must append to existing curriculums as separate lessons, units, or courses. Quite the contrary is true. Multicultural education is more than content: it includes policy, learning climate, instructional delivery, leadership, and evaluation (see Banks, 1994; Bennett, 2003; Grant & Gomez, 2000). In its comprehensive form, it must be an integral part of everything that happens in the education enterprise, whether it is assessing the academic competencies of students or teaching math, reading, writing, science, social studies, or computer science. Making explicit connections between multicultural education and subject- and skill-based curriculum and instruction is imperative.

It is not pragmatic for K–12 educators to think of multicultural education as a discrete entity, separated from the commonly accepted components of teaching and learning. These conceptions may be fine for higher education, where specialization is the rule. But in K–12 schools, where the education process focuses on teaching eclectic bodies of knowledge and skills, teachers need to use multicultural education to promote such highly valued outcomes as human development, education equality, academic excellence, and democratic citizenship (see Banks & Banks, 2001; Nieto, 2000).

To translate these theoretical conceptions into practice, educators must systematically weave multicultural education into the central core of curriculum, instruction, school leadership, policymaking, counseling, classroom climate, and performance assessment. Teachers should use multicultural content, perspectives, and experiences to teach reading, math, science, and social studies.

For example, teachers could demonstrate mathematical concepts, such as less than/greater than, percentages, ratios, and probabilities using ethnic demographics. Younger children could consider the ethnic and racial distributions in their own classrooms, discussing which group's representation is greater than, less than, or equal to another's. Older students could collect statistics about ethnic distributions on a larger scale and use them to make more sophisticated calculations, such as converting numbers to percentages and displaying ethnic demographics on graphs.

Students need to apply such major academic skills as data analysis, problem solving, comprehension, inquiry, and effective communication as they study multicultural issues and events. For instance, students should not simply memorize facts about major events involving ethnic groups, such as civil rights movements, social justice efforts, and cultural accomplishments. Instead, educators should teach students how to think critically and analytically about these events, propose alternative solutions to social problems, and demonstrate understanding through such forms of communication as poetry, personal correspondence, debate, editorials, and photo essays.

Irvine and Armento (2001) provide specific examples for incorporating multicultural education into planning language arts, math, science, and social studies lessons for elementary and middle school students and connecting these lessons to general curriculum standards. One set of lessons demonstrates how to use Navajo rugs to explain the geometric concepts of perimeter and area and to teach students how to calculate the areas of squares, rectangles, triangles, and parallelograms.

These suggestions indicate that teachers need to use systematic decision-making approaches to accomplish multicultural curriculum integration. In practice, this means developing international and orderly processes for including multicultural content. The decision-making process might involve the following steps:

- Creating learning goals and objectives that incorporate multicultural aspects, such as "Developing students' ability to write persuasively about social justice concerns."
- Using a frequency matrix to ensure that the teacher includes a wide variety of ethnic groups in a wide variety of ways in curriculum materials and instructional activities.
- Introducing different ethnic groups and their contributions on a rotating basis.
- Including several examples from different ethnic experiences to explain subject matter concepts, facts, and skills.
- Showing how multicultural content, goals, and activities intersect with subject-specific curricular standards.

Virtually all aspects of multicultural education are interdisciplinary. As such, they cannot be adequately understood through a single discipline. For example, teaching students about the causes, expressions, and consequences of racism and how to combat racism requires the application of information and techniques from such disciplines as history, economics, sociology, psychology, mathematics, literature, science, art, politics, music, and health care. Theoretical scholarship already affirms this interdisciplinary need; now, teachers need to model good curricular and instructional practice in elementary and secondary classrooms. Putting this principle into practice will elevate multicultural education from impulse, disciplinary isolation, and simplistic and haphazard guesswork to a level of significance, complexity, and connectedness across disciplines.

Multiculturalism and Curriculum Development

How can teachers establish linkages between multicultural education and the disciplines and subject matter content taught in schools? One approach is to filter multicultural education through two categories of curriculum development: *reality/representation* and *relevance.*

Reality/Representation

A persistent concern of curriculum development in all subjects is helping students understand the *realities* of the social condition and how they came to be as well as adequately representing those realities. Historically, curriculum designers have been more exclusive than inclusive of the wide range of ethnic and cultural diversity that exists within society. In the haste to promote harmony and avoid controversy and conflict, they gloss over social problems and the realities of ethnic and racial identities, romanticize racial relations, and ignore the challenges of poverty and urban living in favor of middle-class and suburban experiences. The reality is distorted and the representations incomplete (Loewen, 1995).

An inescapable reality is that diverse ethnic, racial, and cultural groups and individuals have made contributions to every area of human endeavor and to all aspects of U.S. history, life, and culture. When students study food resources in the United States, for example, they often learn about production and distribution by large-scale agribusiness and processing corporations. The curriculum virtually overlooks the contributions of the many ethnically diverse people involved in planting and harvesting vegetables and fruits (with the Mexican and Mexican American farm labor unionization movement a possible exception). School curriculums that incorporate comprehensive multicultural education do not perpetuate these exclusions. Instead, they teach students the reality—how large corporations and the food industry are directly connected to the migrant workers who harvest vegetables and pick fruits. If we are going to tell the true story of the United States, multicultural education must be a central feature of telling it.

School curriculums need to reverse these trends by also including equitable *representations* of diversity. For example, the study of American literature, art, and music should include contributions of males and females from different ethnic groups in all genres and in different expressive styles. Thus, the study of jazz will examine various forms and techniques produced not just by African Americans but also by Asian, European, and Latino Americans.

Moreover, educators should represent ethnically diverse individuals and groups in all strata of human accomplishment instead of typecasting particular groups as dependent and helpless victims who make limited contributions of significance. Even under the most oppressive conditions, diverse groups in the United States have been creative, activist, and productive on broad scales. The way in which Japanese Americans handled their internment during World War II provides an excellent example. Although schools must not overlook or minimize the atrocities this group endured, students should also learn how interned Japanese Americans led dignified lives under the most undignified circumstances and elevated their humanity above the circumstances. The curriculum should include both issues.

Relevance

Many ethnically diverse students do not find schooling exciting or inviting; they often feel unwelcome, insignificant, and alienated. Too much of what is taught has no immediate value to these students. It does not reflect who they are. Yet most educators will agree that learning is more interesting and easier to accomplish when it has personal meaning for students.

Students from different ethnic groups are more likely to be interested and engaged in learning situations that occur in familiar and friendly frameworks than in those occurring in strange and hostile ones. A key factor in establishing educational relevance for these students is cultural similarity and responsiveness (see Bruner, 1996; Hollins, 1996; Wlodkowski & Ginsberg, 1995). For example, immigrant Vietnamese, Jamaican, and Mexican students who were members of majority populations in their home countries initially may have difficulty understanding what it means to be members of minority groups in the United States. Students who come from education environments that encourage active participatory learning will not be intellectually stimulated by passive instruction that involves lecturing and completing worksheets. Many students of color are bombarded with irrelevant learning experiences, which dampen their academic interest, engagement, and achievement. Multicultural education mediates these situations by teaching content about the cultures and contributions of many ethnic groups and by using a variety of teaching techniques that are culturally responsive to different ethnic learning styles.

Using a variety of strategies may seem a tall order in a classroom that includes students from many different ethnic groups. Research indicates, however, that several ethnic groups share some learning style attributes (Shade, 1989). Teachers need to understand the distinguishing characteristics of different learning styles and use the instructional techniques best suited to each style. In this scenario, teachers would provide alternative teaching techniques for clusters of students instead of for individual students. In any given lesson, the teacher might offer three or four ways for students to learn, helping to equalize learning advantages and disadvantages among the different ethnic groups in the classroom.

Scholars are producing powerful descriptions of culturally relevant teaching for multiethnic students and its effects on achievement. Lipka and Mohatt (1998) describe how a group of teachers, working closely with Native Alaskan (Yup'ik) elders, made school structure, climate, curriculum, and instruction more reflective of and meaningful to students from the community. For 10 years, the teachers translated, adapted, and embedded Yup'ik cultural knowledge in math, literacy, and science curriculums. The elders served as resources and quality-control monitors of traditional knowledge, and they provided the inspiration and moral strength for the teachers to persist in their efforts to center the schooling of Yup'ik students around the students' own cultural orientations. In math, for instance, the teachers now habitually make connections among the Yup'ik numeration system, body measurements, simple and complex computations, geometry, pattern designs, and tessellations.

Similar attributes apply to the work of such scholars as Moses and Cobb (2001), Lee (1993), and Boykin and Bailey (2000), who are studying the effects of culturally relevant curriculum and instruction on the school performance of African American students.

Moses and his colleagues are making higher-order math knowledge accessible to African American middle school students by teaching this material through the students' own cultural orientations and experiences. To teach algebra, they emphasize the experiences and familiar environments of urban and rural low-income students, many of whom are at high risk for academic failure. A key feature of their approach is making students conscious of how algebraic principles and formulas operate in their daily lives and getting students to understand how to explain these connections in nonalgebraic language before converting this knowledge into the technical notations and calculations of algebra. Students previously considered by some teachers as incapable of learning algebra are performing at high levels—better, in fact, than many of their advantaged peers.

Evidence increasingly indicates that multicultural education makes schooling more relevant and effective for Latino American, Native American, Asian American, and Native Hawaiian students as well (see McCarty, 2002; Moll, Amanti, Neff, & Gonzalez, 1992; Park, Goodwin, & Lee, 2001; Tharp & Gallimore, 1988). Students perform more successfully on all levels when there is greater congruence between their cultural backgrounds and such school experiences as task interest, effort, academic achievement, and feelings of personal efficacy or social accountability.

As the challenge to better educate underachieving students intensifies and diversity among student populations expands, the need for multicultural education grows exponentially.

Multicultural education may be the solution to problems that currently appear insolvable: closing the achievement gap; genuinely not leaving any children behind academically; revitalizing faith and trust in the promises of democracy, equality, and justice; building education systems that reflect the diverse cultural, ethnic, racial, and social contributions that forge society; and providing better opportunities for all students.

Multicultural education is crucial. Classroom teachers and educators must answer its clarion call to provide students from all ethnic groups with the education they deserve.

References

Banks, J. A. (1994). *Multiethnic education: Theory and practice* (3rd ed.). Boston: Allyn and Bacon.

Banks, J. A., & Banks, C. A. M. (Eds.). (2001). *Multicultural education: Issues and perspectives* (4th ed.). Boston: Allyn and Bacon.

Banks, J. A., & Banks, C. A. M. (Eds.). (2002). *Handbook of research on multicultural education* (2nd ed.). San Francisco: Jossey-Bass.

Barber, B. R. (1992). *An aristocracy of everyone: The politics of education and the future of America.* New York: Oxford University Press.

Bennett, C. I. (2003). *Comprehensive multicultural education: Theory and practice.* Boston: Allyn and Bacon.

Boykin, A. W., & Bailey, C. T. (2000). *The role of cultural factors in school relevant cognitive functioning: Synthesis of findings on cultural context, cultural orientations, and individual differences.* (ERIC Document Reproduction Service No. ED 441 880)

Bruner, J. (1996). *The culture of education.* Cambridge, MA: Harvard University Press.

Du Bois, W. E. B. (1994). *The souls of black folk.* New York: Gramercy Books.

Grant, C. A., & Gomez, M. L. (2000). (Eds.). *Making school multicultural: Campus and classroom* (2nd ed.). Upper Saddle River, NJ: Merrill/Prentice-Hall.

Hollins, E. R. (1996). *Culture in school learning: Revealing the deep meaning.* Mahwah, NJ: Erlbaum.

Irvine, J. J., & Armento, B. J. (Eds.). (2001). *Culturally responsive teaching: Lesson planning for elementary and middle grades.* Boston: McGraw-Hill.

Lee, C. (1993). *Signifying as a scaffold to literary interpretation: The pedagogical implications of a form of African American discourse* (NCTE Research Report No. 26). Urbana, IL: National Council of Teachers of English.

Lipka, J., & Mohatt, G. V. (1998). *Transforming the culture of schools: Yup'ik eskimo examples.* Mahwah, NJ: Erlbaum.

Loewen, J. W. (1995). *Lies my teacher told me: Everything your American history textbook got wrong.* New York: New Press.

McCarty, T. L. (2002). *A place to be Navajo: Rough Rock and the struggle for self-determination in indigenous schooling.* Mahwah, NJ: Erlbaum.

Moll, L. C., Amanti, C., Neff, D., & Gonzalez, N. (1992). Funds of knowledge for teaching: Using a qualitative approach to connect homes and classrooms. *Theory into Practice, 31*(1), 132–141.

Moses, R. P., & Cobb, C. E., Jr. (2001). *Radical equations: Math literacy and civil rights.* Boston: Beacon Press.

Nieto, S. (2000). *Affirming diversity: The sociopolitical context of multicultural education* (3rd ed.). New York: Longman.

Park, C. C., Goodwin, A. L., & Lee, S. J. (Eds.). (2001). *Research on the education of Asian and Pacific Americans.* Greenwich, CT: Information Age Publishers.

Shade, B. J. (Ed.). (1989). *Culture, style, and the educative process.* Springfield, IL: Charles C. Thomas.

Tharp, R. G., & Gallimore, R. (1988). *Rousing minds to life: Teaching, learning, and schooling in social context.* Cambridge, UK: Cambridge University Press.

Wlodkowski, R. J., & Ginsberg, M. B. (1995). *Diversity & motivation: Culturally responsive teaching.* San Francisco: Jossey-Bass.

Postnote

Multicultural education is a controversial issue, partly because there is no generally accepted definition. Some people see multicultural education as being divisive, creating separate pockets of different cultures, rather than helping to create a common culture. Others see multicultural education as promoting cultural pluralism, recognizing that cultural diversity is a valuable resource that should be preserved and extended. Geneva Gay rejects both assimilation and separatism as ultimate goals. She recognizes that each subculture exists as part of an interrelated whole. Multicultural education reaches beyond awareness and understanding of cultural differences to recognize the right of these different cultures to exist and to value that existence.

In addition to valuing cultural diversity, multicultural education is also based on the concept of *social justice*, which seeks to do away with social and economic inequalities for those in our society who have been denied these benefits in a democratic society. African Americans, Native Americans, Asian Americans, Hispanic Americans, women, disabled individuals, people with limited English proficiency, persons with low incomes, members of particular religious groups, and gays and lesbians are among those groups that have at one time or another been denied social justice. Educators who support multicultural education see establishing social justice for all groups of people who have experienced discrimination as a moral and ethical responsibility. Extending the concept of multicultural education to include a broader population, however, has also contributed to its controversy.

Discussion Questions

1. In your own words, what does multicultural education mean?
2. In your opinion, should cultural pluralism be a goal of our society and its schools? Why or why not?
3. What examples of multicultural education can you describe from your own education?

Enabling or Disabling? Observations on Changes in Special Education

JAMES M. KAUFFMAN, KATHLEEN McGEE, AND MICHELE BRIGHAM

FOCUS Question

As you read this article, are you persuaded that the pendulum toward full inclusion has swung too far, thus reducing special education services for youngsters who might need them?

TERMS TO NOTE

Inclusion

Individualized education program (IEP)

Mainstreaming

Schools need demanding and distinctive special education that is clearly focused on instruction and habilitation.[1] Abandoning such a conception of special education is a prescription for disaster. But special education has increasingly been losing its way in the single-minded pursuit of full inclusion.

Once, special education's purpose was to bring the performance of students with disabilities closer to that of their nondisabled peers in regular classrooms, to move as many students as possible into the mainstream with appropriate support.[2] For students not in regular education, the goal was to move them toward a more typical setting in a cascade of placement options.[3] But as any good thing can be overdone and ruined by the pursuit of extremes, we see special education suffering from the extremes of inclusion and accommodation.

Aiming for as much normalization as possible gave special education a clear purpose. Some disabilities were seen as easier to remediate than others. Most speech and language disorders, for example, were considered eminently remediable. Other disabilities, such as mental retardation and many physical disabilities, were assumed to be permanent or long-term and so less remediable, but movement *toward* the mainstream and increasing independence from special educators were clear goals.

The emphasis in special education has shifted away from normalization, independence, and competence. The result has been students' dependence on whatever special programs, modifications, and accommodations are possible, particularly in general education settings. The goal seems to have become the *appearance* of normalization without the *expectation* of competence.

Many parents and students seem to want more services as they learn what is available. Some have lost sight of the goal of limiting

---

James M. Kauffman is professor emeritus, Curry School of Education, University of Virginia. **Kathleen McGee** is a special education teacher at the high school level. **Michele Brigham** teaches high school special education and music, Albemarle County Public Schools, Charlottesville, Virginia. "Enabling or Disabling? Observations on Changes in Special Education," by James M. Kauffman, Kathleen McGee, and Michele Brigham, *Phi Delta Kappan,* April 2004, pp. 613–620. Reprinted by permission.

accommodations in order to challenge students to achieve more independence. At the same time, many special education advocates want all services to be available in mainstream settings, with little or no acknowledgment that the services are atypical. Although teachers, administrators, and guidance counselors are often willing and able to make accommodations, doing so is not always in students' best long-term interests. It gives students with disabilities what anthropologist Robert Edgerton called a cloak—a pretense, a cover, which actually fools no one—rather than actual competence.[4]

In this article, we discuss how changes in attitudes toward disability and special education, placement, and accommodations can perpetuate disability. We also explore the problems of ignoring or perpetuating disability rather than helping students lead fuller, more independent lives. Two examples illustrate how we believe good intentions can go awry—how attempts to accommodate students with disabilities can undermine achievement.

"But he needs resource. . . ." Thomas, a high school sophomore identified as emotionally disturbed, was assigned to a resource class created to help students who had problems with organization or needed extra help with academic skills. One of the requirements in the class was for students to keep a daily planner in which they entered all assignments; they shared their planner with the resource teacher at the beginning of class and discussed what academic subjects would be worked on during that period.

Thomas consistently refused to keep a planner or do any work in resource (he slept instead). So a meeting was set up with the assistant principal, the guidance counselor, Thomas, and the resource teacher. As the meeting was about to begin, the principal announced that he would not stay because Thomas felt intimidated by so many adults. After listening to Thomas' complaints, the guidance counselor decided that Thomas would not have to keep a planner or show it to the resource teacher and that the resource teacher should not talk to him unless Thomas addressed her first. In short, Thomas would not be required to do any work in the class! When the resource teacher suggested that under those circumstances, Thomas should perhaps be placed in a study hall, because telling the parents that he was in a resource class would be a misrepresentation, the counselor replied, "But he *needs* the resource class."

"He's too bright. . . ." Bob, a high school freshman with Asperger's Syndrome, was scheduled for three honors classes and two Advanced Placement classes. Bob's IEP (individualized education program) included a two-page list of accommodations. In spite of his having achieved A's and B's, with just a single C in math, his mother did not feel that his teachers were accommodating him appropriately. Almost every evening, she e-mailed his teachers and his case manager to request more information or more help for Bob, and she angrily phoned his guidance counselor if she didn't receive a reply by the end of the first hour of the next school day.

A meeting was scheduled with the IEP team, including five of Bob's seven teachers, the county special education supervisor, the guidance counselor, the case manager, the principal, and the county autism specialist. When the accommodations were reviewed, Bob's mother agreed that all of them were being made. However, she explained that Bob had been removed from all outside social activities because he spent all night, every night, working on homework. The accommodation she demanded was that Bob have *no* homework assignments. The autism specialist agreed that this was a reasonable accommodation for a child with Asperger's Syndrome.

The teachers of the honors classes explained that the homework in their classes, which involved elaboration and extension of concepts, was even more essential than the homework assigned in AP classes. In AP classes, by contrast, homework consisted primarily of practice of concepts learned in class. The honors teachers explained that they had carefully broken their long assignments into segments, each having a separate due date before the final project, and they gave illustrations of their expectations. The director of special education explained the legal definition of accommodations (the mother said she'd never before heard that accommodations could not change the nature of the curriculum). The director also suggested that, instead of Bob's sacrificing his social life, perhaps it would be more appropriate for him to take standard classes. What Bob's mother was asking, he concluded, was not legal. She grew angry, but she did agree to give the team a "little more time" to serve Bob appropriately. She said she would "be back with her claws and broomstick" if anyone ever suggested that he be moved from honors classes without being given the no-homework accommodation. "He's too bright to take anything less than honors classes, and if you people would provide this simple accommodation, he would do just fine," she argued. In the end, she got her way.

Attitudes Toward Disability and Special Education

Not that many decades ago, a disability was considered a misfortune—not something to be ashamed of but a generally undesirable, unwelcome condition to be overcome to the greatest extent possible. Ability was considered more desirable than disability, and anything—whether a device or a service—that helped people with disabilities to do what those without disabilities could do was considered generally valuable, desirable, and worth the effort, cost, and possible stigma associated with using it.

The disability rights movement arose in response to the widespread negative attitudes toward disabilities, and it had a number of desirable outcomes. It helped overcome some of the discrimination against people with disabilities. And overcoming such bias and unfairness in everyday life is a great accomplishment. But the movement has also had some unintended negative consequences. One of these is the outright denial of disability in some cases, illustrated by the contention that disability exists only in attitudes or as a function of the social power to coerce.[5]

The argument that disability is merely a "social construction" is particularly vicious in its effects on social justice. Even if we assume that disabilities are socially constructed, what should that mean? Should we assume that socially constructed phenomena are not "real," are not important, or should be discredited? If so, then consider that dignity, civil rights, childhood, social justice, and nearly every other phenomenon that we hold dear are social constructions. Many social constructions are not merely near and dear to us, they are real and useful in benevolent societies. The important question is whether the idea of disability is useful in helping people attain dignity or whether it is more useful to assume that disabilities are not real (i.e., that, like social justice, civil rights, and other social constructions, they are fabrications that can be ignored when convenient). The denial of disability is sometimes expressed as an aversion to labels, so that we are cautioned not to communicate openly and clearly about disabilities but to rely on euphemisms. But this approach is counterproductive. When we are able only to whisper or mime the undesirable difference called disability, then we inadvertently increase its stigma and thwart prevention efforts.[6]

The specious argument that "normal" does not exist—because abilities of every kind are varied and because the point at which normal becomes abnormal is arbitrary—leads to the conclusion that no one actually has a disability or, alternatively, that everyone has a disability. Then, some argue, either no one or everyone is due an accommodation so that no one or everyone is identified as disabled. This unwillingness to draw a line defining something (such as disability, poverty, or childhood) is based either on ignorance regarding the nature of continuous distributions or on a rejection of the unavoidably arbitrary decisions necessary to provide special services to those who need them and, in so doing, to foster social justice.[7]

Another unintended negative consequence of the disability rights movement is that, for some people, disability has become either something that does not matter or something to love, to take pride in, to flaunt, to adopt as a positive aspect of one's identity, or to cherish as something desirable or as a badge of honor. When disability makes no difference to us one way or the other, then we are not going to work to attenuate it, much less prevent it. At best, we will try to accommodate it. When we view disability as a desirable difference, then we are very likely to try to make it more pronounced, not to ameliorate it.

Several decades ago, special education was seen as a good thing—a helpful way of responding to disability, not something everyone needed or should have, but a useful and necessary response to the atypical needs of students with disabilities. This is why the Education for All Handicapped Children Act (now the Individuals with Disabilities Education Act) was written. But in the minds of many people, special education has been transformed from something helpful to something awful.[8]

The full-inclusion movement did have some desirable outcomes. It helped overcome some of the unnecessary removal of students with disabilities from general education. However, the movement also has had some unintended negative consequences. One of these is that special education has come to be viewed in very negative terms, to be seen as a second-class and discriminatory system that does more harm than good. Rather than being seen as helpful, as a way of creating opportunity, special education is often portrayed as a means of shunting students into dead-end programs and killing opportunity.[9]

Another unintended negative consequence of full inclusion is that general education is now seen by many as the *only* place where fair and equitable treatment is possible and where the opportunity to learn is extended to all equally.[10] The argument has become that special education is good only as long as it is invisible (or nearly so), an indistinguishable part of a general education system that accommodates all students, regardless of their abilities or disabilities. Usually, this is described as a "unified" (as opposed to "separate") system of education.[11] Special education is thus something to be avoided altogether or attenuated to the greatest extent possible, regardless of a student's inability to perform in a general setting. When special education is seen as discriminatory, unfair, an opportunity-killing system, or, as one writer put it, "the gold-plated garbage can of American schooling,"[12] then it is understandable that people will loathe it. But this way of looking at special education is like seeing the recognition and treatment of cancer as the cause of the problem.

The reversal in attitudes toward disability and special education—disability from undesirable to inconsequential, special education from desirable to awful—has clouded the picture of what special education is and what it should do for students with disabilities. Little wonder that special education stands accused of failure, that calls for its demise have become vociferous, and that contemporary practices are often more disabling than enabling. An unfortunate outcome of the changing attitudes toward disability and special education is that the benefit of special education is now sometimes seen as freedom from expectations of performance. It is as if we believed that, if a student has to endure the stigma of special education, then the compensation should include an exemption from work.

Placement Issues

Placing all students, regardless of their abilities, in regular classes has exacerbated the tendency to see disability as something existing only in people's minds. It fosters the impression that students are fitting in when they are not able to perform at anywhere near the normal level. It perpetuates disabilities; it does not compensate for them.

Administrators and guidance counselors sometimes place students in programs for which they do not qualify, even as graduation requirements are increasing and tests are mandated. Often, these students' *testing* is modified although their *curriculum* is not. The students may then feel that they have beaten the system. They are taught that the system is unfair and that the only way to win is by gaming it. Hard work and individual responsibility for one's education are often overlooked—or at least undervalued.

Students who consistently fail in a particular curriculum must be given the opportunity to deal with the natural consequences of that fact as a means of learning individual responsibility. For example, social promotion in elementary and middle school teaches students that they really don't have to be able to do the work to pass. Students who have been conditioned to rely on social promotion do not believe that the cycle will end until it does so—usually very abruptly in high school. Suddenly, no one passes them on, and no one gives them undeserved credit. Many of these students do not graduate in four years. Some never recover, while others find themselves forced to deal with a very distasteful situation.

No one wants to see a student fail, but to alter any standard without good reason is to set that same student up for failure later in life. Passing along a student with disabilities in regular classes, pretending that he or she is performing at the same level as most of the class or that it doesn't really matter (arguing that the student has a legal "right" to be in the class) is another prescription for disappointment and failure in later life. Indeed, this failure often comes in college or on the job.

Some people with disabilities do need assistance. Others do not. Consider Deborah Groeber, who struggled through degenerative deafness and blindness. The Office of Affirmative Action at the University of Pennsylvania offered to intercede at the Wharton School, but Groeber knew that she had more influence if she spoke for herself. Today, she is a lawyer with three Ivy League degrees.[13] But not every student with disabilities can do or should be expected to do what Groeber did. Our concern is that too many students with disabilities are given encouragement based on pretense when they could do much more with appropriate special education.

Types of Accommodations

Two popular modifications in IEPs are allowing for the use of calculators and granting extended time on tests and assignments. Calculators can be a great asset, but they should be used when calculating complex problems or when doing word problems. Indiscriminate use of a calculator renders many math tests invalid, as they become a contest to see if buttons can be pushed successfully and in the correct order, rather than an evaluation of ability to do arithmetic or use mathematical knowledge.

Extended time on assignments and tests can also be a useful modification, but it can easily be misused or abused. Extended time on tests should mean *continuous* time so that a test is not studied for first and taken later. Sometimes a test must be broken into smaller segments that can be completed independently. However, this could put students with disabilities at a disadvantage, as one part of a test might help with remembering another part. Extensions on assignments need to be evaluated each time they are given, not simply handed out automatically because they are written into an IEP. If a student is clearly working hard, then extensions may be appropriate. If a student has not even been attempting assignments, then more time might be an avoidance tactic. Sometimes extended time means that assignments pile up and the student gets further and further behind. The result can then be overwhelming stress and the inability to comprehend discussions because many concepts must be acquired in sequence (e.g., in math, science, history, and foreign languages).

Reading tests and quizzes aloud to students can be beneficial for many, but great caution is required. Some students and teachers want to do more than simply read a test. Reading a test aloud means simply reading the printed words on the page *without* inflections that can reveal correct answers and without explaining vocabulary. Changing a test to open-notes or open-book, without the knowledge and consent of the classroom teacher, breaches good-faith test proctoring. It also teaches students dependence rather than independence and accomplishment. Similarly, scribing for a student can be beneficial for those who truly need it, but the teacher must be careful not to add details and to write only what the student dictates, including any run-on sentences or fragments. After scribing, if the assignment is not a test, the teacher should edit and correct the paper with the student, as she might do with any written work. But this must take place *after* the scribing.

How Misguided Accommodations Can Be Disabling

"Saving" a child from his or her own negative behavior reinforces that behavior and makes it a self-fulfilling prophecy. Well-intentioned guidance counselors often feel more responsibility for their students' success or failure than the students themselves feel. Sometimes students are not held accountable for their effort or work. They seem not to understand that true independence comes from *what* you know, not *whom* you know. Students who are consistently enabled and not challenged are never given the opportunity to become independent. Ann Bancroft, the polar explorer and dyslexic, claims that, although school was a torment, it was disability that forged her iron will.[14] Stephen Cannell's fear for other dyslexics is that they will quit trying rather than struggle and learn to compensate for their disability.[15]

Most parents want to help their children. However, some parents confuse making life *easier* with making life *better* for their children. Too often, parents feel that protecting their child from the rigors of academic demands is in his or her best interest. They may protect their child by insisting on curricular modifications and accommodations in assignments, time, and testing. But children learn by doing, and not allowing them to do something because they might fail is denying them the opportunity to succeed. These students eventually believe that they are not capable of doing what typical students can do, even if they are. Sometimes it is difficult for teachers to discern what a student actually can do and what a parent has done until an in-class assignment is given or a test is taken. At that point, it is often too late for the teacher to do much remediation. The teacher may erroneously conclude that the student is simply a poor test-taker.

In reality, the student may have been "protected" from learning, which will eventually catch up with him or her. Unfortunately, students may not face reality until they take a college entrance exam, go away to college, or apply for a job. Students who "get through" high school in programs of this type often go on to flunk out of college. Unfortunately, the parents of these students frequently blame the college for the student's failure, criticizing the post-secondary institution for not doing enough to help. Instead, they should be upset both with the secondary institution for not preparing the child adequately for the tasks to come and with themselves for their own overprotection.

The Benefits of Demands

Many successful adults with disabilities sound common themes when asked about their ability to succeed in the face of a disability. Tom Gray, a Rhodes Scholar who has a severe learning disability, claims that having to deal with the hardest experiences gave him the greatest strength.[16] Stephen Cannell believes that, if he had known there was a reason beyond his control to explain his low achievement, he might not have worked as hard as he did. Today, he knows he has a learning disability, but he is also an Emmy Award–winning television writer and producer.[17] Paul Orlalea, the dyslexic founder of Kinko's, believes God gave him an advantage in the challenge presented by his disability and that others should work with their strengths. Charles Schwab, the learning-disabled founder of Charles Schwab, Inc., cites his ability to think differently and to make creative leaps that more sequential thinkers don't make as chief reasons for his success. Fannie Flagg, the learning-disabled author, concurs and insists that learning disabilities become a blessing *only if you can overcome them*.[18] Not every student with a disability can be a star performer, of course, but all should be expected to achieve all that they can.

Two decades ago, special educators thought it was their job to assess a student's achievement, to understand what the student wanted to do and what an average peer could do, and then to develop plans to bridge the gap, if possible. Most special educators wanted to see that each student had the tools and knowledge to succeed as independently as possible. Helping students enter the typical world was the mark of success for special educators.

The full-inclusion movement now insists that *every* student will benefit from placement in the mainstream. However, some of the modifications and accommodations now being demanded are so radical that we are doing an injustice to the entire education system.[19] Special education must not be associated in any way with "dumbing down" the curriculum for students presumed to be at a given grade level, whether disabled or not.

Counselors and administrators who want to enable students must focus the discussion on realistic goals and plans for each student. An objective, in-depth discussion and evaluation must take place to determine how far along the continuum of successfully completing these goals the student has moved. If the student is making adequate progress independently, or with minimal help, special education services might not be necessary. If assistance is required to make adequate progress on realistic goals, then special education may be needed. Every modification and every accommodation should be held to the same standard: whether it will help the student attain these goals—*not* whether it will make life easier for the student. Knowing where a student is aiming can help a team guide that student toward success.

And the student must be part of this planning. A student who claims to want to be a brain surgeon but refuses to take science courses needs a reality check. If a student is unwilling to attempt to reach intermediate goals or does not succeed in meeting them, then special education cannot "save" that student. At that point, the team must help the student revisit his or her goals. Goals should be explained in terms of the amount of work required to complete them, not whether or not the teacher or parent feels they are attainable. When goals are presented in this way, students can often make informed decisions regarding their attainability and desirability. Troy Brown, a university dean and politician who has both a doctorate and a learning disability, studied at home with his mother. He estimates that it took him more than twice as long as the average person to complete assignments. Every night, he would go to bed with stacks of books and read until he fell asleep, because he had a dream of attending college.[20]

General educators and special educators need to encourage all students to be responsible and independent and to set realistic expectations for themselves. Then teachers must help students to meet these expectations in a more and more independent manner. Special educators do not serve students well when they enable students with disabilities to become increasingly dependent on their parents, counselors, administrators, or teachers—or even when they fail to increase students' independence and competence.

Where We Stand

We want to make it clear that we think disabilities are real and that they make doing certain things either impossible or very difficult for the people who have them. We cannot expect people with disabilities to be "just like everyone else" in what they can do. The views of other writers differ:

> The human service practices that cause providers to believe that clients [students] have inadequacies, shortcomings, failures, or faults that must be corrected or controlled by specially trained professionals must be replaced by conceptions that people with disabilities are capable of setting their own goals and achieving or not. Watered-down curricula, alternative grading practices, special competency standards, and other "treat them differently" practices used with "special" students must be replaced with school experiences exactly like those used with "regular" students.[21]

We disagree. In our view, students with disabilities *do* have specific shortcomings and *do* need the services of specially trained professionals to achieve their potential. They *do* sometimes need altered curricula or adaptations to make their learning possible. If students with disabilities were just like "regular" students, then there would be no need whatever for special education. But the school experiences of students with disabilities obviously will not be—*cannot* be—just like those of students without disabilities. We sell students with disabilities short when we pretend that they are no different from typical students. We make the same error when we pretend that they must *not* be expected to put forth extra effort if they are to learn to do some things—or learn to do something in a different way. We sell them short when we pretend that they have competencies that they do not have or pretend that the competencies we expect of most students are not important for them.

Like general education, special education must push students to become all they can be. Special education must countenance neither the pretense of learning nor the avoidance of reasonable demands.

Notes

1. James M. Kauffman and Daniel P. Hallahan, *Special Education: What It Is and Why We Need It* (Boston: Allyn & Bacon, forthcoming).
2. Doug Fuchs et al., "Toward a Responsible Reintegration of Behaviorally Disordered Students," *Behavioral Disorders,* February 1991, pp. 133–47.
3. Evelyn Deno, "Special Education as Development Capital," *Exceptional Children,* November 1970, pp. 229–37; and Dixie Snow Huefner, "The Mainstreaming Cases: Tensions and Trends for School Administrators," *Educational Administration Quarterly,* February 1994, pp. 27–55.
4. Robert B. Edgerton, *The Cloak of Competence: Stigma in the Lives of the Mentally Retarded* (Berkeley, Calif.: University of California Press, 1967); idem, *The Cloak of Competence,* rev. ed. (Berkeley, Calif.: University of California Press, 1993); and James M. Kauffman, "Appearances, Stigma, and Prevention," *Remedial and Special Education,* vol. 24, 2003, pp. 195–98.
5. See, for example, Scot Danforth and William C. Rhodes, "Deconstructing Disability: A Philosophy for Education," *Remedial and Special Education,* November/December 1997, pp. 357–66; and Phil Smith, "Drawing New Maps: A Radical Cartography of Developmental Disabilities," *Review of Educational Research,* Summer 1999, pp. 117–44.
6. James M. Kauffman, *Education Deform: Bright People Sometimes Say Stupid Things About Education* (Lanham, Md.: Scarecrow Education, 2002).
7. Ibid.
8. James M. Kauffman, "Reflections on the Field," *Behavioral Disorders,* vol. 28, 2003, pp. 205–8.
9. See, for example, Clint Bolick, "A Bad IDEA Is Disabling Public Schools," *Education Week,* 5 September 2001, pp. 56, 63; and Michelle Cottle, "Jeffords Kills Special Ed. Reform School," *New Republic,* 18 June 2001, pp. 14–15.
10. See, for example, Dorothy K. Lipsky and Alan Gartner, "Equity Requires Inclusion: The Future for All Students with Disabilities," in Carol Christensen and Fazal Rizvi, eds., *Disability and the Dilemmas of Education and Justice* (Philadelphia: Open University Press, 1996), pp. 144–55; and William Stainback and Susan Stainback, "A Rationale for Integration and Restructuring: A Synopsis," in John W. Lloyd, Nirbhay N. Singh, and Alan C. Repp, eds., *The Regular Education Initiative: Alternative Perspectives on Concepts, Issues, and Models* (Sycamore, Ill.: Sycamore, 1991), pp. 225–39.
11. See, for example, Alan Gartner and Dorothy K. Lipsky, *The Yoke of Special Education: How to Break It* (Rochester, N.Y.: National Center on Education and the Economy, 1989). For an alternative view,

see James M. Kauffman and Daniel P. Hallahan, "Toward a Comprehensive Delivery System for Special Education," in John I. Goodlad and Thomas C. Lovitt, eds., *Integrating General and Special Education* (Columbus, Ohio: Merrill, 1993), pp. 73–102.

12. Marc Fisher, "Students Still Taking the Fall for D.C. Schools," *Washington Post,* 13 December 2001, p. B-1.
13. Elizabeth Tener, "Blind, Deaf, and Very Successful," *McCall's,* December 1995, pp. 42–46.
14. Christina Cheakalos et al., "Heavy Mettle: They May Have Trouble Reading and Spelling, but Those with the Grit to Overcome Learning Disabilities Like Dyslexia Emerge Fortified for Life," *People,* 30 October 2001, pp. 18, 58.
15. Ibid.
16. Ibid.
17. Stephen Cannell, "How to Spell Success," *Reader's Digest,* August 2000, pp. 63–66.
18. Cheakalos et al., op cit.
19. Anne Proffit Dupre, "Disability, Deference, and the Integrity of the Academic Enterprise," *Georgia Law Review,* Winter 1998, pp. 393–473.
20. Cheakalos et al., op cit.
21. James E. Ysseldyke, Bob Algozzine, and Martha L. Thurlow, *Critical Issues in Special Education,* 3rd ed. (Boston: Houghton-Mifflin, 2000), p. 67.

Postnote

The movement toward full inclusion of children with disabilities into the regular education classroom has gained considerable support and momentum in the last ten years. Many supporters of full inclusion contend that disabled youngsters have a civil right to be educated with their nondisabled peers. The authors of this article, while supportive of inclusion, believe the movement has gone too far by not always serving the students' long-term interests. The authors believe that many parents, by insisting on the full inclusion of their child in the regular classroom, are denying the child the full range of services that are available in special education settings, particularly for those students whose disabilities are more severe.

Discussion Questions

1. What aspects of inclusion seem to cause controversy, and why is this so?
2. Have you had any experiences working with children with disabilities? If so, describe the circumstances and your successes or failures. If you haven't worked with children with disabilities, are you planning to get this experience? If so, how?
3. What do you think are the strongest arguments made by the authors of this article? If you could ask them a question, what would it be?

Making Inclusive Education Work

RICHARD A. VILLA AND JACQUELINE S. THOUSAND

FOCUS Question

As you read this article, think of the various benefits and challenges that inclusion presents to both the classroom teacher and the disabled child.

Terms to Note

Complementary teaching
Consultation
Coteaching
Differentiated instruction
Inclusion
Least restrictive environment (LRE)
Parallel teaching
Supportive teaching

As an educator, you are philosophically committed to student diversity. You appreciate that learning differences are natural and positive. You focus on identifying and capitalizing on individual students' interests and strengths. But making inclusive education work requires something more: It takes both systems-level support and classroom-level strategies.

Since the 1975 implementation of the Individuals with Disabilities Education Act (IDEA), federal law has stated that children with disabilities have the right to an education in the least restrictive environment (LRE). According to the act, removal from general education environments should occur only when a student has failed to achieve satisfactorily despite documented use of supplemental supports, aids, and services.

During the past 28 years, the interpretation of what constitutes the least restrictive environment has evolved, along with schools' and educators' abilities to provide effective supports. As a result, increased numbers of students with disabilities are now served in both regular schools and general education classes within those schools.

When IDEA was first promulgated in 1975, schools generally interpreted the law to mean that they should mainstream students with mild disabilities—for example, those with learning disabilities and those eligible for speech and language services—into classes where these students could keep up with other learners, supposedly with minimal support and few or no modifications to either curriculum or instruction. In the early 1980s, however, the interpretation of least restrictive environment evolved to include the concept of integrating students with more intensive needs—those with moderate and severe

---

Richard A. Villa is president of Bayridge Consortium, San Diego, California. **Jacqueline S. Thousand** is Professor in the College of Education at California State University-San Marcos. "Making Inclusive Education Work," by Richard A. Villa and Jacqueline S. Thousand, *Educational Leadership,* October 2003, pp. 19–23. Reprinted by permission. The Association for Supervision and Curriculum Development is a worldwide community of educators advocating sound policies and sharing best practices to achieve the success of each learner. To learn more, visit ASCD at **www.ascd.org.**

disabilities—into regular classrooms. By the late 1980s and early 1990s, the interpretation evolved into the approach now known as *inclusion:* the principle and practice of considering general education as the placement of first choice for all learners. This approach encourages educators to bring necessary supplemental supports, aids, and services into the classroom instead of removing students from the classroom for those services.

As the interpretation of least restrictive environment has changed, the proportion of students with disabilities included in general education has increased dramatically. By 1999, 47.4 percent of students with disabilities spent 80 percent or more of their day in general education classrooms, compared with 25 percent of students with disabilities in 1985 (U.S. Department of Education, 2003).

Although the 1997 reauthorization of IDEA did not actually use the term *inclusion,* it effectively codified the principle and practice of inclusion by requiring that students' Individualized Education Programs (IEPs) ensure access to the general education curriculum. This landmark reauthorization broadened the concept of inclusion to include academic as well as physical and social access to general education instruction and experiences (Kluth, Villa, & Thousand, 2002).

Despite the continued evolution toward inclusive education, however, tremendous disparities exist among schools, districts, and states. For example, the U.S. Department of Education (2003) found that the percentage of students with disabilities ages 6–21 who were taught for 80 percent or more of the school day in general education classrooms ranged from a low of 18 percent in Hawaii to a high of 82 percent in Vermont. Further, the nature of inclusion varies. In some schools, inclusion means the mere physical presence or social inclusion of students with disabilities in regular classrooms; in other schools, it means active modification of content, instruction, and assessment practices so that students can successfully engage in core academic experiences and learning.

Why can some schools and districts implement inclusion smoothly and effectively, whereas others cannot? Three sources give guidance in providing high-quality inclusive practice. First, research findings of the past decade have documented effective inclusive schooling practices (McGregor & Vogelsberg, 1998; National Center on Educational Restructuring and Inclusion, 1995; Villa, Thousand, Meyers, & Nevin, 1996). Second, our own experiences as educators suggest several variables. Third, we interviewed 20 nationally recognized leaders in the field of inclusive education who, like ourselves, provide regular consultation and training throughout the United States regarding inclusive practice.

A Systems Approach

Successful promotion and implementation of inclusive education require the five following systems-level practices: connection with other organizational best practices; visionary leadership and administrative support; redefined roles and relationships among adults and students; collaboration; and additional adult support when needed.

Connection with Best Practices

Inclusive education is most easily introduced in school communities that have already restructured to meet the needs of their increasingly diverse student populations in regular education. Initiatives and organizational best practices to accomplish this aim include trans-disciplinary teaming, block scheduling, multi-age student grouping and looping, schoolwide positive behavior support and discipline approaches, detracking, and school-within-a-school family configurations of students and teachers. These initiatives facilitate the inclusion and development of students with disabilities within general education.

School leaders should clearly communicate to educators and families that best practices to facilitate inclusion are identical to best practices for educating all students. This message will help members of the school community understand that inclusion is not an add-on, but a natural extension of promising research-based education practices that positively affect the teaching and learning of all students.

Visionary Leadership

A national study on the implementation of IDEA's least restrictive environment requirement emphasized the importance of leadership—in both vision and practice—to the installation of inclusive education. The researchers concluded,

> How leadership at each school site chose to look at LRE was critical to how, or even whether, much would be accomplished beyond the status quo. (Hasazi, Johnston, Liggett, & Schattman, 1994, p. 506)

In addition, a study of 32 inclusive school sites in five states and one Canadian province found that the degree of administrative support and vision was the most powerful predictor of general educators' attitudes toward inclusion (Villa et al., 1996).

For inclusive education to succeed, administrators must take action to publicly articulate the new vision, build consensus for the vision, and lead all stakeholders to active involvement. Administrators can provide four types of support identified as important by frontline general and special educators: personal and emotional (for example, being willing to listen to concerns); informational (for example, providing training and technical assistance); instrumental (for example, creating time for teachers to meet); and appraisal (for example, giving constructive feedback related to implementation of new practices) (Littrell, Billingsley, & Cross, 1994).

Visionary leaders recognize that changing any organization, including a school, is a complex act. They know that organizational transformation requires ongoing attention to consensus building for the inclusive vision. It also requires skill development on the part of educators and everyone involved in the change; the provision of extra common planning time and fiscal, human, technological, and organizational resources to motivate experimentation with new practices; and the collaborative development and communication of a well-formulated plan of action for transforming the culture and practice of a school (Ambrose, 1987; Villa & Thousand, in press).

Redefined Roles

For school personnel to meet diverse student needs, they must stop thinking and acting in isolated ways: "These are my students, and those are your students." They must relinquish traditional roles, drop distinct professional labels, and redistribute their job functions across the system. To facilitate this role redefinition, some schools have developed a single job description for all professional educators that clearly articulates as expected job functions collaboration and shared responsibility for educating all of a community's children and youth.

To help school personnel make this shift, schools must clarify the new roles—for example, by making general education personnel aware of their legal responsibilities for meeting the needs of learners with disabilities in the least restrictive environment. In addition, schools must provide necessary training through a variety of vehicles, including inservice opportunities, coursework, co-teaching, professional support groups, and other coaching and mentoring activities. After clarifying teachers' new responsibilities and providing training, schools should encourage staff members to reflect on how they will differentiate instruction and design accommodations and modifications to meet the needs of all students. School administrators should monitor the degree of collaboration between general and special educators. They should also include implementation of IEP-mandated activities as part of ongoing district evaluation procedures.

Collaboration

Reports from school districts throughout the United States identify collaboration as a key variable in the successful implementation of inclusive education. Creating planning teams, scheduling time for teachers to work and teach together, recognizing teachers as problem solvers, conceptualizing teachers as frontline researchers, and effectively collaborating with parents are all dimensions reported as crucial to successful collaboration (National Center on Educational Restructuring and Inclusion, 1995).

Achievement of inclusive education presumes that no one person could have all the expertise required to meet the needs of all the students in a classroom. For inclusive education to work, educators must become effective and efficient collaborative team members. They must develop skills in creativity, collaborative teaming processes, co-teaching, and interpersonal communication that will enable them to work together to craft diversified learning opportunities for learners who have a wide range of interests, learning styles, and intelligences (Thousand & Villa, 2000; Villa, 2000a; Villa, Thousand, & Nevin, in preparation). In a study of more than 600 educators, collaboration emerged as the only variable that predicted positive attitudes toward inclusion among general and special educators as well as administrators (Villa et al., 1996).

Adult Support

An "only as much as needed" principle dictates best practices in providing adult support to students. This approach avoids inflicting help on those who do not necessarily need or want it. Thus, when paraprofessionals are assigned to classrooms, they should be presented to students as members of a teaching team rather than as people "velcroed" to individual students.

Teaching models in which general and specialized personnel work together as a team are effective and efficient ways of arranging adult support to meet diverse student needs (National Center on Educational Restructuring and Inclusion, 1995; Villa, 2002b). Such models include

- *Consultation.* Support personnel provide assistance to the general educator, enabling him or her to teach all the students in the inclusive class.
- *Parallel teaching.* Support personnel—for example, a special educator, a Title I teacher, a psychologist, or a speech language therapist—and the classroom teacher rotate among heterogeneous groups of students in different sections of the general education classroom.
- *Supportive teaching.* The classroom teacher takes the lead role, and support personnel rotate among the students.
- *Complementary teaching.* The support person does something to complement the instruction provided by the classroom teacher (for example, takes notes on a transparency or paraphrases the teacher's statements).
- *Coteaching.* Support personnel coteach alongside the general education teacher.

Promoting Inclusion in the Classroom

Several curricular, instructional, and assessment practices benefit all the students in the classroom and help ensure successful inclusion. For instance, in a study conducted by the National Center on Educational Restructuring and Inclusion (1995), the majority of the districts implementing inclusive education reported cooperative learning as the most important instructional strategy supporting inclusive education. Some other general education theories and practices that also effectively support inclusion are

- Current theories of learning (such as multiple intelligences and constructivist learning).
- Teaching practices that make subject matter more relevant and meaningful (for example, partner learning, project- and activity-based learning, and service learning).
- Authentic alternatives to paper-and-pencil assessment (such as portfolio artifact collection, role playing, and demonstrations).
- A balanced approach to literacy development that combines whole-language and phonics instruction.
- Thematic/interdisciplinary curriculum approaches.
- Use of technology for communication and access to the general education curriculum.
- Differentiated instruction.

Responding to Diversity

Building on the notion of differentiated instruction (Tomlinson, 1999), universal design provides a contemporary approach to facilitate successful inclusion (Udvari-Solner, Villa, & Thousand, 2002).

In the traditional retrofit model, educators determine both content and instructional and assessment strategies without taking into consideration the special characteristics of the actual learners in the classroom. Then, if a mismatch exists between what students can do and what they are asked to do, educators make adjustments. In contrast, educators using the universal design framework consider the students and their various learning styles first. Then they differentiate curriculum *content, processes,* and *products* before delivering instruction.

For example, in a unit on the history of relations between the United States and Cuba, students might access *content* about the Cuban Missile Crisis by listening to a lecture, interviewing people who were alive at that time, conducting Internet research, reading the history text and other books written at a variety of reading levels, or viewing films or videos. The teacher can differentiate the *process* by allowing students to work independently, in pairs, or in cooperative groups. Additional processes that allow learners of differing abilities and learning styles to master standards include a combination of whole-class instruction, learning centers, reflective journal writing, technology, and field trips. Finally, students may demonstrate their learning through various *products,* including written reports, debates, role-plays, PowerPoint presentations, and songs.

Thus, students can use a variety of approaches to gain access to the curriculum, make sense of their learning, and show what they have learned. A universal design approach benefits every student, not just those identified as having disabilities.

Differentiating to enable a student with disabilities to access the general education curriculum requires creative thinking. Four options suggest varying degrees of student participation (Giangreco, Cloninger, & Iverson, 1998).

- First, a student can simply join in with the rest of the class.
- Second, multilevel curriculum and instruction can occur when all students involved in a lesson in the same curriculum area pursue varying levels of complexity.
- Curriculum overlapping is a third option, in which students working on the same lesson pursue objectives from different curricular areas. A student with severe disabilities, for example, could practice using a new communication device during a hands-on science lesson while others focus primarily on science objectives.
- The fourth option, and the last resort, involves arranging alternative activities when a general education activity is inappropriate. For example, a student may need to participate in an activity within his Individualized Education Program, such as employment training in the community, that falls outside the scope of the general education curriculum.

Bridging the Gap

Systems-level and classroom-level variables such as these facilitate the creation and maintenance of inclusive education. Systemic support, collaboration, effective classroom practices, and a universal design approach can make inclusive education work so that students with disabilities have the same access to the general education curriculum and to classmates as any other student and the same opportunity for academic, social, and emotional success.

Inclusive education is a general education initiative, not another add-on school reform unrelated to other general education initiatives. It incorporates demonstrated general education best practices, and it redefines educators' and students' roles and responsibilities as creative and collaborative partners. The strategies described here can bridge the gap between what schools are doing well and what they can do better to make inclusion part and parcel of a general education program.

References

Ambrose, D. (1987). *Managing complex change.* Pittsburgh, PA: The Enterprise Group.

Giangreco, M. F., Cloninger, C. J., & Iverson, V. S. (1998). *Choosing outcomes and accommodations for children (COACH): A guide to educational planning for students with disabilities* (2nd ed.). Baltimore: Paul H. Brookes.

Hasazi, S., Johnston, A. P., Liggett, A. M., & Schattman, R. A. (1994). A qualitative policy study of the least restrictive environment provision of the Individuals with Disabilities Education Act. *Exceptional Children, 60,* 491–507.

Kluth, P., Villa, R. A., & Thousand, J. S. (2002). "Our school doesn't offer inclusion" and other legal blunders. *Educational Leadership, 59* (4), 24–27.

Littrell, P. C., Billingsley, B. S., & Cross, L. H. (1994). The effects of principal support on special and general educators' stress, job satisfaction, school commitment, health, and intent to stay in teaching. *Remedial and Special Education, 15,* 297–310.

McGregor, G., & Vogelsberg, T. (1998). *Inclusive schooling practices: Pedagogical and research foundations.* Baltimore: Paul H. Brookes.

National Center on Educational Restructuring and Inclusion. (1995). *National study on inclusive education.* New York: City University of New York.

Thousand, J. S., & Villa, R. A. (2000). Collaborative teaming: A powerful tool in school restructuring. In R. A. Villa & J. S. Thousand (Eds.), *Restructuring for caring and effective education: Piecing the puzzle together* (2nd ed., pp. 254–291). Baltimore: Paul H. Brookes.

Tomlinson, C. A. (1999). *The differentiated classroom.* Alexandria, VA: ASCD.

Udvari-Solner, A., Villa, R. A., & Thousand, J. S. (2002). Access to the general education curriculum for all: The universal design process. In J. S. Thousand, R. A. Villa, & A. I. Nevin (Eds.), *Creativity and collaborative learning* (2nd ed., pp. 85–103). Baltimore: Paul H. Brookes.

U.S. Department of Education. (2003). *Twenty-third annual report to Congress on the implementation of the Individuals with Disabilities Education Act.* Washington, DC: Author.

Villa, R. A. (2002a). *Collaborative planning: Transforming theory into practice* [Videotape]. Port Chester, NY: National Professional Resources.

Villa, R. A. (2002b). *Collaborative teaching: The coteaching model* [Videotape]. Port Chester, NY: National Professional Resources.

Villa, R. A., & Thousand, J. S. (in press). *Creating an inclusive school* (2nd ed.). Alexandria, VA: ASCD.

Villa, R. A., & Thousand, J. S., Meyers, H., & Nevin, A. (1996). Teacher and administrator perceptions of heterogeneous education. *Exceptional Children, 63,* 29–45.

Villa, R. A., Thousand, J. S., & Nevin, A. (in preparation). *The many faces of co-teaching.* Thousand Oaks, CA: Corwin Press.

Postnote

Working successfully with children with disabilities is one of the most challenging tasks facing beginning teachers. About 5.8 million students, 12 percent of the total school population, receive federal aid for their disabilities, so it is likely that you will have students with disabilities in your classroom. It is important that you approach instruction for these children as you would for other students: expect diversity, expect a range of abilities, and look for the particular strengths and learning profiles of each student. If you are a regular education teacher, work with the special education teachers in your school to coordinate instruction and services for your students with disabilities. If you are a special education teacher, you will be expected to work closely with regular education teachers to provide the least restrictive environment and best instruction possible for these children. Only by working closely together can regular and special education teachers ensure that "no child is left behind."

Discussion Questions

1. What concerns, if any, do you have about teaching children with disabilities? What can you do to address those concerns?
2. Is full inclusion a good idea? What limitations, if any, do you see in its implementation?
3. How would you go about ensuring that your regular education students are accepting of and helpful to any students with disabilities who might be in your class?

With Boys and Girls in Mind

MICHAEL GURIAN AND KATHY STEVENS

FOCUS Question

In what ways will schools and teaching practices need to change to address the differences in how boys and girls learn?

TERM TO NOTE

Nature-based approach

Something is awry in the way our culture handles the education needs of boys and girls. A smart 11-year-old boy gets low grades in school, fidgets and drifts off in class, and doesn't do his homework. A girl in middle school only uses the computer to instant-message her friends; when it comes to mastering more essential computer skills, she defers to the boys in the class.

Is contemporary education maliciously set against either males or females? We don't think so. But structurally and functionally, our schools fail to recognize and fulfill gender-specific needs. As one teacher wrote,

> For years I sensed that the girls and boys in my classrooms learn in gender-specific ways, but I didn't know enough to help each student reach full potential. I was trained in the idea that each student is an individual. But when I saw the PET scans of boys' and girls' brains, I saw how differently those brains are set up to learn. This gave me the missing component. I trained in male/female brain differences and was able to teach each individual child. Now, looking back, I'm amazed that teachers were never taught the differences between how girls and boys learn.

New positron emission tomography (PET) and MRI technologies enable us to look inside the brains of boys and girls, where we find structural and functional differences that profoundly affect human learning. These gender differences in the brain are corroborated in males and females throughout the world and do not differ significantly across cultures.

It's true that culture affects gender role, gender costume, and gender nuances—in Italy, for example, men cry more than they do in England—but role, costume, and nuance only affect some aspects of the learning brain of a child. New brain imaging technologies confirm that genetically

---

Michael Gurian is cofounder of the Gurian Institute, and **Kathy Stevens** is Director of the Gurian Institute, located in Colorado Springs, Colorado. "With Boys and Girls in Mind," by Michael Gurian and Kathy Stevens, *Educational Leadership,* November 2004, pp. 40–44. Reprinted by permission. The Association for Supervision and Curriculum Development is a worldwide community of educators advocating sound policies and sharing best practices to achieve the success of each learner. To learn more, visit ASCD at **www.ascd.org.**

templated brain patterning by gender plays a far larger role than we realized. Research into gender and education reveals a mismatch between many of our boys' and girls' learning brains and the institutions empowered to teach our children.

We will briefly explore some of the differences, because recognizing these differences can help us find solutions to many of the challenges that we experience in the classroom. Of course, generalized gender differences may not apply in every case.

The Minds of Girls

The following are some of the characteristics of girls' brains:

- A girl's corpus callosum (the connecting bundle of tissues between hemispheres) is, on average, larger than a boy's—up to 25 percent larger by adolescence. This enables more "cross talk" between hemispheres in the female brain.
- Girls have, in general, stronger neural connectors in their temporal lobes than boys have. These connectors lead to more sensually detailed memory storage, better listening skills, and better discrimination among the various tones of voice. This leads, among other things, to greater use of detail in writing assignments.
- The hippocampus (another memory storage area in the brain) is larger in girls than in boys, increasing girls' learning advantage, especially in the language arts.
- Girls' prefrontal cortex is generally more active than boys' and develops at earlier ages. For this reason, girls tend to make fewer impulsive decisions than boys do. Further, girls have more serotonin in the bloodstream and the brain, which makes them biochemically less impulsive.
- Girls generally use more cortical areas of their brains for verbal and emotive functioning. Boys tend to use more cortical areas of the brain for spatial and mechanical functioning (Moir & Jessel, 1989; Rich, 2000).

These "girl" brain qualities are the tip of the iceberg, yet they can immediately help teachers and parents understand why girls generally outperform boys in reading and writing from early childhood throughout life (Conlin, 2003). With more cortical areas devoted to verbal functioning, sensual memory, sitting still, listening, tonality, and mental cross talk, the complexities of reading and writing come easier, on the whole, to the female brain. In addition, the female brain experiences approximately 15 percent more blood flow, with this flow located in more centers of the brain at any given time (Marano, 2003). The female brain tends to drive itself toward stimulants—like reading and writing—that involve complex texture, tonality, and mental activity.

On the other hand, because so many cortical areas are used for verbal-emotive functioning, the female brain does not activate as many cortical areas as the male's does for abstract and physical-spatial functions, such as watching and manipulating objects that move through physical space and understanding abstract mechanical concepts (Moir & Jessel, 1989; Rich, 2000). This is one reason for many girls' discomfort with deep computer design language. Although some girls excel in these areas, more males than females gravitate toward physics, industrial engineering, and architecture. Children naturally gravitate toward activities that their brains experience as pleasurable—"pleasure" meaning in neural terms the richest personal stimulation. Girls and boys, within each neural web, tend to experience the richest personal stimulation somewhat differently.

The biological tendency toward female verbal-emotive functioning does not mean that girls or women should be left out of classes or careers that use spatial-mechanical skills. On the contrary: We raise these issues to call on our civilization to realize the differing natures of girls and boys and to teach each subject according to how the child's brain needs to learn it. On average, educators will need to provide girls with extra encouragement and gender-specific strategies to successfully engage them in spatial abstracts, including computer design.

The Minds of Boys

What, then, are some of the qualities that are generally more characteristic of boys' brains?

- Because boys' brains have more cortical areas dedicated to spatial-mechanical functioning, males use, on average, half the brain space that females use for verbal-emotive functioning. The cortical trend toward spatial-mechanical functioning makes many boys want to move objects through space, like balls, model airplanes, or just their arms and legs. Most boys, although not all of them, will experience words and feelings differently than girls do (Blum, 1997; Moir & Jessel, 1989).
- Boys not only have less serotonin than girls have, but they also have less oxytocin, the primary human bonding chemical. This makes it more likely that they will be physically impulsive and less likely that they will neurally combat their natural impulsiveness to sit still and emphatically chat with a friend (Moir & Jessel, 1989; Taylor, 2002).
- Boys lateralize brain activity. Their brains not only operate with less blood flow than girls' brains, but they are also structured to compartmentalize learning. Thus, girls tend to multitask better than boys do, with fewer attention span problems and greater ability to make quick transitions between lessons (Havers, 1995).
- The male brain is set to renew, recharge, and reorient itself by entering what neurologists call a *rest state.* The boy in the back of the classroom whose eyes are drifting toward sleep has entered a neural rest state. It is predominantly boys who drift off without completing assignments, who stop taking notes and fall asleep during a lecture, or who tap pencils or otherwise fidget in hopes of keeping themselves awake and learning. Females tend to recharge and reorient neural focus without rest states. Thus, a girl can be bored with a lesson, but she will nonetheless keep her eyes open, take notes, and perform relatively well. This is especially true when the teacher uses more words to teach a lesson instead of being spatial and diagrammatic. The more words a teacher uses, the more likely boys are to "zone out," or go into rest state. The male brain is better suited for symbols, abstractions, diagrams, pictures, and objects moving through space than for the monotony of words (Gurian, 2001).

These typical "boy" qualities in the brain help illustrate why boys generally learn higher math and physics more easily than most girls do when those subjects are taught abstractly on the chalkboard; why more boys than girls play video games that involve physical movement and even physical destruction; and why more boys than girls tend to get in trouble for impulsiveness, shows of boredom, and fidgeting as well as for their more generalized inability to listen, fulfill assignments, and learn in the verbal-emotive world of the contemporary classroom.

Who's Failing?

For a number of decades, most of our cultural sensitivity to issues of gender and learning came from advocacy groups that pointed out ways in which girls struggled in school. When David and Myra Sadker teamed with the American Association of University Women in the early 1990s, they found that girls were not called on as much as boys were, especially in middle school; that girls generally lagged in math/science testing; that boys dominated athletics; and that girls suffered drops in self-esteem as they entered middle and high school (AAUW, 1992). In large part because of this advocacy, our culture is attending to the issues that girls face in education.

At the same time, most teachers, parents, and other professionals involved in education know that it is mainly our boys who underperform in school. Since 1981, when the U.S. Department of Education began keeping complete statistics, we have seen that boys lag behind girls in most categories. The 2000 National Assessment of Educational Progress finds boys one and one-half years behind girls in reading/writing (National Center for Education Statistics, 2000). Girls are now only negligibly behind boys in math and science, areas in which boys have historically outperformed girls (Conlin, 2003).

Our boys are now losing frightening ground in school, and we must come to terms with it—not in a way that robs girls, but in a way that sustains our civilization and is as powerful as the lobby we have created to help girls. The following statistics for the United States illustrate these concerns:

- Boys earn 70 percent of *D*s and *F*s and fewer than half of the *A*s.
- Boys account for two-thirds of learning disability diagnoses.
- Boys represent 90 percent of discipline referrals.
- Boys dominate such brain-related learning disorders as ADD/ADHD, with millions now medicated in schools.
- 80 percent of high school dropouts are male.
- Males make up fewer than 40 percent of college students (Gurian, 2001).

These statistics hold true around the world. The Organisation for Economic Co-operation and Development (OECD) recently released its three-year study of knowledge and skills of males and females in 35 industrialized countries (including the United States, Canada, the European countries, Australia, and Japan). Girls outperformed boys in every country. The statistics that brought the male scores down most significantly were their reading/writing scores.

We have nearly closed the math/science gender gap in education for girls by using more verbal functioning—reading and written analysis—to teach such spatial-mechanical subjects as math, science, and computer science (Rubin, 2004; Sommers, 2000). We now need a new movement to alter classrooms to better suit boys' learning patterns if we are to deal with the gaps in grades, discipline, and reading/writing that threaten to close many boys out of college and out of success in life.

The Nature-Based Approach

In 1996, the Gurian Institute, an organization that administers training in child development, education, and male/female brain differences, coined the phrase *nature-based approach* to call attention to the importance of basing human attachment and education strategies on research-driven biological understanding of human learning. We argued that to broadly base education and other social processes on anything other than human nature was to set up both girls and boys for unnecessary failure. The institute became especially interested in nature-based approaches to education when PET scans and MRIs of boys and girls revealed brains that were trying to learn similar lessons but in widely different ways and with varying success depending on the teaching method used. It became apparent that if teachers were trained in the differences in learning styles between boys and girls, they could profoundly improve education for all students.

Between 1998 and 2000, a pilot program at the University of Missouri–Kansas City involving gender training in six school districts elicited significant results. One school involved in the training, Edison Elementary, had previously tested at the bottom of 18 district elementary schools. Following gender training, it tested in the top five slots, sometimes coming in first or second. Statewide, Edison outscored schools in every subject area, sometimes doubling and tripling the number of students in top achievement levels. Instead of the usual large number of students at the bottom end of achievement testing, Edison now had only two students requiring state-mandated retesting. The school also experienced a drastic reduction in discipline problems.

Statewide training in Alabama has resulted in improved performance for boys in both academic and behavioral areas. Beaumont Middle School in Lexington, Kentucky, trains its teachers in male/female brain differences and teaches reading/writing, math, and science in separate-sex classrooms. After one year of this gender-specific experiment, girls' math and science scores and boys' Scholastic Reading Inventory (SRI) scores rose significantly.

The Nature-Based Classroom

Ultimately, teacher training in how the brain learns and how boys and girls tend to learn differently creates the will and intuition in teachers and schools to create nature-based classrooms (see "Teaching Boys, Teaching Girls" for specific strategies). In an elementary classroom designed to help boys learn, tables and chairs are arranged to provide ample space for each child to spread out and claim learning space. Boys tend to need more physical learning space than girls do. At a table, a boy's materials will be less organized and more widely dispersed. Best practice would suggest having a variety of seating options—some desks, some tables, an easy chair, and a rug area for sitting or lying on the floor. Such a classroom would allow for more movement and noise than a traditional classroom would. Even small amounts of movement can help some boys stay focused.

The teacher can use the blocks area to help boys expand their verbal skills. As the boys are building, a teacher might ask them to describe their buildings. Because of greater blood flow in the cerebellum—the "doing" center of the human brain—boys more easily verbalize what they are doing than what they are feeling. Their language will be richer in vocabulary and more expansive when they are engaged in a task.

An elementary classroom designed to help girls learn will provide lots of opportunities for girls to manipulate objects, build, design, and calculate, thus preparing them for the more rigorous spatial challenges that they will face in higher-level math and science courses. These classrooms will set up spatial lessons in groups that encourage discussion among learners.

Teaching Boys, Teaching Girls

For Elementary Boys

- Use beadwork and other manipulatives to promote fine motor development. Boys are behind girls in this area when they start school.
- Place books on shelves all around the room so boys get used to their omnipresence.
- Make lessons experiential and kinesthetic.
- Keep verbal instructions to no more than one minute.
- Personalize the student's desk, coat rack, and cubby to increase his sense of attachment.
- Use male mentors and role models, such as fathers, grandfathers, or other male volunteers.
- Let boys nurture one another through healthy aggression and direct empathy.

For Elementary Girls

- Play physical games to promote gross motor skills. Girls are behind boys in this area when they start school.
- Have portable/digital cameras around and take pictures of girls being successful at tasks.
- Use water and sand tables to promote science in a spatial venue.
- Use lots of puzzles to foster perceptual learning.
- Form working groups and teams to promote leadership roles and negotiation skills.
- Use manipulatives to teach math.
- Verbally encourage the hidden high energy of the quieter girls.

Boys and Feelings

An assistant principal at a Tampa, Florida, elementary school shared a story of a boy she called "the bolter." The little boy would regularly blow up in class, then bolt out of the room and out of the school. The assistant principal would chase him and get him back into the building. The boy lacked the verbal-emotive abilities to help him cope with his feelings.

After attending male/female brain difference training, the assistant principal decided to try a new tactic. The next time the boy bolted, she took a ball with her when she went after him. When she found the boy outside, she asked him to bounce the ball back and forth with her. Reluctant at first, the boy started bouncing the ball. Before long, he was talking, then sharing the anger and frustration that he was experiencing at school and at home. He calmed down and went back to class. Within a week, the boy was able to self-regulate his behavior enough to tell his teacher that he needed to go to the office, where he and the assistant principal would do their "ball routine" and talk. Because he was doing something spatial-mechanical, the boy was more able to access hidden feelings.

Girls and Computers

The InterCept program in Colorado Springs, Colorado, is a female-specific teen mentor-training program that works with girls in grades 8–12 who have been identified as at risk for school failure, juvenile delinquency, and teen pregnancy. InterCept staff members use their knowledge of female brain functioning to implement program curriculum. Brittany, 17, came to the InterCept program with a multitude of issues, many of them involving at risk behavior and school failure.

One of the key components of InterCept is showing teenage girls the importance of becoming "tech-savvy." Girls use a computer-based program to consider future occupations: They can choose a career, determine a salary, decide how much education or training their chosen career will require, and even use income projections to design their future lifestyles. Brittany quite literally found a future: She is entering a career in computer technology.

The Task Ahead

As educators, we've been somewhat intimidated in recent years by the complex nature of gender. Fortunately, we now have the PET and MRI technologies to view the brains of boys and girls. We now have the science to prove our intuition that tells us that boys and girls do indeed learn differently. And, even more powerful, we have a number of years of successful data that can help us effectively teach both boys and girls.

The task before us is to more deeply understand the gendered brains of our children. Then comes the practical application, with its sense of purpose and productivity, as we help each child learn from within his or her own mind.

References

American Association of University Women. (1992). *AAUW Report: How schools shortchange girls.* American Association of University Women Foundation.

Baron-Cohen, S. (2003). *The essential difference: The truth about the male and female brain.* New York: Basic Books.

Blum, D. (1997). *Sex on the brain: The biological differences between men and women.* New York: Viking.

Conlin, M. (2003, May 26). The new gender gap. *Business Week Online.* Available: **www.businessweek.com/magazine/content/03_21/b3834001_mz001.htm**

Gurian, M., Henley, P., & Trueman, T. (2001). *Boys and girls learn differently! A guide for teachers and parents.* San Francisco: Jossey-Bass/John Wiley.

Havers, F. (1995). Rhyming tasks male and female brains differently. *The Yale Herald, Inc.* New Haven, CT: Yale University.

Marano, H. E. (2003, July/August). The new sex scorecard. *Psychology Today,* 38–50.

Moir, A., & Jessel, D. (1989). *Brain sex: The real difference between men and women.* New York: Dell Publishing.

National Center for Education Statistics. (2000). *National Assessment of Educational Progress: The nation's report card.* Washington, DC: U.S. Department of Education.

Organisation for Economic Co-operation and Development. (2003). *The PISA 2003 assessment framework.* Author.

Rich, B. (Ed.). (2000). *The Dana brain daybook.* New York: The Charles A. Dana Foundation.

Rubin, R. (2004, Aug. 23). How to survive the new SAT. *Newsweek,* p. 52.

Sommers, C. (2000). *The war against boys.* Simon and Schuster.

Taylor, S. (2002). *The tending instinct.* Times Books.

Postnote

The authors of this article argue that for true gender equity to occur in our schools, teaching practices need to address the different needs of male and female brains. They also argue that these brain differences help to explain why girls generally outperform boys in reading and writing, while boys generally learn higher mathematics and physics more easily than most girls when those subjects are taught abstractly. This is a highly controversial position, as Lawrence Summers, the president of Harvard University, discovered in 2005. Addressing a group of faculty members, he made comments suggesting that women don't perform as well as men in higher mathematics and that the reason is at least partly because of innate differences in men and women. His remarks provoked a maelstrom of protests from many faculty members.

The position taken by the authors of this article raises another interesting question. Will both girls and boys perform better academically in a single-sex setting? Can teachers better address the particular needs of boys and girls when only one gender is present in class? Research on single-sex schools by Anthony Bryk and his colleagues demonstrates rather conclusively that girls are more likely to flourish academically in a girls-only setting. Anecdotal evidence suggests that many young boys also do better when taught by male teachers in a single-sex setting.

Discussion Questions

1. Which group, girls or boys, do you believe is shortchanged the most in schools today? Why do you think so?
2. What are your views on the value of single-sex education?
3. What problems or obstacles can you identify in trying to implement teaching practices that address the differences in boys' and girls' brains?

Glossary

Note: Boldfaced terms that appear within definitions can be found elsewhere in the glossary.

Academic freedom The freedom of teachers to teach about an issue or to use a source without fear of penalty, reprisal, or harassment.

Academic learning time Time spent by students performing academic tasks with a high success rate.

Academies A type of academic secondary school popular during the early national period, which stressed the classics as a preparation for college.

Acceptable use policy (AUP) A statement of rules governing student use of school computers, especially regarding access to the Internet.

Accountability movement Reform movement in the 1970s embracing the idea that schools and educators should be required to demonstrate what they are accomplishing and should be held responsible for student achievement and learning.

Achievement gap Differences in educational achievement between students of different socioeconomic or racial and ethnic groups.

Adaptation Changes in instruction or materials made to meet the needs of learners with disabilities.

Added-value approach A system of compensation based on the difference between the actual and the expected academic improvement of a teacher's students.

Aesthetic Appreciative of or responsive to the beautiful.

American Federation of Teachers (AFT) The nation's second-largest teacher's association or union. Founded in 1916, it is affiliated with the AFL-CIO, the nation's largest union.

Assertive behavior The ability to stand up for one's legitimate rights in ways that make it less likely that others will ignore or circumvent them.

Assessment The process of determining students' learning progress.

Assimilation The absorption of an individual or a group into the cultural tradition of a population or another group.

Assistive technology The array of devices and services that help people with disabilities to perform better in their daily lives. Such devices include motorized chairs, remote control units that turn appliances on and off, computers, and speech synthesizers.

At-homeness A sense of awareness of and equanimity with the world in which one lives.

At risk A term used to describe conditions, for example, poverty, poor health, or learning disabilities, that put children in danger of not succeeding in school.

Attendance-zoned school School to which children are assigned because they are of mandatory school age and live within the school's designated neighborhood boundaries.

Autism A developmental disorder characterized by self-absorption, repetitive behaviors, and problems with social and language skills.

Back-to-basics movement A theme in education reform during the late 1970s and early 1980s that called for more emphasis on traditional subject matter such as reading, writing, arithmetic, and history. It also included the teaching of basic morality and called for more orderly and disciplined student behavior.

Behavioral indicators of child abuse Changes or signals in a child's behavior that suggest the child is being abused or neglected.

Behavioral psychology A branch of psychology dealing with human action that seeks generalizations of people's behavior in society.

Behaviorism (behaviorist) The psychological theory that all human behavior is shaped by environmental events or conditions. Behaviorists are people who follow or practice behaviorism.

Benefit maximization An ethical principle suggesting that individuals should choose the course of action that will make people generally better off.

Bilingual education A variety of approaches to educating students who speak a primary language other than English.

Block grants Federal aid to states or localities that comes with only minimal federal restrictions on how the funds should be spent (as opposed to categorical aid, which restricts federal funds to specified uses or categories of use).

Block scheduling An approach to class scheduling in which students take fewer classes each school day, but spend more time in each class.

Bottom fishing A variation of **cherry picking,** where an evaluator selects specific poor-performing subjects (e.g., students, schools) as evidence of failure.

Brown* v. *Board of Education of Topeka U.S. Supreme Court ruling in 1954 holding that segregated schools are inherently unequal.

Buckley Amendment An act passed by Congress in 1974, the real name of which is the Family Educational Rights and Privacy Act. It stipulates that students have the right to see the files kept on them by colleges and universities, and that parents should be allowed to see school files kept on their children.

Busing The controversial practice of transporting children to different schools in an attempt to achieve racial desegregation.

Carnegie Forum (on Education and the Economy) A program of the Carnegie Corporation of New York that was created to draw attention to the link between economic growth and the skills and abilities of the people who contribute to that growth, as well as to help develop education policies to meet economic challenges. In 1986 the Forum's Task Force on Teaching as a Profession issued *A Nation Prepared: Teachers for the 21st Century*, a report that called for establishing a national board for professional teaching standards.

Carnegie unit A measure of clock time used to award high school credits toward graduation.

CD-ROM An acronym for Compact Disc–Read Only Memory, a type of computer disk that stores several hundred megabytes of data and is currently used for many kinds of multimedia software.

Certification Recognition by a profession that one of its practitioners has met certain standards. Often used as a synonym for *licensure,* which is governmental approval to perform certain work, such as teaching.

Channel One A controversial commercial program that delivers ten minutes of high-quality news programming directly to public school classrooms free of cost in exchange for two minutes of advertising.

Chapter 1 *See* **Title I.**

Character The sum of an individual's enduring habits, which largely determines how one responds to life's challenges and events.

Character education Efforts by the home, the school, the religious community, and the individual student to help the student know, love, and do the good, and, in the process, to forge good qualities such as courage, respect, and responsibility.

Charter school School in which the educators, often joined by members of the local community, have made a special contract, or charter, with the school district. Usually the charter allows the school a great deal of independence in its operation.

Cherry picking An error made when particular subjects (e.g., a student, a school) of an experiment are held up to advertise the results of a particular research effort.

Child abuse Physical, emotional, or sexual maltreatment or neglect of a child.

Citizenship education A curriculum that includes teaching the basic characteristics and responsibilities of good citizenship, including neighborliness, politeness, helpfulness, and respect.

Civil Rights Act of 1964 Established that discrimination on the basis of race, color, or national origin is illegal in any program or activity receiving federal funding.

Classical humanism Renaissance philosophy centered on human values and exalting humans' free will and their superiority to the rest of nature.

Class size The number of students in a particular classroom, usually under the direction of an individual teacher.

Coalesced content standard A modest repacking or reworking of a state's existing curricular standards.

Coercive accountability A form of responsibility for results, also called "mean" accountability, that uses incentives and sanctions to ensure that educators and students perform up to expectations.

Collective bargaining A procedure for reaching agreements and resolving conflicts between employers and employees; in education, it covers the teacher's contract and work conditions.

Common curriculum A curriculum in which there is agreement about what students ought to know and be able to do and, often, about the age or grade at which they should be able to accomplish these goals.

Common school Public elementary schools that are open to children of all races, nationalities, and classes. During the nineteenth century, the common school became the embodiment of universal education.

Competency-based testing Assessment strategy aimed at gauging the acquisition of particular learnings.

Complementary teaching A term used in special education when a support person does something to complement the instruction provided by the classroom teacher, such as taking notes or paraphrasing the teacher's statements.

Comprehensive high school The predominant form of secondary education in the United States in the twentieth century. It provides both a preparation for college and a vocational education for students not going to college.

Compulsory education The practice of requiring school attendance by law.

Computer literacy Basic knowledge of and skills in the use of computer technology; considered an essential element of contemporary education.

Conant Report A study of the American comprehensive high school written by James B. Conant, a former president of Harvard University.

Conservation, concept of Demonstrated through Jean Piaget's famous demonstration of pouring water from a narrow container into a wider one and then posing the question to children of various ages, "Is this more water, less water, or the same amount of water?" Used to show the importance of providing children with **developmentally appropriate** learning experiences.

Constructivism A theory, based on research from cognitive psychology, that people learn by constructing their own knowledge through an active learning process, rather than by simply absorbing knowledge directly from another source.

Consultation When support personnel in special education provide assistance to general educators, enabling them to teach all the students in an inclusive class.

Content standards Statements of the knowledge and skills that students are expected to learn.

Conversation gap The disparity between poor and middle classes in the frequency and quality of child-adult verbal interaction.

Cooperative learning An educational strategy, composed of a set of instructional methods, in which students work in small, mixed-ability groups to master the material and to ensure that all group members reach the learning goals.

Coteaching A situation in which two teachers, often a special education teacher and a general education teacher, teach the same class together.

Council for Exceptional Children A national organization of individuals concerned about the education of children with disabilities or gifts. The organization promotes research, public policies, and programs that champion the rights of exceptional individuals.

Creative thinking skills The set of skills involving creative processes as means of analysis and decision making.

Criterion-referenced testing Assessment in which an individual's performance is evaluated against a set of preestablished objectives or standards (for comparison, *see* **norm-referenced testing**).

Critical thinking A general instructional approach intended to help students evaluate the worth of ideas, opinions, or evidence before making a decision or judgment.

Cultural milieu The characteristics of a particular culture, particularly the characteristics that determine one's value or success. For instance, the self-made person is valued in a highly competitive culture such as that of the United States. The cultural milieu is strongly promulgated by the mass media.

Cultural pluralism An approach to the diversity of individuals that calls for understanding and appreciation of differences.

Curriculum All the organized and intended experiences of the student for which the school accepts responsibility.

Curriculum compacting A teaching strategy that first gauges what students know about a subject and then tailors instruction to build on that knowledge.

Curriculum standards *See* **Standards movement.**

Dame schools Schools run by housewives during the early colonial period.

Decentralization The practice of diffusing the authority and decision making of a central individual or agency and allocating these responsibilities and privileges among others. As a restructuring approach in education, decentralization is intended to achieve more responsive and flexible management and decision making; **site-based management** is an example.

Derivative assessment framework A framework gleaned from a state's curricular standards that focuses on a small number of reconceptualized, eligible-to-be-taught curricular targets.

Desegregation The practice of eliminating **segregation;** that is, bringing together students of different racial, ethnic, and socioeconomic levels.

Developmentally appropriate The term used to describe learning tasks appropriate to the child's level of intellectual development.

Dewey, John American philosopher, educator, and author (1859–1952) who taught that learning by doing should form the basis of educational practice.

Didactic instruction A lecture approach to teaching that emphasizes compliant behavior on the part of the student while the teacher dispenses information.

Didactic philosophy The view that teachers should be masters of particular subject areas and that their role is to transmit their knowledge to students. Under this philosophy, teaching methods include lectures and recitations. Students are expected to memorize facts and concepts and practice skills until mastery has been achieved. (For comparison, *see* **constructivism.**)

Differentiation (differentiated instruction) A variety of techniques used to adapt instruction to the individual ability levels and learning styles of each student in the classroom.

Direct instruction Instruction in which the teacher explains the intended purpose and presents the content in a clear, orderly way.

Directive teaching Instructional method in which the teacher leads the students through the learning process rather than allowing learning to be student-led.

Disaggregated data Usually statistical information that has been broken down into smaller parts.

Discipline problems Violations of, or students who violate, classroom rules.

Distance learning The use of technology to link students and teachers who are separated in terms of location.

Dominance The teacher's ability to provide clear purpose and strong guidance regarding both academics and student behavior.

Due process The deliberative process that protects a person's constitutional right to receive fair and equal protection under the law.

Early childhood education Programs that concentrate on educating young children (usually up to age eight). Early childhood education has become an important priority in helping children from disadvantaged backgrounds achieve educational parity with other children.

Edison Project Experiment in entrepreneurial education begun in 1992 that seeks to establish partnerships with the public schools to create schools with a common curriculum and greater use of technology, among other characteristics. Now called the Edison Schools.

Educable mentally retarded (EMR) A classification of individuals who are mentally retarded but capable of learning basic skills and information.

Educated person An individual who is able to see the connectedness of all things.

Education The process of living and not a preparation for future living; a continuing reconstruction of experience.

Educational Testing Service (ETS) A nonprofit organization, located in Princeton, New Jersey, that develops educational tests like the SAT.

Education for All Handicapped Children Act (PL94-142) 1975 federal law that established the right of all students with disabilities to a free appropriate public education.

Elementary and Secondary Education Act The federal government's single largest investment in elementary and secondary education, including Title I. Originally passed in 1965, Congress reauthorizes it periodically, most recently in 2001 as the **No Child Left Behind Act.**

Empathy The capacity to participate in another's feelings or ideas.

English as a second language (ESL) Method of teaching English to non-English speakers.

Epistemic knowledge Representational or symbolic knowledge; the understanding that explicit concepts and domains connect or correspond. Such knowledge is demonstrated by the use of manipulatives such as blocks in teaching mathematics.

Equal Access Act of 1984 Statute making it unlawful for any public secondary school receiving federal funds to discriminate against any students who want to conduct a meeting on school premises during "noninstructional time" (before and after regular school hours) if other student groups (such as clubs) are allowed to use school facilities during these times.

Equal educational opportunity The legal principle that all children should have equal chances to develop their abilities and aptitudes to the fullest extent regardless of family background, social class, or individual differences.

Equal respect An ethical principle suggesting that our actions acknowledge the equal worth of humans (i.e., the Golden Rule).

Ethics A branch of philosophy that emphasizes values that relate to "good" and "bad" behavior; examining morality; and rules of conduct. Proponents believe that an educated person must have these values and that all children should be taught them.

Eurocentrism Term used to describe the heavy focus in school curricula on European history and contributions to Western civilization and the effective exclusion from instruction of the history and advances of other peoples.

"Evaded" curriculum A term coined to describe issues central to students' lives that are addressed briefly, if at all, in most schools; examples include teenage pregnancy and sexually transmitted disease.

Evidence-based research A term for studies that are properly conducted with true scientific rigor.

Excellence movement Education reform movement of the mid-1980s, in which greater academic rigor and higher standards were required of both students and teachers.

Extended school year Provision of education programs beyond the minimum number of school days mandated by law. Often referred to as "summer school."

Extrinsic motivation Rewards or motivation that are external to an activity itself, such as grades, gold stars, and prizes.

Fair use doctrine A legal principle defining specific, limited ways in which copyrighted material can be used without permission from the author.

Family Educational Rights and Privacy Act (1974) *See* **Buckley Amendment.**

Fetal alcohol syndrome (FAS) A disorder caused by a mother's consumption of alcohol during pregnancy, which can lead to retardation and delayed growth in the child.

Flexible grouping The grouping of students according to strength, need, or interest in order to advance instruction.

Formal curriculum Subjects taught in school and the instructional approaches used to transmit this knowledge.

Formative assessment *See* **Formative evaluation.**

Formative evaluation Evaluation used as a means of identifying a particular point of difficulty and prescribing areas in need of further work or development. Applied in developmental or implementation stages.

Fourteenth Amendment Requires that there be no law "respecting the establishment of religion or prohibiting the free exercise thereof." Relevant case law has been applied to keep public schools neutral in matters of religion.

Frontal teaching Traditional teaching method, now much criticized, in which the teacher's primary instructional method is lecturing in front of the classroom.

Full-day kindergarten An extension of the standard initial three- or four-hour introductory educational program for four- to six-year-old children to a full six- to eight-hour program.

Full-service schools Schools where the educational, health, psychological, and social requirements of students and their families are addressed by coordinating the services of professionals from these various disciplines at the school site.

Generational poverty The condition of many poor children whose parents and grandparents have been mired in economically impoverished circumstances.

Globalization The recent move toward heightened connection among nations and people around the world, fed by technology, free markets, and the free flow of information.

Goals 2000 *See* **National Education Goals.**

"Good" school A favorable judgment made about a school based on variable criteria, such as student achievement, test scores, low delinquency, and/or school climate.

Group investigation Form of cooperative learning in which students work in small groups using cooperative inquiry, group discussion, and projects.

Guided reflection protocol Method developed to aid teachers, alone or with colleagues, to think about their teaching practice.

Head Start A federally funded compensatory education program, in existence since the mid-1960s, that provides additional educational services to young children suffering the effects of poverty.

Health and housing gap The disparity between poor and middle children in the quality of health care and comfortable housing available.

Heuristic learning Educational method in which the student is encouraged to learn independently through extensive and reflective trial-and-error investigation.

Hidden curriculum *See* **Informal curriculum.**

Hidden rules A term used to refer to the social cues and language codes of the middle class, which are frequently unknown by poor children.

High-stakes tests The use of standardized test scores as a major determinant of significant educational outcomes, such as graduation, admission, or promotion.

Holistic scoring Grading a student's work as a whole, considering achievement in all relevant skill areas; the opposite of analytic scoring, which involves grading work according to specific, quantifiable achievement criteria.

Home schooling A movement that allows parents to keep their children out of regular public or private school and to educate them in the home.

Home-school liaison An individual who acts as a communications link between the school and students' parents or guardians.

Ideology The integrated assertions, theories, and aims that constitute a sociopolitical program.

Inclusion The commitment to educate each child, to the maximum extent appropriate, in the regular school and classroom, rather than moving children with disabilities to separate classes or institutions.

Inconsequential learning Information taught by another, rather than self-discovered, which has little or no importance to the learner.

Individualized education program/plan (IEP) A management tool required for every student covered by the provisions of the **Individuals with Disabilities Education Act.** It must indicate a student's current level of performance, short- and long-term instructional objectives, services to be provided, and criteria and schedules for evaluation of progress.

Individuals with Disabilities Education Act (IDEA) Federal law passed in 1990, extending and expanding the provisions of the Education for All Handicapped Children Act of 1975.

Informal curriculum The teaching and learning that occur in school but are not part of the formal, or explicit, curriculum; also called the *hidden curriculum.*

In loco parentis The responsibility of the teacher to function "in the place of the parent" when a student is in school.

Inquiry An education method that confronts the learner with an issue or problem and guides the learner toward a solution.

Inservice training Training provided by a school or school district to improve the skills and competencies of its professional staff, particularly teachers.

Institutional perspective The point of view or policy position of a social entity such as a school.

Intelligence According to classical theory, a single and general human capacity to think and solve problems.

Interdisciplinary (curriculum) A curriculum that integrates the subject matter from two or more disciplines, such as English and history.

International Baccalaureate program A rigorous academic curriculum designed to provide an education that would facilitate the admission of students into the universities of their choice in different countries. The program is run by the International Baccalaureate Organization.

Interstate New Teacher Assessment and Support Consortium (INTASC) A project sponsored by the Council of Chief State School Officers that is identifying standards for what beginning teachers should know and be able to do.

Intrinsic motivation Motivation that comes from the satisfaction of doing something, in contrast to **extrinsic motivation,** which comes from the reward received for doing something.

Invented spelling Child's attempt to express in symbols (letters) the group of sounds that make up a word.

Iowa Test of Basic Skills A series of standardized achievement tests that measure learning in reading, mathematics, language, and word study skills in grades K–9.

IQ Intelligence quotient, a measure of an individual's general intelligence.

Jigsaw teaching Form of cooperative learning in which each student on a team becomes "expert" on one topic by working with members from other teams assigned the same topic. On return to the home team, each expert teaches the group, and all students are assessed on all aspects of the topic.

Kohlberg's moral dilemma discussions Values education methodology involving presentation of moral dilemmas as catalysts for student discussions and the development of moral reasoning.

Learning communities A clustering of educators devoted to both professional development and learning-for-learning's-sake.

Learning criteria Specific statements of what students should know and be able to do after having completed a learning experience.

Learning disability (LD) A disability classification referring to a disorder in basic psychological processing that affects the individual's ability to listen, think, speak, read, write, spell, or do mathematical calculations. A learning disability is not primarily the result of visual, hearing, or motor disabilities; of mental retardation; of emotional disturbance; or of environmental, cultural, or economic disadvantage.

Learning style Characteristic way a student learns, including such factors as the way an individual processes information, preference for competition or cooperation, and preferred environmental conditions such as lighting or noise level.

Least restrictive environment (LRE) A requirement of the **Individuals with Disabilities Education Act** that students with disabilities should participate in regular education programs to the extent appropriate.

Lemon test A set of three requirements, established by the Supreme Court ruling in the case *Lemon* v. *Kurtzman,* that limits government action or legislation with respect to religion in the schools. Government action must not 1) have a religious purpose, 2) have the primary effect of either enhancing or inhibiting religion, and 3) create "excessive entanglement" between church and state.

Liberal education A broadly based education that teaches people to think for themselves rather than follow a particular orthodoxy.

Licensure (Licensing) Governmental approval to perform certain work, such as teaching.

Linear thinking The process of thinking through a concept or idea from start to finish by using step-by-step reasoning to reach a logical conclusion.

Local area network (LAN) A method of connecting computers within a relatively small area to allow people to work together and share information. Especially useful for fostering communication among classrooms within a school.

Magnet schools Alternative schools that provide instruction in specified areas such as the fine arts, for specific groups such as the gifted and talented, or using specific teaching styles such as open classrooms. In many cases, magnet schools are established as a method of promoting voluntary desegregation in schools.

Mainstreaming The practice of placing special education students in general education classes for at least part of the school day, while also providing additional services, programs, or classes as needed.

Matched group experiment An experimental method whereby subjects in the control and experimental groups are "matched" according to the focus variables, such as past achievement, IQ, and other characteristics.

McGuffey Readers A six-volume series of textbooks, written by William Holmes McGuffey, that sold over 100 million copies during the nineteenth century. The books contained poetry, moral teachings, and writings of statesmen and religious leaders, as well as grammar teaching.

Median A statistical term meaning the midpoint of a set of scores; that is, the point on either side of which half the scores occur.

Mediation A cognitive activity whereby a person uses certain strategies to understand his or her environment and solve problems.

Melting pot A metaphor and historical theory that suggests that although America takes in a wide variety of peoples (races, creeds, nationalities, and classes), the process of living in this country and being an American melts away differences so that all peoples blend together.

Merit pay The system of paying teachers according to the quality of their performance, usually by means of a bonus given for meeting specific goals.

Mixed-ability (or heterogeneous) grouping A placement approach in which students of different abilities are grouped together. Rooted in the belief that peer supervision, peer teaching, and group learning are effective means of educating all students, this approach is the opposite of **tracking** or ability grouping.

Moral ecology The ethical balance or pattern needed to maintain a society.

Moral leadership Guiding or setting examples in matters of **ethics**, **character**, and right or wrong.

Multicultural education An approach to education intended to recognize cultural diversity and foster the cultural enrichment of all children and youth.

Multiculturalism A concept or situation in which individuals understand, respect, and participate in aspects (such as sports, food, customs, music, and language) of many different cultures.

Multilevel learning stations A teaching strategy typically used to offer individual students an opportunity to select independent study tasks from a variety of options (e.g., exploring a particular topic through music or texts or videos).

Multimedia The combination of various media, such as text, graphics, video, music, voice narration, and manipulative objects; today, the term is often applied to computerized applications that incorporate two or more media.

Multiple intelligence theory A theory of human intelligence advanced by Howard Gardner, which suggests that humans have the psychobiological potential to solve problems or to fashion products that are valued in at least one cultural context. Gardner's research indicates at least eight separate faculties.

A Nation at Risk: The Imperative for Educational Reform A highly influential 1983 national commission report calling for extensive education reform, including more academic course requirements, more stringent college entrance requirements, upgraded and updated textbooks, and longer school days and years.

National Assessment of Educational Progress (NAEP) A congressionally mandated survey of American students that is the primary source on educational achievement, and has become known as "the nation's report card."

National Board for Professional Teaching Standards (NBPTS) A professional agency that is setting voluntary standards for what experienced teachers should know and be able to do in more than thirty different teaching areas.

National Child Abuse Prevention and Treatment Act of 1974 Federal law that defines child abuse and neglect as "the physical or mental injury, sexual abuse or exploitation, negligent treatment, or maltreatment of a child under the age of eighteen, or the age specified by the child protection law of the state in question, by a person who is responsible for the child's welfare."

National Commission on Teaching and America's Future Blue-ribbon panel that in 1996 released the report *What Matters Most: Teaching for America's Future*. The report emphasized the importance of high-quality teaching and recommended the National Board certification of 105,000 teachers by the year 2006.

National Council for Accreditation of Teacher Education (NCATE) Nationally recognized organization awarding voluntary accreditation to college-level teacher education programs. Approximately 600 colleges and universities in the United States are accredited through NCATE.

National Education Association (NEA) The nation's largest teachers' association, founded in 1857 and having a membership of over 2.2 million educators.

National Education Goals Goals for U.S. education, established by the president and the fifty state governors in 1990.

Nature-based approach Basing education strategies upon a research-driven, biological understanding of human learning.

New England Primer An illustrated book of religious texts and other readings that was the most famous basic school text for the period between 1690 and 1790.

New math A mathematics curriculum popular in the 1960s that focused on teaching students to understand the structure of the discipline of mathematics rather than on teaching computation techniques.

No Child Left Behind Act The most recent reauthorization, in 2001, of the **Elementary and Secondary Education Act**, the federal government's single largest investment in elementary and secondary education, including Title I.

Nondiscussables Important topics of conversation that are laden with anxiety and strong feelings.

Norming The process of establishing norms for standardized tests, based on reviews of norm groups and their scores. Most tests are renormed approximately every seven years; the trend has been to raise norms on subsequent evaluations, so that increasingly higher performance has been required to reach the 50th percentile (or normal performance).

Norm-referenced testing Assessment in which an individual's performance is evaluated against what is typical of others in his or her peer group (i.e., norms) (for comparison, *see* **criterion-referenced testing**).

OERI The Office of Educational Research and Improvement, a division of the U.S. Department of Education up until 2003.

Old Deluder Act A Massachusetts law passed in 1647 that strengthened an earlier law that required parents to educate their children by requiring citizens to support schools, which would in turn enable children to thwart the snares of Satan by their ability to read God's word in the Bible.

Oldfield schools An early form of community schools in rural areas, usually built in abandoned, worn-out fields and supported by parents' contributions and tuition payments.

Paideia From the Greek *pais,* meaning "the upbringing of a child"; used as the equivalent of the Latin *humanitas* (from which came "the humanities"), signifying the general learning that should be the possession of all human beings.

Pantheism The belief that there are many gods and that they inhabit all reality.

Parallel teaching A situation in which support personnel (such as a special educator or Title I teacher) and the classroom teacher rotate among heterogeneous groups of students in different sections of the general education classroom.

Paraprofessional A trained aide who assists a professional, such as a teacher's aide.

Parent involvement The situation in which students' parents or guardians play a role in aspects of school life.

Pedagogy The art or profession of teaching.

Peer coaching A method by which teachers help one another learn new teaching strategies and material. It often involves release time to allow teachers to visit one another's classes as they start to use new programs, such as **cooperative learning.**

Peer review A system of evaluation in which the perceptions and judgments of fellow employees (teachers) contribute to salary decisions.

Performance-based tests Tests that require students to actually perform, as by writing or drawing, to demonstrate the skill being measured.

Personalism An approach to life that focuses on the satisfaction of individual desires.

Philosophy The love or search for wisdom; the quest for basic principles to understand the meaning of life. Western philosophy traditionally contains five branches of philosophy: metaphysics, ethics, aesthetics, epistemology, and logic.

Phonics An instructional strategy used to teach letter-sound relationships to beginning readers by having them sound out words.

Physical indicators of child abuse Physical symptoms that suggest a child is being abused.

Politically correct (PC) A term coined to describe thinking that is politically popular. Taken to extreme, such thinking is so euphemistic and generalized as to be opinionless.

Portfolio A collection of a person's work. For students, portfolios are being used as a relatively new form of authentic assessment. They can contain a great range of work, from paper and pen work to sculpture.

Portfolio assessment A means of assessment based on a collection of a person's work. For students, portfolios may contain a great range of work, from paper and pen work to sculpture.

Positivism A philosophy asserting a radical distinction between facts, which can be scientifically proven, and values, which positivism holds are mere expressions of feelings, not objective truth. Positivism provides the philosophical underpinnings for moral **relativism.**

Pragmatism Belief that one tests truth by its practical consequences. Therefore, truth is relative.

Pre–post studies A type of flawed research study in which key variables are measured before and after a treatment (e.g., new math program, longer school day), and the results are attributed to the treatment without accounting for other possible effects (e.g., better teachers, demographic changes).

Presage characteristics Characteristics of teachers resulting from formative experiences, training, and individual properties such as intelligence and personality.

Private-venture schools Schools run by individuals or corporations, which theoretically can generate a profit.

Privatization A movement in which public schools are run by private, often for-profit, organizations.

Problem-solving skills Skills involving the application of knowledge and information to solving a given problem, for example, definition, analysis, comparison/contrast, and sequencing; synonymous with higher-order thinking skills.

Process criteria Learning criteria used for grading and reporting in which teachers take into account effort, work habits, classroom quizzes, homework, class participation, or attendance. (For comparison, *see* **product criteria** and **progress criteria.**)

Product choice An instructional strategy whereby the teacher allows students to select the "product outcome" (e.g., videotaped presentation, mural, research paper) for a particular lesson or unit.

Product criteria Learning criteria used for grading and reporting in which teachers base their grades or reports exclusively on final examination scores, overall assessments, or other culminating demonstrations of learning. (For comparison, *see* **process criteria** and **progress criteria.**)

Professional development Continuous advances in teacher's knowledge and skills; lifelong learning.

Professional development schools Innovative public schools formed through partnerships between professional education programs and P–12 schools. Their mission is professional preparation of candidates, faculty development, inquiry directed at the improvement of practice, and enhanced student learning.

Professionalization of teaching The movement toward establishing or recognizing teaching as a profession, not merely an application of skills toward a particular task. This movement supports such practices as **site-based management** and other efforts that give teachers more authority and control over educating students.

Progress criteria Highly individualized learning criteria used for grading and reporting in which teachers look at how far students have come rather than where they are. (For comparison, *see* **process criteria** and **product criteria.**)

Progressive school A school that focuses on students' personal and social development. *See* **progressivism.**

Progressivism (progressive ideals) An educational philosophy that embraces largely unstructured educational programs, focusing on implicit teaching and individualized instruction.

Provincial Social values that are determined by local traditions and mores.

Pull-out groups Groups of students who periodically leave the regular classroom for special education services. For instance, students with hearing impairments may attend regular sessions of instruction in sign language.

Randomized experiment An experiment in which the subjects are assigned to particular groups by chance, thus eliminating selection bias.

Readiness A judgment that a student is capable of learning a specific topic or skill.

Reading gap The difference between the amount of time spent reading and the quality of reading material to which poor and middle-class children are exposed; disparities in performance on reading assessments between poor and middle-class children.

Reciprocal teaching An instructional procedure designed to teach students cognitive strategies that might lead to improved reading comprehension. Examples include summarization, question generation, clarification, and prediction, supported through dialogue between teacher and students and the attempt to gain meaning from the text.

Reflection An inner process in which the individual thinks back on events, attempting to see them in a more objective matter with a view toward improvement.

Regression analysis A statistical approach that allows judgment regarding the impact of one variable independent of the effects of other variables.

Role model gap The disparity between poor and middle-class children in availability of successful, achieving adults.

Rubric A set of rules for scoring student products or student performance. Typically takes the form of a checklist or a rating scale.

Sabbatical A study leave granted to selected teachers, usually after a number of years of service.

Saxon Math Program A traditional skills-based approach for teaching mathematics developed by John Saxon; it emphasizes repetition of mathematical operations.

School choice Allowing parents to select alternative educational programs for their children, either within a given school or among different schools.

School culture The prevailing mores, values, and rituals that permeate a school.

School within a school In large schools, the establishment of "houses" of teachers and 100 to 400 students who spend much of their time together.

Scientifically based research An investigation employing systematic, objective procedures to obtain valid knowledge.

Scientific creationism A theory of world creation, based on the Book of Genesis, that some Christians have proposed as a counterbalance to the teaching of evolution in science classes.

Secularism An educational approach that ignores religious and spiritual perspectives in favor of a scientific and totally human perspective, excluding, too, the role of religious motivation in historical events (e.g., the movement to free slaves in nineteenth-century America).

Segregation The act of separating people according to such characteristics as race, ethnicity, or **socioeconomic status.** In education, the fact that most students attend schools in the areas in which they live means that student populations will be homogeneous and thus segregated; **desegregation** is achieved when student populations are mixed.

Self-actualization The status of having achieved one's potential through one's own efforts. Providing opportunities for self-actualization greatly promotes self-esteem.

Self-discovered learning Private truths that each individual has personally uncovered and assimilated into his or her consciousness.

Self-fulfilling prophecy Students' behavior that comes about as a result of teachers' expectations that the students will behave in a certain way. Teachers expect students to behave in a certain way, they communicate those expectations by both overt and subtle means, and students respond by behaving in the way expected.

Sexism Discriminatory attitudes and actions against a particular gender group, especially women.

Sexual harassment Acts directed against an individual that are intended to humiliate, intimidate, or oppress. Sexual harassment includes making comments of a sexual nature, propositioning, touching, making unwelcome sexual advances, or making one's successful employment or education contingent upon accepting or tolerating such harassment.

Simulation A technique for learning or practicing skills that involves dealing with a realistic, but artificial problem or situation. Typically, it provides an opportunity for safe practice with feedback on performance.

Single salary schedule The dominant remuneration system in public education, where compensation is based on degrees and years of service rather than demand or competence.

Site-based management A school reform effort to decentralize, allowing decisions to be made and budgets to be established at the school-building level, where most of the changes need to occur. Usually teachers become involved in the decision-making process. Also known as site-based decision making, school-based management, or school-based decision making.

Situation poverty The temporary condition of many poor children due to unforeseen events, such as death, divorce, job loss, or parent illness.

Socialization The general process of social learning whereby the child learns the many things he or she must know to become an acceptable member of society.

Social justice The concept of doing away with social and economic inequalities for those in our society who have been denied these benefits of a democratic society.

Social learning theory The part of psychology that deals with human learning in social situations, including attitudes, motivations, and behavior.

Social promotion The practice of promoting students to the next grade whether or not they have accomplished the goals of their current grade.

Socioeconomic status The status one occupies on the basis of social and economic factors such as income level, educational level, occupation, area of residence, family background, and the like.

Socratic instruction A method of teaching in which the teacher asks questions and leads the student through responses and discussion to an understanding of the information being taught.

Split-brain theory Theory suggesting that certain intellectual capacities and functions are controlled by the left hemisphere of the brain and others by the right hemisphere.

Sputnik 1 The Soviet rocket launched into space in 1957 that threatened American security and thus stimulated educational reform.

Stakeholders People who are affected by the activities within an institution.

Standard Exemplary performance that serves as a benchmark.

Standardized tests Tests given to large groups of students under uniform, or standard, conditions and scored according to uniform procedures.

Standards-based education *See* **Standard** and **Standards movement.**

Standards-based reform *See* **Standards movement.**

Standards movement Efforts at the local, state, and federal level to make clear exactly what students need to know and be able to do and, therefore, what schools need to teach. Implicit in the standards movement is an attempt to increase the academic achievement of students.

Star teachers A teacher with several attributes and the capacity to transcend the limitations of the school environment.

Suggestive accountability Also called "nice" accountability, a soft, accommodating form of responsibility for outcomes or results that depends on educators' cooperation and has few real consequences.

Summative assessment *See* **Summative evaluation.**

Summative evaluation Evaluation used to assess the adequacy or outcome of a program after the program has been fully developed and implemented.

Supportive teaching A situation in an inclusive classroom in which the classroom teacher takes the lead role, and support personnel rotate among the students.

Tao A Chinese term used by C. S. Lewis that combines the wisdom of many cultures to identify a universal path to becoming a good person.

Teacher competencies The characteristics that make a teacher qualified to do the job, including various areas of subject-matter expertise and a wide range of personality variables. Some school reform proposals urge that teachers undergo periodic assessment of their competencies to maintain licensure or earn incentives.

Teacher empowerment The process of giving teachers (or of teachers taking) greater control over their professional lives and how they deliver their educational services.

Teacher expectations A teacher's preconceptions about how a given student will behave or perform.

Teacher voice The quality of a learning community in which teachers have a real "say" in their professional development.

Teach for America An alternative teacher education and placement program for college graduates who have not taken an undergraduate teacher preparation program. After training, recruits are placed in urban or rural schools and make a two-year commitment to stay in teaching.

Teaching for meaning An educational approach that focuses on big ideas and that requires students to inquire and solve problems in authentic contexts.

Teaching portfolio Collection of such items as research papers, pupil evaluations, teaching units, and videocassettes of lessons to reflect the quality of a teacher's teaching. Portfolios can be used to illustrate to employers the teacher's expertise or to obtain national board certification.

Tenure A legal right that confers continuing employment on teachers, protecting them from dismissal without adequate cause.

Tiered assignment An instructional strategy in which the teacher allows students to select assignments of various degrees of difficulty and complexity depending on their abilities.

TIMSS The Third International Mathematics and Science Study, which is the largest and most extensive international study of academic achievement in mathematics and science ever undertaken.

Tinker* v. *Des Moines Independent Community School District The 1969 decision in which the Supreme Court held that the schools cannot prohibit students' expression of opinions when the expression does not materially and substantially interfere with the requirements of appropriate discipline in the schools; to do so would violate the First Amendment of the Constitution.

Title I (Chapter 1) Part of the 1965 Elementary and Secondary Education Act that delivers federal funds to local school districts and schools for the education of students from low-income families. It also supplements the educational services provided to low-achieving students in those districts.

Tracking The homogeneous grouping of students for learning tasks on the basis of some measure(s) of their abilities.

Traditional school A school that seeks to transmit to its students the best knowledge, skills, and values in society.

Transfer of learning Connection or application of learned material to future knowledge or skill acquisition.

Valid research A study that accurately measures the phenomenon it sets out to study.

Values Principles or qualities we like or believe to be good or desirable. Certain concepts, such as responsibility, justice, fairness, and caring, are frequently mentioned as values that form the basis of civil life and morality.

Values clarification A values education methodology advocating the presentation of values to students free from imposed value judgments. Students should then be allowed freedom to choose their own values.

Voucher programs A type of **school choice** plan that gives parents a receipt or written statement that they can exchange for the schooling they feel is most desirable for their child. The school, in turn, can cash in its received vouchers for the money to pay teachers and buy resources.

White flight A response to public school racial integration efforts in which white citizens move out of the central city into the suburbs so their children can attend neighborhood schools with a lower percentage of minority students.

Whole language A progressive approach to the teaching of reading that emphasizes the integration of language arts skills and knowledge across the curriculum.

Zone of proximal development A range of tasks that a person cannot do alone yet but can accomplish when assisted by a more skilled partner. This zone is the point at which instruction can succeed and real learning is possible.

Index

Abington v. *Schempp,* 184
Abuse, 54
  physical and behavioral indicators of, 87
  recognizing and reporting, 85–90
  types of, 86
Academic freedom, 300–301
Acceptable use policies (AUPs), 393
Accommodation, 418
Accountability, 332–340, 355–360, 362, 375–376
  coercive, 349, 350, 351, 353
  nice *vs.* mean, 349–351
  suggestive, 349–350
"Accountability: What's Worth Measuring?" (Raywid), 355–360
Achievement
  class and, 341–347
  classroom management and, 206–213
  cooperative learning and, 251
  voucher programs and, 374
Achievement gap, 199–204
Active learners, 232
Active learning, 9
Adler, Mortimer J., "The Paideia Proposal: Rediscovering the Essence of Education," 163–168
Administrators, as teachers, 114–115
Adult education, 384
Aesthetics, 18
African American students
  achievement gap and, 199, 200
  cultural heritage in curriculum for, 405
  dropout rates for, 117, 118
  resegregation and, 400
  voucher programs and, 373
After-school programs, 132–135
Aggressive students, 210, 211
Allies
  colleagues as, 38–39
  parents as, 40–41
  professional groups as, 41
  professional literature as, 42
  self as, 43–44
  students as, 39–40
  teachers as, 37
  universities as, 42–43
"All Teachers Are Not the Same: A Multiple Approach to Teacher Compensation" (Koppich), 11–13
Alvarado, Anthony, 160
American Academy of Arts and Sciences, 176
American Association of School Administrators, 158
American Association of University Women (AAUW), 75, 76, 77, 436
American Dream and the Public Schools, The (Hochschild and Scovronick), 402
American Educational Research Journal, 35
American Federation of Teachers, 11, 156, 181
American Jewish Congress, 181
Annenberg Institute for School Reform, 118
Apathy, 218
Asperger's Syndrome, 419
Assertive behavior, 208
Assessment, 144. *See also* Grading
Assignments, 216. *See also* Homework
Assimilation, 404–406
Association of School Counselors, 210
At-homeness, 19–20
"At Risk for Abuse: A Teacher's Guide for Recognizing and Reporting Child Neglect and Abuse" (Cates, Markell, and Bettenhausen), 85–90
At-risk students
  for child abuse or neglect, 85–90
  school culture and, 102
Attrition
  rates, 31–36
  teacher preparation and, 35 (fig.)
Authentic standards movement, 155–160
"Authentic Standards Movement and Its Evil Twin, The" (Thompson), 155–160
Autism, 419
Averaging, 240
Ayers, William, 42

Bancroft, Ann, 423
Barber, Benjamin, 411
Barr, Robert D., "Who Is This Child?", 50–51
Barth, Roland S., 37
Barth, Roland S., "The Culture Builder," 99–103
Behavioral indicators of neglect or abuse, 87
Benefit maximization, 295–296
Bennett, William J., 17, 106
Berry, Barnett, 32
Bettenhausen, Sherrie, "At Risk for Abuse: A Teacher's Guide for Recognizing and Reporting Child Neglect and Abuse," 85–90
Bill and Melinda Gates Foundation, 17, 119, 122
Blacher, J., 86
Black, Hugo, 183
Bloom, Benjamin, 95
Bottom fishing, 282
Bottoms, Gene, 119
Boyer, Ernest L., 178
Boyer, Ernest L., "The Educated Person," 271–277
Boys, education needs of, 434–439
Brain research, gender-specific characteristics and, 434–435, 437, 439
Breaking Ranks, 118
Brigham, Michele, "Enabling or Disabling? Observations on Changes in Special Education," 418–425
Brown v. *Board of Education of Topeka,* 399, 400, 401
Buber, Martin, 187
Buderi, Robert, 392, 396
Burney, Deanna, 160
Burnout, teacher, 23, 33
Burstein, Daniel, 391
Bush, George W., 117
Business Roundtable, 118

Cahill, Michele, 118, 119
Calkins, Lucy, 42
Cannell, Stephen, 423
"Can Star Teachers Create Learning Communities?" (Haberman), 21–26
Capital flight, 57
Caring, in curriculum, 186–192
Carmichael, Stokely, 405
Carnegie Corporation of New York, 318
Carnegie Forum, 17
Carnegie Foundation, 119
Carnegie unit, 272
Carper, James C., "The Changing Land of U.S. Education," 286–290

"Case for Being Mean, The" (Hess), 349–353
Cates, Dennis L., "At Risk for Abuse: A Teacher's Guide for Recognizing and Reporting Child Neglect and Abuse," 85–90
Center for the Future of Teaching and Learning, 32
Certification, 329
Cetron, Kimberley, "A Forecast for Schools," 380–385
Cetron, Marvin, " A Forecast for Schools," 380–385
"Changing Landscape of U.S. Education, The" (Carper), 286–290
Character education, 194–197, 310–315
Charter schools, 286, 290, 369, 370, 372
Cherry picking, 282
Child abuse/neglect, 54
  recognizing and reporting, 85–90
Child Abuse Prevention and Treatment Act of 1974, 86
Children's Defense Fund, 54
Churchill, Winston, 179
Civil Rights Project (Harvard University), 118, 400
Clark, Tom, 184
"Class and the Classroom" (Rothstein), 341–347
Classroom management, 206–213
Class size, 121–125, 373, 376
Clifford, Margaret M., "Students Need Challenge, Not Easy Success," 218–223
Clonlara Home-Based Education, 140
Clonlara v. *State Board,* 140
"Closing the Achievement Gap" (Haycock), 199–204
Coalesced content standards, 146
Coalition of Essential Schools, 118, 141
Coercive accountability, 349
Cohen, Rosetta Marantz, "Schools Our Teachers Deserve," 109–115
Coleman, James, 289
Collaboration, 22
Collaborative learning. *See* Cooperative learning
Colleagues, as allies, 38–39
Colonial education, 286–288
"Coming Around on School Choice" (Viteritti), 367–371
Committee of Ten, 122
Committee on Grading, 237
Common school reform, 288–289
Community, 22
Competencies, 14–20
Competency-based testing, 368
Complementary teaching, 430
Computers, 383
  girls and, 439
Conant, James, 177, 191
Conant Report, 122
Conceptually difficult knowledge, 234
"Considered Opinion, A: Diversity, Tragedy, and the Schools" (Ravitch), 404–406
Constraints, 219–220
Constructivism, 231–235
Consultation, 430
Content, 431
Content standards, 145–146, 226, 228, 229
Conversation gap, 343–344
Cooney, Joan, 276
Cooperation, 208–209
Cooperative base groups, 247–248
Cooperative learning, 232, 431
  achievement and, 245–246
  application of, 245–252
  competitive *vs.,* 110
  effects of, 246
  elements of, 245–246
  explanation of, 110, 232
  groups, 246
  home schoolers and, 140
  integrated use of, 248–249
  interpersonal relationships and, 251–252
  outcomes of, 251
  social competence and, 252
  types of, 247–248
Copyright law, 307–308
Corporal punishment, 303–304
Coteaching, 429, 430
Covert students, 210
Creative learners, 232
Critical Incidents in Teaching: Developing Professional Judgement (Tripp), 2, 4, 6
Critical Incidents Protocol, 4–6
Crowley, John C., "Letter from a Teacher," 46–48
Cuban, Larry, 392
Cuban, Larry, "A Tale of Two Schools," 104–107
Cultural diversity. *See* Diversity; Multicultural education
Cultural Literacy: What Every American Needs to Know (Hirsch), 15
Culture
  aspects of, 59–61
  gender and, 434
  school, 99–103, 357–358
"Culture Builder, The" (Barth), 99–103
Curriculum
  achievement gap and, 202–204
  character education and, 194–197
  characteristics of effective, 271
  compacting, 93–94
  formal, 195–196
  hidden, 196, 358
  interdisciplinary, 412–416
  Paideia, 163–168
  quality school, 169–174
  religion in, 181–185
  saber-tooth, 149–154
  Tao to guide, 195
  themes of care in, 186–192
  universal design of, 431
"Curriculum Matters" (Popham), 143–147

Dame schools, 287
Darling-Hammond, Linda, "What Matters Most: A Competent Teacher for Every Child," 318–330
Davis, Allison, 176, 177
Davis, LaShonda, 76
Davis v. *Monroe County Board of Education,* 76
Dead Poets Society (film), 9
Deiro, Judith, 43
Delphi polls, 380
Deming, W. Edwards, 174
Dependency ratio, 402
Derivative assessment frameworks, 146
Desegregation, 400, 401
De Tocqueville, Alexis, 62
Dewey, John, 4, 6, 179
Dewey, John, "My Pedagogic Creed," 261–267
Differentiated instruction, 254–259, 430, 431
DiMartino, Joseph, 119
Disabilities. *See* Students with disabilities
Discipline problems, 79–83
Discrimination, racial, 400–401
Diversity
  assimilation and, 404–406
  contributions from, 408
  educational technology and, 382
  gender-specific needs and, 434–439
  inclusion and, 418–425, 427–432
  multicultural education and, 411–416
  parental involvement and, 136
  racism and, 58
Dodd, Anne Wescott, "Engaging Students: What I Learned Along the Way," 214–217
Doing School (Pope), 385
Dominance, 207
Donne, John, 15
Dowell v. *Oklahoma City,* 400
Dreyfus, Richard, 9
Dropout rates, 117, 118, 218, 400, 437
Du Bois, W. E. B., 411, 412
Ducharme, Edward R., 14
Due process, 302–303

Economic transformation, 57–58
Edelman, Marian Wright, "Leaving No Child Behind," 52–54
Educated person, 271–277
"Educated Person, The" (Boyer), 271–277

Education. *See also* Teacher education/training
 character, 194–197, 310–315
 colonial, 286–288
 essence of, 163–168
 gender-specific needs and, 434–439
 inclusive, 427–432
 lifelong, 384–385
 multicultural, 404, 407–410, 411–416
 philosophy of, 46–48
 special, 418–425
 spending on, 361–365
 standards-based, 356
Educational attainment, 201
Educational philosophy, 46–48
Educational reform
 barriers to, 320–322
 challenges for teaching and, 319–320
 commission recommendations for, 322–326
 economic issues related to, 361–365
 evidence-based, 279–280
 guidelines for, 332–340
 overview of, 317
 school choice and, 367–371
 standards-based, 155–160, 202
 teacher-centered, 111–115
Educational technology
 culture of learning and, 392–396
 evaluating use of, 387–391
 function of, 379
 future outlook for, 380–385
 issues related to, 387–391
Education for All Handicapped Children Act, 302
Education research, judging validity of, 280–281
Education Trust, 200, 204, 376
Egalitarianism, 22
Einstein, Albert, 83
Eisner, Elliot W., "The Kind of Schools We Need," 332–340
Eitzen, Stanley, "Problem Students: The Sociocultural Roots," 56–61
Electives, 164
Elmore, Richard, 157, 160
Emotional abuse, 86
Empathy, development of, 47
Empowerment, 110
"Enabling or Disabling? Observations on Changes in Special Education" (Kauffman, McGee, and Brigham), 418–425
Endangered Minds (Healy), 392
Endsley, Dan, 139
"Engaging Students: What I Learned Along the Way" (Dodd), 214–217
English Language Learners (ELLs), 403
Equal Access Act, 299
Equal respect principle, 295–296
Ethics, of teaching, 293–296
"Ethics of Teaching, The" (Strike), 293–296
Evaluation
 as external constraint, 219
 formative, 222
 summative, 222–223
 of teachers, 12–13
 unobtrusive, 359–360
Evans, Robert, 394
Evidence-based reform, 279–280
Experience and Education (Dewey), 4, 6
Extrinsic motivation, 215

Face-to-face promotive interaction, 250
"False Promise of Vouchers, The" (McDonald), 373–376
Family Matters (Evans), 394
Family structure, 59
Farenga, Pat, 139
Farr, Roger, 147
Farris, Michael P., 140
Featherstone, Joseph, 38
Feldman, Sandra, 156
Ferguson, Ronald, 204
Feuerstein, Reuven, 71
Finders, Margaret, "Why Some Parents Don't Come to School," 126–131
"Finding Allies: Sustaining Teachers' Health and Well-Being" (Houghton), 37–44
First Amendment, 298, 368
Flagg, Fannie, 423
Flexible grouping, 94
Flickering Mind, The (Oppenheimer), 392
"Flickering Teacher, The" (Sky-McIlvain), 395
Florio-Ruane, Susan, 39
"Forecast for Schools, A" (Cetron and Cetron), 380–385
Forecasting International, 380
Foreign knowledge, 234–235
Formal cooperative learning, 247
Formal curriculum, 195–196
Formative evaluation, 222
Foundations, 260
Fourteenth Amendment, 298
Fried, Robert, 7
Friedman, Milton, 368
Fulton, Kathleen, 33
Funding, adequate, 365

Gardner, Howard, 106
Gates, Bill, 394
Gay, Geneva, "The Importance of Multicultural Education," 411–416
Gender, after-school activities and, 134–135
Gender-specific educational needs, 434–439
Generational poverty, 70
Gifted students, 92–96
Girls, education needs of, 434–439
Glasser, William, "The Quality School Curriculum," 169–174
Goldberg, Arthur, 184
Goodlad, John, "Teaching What We Hold to be Sacred," 176–179
Google, 394
Gould, Stephen J., 177
Government policy, consequences of, 58–59
Gow, Paul, "Technology and the Culture of Learning," 392–396
Grading
 benefits for students and, 237–242
 as challenge to educators, 241
 function and methods for, 237–239
 guidelines for, 240–241
 historical background of, 241–242
 learning criteria and, 239–240
Gray, Tom, 423
Graziano, Claudia, 21, 31, 36
"Great Teacher Question: Beyond Competencies, The" (Ducharme), 14–20
Greene, Jay, 118
Groeber, Deborah, 422
Grossman, Pam, 38
Group processing, 250
Guided Reflection Protocol, 2–4
Gurian, Michael, "With Boys and Girls in Mind," 434–439
Guskey, Thomas R., "Making the Grade: What Benefits Students?", 237–242

Haberman, Martin, 21
Hardy, Lawrence, "The New Diversity," 399–402
Hart, Betty, 344
Havighurst, Robert, 176, 177
Haycock, Kati, "Closing the Achievement Gap," 199–204
Haynes, Charles, 184
Head Start, 61, 178
Health gap, 345–346
Healy, Jane M., 392
Healy, Jane M., "The Mad Dash to Compute," 387–391
"Heart of the Matter, The" (Fried), 7–9
Hess, Frederick M., "The Case for Being Mean," 349–353
Hidden curriculum, 196, 358
Hidden rules, 70, 71–73
High-needs students, 210–212
High-performance learning group, 246
High School (Boyer), 178
High schools, remaking, 117–120
High-stakes tests, 155, 156, 158, 159
Hiring practices, teacher, 113–114, 321
Hirsch, E. D., Jr., 15, 16, 106

Hispanic American students
achievement gap and, 199, 200
demographic trends and, 402
dropout rates for, 117, 118
educational technology and, 382
segregation and, 399
voucher programs and, 373
Hobbs, Lois, 400
Hochschild, Jennifer, 402
Hofferth, Sandra L., "Life After School," 132–135
Hole, Simon, "Reflection Is at the Heart of Practice," 2–6
Holmes Group, 17
Home Education League of Parents (HELP), 139
Home environments, 129–130
Home-School Association, 139
Home schooling, 137–141, 290
"Home Schooling Comes of Age" (Lines), 137–141
Home Schooling in Oregon (Lahrson), 139
Home-School Legal Defense Association, 140
Homework, achievement and, 344
Hostile Hallways: Bullying, Teasing, and Sexual Harassment in School (American Association of University Women Educational Foundation), 75, 76, 77
"Hostile Hallways" (Woods), 75–78
Hostile students, 210
Houghton, Patricia, "Finding Allies: Sustaining Teachers' Health and Well-Being," 37
Housing
discrimination and, 400–401
gap in, 345–346
"How to Create Discipline Problems" (Wasicsko and Ross), 79–83
Hudson, Mildred, 36
Hutchins, Robert M., 176
Hyperactive students, 211, 212

Ideas, continual sharing of, 22
Immigration, 58, 399, 403, 404, 411
"Importance of Multicultural Education, The" (Gay), 411–416
Inattentive students, 211, 212
Inclusion, 418–425, 427–432
Inconsequential learning, 269
Index of Dissimilarity, 401–402
Individual accountability, 249
Individualized education programs (IEPs), 419, 422, 428
Individuals with Disabilities Education Act (IDEA), 140, 302, 421, 427
Induction programs, 35–36
Industrial Revolution, 57
Inert knowledge, 233
Informal cooperative learning, 247
Informational feedback, 220
Ingersoll, Richard, 35
Institutional perspective, 126–127
Instruction
achievement gap and, 199–204
challenge as element of, 218–223
differentiated, 254–259, 430, 431
engaging students in, 214–217
Integration, 400
Interdisciplinary curriculum, 412–416
International Baccalaureate (IB) program, 383
Internet, 381, 384, 392, 395, 396
Interpersonal relationships, cooperative learning and, 251–252
Interstate New Teacher Assessment and Support Consortium (INTASC), 323
INTIME (Integrating New Technologies into the Methods of Education), 35
Intrinsic motivation, 215, 219, 338
Iowa Tests of Basic Skills, 228
Islamic Society of North America, 181

Jackson, Jesse, 178
Jankuniene, Zita, "Life After School," 132–135
Johnson, David W., "Making Cooperative Learning Work," 245–252
Johnson, LouAnne, 42
Johnson, Roger T., "Making Cooperative Learning Work," 245–252

Kauffman, James M., "Enabling or Disabling? Observations on Changes in Special Education," 418–425
"Key to Classroom Management, The" (Marzano and Marzano), 206–213
"Kind of Schools We Need, The" (Eisner), 332–340
King, M., 101
King, Martin Luther, Jr., 277
Kline, David, 391
Knestrict, Thomas David, "Memories from the "Other": Lessons in Connecting with Students," 63–68
Knowledge
conceptually difficult, 233
foreign, 234–235
inert, 233
ritual, 233
Koppich, Julia E., 11
Kress, Nancy, 396

Lahrson, Ann, 139
Learners
active, 232
creative, 232
social, 232
students as, 102–103
Learning
active, 9
classroom management and, 208, 209
cooperative, 110, 140, 232, 245–252, 431
feedback to enhance, 220
gender-specific, 434–439
grades and, 239
inconsequential, 269
lifelong, 384–385
meaningful, 3–4, 225–229
personal thoughts on, 268–270
problem-based, 233
self-discovered, 269
technology and culture of, 392–396
transfer of, 337
Learning communities, 21
attributes of, 22
Learning criteria, grading and, 239–240
Learning-profile differentiation, 258
Least restrictive environment (LRE), 427, 428
"Leaving No Child Behind" (Edelman), 52–54
Lee, Chungmei, 400
Lee v. *Wiseman,* 299
Legal issues
related to child abuse or neglect, 88–89
related to home schooling, 137–138
related to teaching, 298–309
Lemon Test, 299
Lemon v. *Kurtzman,* 299
"Lessons of a First-Year Teacher" (Ness), 27–29
"Letter from a Teacher" (Crowley), 46–48
Lewis, C. S., 195, 197
Lewis, Cynthia, "Why Some Parents Don't Come to School," 126–131
Libel, 306–307
Licensing, 325
Lickona, Thomas, "The Return of Character Education," 310–315
"Life After School" (Hofferth and Jankuniene), 132–135
Lifelong learning, 384–385
Lightfoot, Sara Lawrence, 110
Limited English proficient (LEP), 403
Lines, Patricia M., "Home Schooling Comes of Age," 137–141
Literacy, 337, 363–364, 409–410
Living Between the Lines (Calkins), 42
Logan, John R., 401, 402
Loose coupling, 157
Losing Our Language, 408
Lovitt, Thomas, 178
Lundquist, Ernie, 83

"Mad Dash to Compute, The" (Healy), 387–391
Magnet schools, 286, 368
Mainstreaming, 419
"Making Cooperative Learning Work" (Johnson and Johnson), 245–252

"Making Inclusive Education Work" (Villa and Thousand), 427–432
"Making the Grade: What Benefits Students?" (Guskey), 237–242
Malone, Matthew, 119
Manhattan Institute for Policy Research, 118
Manley, Sue, 33, 34, 35, 36
Mann, Horace, 288
"Many Faces of Constructivism, The" (Perkins), 231–235
"Mapping a Route Toward Differentiated Instruction" (Tomlinson), 254–259
Markell, Marc A., "At Risk for Abuse: A Teacher's Guide for Recognizing and Reporting Child Neglect and Abuse," 85–90
Marzano, Jana S., "Keys to Classroom Management," 206–213
Marzano, Robert J., "Keys to Classroom Management," 206–213
Maslow, Abraham, 67
Math/science gender gap, 436, 437, 438, 440
McCauley, Bob, 119, 120
McDaniel, Thomas R., "The Ten Commandments: School Law in the Classroom," 298–309
McDonald, Timothy, "The False Promise of Vouchers," 373–376
McEntee, Grace Hall, "Reflection Is at the Heart of Practice," 2–6
McGee, Kathleen, "Enabling or Disabling? Observations on Changes in Special Education," 418–425
McGuffey, William, 310
McGuffey Readers, 310
McKnight Foundation, 120
McNeil, Linda, 169
McTighe, Jay, "You Can Teach for Meaning," 225–229
Meaning, teaching for, 225–229
Meaningful learning, 3–4
Media, influence of, 60
Median score, 241
Mediation, 71
Meier, Deborah, 37, 106, 123
Melting pot, 404
"Memories from the "Other": Lessons in Connecting with Students" (Knestrict), 63–68
Merit pay, 11
Meyer v. *Nebraska,* 289
Middleton, Warren, 237
Miles, Karen Hawley, "Putting Money Where It Matters," 361–365
Milliken v. *Bradley,* 400
"Mining the Values in the Curriculum" (Ryan), 194–197
Minority students, 399. *See also* Diversity
  achievement gap and, 199, 201
  dropout rates for, 117, 118
  educational technology and, 382
  literacy and, 409–410
  voucher programs and, 373
Mismeasure of Man, The (Gould), 177
Mitchell v. *Helms,* 290
Modeling, 22
Montano-Harmon, Maria, 70
Moral education, 177–178
Motivation
  external constraints eroding, 219–220
  extrinsic, 215
  intrinsic, 215, 219, 338
  success as, 219
Movies, passionate teachers portrayed in, 9
Mr. Holland's Opus (film), 9
MRI technologies, 434, 437, 439
Multicultural education, 195, 404, 407–410, 411–416. *See also* Diversity
"Multicultural Illiteracy" (Stotsky), 407–410
Multilevel learning stations, 95
Multiple intelligence theory, 383
Murdock, Steve, 402
"My Pedagogic Creed" (Dewey), 261–267
My Posse Don't Do Homework (Johnson), 42

Nabozny, Jamie, 76
Nabozny v. *Podlesny,* 76
National Assessment of Education Progress (NAEP), 199, 202, 409, 436
National Association of Elementary School Principals, 139
National Association of Evangelicals, 181
National Association of Secondary School Principals, 118
National Board for Professional Teaching Standards (NBPTS), 11, 323
National Center for Education Statistics (NCES), 32, 118, 199
National Center for Home Education, 140
National Center on Educational Restructuring and Inclusion, 430
National Clearinghouse on Child Abuse and Neglect Information, 91
National Commission on Teaching and America's Future (NCTAF), 33, 318
National Council for Accreditation of Teacher Education (NCATE), 323
National Council of Churches, 181
National Council of Teachers of Mathematics, 323
National Education Association, 11, 31, 77, 181
National Endowment for the Humanities, 113
National Reading Panel, 283
National Research Council, 156, 310
National School Boards Association, 181
Nation at Risk, A (National Commission on Excellence in Education), 317
Native American students, dropout rates for, 118
Nature-based approach, 437–438
Nature-based classrooms, 438
Negativism, 1
Neglect, 85–90
Ness, Molly, 27
"New Diversity, The" (Hardy), 399–402
New Teachers Network, 35
No Child Left Behind (NCLB) Act, 12, 36, 96, 118, 142, 283, 317, 342, 349, 381
  English Language Learners and, 403
  state standards/assessments and, 144–147
Noddings, Nel, 37
Noddings, Nel, "Teaching Themes of Care," 186–192
Nondiscussables, 100
Nord, Warren A., "The Relevance of Religion to the Curriculum," 181–185
Normalization, 418
Numeracy, 337

Office of Civil Rights (Department of Education), 77
Ogbu, John, 345
Old Deluder Act, 287
Oldfield schools, 286
Oppenheimer, Todd, 392
Oppositional students, 210, 211
Orfield, Gary, 118, 400, 401, 402
Organisation for Economic Co-operation and Development (OECD), 437
Orlalea, Paul, 423
Oversold and Underused (Cuban), 392

Paideia Proposal, 163–168
"Paideia Proposal, The: Rediscovering the Essence of Education" (Adler), 163–168
Papert, Seymour, 382
Parallel teaching, 430
Parents
  as allies, 40–41
  involvement of, 126–131
Parent-Teachers Association, 139
Parks, Rosa, 401
Passionate teachers, 7–9

Payne, Ruby, "Understanding and Working with Students and Adults from Poverty," 69–73
Peddiwell, J. Abner, " The Saber-Tooth Curriculum," 149–154
Peer review, 13
People for the American Way Foundation, 374
Perennialists, 168
Perfectionist students, 211, 212
Perkins, David, "The Many Faces of Constructivism," 231–235
"Personal Thoughts on Teaching and Learning" (Rogers), 268–270
Pfeffer, Jeffrey, 110
Pflaum, William, 392
Phillips, D. D., 232
Philosophy of education, 46–48
Photocopies, 307–308
Physical indicators, 87
Pierce v. *Society of Sisters,* 138, 289
Place Called School, A (Goodlad), 178
Pope, Denise Clark, 385
Popham, W. James, "Curriculum Matters," 143–147
Positive interdependence, 249
Positron emissions tomography (PET), 434, 437, 439
Poverty
  achievement gap and, 199, 201, 204, 341–347
  problems resulting from, 54, 57–58, 400–401
  star teachers for students in, 21–26
  teacher turnover and, 32
  understanding students and adults in, 69–73
  voucher programs and, 373–376
Powell, John A., 401
Power of Ideas, The (Meier), 123
PowerPoint, 394
Practical applications, 22
Preinstructional decisions, 247
Pre-post studies, 282–283
Press, Frank, 272
Prime of Miss Jean Brodie, The (film), 9
Private schools, 162
Private-venture schools, 287, 288, 370
Privileges, withdrawal of, 81–82
Problem-based learning, 233
"Problem Students: The Sociocultural Roots" (Eitzen), 56–61
Process criteria, 239
Processes, 431
Product choices, 94–95
Product criteria, 239
Productivity, 22
Products, 431
Professional development, 33, 36, 321, 323–324, 364. *See also* Teacher education/training
Professional development schools (PDSs), 328
Professional literature, 42
Professional organizations. *See also specific organizations*
  as allies, 41
Professional teachers, 46–48
Progress criteria, 240
Progressivism, 104–107
Pseudo learning group, 246
Punishment
  academic penalties as, 303
  consistency in, 82
  corporal, 303–304
  effects of, 81
  strategies for, 80–81
Purposeful reading, 147
"Putting Money Where It Matters" (Miles), 361–365

Quality School, The (Glasser), 169
"Quality School Curriculum, The" (Glasser), 169–174

Racism, trends in, 58
"Raising Expectations for the Gifted" (Willard-Holt), 92–96
Randomized experiment, 281
Ravitch, Diane, "A Considered Opinion: Diversity, Tragedy, and the Schools," 404–406
Raywid, Mary Anne, "Accountability: What's Worth Measuring?", 355–360
"Reader's Guide to Scientifically Based Research, A" (Slavin), 279–284
Readiness differentiation, 257
Reading gap, 342–343
Reality/representation, 414
Recruiting New Teacher (RNT), 36
Recruitment, teacher, 36, 321, 324–325
"Reflection Is at the Heart of Practice" (Hole and McEntee), 2–6
Reflective teachers, 2–6
Reform
  of high schools, 117–120
  standards-based, 155–160
  teacher-centered, 111–115
  test-based, 156
Relevance, 414–416
"Relevance of Religion to the Curriculum, The" (Nord), 181–185
Religion
  in classroom, 298–300
  in curriculum, 181–185
"Remaking High School" (Vail), 117–120
Research, scientifically based, 279–284
Resegregation, of schools, 400
"Return of Character Education, The" (Lickona), 310–315
Rewards, effects of, 80–81, 83
Risk taking, 220–223
  achievement through, 220–221
  by teachers, 18–19
Risley, Todd, 344
Ritual knowledge, 233
Road Warriors (Burstein and Kline), 391
Rockefeller Foundation, 318
Rogers, Carl, "Personal Thoughts on Teaching and Learning," 268–270
Rogers, Will, 21
Role model gap, 344–345
Ross, Steven M., "How to Create Discipline Problems," 79–83
Rouse, Cecilia, 374
Rubrics, 208
Ryan, Kevin, "Mining the Values in the Curriculum," 194–197

Sabbaticals, 112–113
"Saber-Tooth Curriculum, The" (Peddiwell), 149–154
Sadker, David, 436
Sadker, Myra, 436
Safety, 304–306
Salaries, teacher, 11–13, 32, 112, 362
Sanders, William, 12
Saphier, J., 101
Scarpella, Charlotte, 120
Scholastic Reading Inventory (SRI), 438
School choice, 367–371. *See also* Voucher programs
Schools
  charter, 286, 290, 369, 370, 372
  Colonial, 286–287
  cooperative, 249
  culture of, 99–103, 357–358
  dame, 287
  effective, 326
  expectations of, 332–340
  good, 104–107
  high schools, 117–120
  magnet, 286, 368
  oldfield, 286
  parental involvement in, 126–131
  private, 162, 370
  private-venture, 287
  quality, 169–174
  resegregation of, 400
  role of, 178–179
  sexual harassment policy of, 76–77
  single-sex, 440
  size of, 121–125
  supportive environment in, 77–78
  technology, risk management and, 393–394
  that meet teacher needs, 109–115
  traditional *vs.* progressive, 104–107
  urban, 22, 23, 25, 401–402
"Schools Our Teachers Deserve" (Cohen), 109–115
"School's Out" (Graziano), 31–36
School-within-a-school, 124
Schwab, Charles, 423
Scientifically based research, 279–284
Sclafani, Susan, 118

Scovronick, Nathan, 402
Sease v. *School District of Philadelphia,* 299
Seif, Elliott, "You Can Teach for Meaning," 225–229
Self-discovered learning, 269
Sexual abuse, 86
Sexual harassment, 75–78
Single salary schedule, 11
Single-sex schools, 440
Situational poverty, 70
Sizer, Theodore, 118, 191
Sky-McIlvain, Elizabeth, 395
Slander, 306–307
Slavin, Robert E., "A Reader's Guide to Scientifically Based Research," 279–284
"Small Classes, Small Schools: The Time Is Now" (Wasley), 121–125
Small learning communities, 119
Smith, Maggie, 9
Social class, classroom and, 341–347
Social competence, 252
Social justice, 413, 420
Social learners, 232
Socially inept students, 211, 212
Social skills, 250
Special education, 418–425
SRI International, 32
St. Vincent Millay, Edna, 16
Stakeholders, 101
Standards
  achievement gap and, 199
  class size/school size and, 121
  content, 145–146
  gifted students and, 92
  movement, 155–160
  for school performance, 363–363
  setting high, 322–323
  for teaching, 320
Standards-based education, 356
Standards-based reform, 155–160, 202
Standards movement, 155–160
Star Administrator Selection Interview, 25
Star teachers, 21–26
Star Teacher Selection Interview, 22, 25
Stein, Nan, 75, 76, 77
Steinbeck, John, 15
Stevens, Kathy, "With Boys and Girls in Mind," 434–439
Stotsky, Sandra, "Multicultural Illiteracy," 407–410
Strike, Kenneth A., "The Ethics of Teaching," 293–296
Students
  after-school activities of, 132–135, 347
  as allies, 39–40
  at-risk, 85–90, 102
  care in statements about, 306–307
  challenges for, 218–223
  classroom management and, 206–213
  connecting with, 63–68
  discipline problems in, 79–83
  dropout rates for, 117, 118, 218, 400, 437
  due process for, 302–303
  empathy with, 47
  engaging, 214–217
  gifted, 92–96
  goals for, 356–357
  grading and, 237–242
  high-needs, 210–212
  home-schooled, 137–141
  importance of challenge for, 218–223
  as individuals, 50–51
  limited English proficiency, 403
  minority, 199, 201, 399
  recognizing neglect or abuse in, 85–90
  safety of, 304–306
  sexual harassment of, 75–78
  sociocultural roots of problem, 56–61
  strategies to get to know, 50–51, 215–216
  teachers' personal interest in, 209
"Students Need Challenge, Not Easy Success" (Clifford), 218–223
Students with disabilities
  abuse or neglect of, 86
  inclusion and, 418–425, 427–432
Success
  challenge as opposed to easy, 218–223
  motivating through, 219
Suggestive accountability, 349
Summative evaluation, 222–223
Summers, Lawrence, 440
Supportive teaching, 430
Suro, Roberto, 399
Suzaki, David, 276
Swanson, Christopher, 118

Taking Religion Seriously Across the Curriculum (Nord & Haynes), 184
"Tale of Two Schools, A" (Cuban), 104–107
Tao, 195
Teacher education/training. *See also* Professional development
  commission recommendations for, 322–326
  difficulties of, 27–29
  investment in, 362–364
  quality variations in, 318
Teachers
  administrators as, 114–115
  as allies, 37
  at-homeness and, 19–20
  burnout in, 23, 33
  certification for, 329
  classroom management by, 206–213
  competencies for, 14–20, 318–330
  empowerment of, 110
  evaluation of, 12–13, 113
  hiring of, 113–114, 321
  input in budget, 113
  issues facing, 1
  licensing of, 325
  passionate, 7–9
  professional, 46–48
  professional development for, 33, 36, 364
  quality of, 321
  recruitment of, 36, 321, 324–325
  reflective, 2–6
  rewards for competent, 321–322
  risk-taking, 18–19
  sabbaticals for, 112–113
  salaries for, 11–13, 32, 112, 362
  schools that meet needs of, 109–115
  star, 21–26
  support systems for, 35–36
  sustaining health and well-being of, 37–44
  ten commandments for, 298–309
  tenure of, 114
  turnover of, 31–36, 32 (fig.)
  underqualified, 203
Teachers and Machines (Cuban), 392
Teacher Expectations and Student Achievement, 209
Teachers Learning in Networked Communities (T-LINC), 33
"Teacher's Ten Commandments, The: School Law in the Classroom" (McDaniel), 298–309
Teacher voice, 23–24
Teach for America, 27–29
Teaching
  complementary, 430
  ethics of, 293–296
  for meaning and understanding, 225–229
  parallel, 430
  personal thoughts on, 268–270
  standards for, 320
  supportive, 430
"Teaching Themes of Care" (Noddings), 186–192
"Teaching What We Hold to be Sacred" (Goodlad), 176–179
Technology. *See* Educational technology
"Technology and the Culture of Learning" (Gow), 392–396
Technology Fix, The (Pflaum), 392
Tenure, 114
Tests
  competency-based, 367
  high-stakes, 155, 156, 158, 159
Test scores, value-added, 12, 13
Thompson, Scott, "The Authentic Standards Movement and Its Evil Twin," 155–160

Thousand, Jacqueline S., "Making Inclusive Education Work," 427–432
Tiered assignments, 95
Tinker decision, 300, 302
Title I, 363
Title IX, 76
Tomlinson, Carol Ann, 96
Tomlinson, Carol Ann, "Mapping a Route Toward Differentiated Instruction," 254–259
To Teach: The Journey of a Teacher (Ayers), 42
Tracking, 163–164
Traditional learning group, 246
Transfer of learning, 337
Treman, Jim, 34
Trends in International Mathematics and Science Study (TIMSS), 227, 228
Tripp, David, 2, 6
Turnover, teacher, 31–36, 32 (fig.)
Tyler, Ralph, 176

"Understanding and Working with Students and Adults from Poverty" (Payne), 69–73
Unemployment, 401
Unions, teacher, 11, 12, 13
Unitary school districts, 400
Universities, 42–43
Urban Institute, 118
U.S. Department of Education, 32, 36, 117, 122
U.S. federal budget deficit, 381

Vail, Kathleen, "Remaking High School," 117–120
Value-added approach, 12, 13
Values, 52–54, 59–60, 194–197, 277, 311
Vander Ark, Tom, 117
Van Doren, Mark, 277
Verbal abuse, 86
Villa, Richard A., "Making Inclusive Education Work," 427–432
Viteritti, Joseph P., "Coming Around on School Choice," 367–371
Voucher programs, 158, 290, 367–371, 372, 373–376
Vygotsky, L. S., 92

Wasicsko, M. Mark, "How to Create Discipline Problems," 79–83
Wasley, Patricia A., "Small Classes, Small Schools: The Time Is Now," 121–125
"What Matters Most: A Competent Teacher for Every Child" (Darling-Hammond), 318–329
What Matters Most: Teaching for America's Future (National Commission on Teaching and America's Future), 318
White, E. B., 101
White flight, 399, 401–402
Whitehead, Barbara Dafoe, 312
"Who Is This Child?" (Barr), 50–51
"Why Some Parents Don't Come to School" (Finders and Lewis), 126–131
Wiggins, Grant, "You Can Teach for Meaning," 225–229
Wilkins, Roger, 61
Willard-Holt, Colleen, "Raising Expectations for the Gifted," 92–96
Williams, Robin, 9
Wilson, William Julius, 401
Wineburg, Sam, 38
Wisconsin v. *Yoder,* 137
"With Boys and Girls in Mind" (Gurian and Stevens), 434–439
Woods, Jacqueline, "Hostile Hallways," 75–78
Word processing, 394

"You Can Teach for Meaning" (McTighe, Seif, and Wiggins), 225–229

Zabel, Pam, 34
Zone of proximal development, 92
Zorach v. *Clauson,* 299

Article Review Form

Feel free to photocopy this page and use it to help you review each article you read in this edition of *Kaleidoscope.*

Name: ______________________ **Date:** __________ **Article no.:** ________

In your own words, briefly state the main idea of the article.

With what points or arguments made by the author(s) do you agree or disagree?

Agree:

Disagree:

What did you learn from the article that you think is (1) important, (2) interesting, and (3) unclear?

(1) ______________________

(2) ______________________

(3) ______________________

List any new terms or concepts you found in the article, and briefly define them.

Student Response Form

We'd like to make this book as useful as we can for readers, and your views are vital to our task. What did you think about the selection of articles in this eleventh edition of Kaleidoscope? Your comments on the form below will help us revise the book for the next edition. You can use a scale of 1 to 5 to "grade" the articles you've read:

5—Excellent 4—Good 3—Average 2—Below average 1—Poor

Please mail the completed form to College Marketing, Houghton Mifflin Company, 222 Berkeley Street, Boston, MA 02116-3764.

Grade	Author/Title
_____	1. Hole & McEntee, *Reflection Is at the Heart of Practice*
_____	2. Fried, *The Heart of the Matter*
_____	3. Koppich, *All Teachers Are* Not *the Same: A Multiple Approach to Teacher Compensation*
_____	4. Ducharme, *The Great Teacher Question: Beyond Competencies*
_____	5. Haberman, *Can Star Teachers Create Learning Communities?*
_____	6. Ness, *Lessons of a First-Year Teacher*
_____	7. Graziano, *School's Out*
_____	8. Houghton, *Finding Allies: Sustaining Teachers' Health and Well-Being*
_____	9. Crowley, *Letter from a Teacher*
_____	10. Barr, *Who Is This Child?*
_____	11. Edelman, *Leaving No Child Behind*
_____	12. Eitzen, *Problem Students: The Sociocultural Roots*
_____	13. Knestrict, *Memories from the "Other": Lessons in Connecting with Students*
_____	14. Payne, *Understanding and Working with Students and Adults from Poverty*
_____	15. Woods, *Hostile Hallways*
_____	16. Wasicsko & Ross, *How to Create Discipline Problems*
_____	17. Willard-Holt, *Raising Expectations for the Gifted*
_____	18. Cates, Markell, & Bettenhausen, *At Risk for Abuse: A Teacher's Guide for Recognizing and Reporting Child Neglect and Abuse*
_____	19. Barth, *The Culture Builder*
_____	20. Cuban, *A Tale of Two Schools*
_____	21. Cohen, *Schools Our Teachers Deserve*
_____	22. Vail, *Remaking High School*
_____	23. Wasley, *Small Classes, Small Schools: The Time Is Now*
_____	24. Finders & Lewis, *Why Some Parents Don't Come to School*
_____	25. Hofferth & Jankuniene, *Life After School*
_____	26. Lines, *Home Schooling Comes of Age*
_____	27. Popham, *Curriculum Matters*
_____	28. Peddiwell, *The Saber-Tooth Curriculum*
_____	29. Thompson, *The Authentic Standards Movement and Its Evil Twin*
_____	30. Adler, *The Paideia Proposal: Rediscovering the Essence of Education*
_____	31. Glasser, *The Quality School Curriculum*
_____	32. Goodlad, *Teaching What We Hold to Be Sacred*
_____	33. Nord, *The Relevance of Religion to the Curriculum*
_____	34. Noddings, *Teaching Themes of Care*
_____	35. Ryan, *Mining the Values in the Curriculum*
_____	36. Haycock, *Closing the Achievement Gap*
_____	37. Marzano & Marzano, *The Key to Classroom Management*
_____	38. Dodd, *Engaging Students: What I Learned Along the Way*
_____	39. Clifford, *Students Need Challenge, Not Easy Success*
_____	40. McTighe, Seif, & Wiggins, *You* Can *Teach for Meaning*
_____	41. Perkins, *The Many Faces of Constructivism*
_____	42. Guskey, *Making the Grade: What Benefits Students?*
_____	43. Johnson & Johnson, *Making Cooperative Learning Work*

Grade	Author/Title
_____	44. Tomlinson, *Mapping a Route Toward Differentiated Instruction*
_____	45. Dewey, *My Pedagogic Creed*
_____	46. Rogers, *Personal Thoughts on Teaching and Learning*
_____	47. Boyer, *The Educated Person*
_____	48. Slavin, *A Reader's Guide to Scientifically Based Research*
_____	49. Carper, *The Changing Landscape of U.S. Education*
_____	50. Strike, *The Ethics of Teaching*
_____	51. McDaniel, *The Teacher's Ten Commandments: School Law in the Classroom*
_____	52. Lickona, *The Return of Character Education*
_____	53. Darling-Hammond, *What Matters Most: A Competent Teacher for Every Child*
_____	54. Eisner, *The Kind of Schools We Need*
_____	55. Rothstein, *Class and the Classroom*
_____	56. Hess, *The Case for Being Mean*
_____	57. Raywid, *Accountability: What's Worth Measuring?*

Grade	Author/Title
_____	58. Miles, *Putting Money Where It Matters*
_____	59. Viteritti, *Coming Around on School Choice*
_____	60. McDonald, *The False Promise of Vouchers*
_____	61. Cetron & Cetron, *A Forecast for Schools*
_____	62. Healy, *The Mad Dash to Compute*
_____	63. Gow, *Technology and the Culture of Learning*
_____	64. Hardy, *The New Diversity*
_____	65. Ravitch, *A Considered Opinion: Diversity, Tragedy, and the Schools*
_____	66. Stotsky, *Multicultural Illiteracy*
_____	67. Gay, *The Importance of Multicultural Education*
_____	68. Kauffman, McGee, & Brigham, *Enabling or Disabling? Observations on Changes in Special Education*
_____	69. Villa & Thousand, *Making Inclusive Education Work*
_____	70. Gurian & Stevens, *With Boys and Girls in Mind*

Title of course in which you used this book: ______________________________

Name of your school: ______________________________

Your name (optional): ______________________________

Suggestions for next edition (topics, types of articles, specific selections—any ideas you'd like to share with us):

____

____

____

____

____

Topic	Author	Abbreviated Title	Kaleidoscope (pages)	Those Who Can, Teach (chapters)	Foundations of Education (chapters)
Parental Involvement	Finders & Lewis	*Why Some Parents Don't Come to School*	126–131	3, 11, 14	10, 11, 16
Philosophy of Education	Adler	*The Paideia Proposal*	163–168	5, 9	4, 14
	Boyer	*The Educated Person*	271–278	5, 9	2, 4, 5, 14
	Dewey	*My Pedagogic Creed*	261–267	2, 5, 9	4, 5, 14
	Rogers	*Personal Thoughts on Teaching and Learning*	268–270	9	4, 5, 14
Reforming Education	Cohen	*Schools Our Teachers Deserve*	109–116	2, 12, 15	12, 13, 16
	Darling-Hammond	*What Matters Most*	318–331	6, 12, 13, 15	1, 2, 13, 16
	Vail	*Remaking High School*	117–120	12	6, 16
	Eisner	*The Kind of Schools We Need*	332–340	2, 5, 12, 15	2, 13, 16
	Slavin	*A Reader's Guide to Scientifically Based Research*	279–285	12	16
	McDonald	*The False Promise of Vouchers*	373–378	12	8, 16
	Miles	*Putting Money Where It Matters*	361–366	11	8
	Viteritti	*Coming Around on School Choice*	367–372	12	8, 16
Religion and Education	Nord	*The Relevance of Religion to the Curriculum*	181–185	5, 8, 12	3, 9
Schools	Barth	*The Culture Builder*	99–103	2, 3, 11, 12, 14, 15	1, 2, 4, 10, 13, 16
	Cohen	*Schools Our Teachers Deserve*	109–116	2, 6, 12, 14, 15	1, 2, 13, 14, 16
	Cuban	*A Tale of Two Schools*	104–108	2, 12	14, 16
	Goodlad	*Teaching What We Hold Sacred*	176–180	2, 9, 10, 12	4, 6, 13, 16
	Wasley	*Small Classes, Small Schools*	121–125	2, 12	7, 11, 16
	Vail	*Remaking High School*	117–120	2, 12	6, 16
Standards Movement	Haycock	*Closing the Achievement Gap*	199–205	5, 6, 10, 12	11, 12, 16
	Thompson	*The Authentic Standards Movement and Its Evil Twin*	155–162	5, 11, 12	13, 14, 16
Student Motivation and Engagement	Clifford	*Students Need Challenge*	218–224	6, 12	14, 16
	McTighe, Seif, & Wiggins	*You Can Teach for Meaning*	225–230	5, 6, 12	13, 14, 16
	Dodd	*Engaging Students*	214–217	6, 12	14, 16